THROUGH THE EMBERS OF CHAOS

DERVLA MURPHY

THROUGH THE EMBERS OF CHAOS

Balkan Journeys

In all the former Yugoslav territories people are now living a postmodern chaos. Past, present and future are all lived simultaneously. In the circular temporal mish-mash suddenly everything we ever knew and everything we shall know has sprung to life and gained its right to existence.

Dubravska Ugrešić, August 1993

JOHN MURRAY
Albemarle Street, London

First published in 2002
by John Murray (Publishers) Ltd,
50 Albemarle Street, London W1S 4BD

A catalogue record for this book is available from the British Library

ISBN 0-7195-6232 5

Typeset in Monotype Baskerville by
Servis Filmsetting Ltd, Manchester
Printed and bound in Great Britain by
Butler and Tanner Ltd, Frome and London

For Zea, who dictated the shape of this book from the womb and who, since emerging, has continued to dictate to everyone about everything

Contents

Author's Note

A word about acronyms, which throughout the Balkans seem to breed even faster than elsewhere (see list on p. 371). In the numerous lengthy documents circulated by the plethora of international agencies sentences like this are the norm – 'The OECD and the OSCE delegates were joined by an IPTF representative to establish new parameters around the structuring of transport programmes related to previous links between PRIZAD and JUSAT in what is now the NDH.' In an attempt to control this plague I have referred to institutions such as the EU and OSCE by their current acronyms, even when writing about a time when they were otherwise known.

Two new terms are contentious though now in general usage: 'Kosovars' instead of Kosova Albanians and 'Bosniaks' instead of Bosnian Muslims. In the former case 'Kosovars' offends some Serbs who argue that all who live in Kosovo should be so described, that to apply 'Kosovars' only to the Albanians is to deny Kosovo's Serbs the right to exist. However, at least 90 per cent of Kosovo's population are Albanians who do not see themselves as citizens (or potential citizens) of either Serbia or Albania. Therefore to describe them as 'Kosovars' seems fair enough. The Bosnian Muslims' wish to be known as 'Bosniaks' is even trickier. It can be seen to suggest that community's assumption of a right to dominate in Bosnia, relegating Serbs and Croats to inferior minority status. But that is a perverse misinterpretation of the average Bosniak's attitude. The adoption of 'Bosniak' merely signifies their wish to be seen as citizens of Bosnia-Herzegovina rather than as *Muslims*.

As for the phrase 'ethnic cleansing' – I'm minded to start a campaign against its use. It originated in Serbia when the Milošević-controlled media chose the euphemism *čišćenje terena* (cleansing the terrain) to describe the forcible uprooting of non-Serbs from their home areas – then referred to, by the same media, as 'liberated' territories. Quickly foreign journalists adapted the phrase for their own use and 'ethnic cleansing' – a doubly inaccurate term – is by now used all over the English-speaking world.

This abuse of language blunts both thinking and feeling. 'Cleansing' is a wholesome word, conjuring up a process with a healthy outcome. And in the Balkan case '*ethnic*' cleansing is seriously misleading. Apart from Kosovo's Albanians, all those involved in the recent conflicts are of the same stock – southern Slavs to a man and woman. They were not murdering, plundering and displacing each other for ethnic reasons.

The 'international community' is another reprehensible euphemism. As the journalist Diana Johnstone has pointed out, 'The IC is not even a community; the initials could more accurately stand for "imperialist condominium", a joint exercise of domination by the former imperialist powers, torn apart and weakened by two World Wars, now brought together under US domination with Nato as their military arm. Certainly there are frictions between the members of this condominium, but so long as their rivalries can be played out within the IC, the price will be paid by smaller and weaker countries.' When I refer to the 'international community' or IC I mean this condominium rather than the true (but tragically impotent) international community represented by the UN General Assembly.

Finally, two old terms need clarification.

The Ustasha were ferocious ultra-nationalistic Croatians who fought with the Nazi invaders of Yugoslavia, in the expectation that after a German victory they could rule an independent Croatia.

The Chetniks were Serbian royalists and nationalists equally notorious for their ferocity during the Second World War. They at first fought against the Nazis and Ustasha, then became demoralized and divided. They no longer exist as a recognized group; in 1990 the Belgrade authorities refused to register as a political party Vojislav Šešelj's 'Serbian Četnik Movement'. However, recent victims of Serbian aggression in Croatia, Bosnia-Herzegovina and Kosovo habitually refer to the Serbian police, military and paramilitary forces as 'Chetniks' and I have sometimes followed that usage.

Background Information

In the mid-1980s, before Slobodan Milošević gained power, all knowledgeable observers were aware that Yugoslavia might soon fall apart. Tito's ingenious but perilously complicated constitutional devices had ensured the country's peace and stability but without his quality of leadership were no longer effective. They had been based on the gradual strengthening of local authorities, and post-Tito this led to a dangerous disrespect for the federal government. Yet a countrywide referendum, held in 1990, might well have shown a majority in every Yugoslav republic (except tiny Slovenia) in favour of maintaining unity. Most Yugoslavs were proud of belonging to a state well regarded internationally for its non-alignment, its original brand of socialism and – by regional standards – its liberal political and economic policies. The failure of the latter didn't have to prove fatal to Yugoslavia.

However, during Tito's twilight years (he died in 1980), his government unwisely sought prosperity through exports. Finance ministers borrowed wildly from the West, which soon after plunged into a recession and rejected Yugoslav goods, leaving the country debt-stricken. The International Monetary Fund (IMF) then persuaded the government to dump most of the debt-related hardships on the working class. Concurrently the Yugoslav League of Communists spawned several opportunistic leaders eager to ingratiate themselves with Western bankers and entrepreneurs. Among them was Slobodan Milošević – not a committed Communist, or capitalist, or nationalist, but someone dedicated to reinforcing his own and his wife's positions in whatever power structure might best serve their purposes as the post-Cold War world took shape.

In 1984 the Reagan administration accepted the US National Security Council's advice to 'push Yugoslavia towards a capitalist restoration' – whereupon the World Bank imposed a uniquely punitive banking mechanism on Yugoslav industries. In the crucial years of 1989–90, this caused 600,000 redundancies, without compensation, out of a 2.7 million workforce. Another half-million went unpaid during the first quarter of 1990. On 29 November 1990 the *International Herald Tribune* reported that the CIA had warned President Bush's State Department: 'Yugoslavia is heading for civil war within eighteen months'.

As the last of the benefits provided by Tito's 'self-management socialism' were eroded, the IMF's Yugoslav allies assured the masses that if they bore their cross patiently they would soon come to a glorious resurrection within the EU. The Slovenes were the first to indicate that they felt they had carried their cross far enough. In January 1990 they made plain their intention of seceding from Yugoslavia as soon as possible and 'joining the EU'. Meanwhile secessionists in Croatia were reactivating pre-1945 bourgeois nationalism, complete with slogans and symbols that for older people awoke bloody memories and, among the younger generations, stirred new fears.

Since Mikhail Gorbachev's advent, Germany, Austria, Hungary and the Vatican had been seeking to re-establish their traditional spheres of influence and by 1989–90 were vigorously promoting Slovenian and Croatian independence. In 1992 John Zametica, of the London International Institute for Strategic Studies, wrote:

> Austria saw the Yugoslav crisis as an auspicious moment for self-assertion and had a remarkably open and sometimes brazen policy aimed at helping Slovenia and Croatia in their efforts to leave the Federation. By the summer of 1991 the EU was warning Austria that unless it desisted from its energetic meddling in Yugoslavia it would not be considered for eventual EU membership. But Austria only laughed at this empty threat. And Hungary – even keener to see the death of Yugoslavia – covertly supplied Croatia with a large consignment of automatic assault rifles in December 1990. These were being used six months later when Hungary's prime minister, the late Josef Antall, recalled the 1920 Treaty of Trianon [which had humiliatingly dismembered Hungary] and commented that it had been made only with Yugoslavia. 'This historical fact must be kept in mind,' he said. 'We gave Vojvodina to Yugoslavia. If there is no more Yugoslavia then we should get it back.'

Yugoslavia was made up of six republics – Slovenia, Croatia, Bosnia-Herzegovina, Montenegro, Macedonia and Serbia. The two provinces – Vojvodina and Kosovo, parts of the Serb republic – gained a measure of autonomy in 1974. Safeguards were provided to ensure that no one need fear being dominated by anyone else – everyone else had been dominated by Serbs during the inter-war Monarchy. Many Serbs had lived for generations in the other republics and in Tito-time this bothered only the Kosovars (occasionally) because the constitution gave equal rights to the individual as a citizen of a republic and as a member of a nation – a device which could have been used to avert disaster. As Peter Gowan has noted, 'If the Western powers had been interested in putting the interests of the Yugoslav people first, they had adequate levers to play a decisive role, alongside Yugoslavia's federal government, in maintaining the country's integrity.'

Croatia claimed the right to self-determination because the Croatian nation had voted for it in a referendum. But when the Croatian Serbs organized their own referendum, an overwhelming majority rejected the option of living within an independent Croatia. Croatia's leaders ignored this vote, thus denying those Serbs their sovereign national right. Yugoslavia's constitutional principles required a resolution of such conflicting rights and democratic wills. But the EU seemed unaware of the fact that the rights of the Serb *nation* were as valid as the will of the Croat *republic* – admittedly a confusing concept for non-Yugoslavs, yet a vital cog in Tito's peace-keeping machine.

In midsummer 1991, when Germany decided unilaterally to recognize Slovenian and Croatian independence, the Great Powers fell to squabbling among themselves. The US, the UK and France (still passively favouring Yugoslav unity) reminded Germany of the 1975 Helsinki Accords and of the 1990 Treaty of Paris, guaranteeing that all Europe's inter-state borders should be inviolate and that adequate internal arrangements should be made to safeguard minority rights. Yugoslavia presented this new treaty with its first challenge. But the EU, bowing to Germany's will, failed to enforce the relevant principles – having nothing to gain by upholding them. In June 1991 Germany and Austria made fools of the EU Council of Ministers by persuading it to mediate between Ljubljana (Slovenia), Zagreb (Croatia) and Belgrade (Serbia). The EU, though as yet refusing to recognize Slovenia's and Croatia's right to independence, now found themselves, in their role as mediators, implicitly acknowledging the break-away republics' repudiation of Yugoslavia's sovereign authority.

Many international law *savants* (including Barbara Delcouri and Olivier Carten of the Free University of Brussels) consider the secessions from the Yugoslav Federation illegitimate since the principle of 'self-determination' applied to none of those cases. During the turmoil preceding the disintegration, this issue was never openly debated in detail.

How did the Germans bring the other EU members to heel? We know that during an all-night European Political Co-operation meeting, on 15–16 December 1991, Helmut Kohl secured John Major's support by offering the British two important Maastricht Treaty opt-outs, on the Social Charter and Monetary Union. Doubtless comparable inducements were offered to other leaders. Chancellor Kohl promised the meeting that Germany would withhold recognition from Slovenia and Croatia until their minorities' rights had been fully and formally guaranteed in compliance with the Helsinki Accords. As this was not an issue in Slovenia, he was really talking about Croatia's Serbs. Exactly one week later he broke that promise. Apparently the newly united Germany was intent on acquiring a sphere of influence extending over Austria, Hungary, Croatia, Slovenia – and perhaps, later, Poland and Czechoslovakia. How else to explain Kohl's and Genscher's determination to dismember Yugoslavia?

At that time all the emphasis was on Serbia's evil-doing, and the threat posed to other republics by the revived 'Greater Serbia' cult. The demonization of Serbs in general – then and later – was far from spontaneous. Croatian and Kosovar secessionists engaged a Washington DC public relations firm to run their anti-Serb propaganda campaigns – surely an unnecessary expense, given the well-documented atrocities committed by Milošević's militia, his police 'Special Units' and various enlisted criminal gangs. However, these campaigns served to concentrate public attention on Serbian war crimes and deflect the media spotlight from subsequent Croatian, Bosniak and Kosovar atrocities. In Germany few protested when a First World War chant, '*Serbien muss sterbien*' ('Serbia must die'), again became popular. The Green Party leader, Joschka Fischer, likened the Serbs to the Nazis. By October 2000, when Milošević was voted out of power, the simplistic notion that he had caused *all* the Balkan bloodshed was firmly lodged in very many minds.

On 2 January 1992 the Serbs agreed to a 'cessation of hostilities' in Croatia, declaring their willingness to accept UN peace-keeping forces in the battle zones. As these troop were to operate only in Croatia, why did the UN commanders choose Sarajevo in Bosnia-Herzegovina as its command headquarters, while placing its logistical bases in Banja Luka (also in BiH), Zagreb (Croatia) and Belgrade – although Croatia was now a sovereign state? After that, the UN's errors bred like fruit flies, to the angry frustration of the troops from twenty-seven countries, who could clearly see the need to disarm and disband the numerous Serb paramilitary and local militia forces in Croatia, armed by Belgrade. Demilitarization, so crucial to the success of the overall plan, was never attempted. In December Mark Goulding, Assistant Secretary-General 'for political issues' to the UN Secretary-General, had stated that in UN-protected zones 'the laws and institutions of the new Republic of Croatia would not apply'. This encouraged the Serbs to continue their violent domination of those Croatian territories recently seized by force. And the setting aside of Croatian 'laws and institutions' required Unprofor's commanders reluctantly to defer to Serbian local authorities who had usurped the positions of murdered or banished Croats.

Next it was BiH's turn. The Bosnian President, Alija Izetbegović, had personally visited Germany to beg Hans-Dietrich Genscher (then Foreign Minister) not to recognize Croatian independence; he foresaw a consequent BiH separatist movement, led by Belgrade-backed Serbs. The EU-appointed Badinter Commission supported him, advising that Bosnian independence should on no account be recognized without the full and incontestable consent of all three nations. Those, according to the 1981 census, consisted of 1,629,000 Muslims, 1,320,000 Serbs, 758,000 Croats – plus 326,000 Yugoslavs. Many who described themselves as 'Yugoslavs' were partners in mixed marriages and their offspring.

However, by January 1992 Germany's assertiveness had thoroughly unsettled Washington and new actors had arrived on the Balkan stage. Laurence

Eagleburger, President Bush's adviser on European policy, and Brent Scowcroft, head of the us National Security Council, had both served in the us embassy in Belgrade (the former as ambassador) and maintained substantial business interests in Yugoslavia. Eagleburger now warned that when it came to constructing 'the new Europe' Germany was 'getting out ahead of the us'. It was time for Washington to take charge in the Balkans.

As determined by Germany, the position then was that the so-called international community must protect Croatia from Serbia while opposing Bosnian independence. As determined by the us, the position was that Bosnia must be assisted towards independence and then protected from aggressive Serbia. The need to 'project power' in Europe was dictating us policy and this us 'defence of Bosnia's right to self-determination' would show the world who was boss.

In Sarajevo President Bush's envoys confronted Izetbegović, dictating that what he most dreaded – an independent Bosnia and Herzegovina – must happen. Desperately he began to negotiate with the EU. As a result, a three-canton confederal settlement, leaving BiH as part of Yugoslavia, was agreed in March with the Bosnian Serbs and Croats. But this displeased the us, which insisted on his demanding a sovereign, independent state. A week later he repudiated the EU-brokered agreement. us power had been successfully projected and a three-year war followed.

Chronology

Part I gives my impressions of Zagreb at the end of 1991, soon after the secession from Yugoslavia of Slovenia and Croatia and three months before the Bosnian conflict began.

Part II recalls a five-week visit to Serbia in the autumn of 1999, four months after the end of Nato's 'airwar'.

Part III describes my three-month cycle tour, beginning in March 2000, of Croatia, Bosnia-Herzegovina (BiH), Montenegro, Albania and Kosovo.

*

1918
1 December   Formation of the Kingdom of Serbia, Croatia and Slovenia, known from January 1929 as 'the Kingdom of Yugoslavia'.

1945
November   Formation of the Federal People's Republic of Yugoslavia.

1980
4 May   Death of Josip Broz Tito.

1981
11 March   First civil unrest in Kosovo.

1986
February   Slobodan Milošević becomes head of Serbian Communist Party.

1987

24 April — On a visit to the famous battlefield at Kosovo Polje, Milošević intervenes on behalf of Kosovo's Serb minority.

1988

July — Kosovo Serbs set up pro-Milošević committee to organize mass demonstrations throughout Yugoslavia.

1989

28 March — Serbia proclaims its new constitution abrogating the autonomous status of the provinces of Vojvodina and Kosovo. Sustained anti-Serb demonstrations follow in Priština.

28 June — To commemorate the 600th anniversary of the Battle of Kosovo Milošević addresses half a million Serbs on the battlefield near Priština, and threatens 'new fights, even armed conflicts' to keep Kosovo Serbian.

1990

20/21 January — The Slovenes withdraw from the last Congress of the League of Communists of Yugoslavia, ending the Party's existence on the Federal level.

8 April — Slovenia's first free elections.

22 April — Croatia's first free elections.

18 August — Croatia's Serbs hold an autonomy referendum and conflicts begin in many of the republic's Serb-inhabited districts.

11 November — Macedonia's first free elections.

18 November — Bosnia-Herzegovina's first free elections.

22 December — Croatia's *Sabor* (parliament) endows Croatia with 'sovereignty'.

1991

9 March — Milošević sends army tanks on to Belgrade streets after anti-Milošević demo attacked by police, causing violence to spread.

25 March — At Karadjordjevo, Serbia, Croatia's President Tudjman and Milošević hold secret talks about BiH's future.

25 June — Slovenia and Croatia declare independence.

16 December — The EU Council of Ministers decides to recognize Slovenian and Croatian independence on 15 January 1992.

18 December — Germany unilaterally declares its immediate recognition of both states.

1992

2 January	Croatia and Serbia sign a truce in Sarajevo, capital of BiH.
6 April	EU and US recognize BiH's independence. Serbian bombardment of Sarajevo begins.
7/12 April	Law and order breaks down throughout BiH.
20 May	The Yugoslav People's Army (JNA) is declared 'an occupying army' in BiH.
30 May	UN imposes economic sanctions on the Federal Republic of Yugoslavia (FRY).
9 July	President Bush rejects BiH pleas for military intervention.
20 December	In Serbia's federal and republic level parliamentary and presidential elections Milošević re-elected as President.

1993

February	Croatian forces begin hostilities against BiH government forces. Serbian forces intensify campaign against Muslim enclaves.
9 November	Croatian artillery destroy Mostar's Old Bridge. The Croatian government declares its wish to annex part of BiH.

1994

February	Nato declares 'exclusion zone' for heavy weapons around Sarajevo after Serbian mortar bombs kill 68 civilians. In Central Bosnia Croat–Muslim fighting ends.
1 March	An agreement to create a Muslim ('Bosniak')–Croat Federation within BiH is signed in Washington.
29/30 March	BiH parliament ratifies new constitution.
November	Legislation passed in US Congress obliges Washington to stop enforcing arms embargo against government of BiH.
End December	A Jimmy Carter-negotiated cease-fire apparently partially accepted but used by all sides to reinforce troops for spring campaign.

1995

April/May	Renewed heavy fighting in most parts of BiH.
1/2 May	Milošević being no longer willing to support Croatia's Serbs, the Croatian army retrieves key positions in Serb-held Western Slavonia.
25 May	In retaliation for renewed Serbian bombing of Sarajevo, UN authorizes Nato airstrikes in BiH.
June	Serbs take hostage 365 UN personnel, chain them to potential

November/December   KLA uses absence of 'Special Units' to strengthen positions and acquire more arms.

24 December   Cease-fire ends when Serbian forces and KLA clash near Podujevo.

1999

15 January   The contentious Račak massacre reactivates Nato.

19 January   President Clinton's security advisers support back-to-the-wall negotiations threatening airstrikes if Milošević refuses to endorse a genuine Kosovo settlement.

26 January   A joint US-Russian statement demands that Serbia comply with UNSC Resolutions and that both sides cease hostilities and agree on autonomy within FRY for Kosovo. To achieve those objectives the Contact Group announces that negotiations will begin at Rambouillet, in France, on 6 February.

23 February   At Rambouillet Kosovo Albanians agree to sign a peace agreement whose final text stated:

> Three years after the entry into force of this Agreement, an international meeting shall be convened to determine a mechanism for a final settlement for Kosovo, on the basis of the will of the people, opinions of relevant authorities, each Party's efforts regarding the implementation of this Agreement, and the Helsinki Final Act, and to undertake a comprehensive assessment of the implementation of this Agreement and to consider proposals by any Party for additional measures.

Milošević refuses to sign, his main objection being to the stationing of Nato troops in Kosovo, or anywhere in Serbia.

23 March   In Belgrade Holbrooke fails in his final effort to persuade Milošević to sign the Rambouillet Agreement. By a vote of 58 to 41 US Senate authorizes US bombing of FRY as part of Nato's campaign known as Operation Allied Force (OAF).

24 March   OAF begins.

26 March   In UNSC Russia calls for immediate end to bombing of FRY but this draft resolution is defeated by 3 to 12 votes.

30 March   Phase 2 of OAF begins, expanding Nato's target area to include civilian infrastructure.

29 April   By a tie vote (213 each way) the US House of Representatives fails to pass a resolution supporting OAF.

3 May   For the first time ever, Nato's CBU-94 munitions are used, to knock Serbian power-switching stations out of action.

18 May	Clinton announces 'no options are off the table', hinting at a possible ground invasion.
26 May	KLA launches vigorous campaign against Serbian forces in Kosovo.
27 May	The International Criminal Tribunal for the former Yugoslavia indicts, among others, Milošević – for murder, persecution and deportation in Kosovo.
2 June	Viktor Chernomyrdin, President Yeltsin's special envoy in the Balkans, and his co-negotiator, the Finnish President Martti Ahtisaari, dictate Nato's demands to Milošević.
3 June	Peace Plan approved by Milošević and the Serbian Parliament.
3/10 June	Heavy bombing continues, causing more civilian casualties and more damage to Serbia's infrastructure.
9 June	Military-Technical Agreement signed by representatives of the Yugoslav military and Nato, permitting Nato reconnaissance and patrol flights to continue.
10 June	Nato suspends OAF. UNSC Resolution 1244 calls on all FRY forces to leave Kosovo, authorizes the deployment of 45,000 Nato-led troops (K-For) and the presence in Kosovo of international security and civilian personnel for an indefinite period.

Maps

BOSNIA—HERZEGOVINA 1996

BALKAN JOURNEYS

TIA

Vukovar
Temerin
Novi Sad

Derventa
Bosna
Sremska Mitrovica
Pančevo
Tolisa
Sašinci
Sava
Belgrade
Doboj
Drina
Tuzla
Maglaj

SERBIA

Ribnica
Krivaja
Olovo
Kragujevac

GOVINA

Sarajevo
Višegrad
Kraljevo
Jablanica
Konjic
Neretva
Niš
Mostar
Zalomska
Ibar
Radimlje
Trepča
Stolac

MONTENEGRO
Kosovska
Mitrovica
Trebišnjica
Nikšić
Kolašin
Berane
Rožaj
Trebinje
Ostrog
Čakor Pass
Peć
Priština
Dubrovnik
Danilovgrad
Zeta
Cijevna
Hercegnovi
Kotor Pass
Podgorica
Djakovica
Ribnik
Topluga
Cetinje
Tuzi
Drin
Prizren
Koplik
Shkodra
Pukë
Kukës
Skopje

ALBANIA

A d r i a t i c

Durrës
Tirana

MČ

PART I

1991–2
Croatia

1

Croatia in Transition

On 27 December 1991 not many were travelling from Trieste into disintegrating Yugoslavia. The train for Ljubljana, Slovenia's capital, departed at 4 p.m. and in a grimy carriage with frayed upholstery my only companion was Winston, an affable Ghanaian road engineer, resident in Italy since 1980. At the Slovenian border he and his small but expensive suitcase aroused suspicion and an immigration officer requested him to get off and be photographed. On his return he observed, with a twinkle, 'They think all Africans must be drug smugglers. It's best to make allowances for their prejudices. They inherit them.'

We cleaned a window with newspaper, the better to see the sunset. Fragile clouds in layers of the palest pink turning to apricot – bulky orange clouds turning blood-red above the darkness of low wooded mountains – then a final brief glory of high snow peaks, radiantly gold. 'Artists can produce nothing so beautiful,' commented Winston as the carriage light came on.

For an hour or so we talked. In Ljubljana, Winston would celebrate the New Year with a Slovenian friend: 'For him this is a special New Year, in his very new country!' I was invited to stay with the friend on the following night. 'There is space and I see you have a good sleeping-bag. You will be welcome, the family is big-hearted and they like all foreigners.' Then we slept, as the train jolted gently through the night at cycling speed.

In Ljubljana, early on a cold bright Saturday morning, the few people about were exercising status symbol dogs on high-tech leads: Dobermans, Afghan hounds, Irish setters, borzois, emperor poodles. Everywhere new flags were flying – Slovenian flags. All over the city the atmosphere was friendly and most people I chanced to meet spoke English. A bouncy optimism prevailed, a sense of having escaped to where Slovenes belong, in Western/Central Europe – leaving the Croats and the rest to sort themselves out as best they could. Although it cheered me to meet so many happy folk, I was disquieted by the general indifference to the current sanguinary Croat-Serb conflict. Yet one couldn't reasonably condemn

Slovenia's urge to secede; given its homogeneous population there was no 'minority problem' to be sorted out when Yugoslavia was pulled apart. Economically it had been very important to the Federation, a source of subsidies for the poorer republics and the province of Kosovo, and many Slovenes had long resented this 'sharing' role imposed by Tito on their comparatively rich and industrious little land.

In the market I bought bananas from Haris, a Kosovar (Kosovo Albanian) youth who spoke self-taught English. Serbian discrimination had driven him away, his homeland no longer offered worthwhile jobs to Kosovars. An uncle working in Munich might be able to find him a job there. He didn't want to go to Germany without a job – he was afraid of the police: they might think he belonged to the Kosovo mafia.

I asked, 'Is it OK here – no discrimination?'

Haris shrugged. 'Yes, here too is discrimination, Slovenes never like Albanians. They say for forty years too much of their money was given to Kosovo from Belgrade. But now they will like us because in their independent Slovenia we will give cheap labour for jobs they don't want.'

Winston's friends lived in the old city by the river, in what had once been the coach house, stables and laundry of a seventeenth-century Viennese-style stately urban home, one of many such in the area. An extended family had come together for the festive season and independence euphoria suffused the gathering. The only dissenting voice came from the octogenarian mother of Winston's friend – a tiny person sitting in a corner sipping countless cups of herbal tea, wrapped in an Angora shawl handwoven by herself. She spoke five languages and said to me, apologetically, 'English I find the most difficult.' Her reservations were interesting. 'We are so little, in this modern world we cannot in truth be independent. Someone will control us. Now we want to join the EU and then the EU will kill what makes us Slovene. If Yugoslavia had survived, if we had stayed Yugoslav, we could stay Slovene. People forget too much. They don't see what it means, that Tito was half-Slovene, half-Croat. He did terrible, terrible things – cruel things. I remember, I'm eighty-six years old, I was there. My parents were anti-Tito, anti-Communist, never changing. But I saw, after the bad violent repressive time, he made something good. Now foreigners are saying Yugoslavia was a fake and a failure. But for two generations it was a human success – even if the economy didn't work!'

On another frosty sunny day a ninety-mile bus ride took me to Croatia's capital, Zagreb, through a familiar landscape: pine-forested mountains, red-roofed villages tucked away in narrow valleys, each with its tiny, slim-spired church – and then the flatness of the great Pannonian plain. I had first travelled this road by bicycle in 1963 – then by bus in July 1989, on my way to visit my daughter when she lived in Skopje – and again by bus in March 1990 on my way to Romania. Now, at the brand-new border posts between Slovenia and Croatia, a sense of unreality mingled with grief suddenly overwhelmed me. Momentarily, as I showed my passport and rucksack to smartly uniformed Slovenian and Croatian customs and immigration officers, I felt I was participating in some 'let's pretend' game. The formal international recognition of those two countries was still a fortnight away, but already both governments had asserted their independence and I was a mourner at the wake of Yugoslavia.

Croatia was then a country at war – yet not exactly a *country* (until 15 January 1992), and not exactly at *war*, but under attack by the Federal Yugoslav Army (JNA), which had so recently been the Croat army. No wonder a fearful bewilderment was apparent in Zagreb, muting the celebrations associated with independence.

Seeking a cheap hotel, I fell among mercenaries. The Astoria was at that date the ultimate in sleaze: large and dark, reeking of stale cigarette smoke, dirty bedding and greasy kitchens. Here, apart from staff, I was the only woman among 'volunteers' from all over Europe, outwardly rather jolly young men but with frightening eyes. Several were mere adolescents, most were psychopaths ignorant of the politics behind the conflict, only wanting an excuse to kill. One was Irish, from Dungarvan, near my own home town. Declan had tried the IRA, but finding them too squeamishly selective and ideological about their killings had moved on to Croatia, where there were so many easy targets and so few inhibitions. Others came from the UK, Belgium, France, Germany, Switzerland, Sweden, Australia. A surprising number wanted me to understand that they weren't really mercenaries because if they'd stayed at home, receiving the dole from their respective governments, they would be much better off; fighting Serbs earned only £30 a month, paid in DM. But being at home on the dole was *boring* . . . In 1995 I heard that Declan, having joined Karadžic's Bosnian Serb army, had been killed near Pale. I shall never forget those Astoria breakfasts at a long Formica table seating twenty. Everyone was served with a spoonful of lukewarm scrambled egg on a slice of pallid toast and each man kept his personal weapons beside him. Many gloated over their guns, explaining 'special features' to me; some even stroked them as they might stroke a woman. Two years later, in South Africa, I remembered this platoon as I watched other psychopaths fondling their weapons and listened to them boasting about how many Kaffirs could be killed with one squeeze of the trigger.

In Zagreb, as in Ljubljana, new flags were everywhere to be seen. But alas! Croatia's flag is controversial, not to say provocative. Although its distinctive chequerboard design harks back to the medieval Croatian kingdom, people now associate it with the Nazi-sponsored Ustasha régime which first revived it during the German occupation. Therefore it sent a triumphalist and subliminally threatening message to Croatia's Serb minority. So unpleasant are its associations that even I, an outsider, found it offensive.

Apart from those flags, Zagreb at war in midwinter was uniformly drab. All windows were boarded up and every building had its sandbag defences securely in place. Few people were visible and most of those, including the young women, belonged to the National Guard, the Military Police or some paramilitary force. Only an occasional vehicle broke the unnatural city-centre silence which allowed one to hear, at irregular intervals, the distant boom of artillery or the closer crack of a rifle. A few freelance Serb snipers were still recklessly lurking in corners. The Hotel Intercontinental – the media headquarters – seemed to have extra defences; I had to squeeze crabwise between the main entrance sandbags.

A notice directed me to the Foreign Press Bureau, set up in August 1991 by Mara Letica, President George Bush's choice for the new American Embassy in Zagreb, soon to open. A Croatian American herself, she saw a need for a bureau to provide the world's press with 'objective information' about the source and nature of the conflict, and with 'reliable' interpreters and guides to the front line. Most of the staff of seventy or so were second- and third-generation Croats from the us, Australia and Canada. I was greeted by an effusive young man from Cleveland, pony-tailed and wearing a ski-suit, who offered to escort me to Vukovar for $500 all in. I told him it had never occurred to me to visit that pile of rubble, once among the most beautiful Danubian towns. The young man then delivered his anti-Serb spiel and handed me a bulky folder of cleverly wrought propaganda, containing enough truth to hide its 'spin' from the casual glance of a journalist with a deadline.

The cathedral's delicate spires watch over Zagreb; even when you can't see them you know where they are. In 1880 an earthquake did away with what was, by all accounts, a very fine Gothic cathedral. Its would-be 'Gothic' replacement is rather characterless. Somehow, try as they might, late nineteenth-century stone-masons and sculptors couldn't quite bring it off. Nearby are the turrets of the eighteenth-century, ivy-covered, gloomy Archbishop's Palace. In the precinct nuns pattered to and fro, bearing trays.

Above the impressive choir stalls a list of Zagreb's archbishops begins in 1093/94, the date of the city's founding, when the Hungarian king decided to establish an archbishopric at Zagreb, on the site of a Roman city. This was only forty years after the Rome-Constantinople rupture and the affairs of church and state were inextricably intertwined. In 1102 King Kalman summoned the leaders of Croatia's twelve most powerful clans – who had been causing him a lot of trouble – and suggested a treaty. The Pacta Conventa was duly signed, accepting the Hungarian monarch's rule on condition Croatian traditions and customs were respected. Despite many severe stresses and strains, this pact lasted until 1918, though from 1527 the Habsburgs ruled both Hungary and Croatia. Under Croatian and Hungarian landowners, a harsh form of feudalism developed in the twelfth century and kept Croatia in its grip for more than 600 years. Some observers suggest that this bred a people much less straightforward and self-confident than the Serbs. The Balkan peasantry suffered less, on the whole, under the Ottomans than under Christian masters – a fact often overlooked.

The best-known name on the long list of archbishops is Alojzije Stepinac, whose cult has been rapidly gaining momentum since 1990. Notorious for his failure to oppose the Ustasha in public during the Second World War, whatever his private thoughts may have been, he was arrested in September 1946, charged with various forms of 'collaboration' and sentenced to sixteen years' imprisonment. Five years later this was commuted to house-arrest in his home village if he refused, as he did, to migrate to Rome. He was then made a cardinal, to Tito's fury. However, when he died in 1960 Tito astonished the world by allowing him to be buried, with all the appropriate honours, in his cathedral – which gesture of reconciliation helped to heal many wounds. His defenders present Stepinac as a saintly, compassionate, generous man who saved hundreds of Jewish lives after the destruction of Zagreb's synagogue and the killing of most Croatian Jews. He was also, claim the defence, nervous, naive, confused and entrapped by horrible events beyond his understanding or control. Where have we heard that before? Perhaps the most charitable conclusion is that he was 'compromised by association'.

The Stepinac tomb behind the high altar, complete with effigy, was surrounded by plastic floral tributes and big blazing candles inscribed 'Stop War in Croatia!' I noted that the wall plaque honouring His Eminence had been provided by a group of Detroit-based Croats. Children carrying rosary beads were being brought to pray at the tomb and an elderly woman told me, as she looked down proudly at her nine-year-old grandson, 'He wants the war to go on till he's grown up so he can kill Serbs! Croats have no fear of Milošević and his villains!'

On 3 October 1998 Stepinac was beatified by Pope John Paul II at a ceremony in Zagreb Cathedral, to the delirious acclaim of Croatia's Catholics. Hearing of that event, I remembered my encounter in the cathedral on the morning of New Year's Eve, 1991. In 1998 that boy would have been aged fifteen, probably at the beatification ceremony and still wanting to kill Serbs.

Near the cathedral I watched a giant truck of 'Aid from Italy' being unloaded outside a monastery while a young Franciscan in a long brown habit cine-filmed the process. This aid consisted chiefly of dried milk and household appliances: refrigerators, electric cookers, TV sets. When an air-raid siren sounded the few pedestrians around showed no sign of alarm but strolled towards the nearest shelter, beckoning me to follow. Under a small shop an enormous Romanesque cellar – low arched ceiling, thick pillars, a cobbled floor – had been equipped with plank beds, piles of neatly folded blankets, stacks of crates of mineral water, sacks of potatoes and onions, gas cookers and cylinders, rows of chairs and many boxes of candles. Four hours later, when the siren went again, I found myself in a similar, even bigger cellar and reflected that Zagreb was lucky to have all these medieval hidey-holes available in the city centre. But what happened in the high-rise slums around the edges, where live the majority of citizens? Not that this question seemed urgent; the regular bombing of Zagreb would not have suited Milošević's long term plan. During both those subterranean sessions MIGs passed low over the city and were certainly Serb-flown; Croatia lacked access to Yugoslav air force planes. However, there had been no attack since 7 September, when MIG-fired missiles hit the presidential and parliament buildings. It was no coincidence, everyone asserted, that on that very morning the Croatian parliament was voting for full independence.

Zagreb – long recognized, even by some Serbs, as Yugoslavia's cultural capital – has more than its share of English speakers and in both cellars it was easy to steer the conversation towards Croatia's crisis. One man believed that the US could have quickly ended the war, saving Vukovar and much else, by arming Croatia instead of imposing an arms embargo on the whole of Yugoslavia. His friend nodded agreement and complained that American diplomats in Belgrade had been making pro-Serb noises and opposing the dissolution of Yugoslavia. The longing for more weapons was repeatedly and forcefully expressed – not only by men. 'We have many, many brave soldiers,' one woman assured me, 'but never enough guns and tanks and all that electronic battlefield gear the Serbs make for themselves.' Several people voiced gratitude for Germany's support: 'Our best friends, as they were in the last war.' I wondered how many Croatians under fifty were aware of the nature of the Nazi-Ustasha alliance; Titoism blanked out the atrocities committed by all sides during the Second World War.

No one then knew that in March 1991 Croatia's President Tudjman and Slobodan Milošević had met secretly to discuss the partition of Bosnia-Herzegovina (BiH) and the sharing of the spoils. But even leading politicians' public statements about Serb intentions were, inexplicably, being ignored. In 9 October, in Peć in Kosovo, Mihailo Marković, vice-president of Milošević's Serbian Socialist Party, had made a speech stating Serbia's war aims. 'In the new Yugoslav state there will be at least three federal units: Serbia, Montenegro and a united Bosnia and Knin region. If the Bosnian Muslims wish to remain in the new state they will be allowed to do so. If they try to secede, they must know that the Bosnian Muslims' state will be encircled by Serbian territory.' Had Lord Carrington heeded those words he might have been more effective as the EU's negotiator.

In between sirens I visited the university, boarded up and sandbagged with National Guards patrolling the well-kept grounds. I stopped the only student in sight to ask if outsiders were admitted to the library. 'I'm sorry,' the young man replied, 'not just now, because of the war. You see all those guards, we're afraid of Serb saboteurs. But can I help you? You want to consult some special book?'

Karl was tall, big-boned, handsome in a bland sort of way and studying English and economics. ('They go together, for our future!') On discovering my way of life he exclaimed, 'An author! You are the first I have met who writes in English!' Then he realized that I was alone in Zagreb and looked concerned. 'That's no good, today! This evening you must join my family for our New Year and independence party – come at eight, please. You will meet five generations, from my great-grandmother, aged eighty-eight, to my first nephew, aged eighteen months!' He handed me his father's card and I saw an address in the Gornji Grad, the upper city, in an area I already knew where Habsburg mansions, half hidden by chestnut trees, line the street on one side, overlooking the Donji Grad far below. The 1930s saw most of those mansions converted to expensive flats.

A blackout and a sundown curfew were in operation, neither being very strictly enforced. While it was still light I walked up to the Gornji Grad, found Karl's exact address, then visited the church of St Mark – much more congenial than the cathedral, dating from King Bela's time, though the main structure is four-teenth and fifteenth century.

At 8 p.m. Karl ushered me into a long, high-ceilinged drawing room, its tall windows velvet-curtained, its walls crimson-papered and incongruously damp-patched. In contrast to silent Zagreb's outward gloom, the scene was colourful and animated, hectic with American Christmas decorations and noisy with laugh-ter. Opposite the double doors, at the far end of the room, Great-grandmama could be seen occupying a high-backed oak chair, richly carved – quite throne-like on its slightly raised dais. As Karl led me towards her, through the merry throng, my gaze was fixed in horror on the Führer – a life-sized photograph of Hitler hanging directly above her, its baroque gilt frame draped with the chequer-board flag. Graciously she shook my hand, then glanced upwards and said, 'For forty-five years he was down in the cellar, hidden. But now we are free.' From this I deduced that Great-grandmama had lost most of her marbles; otherwise she would scarcely have chosen thus to open a conversation with a visitor from Irska – or anywhere else. The books and pamphlets later presented to me ('you must write honestly, about Croatia') proved that here was a rare (I hoped) nest of Ustasha left-overs. Several had recently returned permanently from North America or Australia, others were briefly visiting their homeland. All belonged to a dangerous sub-species: exiles or the offspring of exiles who had lost touch with recent political developments, spent too long brooding on past wrongs, real and imaginary, and felt bound to contribute some of their new wealth to an outdated cause. They matched Irish-American supporters of the IRA, British Sikh support-ers of 'a free Punjab' and all those paranoid Cubans in Florida and deranged

Hmong in California. However, not everyone was happy with Hitler as the presiding deity; some would have preferred me to see independent Croatia as a reincarnation of the medieval kingdom, untainted by Ustasha atrocities.

A six-course banquet was served in an elegantly proportioned dining room where Great-grandmama sat at the head of the oval mahogany table opposite her great-great-grandson in his high-chair. He had been given some herbal stimulant to keep him awake for the occasion, a device unnecessary in contemporary Britain or Ireland where toddlers seem to retire only when their parents do. His name – you will have guessed – was Adolf. This banquet looked better than it tasted; most ingredients had been imported by the visitors.

At 11.30 the tape concert began and continued for an hour – an old family tradition, Karl explained. Midnight was not directly acknowledged; Beethoven and Mozart marked the merging of the years (I would have expected Wagner) and this was no mere background entertainment. At twelve o'clock we were listening, reverentially, to a Mozart divertimento for strings. I remember that as the most disorientating aspect of a bizarre evening: my sort of music being so appreciated by four generations of a family who thought Hitler was a hero.

By 2 a.m. I was perilously drunk, verging on footlessness, and my condition was not unique. Several men, women and adolescents lay insensible on sofas, or on the floor in corners, some gently hiccupping in their sleep. Karl asked, 'Do you want to lie down? I think your hotel is not possible.' I smiled gratefully at both Karls (there were two by then, each quite distinct), lay down where I stood and never stirred until after sunrise.

Descending from Gornji Grad, inhaling the clear frosty air of 1992's first day, I felt undeservedly vigorous, having imbibed only wholesome homemade wines and spirits. Surprisingly, Dolac market, near the cathedral, was thronged at 9 a.m. Sturdy elderly women from nearby villages, wearing headscarves, voluminous skirts and layers of sweaters and cardigans, beamed cheerfully behind stalls heaped with their own produce: leeks, potatoes, carrots, beetroot, onions, lettuces. No one else looked in the least cheerful; many faces, young and old, were tired and pallid, many eyes wary, many shopping-bags carried home only half-full after long haggling sessions. In one busy corner, little bottles and packets of herbal medicines stood in long rows on trestle tables, some labelled in English: 'To cure Gastrittis – Angina – Bonkitis – Hemeroidi – Cikulation'. Others mysteriously required exclamation marks: '*Masnoća U Krvl! – Žučni Kamenči! – Šećerna Bolesti!*' Several prominent stalls displayed devotional kitsch and plaster busts in various sizes of 'the Father of the Nation', Franjo Tudjman – a domestic adornment then on sale all over Zagreb.

From Dolac market a long, wide flight of steps leads down to the main square where the city's enviably efficient trams have their terminus. (Why did Dublin get rid of its trams?) Here, at noon, I was to meet Dr B——, a relative by marriage of Winston's friends in Ljubljana. Waiting for him under the tail of Ban Jelačić's charger (this giant equestrian statue is an obvious rendezvous) I gazed around at the Habsburgs' Zagreb – not very much altered – and was again overcome by a sense of deep sadness and foreboding. The dissolution of Yugoslavia felt like a monstrous act of vandalism, a regression that could not possibly benefit the majority of Yugoslavs. So Dr B—— found me in a sombre mood, which was not what he needed.

We sat in a small uncrowded café, candle-lit because the electricity had failed and the windows were sandbagged. Dr B—— was elderly, his bald pate contrasting with bushy eyebrows, his face haggard, his unease evident. Tentatively he asked, 'You are here with some international mission?' It seemed he wanted to communicate but first had to suss me out. So I talked about myself at some length, which is not my wont with strangers, and watched Dr B—— relaxing. Eventually he exclaimed, 'It is strange! When first you visited Zagreb, nearly thirty years ago, I was a student! Now how do you see us? Do the Brussels Europeans really, really believe it is good to end Yugoslavia?'

'I don't know what they believe,' I replied. 'But it's certain they and the us will put their own interests first, here as elsewhere.'

Dr B—— nodded. '*Realpolitik* – the same in every century! The difference now is leaders and institutions pretending to be about something else – "democracy", "human rights", "freedom", "development". In Yugoslavia we had no underground dissident movements, no *samizdat* publications. We didn't need them, we were free to write what we thought *above* ground. Yet now the people in Brussels want the world to think Croatians have been liberated from Communist oppression! We have been fooled, what Tudjman gives us is not democracy, we are less free than under Tito. In his time academics, poets, journalists could debate in public. Under Tudjman we have censorship, not by law but by intimidation which is worse. Even a small criticism of his independent Croatia is condemned as "Yugonostalgia", which equals treason. Because I won't lick his boots I've lost my university post after twenty years . . . I wasn't brave, talking out like a dissident. I was only silent, not praising our "Father"' – he glanced at a bust of Tudjman behind the bar – 'and not filling my students with myths. Or reminding them of the cruel things the Chetniks did to their grandparents.'

Then came Dr B——'s family history. 'My father is a Croat, my mother was a Serb, my wife is Vojvodina Hungarian but her mother was Slovenian – you met the old lady in Ljubljana. This is not unusual but now all mixed families must pretend not to be mixed. We must deny what's real for us. There is a new "reality" today for Croatia – all about nationalism. Tudjman tells us we have been victorious, have fulfilled our 1,000-year-old dream by getting independence. This is crazy! Ten years ago most Croats didn't have such dreams. But you can always

stir up uneducated people and drag them back to tribalism and call it "independence" and make them confused and aggressive. And in Zagreb in these days you
can make too many educated people throw away their integrity and look for
power instead. Or maybe they never had any integrity . . .'

When I described my New Year's Eve party, mentioning no names, Dr B——
grimaced and said, 'I think I know this family! Extremists, yes – but not out of
touch with our new Croatia, only beating the drum louder. Horrible things have
been happening here. The Ustasha régime is being white-washed, made to seem
almost OK. We're told it didn't really collaborate with the Nazis but used them for
the most honourable motive – to free Croatia! Our minds are being poisoned.
And is there an antidote? I don't see where to find it. Independent Croatia wants
"purity", to get rid of all non-Croats, even all half-Croats, like Tito and me!
Everyone not "pure" will have a hard time getting passports in this new sovereign
state, even if they and their ancestors have lived here for centuries. Already
bureaucratic arrangements are being made to purge our dream-come-true of
impurities. This year I am emigrating. To get an academic job at my age, with no
connections, will not be possible. But also for me it's not possible to live with what
Croatia has become. We are told to celebrate our freedom and independence
today but wise people are not wishing each other "Happy New Year!" In 1992 no
part of Yugoslavia can be happy – except maybe Slovenia. For Bosnia, too, if it's
given independence, the writing's on the wall and the letters are written in blood.'

Then Dr B—— invited me home to meet his family. As we walked up to Gornji
Grad he confided, 'A main reason for leaving is our children. They are being
infected, they want to pretend to be "pure", they are believing Croatia, backed by
Germany, will soon be rich. In your countries children go against their parents by
taking drugs, listening to ugly music, making stupid hair styles. In Croatia now
they can do it by believing in Tudjman. For me and my wife this is something to
break our hearts. They have a Novi Sad mother, a Belgrade grandmother – they
are Yugoslavs! If they live here, as "pure" Croats, they must build their lives on
lies.'

The B——s' attic flat was just round the corner from Karl's family's bigger
apartment. Mrs B——, a translator of medical textbooks, seemed to be half
expecting me; doubtless there had been a provisional arrangement. Physically she
bore no resemblance to her diminutive mother in Ljubljana, being tall and wide,
but in strength of personality she matched Mamma. To Dr B——'s annoyance
the boys (aged fifteen and seventeen) had not yet returned from their New Year's
Eve party. Addressing his wife in English he said sharply, 'We should never have
let them go with such people!'

When I asked, 'Could you have prevented them from going?' the B——s stared
at me in surprise and I added, 'In Ireland, now, most parents seem afraid to even
try to control teenagers.' Mrs B—— laughed. 'Here is not so, yet. But we plan to

emigrate and in the US this could be a problem for the next few years. Here when we make rules they sulk for a while – some for days, some for hours. But that is normal, I remember the same in my own adolescence. It is something to be ignored, like the pimples they get. Soon the stage is over and then they are glad they were protected.'

At this point the door opened and the revellers entered, pale with exhaustion and smelling strongly of garlic. They shook my hand and mumbled a greeting before retiring. Mrs B—— chuckled. 'They think the garlic hides the whiskey fumes!' Dr B—— glared in the direction of the boys' bedroom and said nothing. I suspected they might have to deal with more than a hangover when they awoke some time next day.

We drank *slivovitz* and coffee and held a post mortem on Yugoslavia. 'Of course it was artificial eighty years ago,' said Dr B——. 'It was mostly left-over bits and pieces of two empires, with Serbia the longest free of imperial rule – long enough to have got imperial ideas itself. After 1918 everything depended on leadership and the monarchy didn't work.'

'It worked for Serbia,' said Mrs B——. 'That's why we had Chetniks versus Ustashas in World War II. It was Tito's leadership worked for everyone as he created the Yugoslavia we grew up in. Now you can say his creation didn't work, was too dependent on one man. But he did give us a genuine shared identity, though now we're told it was an illusion, a Communist plot to repress us! And who tells us that? The same Croats who were the best Communists a few years ago, when power lay with the Party!'

'But,' said Dr B——, 'Tito hadn't the vision or support to set up structures to hold our identity together, permanently. This is the tragedy, even if most are too confused to see it that way. It hurts to think about it but it's hard to think about anything else – the bits and pieces scattered, what we have in common being denied, what divides us being glorified to justify killing and plundering . . .'

I looked at my watch and reluctantly stood up to go; I needed half an hour to get back to my hotel before curfew time.

Mrs B—— held my hand in both of hers for a moment and said, 'Don't get wrong ideas from talking to us. We're not typical. If we were, Yugoslavia couldn't be killed.'

Much bloody water was to pass under many bridges before my return to Zagreb, en route for Serbia, on 18 October 1999.

PART II

1999
Serbia

2

Belgrade as the Dust Settled

In September 1999, when I decided to tour dismembered Yugoslavia, the delightful duties of grandmotherhood dictated the shape of my journey. Because a third grandchild was to be born in Ireland in December, I would spend an autumn month in urban Serbia (Belgrade, Niš, Novi Sad), travelling by bus and train. Then home to welcome the infant, and at the end of February, when the snows were melting, my three-month pedal around Croatia, BiH, Montenegro, Albania and Kosovo could begin.

As Serbia was then in the 'international community's' dog-house, the only passenger flight to Belgrade departed from Prague – so said various reputable travel agencies. But a friend warned me that even starting from there passengers not travelling 'in an official capacity' were forbidden access by air. As a tourist I would have to take a London–Zagreb Eurobus, followed by a Croatian bus to the Serbian border, and a Serbian bus to Belgrade. And my visa, where should I seek it? The same knowledgeable friend directed me to the Cyprus High Commission, which at the time seemed odd. Enlightenment came later; Slobodan Milošević and his cronies had a special relationship with certain Cypriot banks.

Next morning, en route to the Cyprus High Commission, I had a lucky escape. At 11 a.m., while walking through the Hyde Park underpass carrying a small briefcase in my left hand, I was attacked from behind by two large youths. One caught my left leg and jerked it backwards. The other caught my right arm and did likewise while removing a purse, holding only a few coins, from an open jacket pocket. As I fell flat on my briefcase a young man sprinted to the rescue, releasing an Alsatian from its chain. The dog barked, the youths fled, the young man helped me to my feet. Then he handed me my briefcase, containing DM2,000 and US$1,000. Had the youths not attacked me, but seized the briefcase while racing past, their enterprise would have been well rewarded. Going on my way, I discerned a certain parallel with Nato's bombing of Kosovo and Serbia – disproportionate violence proving counterproductive.

In a bleak little corner of the High Commission ('The Yugoslav Special

Interests Section') I was alone. Someone had admitted me by remote control but for long minutes no one appeared. The place seemed to be in a state of suspended animation; no sound could be heard, the windowless walls lacked tourist posters, the little plastic-topped table lacked tourist brochures, two desks behind a glass partition lacked telephones and computers. I sat on a metal camp-chair and registered the fact that my right shoulder socket felt rather sore.

Eventually an impassive middle-aged Serb emerged from a rear office and greeted me unenthusiastically. As he listened to my request for a thirty-day tourist visa incredulity replaced impassivity. He stared into my eyes, searchingly, and asked, '*Why* do you want to be a tourist, *now*, in Yugoslavia?'

Truthfully I replied, 'To see for myself how things are, *now*, for ordinary Serbs. In Ireland many were horrified by Nato's bombing of your country.' This was an occasion for being economical with the truth so I did not add that in Ireland everyone was horrified by Milošević's forces' brutality towards the Kosovars.

'Your profession?' asked the official.

'Retired school teacher,' I blandly replied – a lie tried and tested in several other similarly delicate situations.

The official requested my passport (no photograph required) and £15 in cash, then handed me a form which asked some unusual questions. 'State military rank', 'state position in your firm/organisation/church/government service'. Then came a potential major snag: 'Enclose letter of invitation/introduction from your contact in Yugoslavia'.

I looked up at the official and explained, 'I've no letter, I know no one in Yugoslavia.' Again he stared into my eyes, rather as a doctor might when seeking the first signs of jaundice. After a moment's hesitation he reached forward to take the form and disappeared – to reappear less than ten minutes later with my visa.

The Consul followed: tall, handsome, broad-shouldered, with thick wavy grey hair and a relaxed air. He asked, 'Are you a journalist?'

'No,' I replied.

The Consul gazed at the ceiling and stated, 'Journalism is not allowed. Photography is not allowed.' He lowered his eyes, smiled at me with genuine warmth, bowed slightly and withdrew.

Out on the street, I wondered why my implausible story had been so readily accepted. Did those men really believe I was a retired teacher moved by sympathy for Nato's victims to spend a month in a country where I knew nobody and could expect no tourist comforts or conveniences? Or were they closet opposition supporters scenting a journalist who might put their viewpoint across? Or did they simply covet that modest visa fee?

*

At some stage between 1992 and 1999 Zagreb's squalidly shambolic bus station had become a vast and glitzy terminus-cum-shopping mall. Teutonic in its cleanliness and precise organization, it made Victoria's refurbished coach station seem like a poor relation. Arriving at 2.30 a.m., after a 28-hour Eurobus journey, I was able at once to buy my onward ticket (DM30) for the 5.30 a.m. coach to the Serbian border. Then I stretched out on the floor in a corner, as far as possible from the multiple TV sets, and slept for two hours.

Beyond Zagreb's dreary suburban high-risery, the eastern horizon glowed orange and soon a distended crimson sun was poised on the edge of the world – then seemed to be pulled swiftly up by some invisible string. Hoar frost glistened on expanses of new ploughland, on dark fields of dead maize stalks, on uncultivated patches of wasteland, on small conifer woods and double lines of stately wayside pines. I glimpsed a few long-abandoned, war-damaged homes but most villages lie far from the *autoput*. This boringly straight motorway from Zagreb to Belgrade was officially named 'the Brotherhood and Unity highway' when first constructed in the 1940s. Now it is a smooth toll road sporting the standard EU-type signs seen from Uganda to Laos, from Calabria to Connemara – wherever the road construction industry has seized the landscape in its destructive talons.

Approaching the border many red ribbons appeared, fluttering on sticks stuck in the verge, warning of areas still mined. Our posh new coach was carrying only seven other passengers, all elderly women bound for Belgrade, and at the Croat border each passport was closely scrutinized before we were allowed to cross the mile-long no man's land to a small shabby Serbian bus. Halfway we met its score of ill-dressed passengers, their eyes fixed on the ground as they walked towards our luxury coach. Nearby, between borders, stood a queue of twenty-two white vehicles belonging to the International Committee of the Red Cross (ICRC), mostly enormous articulated trucks but tapering off to minibuses and jeeps. Without them, I was to discover, the plight of the tens of thousands of displaced persons in Serbia (from Croatia, BiH and Kosovo) would be even more desperate.

At the Serbian immigration office I half-expected trouble; owing to a clerical error my visa entry date was 19 October – the next day. Several grim-faced police and immigration officers showed considerable interest in my passport, yet the policeman who took it away to be stamped seemed not to notice the date.

By then I was heartily sick of bus travel and longing to walk; a compact mini-rucksack held my luggage for the month. But probably walking was *verboten* in this area; the newness of these Balkan borders makes them seem extra-precious to their protectors. I therefore pretended, when the conductor came around, that I had assumed my Zagreb-bought ticket to be valid all the way to Belgrade, where dinars awaited me. Scowling and muttering, the conductor at once ejected me in the middle of nowhere. Joyously I walked on, reflecting that this ploy couldn't work in any Asian or African country where an apparently penniless foreigner might well be subsidized by fellow-passengers and would certainly not be put off the bus.

The warm noon sun had energized a glorious variety of butterflies and on my right burning maize stubble made hazy the cloudless sky. Some cultivated fields were scarred by irregular red-flagged mined patches. The traffic flow was bearable, mainly Hungarian holidaymakers going to and from Greece and ramshackle local cars. None of the few trucks was a TRS though this is the main road from northern to southern Europe, *en route* for the Middle East – and indeed for India. Several small roads, linking villages, crossed the *autoput* on stark concrete bridges, spray-painted with Chetnik symbols. Pedestrians avoid the *autoput* and I met only an elderly, heavily moustached shepherd, wearing the ragged remnants of the Montenegrins' traditional garb and lying on the verge beside a small black sheepdog. His fifty or so curly-horned sheep were cropping the short, tough grass of the long acre. Urgently he begged a cigarette and growled imprecations when disappointed. I wondered about his story; on this immense arable plain he and his flock looked ill at ease. The only other visible livestock were an occasional pair of bony black-and-white milking cows tethered by the wayside.

At 1.30 a startling building came into view, dwarfing a one-pump petrol station and a closed mini-market. The external décor was of shiny squares and oblongs of different sizes, painted red, black, green, blue, yellow. This was the Motel Sava, and after two almost sleepless bus nights it tempted me. There was no one around but I found an open door and tentatively explored. A room some twenty feet by thirty had a grey tiled floor and metal bas-reliefs of gigantic mythical fish on the bile-green walls. A small bar, its shelves bare, occupied one corner and opposite the door three plastic garden chairs stood dangerously close to a huge, antique electric fire, all its bars glowing. In the adjacent foyer, high-ceilinged and windowless, hundreds of folding tables and chairs were stacked to one side; evidently the Motel Sava had been designed to double as a conference centre. A wide mock-marble stairway led to large unfurnished landings and long corridors off which opened many stale-smelling bedrooms with naked mattresses. Synthetic carpeting, strewn with dead or dying flies, covered every floor.

Returning downstairs, I became aware of a strange snorting rumble that echoed throughout the empty foyer. On a long table in a far corner my host (I presumed) lay asleep under a rough brown army blanket – why, amidst so many empty beds? It would have been unkind to rouse him, so I returned to the electric fire and awaited developments, wishing the bar shelves were not bare.

Half an hour later the snorer awoke. A tallish, blond, middle-aged man, he was at first completely thrown by my presence but recovered rapidly and proved to be a kindly character. Soon I was drinking very hot Turkish coffee and a generous shot of *rakija*, then Sandar disappeared to make up a bed. No one else was visible in the Motel Sava, either then or during the evening.

From my bedroom window I could see the large village of Sašinci, some two miles away beyond fifty-acre fields where haystacks had been built around tall poles and maize neatly stooked. To the west, a grey-brown smudge above factory chimneys marked Sremska Mitrovica, once among the Roman Empire's main cities – known to Pliny as 'Sirmium' and the birthplace of four Roman Emperors. During the recent forcible uprootings it was overwhelmed by Displaced Persons and became the site of a major humanitarian relief effort.

In an *en suite* bathroom my filthy water was resolutely retained by the hand-basin and all night the lavatory refused to stop flushing itself. The plumbing was original; one pulled on a two-foot-long half-circle of thick rubber sticking out from the wall at head height. Balkan plumbers are renowned for their ingenuity. I decided not to experiment with the shower.

Downstairs again, I was soon revived by a pile of crusty warm white bread and a plate of my favourite Balkan delicacy, thinly sliced smoked raw bacon fat. Then I followed a narrow, potholed road to Sašinci, marvelling at the number of local cars in action; plainly sanctions-busting was not proving too difficult. Around Sašinci's outskirts several large, two-storey houses were being built with family and neighbours' labour, using yellowish bricks, plastered and painted white. All had red-tiled roofs, carved wooden balconies over the hall doors, outside wooden shutters. The general effect – vaguely Swiss/Austrian/ Bavarian – was an improvement on Ireland's pretentious bungaloid rash. An Orthodox church in the traditional style had recently been built on the periphery, but the whole village (population 2,500) was dominated by its grain silo, thrice the height of the church.

The towns and villages of this vast Pannonian Plain enjoy the luxury of space, village streets often extending for a few miles. Sašinci was typical, its roomy one- or two-storey homes surrounded by fruit and vegetable gardens and farmyards with ancient, well-maintained outbuildings. I saw only one hovel, dating from the 1930s, and no luxury 'villas' – which quite neatly sums up Tito's legacy in rural Yugoslavia. A few tiny shops sold such basics as salt, sugar, coffee, cigarettes; even now Sašinci seemed at least semi-self-sufficient. Before 1991, it would have been much more so. Traditionally this region sustained huge flocks of sheep and geese and herds of free-range pigs and numerous working horses.

Nobody smiled at me in Sašinci; only a few awkwardly acknowledged my greetings. Women wearing calf-length skirts and headscarves were helping to unload trailers of maize cobs; those unfit for human consumption were thrown to the ground and collected by children as animal fodder. Serbia's birthrate has long been declining and not many youngsters were visible, but those few looked cheerful and healthy, unlike their urban contemporaries. In most gardens fig trees flourished, hens pecked around shrubs, vines on trellises provided shade for *al fresco* summer meals. One old woman, bent double, crossed the street with her hands behind her back, dressed all in black and looking like a caricature of the Balkan peasant granny with her deeply lined, yellow-brown face and red-rimmed blue eyes – half-scared eyes, as she peered up at the stranger. Stopping outside her home to talk to a neighbour, she got a tremendous welcome from a black-and-white cat who squeezed under the gate and repeatedly stood on his/her hindlegs to head-rub the old woman's knee. Feline ceremonies know no boundaries.

As I returned to Motel Sava wood-smoke scented the air and the red-gold glow along the western horizon seemed infinitely far away. Sandar's friendliness countered the suspiciously staring population of Sašinci. Next morning he brewed me another little brass jug of excellent coffee, yet I was charged only for my bed (DM10) and given a farewell gift of two notebooks advertising 'Fresh International Company, Slovenia'.

The previous morning's hoar frost should have prepared me for that morning's low dark sky and relentless rain, driven by an icy south-east wind. Until 9 a.m. I sat by the heater, waiting for a 7.15 bus that never came. Then Sandar advised me to hitch-hike from the petrol station. Moments after taking up my position under the meagre shelter of its porch I was invited into a cubby-hole office by two men in blue dungarees who offered me the only chair and became effusively friendly on hearing 'Irska'.

One declaimed angrily: 'Nato, the US, the UK are *fascist!*' They spoke enough English to convey that they saw the IRA as heroes and Ireland as the enemy of England and therefore the friend of Nato-bombed Serbia. For once I didn't try to put the IRA in context. As anti-Nato allies we vigorously shook hands while I felt hypocritical, knowing my country to be on the eve of joining Nato's so-called Partnership for Peace (yet another example of the militarists' abuse of the English language).

Forty minutes passed before a car stopped. When my companions asked the driver to rescue me he at first seemed reluctant; both men had to plead hard (I noticed them using my Irishness) before he relented. A lean, dark, handsome Bulgarian, he was driving home from Frankfurt where he worked as a construction company foreman. Although we were able to communicate quite freely he evaded any discussion of Balkan politics, preferring to talk about Northern Ireland and East Timor.

Near Belgrade a few gigantic billboards – mostly in English, advertising cars – could be discerned through the curtain of rain. Novi Beograd looked even grimmer than usual under its dark grey cloud lid. Just beyond the Gazela bridge over the Sava, I was put down amidst raucous traffic and the sick-making fumes of adulterated smuggled petrol. A graffiti-daubed pedestrian underpass, reeking of urine, took me on to a feeder road and twenty minutes later, chilled to the marrow and soaked to the skin, I found a taxi rank. Drivers were sipping coffee in a round yellow kiosk and one young man offered me a cup, then agreed to take me to the Hotel Beograd for 30 dinars (less than £2).

Mika, a maths graduate who could find no appropriate job, spoke almost perfect English and recalled that during the airwar Serbian TV had shown Europe's anti-Nato demos again and again and again. Here my tale becomes improbable but is true. After only a brief conversation Mika glanced sideways at me and exclaimed, 'I think I know your voice! You talked against Nato in some Irish city where that Clinton woman was being given publicity – am I right?'

I affirmed his memory; I had indeed spoken at a protest meeting in May 1999 when Mrs Clinton was being given the Freedom of the City of Galway.

Said Mika, 'Here ordinary Serbs are suffering so much – for what? Who gains by our suffering? What aim does it achieve? Why are we being punished? And what will happen next? Many fear a terrorist campaign run by Nato and the CIA – so they can have Serbia as well as Kosovo!'

The Hotel Beograd (Category B) is huge and old, its shabbiness cosy, its weary-looking staff pleasant in a low-key way, its tariff £9 for B&B. An unvarying break-fast was served from 6 to 9 a.m.: one cup of warm weak tea, a dull bread bun with a pat of margarine and a plastic potlet of synthetic jam. My small fourth-floor room looked on to a badly cracked gable wall scarcely three yards away. At dusk, through its several uncurtained, broken windows, people could be observed cooking on tiny stoves in overcrowded rooms.

The sky had cleared by noon but the wind remained cold as I walked up Balkanska Street towards the Centar. Writing in the late 1960s, J.A. Cuddon, a devoted Yugophile, had to admit: 'Belgrade is really one of the drabbest of cap-itals.' In the interval nothing has happened to change that but a lot has happened to change the people, described by Mr Cuddon as 'delightful: vivacious and ener-getic, hospitable and extremely independent'.

My daily experiences were to confirm the importance of being Irish. Repeatedly, throughout Serbia, my addressing a stranger in English provoked hostility – occasionally extreme hostility (even hatred), sometimes a silent stare of disgust before the person moved on, most often a contemptuous dismissive shrug. This was unsurprising, four months after the end of Nato's bombardment; Serbs cannot be expected readily to identify an Irish accent. In normal circumstances it might be considered eccentric to preface all encounters – asking directions, ordering a beer in a bar, enquiring about train times – with the explanation 'I come from Ireland'. But this did work magic. Tito was a founder of the Non-Aligned Movement and many Serbs were aware of Ireland's honourable record as a non-aligned state. They had not yet heard the news about our desertion to the Nato/arms industry alliance.

My first need was to change money. Peering into a few twilit city-centre banks – hideous multi-storeyed edifices with glass walls – I could see, amidst groves of dusty, towering potted palms, two or three clerks chatting on mobile phones. Around them stretched shadowy empty spaces and lines of closed customer grilles. All the outside doors were securely locked.

At the tourist information office in the Terazije underpass-cum-shopping mall a helpful woman, who was snoozing when I arrived, gave me a free map of the city showing all the embassies. Nato should have contacted her in March 1999 and thus avoided its embarrassing strike on the Chinese embassy. An English-language brochure entitled 'What's On This Week in Belgrade' seemed gallantly optimistic; there were no English-speaking – or any other – tourists visible in Belgrade during that or the following weeks. Apologizing for the locked banks, this underworked woman informed me that the day's rate of exchange was 17 dinars to the DM and a reliable place to change money was the yellow metal kiosk of a locksmith at a nearby street junction. There an obliging young man agreed to 17 without hesitation and the deed was quickly done. A few days later the rate was 15, and a few days after that, 22. This fluctuating unofficial rate became mysteriously known to everyone early each morning while the official rate remained steady at 6 dinars. Haggling was not in order, though usual elsewhere when 'changing on the black', which suggested that the indigenous *mafia* had a firm grip on the economy. Even government departments were changing money on the streets, to my naive astonishment.

At first the many stores displaying expensive goods puzzled me. Elegant gowns, handmade shoes, trendy trainers, Persian carpets, gold-plated bathroom fittings, sparkling cut glass, high-tech tool kits, elaborate leather dog-harnesses, fancy boxes of biscuits and chocolates – sanctions, *what* sanctions? But then I noticed that all such stores were empty of customers, while on the pavements little groups wistfully window-shopped. The effect was surreal: so many pairs of good-looking, chain-smoking saleswomen, the majority English-speaking graduates, sitting idle amidst this abundance of imported (by money-launderers) luxuries. In contrast, the non-luxury stores had almost bare shelves; in one I bought a £4 umbrella from a timid girl who was lunching off a dry bread roll and a mug of instant coffee.

Three young saleswomen in a large, understocked bookshop had no inhibitions about describing themselves as Otpor supporters (anti-Milošević activists); the movement had been started by university students. We talked at length and I invited them to dine with me that evening but the only one free to accept failed to appear. This was the first of several such broken appointments, with no explanation given though all concerned had my telephone number. But I did not take offence. In the autumn of 1999 Belgrade's was a population under stress: impoverished, often to the point of hunger, sometimes doing two or three jobs within twenty-four hours, facing an uncertain (many felt a hopeless) future and too exhausted at the end of the day to enjoy social occasions. Also, in some cases, I suspected a proud reluctance to accept hospitality that could not be returned. My previous journeys through or visits to the Balkans had left me with grateful memories of the ordinary people's spontaneous generosity.

During that night I heard odd sounds – a mournful rattling and sharp discordant flapping noise. Next morning I observed their source: a gusty wind was romping with vast plastic sheets insecurely draped over the bomb-ravaged Ministry of Defence, Ministry of Foreign Affairs and Federal Police headquarters. Hundreds of Venetian blinds swung to and fro in the empty window spaces of an adjacent six-storey apartment block. The government buildings were being slowly repaired but the flats were irreparable; they could only be razed and replaced. Their ruins looked like a major public hazard: huge unstable slabs of reinforced concrete hung over pavements again strewn with glass fragments dislodged by the gale. Along Kneza Miloša Street many tall buildings had boarded-up windows but were otherwise apparently undamaged. Surveying Belgrade's numerous bomb-scars, I marvelled that 'only' 1,000 or so civilians had been killed by Nato. 'Murdered', the Serbs insisted, refusing to concede that 'manslaughter' might be a more appropriate charge. For this one can hardly blame them. As the French army commander, Philippe Morillon, exclaimed during Unprofor's Bosnia campaign, 'Who are these soldiers who are ready to kill and not ready to die?'

By a happy coincidence, Belgrade's International Book Fair was opening on my second day in the city. Given Serbia's pariah status, the '99 Fair was not very stimulating but it did give me an opportunity to meet English-speakers *en masse*.

I followed wide, dreary streets to the Fairgrounds on the right bank of the Sava, passing Belgrade's multi-storeyed Clinical Centre, once the pride and joy of Yugoslavia's medical profession. The bomb damage done to the urology and gynaecology departments and the central pharmacy was still visible. A baby had been born exactly ten minutes before the labour ward was hit by one of Nato's numerous 'straying' missiles, which killed four patients.

Finding myself outside the Fairgrounds with an hour to spare I walked uphill towards Topčider Park through once-prosperous suburbs. Fine houses stood in now neglected gardens, skips overflowing with stinking garbage were parked on every street, weeds and litter blocked the footpaths. There was little motor traffic; those going to work were hurrying down the steep hills to their trolley-bus stops. Passing a nineteenth-century villa, previously the Moroccan Embassy, I noticed on the stucco façade two bas-reliefs representing what seemed at first glance to be couples of naked flirting Lesbians. But doubtless the artist had a cleaner mind than mine.

Punctually at 10 a.m. the Book Fair opened, without speeches or ceremony, in one of a complex of enormous exhibition halls. Entrance was free, though one had to present a pointless ticket, obtained from a roadside stall without any check on ID documents – a prime example of the Balkan countries' lingering addiction to Tito-time bureaucracy. Despite the sanctions constraint the atmosphere was more lively than anywhere else in Belgrade and many with whom I talked were surprisingly open about their longing to get rid of Milošević. Yet there was a dearth of constructive political thinking. As one young man put it, 'We seem to have ten or maybe twenty opposition factions who can't get anything together.' His companion was more prescient. She said, 'Right now we're bomb-shocked. But the Americans are dollar-backing the opposition and Soros is on the scene – I mean his cheque-book is. That sort of intervention unites factions.'

To make up for the withdrawal of foreign support, locally published books had been thinly spread over scores of stalls – often many copies of the same book. Happily a few brave spirits (OUP, Longmans Educational and McGraw Hill) had defied international disapproval and reduced their prices for the occasion. Eager students and medical specialists thronged their stalls, the majority unable to afford even one volume but swotting hard for hours on end to bring themselves up to date on recent developments in their respective fields. No less popular were the numerous volumes giving advice on every aspect of the free market to would-be entrepreneurs. The only other foreign publications came from Iran; in that stall two scholarly young men were happy to discuss Persian and Moghul art in Serbo-Croat or English, though they must have known they had no hope of selling their beautifully produced coffee-table volumes.

Several stalls dedicated to Serbian art attracted little interest. One amiable elderly art publisher, recently reduced to importing second-hand clothes from Austria and selling them on the street, invited me to take a seat and drink coffee. Then his assistant arrived – Sophia, a tall, slender, dark-eyed art student from Novi Sad, of Serb-Hungarian parentage. We talked at length, the publisher lamenting his being unable to enter Croatia without a visa – then almost impossible to get. 'For me and most of my generation this is the hardest thing to bear. We're cut off from what we still think of as part of our own country. How would you feel if you couldn't visit a big part of Ireland where you had many friends and relatives and in-laws? I am one of Tito's children – first a Yugoslav, second a Serb. There are many like me, now afraid to admit it.'

Mr X—— was convinced that the Great Powers had longed to see the break-up of Yugoslavia and had expedited it. 'Our country showed how socialism could work well enough for most citizens without Soviet-style repression. The free market and consumerism and democracy – what have they done for Russia?'

Sophia, aged twenty, flatly asserted that whenever the opposition leaders gained power they would prove to be as corrupt as Milošević & Co. 'Surely not!' I exclaimed. 'But surely yes!' retorted Sophia. 'We've no structures in place to control and punish corruption. And those structures can't be quickly made.' In her view, Nato's attack had done something for the Serbs' morale by giving their favourite 'victim' posture more credibility: all the world knew how unjustly they had been punished for the crimes of their leaders.

By sunset I had a list of eleven addresses and telephone numbers, most of which proved productive over the weeks ahead. And one bore fruit on the following day when Bogdan, a recently graduated chemist, escorted me to Pančevo, his grimly industrialized home town some ten miles north-east of Belgrade.

Should justice ever prevail, and Nato's 1999 leaders find themselves lodging in The Hague Tribunal's guest-wing, Pančevo will head the list of Serbian cities whose bombing constituted indirect chemical warfare and was therefore criminal, according to the Geneva Conventions. Other severely poisoned towns were Kragujevac, Bor and Novi Sad. A report submitted to Kofi Annan by the United Nations Environment Programme (UNEP) and the United Nations Centre for Human Settlements (UNCHS) emphasized how urgently clean-ups were needed because of the airwar's long-term environmental consequences. But Serbia, its state coffers grievously depleted by Milošević & Co., could not possibly afford thorough clean-ups.

Early morning clouds hung low and grey as I walked to meet Bogdan at the 108 bus terminus near the Omladinski Stadium. He was there before me, a slim young man with jet black hair and large brown eyes in a long, thin, sallow face. As No. 108 rattled slowly across dull flat land, he criticized Belgrade's Public Institute of Health, a Department of the Serbian Health Ministry, for making light of Nato's pollution legacy – though local doctors had warned all women who were in Pančevo on 18–19 April to avoid pregnancy for at least two years. And all who at that date had been in the first two months of pregnancy were advised to abort their babies. Vehemently Bogdan declared, 'The government won't admit Nato did so much damage. And it doesn't want to put off foreigners who might invest here when things get normal.'

Pančevo can never have been beautiful and post-bombing it looked like the Tenth Circle of Hell. First we walked by a reeking, litter-clogged canal linking the South Zone Industrial Complex to the Danube. Into it were released, on that April night, 300 tons of sodium hydroxide and 100 tons of carcinogenic vinyl chloride monomer from the Petrohemija factory. It has been estimated that to decontaminate the canal and its banks would cost at least DM43 million.

'Nato wasn't punishing only *us*,' said Bogdan. 'More than ten millions in different countries depend on the Danube for drinking water. Fish died all the way down to the Black Sea. On 19 April the sun never got through the thick fog all over Pančevo – not a natural coloured fog. Our ecotoxicologists tested it. They found concentrates of vinyl chloride, naphtha, dioxins, ammonia – 10,600 times above human safety limits. That day thousands of people were falling around dizzy and vomiting. We were told to soak our scarves in sodium bicarbonate and use them for face masks. The vinyl chloride plant was bombed twice. Clouds of gas and smoke went up hundreds of metres and also held phosgene, hydrochloride acid and ethylene dichloride. And 250 tons of liquid ammonia were thrown into the air.'

By then we had left the canal and were passing the grotesquely twisted remains of one of Europe's biggest fertilizer factories. By chance Nato's bombers missed some of its gigantic warehouses. We paused and Bogdan pointed out the colossal storage tanks, holding 20,000 tons of ammonia. Had those been hit the scale of the disaster would have decisively exposed OAF's 'humanitarian' label as counterfeit and abruptly ended the airwar.

As we lunched in Bogdan's parents' flat his chemical engineer father mentioned an even narrower escape. Thirteen massive oil and petrol slicks on the Danube – one fifteen miles long and 400 yards wide – had threatened Europe's least reliable nuclear power plant at Kozloduy, in Bulgaria. The workers had only thirty minutes to avert a meltdown caused by oily sludge thickening the cooling water.

Father's main personal concern was the eight tons of mercury saturating the soil around the petrochemical plant. Its employees were frantically attempting a clean-up with pumps, to prevent the mercury sinking deeper, into the underground water system. But in four months they had recovered little more than a ton.

Bogdan's mother, also a chemical engineer, described the widespread sense of shocked disbelief when Nato began to bomb indiscriminately – oil refineries, power plants, civilian factories, road and railway bridges. Then, all over Serbia, damage limitation became the priority; plants were closed, chemicals neutralized if possible. However, in Pančevo and elsewhere more desperate remedies were sometimes needed – such as releasing 1,400 tons of carcinogenic ethylene dichloride into the Danube lest a bomb might cause it to explode. Apartment blocks stood less than 150 yards from its storage site. From the same petrochemical plant, 800 tons of hydrochloride acid, 3,000 tons of lye and large deposits of mercury also entered the river. Could there be any connection between those catastrophes and the case of the Lechevo babies? Between October 1999 and July 2000 ten babies were born in the Bulgarian village of Lechevo, near the Serbian border. Eight were 'imperfect' – *very* imperfect. Two died, mercifully, during their first month.

I well remember Nato's excuse for attacking Pančevo so relentlessly. Such 'strikes' were necessary to 'degrade' Milošević's 'war-machine'. By then Nato's commanders were no longer 'protecting' Kosovars but tearing Serbia apart. And their *degraded* form of militarism, using cluster bombs, depleted uranium and indirect chemical warfare, means that for decades to come the Serbs and their neighbours will continue to be punished for the crimes of the Milošević régime.

On our return journey I told Bogdan about a World Service broadcast heard at 1 a.m. on 18 June, eight days after the end of the airwar. Three political commentators were considering how 'the Balkan war' had affected various Alliance leaders' reputations. For President Clinton, after that initial trying controversy about ground troops, it had been 'a good war', casualty-free and 'impressively projecting US power'. For Prime Minister Blair it had been 'a *very* good war', he had stood out as the most resolute and inspiring Alliance leader. For Herr

Schröder it had been 'a good and timely war', enabling him to prove himself 'master of the German Greens'.

'Where are we at,' I demanded despairingly of my companion, 'when "success" in international affairs is measured by the image-enhancement of national leaders, regardless of human suffering?'

'We're at somewhere very frightening,' Bogdan sombrely replied. Then he added, 'Now only nuclear weapons can protect countries from the us. I thought before the bombing India and Pakistan were wrong to make those – after '89 I wanted nuclear disarmament. Now I know they were right. If we'd had even one small Hiroshima-sized bomb – the sort we could get to Rome or Munich – Nato would never have attacked us.'

In Serbia I often felt again that heart-clutching fear first experienced during the airwar. It was (is) a rational fear of an out-of-control rogue superpower. And it is heightened by the ease with which most people were misled into accepting the relentless bombing of Serbia as 'a humanitarian intervention'. We were being shocked and angered by TV-reinforced graphic accounts of the suffering of Kosovo's Albanians. What to do? How could it be right to allow that suffering to continue? Those misfortunates needed help and surely it was Nato's duty to ride (fly) to the rescue? Yet on 27 March (Day Three) Nato's Commanding Officer, General Wesley Clark, admitted that it was 'entirely predictable' that Serbian attacks on Kosovo's Albanians would increase once the bombing began. He said, 'The military authorities fully anticipated the vicious approach that Milošević would adopt, as well as the terrible efficiency with which he would carry it out.'

Here we see the sheer absurdity of the Alliance's political leaders' claim that Operation Allied Force was launched 'to avert a humanitarian catastrophe'. Or are we to deduce that those leaders didn't listen to their own military authorities?

Recalling the confusion that prevailed at the time, among both pro- and anti-Nato commentators, one marvels at our failure to perceive relevant inconsistencies. Turkey, a Nato member, has over the years inflicted on its Kurdish minority cruelties similar to but far exceeding Milošević's forces' cruelties in Kosovo. The us has supplied Turkey with weaponry specific to the task of forcibly uprooting Kurdish villagers – and successive us administrations, through their embassy in Ankara, have vigorously dissuaded outsiders from investigating this brutality.

As for 'What to do?', Noam Chomsky recommends following the Hippocratic principle. If nothing constructive can be achieved through action – *do no harm*. Have the wisdom to *do nothing*. Had oaf not happened, the extent of human suffering would have been far less. In Vietnam, today, thousands born since 1975 are the permanently disabled victims of the Pentagon's campaign of deliberate environmental pollution.

*

When I first met Milica at the Book Fair she wryly described herself as a 'Serb half-breed', before introducing me to her octogenarian mother – in charge of a Belgrade publisher's stall and charming in a twinkly downright way. Later we met for a beer in the Fairground restaurant and it emerged that Milica's Croat father came of a rich bourgeois family, asset-stripped by the Communists in 1945. Having escaped to Canada, he in due course met his Serb wife and begat Milica. But a war wound went wrong ('something internal') and after his death in 1960 mother and daughter returned to Belgrade. 'My mom had never settled in Toronto, was always homesick for Yugoslavia – and now it's taken from her.'

A few days later I visited mother and daughter in their cramped untidy home, a solitary stone cottage in a street of concrete apartment blocks. The date 1895 was still legible above the hall door. 'Why was this not knocked down?' wondered Milica. 'Who can tell? Maybe there's some superstition tied to it, protecting it. Even when they became Communists the Serbs stayed superstitious – it's easier to scare them with a ghost-story than a machine gun!' As I enjoyed a wedge of apple tart and a glass of cherry juice, both made by Mom, an over-fed, meticu-lously groomed golden collie laid his head hopefully on my knee and ingratiat-ingly wagged his feathery tail.

'I should confess right off,' said Milica, lighting yet another cigarette. 'I work for State TV, so I support Milošević as well as hating him. I help to lie to the public to make it easier to control them. I'm not proud of that but what to do? If I left this job on principle us two would be eating out of trash cans. As it is, we've not been paid for two months. But being in jobs we can borrow from Romanian money-lenders. Most professional people are unemployed now. The government can't or won't pay them and private sector jobs are limited.'

'Usually limited to our *mafia* members,' added Mom, who had been an active supporter of 'Women in Black'. Throughout 1998 groups of black-clad mothers organized angry street protests against Milošević's counter-insurgency methods in Kosovo. 'For a while we rattled the government,' Mom recalled. 'They could see the significance of mothers of young Yugoslavs not wanting them to lose their lives killing and terrorizing other Yugoslavs. But we lost support when Nato's bombing threats started, last autumn, just a year ago. Surely that wasn't what Nato expected! But most of us didn't want to be seen siding with people who were shouting about attacking us.'

During the bombing, Milica couldn't use the crowded shelters because dogs were not admitted. A similarly constrained neighbour, owner of two cherished beagles, was one night flung out of his bed by the force of a nearby blast. Milica was then on duty at the TV station where the night staff made Shep the collie welcome. Most people, she said, became remarkably stoical or fatalistic as the bombing intensified. 'We soon learned how to "place" the sites of explosions, then family and friends kept ringing one another to check if all were safe. We could hear glass shattering from a long way off, I don't know why that sound travels such distances. No one needed official pressure to make them lead as normal a life as possible, that was our own reaction. But the hurt feeling is with us till this minute. Serbs fought with the British in two world wars! We'll never forget those months though in a funny way it's hard to believe they ever happened. For three months in '96 tens of thousands marched and protested against Milošević. Why didn't the West then invest in Yugoslavia all the money spent this year on bombing? Why didn't they support the Opposition?'

'We know why!' said Mom. 'That was only months after Dayton and Milošević was someone they could all do business with!'

Milica continued, 'No one explains why they thought they had a right to change our government by force. Millions everywhere don't think much of Clinton but how would the Yanks react if some military alliance tried to *bomb* him out of office?'

We talked then of the many mixed families split by the Nineties conflicts. 'In some cases the separation was enforced,' said Milica. 'In others relationships couldn't take the various strains. My parents' generation thought of Yugoslavia as their shared home. And Yugoslavs loved to travel, to get out on vacations and look at the rest of the world. I don't know how the present lot of students and school-kids will react to being so confined. They've no passports and anyway under sanctions no one will give them visas. So they can't travel even if they could afford it. This will make Serbs more nationalistic and xenophobic and deluded about our historic importance as defenders of European culture and Christianity – what bullshit, if I may say so in front of Mom!'

Mom chuckled and poured me another glass of cherry juice. Then she observed that the Federation of Serbia and Montenegro should still be referred to as 'Yugoslavia'.

'In Montenegro a big minority want independence. And they might be encouraged if everyone now calls the Federal Republic of Yugoslavia "Serbia", making it seem Montenegro is not important. Some say the US wants to take over Montenegro, make it seem independent but keep it dependent on them.'

Mom disapproved of my walking around the city after dark so Milica and Shep escorted me to a trolley-bus stop. As several Mercedes and Rovers and Volvos swept past, I commented on Belgrade's astonishing population of expensive cars.

'No mystery!' laughed Milica. 'Five or six years ago stolen cars from Western Europe could be bought for DM10,000 or so and given false registration plates for DM100. The snag is they can't be taken abroad to countries where Interpol is effective.'

*

Belgrade's three-track commerce was visible on many of the main thorough-fares. Luxury stores opened – one wondered why – at 8 a.m. An hour or so later numerous pavement stall-holders arrived and the pop music ordeal began – rival tape-merchants inflicting too many decibels on the defenceless passers-by. Soon after, cars parked up the adjacent side-streets and the drivers (male and female) spread their shoddy wares on the vehicles' roofs and bonnets – garments and shoes, little plastic toys, cutlery sets, saucepans, china ornaments, combs and razor blades and trinkets. Most of those hawkers were diffident and amateurish and plainly in the wrong job. For 15 dinars I bought a pair of socks from a slim, well-dressed fiftyish woman who spoke fluent English and seemed embarrassed to find herself selling tacky socks to a foreigner. Impulsively I asked, 'What's the story?' Momentarily she was silent, considering me. Then she said, 'Why do you care?' Briefly I explained myself: an Irish writer, trying to understand what was happening in the Balkans. She laughed – a sympathetic laugh – and exclaimed, 'You'll be lucky! *We* don't understand what's happening!'

Then another customer arrived, interested in a T-shirt inscribed 'LOVE IS LOVELY BUT DON'T TRUST IT'. Svetlana handed me her card and said, 'If you really want to know the story, visit us this evening for a coffee.' She lived quite near the Beograd, in a once-affluent street of four-storey houses built between the wars. In her pre-hawker existence she had been a university lecturer.

The sun was setting as I skirted piles of rubble to reach the hall door; the next house had been partially demolished by a rogue missile. In a roomy, sparsely fur-nished flat, Svetlana introduced me to her clinically depressed husband; all evening he chain-smoked, stared at the floor, said nothing.

Svetlana offered me the only easy chair and explained, 'We sold most of our furniture last year to fund our three children going abroad. They're in their teens and have no future here. My brother in Sweden is looking after them. They'll be OK, they're sensible, they won't go crazy on sex and drugs – and they're quite talented, in different ways. But we miss them, especially their father misses them.' She glanced at her withdrawn husband, a glance of mingled affection and exasperation.

The 'story' was all to do with academic freedom, perceived by Milošević as a threat to his régime. University autonomy was abolished on 26 May 1998 when the Serb parliament passed the University Act, designed to bring Serbia's six state universities to Milošević's heel. It gave the government total control over the appointment of Boards of Governors and the selection of lecturers and profes-sors, who could be appointed only when approved by the Minister of Education. Moreover, all the academic staff were obliged to sign new employment contracts. 'And that meant' – said Svetlana – 'allowing ourselves to be muzzled.' Six non-academic Milošević cronies were among the fifteen members of Belgrade University's new Board of Governors and three of the newly appointed professors were simultaneously serving as government ministers. Jagoš Purić, one of the cronies, was appointed President of the university; he had been among the Serb 'intellectuals' who signed a demand for the withdrawal of Radovan Karadžić's indictment as a war criminal.

'So that's our story,' said Svetlana. 'Article 165 of the University Act ended our academic careers and many others. As it was meant to do. Jovo Todorović, the Education Minister, decreed that professors who refused to be muzzled couldn't hold classes or conduct exams. When my husband defied this the police physically removed him from his lecture hall. Education has become impossible at university level. Our graduates once had a high reputation abroad – this crop won't impress anyone. Half-cooked new graduates – youngsters allowed "easy" finals last year – are the present lecturers.'

Svetlana accepted my invitation to dinner but when urged to join us her husband silently shook his head. In the Beograd's restaurant the waiters seemed to recognize my companion and I sensed myself going up in their estimation. Later I learned that Svetlana had distinguished herself as a Women in Black leader.

Throughout the Balkans there is no escaping cigarette smoke – even at a Book Fair, even on the streets if the air is still. My hotel room reeked of it (maids smoke while cleaning) and in restaurants everyone smokes when not in the act of chewing. For this Svetlana apologized, then added, 'You must forgive us, it's the only cheap comfort for most.'

Svetlana found reassurance in the fact that the leadership of the Federal Yugoslav Armed Forces (JNA) was not united behind Milošević. 'We know that's so because we have relatives rather senior in the service. They are bothered, they've seen how little stomach the conscripts had for fighting in Kosovo. When that conscription started, thousands fled abroad – two of our nephews are still in Hungary, afraid to come home. The most chauvinist Serbs think we should fight to regain Kosovo – all the world knows UN troops run away if even a few are killed. Others think we should wait for the KLA [Kosovo Liberation Army] to kill K-For soldiers when they begin to resent being bossed around, not allowed to murder Serbs and burn down our churches and monasteries. You'll have noticed how many Yugoslavian leaders inflamed bigots and psychopaths just to keep themselves in power. We've got Milošević's Special Police, neo-Chetniks in Montenegro, KLA gangsters swapping guns for drugs in Kosovo, warmed-up Nazis in Croatia, Muslim mercenaries fighting on the Serbs' side in Bosnia. Every country has those types but in stable conditions they surface as criminals who can be dealt with. Or even if not directly dealt with, they can't find space to run amok and destroy society – blow a country apart.'

Before we parted, I asked Svetlana how I could contact representatives of Belgrade's refugee communities, but she claimed to know nothing about them. This problem had been so successfully concealed that most people seemed unaware of its magnitude – or could choose not to think about it, reckoning 'We've enough problems of our own.'

By October 1999, when 193,000 Serbs from Kosovo had joined those previously uprooted from Croatia and Bosnia, Displaced Persons made up 9 per cent of Serbia's ten million population. On 10 August 1999 the UN 'advised' Western countries not to distribute humanitarian aid to Serbia through the International Committee of the Red Cross, an organization required by its charter to co-operate with governments. The UN named the Serbian Orthodox Church and its international relief organization as the only institutions through which aid should be distributed. Hence that long line of ICRC trucks seen between the borders, awaiting Church representatives.

None of the victims of forcible uprooting had been made officially welcome in Serbia and the Kosovo Serbs were even less welcome than the rest. As migrants in retreat from vengeful Kosovar returnees – K-For having proved unable adequately to protect Serbs – their presence contradicted Milošević's risible claim to have defeated Nato. Yet most were lucky enough to have been given shelter by relatives or friends. And a minority, foreseeing unrest within Kosovo, had already built themselves new homes near Belgrade. Thus 'only' 20,000 or so were enduring appalling conditions in sports halls or schools, prevented by their police guards from receiving visitors or leaving the immediate vicinity of their accommodation. According to the Civil Protection Headquarters, the government agency in charge of Displaced Persons, those Serbs were illegal immigrants. 'How come?' I asked Pavle, my informant. 'If Kosovo is part of the Federal Republic of Yugoslavia, how can its Serbs be illegal immigrants?'

Pavle shrugged. 'This is how we are now. We have no more sane thinking. Our Serb people from Kosovo are illegal immigrants and our army defeated Nato. We live with madness.'

The location of the refugee 'settlement centres' was not public knowledge and but for my chance encounter with Pavle, who had a policeman brother, I might never have discovered that one camp was near the ancient town of Zemun, now a northern suburb on the right bank of the Danube.

I took a bus to the port area, then walked across the Brankov Most high above the sluggish brown Sava near its confluence with the dull green Danube. This bridge had considerable lewd entertainment value. Gifted graffiti artists had been at work, their chief inspiration Bill Clinton in situations requiring the unconventional use of cigars. And Madeleine Albright was depicted naked as a latter-day St Sebastian, bristling with arrows.

Beyond the bridge I followed a bicycle track along the rivers' willowy banks – first the Sava, then the Danube, for here is the exact spot of their union. This track led to the seriously bombed Jugoslavija Hotel – well known to the world's journalists, a favourite rendezvous of Belgrade's *mafia* and the scene of several spectacular assassinations. Skirting it, I found a footpath, popular with fishermen, which brought me to my first goal – a medieval fortress, its splendour sadly diminished by unfunny graffiti and mounds of garbage. These Gardoš fortifications are all that remain of Zemun's walled town; nothing remains of the original Roman settlement.

Pavle had told me how to find the refugee camp. 'You might be OK,' he said. 'A few guards, like my brother, turn away when visitors come. It's good you don't look like a tourist, you could be a Serb.' (Words I had reason to recall six months later, in Kosovo.) But I wasn't OK. The track to the camp ran between fields of maize and well-tended market gardens and patches of reedy swamp fringed with rusted car skeletons. No one else was in sight when a police van overtook me and stopped. The front-seat passenger, a hefty Federal Yugoslav Police Force (MUP) officer, emerged and demanded my ID card. I greeted him cheerfully and produced my passport. He glanced at it, shouted angrily and pushed me into the back of the van. There two colleagues echoed his shouts. Ten minutes later I was dumped at a bus stop where the police waited until a bus arrived, which caused me to be viewed with some unease by my fellow-passengers.

From the Brankov Most I returned to Kalemegdan, my favourite – surely everybody's favourite – bit of Belgrade. Covering many acres on a high grassy bluff above the meeting of the rivers, it is among the world's biggest fortified networks. The Romans began it, the medieval Serbs extended it, the Austrians completed it in the early eighteenth century. Most of what we now see is Austrian; only two deep Roman wells recall the founders. Criss-crossing the bluff, one walks for miles. Here are two small churches (locked), a zoo (closed), a modern art pavilion (temporarily abandoned) and an awesome moated citadel. Within the citadel's ramparts is the unique Military Museum of the Yugoslav People's Army where, on the previous day, I had spent six solitary hours. The name misleads; though war is the central motif, this museum in fact presents the history of Yugoslavia, from the Bronze Age to Nato's bombing, with a blend of precise scholarship and imaginative *élan* that justifies 'unique'. All the histories I had read came to life in those fifty-three rooms.

From Kalemegdan's highest ramparts one looks beyond the wide Danube to the strangely moving immensity of the great Pannonian Plain, stretching away and away to Hungary and beyond. Standing here, some 1,500 years ago, Roman sentries watched the barbarians advancing in their thousands to camp on the far bank before seizing Kalemegdan. The decline had long since set in, the fall was imminent.

In this corner of Belgrade, on those sunny windy autumn days, with golden-brown leaves dancing and rustling across green grass, it was hard to remember what this city had so recently suffered. Many citizens were strolling amidst the glowing trees – planes, chestnuts, beeches – throwing sticks and balls for bounding dogs (all pure-bred). Young couples canoodled on benches overlooking the rivers, grandparents tended toddlers, older children raced and jumped and played football, some youths were stunt-riding mountain bikes, others sped past on roller-blades. That morning I had seen one boy on blades descending a long steep wide boulevard, suicidally weaving between fast cars – the very epitome of anarchy.

Elsewhere, however, one's impressions were different. In cafés and restaurants solitary men sat around for hours, scruffy and unshaven, making small beers last a long time, looking depressed or tense, not waiting for anyone, not reading news-papers. As I wrote my diary one evening in the Beograd restaurant two men in their thirties sat at neighbouring tables, by the windows overlooking Gavrila Principa Street, sipping *rakija*, apparently absorbed in personal problems. They were not eating or intending to eat yet each remained at his table as I went upstairs. In Ireland they would be in a pub where such sad isolation is not pos-sible, where they would find themselves involuntarily getting into conversation, on however superficial a level. Similarly depressed women were to be seen slumped on park benches, weather permitting, or – more rarely – dawdling over tiny coffee cups in the smarter cafés.

Beggars were numerous – some pathetic aged wrecks, blind or crippled, shiv-ering in threadbare rags. Others were severely maimed young men, many legless with wellies clumsily tied over their stumps. I heard bitter complaints about those injured conscripts being given no support of any kind. One morning, on the steps of St Marko's, I watched a young priest – his black beard long and bushy – using verbal abuse and threatening gestures to chase away two Gypsy women. Both had tangled tinted hair, filthy voluminous ankle-length skirts and small lethargic chil-dren suffering from pink-eye. In contrast, I witnessed a touching sight outside another church when four boys, aged nine or ten, came upon an ancient beggar-woman crouching in a corner and paused to give her a few one-dinar coins – of which they cannot have had many, for they themselves looked ill-fed.

Despite the Serbs' courageous resurrection after the bombing, there was a dis-orienting sense of normal life being in abeyance. And indeed, in legal terms, the state itself was in abeyance: unrecognized as such by the UN, therefore a non-entity. But apart from that a curious ambiguity blurred the picture, as it had in the Yugoslav Section of the Cyprus High Commission. Pairs of uniformed police were occasionally to be seen on Belgrade's streets and around certain installations, and the secret police must have been going about their snooping, but I had no feeling of being in a police state. True, political opponents of the régime were being assassinated at irregular intervals and the media were being censored/per-secuted and the universities and judiciary were being 'controlled'. Yet one sensed anarchy rather than totalitarianism – and anarchy allows space for open dissent. In the Soviet Union, as I remember it in the 1970s, dissidents wouldn't have dared to plaster Moscow with posters mocking their leaders. Nor would pavement stallholders have dared to sell anti-government pamphlets and badges and tapes of defiant lyrics. And ordinary citizens never talked openly to strangers.

In Serbia under Milošević, they did. When I paused early one morning to view the bomb damage around a military hospital near the Beograd (was that, too, an 'error'?) a friendly young man emerged from the security guards' hut, chewing his breakfast slice of *burek*. He was slim and pale and his crew-cut exposed nasty sores on his scalp – the sort associated with malnutrition. Politely he asked for my ID and I explained myself, as usual gambling on being honest. Vojislav then told me that this hospital catered not only for serving and retired soldiers but for their wives and families. He seemed pleased to have a chance to practise his excellent English. At university he had been studying Classics and English Literature – 'For the love of learning, not to earn a living. When my mind was full of good things I would be able to work at something dull without getting bored.' But halfway through his course his grant was cut off when sanctions were imposed. Now he was doing three jobs a day, striving to save enough to continue his studies. 'Here I'm night-watchman, in the day I wash bus windows, in the evening I'm a waiter at a luxury hotel – but now it's not luxury and I get no tips from foreigners. Tourists don't like us and journalists are bored writing about us, they never really understood what was going on here and in Kosovo. For me it is important to keep our culture and be proud of it. We should be what the past has given us – has made us. But believing this doesn't make me a Chetnik. I hate Milošević's nationalism, his way of stirring people up to keep himself in power. And *she's* even worse. But how to get them out of our way? We are too tired, after the struggle against sanctions and then the bombing. That is sad. Without Milošević we could quickly rebuild our country.'

Another example of open talk – in Topčider Park, near Tito's tomb, an ebullient Dalmatian, in hot pursuit of his ball, almost tripped me up. His owner apologized profusely and we got into conversation. This young woman from Vojvodina, recently qualified as a gynaecologist, couldn't get a job that would support herself and her retired but now pensionless parents. So she was working as a salesgirl while continuing her studies. 'If I drop off the medical scene all my years of work are wasted, things change so fast. For this reason friends smuggle in from Hungary a few new publications. Is it not cruel to cut us off from knowledge? For what motive does the world want to make us more weak and ignorant and helpless? But we whine too much, I must stop! Here everyone has enough bread, all over the world millions are worse off, I try every day to remember this. Our life's only intolerable compared with what it could be if Milošević hadn't destroyed us. Our biggest problems are not material – those can be fixed, we're a modern developed European country. The real problems, moral and ethical, are all inside our heads. Can the IMF, EU, OSCE, UN cure such problems? Imagine one day Milošević is gone – one day soon, we hope! Then what do we do? Where are our models for responsible, constructive, honest leadership? If such people existed, they would by now have led us away from Milošević.'

And a third example – an encounter which developed into a friendship. Olga, a twenty-three-year-old student (English Language and Literature), lamented the disruption of her studies by a professors' strike in 1998, when the students had supported the academics, and then by the bombing.

Olga and I first met near a three-quarters-built Orthodox cathedral where two decrepit giant cranes were still in place though work had stopped decades ago when someone made off with the dinars. Her parents – neurologist father, psychologist mother – lived in a large town some 200 miles from Belgrade. An adored twenty-five-year-old brother, Leo, was in his final year studying electronics and they shared a flatlet in the dank basement of an apartment block. Having been brought up to revere 'Western Culture' and detest Titoism ('not much better than Stalinism') they were now, post-bombing, bitterly anti-West. Leo had escaped conscription, electronic skills being of use to the military, but Olga dreaded some dire development that would take him away to be killed. 'Our future is so uncertain! Even a year ago, when Not-so-Bright started her threats, no one foresaw the bombing, no one believed it would be more than bluff because bombing is part of warfare and Yugoslavia was threatening no Nato country.'

Leo laughed – by this stage we were drinking a vile coffee-substitute in the flatlet – and reassured his sister. 'No one can make me kill Yugoslavs! And Hungary is close.'

These two were the only young Serbs I met who seemed entirely uninfluenced by Milošević's propaganda campaigns. When I remarked on this Olga said, 'That's because most of our generation who think like us have gone abroad. Or they're dead. A cousin we loved very much – like a brother – was killed in Kosovo. And four friends from childhood were killed. We don't know who killed them – maybe the KLA, maybe Nato bombs, their families have no information.'

'One superpower is more dangerous than two,' observed Leo. 'That's what Nato's bombing taught us.'

'But why so?' wondered Olga. 'It shouldn't be so – weren't people more afraid during the Cold War – afraid of nuclear death?'

Looking at the two – aged fifteen and thirteen when the Wall came down – I realized that they represented the first generation of post-Cold War adults. But for Yugoslavia's young the brief euphoria of 1989–90 was soon replaced by tension and tragedy.

I replied, 'We were very afraid of a nuclear death – some of us still are. But now we're facing a triple threat. Rampant militarism, globalization and environmental/ecological disaster – all closely linked.'

A brief silence followed; Leo and Olga had grown up deprived of the sort of information that would have made my comments comprehensible.

Then Olga said, 'When all those tens of thousands of students marched on Milošević's villa in '92 Leo and I were still at school. I remember feeling so excited thinking of all those brave crowds calling for him to resign. We longed to be here ourselves, joining this movement to reform politics.'

'But before we got here,' said Leo, 'Milošević had used the fighting in Bosnia to stir up nationalist feelings that divided the students. Then in '96, after Dayton, the government looked a lot weaker and for a time the opposition seemed united. We all worked so hard – thousands and thousands of new students just come from schools. We made the Dean of Belgrade University resign and closed down all the faculties and for months stopped lectures all over Serbia. We thought we might be winning but Milošević was too smart for us – got us disunited again. He had campuses renovated quickly, paid out grants on time by printing lots more money and said, OK, we wouldn't be punished for closing the universities. Exam dates were changed to give us time to catch up on our studies and the movement fell apart. Hundreds of the leaders went away all over the world – they're gone for good. Refugees from Croatia and Bosnia were given their places, and kids from villages who didn't understand what was going on and backed Milošević because they liked ranting about a Greater Serbia. It's a problem that so many went away, they were the most active and determined organizers.'

'You should visit Studentski Grad in Novi Beograd,' said Olga. 'It's a colony for about 11,000 students from rural areas. Milošević sends his demagogues there to get everybody wound up and all sessions begin with Serbian folk songs and military anthems. When you hear about all the messages of support our Slobo gets, you'll find most of them come from Studentski Grad. Those students are from hungry homes and glad to get three free meals a day on campus.'

Both Olga and Leo admitted to still reacting fearfully for an instant on hearing any aeroplane. Olga said, 'We're told so often about Serbs being so strong – our so-called leaders tell us. But we're strong only as others are, humans *in extremis* always turn out to be strong. Propaganda about super-tough Serbs is only propaganda. Look at us now, we manage to keep going – studying, working – only by not thinking about the future and trying to forget the past. Most of my friends live from day to day studying like automatons and making escapist distractions though that's difficult with so little money. And we're dreading this winter, it's not too bad if the electricity is off only two hours but after the bombing it may be four or even eight. I believe most are against Milošević now, but his gang have discovered how much profit you can make in a broken-down country with a scared judiciary – they don't want political or social stability, they do better as things are. I'm not blaming small law-breakers without jobs doing smuggling and selling on the streets to keep alive. But when everyone sees well-respected professional people living off petty crime in public that makes a pattern of contempt for laws.'

'After the bombing', said Leo in his soft slow voice, 'we'd just enough energy left to start Otpor. A few brave students started it and already we've thousands of supporters – all age groups. Also many from Studentski Grad, they see now Milošević can't keep his promises, their three meals have got very small! Their families are very angry too, in the small towns and rural areas. I think more angry than Beograd people. They trusted Milošević more so now feel more let down. And it was harder for their sons to escape conscription, without our sort of resources and contacts. Tomorrow Otpor is marching in support of a student strike – will you join us?'

'Of course she will!' said Olga, suddenly looking animated. She had helped to organize this demo, which would culminate in a four-kilometre march and was seen as a taking of Belgrade's political temperature. With the prosperous *mafia* minority not needing to think about politics and the hungry majority busy devising survival strategies, Olga wasn't optimistic. She said, 'If less than 10,000 of our 60,000 students boycott lectures and come marching, we'll have a failure.'

By 12.30 next day I had acquired my very own Otpor banner, showing a stylized drawing of a white fist against a black background. In the city centre's Terazije Olga and her fellow-organizers were already sitting on the circular seat at the base of a drinking fountain erected in 1860 to celebrate the return from exile of Prince Miloš Obrenović, who soon after died at the age of eighty. A Serb prince only to the extent that Zog was an Albanian king, he set certain unfortunate precedents and is sometimes known as 'Milošević's patron saint'. In Barbara Jelavich's words:

> Miloš, rising from his origins as a poor peasant, became one of the richest men in Europe. Since the public money and his private funds were not clearly separated, he did not hesitate to use his advantage in his speculations. He took possession of state lands and property that had been confiscated from Ottoman owners. Using the state labour taxes, he had the peasants work off their obligations on his private undertakings. He held a monopoly on livestock exports and on the sale of salt. He also owned large estates and seventeen villages in Wallachia. Despite his obvious corruption, Miloš was a popular and respected leader among the population at large. He was a figure that the peasant could understand . . . With the assistance of his relatives and friends, he was able to maintain his control of the state. Although there were frequent conspiracies against him, he suppressed them by direct and brutal methods.

During the next half-hour a crowd of some three or four thousand assembled in the Terazije, including many colleagues, friends and relatives of the academic victims of the '98 purge. Oddly, there was not a uniformed policeman in sight though on 30 October – only three days previously – MUP officers had confiscated 35,000 Otpor leaflets and several student distribution teams had been ungently arrested and detained overnight – Leo among them, which explained his stiff gait.

Also, on the previous evening the government television station had condemned as 'friends of Nato' all who might assemble on Terazije.

As we moved off towards the nearby site of the demo proper, I found myself walking beside a young man wearing a Nato-mocking shirt and carrying a map which he unfolded to illustrate his argument that the US were building a military base in Kosovo as part of their strategy for controlling the flow of oil from the Caspian Sea. 'By now,' he said, 'Serbia is the only Balkan country not in the American camp. That's why they want to get rid of Milošević and have another puppet here. We also want to get rid of him but we won't accept a Yankee stooge instead.'

Outside the university's long and multi-storeyed Mathematics and Natural Sciences Faculty we were joined by another thousand or more, many groups marching behind enormous, variously inscribed banners – THE TIME IS RIPE – WE ARE LOOKING FOR A PRESIDENT – LET'S BURY THE WAR HATCHET AND SMOKE THE PEACE PIPE – PETITION AGAINST REPRESSION, AGGRESSION AND TYRANNY. Other groups were visible or audible in the distance and as we waited for them Olga introduced me to Leo's former professor – tall, rugged-featured, his grey hair collar-length, his well-cut worn suit of fine tweed. He gave me an Otpor lapel badge and denounced the 'cohorts of stupid peasant people' who remained loyal to Milošević. This goaded me into suggesting that 'ignorant' might be more precise than 'stupid'. But the former professor insisted that everyone had had ample opportunities to inform themselves accurately before threats of Nato aggression inspired the Serbian Law of Public Information, passed on 20 October 1998. He added, 'The majority in towns and villages were too lazy to make the effort to understand what was going on. That's why no real democracy is possible for us, yet. We're politically immature, incapable of discussing and debating rationally, afraid of making reasonable compromises. Generations have been conditioned to follow their leaders unquestioningly – or certainly not to question in public. Only the universities and the independent media tried to break that mould – you know the result! Can you remember how comfortable people felt with Tito's dictatorship, even when our economy was terminally ill? He gave Serbs more than their share of top jobs in every republic. That compensated them for all nations in the Federation being equal – Kosovo's Albanians included – under the constitution. But you can't build lasting stability on one man – human life is too short for that. And now the world excludes us, humiliates us. We have a writer called Latinka Perović who recently said: "Having been realized, Serb nationalism threatens the very survival of the nation." Too right!'

Before I had time to ask any of the questions bubbling in my mind, all conversation was brought to an end by what are known in Ireland as 'rebel ballads'. The music-makers stood on a large platform and on either side Otpor flags were held high by groups of students. Several Otpor banners, five metres long, hung from the Faculty buildings' upper windows and every window served as a vantage point for cheering students. 'Those are the ones afraid to come on the street,' said Olga scornfully. Then she added, 'No! I'm unkind – maybe at other demos they've been beaten up.'

Now the crowd was being packed tighter and tighter, as the whole long wide street filled up. Every other person seemed to be blowing a whistle or horn, creating a tension-free mood of jolly defiance. Looking around me, I suddenly realized that this was the first time I'd seen smiling faces in Belgrade's post-airwar streets.

When the speeches began Olga translated for me; pre-airwar, she had worked as a journalists' translator.

One impassioned retired physicist, with an international reputation, told us that he had resigned in 1997 when the departure of nine of his colleagues left him unable to do any work of significance. All those highly qualified men and women had emigrated but he himself was too old for that solution. Quite soon, he foretold, Serbian university degrees would be worthless. Meanwhile more than 50,000 graduates were unemployed or doing menial jobs. This I could well believe, having met so many – including, that very morning, a young economist serving in a greengrocer's shop who thought herself lucky to have this ten-hour job six days a week, plus washing-up in the Moskva Hotel on Sundays.

A middle-aged woman professor of electrical engineering was equally passionate and idolized by the crowd; their cheering delayed the opening of her speech by minutes. She declared that her generation should be ashamed of itself because in 1991 and 1995–6 they had offered only passive support to the students. Not until personally victimized did they become activists, prepared to protest publicly and 'march for change'.

One of several fiery student leaders ended her speech with a flourish: 'All that's needed is one gun and one bullet.' This daring earned loud applause – clapping, whistling, shouts of delight and clenched fists waved in the air. A young woman standing on my left muttered in English, 'No – *two* bullets!' Mirjana Marković, wife to Slobodan and founder-leader of her own political party, was even more detested than her husband – and, by all accounts, even more destructive from the ordinary Serbs' point of view.

In between speeches, recordings of some of the President's more abusive and threat-laden anti-opposition diatribes encouraged the crowd to express their loathing and contempt ever more vigorously. Light relief was provided by an actor, wearing the appropriate wig, who derisively imitated Milošević delivering reams of false statistics about rapid repairs to Nato-inflicted damage. According to one mathematician from the nearby faculty, at the current rate of progress those repairs would take 125 years.

Another student leader complained that the 1995–6 campaign – those miles of marchers that won global attention – had achieved nothing because there was no follow-through, no long-term plan to destroy the régime, no real revolutionary thinking. He exhorted Otpor's followers to form discussion groups and seek new leaders, since the opposition parties offered no leader figure worthy of much respect. Later, as we analysed the day's events, Leo deplored this criticism of the opposition. In his judgement it had merely confused certain sections of the crowd and would have been better left unsaid, however true.

Our forty-minute march around the city centre blocked traffic at all intersections but attracted no discernible animosity and much vociferous support. Citizens of all ages and conditions crowded their block balconies or hung out of high windows throwing wrapped sweets and packets of cigarettes into the marching throng. And they too blew whistles and horns. Our own whistle decibels increased as we passed Party headquarters – the building apparently deserted, the faded Party flag, still incorporating the hammer and sickle, hanging limply from one window. Even there, not a policeman or security vehicle of any sort was visible. How to interpret this? Did Milošević feel so secure he thought 'Give them a chance to let off steam – no harm done!', or so insecure he dared not risk a confrontation that might run out of his control and allow some rival to pounce? 'Who knows?' said Leo. 'He's off the scene – we can't judge how it is for him. That's one reason we're all so nervy now. Having an invisible president is sort of sinister.'

Olga observed that if riot police appeared the demo would cease to be peaceful – a lesson the security forces had learned the hard way – and Milošević must know that public police aggression would swell the ranks of Otpor. 'This time,' she said, 'it's like what you have in Ireland – NO SURRENDER!'

Six months later, in the Croatian town of Knin, I remembered those words when news came from Belgrade about the closing of all Serbia's universities at twenty-four hours' notice. By then Otpor had gained mass support and organized numerous student strikes and protest rallies more successful than their 2 November effort. The state was in a panic; before the closure police squads were invading all the faculties, indiscriminately assaulting students. More than one thousand Otpor members (including Leo) had been detained and hundreds had been badly beaten up by nameless gangs wearing surgical masks and wielding baseball bats. Otpor still didn't have 'a plan' but its 'No surrender!' spirit undoubtedly contributed to Milošević's defeat in October 2000.

3

Damage – Collateral and Otherwise

Pre-OAF, the Belgrade-Niš train journey took three hours. Post-OAF it took five and a half – bomb damage to the line had been only 'temporarily' repaired. In my clean and comfortable carriage two talkative ragged old men, slightly stooped and very weather-beaten, with huge hands and merry eyes, sat by the door. A wordless elderly couple occupied the window seats, he dozing most of the way, she knitting, both looking soured by life (or by each other?).

This railway follows the Morava Valley, Serbia's heartland, where independent peasant-farmers have enjoyed possession of their land since the Ottoman estate owners withdrew in 1830. All afternoon the mellow light of a prolonged Indian summer lay on the tranquil landscape. Numerous farmsteads – mostly newish dwellings – were scattered on gentle hillsides or along the valley floor. Men and women loaded sugarbeet and stooks of corn into trailers by hand. Mini-tractors were preparing the ground for winter wheat, outnumbering the horse-ploughs by ten to one. Ripe pumpkins glowed along the verges of stubblefields, disturbed cock pheasants became iridescent streaks against a deep blue sky. Further south the older women wore traditional garb and were harvesting maize with billhooks. Those hours passed pleasantly; as a form of transport, slow trains are the next best thing to bicycles.

Not far from Niš we entered the narrow valley of the jade-green River Morava, rushing strongly between low hills, steep and densely forested – a glory of crimson and yellow, ochre and russet, occasionally broken by black stands of pine. I moved out to the corridor, the better to appreciate an unashamedly gaudy sunset, a tumultuous display of shifting shapes and changing colours filling half the sky. Long strips of old gold, ragged fragments of scarlet, frail wisps of primrose yellow, bulky banks of pale pink turning to carmine against a blue-green background. Then quite suddenly all was monochrome and the first stars twinkled.

In ebony darkness the train pulled in to Niš's long, unlit, deserted platform. Three passengers got off and immediately disappeared into the gloom; the restaurant and waiting room were locked and shadowy. As I sought the exit, carrying my rucksack in one hand, a taxi driver came running after me, made to grab it and asked, 'Where to?' By torchlight I showed him the address (another Book Fair contact) and he said, 'Fifty DM, OK!' '*Not* OK,' I retorted, tightening my grip on the rucksack and hastening towards the street where a light shone faintly from a kiosk on the far side. A youth was buying cigarettes and chewing-gum; both he and the friendly young saleswoman recognized my contact's name and offered me the use of the kiosk's telephone. 'She lives near but in darkness you can't find.'

Dubravka answered – she was expecting me – and said her son would be at the kiosk within minutes. I knew nothing about her, except that she had volunteered to find me lodgings in Niš.

Soon a Volvo came speeding along the empty street and stopped with a squeal of brakes. Vojislav opened the passenger door, muttered a greeting and thereafter said nothing. He wore a garish, glossy designer tracksuit – very fashionable in the Balkans that season. In a ten-storey apartment block we ascended a bare concrete damp-smelling stairway. Halfway up the time-light went off, leaving us in total darkness, but even then Vojislav didn't offer to carry my rucksack. In the open doorway of a small sixth-floor flat Dubravka was awaiting us – diminutive, wiry, dynamic and obviously rather taken aback by my unprepossessing appearance. In the Balkans appearances still matter as much as they did in western Europe seventy years ago. Doubtless she had been informed that I am an established author of mature years and therefore expected someone who looked more *successful*. However, she recovered quickly, welcomed me effusively and within ten minutes had told me all about her academic honours, her internationally recognized scientific achievements and her ambition to fundraise abroad and set up IT colleges in Niš and Belgrade for poor students – perhaps I could mention that in my book.

Then I found myself viewing a video of her son's eighteenth birthday party in 1997 when sixty guests had assembled in Niš's most prestigious (her word) hotel. The wine had been put down the day Vojislav was born, the cake was cut at the hour he was born (11.17 p.m.) and the dancing continued until dawn. His parents had presented him with a bright yellow semi-sports car and I was given to understand that both came from moneyed backgrounds.

Another video followed, of Dubravka abroad at an international conference where she had been an honoured guest; three times she stood up to point to herself amidst the throng. Then we heard four colleagues fulsomely praising her achievements at considerable length, in languages incomprehensible to me.

Mercifully, Balkan hospitality was simultaneously operating. The *rakija* was special, its golden tint matched by a golden bow around the bottle's neck. The wide range of delicious titbits had been made by Dubravka's mother who lived next door: 'It's necessary for a very busy woman to have the granny close by!' Because of her career, explained Dubravka, she couldn't have more than one child, though all Yugoslav mothers had been granted a year's paid maternity leave. 'That was to encourage us to have more babies, we know we must raise our birthrate or we'll be taken over by Albanians and Gypsies. The last statistics, in '94, alarmed us. In Serbia, not counting Vojvodina and Kosovo, we had 214 abortions for every 100 live births. Our women are too careless, using abortion instead of contraceptives – it was cheaper when hospital treatment was free. They didn't care about wasting our medical resources. For years past our average family is less than two, most mums work if they can, leaving babies with grandparents or at crèches – but now those are no longer free. Or you can have a nanny like the British if you are rich enough!'

I angered Dubravka by asking if she knew Serbia's home-birth statistics.

'You mean having babies in the home? No, we are not so primitive – why should the West think we are like Africans? Our mothers stay in hospital on average five days.'

When I tried to explain that in the West home births are returning to favour among the more sophisticated, Dubravka looked blank – then disbelieving.

For the duration of the airwar Vojislav had been despatched to the safety of Skopje. 'I know nothing about politics,' asserted his mother. 'I just wanted to protect my boy. I've no time to think about that game but most Serbs seem to support our government. They need so little, give them a bit of bread and sausage and *rakija* and they're content. They only wash once a week and never read so they don't miss hot water or electricity. We're the ones who suffer from bombings and sanctions!'

The electronic wall-clock, surmounted by a silvery model of the Statue of Liberty, had ceased to function. I glanced at my watch; it was 11.20. As my hostess searched for a third video (a family holiday on the Montenegrin coast) I murmured about departing. Alas! it had proved impossible to find lodgings. 'Since the bombing, it's got awkward to ask anyone to receive foreigners the way they used to – the rest of the world is bad news! Please sit down for this video, it is not late. After, Voljislav will drive you to the Ambassador, it is a fine hotel.'

Next day I learned that the construction of the Ambassador, a monstrous eyesore dominating Niš's city centre, had provoked much political controversy. The twiggy platinum blonde at reception was so heavily made up one fancied her mask would crack and fall off if she smiled – though it seemed unlikely she ever would smile, under any circumstances. Wordlessly she pointed to the tariff list: DM70 for a single room. As I only had dinars she pouted and said '420' – precisely DM70 at the official rate of exchange. Next two forms had to be filled in and my passport was locked in a safe – as a hostage, lest I might run away with the bedding? (In the Beograd there were no forms, no one asked to see my passport and no payment was requested until the moment of my departure – when the kindly men at reception agreed to look after the impractical number of heavy books I had just acquired.)

On the eighth floor my large room had no bath, a defunct shower, peeling walls and damp sheets with multiple holes. A half-moon lampshade over the bed had been put on the wrong way round and as I switched off my right thumb was burned. Viewing that nasty little blister next morning, I wondered how much it would be worth in the US . . .

The Ambassador's buffet breakfast was astonishing – and disconcerting, when most of the city's population seemed underfed. The spread included a selection of cereals imported from Austria, crusty hot bread, real butter, hard-boiled eggs, two sorts of salami, cold roast pork and chicken, smoked bacon fat, *burek* (pastries with savoury filling), cheeses soft and hard, stewed plums, tea, coffee, orange juice. My fellow guests – a taciturn lot – were probably pillars of the state. The restaurant windows overlooked Trg Oslobodjenja, Niš's main square, 'developed' during the Sixties in that bureaucratesque style which banished charm from so many of Yugoslavia's cities.

Before retrieving my passport I made several telephone calls to the contacts provided by Belgrade friends. Janko and Jasminka (a businessman and his radiographer wife) were friends of Milica, as was Mrs Rakić. Karen and Alek were Otpor activists. Mrs Maček, a cousin of the pavement hawker Svetlana, was an oncologist whose son Alek could certainly introduce me to some of Niš's refugees. As Janko's business activities were in abeyance he suggested a noon meeting and gave me accommodation advice. All Niš's Category B hotels and motels had become refugee centres so there was no alternative to the Deligrad Motel, a brisk hour's walk from Trg Oslobodjenja.

Even in 'the good times', guidebook writers were hard on Niš. J.A. Cuddon described it as 'a large, dull and dirty town'. The *Rough Guide to Yugoslavia* (1985) remarked that 'the surrounding heavy industry has left a thick layer of dirt and depression over the town'. By November 1999 it looked utterly forlorn – much more run down than Belgrade. Many bomb-damaged shops were closed and boarded up; others, half-empty, made no effort to disguise their shortage of stock. For many years a giant electronics factory, covering square kilometres at the foot of wooded hills, had employed 30,000 – one-tenth of the population. Special trains used to take workers to and from their pollution-darkened blocks and a vast car park, now carpeted by vigorous weeds, separated the road from a sprawling complex of deserted buildings. Post-bombing, only 3,000 were employed and the local economy had been killed.

Things were different under the Romans, when Belgrade was merely a fortified trading centre and Niš ranked among the empire's most important administrative centres. Being at a major road junction (turn right for the great Aegean port of Thessaloniki, turn left for Constantinople), the city provoked much blood-letting. In 269 the Emperor Claudius defeated the invading Goths, then the Huns arrived and left not a stone upon a stone. Justinian did the rebuilding and in Nemanjić times Niš again became a place of consequence, until captured by the Ottomans in 1386. In 1689 Austrian troops took over, only to be ejected a year later. In 1737 the Habsburgs were back, but again the Ottomans drove them out. And so it went on – and on – culminating in fierce fighting around Niš during the Second World War as the Germans attempted to secure their grip on Yugoslavia. And who caused all this bloodshed, over the millennia? Not the natives – allegedly so prone to slaughtering one another – but empire-building outsiders.

From the square, a bridge spanning the River Nišava leads directly to the Tvrdjava, a massive fortification built 300 years ago by the Ottomans, probably on the site of a Byzantine citadel. The ramparts rival Dubrovnik's in size, though not in magnificence, and now enclose a public park scattered with decaying Ottoman tombs, dignified old trees, a handsome Ottoman arsenal in poor repair, a neglected mosque and what used to be an open-air cinema-cum-volleyball pitch. Under the imposing main gateway of finely cut stone Janko was awaiting me at noon: a small sallow man, his jeans and anorak shabby, his expression permanently anxious, his manner gentle.

We strolled around the polygonal ramparts in hot sunshine. 'Too hot, not normal in November,' said Janko uneasily. But I wasn't complaining; Niš needed to be viewed under a clear blue sky. Then suddenly the wide central path was busy as university students streamed towards the gateway. Janko observed, 'Their canteen food has got so bad they go to buy something in the market.' He added, 'All our schools and universities were closed during the bombing and for long after but students did their exams on time, though concentration was hard. My son got a good mark and praise.' This sixteen-year-old had planned to go to London in 2002, to study 'tourism management'. (An odd choice of subject, I thought, in view of the Balkans' new unappealing image, but it was good to hear of one optimistic teenager.) 'And now,' continued Janko, 'all his plans are dead. I have no more business, Serbia has no more tourists. Then his mother and me, thinking more about it, said maybe this is best. In London I read terrible things in newspapers!' The recollection prompted him to cross himself quickly. 'A young man could be destroyed there – drugs, gambling, fights with knives, bad behaviour in the streets between boys and girls. Even if I had money, it could be a sin for me to put him in such danger!'

I hesitated, then asked, 'But was there much difference, in normal times, between the young scene in London and in Belgrade?'

Rather sharply Janko replied, 'Yes, our cities can be bad – but here parents can protect children, even grown-up children, if we decide that way.' Which reminded me of a New Year's Day conversation, eight years previously, in Zagreb.

In 1996 Janko, visiting London on a business trip, had been dismayed by the cultural gulf he discerned between 'Balkan people and you people in the hurry-up West'. The exporter with whom he was dealing 'wanted to talk business straight off and showed angry because I was ten minutes late. Ten minutes – and I was travelling through a big strange city by myself! That was not a kind way to treat me! Here we spend time talking about family, health, sport – then business. That way you get to know the person a little and can make a better business talk.'

We were now walking along the embankment above the Nišava, a junior among rivers, swift, shallow and clear. On our right rose the University of Niš Rectorate, a long stately building with a Habsburg flavour. Ahead was another bridge, bombed and sketchily repaired. (CARS ONLY, said a large notice.) This district, near the huge covered market, is pleasingly undeveloped. We turned into Ljubomira Nenadovića Street, quiet and tree-lined, its residences a mix of two-storeyed, semi-detached houses and newer bungalows in ample gardens. Here, between 11.30 and 11.40 a.m. on 7 May, Nato dropped two containers of cluster bombs.

Said Janko, 'Those bombs are for killing *people*, not for destroying military or industrial places. Why drop them in crowded streets around a market at midday?'

And kill people they did, in Niš – fourteen people, including a twenty-five-year-old woman, seven months pregnant, whose photograph overlooked the scene, tied to a telegraph pole. On other poles hung the photographs of a waitress killed outside a café and several other victims. On the following day, when alone, I paused at that café for a *pivo* (beer) and found being from Irska no help. Generally, in Niš, this thawing mantra worked less well than in Belgrade.

The distinctive holes in that road were to become too familiar to me as I cycled around Kosovo. Stricken cars still stood by the kerbs, beside houses with deeply scarred façades. Janko had been walking in the next street when those bombs caught the citizens of Niš completely off guard. His wife Jasminka was then crossing the square and recalled people looking at one another, puzzled, wondering 'What's that?' – not taking it too seriously until moments later deaths were reported and panic set in.

We met Jasminka for a late lunch in a tiny Turkish eating-house opposite the market. She wore a tight-fitting black trouser-suit and was several inches taller than her husband, with copper-tinted hair, sharp features, tired eyes. Her face was set in hard lines yet when occasionally she smiled she seemed a different sort of person – perhaps the sort she might have been if born in another time and place. Her voice trembled with hatred as she condemned those who deliberately attack civilians. Scornfully she rejected my alternative explanation that Nato lies about the 'smartness' of its weapons. Her scorn was understandable. Nato wishes to be feared as an invincible military machine possessing the most advanced weaponry systems. Having projected this image, it can't reasonably expect to be believed when it explains that the demolition of hundreds of dwellings, clinics, schools, churches, museums, hotels, shops and holiday resorts – plus a few passenger trains and buses – were 'mistakes'. And maybe they were not mistakes. An institution unscrupulous enough to use cluster bombs and depleted uranium (DU) can't have a very tender collective conscience.

As we enjoyed our *chorba* (soup) and fresh bread rolls, Jasminka continued predictably: 'Nato is the world's biggest bully!'

'Anyway the biggest since Ghengis Khan,' interposed Janko.

'Why did they attack a country that couldn't defend itself from high-altitude bombers? How could they forget we fought with them against Hitler?'

Everywhere in Serbia I found this last point giving rise to an acrid disappointment, a genuinely baffled sense of betrayal. By way of uniting the new socialist federation, Titoism presented Yugoslavs with a selective history of the Second World War, concentrating on the Partizans' heroic deeds (which were truly heroic) and scarcely mentioning those other Yugoslav fighters, including thousands of Serbs, who sided with the Nazis.

Janko then announced that he would borrow a friend's car next day and show me many more 'war crimes' in and around Niš. When offered similar tours in Belgrade I had pleaded 'lack of time' but Niš provides insufficient diversions for that excuse to be plausible.

On my way to the Deligrad Motel, I brooded on the 'international community's' 'new idealism'. To the Serbs, whether or not they condoned or condemned their government's brutal counter-insurgency methods in Kosovo, that campaign was their own business – a domestic matter, not an excuse for Nato to violate their sovereignty, without declaring war, and shatter their economy. The airwar apologists' attitude they would have found incomprehensible, had they been aware of it. When your own human rights are being literally hammered into the ground, you are unimpressed by the argument that our world has moved into a new era and henceforth the 'defence of human rights' must take precedence over respect for national sovereignty. Who can imagine Nato disregarding, on behalf of their afflicted minorities, the sovereign rights of China or Russia, or Turkey or India?

Beyond an agreeable residential suburb the road to the Deligrad crosses cultivated farmland with low hills in the middle distance. Unfortunately this is a 'feeder' road for Pirot, Skopje, Priština and Belgrade – the junction is nearby – and non-stop car traffic (not many trucks) emphasized the limitations of oil sanctions.

Evidently the Deligrad was not built as a motel; a wide lawn, sheltered by tall pines, separates it from the road and its eccentricities include mock-Gothic windows and long, wood-panelled corridors with vaguely baroque mouldings on the high arched ceilings – as though some apprentice had once practised his craft here. My bedroom walls were beginning to crumble, the handbasin taps were waterless and the lavatory provided a gem for my 'Balkan Plumbing Anthology'. To flush it one had to stand on a stool, reach up and grope within the cistern for a length of wire. I seemed to be the only guest though the restaurant was popular for men's luncheon gatherings – business or political conferences which went on for many beery hours. The underworked staff were friendly though gloomy and the standard breakfast was adequate; a cheese omelette, a hot bread bun, a cup of rose-hip tea.

At 7.30 next morning Janko picked me up in a twenty-year-old car that made strange noises. 'You must be careful about cluster bombs,' he cautioned, as we drove towards Niš's north-western industrial area where many apartment blocks and houses had been damaged beyond repair. We paused close to the century-old Niš tobacco factory, 'listed' in Tito-time as a fine example of pre-1914 industrial architecture. Its ruins overlook a mini-park planted with conifers, their trim rows contrasting oddly with the surrounding chaos. Further up the wide Boulevard 12 February, amidst flat green grassland, the NIŠ Jugopetrol oil storage tanks and pumping station once stood. On 5 May both had been flattened to the ground and replaced by a gigantic crater. On the same date four missiles hit the nearby Energogas complex, demolishing the gas, air and water tanks and the compression pump station.

'In what way did all this help the Albanians in Kosovo?' Janko demanded rhetorically.

'Quite so,' I replied. 'But by then Nato had lost the run of itself, as we say in Ireland. It only wanted to defeat Milošević at any price. This is what happens when militarists try to solve political problems.'

By then I had realized that this tour – displaying to a foreigner the punishment inflicted on *his* place – was therapy of a sort for Janko. Back in the centre, he showed me many more Nato victims, including a partially shattered early Byzantine tomb – one of Niš's few 'ancient monuments' – in a densely populated district heavily bombed on 23/24 April. On 12 May, during the twenty-third attack on the city, 1,300 bombs fell around the residential districts of Duvanište and Lenin Boulevard, damaging a museum, the symphony orchestra's concert hall, the Niš Stock Savings Company and a riverside block incorporating Niš's synagogue – now an art gallery. In the old university complex near the market ten listed buildings had been either seriously damaged by shrapnel or totally destroyed. On the city's eastern outskirts the Mediana Archaeological Park, site of Niš's Roman ancestor, received a deluge of cluster bombs and remained closed to the public. On the opposite side of the Boulevard Veljka Vlahovica, a KV 400 electricity installation had been disabled by an innocuous-looking gauzy substance still hanging in filaments on the transformers. Here skilled men had been hazardously at work for months, strapped to pylons high above the ground. 'Nobody knows when they will finish,' observed Janko. 'Their work is so important they get paid every week, not like other people.'

Serbia was the testing-ground for this substance, as Laos was for cluster bombs in the 1960s. It belongs to a new generation of highly specialized weapons and – I quote Paul Rogers –

> disperses large numbers of carbon fibre filaments to short-circuit electricity-switching stations and transformers. A variant of this, distributed by a new 'bomb' called the Wind Corrected Munitions Dispenser (WCMD) disperses thousands of microscopic fibres that form an almost invisible cloud that will get into a wide range of electronic and electrical devices, including personal computers, and short-circuit them . . . In the airwar against Serbia it proved extremely difficult to detect and destroy Serbian military facilities [but] such weapons, provided there is appropriate targeting, can be used alongside conventional munitions to do massive damage to the economy of a target state.

It was now time for Janko to return his friend's car and for me to continue on foot to Niška Banja where I was to meet Karen and Alek. I had a particular reason for wishing to walk alone over those few miles; thirty-seven years previously, I had cycled along this very road *en route* for Sofia and New Delhi.

Niška Banja, once a thriving spa resort, covers the lower slopes of a wooded ridge and is chiefly memorable for its avenues of magnificent trees. However, Karen and Alek thought it beautiful and clearly expected me to utter exclamations of wonder and delight, which I dutifully did. A maze of laneways and winding paths linked six hotels (all closed), the pump room, school, post office and staff quarters. Shallow streams of hot water, crossed by footbridges, raced over cobbled beds towards a high concrete 'waterfall' – steaming hot – surrounded by tropical shrubs and creepers. What most impressed me was the effort still being put into maintaining these grounds, despite the empty hotels. Serbia was down but not out – a message also conveyed by Belgrade's well-kept parks.

Alek was square-faced, dark-browed, tense and, to begin with, slightly ill-at-ease in the company of a foreigner. Karen seemed much more relaxed and self-confident and was strikingly good-looking – long, glossy raven hair, an olive complexion, almost black eyes, an aquiline nose. As we lunched in the one open restaurant I discovered that she was a Gypsy – and a Gypsy who gets to university in Yugoslavia, and acquires a Serb partner, has to have above average self-confidence.

In January 1999 Belgrade's Humanitarian Law Centre reported: 'Federal, republican and municipal authorities have not invested effective efforts to improve the living conditions of Roma.' Always this minority has endured a level of poverty unknown in normal times among their fellow-citizens. And, as in neighbouring Romania, prejudice against them is widespread and virulent. Yugoslavia's 1991 census showed a Gypsy population of 143,519. The real figure, said Karen, is reckoned to be about half a million; during census-taking many claim to be Serbs, Croats or whatever. 'My family pretended to be Serbs. Now I can stop pretending. I've proved we can compete academically — therefore every other way. I'm fluent in English, German, Italian and I want everyone to know where I've come from.'

In 1998 Karen and Alek were arrested while distributing Anti-War Campaign leaflets and continuously interrogated for six hours. The police demanded, 'Who from outside backs you? Who paid to print those leaflets? Who wrote them?' Alek insisted that no one was backing them, that the campaign was a spontaneous protest, organized by ordinary decent Serbs.

'An interesting thing happened then,' said Karen. 'It looked like those police believed us and even were a bit sympathetic after they listened to our arguments. We were released without charge and so were many other campaigners in Kruševac, Kraljevo Kuršumlija, and Novi Pazar.'

In October 1998, when the Great Powers first threatened bombing, the Serbian Ministry of Information outlawed the retransmission of BBC, Voice of America and Radio Free Europe programmes — described as 'vehicles of propaganda and psychological warfare by the Western powers, which are pursuing a distinctly hostile and aggressive policy towards Serbia and Yugoslavia'. The Serbian Law on Public Information, passed by Parliament in Belgrade on 20 October, deprived citizens of all the 'freedom of speech and information' rights they had enjoyed under the Federal constitution. This was, Alek argued, a good example of one side's 'managed' news reports spawning the other side's censorship.

Karen said, 'Before the bombing, people like us thought we knew the right way to think and act. The counter-insurgency methods used in Kosovo were wrong, the Albanians and ourselves were united in a new way — all victims of Milošević. Now we're divided again, the Albanians gone over to Nato and looking like traitors. The KLA wanted the airwar to get independence for Kosovo some time soon. They were glad the bombing wrecked Serbia. And Nato's propaganda has demoralized us — in a way more than the bombing did. Too many Serbs are seeing all the world as their enemy.'

Niš, unlike Belgrade, did not isolate its displaced Serbs and as we waited for a city-bound bus Karen suggested stopping off at the former Motel Mediana, now a refugee centre. Alek frowned, seemed unhappy with the idea, then explained: 'Before the bombing crowds of journalists visited refugees looking for good stories and promising to organize much more help from outside — but they never did. So these poor people are not pleased any more to see visitors who only want to use them to make money for themselves.'

Fair enough, I thought — but Karen argued that as I didn't have a camera, and looked too old to be a journalist, our visit would be a kindness, a break in the crushing monotony of their lives. She won (I suspected she usually did) but Alek chose to stay on board the bus when we disembarked opposite the ramshackle motel. 'He gets too upset about these sad places,' said Karen. 'And then he gets into a rage about the billions of dollars the IC is spending in Kosovo while displaced Serbs who did no wrong get one DM per person per day – *one!*'

The motel, built where the suburbs merged into the green Archaeological Park, was augmented by a colony of rusty mobile homes and broken-down trucks, buses and army lorries. Most of the eighty inhabitants were from Croatia and BiH, a few from Kosovo. There was no running water, no sewage, no heating except what individuals could provide for themselves; groups pooled their resources to buy calor gas cylinders. The ICRC delivered some clothing (not always suitable) and bedding but during the 1998–9 winter seven elders and two children had died of hypothermia. Food donated via the ICRC and Orthodox Church distributors consisted only of pasta and tinned beans; Karen speculated about the likelihood of other – perhaps more interesting – foods being 'confiscated' by nameless people in unknown places. Some of the younger refugees had found casual labour, paid piecemeal, in the city, despite the general hostility to displaced Serbs. I noticed several mobile homes sporting TV aerials and almost everyone was smoking what appeared to be Rothmans cigarettes. 'Clever imitations,' explained Karen, 'made in Montenegro and smuggled into Italy and elsewhere by the trillion. Montenegrin tobacco is top quality – famous for centuries.'

The Croatian Serbs had been in Niš for four years or more and were pitiably apathetic – entirely without hope. When I suggested that Tudjman's death (then known to be imminent) might improve returnees' chances they merely shrugged and shook their heads. 'Sometimes,' commented Karen, 'they've seen and suffered such horrible things they don't really want to go back.'

One elderly Bosnian Serb woman described returning to Sarajevo, her son, daughter-in-law and two small grandchildren having preceded her. She found them living in one small room because 'Their big flat was taken over by a Muslim family. They were looking after it well but they wouldn't leave until they had built their own new house. They said Serb mortar bombs had destroyed their home and Serbs must take the consequences.'

Another Sarajevo granny told a similar story. Pre-1992, she had been secretary to a hospital director, enjoying a reasonable salary, her own car and a three-roomed flat ('a bright place, overlooking the river') also destroyed by Serb mortars. 'It was in a mixed area, Serbs living in a Serb enclave were safer.'

A seventy-six-year-old peasant woman from a village near Knin, in what was the Serb Krajina, told us her seventy-four-year-old brother was the only relative left out of an extended family of sixteen. The rest were killed during Operation Storm in August 1995 when the Croatian army drove some 200,000 Serbs out of their homeland.

Karen asked me, 'Do you want to hear exactly what happened to this family?'

I shook my head. 'One can too easily imagine it all. I'd hate to stir up nightmare memories.'

'Yet sometimes,' Karen reminded me, 'it's good for them to talk, not to keep it all hidden inside, hurting like a stone in a shoe.'

'No doubt,' I said, 'but how can strangers know which of them might benefit from talking?'

We spent nearly three hours with those forgotten people and I saw that Karen had been right; they did relish this break in the monotony.

Back on the bus, Karen remarked, 'The population shifts we've had are disastrous for Serbia's future. Thousands and thousands of qualified young people, and older academics, are gone and replaced by traumatized, pauper peasants. Without land, they can't contribute to putting Serbia together again after Milošević. But they have to be fed and housed and clothed and this state can't afford to look after its own people.'

Again, I marked a contradiction at the heart of Serbdom: Serbs from Croatia, BiH, Kosovo – 'Greater Serbia', in fact – were regarded as 'outsiders'.

A few days later, in the city centre, I noticed cartons of flour, cooking oil, tinned beans and vitamin biscuits – all conspicuously marked with a Red Cross – being unloaded from a taxi by three well-dressed, robust youths who carried them through an ancient stone archway to a weedy littered courtyard where the stink of stale urine prevailed even over Niš's traffic fumes. Derelict four-storey brick and wood buildings rose on four sides; this seemed to be a fragment of the old Ottoman town. When I entered the courtyard a neatly suited man carrying a briefcase challenged me in English but responded well to the 'Irska' mantra. Here lived 115 Serbs from Croatia and BiH, mostly old people who had lost contact with their families or seen them killed. The youths were church volunteers whose distribution task was sometimes dangerous. 'These old men are so desperate they'd stab you for a packet of biscuits,' said my informant. 'Don't go in on your own, they might try to rob you.'

All over Niš similar displaced groups were subsisting in half-ruined or abandoned houses, apartment blocks, factories, offices, their needs unpublicized either at home or abroad, most citizens hardly aware of their existence.

Daily I witnessed the arrival from Germany, via Hungary, of at least two (often three) giant sanctions-busting tourist coaches towing closed trailers. In some quiet street the goods were unloaded on to the pavement, then reloaded into cars, tractor-trailers, vans, horse-carts. The ubiquitous and miraculously expandable nylon hold-alls (nylon fertilizer sacks rewoven: a Balkan invention, I'm told) were roped to vehicle roofs and inside went all manner of household appliances, cases of Scotch whisky and Gordon's gin, American cigarettes intended for Nato troops, cooking oil, paints, tools, folding beds, kitchen sinks, synthetic carpeting, flooring tiles, bicycles. Those last surprised me; one sees very few in and around

Niš – just the occasional rheumaticky farmer on a rattling sit-up-and-beg or schoolboys in the park on mountain bikes.

Although horse-carts are forbidden within the city, many intrude – farmers delivering produce, Gypsies collecting cardboard and rags. The horses and ponies were in surprisingly good condition (healthier looking than most Niš residents) and might be seen tethered to electricity poles, munching their way through generous nose-bags while their owners refreshed themselves in one of the many small *lokantas* around the market. I enjoyed seeing Gypsies in their light pony-carts inconveniencing motorists by trotting smartly along the main boulevards – sometimes even galloping, like charioteers, the driver standing erect with his feet apart and his head thrown back defiantly. In the few remaining corners of Ottoman Niš, Gypsies had taken over the rickety but attractive old houses and these scavenging families helped to reduce the city's garbage problem. Downstream from the almost litter-free centre, where the river flows through industrial areas, tons of garbage were regularly dumped on the high sloping embankments and jagged remnants of cannibalized vehicles lay half-submerged – providing seats for fishermen, whose catches were never more than six inches long.

Many walls were covered with posters advertising Otpor rallies past and to come, or showing photographs of Mr and Mrs Milošević 'deleted' with two broad red streaks. In Belgrade similar posters were often (not always) half-torn down; but Niš's municipal authorities – themselves strong opposition supporters – ignored them. The graffiti almost rivalled Belgrade's in density and daring. Numerous English-speakers had been at work: 'Slobo Go Away!' – 'Slobo Know Won Want You!' – 'Slobo Get Last!' One gable wall offered light relief. Its announcement, in large white capitals – ANALFUCKS ARE GOOD – was complemented by a vivid red illustration of the relevant orifice. That masterpiece had a wall to itself in the centre and may have survived because not comprehensible to the masses. Less entertaining was the profusion of Chetnik symbols but Mrs Rakić said reassuringly, 'It's only because that sort of swaggering with spray-paint is part of their psychosis.'

Mrs Rakić, Milica's friend, was headmistress of a small private school for 'lucky' children of all ages whose parents aspired to get them, somehow, into western universities. After the bombing the fees of pupils whose families had suffered most, in terms of lost business, had been reduced – 'In the IT age Serbia must have a generation of fluent English-speakers, it is the language of the third millennium.' The identity of the school's philanthropic patriotic owner was not revealed.

Only later – after four months' exposure to Balkan emotions – did I realize how rare was Mrs Rakić's quiet acceptance of the fact that 'there are villains on all sides, atrocity stories to be told about all factions'. As we lunched in the Ambassador restaurant, she spoke of her radiologist brother who, after the airwar, attempted to tour Kosovo with a geiger-counter but was thwarted by K-For.

'Ando is my only sibling and he still lives in Zagreb, married to a Croat dentist. Our families are very close, we visit each other for long periods and together bought a holiday house on one of the islands. Now we can't see each other and all are devastated – especially our children, the cousins.' Suddenly this calm, self-possessed woman was almost overcome – tears glistened. 'It's as though jail bars separate us – we the Serbs are in prison, the criminals, and we're not even allowed visitors! Before, no one asked a question if a Zagreb car was parked outside our home for a week, now that would be a crime! So many families share this sort of sorrow, torn apart . . . People whose only fault was to behave like Yugoslavs and have the other nations as marriage partners, friends, business colleagues. But those relationships will survive. Politicians and generals and Special Police can't turn civilized people against one another – *never!*'

Lamely I said, 'It won't be much longer now, soon he'll be gone. The writing is on the wall – literally, on many walls.'

Mrs Rakić looked uncheered. 'Saddam is still there, eight years after the Gulf War.' She then advised me to meet 'some of Niš University's most distinguished academics, our "intellectual mis-leaders". Talking with them, you'll understand better the trap we're in. Even when *he's* gone, Serb nationalism won't go away. I can arrange appointments for you. They're keen to brainwash foreigners.'

On the following evening I was wined and dined by four 'distinguished academics'. And they were frightening. Suave gentlemen, internationally respected, but with tunnel vision. If such men remain influential, Serbia faces a turbulent future.

Through no fault of my own, I was becoming a regular patron of the Ambassador restaurant; one couldn't invite people like Mrs Rakić and Mrs Maček to a meal in a *lokanta*.

Mrs Maček, Svetlana's oncologist cousin, looked alarmingly exhausted when she joined me for dinner. Sanctions, she said, had wrecked Serbia's hitherto adequate health service. She wondered why pharmaceutical drugs and medical equipment could not be smuggled in as easily as whisky and gin, luxury cosmetics and video games – not to mention the other sort of drugs.

'Milošević's supporters,' continued Mrs Maček, 'don't understand the rationale behind the sanctions system so he can turn it to his own advantage, telling them the UN is cruel to innocent Serbs. UN people sitting in New York don't understand how life is in a censor-controlled mental ghetto. Those of us who know the point of sanctions were already against him – why must we suffer under the UN whip? Last year Niš's Oncology Clinic celebrated thirty years of first-rate, world-class work. It's one of the three major oncology clinics in Serbia with fifty physicians, forty-two of them specialists. We're very proud of it. We use the most advanced diagnostic and therapeutic methods and procedures. How can it be "humanitarian" to harm such a place? Staff morale goes down when you can't do what you should. For me it's specially hard to send convalescent patients back to refugee holding centres where conditions are so against their recuperation. In the case of children it's *very* hard – and in this area the rate of childhood leukaemia has risen by more than 200 per cent since Chernobyl. Foreigners mock our self-image, Serbs being always in the right, always discriminated against. And it's true we're a bit neurotic that way. But Nato's bombardment and the UN's sanctions aren't helping to cure us.'

At one end of the covered market I watched a policeman controlling a few hundred shabbily-dressed men and women seeking their ration of half-litre bottles of cooking oil. Each household, Karen had told me, was entitled to five bottles for three months, regardless of the number in a household – which sounded daft but was reckoned to reduce paperwork in the relevant government department. Around three steps leading to a narrow doorway from which the bottles were being handed out, everyone crowded eagerly, wedged together but good-tempered or at least patient. Again it was a hot day and the policeman, wearing a tight thick uniform, dripped sweat. He was short, big-bellied, double-chinned, with pudgy hairy hands, a hoarse hectoring voice, a long baton and a large revolver in his belt. When a frail old woman tried to peer into the store he pushed her so hard that she fell off the middle step and was saved from the stony ground only by the quick reaction of a crew-cut, pimply youth. Obviously she had merely wished to estimate if enough oil remained to make it worth her while waiting.

Nearby a tiny boy was pleading for a cheap (two dinar) windfall apple; when his mother showed him her empty purse he fell silent. I thought then of the tons of rotting apples lying at that moment in orchards all over Ireland while mindless Irish shoppers bought less flavoursome imported fruit – in the worst case imported from New Zealand. Having given the little fellow five apples (all there were on the trestle table) I went on my way calculating that his mother, who bore all the marks of a chain-smoker, could have bought nineteen windfalls for the price of twenty cigarettes. Incidentally, throughout the Balkans I noticed few cigarette advertisements – an unnecessary expense in a region of heavy smokers. So much for the tobacco industry's claim that they advertise only to influence brand choice.

Briefly back in Belgrade, on my way to Novi Sad, I met Olga and Leo for lunch. They had just returned from a week with their family to celebrate an Orthodox religious festival; both had been baptized when about a year old, quite an unusual parental decision in those days, Leo said, among the professional classes. Olga added, 'Now many of our age-group are becoming more and more religious – maybe it's a desperate way to look for comfort. I don't understand it but definitely it's happening. I'm hoping it's not the same among the Muslims – they get dangerous when they're religious!' Olga's intense dislike of Muslims took me aback: she seemed otherwise such an eminently civilized young woman. On a previous occasion she had said, 'I really hate them and everything to do with their way of thinking. No, that's not true, I don't actually *hate* them, I wouldn't be nasty to a Muslim just for his religion. But it makes me very upset when I hear about our people *marrying* them.'

Olga was not looking well and admitted to feeling 'tense and frustrated'. During her time at home she had longed for one night out with her old school friends but 'None of us had one dinar to spare, we've never been so poor before, we're not used to it. My parents haven't been paid since April, if they didn't have private patients they'd be hawking on the streets. Even those patients can pay very little, sometimes nothing until they get paid!'

Leo, too, seemed subdued and eventually it emerged that their holiday week had been dominated by a friend's mental breakdown. Olga said, 'We both feel he's our best friend, he's very precious to us, very gentle but very macho at the same time – not a silly soft person. But when he came back from Kosovo in June he was crying and moaning every night in his sleep – his mother told us. At first we couldn't get him to talk – not until now, last week. Then he was sobbing while he was telling us about seeing Albanians leaving their shelled villages and burnt homes and shot cattle and maybe dead relatives. He said he had to turn away at the time to hide his tears from the men he was leading. He used to give the Albanians nearly all his rations and cash. Then he was forced to do savage things himself when his platoon was put under the paramilitary police. They'd have shot him if he didn't obey orders. Now he says he wished he'd had the courage to let himself be shot and we're afraid he's going to shoot himself. We can see how he's been changed by Kosovo, he's so damaged I can't describe it but when you love him it's terrible to see.'

Leo said, 'Why didn't your media tell the West, in 1998, about Serbs like Dušan? Then people might have seen Milošević as a *political* problem, for Serbs to deal with.'

'But we weren't dealing with him,' said Olga. 'And we still aren't.'

'Yes we are!' retorted Leo, pulling back his jacket to reveal the Otpor badge on his shirt.

Walking to the bus terminus, I wondered how many JNA conscripts had been similarly damaged in Kosovo. And I remembered those journalists who hung around the refugee camps during the airwar, craving atrocity stories. Had an Albanian family given them a 'kindness story' about a young Serbian officer, would any of their editors have used it?

4

Where the River Flowed Over the Bridges

It has been estimated that the prodigiously fertile Vojvodina, north of Belgrade, provided enough crops to feed all of the former Yugoslavia, with some left over for export. I could believe this, gazing from the bus across limitless fields, unhedged and unfenced. For miles the southern fringe of the Pannonian Plain offered not the slightest variation until, near Novi Sad, a wooded ridge rose in the middle distance. This is the Fruška Gora nature reserve, repeatedly bombed by Nato to the detriment of many of its rare species and currently off the tourist trail because of unexploded ordnance (UXO).

When the Ottomans withdrew to Belgrade after the 1683 Siege of Vienna this region became a dukedom ('Vojvodina') within the Austrian Empire. By way of establishing a buffer-zone, its new rulers drained vast areas of marshland and encouraged settlers from elsewhere in the Empire to join the 40,000 Serb families who, fearing a revival of Ottoman militarism, had recently migrated north. Before long a cluster of six Orthodox monasteries had been built within a few miles of Novi Sad. However, the Serbs soon discovered that as enserfed peasants they were far worse off than they had been under Ottoman rule. In contrast to its uniform landscape, the Vojvodina remains to this day a human mosaic, a microscopic fragment of the Austro-Hungarian Empire including Croats, Slovaks, Gypsies, Ruthenians, Romanians and (the biggest minority) Hungarians.

Serbo-Croat soon became the common language, but in Tito's time primary and secondary schools were provided for Hungarians, Slovakians, Ruthenians and Romanians, at considerable expense to the state. Tito, while assiduously cultivating political unity, respected the cultural traditions of each strand in Yugoslavia's society. Not so Milošević. In 1989, when the Vojvodina (like Kosovo) was deprived of its autonomy as a province of Serbia, most of its minority state schools were closed.

I was sharing the bus's front seat with a youngish Novi Sad woman who complained about Hungarian children now being discriminated against by the centralized education authorities. As the only surviving Hungarian-language secondary schools are fee-paying, most children must attend Serb schools from the beginning which endangers that minority's culture. The Budapest government, my companion angrily asserted, refuses citizenship even to well-educated Hungarians from the Vojvodina, Transylvania, the Czech Republic. Seemingly they want to maintain their influence in those areas, as the French do throughout the Francophone countries of Africa. My companion continued, 'Many of our students now commute weekly to Budapest university, something not easy to pay for. But isn't it worth paying, if you can, to preserve your own culture? Would you like to be British? No! And so we don't like to be Serb!'

On my two-mile walk from the bus terminus to the central Trg Slobode, the first thing I noticed about hill-free Novi Sad was its civilized provision of wide, much-used cycle-paths. Nato's destruction of the three bridges had greatly reduced motor traffic, and anyway the city centre had long been 'pedestrians only'. Elsewhere, parking on pavements was prevented by iron spikes or bollards.

Nineteenth-century dual-carriageway boulevards, long and straight, lead to narrower, older, curved streets – then suddenly I was in the spacious main square where a porticoed town hall, architecturally eclectic but pleasing in its proportions, faces a brick-clad Catholic cathedral (standard would-be Gothic) with 'SLOBA MOTHERFUCKER' spray-painted in huge letters along one wall. Here too was Novi Sad's only functioning hotel, two-storied and sixty-three-bedroomed. Built in 1854 and then named 'Empress Elizabeth', it was renamed 'Queen Maria' during the inter-war royal dictatorship and is now more prosaically known as the Vojvodina Hotel. My £9.50 suite (including an excellent breakfast) consisted of a little hallway, a loo and shower and a large bedroom with a tall balconied window overlooking the baroque-flavoured Trg Slobode. In the evenings I could hear the cheerful chatter and laughter of the *Korzo*, sounds never heard in Belgrade or Niš during the autumn of 1999.

I quote from the leaflet on my bedside table: 'With its architecture, its compositional characteristics and the decorational elements, this hotel ranks among the most outstanding works of bourgeois architecture.' Yes indeed – and 'bourgeois architecture' is positively endearing when compared with the sky-scraping, gold-tapped, hermetically-sealed, artificially-ventilated and electronically-managed hotel chains created by a post-bourgeois 'hospitality industry'. The Vojvodina's wide white marble staircase had a crimson carpet, bright brass stair-rods, elaborately carved oak banisters and a gaudy twelve-foot-high stained-glass window on the landing. The receptionist's mahogany counter occupied one end of an enormous first-floor foyer. At the other end a pewter mini-fountain, tastefully illuminated, splashed water into a clear pool lined with multicoloured stones and overhung by a variety of tall jungly-looking plants. The dining room (or banqueting hall) was all gold and brown striped pillars, high white arches, red plush upholstery, discreet lighting. Scores of attractive crayon sketches of local scenes included the three bombed bridges, to which a waiter drew my attention.

Coming from Belgrade and Niš, one is perhaps extra-susceptible to Novi Sad's charm. The car-free district around Trg Slobode – unchanged since the town was 'modernized' in 1745 – enchanted me. From its narrow, winding streets no high-risery is visible and several old public buildings and small dwellings were being carefully restored instead of demolished. Near the Danube, a line of six-storey apartment blocks, handsomely designed, had been painted in strong contrasting colours – a good antidote to the dereliction of surrounding bomb sites. Civic pride has always played an important part in Novi Sad's development. Even McDonald's, with its brash street signs prominently displayed all over the city ('5000 metres to McDonald's – 2500 metres to McDonald's – 1000 metres to McDonald's – 200 metres to McDonald's') – even that dire institution had been compelled by the municipality to modify the external vulgarity of its Trg Slobode 'outlet'. But of course Novi Sad has not entirely escaped the bureaucratesque and some boulevards run between hideous blocks with cavernous department stores at ground level. Exploring one, I observed many people wandering around gazing at the limited stock, but not buying. Café and restaurant prices were significantly higher than in Belgrade, which possibly explained why such an abnormal percentage of the citizenry ate on the hoof, munching meat rolls or *burek* or pizza from paper bags. However, Novi Sad seemed to have come through the past decade of misery, culminating in the bombardment, with its chin up. As one woman remarked, 'We weren't on any front line and this was always Yugoslavia's richest city. Many families have resources to get them through inflation and sanctions and so on. It's different for the 60,000 workers bombed out of their jobs and getting no government money to help them. Now they are hungry like never before. We can't see why Nato attacked this peaceful place where nobody had been fighting anybody!'

Thus spoke a Serb. Among the large Hungarian minority more ambivalent attitudes were discernible. After all, their ancestral homeland is now a Nato member and collaborated in the airwar. One comment went like this: 'The Americans wanted to rouse up the Serbs to get rid of Milošević and if Serbs weren't so dumb the bombing would have worked. They just weren't clever enough to get united and organized in opposition.' Several of the Hungarians I met revealed, directly or indirectly, disdain for what they saw as the 'crude' Serb way of being and thinking.

Stana, my Novi Sad mentor, came of an old Serb family settled in the Vojvodina for centuries. Wryly she noted that many of her Hungarian fellow-citizens had an imperial cast of mind. Our badges had brought us together – my anti-Nato badge, her CND badge. She had joined CND in 1984, during a post-graduate year in England. 'Ever since I've been a Peacenik – but I believe that word's not used any more. And CND is dying – yes? But our story this year should revive it. With a new name, perhaps, to match the "new world order". Now nuclear disarmament can go down the agenda. People need to look at our country and agitate about the crimes one superpower can commit *without* nukes.'

That evening we met again, in a recently opened but congenial restaurant (much wood and stone, no plastic or chrome) occupying the ground floor of an eighteenth-century terraced house in a quiet laneway. Our excellent mixed grills, with elaborate salads, were accompanied by a pleasantly harsh Kosovo red wine. In that cosy, candlelit room we were the only diners. Sadly the young proprie-tor/waiter/chef explained, 'After the war started, all evening business stopped. Since then, people come for dinner only at weekends. Also I have some regular custom every lunchtime – but how long before I pay back what I borrowed and make some profit?'

Stana's face hardened as she said, 'Željko is another Nato victim, the sort not put in statistics.'

By then I had heard Stana's story. She was herself a Milošević victim, the ex-wife of a Vukovar-born doctor who had been a Yugoslav when they married but became a Croatian nationalist in 1991. 'What the Serbs did to Vukovar made him a nationalist. I could understand that but I couldn't live with it. We weren't communicating any more and a year later he left. He took our boys away, aged three and five. He kidnapped them, I woke up one morning and my family was gone. I went to Zagreb, searching. I found them, but he wouldn't let me see my children. They had to grow up pure Croats, not be confused having a Vojvodina Serb mother. For me, then, was a horrible choice. To fight to have my sons – we couldn't *share* them – or never to see them again. If I fought, they would be inse-cure and upset. Nik is a loving father, he would do everything right for them except let them have a non-Croat mother. I felt not to fight was best. At their age then, losing a mother is not so important – quickly they forget. The mother never forgets. My own mother and some of my friends despised me for not fighting and rescuing them from nationalism, which in Croatia now is fascism. But I knew Nik would make it a long bitter fight and I didn't feel I could have won. Now they are aged ten and twelve and have a kind stepmother and a half-sister. So I know I did right. But still their grandmother – my mother –won't admit that. Still she thinks they should have been rescued and brought up in our family's liberal tradition, even if they got emotionally hurt in the fighting.'

As Stana fell silent Željko appeared in the kitchen doorway and I wondered if he had been eavesdropping. By then I was moist-eyed and only capable of utter-ing incoherent banalities. After a chat with Željko we arranged to meet next day to view a photographic exhibition entitled 'Novi Sad – The City where the Danube Flows Over the Bridges'. As we said goodnight outside the hotel I hugged Stana – whereupon she burst into tears.

*

At sunrise next morning I was walking towards the tangled remains of the Varadin Bridge, an apocalyptic mass of jagged metal blocking the broad Danube. This colossal structure, first built in the 1920s, was wrecked by German bombs in April 1941, reopened by Tito in January 1946 and totally demolished by Nato shortly before sunrise on 1 April 1999. Downstream, I could also see a sprawl of shattered concrete and twisted steel, once a railway bridge linking Novi Sad and Petrovaradin. On 5 April two missiles destroyed it. Further upstream was the site of the magnificent Žeželjev Bridge, of which all Novi Sad had been justly proud since its opening in 1961. Its destruction by Nato on 26 April broke the last link between central Novi Sad and the Srem side of the city. Only one section was visible, near the right bank: a gigantic lopsided concrete cliff, rising fifty feet above the surface, from which lengths of pipes (water and gas) protruded like severed guts. Walking along the right bank one could see numerous treacherous whirlpools created by Žeželjev's underwater bulk. These had stopped all small craft traffic on a stretch of river where it was central to the local economy.

More than anything else seen in Serbia, the ugly ruins of Novi Sad's three mighty bridges seemed to testify to the power of modern weaponry and the wanton destructiveness of modern man.

An ingenious substitute bridge (for light vehicles only) took me to Petrovaradin Fortress on the right bank. Four gigantic Danube barges had been tied together with steel hawsers to serve as a platform for rattling planks. Stana had boasted about this improvization, then added that it could not possibly survive the imminent winter floods.

Petrovaradin Fortress, Novi Sad's most notable structure, stands on a low wooded ridge directly above the bridge – a site fortified since Roman times. The fortress, designed by a French military architect and begun soon after the unnerving Siege of Vienna, took almost a century to build and became known locally as 'the Castle of Death'. A daily average of *sixty* convict labourers died of diseases, injuries or sheer overwork – which prompts speculation about the numbers convicted (of what?) by the Habsburg regime. Seen from afar, Petrovaradin looks deceptively unimpressive. Yet ten miles of tunnels link its four independent subterranean levels, with accommodation for 30,000 troops, and all the surrounding land was covered by its 18,000 loopholes. Ironically, by the date of its completion the Ottomans had retreated so far south that Belgrade was the strategically important place and Petrovaradin's impregnability remained untested. Eventually it was converted from white elephant to jail and one day received a young Austrian army NCO named Josip Broz, better known by his nickname of Tito; he had been given a short sentence for preaching socialism.

The fortress is normally open to tourists but I found it closed, as was the nearby terraced restaurant and café. However, a cautious stroll along the battlements, keeping an eye out for bomblets, gave me a fine view of Novi Sad and a depressing view of Serbia's wrecked oil refinery. Between 5 April and 9 June this was repeatedly bombed, struck by more than 100 missiles. On 2 May twenty-seven oil tanks, storing 38,645 tons of oil and side-products, were hit. The consequent fire burned for three days, producing a thick cloud one mile wide and two and a half miles high – all this only a mile and a half from Novi Sad. Thousands of Šangaj district residents had to be evacuated. According to the Balkan task force, set up by UNEP, the city's water supply was rendered unusable and the surrounding land and the Danube were heavily contaminated. Six months later the polluted water still could not be ingested, even after boiling, which inflicted much hardship on the poor. One litre of scarce bottled water cost the equivalent of forty pence. At the end of July 1999 the World Wide Fund for Nature dispatched a six-man team to Serbia and on 14 September they reported

> the presence in soil and water of notable quantities of mercury, polycyclic aromatic hydrocarbons, ethylene dichloride and other highly toxic substances including dioxins. Pollution is now threatening groundwater drinking supplies and natural resources in several countries of the area.

'Several countries . . .' – that feature of Nato's airwar needs emphasis. In September 1999 the Romanian Shippers' Association, supported by their Bulgarian colleagues, blockaded the Danube, demanding the clearing of the river. They reminded the world that since 24 March more than 3,500 Romanian shipping workers had lost their jobs and Romania's traders had lost some $50 million while 174 of their vessels were trapped in Austrian and Hungarian ports. However, as the bill for removing airwar debris was estimated at $100 million, Belgrade insisted that the Romanian and Bulgarian governments, which had allowed Nato to use their airspace, should make a substantial contribution to the clearing costs. In response, Bucharest pointed out that Romania's economy had been shattered by the Kosovo conflict (sanctions plus bombardment), its losses amounting to $915 million. We need to remember such facts and figures. Increasingly often, as time passes, Nato's 'humanitarian' intervention in the Balkans is referred to as a 'success'. Talk of 'proportionality', one of the requirements for a war to be deemed 'just', is dismissed as wimpish waffle.

Petrovaradin, though sometimes referred to as a suburb of Novi Sad, is in fact a separate and very attractive small town. Descending from the fortress, I walked up Beogradska Street where, during the 'surgical' strike that destroyed the Varadin Bridge, most of the eighteenth and nineteenth century buildings were badly damaged. As were the university's Faculty of Philosophy, a hospital and primary school, the roof of the monastery church of St Juraj and the Vojvodina Museum – said to be the finest in Serbia. On my way back to the temporary bridge I passed several two-storey family homes levelled on 29 May. All of which rather blunted my appetite for viewing 'Novi Sad – The City Where the Danube Flows Over the Bridges'.

This exhibition had as its patron the anti-Milošević City Council and its sponsors included Novi Sad's Ecumenical Humanitarian Organization, founded in 1993 by a group of churches which had since provided 1,500 tons of food and 400 tons of medicines to those fleeing from conflicts, whatever their religious or cultural backgrounds. Another sponsor was the Independent Association of Journalists in Vojvodina, founded in 1990; its 400 members published an independent weekly magazine 'as a voice of conscience and rebellion' and had been among the first to be threatened by Milošević's censorship-cum-intimidation campaign. The famous photographer, Martin Candir, born in Novi Sad in 1958, had used his camera to illustrate the haphazard cruelty of a bombardment conducted from 15,000 feet up.

When the NIŠ oil refinery was bombed on 12 April the nearby Šangaj suburb suffered the whole or partial destruction of numerous dwellings, a primary school, a crèche and a community centre. Candir shows us groups of children standing by the ruins of their homes, hands in pockets, their expressions frightened and puzzled, their dogs gazing at them anxiously.

On 19 April a missile struck the Executive Council building, formerly the Ban's (governor's) Palace, designed by Dragisa Brašovan and listed in all international architectural encyclopaedias. And so on and on, until two days before the end missiles struck the Šangaj district yet again, killing a thirty-seven-year-old man and severely injuring others including an eleven-year-old boy who is permanently maimed. Next day (9 June) more oil storage tanks and pipeline installations were destroyed, though Nato's leaders knew the Military Technical Agreement was being signed that day and the UNSC Resolution 1244, ending OAF, was to be adopted within twenty-four hours.

Leaving the exhibition, Stana and I wondered how it has come about that most people now regard the militarists' approach to problem-solving as acceptable – or at least inevitable – despite all the evidence that this ideology is dangerously disconnected from either rationality or morality.

Every evening that week, punctually at 7.30, a pro-autonomy rally was held in Trg Slobode, just below my bedroom window. The four orators – all soberly dressed solid citizens – spoke eloquently for an hour or so from their high, well-equipped platform to meagre gatherings of mixed ages. They earned only a few claps and whistles and muted cheers and were ignored by the slowly strolling *Korzo*. On my second evening I joined the gathering and was welcomed by a tall, lean, elderly man with a nut-brown tan, a grey goatee beard, a tweed cap and a pipe. Dr Vezi, a law professor, set about informing me while the orators' minions adjusted the equipment. First I had to understand that the Vojvodina was free of separatists. Nobody wanted independence but at least 60 per cent wanted the province's full autonomy restored. Between 1974 and 1989, when it enjoyed economic independence under its own constitution, the provincial income equalled Slovenia's and Croatia's and exceeded Serbia's. But when Belgrade took control of its finances incomes fell, and soon after came the disintegration of Yugoslavia, leading to the Vojvodina's loss of its traditional markets in Slovenia, Croatia and Western Europe.

When I remarked on the crowd's smallness Dr Vezi said, 'This is a missile-shocked city, it's hard to get people enthused. But I like to see these rallies keeping the autonomy embers glowing. That's why I'm here waving my flag. Novi Sad people are resilient. We've always bounced back and we will again.'

After the rally, Dr Vezi and I drank beers by starlight at a pavement café in a narrow cobbled street, marvelling at the warmth of this November evening. My companion had didactic tendencies and tried to explain the intricacies of the Vojvodina's politics in relation to Belgrade's tyranny. I listened apparently attentively, nodding at intervals, but got lost after five minutes. Before we parted, Dr Vezi suggested my visiting the Refugee Reception Centre at Temerin, a little town some ten miles north of Novi Sad. 'It's good for them to have foreign visitors, makes them feel less cut off and forgotten. But you need permission from our local ICRC who can be a bit prickly. If you wish I can take you to their office tomorrow.' I did wish.

The office, on the first floor of a converted mansion, overlooked one of Novi Sad's several pleasant parks, its rippling stream shaded by Habsburg-planted chestnut trees and towering pines. Numerous young women who seemed to have not much to do took it in turns to scrutinize my passport, then held prolonged muttered conversations with Dr Vezi. But when someone rang the Temerin office there was after all no problem: the Commander of the Centre would be delighted to introduce me to his charges.

On the Temerin bus my bucolic fellow-passengers eyed me with an odd sort of furtive sullenness. They knew where I was going – Dr Vezi had asked the driver to put me down outside the ICRC office – and the refugees are not their favourite neighbours.

Temerin is a long one-street town with the air of an overgrown village. In the ICRC's minimally furnished office I found an amiable elderly man eating a bread roll and a pot of yoghurt and reading the soccer page of a tabloid. He spoke no English but at once rang Commander Borislav, who arrived ten minutes later almost in tears; during the night his car window had been smashed and the radio stolen. On hearing that this crime occurs hourly in Ireland he looked incredulous. 'Here it is very, very new, to have such things happening. Is it that our people go to outside countries and learn how?'

'Probably,' I replied. 'All the ex-Communist countries have a fast-rising crime rate, it goes with uncontrolled capitalism and consumerism.'

Marijana, the interpreter, couldn't join us because this was Saturday and on Saturdays and Sundays she gave private tuition all day. Had I come the day before, her state-school pupils could have been abandoned. However, her younger sister Mladjanka (studying Serb literature at Novi Sad university) proved an adequate substitute.

Temerin's 6,111 registered refugees had fared better than average, partly because so many had local friends or relatives who offered accommodation – usually very cramped but at least allowing people to live non-institutional lives. Others found jobs in Novi Sad and could pay for lodgings. If their employers were big construction companies it was possible gradually to 'acquire' enough breeze-blocks, wood and roof tiles to build two-roomed houses on sites given free by the municipality. Those with relatives settled in Western Europe were also given sites and could afford to build bigger houses. But as land prices were soaring this municipal generosity had aroused considerable indignant envy.

The unlucky residue lived in what had been a Cultural Centre for Children until 1990, when such state-funded facilities began to close. Forty-eight Displaced Persons of all ages shared one big hall lined with iron bunk-beds set two yards apart. The stage opposite the entrance – on which Mladjanka could remember performing as a child – served as the single males' dormitory. Such a lack of any personal private space would utterly demoralize me; I would far prefer solitary confinement in a prison cell. Overcrowding usually promotes, among other things, extreme tidiness – as in a caravan or submarine – and here not a hairbrush was out of place. From the stage a steep, narrow stairway led to a smallish kitchen with three electric cookers, a few plastic tables and chairs but no sink, no work-tops, no refrigerator. But then, what would be kept in a refrigerator? The ICRC's sources had donated enough clothing and bedding but the food ration was no more than one tin of beans with morsels of pork per day per person. Year after year this had been their staple diet, supplemented by whatever fresh vegetables individuals could afford – usually cabbage, the cheapest. Most complaints centred on the failure to install running water, washing facilities and indoor lavatories. The outdoor Portaloos were too few and punishing for the elderly to visit on a winter's night. And there were many elderly, including a couple aged eighty-eight and eighty-three – the wife's rosy cheeks and clear blue eyes suggesting a healthy way of life in happier times.

Mladjanka explained that most of those at the centre had been able to salvage nothing when the Croats drove them out of their homes. They had left behind substantial dwellings, fertile fields, thriving fruit orchards and/or vineyards and enough livestock to feed a family, with produce to spare for sale.

'We were not rich but we had all we needed, now we only have worries,' said the fifty-three-year-old daughter of the octogenarians, whose husband had been killed during a battle to defend his village. Croat Displaced Persons forcibly uprooted from Bosnia were now living in their home and a family member would be allowed a temporary visit to sell it to them for DM35,000 – its real value being about DM150,000. However, this family, and others, were resolved to get their property back. 'Even if it takes ten or fifteen years, we'll wait to go back to our land. We're Serbs, but Serbia isn't our home.' (Is this a Balkan manifestation of 'the myth of return' once so common amongst Pakistani immigrants to Britain?) The tendency was to claim that all in their neighbourhood had lived together in peace until 'bad leaders' and 'outsiders' made trouble. 'Outsiders' were the favourite villains, rather than local 'bad leaders'.

One woman recalled her elderly mother returning home from Germany in March 1991, for a family wedding, and being killed by a reckless Croat driver. When her husband protested about the police failure to arrest the culprit, whose vehicle number they had been given, he was told by a senior police officer 'That's one Serb less, that's OK!' For us this is hard to believe but such words spoken in such circumstances are consistent with the deeds that followed.

Anti-Nato propaganda stories abounded and were not questioned, however outlandish – for instance, the tale of a bridge being bombed to create a dam to flood cellars near the Danube where hundreds sheltered nightly. There was also talk of anti-Nato postcards not being delivered by the postal authorities in Nato member countries – which reminded me of the warnings I had been given in Belgrade about Serbian postal officials burning letters addressed to such countries. For a visiting foreigner to challenge those tales would have been inappropriate. Truth being the first casualty of war is, I suppose, inevitable; but unless the truth is afterwards revived and exposed, propaganda continues to poison the atmosphere and endanger the peace.

These refugees had possessed no cash for years past and several referred to the humiliation of not being able to *choose* what to wear, what to eat, where to go for recreation. It must be hard to feel grateful for 'aid' when you have done nothing to deserve your misfortune. Yet the centre's residents, if in good health, looked happy enough; human adaptability is awesome. It cheered me to hear that most of the young men had jobs but chose to spend their wages on food for destitute parents or grandparents instead of renting accommodation.

As we left the centre I wondered if the President-in-Hiding could appreciate the underlying irony of Serbia '99. After almost a decade of bloody turmoil, ostensibly engineered to protect or enhance Serbs' privileges, thousands of unwanted and dispossessed Serbs were amongst the *most* unfortunate of Milošević's surviving victims.

By then the sun was setting and Mladjanka invited me to a meal. When I hesitated she reassured me – 'My mother has cooked some pig and there is enough.'

The Filipovićs' two-storey house had been built with family labour over a three-year period when times were good (1972–5) and a hard-working couple could save money. 'Now that would be impossible,' said Mladjanka. Her father had died of cancer in 1984, her mother had worked until April as a laboratory assistant in the chemical department of a factory obliterated by Nato. The eldest of the family, Mirko, was married with two small children and lived next door; he, too, had been bombed out of his job. When introducing us Mladjanka said, 'He now does unofficial translating.' I forebore to ask what that entailed but Temerin is close to both the Hungarian and Romanian borders and not all smugglers are multilingual. Happily, in this semi-rural area being jobless did not involve hunger on the urban scale. Seen from the street, Temerin's dwellings seemed prim suburban homes with tidy front gardens. There was no sign of their agricultural hinterland yet behind each house big back gardens merged into the surrounding farmland and most families kept a pig, a few goats, some poultry.

Mrs Filipović's lack of English did not deter her from quizzing me about my family circumstances and I suspected that a solo wandering granny offended her sense of propriety. As the dining room had been given over to Marijana's tuition classes we ate off coffee tables in the sitting room, perched on the edges of a sofa and fat armchairs upholstered in lime-green nylon. Mirko and Marijana had joined us for supper (casseroled pork and boiled potatoes) and, idiotically, I assumed a charming family of fluent English-speakers to be anti-Milošević. But even as I uttered that name in a critical tone I realized my error. This whole family had been thoroughly brainwashed by those neo-Chetniks who began to exert a widespread influence in the mid-1980s. Mirko was ready and positively eager to fight to keep Kosovo Serb and all his womenfolk supported him; even his mother seemed willing to sacrifice her only son for 'the cause'. Here were people convinced that Milošević's forces were merely biding their time and quite soon would launch a counter-offensive to dislodge Nato from the 'Sacred Soil of Kosovo'. But after Nato's battering of Serbia – causing $60 billion worth of damage to the economy and leaving this country the poorest in Europe – how could any Serb believe it possible to regain Kosovo by force? As we talked on, it became clear that my companions had been addled by the UN's confused and confusing stance, which opposed independence for Kosovo while denying Milošević's government the right to rule the province – an addlement compounded by misunderstanding of the UN/Nato relationship.

Marijana said, 'It's Milošević the UN is against. If he loses the next election they won't stop our army going in to throw out Nato.'

Mirko added, 'The UN represents the whole world, every country. The whole world is not against us, only Nato is. When we fight for Kosovo most of the world will be with us. Nato is only nineteen countries.'

I made no comment. The Filipovićs' misunderstanding of the 'international community' – their concept of the UN as an institution more powerful than Nato – could not be easily remedied.

When Mirko escorted me to the bus stop I asked, '*Why* is Kosovo so important to you? Important enough for you to risk your life to regain a territory mainly inhabited by Albanians. Why are your wife and children not *more* important?'

Mirko smiled kindly at me – he was a disarming fanatic – and replied, 'The Albanians got in by deceit. They don't matter, they're like rats in a house, not part of the family. The land matters, with all our holy places. It is sacred for us, it is part of our soul, it is where Serbs became great and strong.'

I chose deliberately to over-simplify and said, 'Perhaps you're thinking too far back? Surely Kosovo's significance 600 years ago isn't genuinely relevant to Serbia *now*? Why not live in the present? Centuries ago Spain owned the Netherlands, England owned a bit of France, Venice owned Dalmatia, Russia owned part of Poland and so on. It makes no sense for states to claim past possessions – past ownership – when a region's contemporary inhabitants want independence. There are six centuries between now and the days when Serbia became "great and strong" in Kosovo.'

Mirko shook his head and sighed. 'Foreigners can't understand our *love* for Kosovo, how we depend on it with our emotions. These others you talked about don't have their souls tied in our way. They can forget the past. Serbs can't. We have suffered so much it's not possible for us to go on without nourishment from Kosovo.'

At which point the bus arrived.

Back in Belgrade, I invited Milica and Mom to a meal on the eve of my departure for Zagreb. But only Milica came; it was Mom's evening for playing bridge with the neighbours. 'This,' said Milica, 'is one good thing Nato has done for us. Before, people were so depressed by their poverty they withdrew even from their friends and social life atrophied. The bombing reawakened a sense of interdependence and camaraderie. I believe some visitors don't see how impoverished we've become – they're fooled by all the signs of wealth. Yet we're talking *real* poverty, you can't live on dry bread. Many have to think three times before spending one dinar. They're often *hungry*, though that's hard to believe in a European country in 1999. The government subsidizes milk, bread and meat but milk and meat are very scarce. Farmers don't like government-controlled low prices so they smuggle most of their livestock to Romania, Hungary or Greece. That could be why not so many turned out for Otpor's demo. The young have lost their energy, they need more food than we do. Students everywhere enjoy demos but when your energy levels are down it can seem like too much effort. As for the rest of us, after seeing our country bombed to hell it's surprising so many have kept their balance with so much destabilizing propaganda going on now. Most folk I know don't believe Nato was trying to kill civilians. They know why Nato's leaders chose an airwar – to protect their own soldiers. Dead Serbs matter less. But that wasn't exactly what Milošević describes as "Murder".'

When I mentioned the Filipovićs' mindset Milica became fiercely anti-Orthodoxy, as it operates in Serbia. 'Milošević had no difficulty using the Church's authority – still strong among the uneducated. He used it very slyly when he chose Kosovo as his ladder to power. Then we heard all about the "sacred soil of Kosovo" – its holy buildings being "the most revered in Serbdom" – Kosovo being for all time the fountain of Serb spirituality, culture, art and much more of the same. When you get a power-hungry politician and a power-hungry national church in collusion – then you sure have a problem! Until that alliance took off, most Serbs didn't give a dog's fart for Kosovo as the fountain of their culture. Few ever visited all those revered buildings, they preferred the ski-slopes and the beaches.'

Our consideration of Serbia's multiple miseries led to inebriation. At midnight Milica incoherently rang Mom, then slept in my bed while I slept on the floor. Friends who had observed me packing a sleeping-bag had queried the need for it, given my urban destinations. But I have a snailshell relationship with my flea-bag and lacking it I feel handicapped. When unforeseen crises arise, it facilitates adaptability.

I returned to Zagreb in a very slow, rather dingy and almost empty train. For the last hour I had company, a chatty young army conscript who responded thus to 'Irska' – 'Ah! is good, Ireland is holy, like Croatia, yes? You are Catholic, is better than England, all Protestants and nothings. Our Papa visited you too and every-one listened to him. I have a book of his journeys with pictures of your beautiful country and so many millions listening to the Papa!' I didn't disillusion him by saying that twenty years on far fewer would listen.

After five weeks in Serbia, Croatia's capital felt like London or Paris. And I con-trasted it, too, with the dark, edgy Zagreb of that transition time in December 1991. In November the city-centre stores had their Christmas lights and decora-tions already in place and the toyshops were no less disquieting than our own. In one I watched a fur-coated woman paying the equivalent of £400 for a toy police motorbike, complete with radio. The many large bookshops stocked an impres-sive array of English, Italian, German, French and US publications, those last devoted to the learning needs of people in a hurry to succeed as free marketeers. All the bookshop windows had prominent displays of a recent hardback Croat translation of *Mein Kampf*, with a large photograph of the author on the jacket. It was selling fast at £45 a copy. 'Now it's history and we must study it,' said one bookseller, not very convincingly, in reaction to my surprised look. Nearby were copies of *Hitler and Israel*, in Croat – a thick volume and I wished I could read it.

As my London-bound coach pulled out of the terminus at 8 p.m. I realized that I had seen no bicycle shops. But the young man beside me was reassuring; on my return in February I could certainly find a very good machine in one of the new hypermarkets.

A few weeks later I became the happy washer of a third granddaughter's nappies.

PART III

2000
Croatia, Bosnia-Herzegovina, Albania, Montenegro, Kosovo

5

Carnival Time in Pokupsko

On 28 February 2000, back in Zagreb, I considered the bicycles displayed in an out-of-town hypermarket – a cut-price Harrods, acres wide, where you could buy anything from a needle to a DIY summer-house. But nothing on offer looked equal to the task ahead. Then a friend guided me to a small city-centre bicycle shop and there, amidst the frail racing models, stood one sturdy mountain bike. (Painted red, therefore named 'Ruairi' after a very young red-headed Irish friend.) He was a bargain at £240, plus £18 for the essential modification of a woman's saddle. Pedalling through central Zagreb I rejoiced; Ruairi and I were instantly compatible – not always the case with a new bicycle. At Luby's house I attached my veteran pannier-bags without difficulty and felt impatient for the morning.

It was below freezing at dawn, as I thrice went astray in look-alike suburbs, their high-rise dreariness alleviated only when the sun rose and factory smoke turned to flamingo-pink plumes drifting across a blue-green sky. I was seeking a secondary road to the Bosnia-Herzegovina border and there were no signposts. Yet within an hour I had escaped; fields surrounded me and even if this was the wrong little road it couldn't be very wrong because it led south-west.

All morning an icy cross-wind blew and the air tasted of snow. Here was mildly hilly terrain: lots of short steep slopes, the wide sunny pastures interspersed with beech woods still clinging, as beeches do, to last year's dull brown leaves. Despite clusters of wayside farmhouses the region felt deserted. My Zagreb friends had alluded to this rural depopulation, accelerated but not caused by recent conflicts. From this region, the younger generation now buses or drives to city jobs, leaving its elders to milk a cow or two, prune a few fruit trees, grow a few vegetables, keep a few hens, look after small grandchildren. Before the First World War rural over-population was seen as a serious Balkan problem and between the wars Yugoslavia's average rate of population growth was more than three times that of France and Britain – hence the post-war *Gastarbeiter* exodus. When the 1971 census showed some 790,500 Yugoslavs working temporarily abroad, officialdom reacted ambivalently. *Gastarbeiter* earnings boosted the economy but the desertion of the countryside had become a major worry, especially in Croatia. Although only 21 per cent of Yugoslavs were Croats, that republic supplied 34 per cent of the *Gastarbeiters*.

On a wooded ridgetop I paused to rest beside the lonely grave of a local hero, killed in October 1991 at the age of thirty-one. Croatia's chequerboard emblem had been engraved on his tall marble headstone and at its base someone (mother? wife?) had recently placed a carefully arranged tray of plastic flowers and two unlit candles. I was now on the periphery of the war zone created in September 1991 when the Krajina Serb militia captured this area of Croatia on behalf of Milošević – who at the time blandly denied having anything to do with these 'local disorders'. In August 1990 Milan Babić, leader of the 600,000 Croatian Serbs, had proclaimed the 'Autonomous Province of the Serbian Krajina' with Knin as its 'capital' – though in fact that town had never been part of the Habsburg Vojna Krajina. Exactly a year later – a memorably tense year – the Sabor (Croatian parliament) accepted the inevitability of full-scale war with Serbian forces, reconstituted many of its police units as the National Guard and forbade Croats to join the Federal Yugoslav Army. Now, fewer than 100,000 Serbs live in Croatia.

On the descent from that ridge I passed four other graves, marked only by small crude wooden crosses thrust askew into the leaf mould, the names already indecipherable. Then the sombre rustling beeches were left behind and ahead stretched bright miles of spring-green grass, clothing gentle slopes and shallow valleys. Several small churches could be seen in the distance, indicating villages invisible from the road; my binoculars revealed shell damage on all those church towers. Having guessed correctly at three signpostless junctions, a wrong guess took me up to a wide, high plateau of miles of grassland, unstocked and uncultivated, with more woods along the horizon. Here the road became a muddy track leading to an isolated three-storey farmhouse, a gaunt ruin, fire-blackened, its barn and stables shelled. As I turned back dark clouds were gathering swiftly to the north; then came a passing flurry of powdery snow, leaving the landscape all a-sparkle as the noon sun came out again. I was by now operating on two separate levels – the egocentric me exultant, pedalling on a traffic-free road through a quietly beautiful countryside in perfect cycling weather, the other me unsettled by this region's vibes.

Soon Pokupsko appeared, a large straggling hilltop village overlooking the river Kupa. My arrival astonished the few folk visible at lunchtime on a Sunday. A beer logo display in a bungalow window drew me into a tiny bar, previously the family's living room, where two teenage girls sat on high stools drinking Cokes and chatting with their contemporary behind the counter. All three spoke just enough English to understand that my secondary need (after *pivo*) was somewhere to lodge for the night. They discussed this problem between themselves at considerable length, giving me time for a second *pivo*. Then one smiled at me reassuringly before moving to the public phone with her phone card. The organizing of my accommodation took four calls yet payment was indignantly refused.

As I followed the main road towards my lodging a brass band was playing outside the village hall and groups of laughing children, wearing comic masks, were prancing and dancing towards it – celebrating the traditional pre-Lent carnival recently revived in Croatia. Pokupsko had the air of a village once prosperous but now in reduced circumstances. The war damage shocked me then though in fact it was comparatively slight: several homes bullet-pocked and with boarded-up windows, several others shelled and roofless, a few half-burnt. The small Catholic church had been bombed but not too severely; no one was attempting restoration – it seemed to have been neglected for many pre-war years.

The Veselicas' home stood alone beyond the village, a three-storey brick dwelling built in 1956 for the newly-wedded Mr and Mrs Veselica. The bride had planted four pine trees, now as tall as the house; to have trees growing with a young family was supposed to bring good luck – but it hadn't. Mr Veselica and his elder son were killed by the Serbian militia in 1991. The ground floor was divided between a large café-bar, closed since the war, and a disused store-room – a shell had knocked a very big hole in its gable wall. The hall door, in the other gable wall, had a Yale-type lock reinforced by an inner chain, always kept on its hook. Before the war, Mrs Veselica recalled wistfully, no one in Pokupsko locked doors. But now – well, with so much poverty around, and so many guns, it was best to take precautions.

I found Mrs Veselica and her aged aunt brewing herbal tea. My hostess was tall and sturdily built with a ruddy complexion and a wide smile. Aunty had been born deaf and dumb but gave me a welcoming hug and seemed serene and happy. Her tapestries and embroidery brightened the drab walls, were spread on the sofa and chairs and served as table-mats. Once she had regularly sold them in Zagreb market; now her failing sight precluded such close work, just when the family urgently needed that income.

Ruairi's safety was of immediate concern and Aunty led us to an enormous stone barn, generations older than the dwelling, where hens roosted on high perches, onions and pumpkins hung from the rafters, two horse-ploughs rusted in the shadows and the current distillation of *rakija* dripped quietly in a far corner. Here, behind a padlocked door, Ruairi would be very safe.

In this shabby but comfortable home a prototypical washing-machine stood idle in the bathroom (where water no longer flowed) and cooking was done on a wood-stove which also heated the large living-room-cum-kitchen and its curtained annexe. There I slept on a divan, beside a huge but happily out-of-order television set.

As I ate the remains of Sunday lunch (potato salad, a hard-boiled egg, bread), Mrs Veselica asked my age, using sign language, then chortled and shook hands on discovering that we were almost twins, born within the same week in 1931. Soon Melita arrived, the only Veselica daughter, accompanied by her three children – girls aged ten and eleven, an undersized six-year-old boy with a shaven head ('Ringworm', his mother whispered apologetically). In August 1991 Melita took her toddler and baby to stay in Munich with a *Gastarbeiter* uncle; five years later they returned, speaking adequate German and basic English. The children's initial shyness was quickly dispelled by my trying to learn how to count to ten in Serbo-Croat. This endeavour made them giggle convulsively and then they invited me to walk to the river to see the boat their father had built. He worked in a Zagreb factory and came home only every other weekend.

A rough track took us to the left bank of the Kupa. In September 1991, after the fall of Petrinja – a half-Croat, half-Serb town twenty-eight miles from Pokupsko – this river became the new frontier of one of the two largest Serb-conquered enclaves in Croatia, the other being the Knin Krajina. By a disconcerting coincidence, the Kupa hereabouts almost replicates my favourite stretch of the Blackwater River near my home town, Lismore. On our side small fields sloped slightly up to the base of Pokupsko's hill, on the far side a long, densely wooded ridge rose steeply from the water's edge. High on this ridge stood a solitary, ancient church, half-hidden by trees; from its tower the Krajina militia had shelled Pokupsko. For Melita and her mother, I realized later, that made the hole in their gable wall seem like an act not merely of aggression but of sacrilege. Their home having been attacked from their church – a church for centuries revered as *specially* sacred – added to the family's demoralization.

My companions thought of the war as that time when they lived in Germany while Serbs killed their grandfather and uncle and several neighbours. After our stroll by the river they showed me four abandoned homes (their idea, I didn't need this experience) and described in some detail the families' fates. Some had been shot, some stabbed to death. A young couple, their two small children and the husband's father had allegedly been decapitated and their heads stuck on the poles of their tiny vineyard above the river. Here I felt some scepticism; this story had the flavour of those Serbian legends about Bosniaks crucifying Serb babies before throwing them into rivers. But who knows? When leaders work hard to bring out the worst in their followers they can be gruesomely successful. True or not, such details having been told to children appalled me. Surely this was the sort of damage no 'international aid package' or 'reconstruction and development programme' could undo – a generation being initiated into hostility, conditioned to fear, hate and despise those who once were their fellow-Yugoslavs. Throughout this macabre tour both girls remained very matter-of-fact and their apparent detachment, while recalling throat-slashings and disembowellings, was in itself disturbing.

Back at the house, Mrs Veselica, Melita and Aunty were preparing costumes for that night's carnival masked ball, to which I was warmly invited. As the three women experimented with preposterous garments and grotesque masks, I marvelled at Aunty's participation. Her disability seemed much less of a handicap than it would be in our society. We provide special schooling, and nowadays advanced technology, for the deaf and dumb and make various 'politically correct' efforts on their behalf. Here Aunty's misfortune was accepted unselfconsciously; she simply fitted in to family and village life, loved for herself and admired for her talent. At first I wondered if she seemed so serene because her disability had somehow reduced the impact of the wartime horrors. But no, she was not unaware or isolated in her own world. Melita said, 'When the Serbs killed my father, and I went away with the babies, and my husband was in the National Guard, Aunty gave my mother courage. She is very strong.'

After dark, as we walked up to the village, I asked my companions, 'Are you pleased to be living in an independent Croatia?'

Melita said 'Yes', Mrs Veselica said 'No'. Then Melita explained, 'My mother remembers in Yugoslavia we were not poor. With independence village people will always be poor because that is the new way our government wants to run the country. But for my children I hope they live always in Germany, like our uncle. And that will be easier for them if they come from Croatia – not from Milošević's Yugoslavia!' She complained then about Pokupsko being 'forgotten' though in BiH foreigners were pouring millions of dollars and marks into villages for every sort of 'scheme'. Perhaps, she suggested ironically, Croatia hadn't suffered enough for long enough . . . I felt unqualified to comment, though already I had asked myself why Pokupsko looked so neglected when lavish spending had given Zagreb's centre a Rich World façade.

In the village's main café – a tawdry 1980s structure – the floor had been cleared for dancing by stacking most tables and chairs along one wall. Younger people were in a minority though what passed for music was geared to their taste. Truly dreadful cacophonies were exacerbated by shrieking men and women who, if heard in another context, would immediately be identified as torture victims. Although I made no remark Melita intuited my allergy and said, 'Here this is new, I'm sorry you don't hear our own old music.' Then Mrs Veselica murmured something and Melita translated. 'My mother says in Tito's time we were liking best our own music. In these days we want to seem like everyone else. She says many old people think same as you but it doesn't matter. In this new century only what young people want is important.'

The hours passed, the cigarette-smoky fug became eye-stinging, the pile of empty beer-crates outside the entrance to the loo rose rapidly. By midnight I was wearing a pair of outsize shiny plastic boobs with ostentatiously erect nipples and was balancing a chair on my head while a man sporting waist-length golden ringlets stood on a stool trying to thrust his plastic mega-penis into my left ear. This is known as 'entering into the spirit of the thing'. Mrs Veselica was running around with a plastic axe pretending to castrate young men who feigned terror at her approach. And Melita, wearing a bearded mask, was attempting to 'rape' a teenage girl clad in a transparent pink nightgown augmented by a knee-length, shawl-like black wig. It could all be described as good dirty fun, peasant-style – hilariously vulgar but not even slightly salacious. This is a community, I was later informed, where even in the year 2000 pre-marital sex is OUT; so perhaps these carnival capers serve as a safety-valve of sorts.

A long time after midnight we wavered home, all drunk – Mrs Veselica, Aunty, Melita and I linking arms and giggling and stumbling. Then we ate vast amounts of blotting-paper bread and cold sausage, followed by mugs of an excellent chicken broth prepared by the children while their elders were misbehaving. And so to bed, after goodnight kisses all round.

Despite those carnival capers, I was on the road soon after sunrise, crossing an ugly new bridge over the Kupa. Melita had showed me a photograph of its handsome predecessor, when pointing out the exact spot on the slope above where her father had been killed. She seemed to need to talk about his death and as she spoke I realized that she was trying to persuade herself that it had been an accident.

For fifteen miles a narrow unused road wound through mixed woodlands and over low mountains to join the main road near Glina. Previously this town's police force, Communist Party and few inconspicuous industries had been controlled by Glina's Serbs – the majority solid social democrats, untainted by nationalism and with no ambition to join a Greater Serbia. In the April 1990 elections most voted for the Party of Democratic Change (formerly the Communist Party). But a year of exposure to Serbian extremist propaganda and Tudjman's vicious Croatian police moved them to fight on the Serbian side in 1991. Thereafter various militias repeatedly attacked Glina as the fortunes of war seesawed. Yet the town retains a ghostly Habsburg flavour, emanating from a few public buildings of imperial gravitas and classical proportions.

At 8.30 that morning only one café was open and I couldn't have an omelette because the day's eggs had not yet been delivered. The bleary-eyed young waiter (also suffering from a post-carnival hangover?) seemed to enjoy giving me this bad news. From my table by the window I could see the locked Orthodox church which I had already tried to enter. In 1941 the Ustasha herded 800 Serbs into that church before killing them – an event pre-figuring some of Rwanda's 1994 massacres. Also, more than 1,000 civilian Serbs – men, women and children – were slaughtered on the edge of the town. A similar war crime is said to have been committed on the edge of Knin by some of the US-backed Croatian troops who forcibly uprooted the Krajina Serbs in August 1995.

A terrifying few miles on the main road – not nearly wide enough for its countless impatient truck-drivers – took me to the turn-off for Velika Kladuša just over the border in BiH (the Serbo-Croat acronym for Bosnia and Herzegovina). There I was to stay with Nurvet and his family, friends of my Zagreb friends. For thirty miles the road wandered through depopulated farmland, following the erratic course of the river Glina and passing only one village – Topusko, renowned as the Partizans' regional headquarters during the Second World War. Hereabouts 60 per cent of Tito's guerrillas were anti-Nazi, anti-Ustasha Croats, their stronghold the wooded hills now all about me.

Near Topusko many unlovely traces remained of the enormous open-air emergency camp for Displaced Persons set up by the river in August 1995. There thousands of dispossessed Krajina Serbs awaited UNHCR transport to already overcrowded camps in Serbia.

For the last few miles the narrow Glina marks the border and the road runs just above the riverbank; on the BiH side I could see two young Bosniak women planting potatoes in heavy clay soil – they dug with difficulty. Both wore headscarves and baggy trousers, no longer usual garb in BiH. In general, throughout Tito's time, individual peasant farmers retained control of animal husbandry and supplied most of Yugoslavia's poultry and dairy products, fruits and vegetables. But agri-businesses also existed and now a relic of the most notorious of these, Agrokomerc, appeared beyond the river – several abandoned battery hen units. Agrokomerc has entered the history books because of its founder's triple career as entrepreneur, political wheeler-dealer and warlord. His tale is worth a digression. When first I heard the details these sounded familiar – naturally enough, Fikret Abdić being a magnified version of some of Ireland's more inglorious political leaders.

Abdić was born in 1939, in an impoverished hamlet near Velika Kladuša, the third of his parents' many children. On leaving school he found a job with the local agricultural co-op, which then had twenty-six employees. In 1959 he joined the League of Communists and was elected a Deputy at the age of twenty-four, becoming a member of the Bosnian Communist Central Committee four years later. Already he was seen as one of Bosnia's most powerful men; that little co-op had become Agrokomerc – Abdić's empire. The industry quickly grew to employ 13,500 men and women, run 430 farms in fifty villages, hold the monopoly on Yugoslavia's chicken and turkey market, produce a variety of processed foods in fifty-two factories and export enough to the Middle East significantly to assist Yugoslavia's purchase of oil.

In 1967 Abdić's entrepreneurial genius earned him the Bosnian government's most coveted mark of honour, the King Faisal Award. Agrokomerc was transforming what had been an extremely poor region, half-forgotten by Tito's developers, and the locals idolized Abdić – known to all throughout his fiefdom as 'Babo' (Daddy). Another generation was to grow up before the sensational allegations, in 1987, of Agrokomerc's rotten foundations. It was alleged that for decades Abdić had been juggling with Yugoslavia's unique 'bank bond' system on a scale that amounted to printing money – us$300 million, to be exact. He was then charged though never actually convicted on numerous counts of contract-linked corruption and imprisoned for more than two years while investigations proceeded.

Now the whole Agrokomerc-dependent economy of north-west Bosnia (the Bihać area) teetered on the brink of collapse. But the police investigations led, predictably, to no indictments and on Abdić's release in 1989 certain skilful negotiations rapidly revived his empire – without restoring it to full health. It was rumoured that he looked back on his imprisonment, which had involved the minimum of hardship, as fortuitous. It gave him time for rest and reflection – reflection on how he could most profitably react to Slobodan Milošević's increasingly convoluted manoeuvrings. Also, he had become even more popular while 'inside', the Bosnians having persuaded themselves that he was the innocent victim of an anti-Bosnian conspiracy.

Soon Abdić was appointed a delegate to the (dying) Assembly of Yugoslav Republics and could be identified as the main political rival of Alija Izetbegović, the Bosnian President. In Bosnia's first multi-party elections at the end of 1990 he received 48 per cent of the vote as against Izetbegović's 40 per cent but, for reasons unclear, he chose not to take on the responsibilities of leadership. Instead, he nominated a close colleague, Alija Delimustafić, as Interior Minister. A Serb was then named as Speaker of that doomed parliament and a Croat as Prime Minister.

In 1991 Abdić was recruited by General Aleksandar Vasiljević, head of Yugoslavia's military counter-intelligence (kos) to provision the Federal Yugoslav Army (jna) during the war in Croatia. When the Serbs launched their terrorist campaign against BiH in the spring of 1992 a series of enigmatic events stirred suspicions that Babo, supported by Belgrade and a clique of jna generals, now wished to replace Izetbegović. Abdić argued that Izetbegović could only inflict more suffering on his own people – and on all Bosnians – by refusing to concede victory to the Serbs. However, around besieged Sarajevo his popularity was waning and in September 1992 he returned to his home base, by then known as 'the Bihać Pocket', determined to keep Agrokomerc productive despite the war. To regain his grip on regional affairs he took on an advisory role in the District Assembly and used all his wheeler-dealer dexterity to keep the Pocket out of the fast-spreading conflict. The un's inclusion of Bihać on its fatally misleading list of six Muslim 'Safe Havens' gave him no comfort; as he well knew, the Great Powers lacked the will to provide the means to protect those areas. When it became obvious that the Bosnian Government's 5th Corps could not possibly defend Bihać, Abdić resolved to negotiate with the Serbs. He then publicly condemned Izetbegović's refusal even to consider the partition of BiH – something ultimately inevitable, in Abdić's view, since the Serbs had seized 70 per cent of the republic's territory. An Open Letter to Izetbegović ended with stern words:

Before our country takes on the fate of a still-born child, and the Muslim people are forced into reservations and condemned to slow death, we have to turn the situation to our advantage and finally become seasoned partners, mature enough to deal with the historic cataclysm which we now face.

Shortly afterwards, Abdić was observed on the island of Brioni, demonstrating his 'maturity' by advising President Tudjman on how he should bargain during the next round of peace talks. He then began to echo the outrageous Serbian and Croatian accusations that Izetbegović was playing the Islamic fundamentalist game, a 'spin' that deceived certain Great Power representatives who should have known better.

By this stage the Bosnian Serbs and Bosnian Croats had kissed and made up and decided to unite against the Muslims. Therefore Croatia, now at war with Izetbegović's Sarajevo government, was as keen as the Serbs to divide the Muslim leadership and Tudjman granted Agrokomerc the valuable concession of a duty-free area in Rijeka, Croatia's main port. Other deals guaranteed a nourishing cash-flow for the convalescent Agrokomerc and steady jobs for its employees. Soon Abdić was being praised in Belgrade, Zagreb and Pale (the headquarters of Mladic and Karadžić) as 'a man of peace' – while in Sarajevo, his home capital, he was being reviled as a traitor.

In the summer of 1993, as Sarajevo's besieged citizens continued to endure extreme deprivation and terror, representatives of BiH's three communities luxuriated in five-star Geneva hotels during the peace talks mediated by Lord Owen and Thorvald Stoltenberg. When Abdić was summoned to attend he gladly joined the Bosnian Presidency delegation, which viewed his arrival with considerable unease. The mediators had identified him as a Muslim who at this stage could depose Izetbegović and would then 'do the sensible thing' by agreeing to partition along 'ethnic' lines, thus ending the conflict by rewarding Serbian aggression. But Izetbegović proved less deposable than expected; the mediators had overestimated Abdić's cunning. Meanwhile, back on the battleground, the fighting became ever more ferocious as each army, foreseeing a carve-up, strove to grab as much territory as possible before peace was imposed.

On 30 July it seemed that the mediators/appeasers had won. Izetbegović, feeling increasingly trapped by the Great Powers' shameless backing of the Serbs, had reluctantly accepted the 'Joint-Action Plan'. This gave to the Serbs 53 per cent of BiH's territory, to the Bosniaks 30 per cent, to the Croats 17 per cent – though the 1991 populations were 44 per cent Bosniak, 31 per cent Serb, 17 per cent Croat. These of course are approximate figures; in urban areas, by the late 1980s, some 30 per cent of marriages were 'mixed'. (So much, incidentally, for 'ancestral tribal hatreds'; where those exist, as in Northern Ireland, mixed marriages are rare.)

A triumphant Milošević then declared, 'This Plan completely affirms Republika Srpska'. A member of the Bosnian Serb delegation announced that the Serbs had won the war 'and now the Turks [an insulting sobriquet for Bosniaks] are going to be like walnuts in a Serbian-Croatian nutcracker'. But he spoke too soon. At the very last moment Izetbegović backed off, as so often before – quoting from UN Security Council Resolution 242 which refers, in the Palestinian context, to 'the inadmissibility of the acquisition of territory by force'. He could not bring himself to accept the defeat of a people who had done nothing to provoke aggression and had been prevented from defending themselves by the Great Powers' arms embargo.

As the exasperated mediators and thwarted (in different ways) delegations dispersed, Abdić returned to Velika Kladuša with a new idea. Emboldened by the Great Powers' recognition of his potential usefulness, he proclaimed the 'Autonomous Region of Western Bihać (ARWB) on 29 September 1993, appointing himself as President of the flourishing enclave that soon formed around Velika Kladuša. Here was the Abdić heartland, the northern half of the Bihać Pocket which, since August 1993, had been completely surrounded by Serbian troops.

Having acquired a territory mainly inhabited by loyal 'subjects', Abdić's next requirement was an army to defend it and, with luck, extend it over the entire Pocket. He found recruitment easy. By the autumn of 1993 the ordinary Bihać folk cared nothing for the ideas or ambitions of *any* politicians, diplomats or generals; day-to-day survival absorbed all their energies. Most men from northern Bihać, then serving with Bosnia's 5th Corps or the Territorial Defence Forces, saw Agrokomerc as a much more reliable paymaster than the destitute Sarajevo government and eagerly switched their allegiance to Abdić's militia, known as the APWB forces. Not of course to be confused with those other forces then operating in BiH – the Armija (Bosnian Muslim Army), the BSA (Bosnian Serb Army), the HV (Croatian Army), the HVO (Bosnian Croat Army), the JNA (Yugoslav National Army) and the SARSK (Serbian Army of the Republic of Srpska Krajina). It is sometimes argued, only half-jokingly, that the Great Powers betrayed BiH not for any sinister political reasons but quite simply because they couldn't get a handle on who was fighting whom – and when, where and why.

Abdić's militia consisted of six brigades armed with heavy machine-guns and new light mortars bought from SARSK. By mid-October the town of Cazin had become the first casualty of a new conflict: Abdić's APWB forces versus Izetbegović's 5th Corps, Bosniak versus Bosniak. In Cazin, on 4 December, General Atif Dudaković, commander of the 5th Corps, met a UN Military Observer team and excoriated Unprofor for allowing SARSK forces to resupply Abdić's militia and grant them unrestricted access to the Krajina. General Dudaković was not alone in his failure to understand the UN's 'peace-keeping' ethos which dictated that a United Nations Protection Force, dispatched to a country at war, was mandated only to protect itself. In Bihać, as elsewhere, Unprofor troops had to sit around watching the slaughter and waiting for the combatants to withdraw – at which point the Blue Berets were free to collect corpses and drive the wounded to hospital. On Christmas Day 1993 there were more than a thousand of the latter, after the 5th Corps had dislodged Abdić's militia from the Skokovi Pass and the town of Pecigrad.

On all sides, including Unprofor, military commanders either pretended not to notice the flourishing black market or, more usually, participated in it – as did the Croatian police and army who, though officially at war with SARSK, never checked the flow of contraband into their territory. Once these goods were over the border, in the hands of the SARSK Kordun Corps, Abdić could buy whatever luxuries he fancied. Meanwhile, the SARSK Lika Corps were supplying both essentials and luxuries to their own enemy, General Dudaković and his 5th Corps men. And, because Abdić could afford not to haggle, a relative of the Croatian Defence Minister was furtively selling to the APWB a wide variety of weapons for which the ammunition had been donated by the Bosnian Serb Army.

During the ARWB's brief existence, sanctions-busting became very big business. Central to the Abdić-Tudjman deal was the sale to Agrokomerc of fuel and other essentials, ostensibly for use only in the ARWB. However, long convoys of oil-tankers traversed the Krajina every day to supply both the Bosnian Serbs and Serbia itself. In a conflict notorious for its scams, this was the greatest. And the region's swarming military expats (bureaucratic, diplomatic and legal) regularly witnessed this lucrative trading. Yet nothing was done to enforce UN sanctions until, in August 1994, the 5th Corps drove Abdić and his militia out of Bihać.

More than 30,000 Muslims, so loyal to Babo that they feared reprisals when the 5th Corps took control, at once followed their leader over the border to Croatia. But these wretched people, soon to be known internationally as 'Abdić's refugees', were refused admission to Zagreb-held territory. Croatia, having yet again turned its coat, now spurned Abdić who was no longer in a position to engender war profits all round. Thus, by a bizarre turn of Fortune's wheel, some 20,000 Abdić worshippers found themselves crammed into the foetid buildings of a disused Agrokomerc chicken-farm

In October 1994, when Izetbegović's 5th Corps moved south from the Pocket, SARSK began hurriedly to arm the males among 'Abdić's refugees' and then deployed them to attack the 5th Corps from the rear. As General Dudaković was not equipped to fight on two fronts, the Serbs quickly recaptured Velika Kladuša though the 5th Corps successfully defended the rest of the Pocket. Ten months later the Croatian army defeated SARSK and Abdić's militia disintegrated overnight. Retreating to Rijeka on the coast, he promptly founded another commercial enterprise, FINAB food company, which was soon employing 1,200 grateful Croats. In 1996 the Bihać authorities tried him, in absentia, for war crimes. But he took that as rather a joke and when last heard of was still interested in resuming his political career in BiH and resurrecting Agrokomerc.

To return to my narrative – I found a row of concrete-filled tar barrels blocking the BiH border, which explained the blissful lack of motor traffic all the way from Glina. Ruairi could have been wheeled between the barrels but a surly young man, emerging from a nearby shrapnel-scarred house (the only building in sight) wordlessly discouraged this illegality. He pointed to an earth track leading to the main Vojnić to Velika Kladuša road and the official crossing. Thus I came by chance upon Batnoga, the infamous Agrokomerc chicken-farm refugee camp described by Tim Judah as 'the epitome of the Bosnian nightmare'. Here my imagination didn't merely boggle, it cravenly swerved away from the image of 20,000 frightened human beings enduring confinement for four months in a few battery-henhouses within sight of their own hilltop homes in Velika Kladuša, less than two miles away. Not until the end of December 1994 were those thousands released from their torment.

Eight months later a European Community Monitor Mission (ECMM) was reporting:

> The refugees from Velika Kladuša are now living in Kuplensko [Croatia] under miserable conditions and they refuse to return home. The Abdić refugees are jointly accommodated in the primary school and empty houses. The Croatian military commander in Vojnić stated that these refugees who formerly lived in Turani and Batnoga were looting and stealing from local properties. To prevent this a joint Croatian police/military presence had been strengthened and ECMM and the ICRC were asked to leave the area.

Most 'Abdić refugees' eventually returned to Velika Kladuša (what choice had they?) where it did not surprise me to find the atmosphere uncheerful. It takes more than four and a half years for people to recover from such a sequence of severe communal traumas.

Overlooking Velika Kladuša is an imposing fortified castle (900 years old, say some: but that seems improbable) which Babo was in the process of converting to a presidential palace when fate intervened. Walking through the moribund town centre, I several times sought guidance, showing Nurvet's address written in block capitals. All those I approached stared at me incredulously, saying nothing, then shrugged and went on their way. I had almost given up hope when a smiling young woman ran across the street and exclaimed, 'You must be the person from Ireland! We are waiting for you, my father likes writers, he is excited to meet you – come!'

As we walked between high-rise residential blocks, not much war damaged, Flora (aged twenty-one) talked rapidly in American-tinged English. 'I was never a teenager,' she informed me, 'not in the Western way. In war you have to stay a child, not trying to understand, or grow up fast. I grew up fast. After primary school I had no more education but that didn't matter. My parents could educate me. For other young people it matters a lot and here many are angry. Having no education means no hope and it's not fair. They didn't make the war. Velika Kladuša had no conflict until outsiders made it. We were lucky, in '93 we ran away like everyone else when the area got too dangerous but we could get beyond Batnoga! We bribed the Croats and stayed with our friends in Zagreb. After two months we came home and next time didn't run away. We were never Abdić people, always we supported Mr Izetbegović.'

At the entrance to a block on the edge of town, Flora apologized for the non-functioning lift and I removed the panniers before carrying Ruairi upstairs – to Nurvet's mortification, when he opened the hall door. Sharply he reprimanded Flora for not having summoned him to do the porterage. She laughed and said, 'But our Irish friend is a liberated lady, she doesn't need men!'

The windows of this roomy sixth-floor flat gave fine views of green hills and wooded valleys stretching away to the south. One living-room wall was shelved from floor to ceiling and never have I seen a more comprehensive display of Penguin Classics, dating back to the 1950s. 'How did you keep them safe?' I asked.

Nurvet smiled, put a finger to his lips, then whispered, 'Now I must shock you! I paid a friend in the 5th Corps, a senior officer, to keep an armed guard here! That was good for everyone in this block. There were no torchings though other flats were looted.'

Nurvet – tall, thin, silver-haired, slightly stooped – spoke fluent English but at first I found his accent difficult. While Flora was brewing coffee he echoed what she had already said: 'For us, in this Cazin-Bihać area, the war was such a *shock*! We never thought about this person being Muslim, that one Serb, the other Croat. We were all Bosnians. Our war was something false, from outside, not something waiting fifty years under the surface like outsiders wanted to see. Every day in Zagreb I got into rages reading what some journalists were writing – in important papers, papers that influence thinking and then acting. If the West tried to understand Bosnia they couldn't have forgotten justice and only looked for peace at any price. They didn't want to understand, they only wanted peace to give themselves an escape. They were afraid of the Serbian aggressors. They didn't think about the other sort of Serbs who would have liked them to defend Bosnia. Serbs are the same as the rest of us, all are not *bad people*.' At that moment, as though on cue, we heard footsteps in the hall and Nurvet said, 'My wife comes, now you'll meet a *good* Serb!'

Vesna was small, plump and exhausted-looking, a physiotherapist who had spent a long day working with war-maimed children. She sat beside me on the sofa and Flora brought more coffee as her mother said, 'I'm not as simple as a good Serb, my mother was a Croat.'

Flora chuckled and said, 'So what am I? I know there's an English word for it, when a dog is all mixed up – what is it?'

'Mongrel,' I replied. 'Knowledgeable dog-lovers prefer mongrels, they've more character and intelligence than pure-breds.'

Nurvet feigned distress. 'Am I not having much character and intelligence? I'm a pure-bred Muslim – I think. No one can be sure, in Bosnia, if you go back far enough.'

Abruptly Vesna turned towards me and remarked, 'You look depressed – are you?'

Taken aback, I hesitated. Then Nurvet said dryly, 'You don't have to be polite. We don't expect foreigners not to be depressed in the dead Yugoslavia. Why have you come here? It's not now a holiday place.'

I fumbled my reply, dithered about wanting to see for myself the results of outside interventions in the post-war Balkans.

'So you must be feeling guilty because your side behaved so badly,' diagnosed Nurvet. His wife and daughter nodded agreement.

'To me it's strange,' said Vesna, 'how argumentative and *emotional* foreigners get amongst themselves about the Balkans. Is it because they're using this bit of Europe as a laboratory, testing things out here? Like new ways of "peace-keeping" and delivering "impartial" humanitarian aid. And doing "human rights" and "war crimes" experiments. And here and in Kosovo practising how to set up civil administrations and police forces and "democratic" governments. That gets so many different sorts of ex-pats involved here, all trying to prove their own systems and methods are best. And some trying to turn Balkan history this way and that to suit their own theories.'

Nurvet picked up the theme. 'Also being *so* superior! How dare they criticize Balkan corruption! Some of their own most respected men tried to use a criminal like Abdić to get their way in Bosnia.'

'Hey dad, that's how *realpolitik* works!' Flora winked at me, enjoying playing devil's advocate.

Her father cracked his knuckles and said, '*Realpolitik!* You know what it is? It's the notion leaders use to bully people, make them think they're being silly when they look for justice and honesty. All this new talk about "human rights" – offices being opened all over the world, teams sent here and there – if it meant anything it would kill *realpolitik*. You can't have both.'

'I'm hungry,' said Vesna. 'We must eat. That's my *realpolitik* for now.'

Flora went to the kitchen and Nurvet continued, 'Donors complain about our corruption then feed it with their aid programmes. They pretend they can control the spending but they can't. If they really tried they'd start another war – gang warfare – and lose their jobs. Every day they condemn Balkan corruption but always in a general way to excuse their own failures. They hardly ever name guilty individuals or send the UN police after them. The money they throw around makes the criminals so strong the donors daren't confront them.'

Vesna intervened. 'Here in this region thousands could never have rebuilt their homes without aid.'

Her husband said something in Serbo-Croat that sounded as though it might have had four letters in English. Then he asked, 'How do you know that's true? We've had wars before there were aid programmes and always people rebuilt. Maybe so many wouldn't have run away from here, leaving homes to be looted and torched, if they didn't know foreigners would feed them over the border.'

The gathering cloud of acrimony was dispelled by Flora's reappearance; she placed an enormous casserole on the dining-table and I pleased everyone by putting away three helpings of *djuveć* – mutton stewed with rice, carrots, peas, tomatoes, peppers. Afterwards I could scarcely keep awake; the masked ball was taking its toll. As I unrolled my flea-bag Vesna and Nurvet wrote the names and telephone numbers of several of their Sarajevo friends into my notebook.

6

Crossing a Shameful 'Border'

From Velika Kladuša there was no alternative to the main road to Ostrožac – thirty traffic-plagued miles against a strong, relentless headwind. As on certain Kenyan highways, not only was I at risk – so were the drivers who might have crashed while trying to avoid me. I pedalled past hamlets and villages devastated by Serbian 155-mm shells, cluster-bombs and ORKAN rockets, which last had dispersed anti-personnel mines over wide areas. Here was much reconstruction, including new mosques provided by Saudi Arabia, and other oil-rich donors, immediately after the signing of the Dayton Agreement. Given the statistics – less than 20 per cent of Bosniaks are practising Muslims – this instant replacement of mosques seemed a proselytizing rather than humanitarian enterprise. In shattered Cazin I stopped for a coffee and the young waiter voiced similar thoughts: 'More than mosques we need factories, clinics, schools, houses.'

I asked, 'Would you like Mr Abdić to come back?' He looked startled, then said defensively, 'I don't know this Mr Abdić.'

Cazin lies in a hollow, between steep hills; it used to be a busy, unlovely industrial town. As I pushed Ruairi up and up, I was overlooking yet another abandoned Agrokomerc industrial estate. Beside this region's countless ruins were new bridges, houses, cafés, petrol stations, post offices, shops, schools, clinics, even a few small factories. The visual effect of so much rapid breeze-block reconstruction was not pleasing (angular shapes, garish colours, brash plastic façades) but at least these villages had been given a chance to resume a normal existence.

At 8.30 a.m. the road had been thickly iced but by noon the brilliant sun felt warmish, even on a high pass where snow was piled along the verges. The traffic included countless speeding 'aid' vehicles whose drivers tend not to set indigenous populations a good example. Within two hours I saw the ubiquitous white 4 x 4s of the UNHCR, UNICEF, WFP, ICRC, EU, OSCE, I-for police – not to mention a convoy of Canadian S-For military vehicles bristling with long menacing guns. Those made me wonder – not for the last time – why, more than four years after Dayton, S-For continued to display its weaponry. Such displays can't be intended to reassure the populace, given the force's commitment to protecting only its own troops. And they certainly don't help to restore a tranquil atmosphere.

The headwind, and many formidable gradients, made me realize how unfit I was. By 2 p.m. I had decided to abandon Bosanska Krupa, my original destination for the day, in favour of Ostrožac's hotel, advertised outside Cazin – which fact should have warned me off. By the time the monstrosity appeared I had freewheeled down to the Una valley, a steep three-mile descent through a forest of towering pines. Not feeling like a steep three-mile ascent, I resigned myself to a £30 room in this 200-bed mutation of a Swiss chalet. Its architect must have been peculiarly perverse; he took no advantage of a superb riverbank site. Moreover, the bedroom balconies – each furnished with a plastic table and chairs – were so designed that one could admire the Una valley only when standing up.

Next morning a dense river mist delayed my start; on the very narrow, very twisting Prijedor-Bihać road no mist-obscured cyclist could long survive. Here the Una valley is almost a gorge, through which wriggle the road, the racing river – violently white in springtime – and the strategically important Split-Zagreb railway. Largely because of the railway, this became a much-fought-over region as BiH's triangular conflict developed.

That conflict's shifting alliances – and the proliferation of local militias – owed much to us military input, official and freelance. In preparation for Operation Storm, when Tudjman's army launched a forcible uprooting campaign against the Knin Krajina Serbs, help came from the Virginia-based Military Professional Resources Inc. This private enterprise, set up by former us Marines and other 'special forces', supplied sophisticated weaponry to the Croatian army. And sometimes it subcontracted – for instance, to two British private 'security' companies which in 1998 didn't do much for Kosovo's 'security' by helping to arm and train the Kosovo Liberation Army. More recently, in the spring of 2001, Military Professional Resources Inc. provided training programmes for both the Macedonian army and the KLA. 'Privatized' militarism thrives on armed conflict and directly discourages political settlements.

The very beautiful Una valley had a litter problem spectacularly exacerbated by looters. The usual roadside deposits of household waste, spilling out of burst plastic bags, were here augmented by armchairs, dressers, beds, tables, 'white goods' – all seized in some frenzy of hate and greed, then dumped when no longer easily transported.

Where the valley opens out, near Bosanska Krupa, I saw the first of countless hoardings erected by aid agencies to demarcate their territory. This one said: RECONSTRUCTION OF HOUSES IN BOSANSKA KRUPA MUNICIPALITY. EC HUMANITARIAN OFFICE. IMPLEMENTED BY EDINBURG (*sic*) DIRECT AID. In a bottom corner some ingrate had neatly inscribed 'Fuck Of!' The reverse side, carrying the same information, had been temporarily obliterated by a large Croatian Democratic Union (HDZ) election poster.

Bosanska Krupa is close to the 'border' between the Bosniak-Croat Federation 'entity' and the Republika Srpska 'entity' – as the Dayton Agreement describes those artificially separated regions into which it divided BiH. The town was doomed as early as July 1991 when the three leaders of its Serbian community (27 per cent of the population) boycotted the legally elected municipal body, established the Serbian Municipality of Bosanska Krupa and displayed a new map illustrating their appropriation of 60 per cent of the town. Force would be used against any Bosniak or Croat who opposed this partition. From then on, all male Serbs wore paramilitary or police uniforms. During the next nine months the Bosniak members of the local Territorial Defence Force did what they could (not much) to arm themselves.

Typically, in the course of this well-planned terrorist campaign, Chetnik para-militaries overran a town, murdered many Bosniak and/or Croat civilians and expelled the rest. Surviving Bosniaks of military age were either used as slave labourers or held in concentration camps under unimaginably cruel conditions. Next the JNA-protected local Serbs were put in charge, with orders to demolish their town's mosques, madrasas, hammams and other centuries-old relics of Ottoman civilization. Many of the Chetniks were criminals who had been released early on condition they 'fought well'. Milošević's secret police controlled their military activities and colluded in their black-marketeering.

In mid-April 1992 the Bosniak Mayor of Cazin and his Chief of Police pleaded pathetically for the UN to take over the administration of this whole Bihać Pocket and eject the JNA. By then Bosanska Krupa's Bosniaks knew an attack was imminent; the town's Serbian women and children had been temporarily evacu-ated. At about 5 p.m. on 21 April the first shell was fired and the Chetnik gangs went into action with assault rifles and machine guns. For three days the shelling continued, until all the Bosniak buildings on the right bank of the Una had been reduced to irreparable ruins. Then the 'cleansing' began. Prisoners from the town jail were used to collect corpses and clear rubble. No one will ever know how many men of military age were murdered. More than 3,000 women and chil-dren, from Bosanska Krupa and surrounding villages, were dispatched to con-centration camps.

At first, in BiH's mixed villages (and most were mixed), the Chetniks could not rely on local Serbs to kill or evict their Bosniak friends, neighbours, work-mates – sometimes in-laws. The solution for this problem was also used by the Interahamwe leaders of Rwanda's genocide. A gang would arrive in a village, approach a Serbian home and compel the head of the household (or his grown-up son) to accompany them to a Bosniak home where any available male was bidden to join the party. Those neighbours were then taken to a public place where the Serb was ordered to kill the Bosniak and provided with an AK-47 or – more usually – a knife. The many Serbs who refused to co-operate when this campaign opened were instantly shot dead. Soon all Serbs could be relied upon to obey Chetnik orders to 'cleanse' their villages.

From the outskirts, Bosanska Krupa looked deceptively intact: stretching along the riverbank, semi-encircled to the west by lowish ridges, overlooked from the east by highish mountains. Slowly I wheeled Ruairi through reconstructed streets where aid programme hoardings jostled each other. Eight occupied one grassy patch at a junction: RECONSTRUCTION OF ELECTRICAL NETWORK – Donor: Echo – Implementing Party: Mercy Corps, Scottish European Aid. WATER SUPPLY IMPROVEMENTS – Employer: European Union Representation Office of the European Commission to Bosnia and Herzegovina – Beneficiary: JKP '10 Juli' Bosanska Krupa – Engineer: Rodeco GmbH Fed. Rep. of Germany. Contractor: GMC Engineering Sarajevo. RECONSTRUCTION OF HOUSES IN BOSANSKA KRUPA MUNICIPALITY – Impact. And so on and on . . . Despite all these efforts, the town seemed to be in a state of suspended animation. At 9.15 on a crisp sunny morning few citizens were visible, the traffic consisted entirely of aid vehicles and the poorly stocked shops were not yet open. Coming within sight of the old Bosniak quarter, now all ruins, I stopped – then turned back, sickened by that glimpse.

Normally I eschew alcohol until the day's cycling is done but Bosanska Krupa drove me to order a *rakija* with my coffee. In an empty new café, smelling of cement dust and shiny with plastic tiles and metallic furniture, the one-eyed proprietor was stiffly unwelcoming. But when I pretended not to notice this he quite quickly unstiffened, then summoned his English-speaking daughter who arrived with babe in arms. Violeta worked part-time with a Canadian NGO and for an hour served as our interpreter while her four-months-old son conveniently slept.

Violeta's mother had died of general septicaemia in the Jasenica concentration camp, aged forty-two. Her only brother had died on the nearby hills, aged seventeen, trying to fight the Chetniks with a shotgun. Zlatan, her father, had spent six months – and lost an eye – in a concentration camp near Prijedor. Before the aggression (as Violeta phrased it) he had owned a small factory; on 22 April 1992 Serbian shells destroyed both it and his home. Yet he considered himself relatively lucky; two brothers with permanent jobs in Austria had helped to build the café and the four-roomed flat above it. Violeta's husband worked full-time as an interpreter in a Bihać EU office.

Zlatan admitted to having confused feelings about foreigners. They had kept off the scene while it was dangerous, while the Serbs were savaging the Bosniaks (and some Croats) – then had arrived in their multitudes when it was profitable to intervene. The reconstruction of BiH, he argued – as had Nurvet – brought big bucks to the donors' corporate buddies. The deconstruction of BiH, he believed, could have been prevented, and many thousands of lives saved, by a short sharp

Great Powers military intervention early in 1992. He recalled European Union Monitors frequently visiting Bosanska Krupa during that fateful April, observing what was happening, trying to organize 'peace talks' and writing detailed daily reports which prompted no action. Then he recalled how it was *before* . . . He grew up – as did Violeta, to the age of fifteen – in a town free of all but the most minor tensions. Bosniaks, Serbs and Croats shared a sense of belonging to Bosanska Krupa. What had shattered that? He couldn't fully understand, though the topic was so much discussed. But he knew the shattering was for ever; 'reconciliation' could never be on his agenda. At which point I requested another coffee and *rakija*.

In silence Zlatan brought the tiny cup and tiny glass and topped up my water glass. Then he went to stand in his doorway and looked up and down the street – a little busier now, though scarcely bustling. Violeta translated, 'He says please don't think he's not grateful for all the foreign help. He has to say "thank you" for bringing back water, electricity, medicines, X-rays, phones – everything! Without outsiders, we'd still be living like Gypsies!'

The map showed a choice of routes to Prijedor: the main road, via Bosanski Novi, or minor roads through the mountains via Sanski Most. I didn't have to hesitate and soon was panting up a steep mountainside between tall, roofless nineteenth-century buildings and heaps of rubble half-concealed by weeds and saplings.

That climb ended on a wide, uneven plateau of extraordinary beauty and heart-breaking devastation. In 1991 this fertile expanse was quite densely populated; I was rarely out of sight of villages on gentle grassy slopes, or ridgetop hamlets, or roadside farmsteads – all shelled, burnt, looted. The looting had been systematic: everything movable taken, including doors, windows, guttering, electric wiring. Then the roof was shelled or the whole building set alight. Half-built houses had also been attacked; it was the custom to build in instalments, as *Gastarbeiters* saved the necessary funds, and families sometimes lived in ground-floor rooms before the structure had been completed. In many yards stood the incinerated skeletons of cars, vans, a few trucks – but, oddly, no tractors. Were these taken as loot? But then why not take every vehicle? Perhaps there were not enough looters to drive them all away. From the top branches of a tall lime tree hung the rusted frame of a bicycle, no doubt flung there by the blast that demolished the adjacent house. Over twenty-five miles I saw only three aged couples, surviving in some clumsily restored corner of a once-comfortable dwelling.

I like the silence of naturally uninhabited regions – in fact I need it, the blessing of silence draws me to remote places. But here the silence felt like a curse.

In BiH the killing and expulsion of non-Serb populations, and the destruction of their property and livestock, was not an incidental consequence of warfare – which is why I found this battlefield that was not a battlefield so peculiarly distressing. As Brendan O'Shea has recorded, in his carefully documented *Crisis at Bihać*:

. . . the Muslims were barely able to defend themselves because of a deliberate policy that the JNA had implemented as they withdrew from the area earlier that month [April 1992]. While they handed over huge quantities of arms and equipment to both the Krajina and Bosnian Serbs, the Muslims and Croats were given nothing. From then on the local Serb militias were at liberty to use tanks, artillery, mortars, anti-aircraft guns and helicopters more or less at will.

Why, then, did the 'international community' react as though a *real* war were being fought? A war out of which they were determined to keep, while even-handedly providing humanitarian relief? In *Bankrupt in the Balkans*, J.M.O. Sharp quoted from a US report, dated January 1993, noting that 'Serbian warlords were allocated 23 per cent of UN relief supplies'.

The IC undoubtedly saved lives by sponsoring humanitarian relief on a massive scale, yet by November 1992 Sadako Ogata, the UN High Commissioner for Refugees, was asking:

To what extent do we persuade people to remain where they are, when that could well jeopardise their lives and liberties? On the other hand, if we help them to move, do we not become an accomplice to 'ethnic cleansing'?

Different questions should have been asked: Why are we sending the wrong message to the 'cleansers'? Why are we granting their criminal campaign the status of a 'war', a legitimate activity requiring 'impartial' humanitarian responses from 'concerned' neutrals? (Some of us think it odd that at this stage of humankind's development *any* war can be considered legitimate: but that's beside the present point.)

At 3.30, from the edge of the plateau, I was looking down on Lušci Palanka, a small forlorn town, apparently abandoned in its wide green valley far below. But no, not quite abandoned. As I bumped down on a shell-roughened road, passing ruined homes with the 'Chetnik' symbol spray-painted on their surviving walls, I saw a few smoking chimneys. Eagerly, hungrily, I pedalled around the people-less streets seeking a shop, kiosk or market stall. But I could find only a bizarre café, set up in a reconstructed corner of what had been a supermarket and furnished with six video screens. Four surly teenage boys, wearing tracksuits and baseball caps, were obsessively playing war games. This seemed surreal yet hideously logical: in a town totally wrecked by violence, the only visible inhabitants were playing war games.

From an empty bar behind this video salon came the proprietor: small, sallow, fortyish and icily hostile. For a moment I thought he was going to order me out. But he spoke a little English and a lot of German and by this stage my Engman (or Gerlish) had become almost fluent. When he realized that I was a tourist on a bicycle, not an expat in a white vehicle, his ice thawed. Tentatively I suggested 'Food?' There wasn't any, nor was there any coffee – he could offer only beer.

•

Emin was a displaced person from Prijedor, his home town, where he had been a garage mechanic since his marriage. Before that he had worked for a Munich bus company in Zagreb – hard work, big money! During the attack on Prijedor, while he was fighting the Chetniks, his wife had disappeared. He supposed she was dead. He was glad they'd had no children. UN staff had told him the ICRC could find out what had happened to her but that was not true. In BiH so many were missing the ICRC couldn't possibly find them all.

At sunset I suggested my sleeping on the video salon floor, when the establishment closed. I had a warm sleeping-bag, I explained, and I often sleep on floors, it wasn't a problem. But this suggestion outraged Emin's code of hospitality. He would somehow find me a *bed*. Suddenly the four boys were detached from their war games and sent off in different directions to make enquiries.

Within ten minutes one lad returned accompanied by a tall, shabbily-dressed youngish man with curly hair, a week's beard, a badly broken nose, only one front tooth and a disabling limp. In 1992, when his home town of Kozarac was razed, he had been 'detained' in the infamous Omarska camp and repeatedly beaten up. Now he earned an uncertain living as a smuggler. (Smuggling what, from and to where, was not explained.) Eso spoke no English but could provide a comfortable bed for DM10 if I didn't mind sharing a room with him.

Thanking sad Emin for his help, I followed Eso through empty, haunted streets (in the dusk and the silence they felt seriously haunted) to a small breezeblock house that had chanced to escape both arson and artillery. He occupied one ground-floor room, furnished with a sofa (my bed), a shaky little table, a sink and a primus stove. Three other displaced young men were his fellow-squatters; soon they had joined us and were staring at me and Ruairi (parked near the sink) with amazement. They sat silently on the kelim in the centre of the concrete floor while Eso made herbal tea before fetching from the yard an eight-weeks-old pup, an already formidable Rottweiler/Doberman cross, which he hoped to sell in Prijedor to some NGO in need of a guard-dog.

Then Emin's English-speaking half-brother arrived with a bottle of *rakija* and my unexpected supper (three delicious home-made sausages and a hunk of stale bread). Rezak had driven UNHCR aid trucks throughout the conflict, a dangerous job. Often his convoys were refused access to the most needy camps or robbed at gunpoint.

'What about Unprofor?' I asked. Rezak smiled. 'The French killed a few Serbs and the British killed a lot of Croats, more than they ever told about to the journalists. But that was when they could fire at them from a safe APC. The UN chiefs would be angry if their soldiers got hurt. That's why for years Nato couldn't help us by bombing Chetniks. Karadžić and Mladić liked having Unprofor here, protecting all the Serbs from Nato. In '95, when the UN moved their troops from Serb areas, we knew the bombs would be used. How many lives did the delay cost?'

His question was rhetorical, but I answered it. 'According to Zimmermann, 200,000.' (Warren Zimmermann was the last US ambassador to Yugoslavia.)

We used our cups instead of glasses and, once provided with *rakija* and an interpreter, Eso and his friends became conversational. Lušci Palanka, they told me, had been a mixed town of some 3,000 inhabitants, with two small factories. I asked about the undamaged houses, a few recently redecorated. These had belonged to Serbs, now living in the other 'entity'. 'They can never come back,' said Rezak. 'It wasn't only Bosniaks and Croats had to leave their homes. It was all crazy! Now our people can take those houses. But only a small number want to live here without factory jobs. You can't grow much on the mountains around. Ten years ago we were all better off – all except the politicians and army generals who got rich on war.'

Eso and his three friends were men who had depended, as we all do, on their place in a community – and suddenly that was gone. Lacking Emin's and Rezak's mental and economic resources they were lost, wandering in the wilderness, laden with memories of their own and their families' sufferings, exuding a false cheery macho-ness as they postured about smuggling arms, shooting Chetniks, reclaiming Republika Srpska . . . That was a sad ending to rather a stressful day.

As I set out at dawn, leaving Eso still asleep, a mangy cat devouring a mouse was the only sign of life. The calm, frosty air tasted good, the pale sky was clear, my narrow road climbed steeply away from Lušci Palanka around a bare stony mountain – and I noticed that I was fit again. The suddenness of this transition always surprises me: from poor condition to prime condition within a few days.

The twenty mountainous miles to Sanski Most inspired several paragraphs of purple prose in my journal – too purple for the transfer to print. I was now in S-For's British zone and on the edge of badly battered Sanski Most a temporary bridge over the Sana had been built in 1996 by the Gurkhas – so said a discreet little plaque. None of the few open cafés served breakfast but in a well-stocked supermarket I bought bread, sardines and a litre of milk imported from Slovenia.

Beyond Sanski Most piles of household rubbish reeked on the verges and a slight movement caught my eye. Amidst the garbage lay a dead Labrador bitch, being nuzzled by three tiny whimpering pups, still blue-eyed, not yet walking. It was evident that she had died of hunger. I couldn't cycle on; no one would rescue those pups – they'd need bottle-feeding – and if a predator didn't get them death would come slowly. I looked for a suitable plastic sack, replaced its contents (Pampers) with a few big stones, returned to the Gurkhas' bridge and dropped the pups in the Sana. After that I needed a *rakija*. The young waiter in the café looked at me anxiously and asked, 'You sick?' 'No,' I replied, 'I'm just being feeble.'

Soon I came to the 'border' and winced to see a huge blue-on-white hoarding saying in Serbo-Croat and English: WELCOME TO REPUBLIKA SRPSKA. In BiH one can't be – and one shouldn't be – impartial. Beyond that marker lay territory to which its triumphalist new Serb rulers had no *exclusive* right. I pedalled on very fast, anger-stimulated adrenalin giving me extra energy. And I remembered Warren Bass's comments in *Foreign Affairs* (September/October 1998):

> Milošević and Tudjman were not vanquished by Dayton but emboldened. Many of the agreement's imperfections relate directly to the failure to confront the scourge of Ultra-nationalism. Letting the Bosnian Serb entity be called Republika Srpska, in whose name ethnic cleansing was perpetrated, is ghastly. Dayton's core logic rests on a military balance of power and adheres to an ethnic territorial division – 51 per cent for the Muslims and Croats, 49 per cent for the Serbs – that codifies Serbian aggression.

Here was mildly hilly, lightly wooded country with the blue bulk of the Majdan Planina range quite close on my left. In the orchards fruit trees were just beginning to bud and last year's haycocks still stood beside trim red-tiled houses. Fat glossy horses pulled long carts of manure to fields where both sexes and all the generations were working together. Over the last twelve miles to Prijedor the road accompanied the Sana – wide, shallow, greenish and choked with every sort of litter from the ubiquitous bundles of Pampers to mounds of broken glass and half-submerged cars. Throughout this wide densely populated valley much rebuilding was in progress; the contrast with yesterday's deserted but equally fertile plateau could not have been more stark. I felt an upsurge of irrational but understandable anti-Serb emotion – then reproached myself. As Rezak had remarked, every community suffered when BiH was shattered. Some of those peasants whom I was now tempted to view with hostility must themselves have been uprooted. In 1990 this Prijedor region was 44 per cent Bosniak, 42 per cent Serb and 8 per cent 'Yugoslav'.

Prijedor became notorious for the extreme savagery with which the Chetniks set about its 'purification'. In BiH's 1990 election, Radovan Karadžić's Serbian Democratic Party (SDP) lost control of the Prijedor district because Ante Marković had split the Serbian vote by running a civilized candidate representing his new Reformist Forces Party. With Izetbegović's party in control, the SDP could not include Prijedor in their 'Autonomous District of Bosanska Krajina'. This made them writhe with frustration and hyper-tension was afflicting Prijedor long before the terrorist campaign started in May 1992.

When it did start, some Bosniak villagers refused to flee; they believed that one day – soon, surely! – outsiders would intervene on their behalf. Thus, in February 1994, six or seven thousand remained in the Prijedor/Banja Luka area. Then came yet another sequence of burnings, bombings and sadistic murders; among the Chetniks many psychopaths were now running amok – officially diagnosed psychopaths, released from mental hospitals or prisons. In response, the UNHCR decided to evacuate to Croatia all the remaining Bosniaks and Prijedor's local authorities at first seemed willing to co-operate. But then Karadžić spoke from on high, from his Pale 'seat of government'. The Serbs had grown used to acquiring their share of that 'aid' which would be diverted to Croatia if all the Bosniaks left. They must stay, insisted Karadžić. There would be no more killings – he, Radovan Karadžić, would protect everyone's human rights! That was a guarantee! The UNHCR could not force the issue. Karadžić Ruled OK.

A short peaceful interlude followed but when the journalists had moved on the killing was resumed. At which point Larry Hollingsworth, a former British army colonel described by David Rieff as 'one of the most effective and certainly the most outspoken UNHCR official in Bosnia', explained to the *Sunday Times* – 'We should have been much tougher from the beginning. The UN missed the chance to seize the initiative and be forceful, and we have seen a gradual chipping away of authority ever since . . . If we had said from the start, "Either you stop this hassle or we're off and no one will get anything", we would have established some power.'

In Prijedor I heard an alternative explanation for the failure of this particular evacuation: allegedly the Prijedor Serbs were dissatisfied with the UN bribe (in effect the ransom) on offer for the release of their Bosniak 'hostages'. Karadžić's self-appointed SDP 'authorities' were not of course legally entitled to dictate anyone's movements. By then, however, the UN's authority had been so 'chipped away' that the SDP were free to keep their hostages and murder a certain number at frequent intervals by way of persuading the UNHCR to open wider its unofficial purse.

Not far from Prijedor a colossal white elephant motorway bridge spanned the Sana, with no trace of a motorway at either end. In its shadow a mill-wheel, tended by two children, was grinding corn. At noon the multi-storey Prijedor Hotel loomed ahead, overlooking the river – its ugliness banal, replicated on every continent. A faded forecourt hoarding boasted of DISCO, SAUNA, FITNESS CLUB, FAST FOOD. Irritably I reflected that if people abstained from fast food they wouldn't need fitness clubs. Of course none of these delights was currently on offer – and the slow food was very slow and might have seemed unappetizing had I not been so ravenous. The town offered no alternative accommodation and my room (*sans* table, chair, central light, towel, hot water) cost £32 paid in DM. BiH had recently created its own 'funny money', misleadingly known as 'the Konvertible Mark' and equal to the DM on its home ground. But it was not 'konvertible' anywhere else nor would any BiH hotel accept it from a foreigner.

In the Hotel Prijedor the UN police regional headquarters occupied the whole floor below mine – sixteen rooms. I was therefore able discreetly to observe them in action and one helpful Englishman explained the nature of the operation. British police and Irish gardai were not training the local police but training the UN's multinational police force, from nine non-European countries, who were supposed eventually to be capable of training the BiH police. Edward explained, 'In places like Mozambique the UN learned that multinational police don't work well without co-ordination. So now there's this British and Irish top layer trying to achieve some degree of consistency. It's not easy! And made no easier by two of your compatriots from West Cork. Even the other gardai can't always understand them! So pity the poor Jordanians, Bangladeshis, Ugandans, Nepalese and so on. . .'

I made sympathetic noises and told Edward I'd seen this problem for myself – in Mozambique, as it happened, where Paraguayan policemen, from one of the world's most corrupt and brutal forces, were supposed to be 'training' the locals. I did not tell him in so many words that I considered the whole enterprise a disgraceful waste of resources.

Edward kindly gave me a map showing the mined areas between Prijedor and Sarajevo and my pre-planned route was modified accordingly. As I remembered from Laos, defective mines or cluster bombs can remain dormant for years, being driven over by countless vehicles – before one day being activated by some unlucky pedestrian or cyclist.

Surprisingly – and reassuringly – this UN unit seemed to have no security of any sort and I was free to ramble around seeking the gardai, looking forward to hearing West Cork accents. My discreet observing (otherwise known as snooping) revealed that some of the British and Irish officers showed towards their colleagues attitudes describable as 'colonial' rather than 'racist' – which did not unite the nations. Multiple tensions and animosities were evident – and inevitable, when certain non-European officers were being lectured rather patronizingly, or even reprimanded sharply, by European officers holding a lower rank.

That afternoon felt summery – the sun freakishly hot, café tables outside, customers sitting in shirt sleeves and blouses, licking ice creams. Prijedor, though ignored by most guidebooks, was in Ottoman times an important fortified northern outpost, graced by several mosques of note. Now, around every corner, I passed heaps of garbage matching the visual pollution of crude and threatening Chetnik graffiti. Huge brightly-coloured SDP election posters, depicting all the kings of Serbia from the Nemanjićes to the Karadjordjevićes, had the virtue of relieving the general drabness. Beside them hung placard photographs of the Bosnian Serb Duško Tadic, soon to be convicted in The Hague of multiple crimes against humanity, including membership of a killer mob while they were killing the man who had been his closest friend since kindergarten days. On the ground below those photographs lay plastic bouquets with 'Good Luck' cards attached, wishing Duško a safe return from The Hague.

The traffic consisted mainly of expat vehicles. Along the wide main street – most of its buildings intact but its commerce limping – I met few pedestrians while shopping for picnic foods. A two-kilo bag of excellent Austrian muesli cost DM30 and all the imported foods were by local standards expensive. The bigger shops opened for only a few hours daily and displayed their sparse goods ingeniously, to avoid empty shelves. Many businesses had simply given up, locked their doors and taken down their signs – or converted the premises to apartments if the deeds difficulty could be overcome. (Burning deeds was a crucial part of the uprooting programme.) Yet in the central square designer-labelled young people crowded several large cafés, conversing in shouts above pop-group wailings. The majority were, ostentatiously, mobile-phone owners. Later a friend dryly remarked, 'Here we have two economies.'

Eventually I came to the devastated Old City, the Bosniak heart of Prijedor at the confluence of the Sana and the little river Berek. But again, as in Bosanska Krupa, I could tolerate no more than a glimpse.

From the hotel I walked upstream into open country on a litter-lined path; multicoloured plastic bags fluttered in the branches of the willows and flotillas of Coke bottles and beer cans bobbed in midstream or had been beached below the banks. Yes, I am sounding obsessional – when litter's omnipresence means that no prospect pleases, paranoia rises above the horizon.

I thought again about the legalizing of this ridiculous, impractical, brutally created 'entity'. In Lušci Palanka Rezak had asked, 'Why did Clinton and Nato act in '95 when they wouldn't before? What changed them? The UN Americans told me it was Srebrenica but why *then*? We had so much suffering so long and they never noticed – how would Srebrenica change them?'

I had dodged those questions because they demanded such convoluted answers – one of which has a comical aspect.

In June 1995 the US State Department's senior officials, and the President himself, were startled by the news that soon 20,000 US troops might be deployed in BiH. How had this contretemps come about? Apparently because of a bureaucracy's infinite capacity for making muddles.

Several months previously, Clinton's administration had rashly promised to provide Nato support should Unprofor ever have to retreat rapidly from BiH. Nato's planners therefore got to work on Op-plan 40104, requiring 20,000 US troops to make up one-third of the proposed 'withdrawal mission'. Early in 1995, without the White House realizing what was going on, the US military planners in Brussels and the US ambassador to Nato sanctioned Op-plan 40104.

Then came the July massacres, in the UN-guaranteed 'safe areas' of Srebrenica and Žepa. The humiliated European contributors to Unprofor now began seriously to discuss an imminent withdrawal, which meant that Op-plan 40104 might soon be coming off the drawing board on to the battlefield. This put President Clinton on the sharp horns of a dilemma – and the dilemma was bucking. Nato's already wobbly credibility would topple over if the White House broke its promise. Yet keeping that promise might produce body-bags and the next presidential election was not far off.

Madeleine Albright, then US ambassador to the UN, and Anthony Lake, then

National Security Adviser, now took charge, flanked by other Clinton administration gurus. To avoid US troop deployment in BiH, the gurus quietly urged their President to seek a political victory, rather than have the world watch the US army ingloriously assisting its allies to run away – and possibly 'taking casualties' in the process.

There followed Nato's two-week bombing of the Serbian military assets near Sarajevo, in response to a mortar attack on a city-centre market which killed thirty-seven shoppers and wounded eighty-eight. This cowed the already seriously demoralized Serbian forces. Next came Richard Holbrooke's yo-yo diplomacy, leading to the ceasefire of 5 October – and to the Dayton Accord, signed in December, establishing the two 'entities' of the Bosniak-Croat Federation and Republika Srpska. Without the trap accidentally set for President Clinton by Opplan 40104, would the US have had sufficient incentive to seek a political solution? And without the Dayton Accord, would BiH be a more stable region today?

After the Croatian army's defeat, in May 1995, of the Croatian Serb forces in Western Slavonia, and after its forcible uprooting, in August, of the Krajina Serbs, the BiH conflict had by September come very close to a military resolution which would have deprived the Serbs of their ill-gotten gains. Noel Malcolm has commented on the fact that

> it was the Americans who had halted that military process and imposed quasi-partition instead, having spent the previous three years criticizing European governments for their pursuit of diplomatic solutions derived from very similar principles. In the end it seemed that American policy had succumbed to the false analysis which had so poisoned European policy since the start of the war – an analysis which saw "ancient ethnic hatreds" as the origin of the conflict, and therefore favoured some kind of ethnic separation as the solution.

Given its reputation, I would have avoided Prijedor but for Laszlo and Phyllidia, two Serb academics temporarily based there while doing research into the post-conflict mindset of the Bosanska Krajina Serbs. We had first met at the Belgrade Book Fair in October 1999 and thereafter spent a few evenings together. The Medićs were a lovable couple belonging, as Phyllidia ruefully put it, to an extinct species: the 'Yugoslav'. Their son, their only child, had been killed at the age of eighteen while the JNA were 'liberating' (razing) Vukovar. They blamed themselves for not having sent him abroad in 1990. He had been called up without warning, they were still thinking of him as a schoolboy – but that was so *stupid* of them! And so they went on, torturing themselves, on that October evening when I dined in their flat. As I left Laszlo said, 'You must forgive us, we're not always like this – but today is the anniversary of Ante's death.'

At 6 p.m. the Medićs joined me in the hotel's vast, dimly lit foyer-bar where we sat – just the three of us – amidst serried ranks of long, puce-upholstered seats and long, low glass-topped tables. As we talked the unfriendly young barman – thin-lipped, with bad acne and a blond ponytail – leant on the counter, chain-smoking and staring at us.

It was apparent that close encounters with the local mindset were doing my friends no good. 'This is a *sick* place!' diagnosed Laszlo. 'The people in control are manic. They live on hatred. And now they hate Milošević too because he ditched them at Dayton. He just used them and threw them away. When he thought he could get his Greater Serbia he provoked them to fight for it – and destroy their own homeland in the process. When his strategy failed he went along with the Americans, agreed not to listen to Karadžić, gave Sarajevo to the "enemy" – for that he'll never be forgiven!'

I asked how many of the moderate local Serbs – those who voted for Ante Marković's party in 1990 – had been able to preserve their moderation.

'Most have left,' said Phyllidia. 'Our work here is showing us Republika Srpska is a reservation for fanatics.'

Laszlo explained, 'The moderates were usually outsiders from Serbia or Croatia. Now the place lacks any educated element. Historically Muslims were the landowners in BiH, the ruling cultivated class. Generations ago the big estates disappeared but an educational difference remained – a class difference, really. Tito didn't entirely do away with that sort of thing. As sociologists we can see it in BiH – the way archaeologists can see prehistoric villages from a plane.'

Phyllidia said, 'This entity smells like a failure. But there's a sense of expectancy, too – of *waiting*. Maybe waiting for union with Serbia?'

Laszlo nodded. 'And in a way, why not? Dayton gave in to Serbian aggression – why not admit total defeat? Wouldn't that be more honest? Republika Srpska is only playing at going along with bits of Dayton to collect aid and subsidies. There will never again be a united BiH, all the discernible influences will keep angers and contempts alive. Lord Acton was right: "The principle of universal national self-determination is a retrograde step in history".' Quickly Phyllidia added, 'Also Hannah Arendt was right – you can manufacture *fact* through lies accompanied by violence. That's exactly what's happened in Yugoslavia.' I had noticed in Belgrade how much these two enjoyed capping each other's quotations/allusions.

Soon we moved to the Medićs' bed-sitter above an empty, thoroughly vandalized lawyer's office near the town centre. The lawyer had been murdered and his wife and two teenage daughters held for months in a nearby concentration camp. 'But they were not raped,' Phyllidia added reassuringly. 'They moved to Ljubljana in '95, to live with the Slovenian mother's family.'

Our supper was ready: raw smoked bacon fat, pickled cucumber, potato salad and a two-litre flagon of almost black wine. 'It's rough but real,' said Laszlo. 'No chemicals!'

The news from Belgrade was mixed. Laszlo felt cheered by increasing government repression of the (then) opposition media. 'When Milošević is sure of himself he likes to show off his "free press" to visitors. Coming in heavy with censorship must mean he's losing his nerve.'

Phyllidia speculated, 'Without him, would Yugoslavia have held together? No – one man isn't that powerful! But why were we so easily manipulated? Every day, since coming to Prijedor, I ask myself – could the West's pet theory be right? Did "ancient hatreds" undo us?' She looked at me over the flame of her cigarette-lighter. 'You seem puzzled – do you imagine intelligent Yugoslavs must know all the answers? But we don't have any answers if we're not extremists – we're the most confused and frightened of all!'

Laszlo laughed. 'Speak for yourself! I'm frightened, yes, because we don't know where we're going. But I'm not confused, it's easy to see where we're coming from. And I'll only allow a *soupçon* of those "ancient hatreds" imagined by journalists to explain the sort of violence they couldn't understand. I mean butchering whole families rather than fighting a war – here we need to factor in alcohol. The media regularly wrote up drunken troops without connecting them to the *chemistry* of *terrorism*. Journalists used the phenomenon to underline how unruly and decadent and *different* the Balkans are – I could see their mental cogs turning! "Civilized security forces don't drink on duty." We know that, after three years living in London. But here was a deliberate use of alcohol by Mladić, a horrible pattern. Survivors we interviewed in '96 described what it did to them, never knowing when drunken men might appear, armed with knives and guns and hand grenades – people you couldn't reason with or guess their next move. At the time that completely unnerved them and afterwards gave them the worst nightmares. Next year we interviewed ordinary Serb conscripts and some said they were never sober for months on end. They claimed without *rakija* they couldn't have done the things they were ordered to do. I believed them. They also have nightmares. For about a year they got no pay – only free *rakija*, a present from Uncle Mladić in Pale.'

Phyllidia said, 'That's why I think it's unfair to say all Bosnian Serbs are full of hate. In my interviews I'm finding guilt – remorse – shame. Some of these Serbs risked a lot to protect Bosniak neighbours, even gave them money to escape.'

'You're misquoting me!' complained Laszlo. 'I said their *leaders* are full of hate.'

I commented then on the contrast between Prijedor's ill-stocked shops and affluent café clientele. Phyllidia laughed. 'It's Belgrade in miniature! Two of our colleagues, writing about crime in Yugoslavia, compared Belgrade in the 1990s to Chicago in the Twenties, Berlin in the Thirties, spy-infested Casablanca in the Forties, war-wealthy Saigon in the Sixties. The bad mid-Eighties scene became hell after the UN's '92 sanctions. I mean hell for us, heaven for the *mafia*. "There's no business like sanctions-busting business." Then our First League criminals came racing each other back from Western Europe, men like Arkan and Beli and Giška. Luckily they tend to die young – assassinate each other.'

'Unluckily,' said Laszlo, 'their way of life doesn't die with them. In BiH nobody's restoring law and order and the chaos is making corruption seem *respectable*. It's not even recognized as corruption or crime. This town's police chief, Bogdan Delić, admitted in '93 that *several billion* DM had been collected as the assets of 50,000 Bosniaks and Croats driven out of the area. The wives of interned men were lied to, told they could get men out by signing over their property to Prijedor municipality in exchange for an exit permit – exit from the prison camp. What the wives really got was an expulsion order – expulsion from BiH. A bureaucrat sat in the town hall organizing all this; he made a fetish of keeping tidy files, every tiny detail correctly filled in – he'd have done well at Dachau.'

I asked, 'And the several billion DM?'

'Stolen,' came the crisp reply. 'Some grabbed by the new local authorities – police, military, civilian. Some – who knows how much? – taken to Serbia by senior army crooks. That's one reason why the Serb troops were so easily routed in '95. By then conscripts knew how it was – no pay for them, luxury holiday homes for generals.'

'Even worse,' said Phyllidia, 'the local economy is crippled because of what happened to Prijedor's public resources. Gangsters disguised as "officials" seized and sold most farming and industrial assets. They stripped the Ljubija mine, left it inoperative. Over 7,000 cattle were looted, taken to Serbia, so this area still imports milk from Slovenia. The local paper compares them to the Sicilian *Mafia* – that proves how desperate the situation is, it's not a radical paper.'

'So why,' demanded Laszlo (echoing Nurvet), 'is the international community pouring millions into Republika Srpska? They're boosting our *mafia*, fostering the cult of impunity.'

By this stage we were on the way back to the hotel, passing a large blue and yellow EU hoarding. Laszlo shone his torch on it and ordered, 'Read that!' I told him I had already done so and been suitably unimpressed. It proclaimed yet another:

EU PROGRAMME OF RECONSTRUCTIONS: INTEGRATED REHABILITATION PROGRAMME FOR THE COMPLEMENTARY REGIONS OF WESTERN REPUBLIKA SRPSKA & UNA-SANA CANTON.

Laszlo made a strange sound, between a snort and a hiss. 'Who are these people who earn a living by daydreaming? "Integrated"! "Complementary Regions"! This whole programme, nowhere does it touch reality!'

'There's no harm in hoping,' protested Phyllidia. 'At least it's an idealistic day-dream, setting standards.'

'Nonsense!' snapped Laszlo. 'It's only pretending Dayton makes sense by feeding fantasies to Washington and New York and Geneva. And opening up nourishing new pastures for the BiH *mafia* to graze on.'

At the hotel entrance we said goodbye and Phyllidia warned, 'Be careful tomorrow, you're going into mineland.'

7

Minefields and a Blizzard

While dressing next morning I heard a nostalgic clip-clop of hoofs and creaking of carts, sounds more common than car engines in the Lismore of my childhood. From the window I could see three high-stepping horses crossing the long bridge above the Sana, wearing scarlet bobbles on their right ears and drawing loads of vegetables and firewood to Prijedor's market.

In my anxiety to avoid the main Karlovac–Banja Luka road I went slightly astray and found myself bumping along an undulating earth track through a tranquil landscape where fields of young crops separated undamaged farmhouses surrounded by well-tended orchards. This was blissful, until I realized that my track was doing a loop and would soon have me back in Prijedor.

Stopping to consult the map, I was hailed by a white-haired, ruddy-cheeked Serb, standing in his doorway looking astonished and friendly. Beckoning me with a big smile, he suggested '*Šlivovica*?' It can't have been a coincidence that this spontaneous hospitality, once normal throughout the rural Balkans, was offered in an unscarred corner of BiH.

Mr Jović ushered me into a small living room, very clean and tidy, where a photograph of Tito in Partizan uniform still had place of honour, surrounded by family photographs going back to my host's wedding fifty-five years before. Now he and his brother, both widowers, shared this house. Their children and grandchildren, having no stomach for 'ethnic' conflict, had fled to Belgrade in the spring of 1992 and none wanted to return. In Mr Jović's opinion, Republika Srpska would not survive since most of the ordinary decent Serbs had chosen to leave. Declining a second *šlivovica* (it was 8.30 a.m.) I went on my way, following another track, its banks aglow with primroses, which eventually joined the road to Kožarac – or what had been Kožarac.

The setting is beautiful; here the wide, fertile Sana valley ends at the base of the Kozara range – low, darkly forested mountains. Many of Kožarac's new ruins are scattered amidst pine trees where the land begins to slope upwards. This used to be a widespread, uncrowded town, the surrounding fields always visible.

One night in 1942, when 500 Serbs were massacred here by the Ustasha, their

Bosniak neighbours were not harmed – a sure sign, say the Serbs, that they were pro-Ustasha. Which is probably true; during that war Bosniaks fought on both sides. Exactly fifty years later the majority of the town's 20,000 inhabitants were Bosniaks who surrendered without firing a shot when they saw Kožarac being surrounded by JNA units, Chetnik militias and paramilitary police. The Serbs then murdered thousands of civilians and interned the rest. Until the slaughter of Srebrenica's male population three years later, this was BiH's best-organized massacre.

Battered, shattered, devastated, demolished, ravaged, razed, levelled – I am running out of adjectives. Even in combination, those words hardly describe what was done to Kožarac. They relate only to structures (none was spared) and don't begin to convey the immense melancholy of the place eight years afterwards – the terror and suffering and grief held in the atmosphere, suspended above the scene like a cloud of emotional dust.

Only a few elderly Serb peasants had drifted back to the ghost of their home town because they had nowhere else to go. When I stopped to photograph a dynamited mosque one of them shouted at me angrily, waving a clenched fist. The Madrasa was too big for its seventeenth-century magnificence to have been totally obliterated by JNA artillery. Some construction had been started by an EU-sponsored Austrian company but they seemed to have abandoned the project.

I spent half an hour in the enormous graveyard, covering acres. (All my life I've been addicted to graveyards.) The earliest legible headstone, exquisitely carved, was dated 1688; the latest was dated 2000 – not a headstone, just a simple wooden memorial to a Bosniak brought back (from where?) to lie in the earth to which he belonged. This was a mixed community of the departed, Bosniaks and Serbs lying together in death as they had lived together until their leaders divided them.

Slowly I pedalled away, into the mountains. If Western TV crews had filmed Kožarac's day of destruction, would their footage have altered the Great Powers' perception of and reaction to BiH's 'civil war'? Probably not. I remembered Alija Izetbegović's response to their publicly announced decision, in May '93, not to intervene militarily in BiH. The then President said:

> If the international community is not ready to defend the principles which it itself has proclaimed as its foundations, let it say so openly, both to the people of Bosnia and the people of the world. Let it proclaim a new code of behaviour in which force will be the first and the last argument.

At every opportunity 'we, the people' should challenge militarism's inconsistencies. The Great Powers, to support their arms industries, encourage international violence. Nato's political leaders claim the Alliance is needed to 'defend our Western values'. Then comes trouble in BiH, where Western interests do not require action – so Nato looks on for three years while Milošević's 'coalition' of drunken conscripts, Arkan-led criminal gangs and released psychopaths forcibly uproot hundreds of thousands of unarmed civilians.

Soon a faded and bullet-holed notice informed me that I was entering the Kozara National Park, a tourist attraction in times past. These mountains are not as trivial as they seem from a distance and Ruairi had to be pushed for eight miles on a small unused road through dense beech woods, overlooking deep narrow valleys – almost ravines. The pass, a wide grassy saddle, is defaced by an incongruous expanse of concrete steps leading up and up to the highest point, where a dismally ugly cenotaph honours the victims of a Second World War crime. A junior intelligence officer named Kurt Waldheim was later decorated by Ante Pavelić for his 'achievement' as a supervisor of this crime. It involved four armies (Ustasha, German, Italian, Hungarian) which rounded up 10,000 Serbian Partizans and displaced persons, including 4,000 children. All were driven, like so many hunted animals, into a *cul-de-sac* valley below the pass where the Ustasha, obeying their German masters, massacred most of them. (One wonders – how many of the Ustasha were drunk on duty?)

The pass was once a picnic site; chunks of concrete tables and toadstool seats, scattered over a wide area, marked its transition to a battlefield. Just below the saddle reared the ruins of a many-roomed hotel. It had been taken over in 1993 by Bosnian forces (I was told that evening) and then attacked by the Serbs.

Here ended the tarred road and as I began a ten-mile descent the weather changed abruptly. A storm-force wind blew up and under low charcoal clouds it was dusky at noon. On this side of Kozara ancient pine forests replace the beech woods – mighty trees, giants moaning and creaking in the gale.

The track, unfriendly to anything on wheels, severely tested Ruairi. Its surface of deep leaf-mould, loose boulders and erratic erosion channels seemed to have been neglected since the Axis armies marched this way fifty-eight years previously. It took me three hours to cover those ten downhill miles.

Tar reappeared where the forest thinned and betweeen the trees stood a few isolated mortar-bombed homes – traditional dwellings, built of alternate layers of stones and beams. Then came twenty miles across level open farmland; half the houses in a string of roadside hamlets seemed abandoned though undamaged. The few inhabitants I met were suspicious and surly.

Bosanska Gradiška is a smallish shell-struck border town on the right bank of the Sava. Never a lively place, in its depopulated Republika Srpska incarnation it felt positively paralysed. The only hotel overlooked the bridge (TEMPORARY RECON-STRUCTION: DRIVE SLOW said a rather alarming notice). At first this bleak, grey, eight-storey edifice seemed closed and my spirits rose; that would give me an excuse to seek lodgings with a family. But then the main door opened and two children emerged, each carrying a crate of empty Coke bottles. Locking Ruairi to the metal banisters I climbed two flights of cracked concrete stairs to a deserted reception area: no hanging keys, no ledger, no telephone. 'Banket Hall' was inscribed over one door and within I found an Olympic-sized restaurant, all its windows boarded up. In a far corner, beyond scores of bare plastic tables, sat the manager and his staff, two gloomy white-coated women, eating an early supper of mutton stew and bread. They peered at me through the twilight with incredulity and apprehension. As I walked the length of the Banket Hall several bursts of rifle-fire could be heard nearby. The manager said soothingly, 'Is OK, we have no more war, don't be feared. Is our *mafia*, they shoot each other sometimes about contraband.'

Alas! there was no mutton stew left; I had to settle for bread and pickled onions and ersatz salami made from who knows what. The manager proved to be a lugubriously amiable character and the women cheered up on being shown photographs of my granddaughters.

Then – tension. Three policemen arrived, demanding to see my passport. The oldest, balding and obese, could easily be imagined organizing a massacre. The fortyish one obviously hated foreigners. The young one, their interpreter, seemed pleasant enough but was not allowed to converse with me.

Baldie angrily accused me of having an expired Serbian visa. I retorted that that was irrelevant: I was in BiH. Baldie insisted that tourists must have a Serbian visa for Republika Srpska. 'Rubbish!' I scoffed. 'This is not part of Serbia.' Baldie, red with rage, pocketed my passport and said the visa fee was DM50. I laughed at him and said 'No deal!' He shouted something which was not translated, buttoned the pocket holding my passport and lumbered away, followed by his subordinates – the junior giving me a furtive sideways glance that might have been of admiration.

'Bad men!' muttered the manager. 'Very rich, after the war, everyone running away to Croatia over the bridge must pay them. Anyone don't give them all their marks can't cross.'

An hour later Baldie and the youth returned. If I paid for my visa next morning in the police station my passport could be retrieved.

Cheerfully I lied. 'In Sarajevo I can easily get a new passport – now I'm going to bed.' Standing up, I collected my journal, pens, photographs, maps, then said goodnight to the manager, ignored the police and departed the scene.

I was brushing my teeth when there came a knock on the door. The manager, beaming, handed me my passport. 'You too smart for them!' he chuckled.

The fifty miles to Derventa were mostly level, on a quiet secondary road accompanying the Sava around the base of the Motajnica hills. By 9 a.m. the sun was hot and thirst became a problem. The three sparkling Ottoman fountains passed *en route* were behind mine-warning tapes: they might well have been safe but the Serbs often mined Bosniak water-sources and S-For had not yet got around to checking them all. Many other mine-warning tapes, running for miles by the roadside, partly explained the uncultivated land surrounding scores of bombed or burnt farmhouses. In contrast to this silent desolation I could often see, on the Sava's far bank, smoking factory chimneys – and sometimes heavy trucks were faintly audible where the Croatian road closely followed the river's curves.

At Dubočao, another sad village, the road leaves the Sava and climbs for a few miles around open hillsides, past traces of industrial activity and countless ruins. Two new red-brick dwellings stood out conspicuously and I asked myself, 'Who would want to live here, within sight of dozens of roofless homes?' Near both houses low plastic tunnels (EU-funded, not yet in use) had been set up on pale brown fields.

Derventa is quite a large town and its site, on a bluff above the wide river Ukrina, less than two hours' drive from Serbia, gave it 'strategic value'. I paused on the new bridge, staring at acres of rubble, skeletons of factories and schools, a burnt and mortar-bombed Orthodox church, half-burnt roof-beams hanging from jagged fragments of walls. Two narrow twelve-storey apartment blocks, built close together, were missing their gable ends.

For some reason, at that particular moment, the sheer *insanity* of the Serbs' campaign overwhelmed me – insanity as distinct from brutality. To get rid of the Bosniaks they had destroyed what they longed to possess. Now they were left with a crippled pretend 'Republika': its farmland mined, its industries and infrastructure wrecked, its towns and villages devitalized, its *Serb* population disastrously diminished by emigration. Some argue that Milošević, Karadžić, Mladić *et al.* simply could not imagine their campaign failing. And in one sense it didn't fail. Republika Srpska is recognized as an 'entity' by the 'international community' and generously funded. The campaign has achieved a Serb-controlled 'pure' entity that is in fact a malignant growth within the Balkan body.

I wandered up and down Derventa's steep streets, pushing Ruairi. Most town-centre buildings were still standing though damaged. Few shops were open, few people visible. In a cavernous café a dozen shabby unshaven men, young and old, were huddled over ash-strewn tables, silently seeking solace from *rakija*. Ordering a *pivo*, I asked about accommodation but no one was helpful.

I wandered further, hoping to find a restaurant, my tummy plaintively rumbling. There was no restaurant. In 1995 people described Derventa as 'a ghost town' and since then the wraith had not gained much substance. One of the numerous donor advertisements said: REPUBLIKA SRPSKA – RECONSTRUCTION ASSISTANCE PROJECT – FUNDED BY THE WORLD BANK. Nearby a solitary recently finished apartment block, with a draper's shop on the ground floor and potted plants on the balconies, seemed an unconvincing herald of affluence.

Then I spotted a small wooden sign pointing towards a '*Pension*'. In January 2000 a newly built, donor-subsidized twenty-bed *pension* had been optimistically opened by a Serb father and son, natives of the town, who claimed to believe in its future.

'We must work hard to restore Derventa,' said father. 'It can be a busy place again.'

'If people have nowhere to stay,' said son, 'they won't come to help us reconstruct. We must co-operate with the international community, it is important.'

My fellow-guests were three pseudo-sophisticated young Serbs (one female, two male) working for a Banja Luka-based UN agency and now doing an 'assessment' in Derventa. Their standard issue 4 x 4 vehicle left little space for Ruairi in the garage. They spoke near-perfect American English and were expensively dressed and scented. Their disdain for 'ignorant peasants', and their faith in economic growth as a global cure-all, were typical of the young Balkan élite who ride on 'aid' bandwagons. All three were planning, at the end of their present contracts, to settle in the US; their American colleagues could fix that. 'Good riddance' said I to myself, thinking on behalf of the Balkans.

That *pension*, its sights fixed on expats, scorned the routine tourist hotel breakfast of omelette and roll and tried to imitate a five-star hotel by laying out an array of processed foods, plus soggy factory bread and Thermos flasks of weak lukewarm instant coffee made with powdered milk. The cheeses, chicken paté, marmalade, butter-substitute and 'individualized' containers of orange juice all tasted like airline foods. And, on scrutinizing their labels, I saw that that's exactly what they were.

The first five hellish miles out of Derventa, on the busy main road to Sarajevo, were more than compensated for by the next forty miles, on gravel roads twisting through almost ruin-free mountains. Traditionally this has been a mainly Serb district of small villages and farms in shallow valleys. Sheets of white and purple crocuses vied with banks of primroses. Willows – their catkins furry – shaded swift little streams. Around the villages black-and-white pigs grunted and rooted beneath beech trees; long-horned golden-brown cows, soon to calf, were tethered in many yards, chewing maize cobs and stalks; pairs of plough-horses were at work in sloping fields – rare is the region where they still outnumber tractors and I often paused to admire the ploughman's skill.

By early afternoon I was crossing terrain too broken for farming, with miles of scrubland all around. As I coasted down a slight slope, enjoying the birdsong, another sort of noise intruded – a weirdly piteous screaming. Even before identifying its source, I identified it as panic-stricken – a lost toddler, was my first wild surmise. In fact it was an abandoned puppy, crouching shivering on the verge – large, fat and fluffy, not more than two months old, clearly well looked after, all black but for four symmetrically white paws. When I called her quietly she rushed to me at once, too young to be shy, squeaking with joyous relief. I picked her up and cuddled her and she licked my face. She had a slight hernia and no tail (not cropped, just absent). Finding her miles from anywhere, I knew she couldn't possibly have strayed and anyway puppies of that age don't wander off on their own. '*Now* what?' I desperately asked myself. She was too big to fit in a pannier (the shape of her head suggested mastiff genes) and my efforts to attach her securely to the carrier were in vain.

I turned back towards the nearest hamlet, some five miles away, where I had noticed an elderly man digging his field. The puppy didn't have to be encouraged to follow me; delightedly she wobbled along by my side for a mile or so – then collapsed, exhausted, and had to be carried the rest of the way. She may well have been less than two months old. Parking Ruairi, I approached the old man – mercifully, he had a kind face. In sign language I tried to explain the situation, placed the puppy at his feet and hastened away, hoping her adorableness would appeal as much to him as to me. But on reaching the road I heard shrill anxious squeals and glanced back to see her struggling through the high rough grass, trying to regain me. I hesitated, then the old man waved reassuringly and hurried to pick her up. Mounting Ruairi, I sped away with a lump in my throat.

A touching incident occurred on the main road near Doboj. Four Swedish army (S-For) vehicles overtook me on a very long, very steep hill and the last one slowed to accompany me all the way down. It stopped as I dismounted to walk up the opposite hill and a worried-looking young soldier emerged. In perfect English he informed me that I had been travelling at 65 k.p.h. and he thought on such descents I should use my brakes – especially, he added reprovingly, as I wasn't wearing a helmet. Thanking him, I explained apologetically that one doesn't realize the speed gathered by a loaded bicycle on a long descent.

One leaves Republika Srpska on the edge of Doboj, a place strategically important to the Ottomans who massively fortified an outcrop of rock high above the town. Under Tito Doboj became industrialized, ugly and prosperous – a prosperity now in the past. It was one of three towns bombed by the Yugoslav air force in 1992 while, according to Milošević, the JNA was 'peace-keeping' in BiH, trying to separate the 'violent factions'. However, the place felt more alive, friendly and cheerful than anywhere I had visited in Republika Srpska. As I attended to my first need in an open-air café, facing the mangled remains of a municipal garden, a group of elderly men, curious about my journey, invited me to their table and insisted on paying for my *pivo*. They told me the fortress was out of bounds – possibly mined – then admitted it was Doboj's only tourist attraction.

Dr Nezirević, a retired professor of economics, had done a postgraduate course in the US then spent fifteen years in Belgrade. 'There I made many good Serb friends but today that time feels like another existence.'

In 1941, when Dr Nezirević was an adolescent, the Ustasha shot several hundred local Serbs and dumped their bodies in the Bosna and Spreca rivers whose confluence is nearby. His family had tried to shelter Serb neighbours in their basement but the Ustasha found them and then murdered his father and uncle. He remembered German officers being sickened by their Croat allies' manic ferocity and attempting, unsuccessfully, to restrain them.

'The Balkans *are* different,' pronounced Dr Nezirević. 'We're not "all Europeans together". The difference is *time*. We need a few hundred years to catch up, which is another way of saying we're primitive and a lot of my friends would be angry to hear me! But see if this makes sense. In distant centuries the Germans and French and English killed their own people inside their own countries, like us now. In the last century's two big wars they killed other people – which *is* different. That's why no one would help Bosnia. They thought, "Let those Yugoslav tribes fight it out the way they like to." Look at your own country, suppose Northern Irish Protestants decided to ethnically cleanse, to murder all the Catholics or loot and burn their homes to drive them out, to have Northern Ireland part of Britain without argument – would the UN, US, EU stand watching, letting it happen? How can they say they see us as just another part of Europe? It's a lie!'

Several *pivos* later Dr Nezirević escorted me through the dusk to Doboj's scruffy multi-storey hotel, where the receptionist kindly offered Ruairi the hospitality of his ground-floor bedroom.

From Doboj to Maglaj I followed the old road, with a railway close by on my left. On my right, the garbage-clogged Bosna flowed between me and the main road – noisy even at 7 a.m. During the conflict British Unprofor troops tried to keep this important transport route to Sarajevo open, taking more risks than their mandate permitted. But they failed; Serb gunners, dug in on the hills above, retained control by attacking first and asking questions afterwards.

To my puzzled delight I met no traffic, saw only groups of peasants carrying sacks to market. Soon I discovered why. A bridge over the railway was missing, or rather displaced, lying all over the track far below. That explosion also demolished several wayside trees, leaving high jagged stumps on which Unprofor had hung skull-and-crossbones mine warnings. Beyond this deep cutting a few cars, horse-carts and tractors had been parked (or tethered) by those trudging peasants and a family was cautiously descending a precipitous path. Removing the panniers, I concealed them in the undergrowth and slithered down with Ruairi – acquiring a nasty gash on my left hand from a piece of sharp rock. The approaching family greeted me shyly, oozing curiosity. When I had explained myself in Gerlish the father volunteered to haul Ruairi up to the road while I fetched the panniers, reciprocating his good deed by carrying one of his wife's sacks of onions.

Riding into Maglaj, my spirits rose: here was a town intact – and very beautiful, too, gathered around its famous Kuršumli Džamija, an unusual mosque with a polygonal minaret and a clock tower. Narrow cobbled streets lead up to a time-ruined castle on an isolated rocky hill, the most imposing of Maglaj's many crumbling castles. No one could tell me why there was such a flurry of castle-building around here. However, the numerous ancient Muslim cemeteries (which considerably delayed me) suggest that this may have been a more populous and important town in the distant past. In the recent past its two hotels (now closed) had a loyal clientele of hunters, fishermen and tourists seeking 'undeveloped' mountains. But the locals foresaw no rapid revival of that sort of tourism – 'too many mines'. Also, war and hunger have drastically depleted the hunters' prey (bear, deer, lynx, wild boar).

The Maglaj enclave, defended by Bosniak forces, suffered a long siege and though the structural damage was slight its 19,000 inhabitants endured hardships akin to Sarajevo's. Serbian guns in the nearby mountains blocked UN aid convoys and throughout 1993 most of the town's UNHCR-supplied food was airdropped by US planes; many of those 'drops' inadvertently fed the Serbs. In the spring of 1994 aid workers foretold countless deaths from starvation. But then the siege was lifted by the well-armed Bosnian Croat forces, though the Serbs remained behind their mountain guns for several more months, hoping that when the inevitable negotiations happened they could include the Maglaj enclave, and Doboj, in Republika Srpska.

Another bombed bridge guaranteed fifteen traffic-free miles to Zavidovići, with mine-warning tapes laid along the verges. This time no rustic knight appeared and the 'porterage' took longer though the paths were less steep. All around rose patchily forested mountains; their flanks looked untidy from a distance, wounded from close up. Balkan winters are very cold, the various peripatetic armies had to keep warm, trees were the victims.

I avoided Zavidovići (too shelled) and turned on to an even smaller road, hewn out of the base of towering rock cliffs. The opposite cliffs rose sheer from the swift clear waters of the troutful Krivaja, once a fisherman's paradise. Beyond this gorge the road ran for twenty miles between the bulky Velež range, nearby to the south, and smooth-crested terraced hills in the middle distance.

Ribnica, where I arrived at 4.45, had suffered its share of forcible uprootings. Here the valley is wide and the terrain broken: not fertile land but gloriously beautiful. A mile or so from Ribnica the Velež and Konjuh ranges converge, semi-encircling the small spread-out town. To rehouse Bosniak returnees from Croatian refugee camps, there had been some self-help reconstruction. As I wandered to and fro, faintly hoping to find a café, groups of little boys gathered behind me, not sure how to react, simultaneously showing shyness, hostility, curiosity, mockery. The one tiny shop sold salt, soap, pasta, tinned foods (sardines, spam, soup, rice pudding(!), apricots, peaches), biscuits, potato crisps, Coke of course and – hurrah! – *pivo*. The owner was warily welcoming. A man in his late forties, with tired eyes, he spoke no Gerlish/Engman: nor did anyone else in

Ribnica. I thought enviously of my several English and Irish friends who seem to have learned Serbo-Croat almost overnight. To be linguistically challenged is a sad handicap for a traveller. However, for basic needs sign-language suffices and Ilija was happy to offer me a sofa for the night.

Evidently the Krak family was not economically dependent on that shop. Upstairs, their comfortably furnished home sported a luxuriance of indoor plants – Mrs Krak's pride and joy. She told me their names and asked if we have them in Irska? As I'm not an indoor plant person, and all my outdoor plants are weeds, I couldn't answer that one.

Here, as so often elsewhere, I found that, given a mutual will to *relate*, people can enjoy an animated (though not very informative) evening in defiance of the language barrier. Photographs help a lot. I brought out the full range, not only granddaughters but my slightly eccentric home and my numerous animals. The three Krak sons, aged fifteen, twelve and six, had been uneasy with me until seeing the animals. Then suddenly they relaxed and laughed and made appropriate noises (woof-woof! mee-ow!). We ate in the living room, where long coffee tables accompanied each of the three sofas. Vegetable soup (not tinned) and pasta with a sardine and tomato sauce were followed by bottled cherries and biscuits.

At dawn the boys came to watch me packing the panniers and each presented me with a farewell gift: a packet of crisps, a bar of chocolate, a tin of Coke. Then Ilija appeared in his pyjamas and I did wrong; my proffered DM gave great offence. I pedalled away accusing myself of insensitivity. I should have realized that I was an honoured guest – but it's tricky, one doesn't want to batten on people's good nature . . .

Soon I had something else to worry about. At first the sky was clear though a piercingly cold headwind slowed me. Not far beyond Ribnica I nervously crossed a home-made wooden bridge and soon was amidst snowy hills, their pine woods crowding close to the River Krivaja and unmolested by armies. The same could not be said for the road; often I had to dismount to drag Ruairi into and out of anti-tank mine craters. Then, as I approached the awesome Krivaja gorge, the wind dropped and the rain came in an icy torrent. Miserably I pedalled on, the downpour relentless, a stringent test for my new cycling cape. It passed with honours: soon after midday I arrived in Olovo dry from the thighs up.

Olovo was a Bosniak army headquarters town and suffered the consequences. Once it must have been exceptionally attractive, standing where three narrow valleys and two noisy mountain torrents meet at the base of a solitary pointed hill, its lower slopes the old residential district. By mid-March the sheer encircling rock mountains had lost their whiteness but the streets were lined with high ridges of blackened snow. Without any dramatic altitude change, I seemed to have moved into another climate zone.

In Olovo's sprawling low-rise hotel the receptionist, observing my numb hands failing to open the panniers, at once provided thawing *rakija* on the house. Soon after, the rain turned to snow – I had felt all morning that it wanted to be snow – and at suppertime a waiter told me more snow was forecast for the morrow, when the temperature would remain below freezing.

From my bedroom window I could see the old town, older than any of the Ottoman towns or cities, on the pointed hill. When Sarajevo was a mere village, Olovo was a place of consequence, its lead mines one source of medieval Bosnia's prosperity. (The ore was shipped to Sicily and Venice.) German miners and Ragusan merchants forged links with the wider world and by 1385 a Franciscan monastery was well established. Now its descendant is visible from afar, a high grey featureless block, sternly dominating the narrow streets below.

In 1695, by which time Islam was the prevailing culture, the monastery's 'guardian' Franciscan reported that its church was 'held in the highest veneration by the Muslims, because of the continual succession of prodigious miracles which God works there by the intercession of the Holy Virgin'. Other reports mention Muslims entering that church to kiss a revered icon. And throughout Bosnia it was common for dangerously ill Christians to request Muslim dervishes to recite passages from the Koran by their bedsides. In the nineteenth century afflicted Muslims often had Catholic Masses said for them in front of statues of the Virgin. None of which reinforces the 'ancient hatreds' theory.

By nine next morning the sun was shining unwarmly and I decided to walk up the Krivaja Gorge, having been cheated of its finer points by the deluge. In fact such a gorge is best appreciated on foot; cyclists must give too much attention to not skidding into the river. Sometimes I could see only a strip of sky between the rock walls hundreds of feet above. The low, narrow tunnels – mere archways blasted through massive outcrops – had affected the outcome of recent local battles by deterring tank traffic. Confined within this chasm, the tumult of the thaw-flooded Krivaja at times became a roar, echoing and re-echoing off the rock walls, a strangely thrilling sound that seemed to take over one's whole being – scary in an atavistic way though presenting no threat.

Back in Olovo, I observed a USAF helicopter landing on the soccer field where two Unprofor mini-buses were waiting to transport off-duty US soldiers to the hotel (*six* minutes' walk from the field) where they lunched before being bussed to a bridge (*eight* minutes' walk from the hotel) to photograph the beginning (or end) of the Krivaja Gorge before being bussed back to the 'copter. No wonder the US hesitates to deploy ground troops. Those obviously McDonald-fed warriors would probably drop dead halfway up the first hill on their route.

When the sun vanished at noon Olovo shivered under a low grey lid and at 4.15 came the predicted blizzard. I was writing in my room, sitting at a wide window facing a mountain scarcely 200 yards away, when suddenly a gale blew up and over the summit poured a cascade of snow, a most wondrous sight, like some sinuous mythical creature swiftly embracing the town. Five minutes later I couldn't see the building opposite; nothing existed but frantically whirling snowflakes. Yet within two hours all was quiet, still, luminous in the dusk. That evening's forecast sounded reassuring and I planned an extra-early start to mini-mize traffic hazards on the perilous main road to Sarajevo.

Snow-ploughs had been at work during the night, leaving the road apparently clear but dangerously black-iced. Every new-burdened roof and tree glittered and sparkled as I pushed Ruairi up – and up – and up. Around the second hairpin bend pine woods replaced Olovo's burnt-out suburban homes and before long I was looking down on the Krivaja Gorge's jagged walls. Here lived a colony of ravens, sleek ebony forms strutting and pecking through the snow, raucously con-versing, pausing to glance at me, then getting on with their breakfast quest. The traffic was light: two snow-chained trucks, a few cars – the only Balkan vehicles I ever saw being driven slowly on an open road.

At 9.15 came another weather *volte face*. As the brilliant sun was extinguished a gale howled through the pines, sweeping pale grey clouds across the sky. At this altitude the wind-chill factor is not to be disregarded and I paused under a tree to put on all my garments. Soon the pine woods ended, the gale blew unimpeded over an immense expanse of open country and, as it began to snow lightly, I felt myself becoming dangerously cold. An attempt to use my space-blanket was defeated by the strength of the wind. No inhabited dwelling appeared, only an occasional ruined farmhouse – and hereabouts, I had been warned in Olovo, many farmyards were mined before the Serbs withdrew.

The light snow became a blizzard, half-blinding me. At once Ruairi's mud-guards were clogged and the effort required to drag him through the deepening snow should have warmed me but didn't. I had been ill-advised in London that Irish midwinter clothing would suffice in springtime BiH. The slight relief of another pine wood was counteracted by such a severe gradient that Ruairi began to feel like an enemy – an ominous symptom of disorientation and panic. Then suddenly that climb ended on the pass. And there stood a building, just discern-ible through the swirling flakes, with a light in the window. It was an ugly little breeze-block tin-roofed edifice, one side a café, the other a mini-shop – a lamen-table blot on the landscape, I would certainly have thought had I passed that way in midsummer. Before entering, I removed my snow-laden cape and banged my shoes on the doorstep.

The two women huddled beside a red-hot woodstove were startled, then con-cerned. The sudden warmth left me speechless with pain as my extremities thawed, a phenomenon they well understood. *Pelinkovac* was poured and coffee brewed before any questions were asked. (*Pelinkovac* is a *rakija* distilled from wood, best drunk when circumstances have deadened one's taste buds.) Then a shout summoned Mujica, an English-speaking twenty-one-year-old employed to run the shop. 'All day it will snow,' he announced. 'I know, the wind tells me – the TV weather-men should listen to the wind.' However, I could sleep that night on the café floor if the owner gave permission when he returned from Olovo where he worked on a UN forestry scheme. I remembered then the hoarding outside the Olovo hotel:

EU PROGRAM REKONSTRUKCIJE – IMPLEMENTING PARTNER: UNITED NATIONS DEVELOPMENT PROGRAMME – UNDP. VILLAGE EMPLOYMENT AND ENVIRONMENT PROGRAMME – VEEP. PROJECT: REFORESTATION. MUNICIPALITY: OLOVO

By a happy, inebriating coincidence, this was both St Patrick's Day and Bairam, an important Islamic festival. As the Bosniaks are far removed from orthodox Islam they celebrate the first day of Bairam by standing each other strong drinks, much as the Irish celebrate St Patrick's Day. It's as well the weather prevented through traffic; we three women all got merry enough on a few locals dropping in, instigating refilled glasses.

Mujica, unusually, didn't drink alcohol or smoke. He was an unusual young man in many ways, not least in his dislike of urban life and preference for 'the silence and beauty on my mountains'. He had learned English in a Displaced Persons' camp near Olovo; improbably, Pearl Buck was his favourite author. When his mother died of leukaemia he was only six. 'I have many sweet memories of her. The father's love is not the same as the mother's love.'

Mujica's family – father, step-mother, twin half-sisters then aged three and himself – had fled to the camp before their house was mortar-bombed. 'A Serb friend warned us, we were lucky. Most were not so lucky. I can't forget the women and *children* I knew getting killed in their homes, inside the rooms I knew. But I try to forget. Most of us want to forget. We want to live in the future, in peace like before. I blame more than Milošević and Mladić and Karadžić – I blame *all* our leaders. I don't blame all the Serbs. Some tried to help, we don't forget. But their leaders made it too impossible for them. I am sorry for the young Serb soldiers who had to join the army. Most didn't want to fight us. A lot ran away, trying to get into Hungary and Austria.'

By mid-afternoon the wind had dropped and the snow was falling only lightly. Mujica and Ana, the younger woman, went out with shovels to clear a path from road to shop. Not long after, another English-speaker joined us, a good-looking Bosniak woman in her forties, attired in Alpine gear and accompanied by an affable dog of gigantic proportions but uncertain lineage. Over-optimistically she had come to buy bread, then finding a foreigner in the café was happy to sit talking by the stove – though she declined a Bairam *pelinkovac* with a barely repressed shudder. It was my turn to be curious – what was she doing wandering around on this depopulated, blizzard-stricken mountaintop?

Mrs B—— laughed. 'Who are *you* to be surprised? At least I haven't arrived by bicycle!' A teacher, she had come up from Sarajevo for the Bairam holiday. Previously she had taught in a nearby village a little way off the main road (Mujica's village). Now it was '90 per cent destroyed', the school dynamited, her home shelled. But she so loved this region she had restored one room. 'It's a holiday home with a difference,' she said wryly. Then she wanted to talk only about me and my journey. When she left, Mujica told me that her husband, a doctor, had been 'killed by a sniper in Sarajevo'.

Mujica was rather unsuccessfully cultivating a goatee beard and looked closer to thirty than twenty – his narrow face too pale and too thin, his mousy hair receding, his teeth decaying. But chiefly one noticed his clear grey-green eyes and engaging smile.

I asked, 'What are you going to do next? You can't spend the rest of your life tending a mini-shop.'

'Since the war we have no choices,' said Mujica. 'I want university time, to have course in philosophy, to learn more about thinking. But without money that is too impossible. Because I have no money I will stay here, teaching myself about thinking. This is my place. If I could have university in Sarajevo, that would be good. I don't want life in the city where I am one more poor boy. It is better to be here, quiet, trying to think.'

Sunset reactivated the blizzard. In the cubby-hole loo behind the bar, where the window was broken, a snow-drift blocked the door. A family who, deceived by the lull, had set out to drive to Olovo, got stuck somewhere down the road and stumbled in as scared and frozen as I had been. Their two small children howled as they thawed.

At 8.15 a snow-plough parked outside and its three-man team sought *pivo*. Ana had a special relationship with one of them; she sat on his lap and shared his tin of *pivo* and wriggled suggestively, provoking ribald remarks from his mates. Mujica, deeply embarrassed, glanced at me and muttered, 'This is not nice!' An hour later two Sarajevo traffic police arrived in a snow-chained jeep – with a specific purpose. The snow-plough team was their target. They shouted and flourished batons and the three mumbled defensively, then hastened back to their machine. 'This is good,' said Mujica. 'People should not stop work time to have play time.' The stranded family then appealed, timidly, to the police: could they get a lift home? The officers, attaching their batons to their belts, smiled kindly and said 'Yes'.

Not surprisingly, the forestry worker owner never returned from Olovo. This caused Ana and her aunt some anxiety, they being responsible for the café's relatively valuable stock of booze. 'They don't think you thief it,' explained Mujica, touchingly worried about my feelings. 'It's the way that in Yugoslavia people was used to get permits from the boss. When this boss never meets you, to see you're a nice lady, maybe he gets angry with them. But we have no nice homes to give you bed. We are shamed for you to look at the way we live now. Before, we had all you need – now nothing . . .'

The problem was solved by my being locked into the café. Thus the boss could be assured that the stranger had had no opportunity to make off with the booze – which anyway, he must surely realize, could not be transported in any significant quantities on a bicycle through a blizzard. As the one long window had neither curtain nor blind I was asked to bed down in the dark lest any passer-by (but who would be passing, on such a night?) might observe the irregularity of my presence. While unpacking, I registered a disquieting feature of that day; between my arrival at 11.30 a.m. and the closing of the café at 10.30 p.m., Mujica, Ana and her aunt had eaten not one morsel of food.

I slept soundly in a high-altitude flea-bag equal to the occasion; my space-blanket cancelled out the damp concrete floor. Next morning I noticed that a lump of snow near the door had not even tried to thaw during the night.

I remained warmly bagged until Ana and Mujica arrived at 7.15 to light the stove. It was still snowing, there could be no question of my cycling on. But, said Mujica, the Sarajevo bus would eventually follow the snow-plough from Olovo and he promised to cherish Ruairi and the panniers until my return. Two hours later I boarded that over-crowded bus carrying the essentials: journal, passport, money-belt, camera, binoculars, toothbrush.

8

Transformed by a Siege

From my improvised beer-crate seat beside the grumpy bus driver (his grumpiness perhaps attributable to the weather) I could see the speedometer; it never went above 25 k.p.h. (15 m.p.h.) as we descended through fine snow driven horizontally across an invisible landscape. When conditions allowed me to collect Ruairi, four days later, I was awed by the depths of those valleys between pine-clad mountains with every tree snow-laden, coruscating in the morning sun.

At Sarajevo's level the snow stopped but clouds hid the surrounding mountains. Then came predictable squalor: miles of Tito's apartment blocks – new garbage and old war debris – gutted skyscrapers and unlovely reconstructions – skeletal factories and lines of rusting machine-gunned railway wagons. In Prijedor my friends had warned me, 'Sarajevo is a bit of a touristical con-trick. The 1940 population was 80,000, fifty years later it was nearly half a million. That sort of expansion doesn't leave much "tradition" around! And now, after the war – well, you'll see how it is.' Then Laszlo had quoted what Rebecca West's husband said of Istanbul in 1938: 'They are reformists and are trying for excellent motives to uproot their own charm.' He added, 'By 1968 our reformists had done that for most Yugoslav towns.'

Mujica had asked the bus driver to put me down in the centre, near the Presidency. From there I walked up Vojvode Stepe Obala, along the Miljacka embankment, and within five minutes found myself standing on what will always be Sarajevo's most significant spot, where the nineteen-year-old Gavrilo Princip started the First World War by assassinating the Archduke Franz Ferdinand and his morganatic wife. (The war would have started anyway, if at a slightly later date; for years the Austrians had been fixated on attacking Serbia. But let's not spoil the tourist trade's best Sarajevo story.)

Another five minutes took me to the Austro-Spanish-Moorish Town Hall where the odious Archduke and his unappealing wife listened to a Mayoral address of welcome during their last half-hour. This building, later converted to the university library, is now a shell. Since 25 August 1992, when the Serbs repeatedly bombarded it, foreigners have stopped being rude about Herr Wittek's attempt to design a Town Hall congruent with the adjacent Turkish quarter. (The Sarajevans, it seems, always admired it.) In the annals of infamy, this conflagration shares a page with the Croatian army's bombardment of Mostar's bridge. Only a minority of the library's 3.6 million titles could be rescued, though the staff had been moving the most precious manuscripts and books, using their own cars, since the previous April. They also rescued the entire *Bosniaca*, a collection to do with Bosnia or originating there. Repeatedly the librarians had begged the municipality to let them use one of the city's unused nuclear-proof shelters and to provide transport. The authorities ignored them.

Not far from the library (soon to be restored, said a notice) one comes upon the Markale market place. Here, on 5 February 1994, a Serbian mortar bomb killed sixty-eight civilians, injured more than 200 and knocked the IC off the fence. (Bosnian Serbs maintain to this day that the mortar was fired by Bosnian government forces to provoke IC involvement.) At last Unprofor insisted on the Serbs withdrawing their heavy artillery from the mountains overlooking Sarajevo. But why did it take the *simultaneous* death of sixty-eight people to stimulate action when the Serbs' artillery and snipers had killed some 10,000 civilians, including 3,000 or so children, since April 1992? Evidently 'the world media' regarded sixty-eight as a morbidly exciting 'massacre'; the ten killed and eighteen seriously injured only the day before didn't quite 'impact'. After 5 February cameramen and journalists arrived by the score and worldwide sympathy for Sarajevans shamed Unprofor *et al.* into action.

The Ottoman quarter around the Markale, the famous Baščarsija, was heavily bombed in 1941 when fires destroyed most of the tiny wooden shops. Their replacements had been destroyed during the siege and now the new replacements are choc-a-bloc with kitschy tourist – or expat – bait. In a Markale café I watched four young US S-For troopers, their rifles stacked in a corner, drinking *pivos* while comparing the souvenirs just bought around the corner. Here in Sarajevo *pivo* – and everything else – cost two and three times the normal price, an inevitability where dollar-laden expats dwell.

I surprised the elderly waiter by requesting a *rakija* with my coffee. 'No want London gin, Bourbon, French brandy, best vodka, rum with coke? We have all! You don't like *šlivovica*, it is not for visitors!'

'But I do like it,' I insisted – adding, a trifle enigmatically, 'I even like *pelinkovac*, if I'm cold enough.'

The waiter stared and marvelled. 'You know *pelinkovac*?'

'Too well!' I replied feelingly, not having quite recovered from the day before.

When I sought advice about lodgings the waiter directed me to a nearby embryo tourist agency, a tiny dusty room devoid of the usual literature. I was warmly welcomed and offered coffee by a friendly middle-aged woman, a Serb refugee from Kosovo. A telephone call booked a room for DM42 nightly, to be paid to the agency. Later, when I discovered that Mrs Simić, my hostess, received only 20 of those DM, she and I came to a private arrangement.

Sarajevo's charm has not everywhere been uprooted. Clutching a street plan drawn by the tourist agency assistant – a one-armed young man, also from Kosovo – I rambled happily through a maze of cobbled laneways too narrow to be car-friendly and so steep one had to walk slowly when descending. Viewed from the heights above, the tiled roofs of small but substantial terraced houses, either undamaged or skilfully restored, seemed to form a stairway. Minarets rose in every direction; many grassy corners were occupied by a dozen or so grave-stones, some ancient and anonymous, others contemporary. I like this Muslim tra-dition of burying the dead in little groups among the living, instead of banishing them to cemeteries.

A wicket in the Simićs' high double gateway gave access to a passageway between two houses, their blank gable ends facing the street; one was the family's residence, the other for guests. A large vegetable garden, expertly terraced, was separated by a deep valley from the Ottoman fort on its high bluff – not a roman-tic ruin, because the Austrians modernized it, but a sad ruin because somebody (everybody?) attacked it during the seige. Behind that bluff are traces of the iron mines exploited by Ragusan merchants long before the Ottomans took over in 1464 and renamed the little mining settlement Sarajevo – 'Palace in the Fields'.

Mrs Simić was a wide-smiling, grey-haired, fubsy woman, excited by the arrival of her very first guest. She hugged me as though we were old friends and, talking volubly, led me into the family living room, switched on a giant television set and began the coffee-making ritual. Apologetically I indicated my language handicap but she had faith that it could be overcome by her speaking ever more loudly. My lack of luggage worried her a lot and could not be explained until the arrival of an English-speaking radiographer daughter, Lejla.

A mutual exchange of information followed. Mr Simić's wages as a UN driver had made possible the refurbishing of his deceased parents' home as the guest-house. Mrs Simić worked for four hours early every morning as a cleaner in the OSCE offices. A thirty-year-old son did not work because he had had bad experi-ences during the siege – not physical injuries but, as was pathetically evident, mental/emotional damage. Twice he had been with close friends when they were killed: one by a shell, one by a sniper. When Lejla looked at him, sitting staring fixedly at the TV but not really watching it, her sadness showed.

'My brother was born normal,' she said. 'He was a good kind brother for me, always happy. I think he could be normal again with help. In my hospital a very good American gives help for mental trauma but Alija won't go to him. He is afraid of everything, he stays here and works in the garden. He worked well making the guesthouse but he won't talk to anyone or go outside. He is not listening to anyone. He is living alone with himself and his fear. We tell him now everything is safe, no more war, but he doesn't hear us. Some people who had bad injuries to their bodies are more lucky. The American trauma doctor says it is making guilt for people like Alija when they escape and their friends and relatives are killed.'

Mother and daughter showed me to my quarters: a bathroom (but the bath taps didn't work) to the right of the hall door, then up carpeted wooden stairs to the bedroom, parlour and kitchenette, leading off a landing where hung a gilt-framed, signed photograph of Tito – taken out of doors, in old age. Lejla commented, 'My grandparents admired him very much. My grandfather knew him, fought with him in the forest, sometimes ate with him.'

Mrs Simić panicked when Lejla discovered the antique radiator's demise. To me this didn't matter – several quilts were piled on the sofa-bed – but it took time to persuade my hostess that I really do like a cold bedroom. By then it was snowing again and my window looked across a magically beautiful roofscape, all gleaming softness, to the irregular bulk of Mount Trebević beyond the River Miljacka.

Later, I telephoned Serb friends of Nurvet (from Velika Kladuša) who invited me to lunch next day in their Dobrinja flat near the airport.

The UN recognized Bosnia-Herzegovina's independence on 22 May 1992, some six weeks after the Serbs began to attack Sarajevo. As a sovereign state BiH was entitled to defend itself, yet the UN arms embargo laid on Yugoslavia in September 1991 was not lifted. This exposed international law to ridicule. If the rights of sovereign states can be denied when these don't suit the Security Council's agenda, how can the same Council demand respect for international law in other contexts? I deplore arms trading, but to halt it selectively is indefensible when a ruthless army (in 1991 among Europe's strongest) is attacking a state only lightly armed.

Referring to events in BiH during the autumn of 1991, Noel Malcolm has written:

> The steps taken by Karadžić and his party – 'Autonomous Regions', the arming of the Serb population, minor local incidents, non-stop propaganda, the request for federal army [JNA] 'protection', the Serb 'parliament' – matched exactly what had been done in Croatia. Few observers could doubt that a single plan was in operation . . . Such clear declarations of Serbia's war aims were ignored, however, by most Western leaders.

As Zlatan had bitterly pointed out in Bosanska Krupa, when the region was attacked numerous international observer missions did observe exactly what was going on and reported the facts to their headquarters. The Great Powers could not plead 'lack of information' but their representatives chose to evade the facts and, in some cases, to use Milošević's fabrications to excuse their own inaction. According to him, all Serbian and Montenegrin soldiers were leaving BiH –

where, unfortunately, a 'civil war' had just broken out. The Bosnian Serbs were rebelling against their new government only to defend themselves from the Bosniaks who, allegedly, were conspiring with persons unknown (Middle Eastern by implication) to set up an Islamic state which would repress its Serb minority unless they succeeded in establishing 'Republika Srpska'. This web of lies could not have deceived any Great Power representative who did not wish to be deceived.

As time passed the media showed some ambivalence. Their angry coverage of horrific war crimes embarrassed the Great Powers but their reluctance to expose the political roots of those crimes left the public bemused – and really rather bored. Few were interested enough to challenge the BBC's repeated references to 'warring factions' or the politicians' glib elisions. Douglas Hurd, then Britain's Foreign Secretary, maundered on about 'Bosnia's civil war'. In the House of Commons John Major fatuously fantasized about 'ancient hatreds'. Lord Carrington, speaking as an EU negotiator striving for a cease-fire, spectacularly demonstrated his unfitness for this job by pronouncing 'Everybody is to blame for what is happening in Bosnia and Herzegovina'. And when Lord Owen succeeded Lord Carrington he stopped advocating Nato airstrikes against Serbian positions and conducted negotiations as though the Serbs' claims were as valid as anybody else's.

When crises end, and the media turn their attention elsewhere, most after-effects are lost to general view. In Sarajevo I encountered, at least once every day, the residual bitterness bred of a sense of justice denied. And that was in conversation with 'average citizens'; I met no politicians or factional extremists. Those ordinary Sarajevans asserted that they had not wanted the 'international community' to rescue them; they were well aware of the possible long-term implications of such an intervention. They had only wanted to be allowed immediately to acquire weapons to defend themselves. 'Immediately' is the key word: arms can always be acquired and eventually a steady supply was passing through Croatia, the arrangement being that the Croats would keep 30 per cent and dictate the grade of arms allowed; they banned all heavy weapons such as might one day be used against their own army.

The Great Powers' reaction to the Bosniak evasion of the arms embargo illustrated their shambolic disunity and the inconsistency of individual government policies. Post-Dayton, *Newsweek* reported (15 April 1996):

In early 1994 Croatian President Franjo Tudjman asked US diplomats how Washington would react to an Iranian offer to smuggle weapons to Croatia and Bosnia. That would violate the UN arms embargo and increase Iran's sway over the Muslim-led Bosnian government. But Washington decided that levelling the military field was its top priority – even at the expense of its own policy of isolating Teheran. Tudjman was informed that Washington had no views on the matter, a diplomatic signal to let the weapons shipments proceed.

This revelation explains the role of those retired (or reserve) USAF pilots who in defiance of Nato's 'No Fly Zone' flew modified Hercules C-130s from bases in Europe and the UK to northern Cyprus where Iranian 'aid' was loaded up and bolted to pallets, ready for parachuting into BiH. Unprofor's Zagreb-based Intelligence Section knew that US Special Forces were, in Brendan O'Shea's words, 'operating openly in Tuzla . . . At Split airport USAF Colonel Ray Shepherd . . . made no secret of the fact that US personnel scattered throughout the region were operating to specific US agendas.'

While Sarajevo burned, all concerned were working to separate agendas: the US ignoring the UN arms embargo – Nato imposing a 'No Fly Zone' that somehow couldn't exclude US-piloted Hercules C-130s – the Security Council hamstringing Unprofor – the EU, led by Britain and France, vocally supporting the arms embargo and pretending not to notice violations. Meanwhile the Bosniaks were intent on enticing Nato to come in on their side though Ejup Ganić, the BiH vice-president, often visited Teheran to discuss Mr Rafsanjani's agenda which remained opaque to the end. And under the influence of different commanding officers Unprofor unpredictably mutated throughout the siege.

On the night of 4 December 1994 a helicopter overloaded with explosives and ammunition took off from Luka airport, near Zagreb, couldn't gain altitude and crashed spectacularly. 'An exploding petrol tanker,' explained the Croats. But the UN and the EU soon discovered the truth: it was President Izetbegović's personal helicopter, an Mi-8 MTV-1. This discovery was not publicized at the time.

In February 1995, when Brendan O'Shea, an EC Monitor, visited Zenica with his team they found part of its colossal steel factory, supposedly completely closed, swarming with workers and producing quantities of industrial gases and artillery shells. Mr O'Shea was shocked to observe

. . . the deployment throughout the factory grounds of several hundred Turkish UN troops complete with their battalion headquarters . . . [They] were there because this was the site offered by the local municipal leadership, but by now they had become little more than human shields behind which the Muslims could manufacture whatever they wanted. And all of this . . . with the total compliance of both the Turks and UNPROFOR headquarters. The manner in which the UN was being manipulated in Zenica was cynical in the extreme . . . These UN troops could be viewed either as sitting ducks if the Serbs chose to attack, or alternatively as partners in the proliferation of the Muslims' armaments industry.

From June 1994 to July 1995 the Bosniaks were, as the jargon has it, 'on the strategic offensive'. By the summer of 1995 their army, mainly recruited from the Displaced Persons population, was said to number at least 150,000 ill-trained men and boys. (Like all numbers related to recent Balkan conflicts, this figure is hotly disputed.) As Displaced (forcibly uprooted) Persons – in no mood to respect any Geneva Convention – these Bosniaks committed their share of atrocities, notably in the Croatian enclaves around Vitez and Kiseljak where Catholic churches were among their favourite targets.

By May 1995 Sarajevo was again being shelled, after a year of comparative calm. The Serbs had taken back some of the heavy guns previously handed over to Unprofor for 'safe keeping' and had closed the airport in March. Nor was any food getting through to the city by land. In a letter to a friend, dated 25 May 1995, Elma Softić, a young Sarajevan writer, commented bitterly:

> They say: The mandate of UNPROFOR is not to establish peace, to wage war, but rather to safeguard peace. What peace? Here there hasn't been any for three years. You can't guard a safe that doesn't exit. UNPROFOR has the right to defend itself if attacked. Well, then, how come at least 120 of them were captured and tied to stakes like village mutts? Those poor sods are in Bosnia for one single reason: to ensure that the interested parties have a place in the arena of world politics. They're there in service of the great powers' settling of accounts. Just as this war is finally nothing but a chessboard for the grand masters of power.

Soon after dawn I descended slowly to river level: the sky was clear but frozen snow made the steepness limb-threatening. Along the embankment men with shovels were clearing the tram tracks because – I heard later – the snow-ploughs had broken down. This was said to be the coldest March in Sarajevo since 1963.

Crossing the shallow Miljacka by a half-repaired bridge restricted to pedestrians, I soon found the paved beginning of the famed Stambul Djol, the Ottomans' military road to Constantinople, along which Tatar relay-runners carried the Sultan's mail more swiftly than our twenty-first century postal services carry letters from London to Lismore. Here in Bistrik old Ottoman houses line laneways – often becoming mere paths – that curl around the steep flanks of 5,000-foot Mount Trebević. Sometimes those gradients demand stairways instead of paths – hundreds of rock steps, less treacherous on that icy morning than the precipitous slopes. This surprisingly undamaged and wholly unmodernized quarter of Sarajevo is without shops or offices. Traditionally, Muslim neighbourhoods were more or less self-sufficient in food – a tradition revived during the siege. Small open-air markets offered what families didn't produce in their hidden gardens and communities needed only a bakery, to which women brought their daily mix of dough, ready for the oven. This excursion, and the fetching of water from communal wells, provided most women's main escape from house and courtyard.

From Bistrik I took the high road to Dobrinja, walking above the little river Lukavica through a severely punished semi-rural district where many Bosniaks had been eliminated as it became part of 'Srpsko Sarajevo', territory Serb-held throughout the siege.

Dobrinja is a dull suburb of high-rise flats and short streets of older but undistinguished houses. It is also a contentious suburb, having been left dangling in a legal/constitutional vacuum at the end of the siege, during which it formed part of 'Srpsko Sarajevo'. Somehow, it fell between the cracks of the Dayton Accord and for four years the 'entities' fiercely disputed ownership. Since December 1995 the 2,000 or so Dobrinja Bosniaks had been claiming the right to return but their homes were now occupied by Serbs displaced from elsewhere in Sarajevo – whose homes were now occupied by Bosniaks . . .

Nurvet's friends, Angelina and Josip, had retired involuntarily because of the siege. They made no secret of their present poverty but conveyed that had Yugoslavia survived they would have been reasonably well off in middle age.

When I remarked that the windows of their ninth-floor flat afforded a fine view of the airport Angelina smiled and said, 'Too fine! In siege time we didn't really want to know what was going on.'

Josip asked, 'Did Nurvet explain us?' I shook my head. 'Well,' said he, 'we felt Sarajevan first, then Yugoslav, then Serb. So we stayed, when many of our Serb friends left. Sometimes we were able to send secret messages to other Sarajevo friends saying, "We're still here, thinking of you every day." We had more food on this side of the conflict line – the Chetniks stole it from the UN. Now and then we could send packages across – but not often, it was too dangerous for the messenger.'

This was a roomy flat; the Yugoslav housing authorities were more generous with space than their Soviet, Romanian or Polish counterparts. It was comfortably – bookishly – untidy and two elegant smoky grey cats lay in the sun on the back of a sofa. 'They're roof cats,' said Angelina. 'From our balcony they can get on to the roof and then on to other roofs. I don't think their paws have ever touched terra firma.'

I remarked on the numbers of cats I had seen in Sarajevo, especially in Bistrik, and Josip said, 'Muslims dote on cats. You know about the Prophet? One day he had to attend to some urgent business while his cat was asleep on the end of his robe – so he cut off the end. What you won't see are many dogs, few survived the siege. It's true – though now denied – that some people ate them. So would you, if you were hungry enough. I don't understand the denials.'

'You'll put Dervla off her lunch,' said Angelina, carrying in a tray of steaming bowls of vegetable soup.

As we ate I asked if the Dobrinja controversy bothered them personally. 'Yes,' said Angelina, 'very much. It's stopping the sort of reconciliation we'd like to see. It keeps tension going. All the Serbs who moved into Muslim homes here feel horribly insecure. Even when their own homes in what have become all Muslim areas are empty, and they have ownership papers, they're afraid to go back. A few did and got hand grenades through the windows.'

'For ordinary people it's too soon for reconciliation,' said Josip. 'They were taught too well how to hate and then they did the things people do when they hate – making real reasons for hate that weren't there before.'

Angelina disagreed. 'Even after all that's happened, I believe here we could come together quite quickly. I mean, if the Chetniks didn't interfere. They still make the trouble in Dobrinja, they don't want to see friendly mixed communities. They tell us Serbs must never agree to Dobrinja 1 and 4 being given to the Federation, who'd persecute them. We must never let Bosniaks come back because they'd murder us in our beds. And so on . . .'

Josip said, 'That's a special feature of our problem, all over former Yugoslavia – millions of Displaced Persons. After the World Wars most armies had homelands to go back to. You can't imagine how much *displaced* suffering goes on here, long after a kind of peace came.'

Four enjoyable hours later, as I was leaving, Angelina rang Merima – one of the recipients of 'secret messages' – and arranged for us to meet next afternoon. Angelina and Josip were to dine with me in a restaurant of their choice a few days hence, when I had fetched Ruairi from the pass and changed into clean clothes.

Without Nurvet's introduction as a first link in my chain of Sarajevo contacts I would have fared ill, socially, in this uneasy city. Twice I experimented by spending half a day wandering around trying to get into conversation with strangers. This approach, successfully tested in many countries, only worked here with fellow-expats – not my targets. One can understand why it didn't work, the surfeit of expats being one reason. They were disconcertingly evident, assertive and affluent. I visited several of their offices but sampled their off-duty milieu only once, when the Irish tricolour, flying high outside a large pub, tempted me to enter. There Guinness cost £5.50 per pint and the cheerful Irish staff naturally identified with the expat colony.

One fellow-drinker was a garrulous, grey-bearded demining expert from Pretoria; the South African government had hired his firm to 'aid' the Balkans. This familiar merry-go-round is bad for my blood pressure. Firstly South African companies profit by selling mines to all and sundry, then the same companies profit by running demining teams. 'Liberating' countries from anti-personnel mines, anti-tank mines and unexploded ordnance has become very big business, as was obvious when Mr Greybeard and a colleague began to discuss the increasing competition for contracts.

Then Dwight arrived, a young US army officer in Sarajevo to teach BiH's army how to use sophisticated weaponry made in the USA. He worshipped Madeleine Albright, which reduced our chances of becoming soul-mates. 'Hey, she's so great it don't matter who wins the next election! She's *genius* stuff, the Republicans would use her, couldn't afford to waste her – she saved Kosovo!'

Tapes of Irish pop groups were vying with Sky TV so I took my second pint out to the garden and sat in warm afternoon sunshine, eavesdropping on conversations which might have been taking place in any expat-infested city on any continent. The atmosphere generated by such gatherings always prompts the question: 'Should this Aid Industry be "downsized"?' And somehow, in Sarajevo, it was extra-hard to take the inter-agency bickering and back-biting, the remoteness from and indifference to ordinary local folk.

On a sunny morning I revisited enchanting Bistrik, then continued upwards on a little road that might lead to Trebević's summit. Here was open ground, less steep than lower down, where a few new dwellings had risen among the shelled farmhouses, burnt-out cars, mine-warnings and defaced Ottoman wayside fountains – the water still flowing but the handsomely carved stone embrasures and surrounding seats shattered and spray-painted. Post-siege, not many remained of all the pines and poplars that for centuries had made this slope a favourite retreat of Sarajevans during their long hot summers. Eventually the road became an unused grassy track leading through the corpse of a wood – tree tops blasted away, leaving only blackened trunks. Not far off the track stood a large ruined farmhouse, near a 200-foot outcrop of jagged rock overlooking all of Sarajevo – to the east the Miljacka emerging from its gorge, directly below the many minarets of Old Sarajevo; to the west New Sarajevo, uglifying the widening valley.

I noticed then that this shell of a house was occupied. Part of the roof had been replaced with blue UN plastic sheeting, cardboard replaced a few of the missing windows and the hall door was brand new. Suddenly an elderly woman, her garments dirty and frayed, appeared around a corner carrying a bundle of twigs. When she stood still and shouted at me I imagined for a moment that she was angry, then recognized her alarm. I must go no further – she dropped her twigs to use both arms in an eloquent gesture saying 'explosion!' Yet here was no mine-warning tape – and then I saw it, tethering a bony cow to a picket. The woman collected her twigs and hurried indoors, not looking at me again. I have never forgotten her face, ravaged by suffering, and her haunted eyes.

Merima had invited me to visit her Vratnik home, below the Ottoman fort, that afternoon. A fifty-year-old, one-legged music teacher (fragments of a mortar bomb removed the other leg in 1993), she was small and chunky with sea-green eyes and long, coarse, shaggy black hair like a Shetland's mane. During our first meeting she had had sad things to say about her beloved Sarajevo.

'Pre-war, we were so creatively mixed: Muslims, Serbs, Croats, Jews – and nobody ever *thinking* in those terms. You could have work colleagues for years and not know or care what their label was. Now we're destructively mixed, with an alien population imported from countries who let Sarajevo rot and bleed for three years. Sure, fine, they have reconstructed – you couldn't picture now the way this city looked only five years ago. But what they don't understand is they can't reconstruct the *spirit* of Sarajevo – that's gone, with the trees. We had to kill the trees to keep ourselves alive during those siege winters. And the siege killed the essence of Sarajevo. People praised our wonderful courage and resilience and ingenuity – it felt to us like if they praised us enough that let them off the hook, they need do no more. And we knew it was sentimental rubbish. To survive we had to act brave – so what? That's an animal instinct, self-preservation – not a virtue. We've yet to prove our resilience. Looking around visitors might think it's all normal now, everything working fine, a remarkable recovery. They can't know how many – I'm one – will never recover inside themselves. I'm not talking about my leg, you soon get used to that. I mean myself as a Sarajevan. I lived *as a Sarajevan*. Now I have no place, there is only the husk left – or the ghost. I suppose I think it's a ghost and that's why I stay here. Loyal to a ghost! Has it all done for my sanity, you must be wondering!'

In an odd way, Merima's passionate lament helped me to come to terms with my own negative feelings towards the husk of Sarajevo.

For centuries, patrician families dwelt in the Vratnik quarter and traces remain: eighteenth-century houses with alarmingly cracked walls and wide latticed purdah balconies – other cracked walls, very high, enclosing what once were shaded gardens with cool streams and tiled paths – a few magnificently wrought iron door handles. Merima's home was half a house: 'The bomb that took my leg took the other half. No matter, now half is enough. My husband divorced me in '96 – went to America with one of his students. A male student, which didn't surprise me. He was a science teacher. Now I hear he's running a kiosk selling hot dogs.'

In 1950, the year of Merima's birth, her mother was deeply distressed when Tito forbade women to wear veils. The same legislation forbade men to have more than one wife, though those already multi-wived were not required to cull their harem. Merima recalled her maternal grandfather, who died in 1970, having three wives. 'By then that was most unusual, really quite eccentric, in Sarajevo. For a long time – long before Communism, maybe always – Bosnia's Muslims have been atypical, unorthodox.'

At 4.30 Merima's evening's work began, a series of music lessons in different districts – not easy, with a handicap, when you are dependent on public transport. I suggested, 'Couldn't the children come to you?'

Merima laughed. 'They're all rich kids – newly rich, the offspring of our post-war *mafia*. Their convenience must get priority.' We walked together to the nearest tram stop on the embankment and Merima gave me the telephone number of her nephew-by-marriage, Rusmir, who had expressed a wish to meet me.

Small children giggled unkindly on seeing me pushing Ruairi up that hill to the Simićs' – a feat almost in the circus-trick category. The minimalism of my luggage sent Mrs Simić into another of her soft-hearted tizzies and there was no Lejla around to help me calm her down. Five days later, when I was leaving Sarajevo, she beamingly presented me with a carrier-bag containing a pink-and-yellow striped cardigan, a voluminous, flowery summer skirt, two blouses to match and a pair of plastic sandals. My gratitude was genuine; she would never know that her gift was passed on within thirty minutes to a Gypsy family squatting in a ruin.

That afternoon I deserted the Simićs for two nights, to stay with a New Sarajevo family in the unusually pronounceable Hum district. Zejnil, another in my rapidly lengthening chain of local benefactors, was the eldest surviving son. His two older brothers had been killed on successive nights in December 1992, in the battle for Grabež plateau. Zejnil, then aged seventeen, had reluctantly heeded paternal orders and maternal pleas not to join the Bosniak forces as a replacement. He was now an army captain, being trained by that Albright-worshipping American.

Hum is a mountain with a TV mast on its summit and a Tito-time suburb on its steep slopes. The long streets behave oddly, some forming almost complete circles, leaving you back where you started two miles later. Others end abruptly on a patch of rubbly wasteland or a wide grassy ledge. The two- or three-storey detached houses (many being repaired) recall past contentment, showing signs of neither affluence nor poverty – all very Yugoslav.

The Landžos lived near the summit, where Hum's suburb merges into old farming hamlets and some families keep a cow, as often as not stabled in a ruin and fed with hay from adjacent conical stacks. This district's open position had left it especially vulnerable to the nearby Serbian artillery and as yet reconstruction was minimal. However, the bureaucrats had been doing their best; each house ruin bore a new number disc (the effect was quite eerie) and the owners' names, Zejnil informed me, had been carefully recorded.

I asked, 'Where are the owners now? Will they come back?' As I spoke I registered – too late – my tactlessness.

'Many are dead,' replied Zejnil. 'Killed in their houses – didn't you hear about it at the time, in your media? Others ran away. Who knows where are they now? They could have such bad memories they don't want to come back. That is our sadness. The memories are very bad. Here was a happy place when I grew up. You can see it was a good place, all those ruins comfortable homes, no big problems. Even when the economy went wrong and the dinar was no good we could be OK here, growing food and having cows and hens. We didn't need a war. It wasn't like oppressed people making a revolution to get a better life. Our war only made life worse for everyone. The Serbs in Republika Srpska have a worse life now than they had in Yugoslavia. Nobody won our war.'

The Landžos' small bungalow had suffered only minor damage, being protected by a six-storey apartment block between it and the gun emplacements. That block was beyond restoration and soon to be demolished. 'They won't replace it,' said Zejnil. 'All that in Dayton about everyone coming home to safety was *bullshit*!' He smiled, pleased with his colloquialism. 'Those apartments had everyone mixed in – Bosniaks, Serbs, Croats, Montenegrins. Now it's all Bosniaks here. Others would fear to come back.'

'And if they did, what would happen?'

Zejnil hesitated. Then, 'I wouldn't like it, I loved my dead brothers. I wouldn't hurt them but I wouldn't smile at them. Other people might hurt them – and a few can make much trouble.'

'But you must have known many of those Serbs, been at school with them and so on – is it fair to blame *all* Serbs?'

Angrily Zejnil said, 'They moved out before any attack, taking what they had – they knew the plans!'

'But they didn't make the plans – and they also lost their homes.'

Zejnil gestured impatiently. 'You can't think that way, after a war.'

I received a warm welcome from Zejnil's parents, a peasant couple who spoke no English. Mr Landžo was small and wiry with a crushed expression. His wife, taller and wider, wore a kerchief day and night and seemed the stronger of the two, in every sense. My heart ached for them; they weren't going to 'get over' their sons' deaths. Next day, when I talked again with Merima, she commented, 'It's easier, I think, for parents to be resigned if something is gained, if you can see some *purpose* . . . When you lose your sons *and* your country, what's left? As we are now, all disconnected from the culture that sustained us, we're *weakened*. Then personal grief can become an obsession, time doesn't do its normal healing. This is happening a lot here.'

At dawn on a cold, foggy Sunday morning I set off for Pale, the small town some fifteen miles from Sarajevo which became internationally notorious as the headquarters of Mladić and Karadžić. 'A sinister place,' observed Merima. 'You don't want to hang about there.' So I had decided on a daytrip.

Gradually the road climbed, following the course of the Miljacka, and I paused to photograph a very beautiful little Ottoman bridge, marvelling at its survival. Another WELCOME TO REPUBLIKA SRPSKA hoarding soon appeared and all around were mine-warning tapes and triangular skull-and-crossbones signs nailed to stakes. The few roadside dwellings seemed to be deserted, even when intact, but beyond the river, on mountains where snow-drifts persisted, my binoculars revealed a scattering of new houses amidst many ruins. Then, rounding a corner, I came upon a huge heap of rock blocking this main road. I looked at the cliff-face above: here was no rock fall or landslide – the top half of the cliff had very recently been blown off, by accident or design. The hairs on the back of my neck stirred. It would have been possible for a cyclist to continue but – forget Pale! (I often wonder why people describe me as 'brave'; at the slightest hint of danger I turn tail.)

My swift retreat was halted by an S-For minibus full of young Spanish troops and their skiing equipment. The driver spoke a little English and sought directions to the ski slopes – they had arrived only two days previously – didn't yet know their way around. I told him they were leaving their destination behind and anyway an explosion blocked the road ahead. He looked confused, then terrified. I begged him to be careful when he was turning, to avoid the taped verges. Two youths in the back seat hastily crossed themselves – an old-fashioned precaution, curiously touching. Those two looked as though they might be slightly missing their mothers.

That afternoon I met Rusmir in my favourite dingy but friendly Markale café. He was conspicuously tall ('a Montenegrin mother', explained Merima) and handsome in rather a forbidding way. Since 1996 he had been employed as a UN interpreter (his salary sustained three generations) but he had not 'deserted' to the expat camp. During the siege, Merima told me, he had retreated to the cellar of his block with a stack of history books in four languages and hardly ever emerged, to the chagrin of his parents who needed help when fetching water and firewood.

I soon realised that Rusmir had wanted to meet me because he disapproved of outsiders writing about the Balkans in general and BiH in particular. He was a very angry and articulate young man. To justify his stance, he carried a folder of articles by American journalists and self-styled 'experts', all insinuating that had the Bosniaks been powerful enough, militarily, they too would have practised 'ethnic cleansing'. Obediently I read the relevant passages and my reaction mollified Rusmir. He conceded, 'You have tried to understand our problems – but of course you can't.'

I suggested a walk to the heights above the Simićs' district – thus precipitating a ninety-minute disquisition on military strategy and tactics, and what the Bosniak forces should not have done, and where the Serbs moved various artillery pieces when Unprofor put the boot (or the slipper) in after the Markale massacre. We followed a winding tarred road and on some sections of the ridge (its crest over 4,000 feet) were standing beside a gun emplacement looking directly down into gardens and yards at river level. Rusmir said, 'Now some people believe Sarajevo was created not by God but by Satan. A team of landscape engineers, paid to design a city where besiegers could torture defenceless citizens, would give you – Sarajevo!'

On this repopulated ridge many new or half-built houses stood amidst the ruins, two cafés and a restaurant were open and litter abounded. (The city centre was admirably litter-free; every morning householders put out their garbage for collection and men wielding twig brooms swept the streets.)

We stopped for *pivos* and sat in warm sunshine looking across deforested slopes towards the Hill of Hum. According to the café owner, from where we sat the homes of 132 civilian victims, including twenty-eight children, were visible. Many had been killed by snipers while perforce collecting firewood – the alternative was certain death by hypothermia. Those statistics, so promptly offered, discomfited me. I didn't doubt their accuracy but they sounded prepared – ready for what Dubravka Ugrešić acidly describes as 'catastrophe tourism'.

Over our second *pivo* Rusmir said, 'It's strange to look back – I was twenty in '91. How naive Sarajevans were then! We couldn't imagine the fighting in Croatia spreading to us. Our leaders even handed over what weapons we had to the UN, trusting Unprofor when they promised to protect us. Instead, we should have expected the West to let the Serbs set up their Republika Srpska. In 1923 the Great Powers thought it was clever to "exchange populations" in a big way – sending Turks from Europe to Turkey, people who'd never been there, or their fathers or grandfathers. And uprooting from Turkey a million Greeks settled there for *3,000* years! The League of Nations organized that and everyone thought it was fine – except the Turks and Greeks who weren't asked what they thought. Britain's Churchill called it 'the disentanglement of populations' and it came in handy again when the Jews took over Israel. What's the difference between that and Serbs uprooting Bosniaks and Croats uprooting Serbs?'

I said, 'The hypocrisy level is different. Much higher now, with the "international community" fussing about "human rights". There's another fast-growing industry!'

Rusmir laughed. 'Too well we know! In the middle of our siege the UN set up a new High Commission for Human Rights – we heard about it as UN troops were watching us being deprived of *every* human right! The notion is used as a smokescreen. Smoke-talk about human rights comforts kind people, makes them think the world is moving their way. Then it's easier for top people to do what suits them.' As he spoke I remembered Nurvet's comments on *realpolitik*, a variation on the same theme of thought control.

We descended by laneways so steep that every little house needed front stilts. On both sides stout metal handrails were set in concrete and even young women used these when toiling upwards laden with shopping-bags. I remarked to Rusmir that one rarely sees Balkan males similarly laden. He glanced at me in surprise and said vaguely, 'I suppose we have other customs here.'

*

On the eve of my departure for Mostar, Kamila and Mevlida (Merima's friends) invited me to supper in their flat. Both were unmarried doctors in their late thirties who had worked seven days a week throughout the siege.

We wined better than we dined. In post-siege Sarajevo, explained Mevlida, good wine was cheaper than good food – expats being uninterested in local vintages. After the meal, a Croatian cherry liqueur moved Kamila to vehemence.

'Sarajevans are proud people,' she declared. 'I can't describe how much pain our *humiliation* caused. That pain can't be measured, like you can count bodies and missing limbs. The presence of foreign troops, driving around safe in armoured vehicles while every day we were being killed – that felt like an insult, a mockery. It told us UN lives were more important than Sarajevans' lives. Armed soldiers keeping safe as our children were being killed – think how we felt! I do understand the *politics*, I don't blame the *soldiers*. But it's *now* I can say that. *Then* I could only feel angry. And we knew how much aid went to the Chetniks, the UN made deals with them, giving them a percentage – the only way, they said, to get the rest to the starving. You won't read that in any official report! For sure it made the war longer. I want someone to research this but the UN must protect itself by hiding facts.'

'It's often been mentioned by responsible journalists,' I assured her. 'They called it "blackmail" or "a sensible compromise", depending on their sympathies.'

'But a serious study is needed,' insisted Kamila. 'Also taking in other war zones, like the Sudan.'

'I question Kamila's argument,' said Mevlida. 'Anyway even if Chetniks got one-third, the starving got the rest.'

'*Why* were they starving?' challenged Kamila. 'Because the Chetniks organized hunger to attract aid convoys! People don't starve in modern Europe. Without that aid, *Serbs* and *Croats* would have been selling food to the displaced. And making it possible for them to earn enough to buy food. "Humanitarian relief" was part of one big damaging package. All wrapped up with the arms embargo, and Unprofor mandated to keep a non-existent peace, and ignorant "senior statesmen" flying around in circles making silly plans. The West complicated everything, while complaining about "Byzantine" Balkan politicians. Their interests muddied our waters. By the summer of '95 the Chetniks were retreating – suppose we'd been well armed from April '92? We had one big advantage – the JNA's poor morale. Those ordinary conscripts had no motive for fighting but we had, once the Chetniks attacked – all we needed was weaponry.'

I said, 'This sounds like one of those big "IFS" of history. Without the package, mightn't Milošević and Tudjman have carved up Bosnia?'

Kamila suddenly looked weary. She shrugged and said, 'But now it's carved up anyway. And outsiders stay here, ruling us. We've gone back a century, to imperial times!'

As I was leaving, Kamila remembered something. She went to her desk, rummaged in a drawer, then handed me a bumper sticker and a leaflet. 'Thousands of these were distributed around Bosnia. Most people burned them but I kept a bundle – lest we forget!'

The sticker simply read: 'UNPROFOR: Working for Peace'. The leaflet, aimed at schoolchildren, was headed: 'WHAT THE UN DOES FOR PEACE'. It explained: 'UNPROFOR is a big group of people from a lot of different countries who have come to the former Yugoslavia to try to stop the war. UNPROFOR stands for United Nations Protection Force. It tries to protect people from getting hurt in the fighting, just like a teacher who stops bullies from hitting you at school.'

9

Threatening Tunnels and a Fractured City

South of Sarajevo a strong, squally headwind at intervals carried sheets of icy rain. My map designates this a 'route with beautiful scenery' – as once it was, before industrialization and new stretches of motorway on concrete stilts. Between Sarajevo and Mostar the karst terrain permits no alternative road and I was prepared, I thought, for the worst: heavy traffic thundering to and from the coast. None of my Sarajevan friends was a cyclist, so none had warned me about the tunnels.

These presented a multi-faceted hazard. All were low and narrow in relation to the bulk of modern trucks, all were unlit and unventilated, with deep, wide pot-holes that caused car drivers to swerve wildly. At either side was a slightly raised path for pedestrians, one yard wide and made of concrete slabs. Many of those had disintegrated, leaving holes two or three feet deep. Over the forty-eight miles to Jablanica there were eight tunnels – a few quite short, some longer and curving so that the middle section was pitch dark but for vehicles' headlamps and one more than a kilometre long according to the warning sign at the entrance. The trucks' loads almost touched the sides and I wondered how (if at all) the drivers would react to my glow-vest. Soon my nerve broke and as each truck approached I pulled Ruairi on to the path and flattened myself against the dank, greasy wall.

Five minutes after entering the longest tunnel my torch gave out – and this was the most broken of all the footpaths. In the brief intervals between headlamps, I walked on the road in total blackness. The confined noise became terrifying, an indescribable threatening reverberating roar. The trucks travelled slowly, their fumes gathering menacingly around me; I first registered this danger in mid-tunnel, when it was too late to turn back. My heart began to race and I was panting, though moving so slowly. Then I felt dizzy and wanted to vomit. Soon after the compulsion to lie down and sleep became almost overwhelming, I seemed to be losing my grip on reality. Fuzzily I thought, 'Must keep moving, keep moving, keep moving.' As another truck came from behind I did keep moving and the driver blasted his horn – but still I kept moving as the lesser of two perils. Most frightening episodes are brief; this one seemed interminable. I stumbled a few times and once lost my grip on Ruairi and found it hard to pick him up. Then a limp cliché acquired vitality as a light appeared at the end of the tunnel – a mere pinpoint, immediately extinguished by the glare of approaching headlamps, but enough to stimulate the resolve to survive.

A few yards beyond the exit I collapsed on the stony verge and was unconscious for perhaps ten or fifteen minutes. It can't have been longer or I would have been colder when I came to, sprawled across Ruairi with vomit all over his handlebars. My mouth and nose reeked of fumes, I had a hangover-type headache and I wanted to vomit again but didn't. Luckily Jablanica was quite close. My memories of that newish, war-battered town are dim; it stands near the shore of an artificial lake created by a hydro-electric scheme and is known only for its colossal power station. Mentally, I wasn't fully functioning until next morning, when I realized the sociological significance of my wayside mini-coma. All drivers had to slow down on approaching that tunnel and obviously I wasn't having a rest; one doesn't lie on a bicycle while relaxing, nor indeed does one relax on an exposed rocky verge in an icy gale. It seems the car culture does not produce many Good Samaritans.

I dreaded the remaining thirty-five miles to Mostar through the Neretva Gorge – through how many more of those nineteenth-century Austrian tunnels? Happily, four of the five were short or shortish and the other was endurable with my recharged torch. However, that was a joyless ride; the headwind still blew, the rain never ceased, the soaring cliffs of this 'route with beautiful scenery' were defaced by giant advertisement hoardings and belligerent graffiti. From Sarajevo a narrow-gauge railway (another Habsburg bequest) accompanies the road and must also tunnel through the mountains. Both sets of tunnels are too low to take modern military tanks, which limitation – as around Olovo – influenced the conduct of recent wars.

On my return home I reread *The Iron Gate of Illyria*, a Swedish traveller's account of his 1953 Yugoslav journey, first read in 1962. Torgny Sommelius took the train to Sarajevo and wrote: 'The second day in Bosnia was the day of the poisonous tunnels. Two soldiers lay stretched out on the wooden benches of the compartment, and in the darkness of the tunnels they coughed and wept.'

Beyond the Neretva Gorge stretched destruction on a scale I hadn't yet seen. Hamlets, villages, little towns – totally obliterated. No reconstruction to speak of – no resettlement – no cultivation – bomb craters in the fields, shell craters on the road, bulletholes in the very tree trunks. Hereabouts people fought two real wars, the second Croats versus Bosniaks, with some input from Serbs. Misha Glenny gives the flavour:

At this stage, the fighting in BiH began to break the bounds of imagination. Around the Konjic [near Jablanica] area, Serb units guaranteed the Croats safe passage as they were retreating. When Gomji Vakuf was being contested, a fight between Croats and Muslims was being monitored by a nearby Serb unit. After some hours, the Muslim guns fell silent. The Serb commander radioed his Muslim counterpart. 'Why have you stopped firing?' he asked. 'We've run out of ammunition. Give us some ammunition', the reply came. Instead, the Serb commander requested the Croat coordinates which the Muslim commander duly supplied. Over the next four hours, the Serb unit pounded the Croats into surrender. The following morning at dawn, the Muslim commander ordered his men to run up the Yugoslav flag instead of the Bosnian ensign in order to thank the Serbs.

It takes concentration to unravel BiH's triangular war, especially in Herzegovina. When the Serbian forces first attacked, their main opponents were *Croats*. The Croats of Herzegovina had been preparing for this Serbian move and were reinforced by the HOS from Croatia. Those paramilitaries had migrated to Herzegovina, at the end of the Serb versus Croat 1991–2 war, to avoid being merged with and disciplined by the Croat government army (HV). They contributed approximately 5,000 men to the 15,000 gathered in Herzegovina by the end of April 1992. A month later, when those numbers had been doubled by HV troops, they launched their counter-offensive, fought hard for some five weeks and drove the Serbs away from the Mostar region.

In the middle of this campaign, on 16 June, Presidents Izetbegović and Tudjman had signed a military alliance which regularized the use in BiH of both HV (Croat government) and HVO (local Croat) forces. Tudjman's motives were obvious but the arms embargo had left Izetbegović in no position to reject Croat assistance. However, by May 1993 the Vance-Owen Plan had dynamited this military alliance and when the Great Powers replaced that Plan with the 'Six Safe Areas' scheme – suggested by Russia's Foreign Minister, Andrej Kozyrev – the Croats at once set about fighting the Bosniaks. This nine-months' war (May 1993 –February 1994) left Mostar both the most physically damaged and the most politically divided city in all of BiH.

The war zone I pedalled through on my way to Mostar had also suffered immensely fifty years earlier, when local Serb peasants rose against the Ustasha and then attacked their Croat and Bosniak neighbours, whose reluctant acceptance of the new Nazi-sponsored régime they mistook for collaboration. In mid-August a Partizan leader wrote despairingly from Sarajevo: 'In the Mostar region the insurgents have plundered Muslim villages and thereby turned the entire Muslim population against themselves.'

A few generations before that, during the 1875 and 1882 peasant uprisings which shook three empires, Herzegovina's Serbs proved the toughest of several tough guerrilla forces. A Mostar university professor, retired because his department was a bombed ruin, told me: 'Herzegovina's Serbs, you can always depend on them to put up a good fight. They're genetically programmed to fight, like the

Montenegrins.' As descendants of the Orthodox peasants who inhabited the Serb-ruled principality of Hum (Herzegovina's medieval name), one would expect these Serbs to be of much the same stock as the Montenegrins, and they are bred in the same sort of sharp, arid, rocky mountains. BiH first became a single political entity in 1326, during one of medieval Bosnia's comparatively short periods of independence, when Hum was annexed by the Ban of Bosnia, Stephen Kotromanić.

For a few miles beyond its gorge the Neretva is lost to view – then suddenly it re-appears, entering the narrow Mostar valley, flowing greenly through the little city between steep rock cliffs. The high main road took me around a mountain from which Mostar was repeatedly attacked until the autumn of 1995. Directly below, on my right, acres of ruins marked the 400-year-old Ottoman town. Then I freewheeled down to winding streets, partially restored, where only the younger Bosniaks looked cheerful.

Across the Carinski Bridge everything was different: the Croat population better dressed and much less friendly, the shops and cafés bigger and busier, the wider streets lined with Austrian or Tito-time buildings, the war damage much less – though considerable. I was soon to discover that the East Side (Bosniak) and West Side (Croat) demand capital letters to emphasize their newly acquired sectarian significance.

I spent a week in Mostar, devoting much time to sorting out the difference between the HDZ, HNS, HOS, HSP, HTV, HV, HVO, HZHB, HZP, HDZ-BiH, NDH, SDA, SDP, SDS. Those acronyms, and many more, were being tossed about, two and three to the sentence, by everyone working for the city's present and future wellbeing. Luckily I had an ally, an unusual expat willing to guide me through the maze of Mostar's peculiarly tortuous problems. I describe him as 'unusual' because he was hanging in there, trying to help, long after it had become obvious that helping Mostar would not help him, career-wise. He was a Very Important Person so let's call him Mr Vip.

More than anywhere else in the Balkans, Mostar distressed me *personally* because of its recent decline into the bitterness from which Northern Ireland has begun gradually to emerge. It was heartbreaking: separate schools – people wary of being in the 'other's' territory – prejudice and suspicion – intimidation and racketeering. All new, in Mostar – not, as in Northern Ireland, having centuries-old roots. That however was merely my own gut-reaction. It never helps to draw such analogies; every conflict is unique, symptomatic resemblances are superficial.

The Bosniaks now want to restore a united city – Mostar 'as was'. The Croats want a divided city, its Croat-controlled West Side purged of Bosniaks. Listening to their arguments, I despaired; they insisted that a united city would be Bosniak-dominated. When I reminded them that in 1991 the census showed 35 per cent Bosniak, 34 per cent Croat and 19 per cent Serb, and power-sharing then caused no abnormal hassle, they gestured dismissively and said, 'The future must be different.' I remembered then a similar sentiment being expressed by the Bosniak Zejnil in Sarajevo: 'You can't think that way, after a war.'

To oversimplify slightly, BiH's present-day Croats come in two varieties: Herzegovina's nationalists who would like to secede to Croatia, and Bosnia's Croats who, on the whole, if unprovoked, would be content to live in peace in the new state of BiH. Mostar, the capital of Herzegovina, is also the Croat hard-liners' command and control centre. Therefore the Washington Agreement of 16 March 1994, which set up the Bosniak-Croat Federation, recognized that this 'entity' couldn't work without a 'stabilized' Mostar. Accordingly the city received special treatment appropriate, in theory, to its special needs. It was decided, with the approval of BiH's Bosniak and Croat leadership, that for two years from July 1994 Mostar should be administered by the EU.

Up pop two more acronyms: EUAM (European Union Administration of Mostar) and MoU (Memorandum of Understanding) – to be followed in due course by OSEM, but we'll leave that until later. The Memorandum was signed by the EU, the Presidents of the Republic of BiH, the representative of BiH's Croats and the Mayors of Mostar East and West. It defined EUAM as a political, *not* a humanitarian organization and a former Mayor of Bremen, Herr Hans Koschnick, was appointed Administrator with a political mandate to unify Mostar within two years. It seems no one publicly questioned the sanity of this mandate. But by what methods was the ex-mayor of a German city supposed to unify a Balkan city torn asunder by every sort of dissension? For an account of this tragi-comic experiment, see Appendix I.

As a fluent Serbo-Croat speaker, six years resident in Mostar, Mr Vip was sensitive to every local nuance and not optimistic about the city's future. There had of course been some improvements since January 1997, when Mostar had to endure extreme public disorder, including many murders of the sinister, shudder-making sort. At the end of that February a squad of police from Croatia, and the BiH Croatian authorities, together ran a major operation which captured Herzegovina's two most feared 'warlords' and many of their gangster followers. The result, unsurprisingly, was a dramatic decrease in the crime rate and intimidation of Bosniaks. One wonders why this literally life-saving operation was not carried out under EUAM's aegis.

Mr Vip lamented the exodus of the young from BiH; in the first three months of 2000, more than 30,000 had left for western Europe or north America. He said, 'The hard men are driving the youngsters out – they don't want to live in this new atmosphere of hate and fear.' What troubled him most was the Croat extremists' determination to maintain a poisoned atmosphere. Recent attempts to organize an informal meeting of Catholic and Muslim religious leaders, to sow a few seeds of reconciliation, had been approved by the latter but spurned by most of the former.

My comfortable Mostar lodging, on the lower slopes of the West Side mountain ridge, catered for the minority of expats who eschew expensive hotels and was owned by a 'mixed' couple – Bosniak wife, Croat husband. Mostar has one of the highest inter-marriage rates in BiH (around 30 per cent) and for all such families recent events had an added dimension of tragedy and danger. Suddenly, what might be described as 'political sectarianism' (as distinct from genuine religious bigotry) had left thousands in a no man's land, after generations of taken-for-granted mixing. The Jačsićs' son and daughter (in their early thirties, one married to a Croat, the other to a Serb) were insecure, tense, feeling under constant pressure to redefine themselves. Many 'young' marriages were falling apart. However, older people told me that in their age group couples were usually drawn closer together by the need to resist the fierce fracturing forces all around them. For the Croat hardliners, it was easy to whip up a quasi-religious bigotry; they had influential allies within their church. But BiH's Muslims had never, at any point in their history, been into *religious* prejudice and they didn't want to start now – much to the disappointment of those Islamic warriors who had come from points east during the wars, hoping to advance their cause.

The Bosniaks of Mostar and Sarajevo, I soon realized, had different sets of apprehensions about the future; Serbs smashed Sarajevo, Croats smashed Mostar (with some Serbian assistance). The Sarajevan Bosniaks suspected Republika Srpska's intentions, the Mostar Bosniaks feared Bosnian-Croatian nationalist (HDZ) attempts to set up a two-canton Croat Republic with Mostar as its Bosniak-free capital – a development that could only lead to unification with Croatia. This threat to BiH the Sarajevans did not take seriously, but then they weren't living in a city bullied by HDZ's hardliners. However, I rather agreed with them; too much bullying is counter-productive and amongst Mostar's ordinary Croats I detected little support for HDZ ambitions.

The Sarajevans seemed more trusting of the Great Powers' will and ability to hold BiH together. The Mostarians, having observed (and suffered from) the EU Administration's impotence, despised and distrusted the Dayton-created 'Office of the High Representative'. Neurotic misperceptions flourished on both Sides. Some Bosniaks assured me that the HDZ had 'powerful Catholic supporters' in Germany and France, fanatics who hated all Muslims everywhere. Some Croats were equally convinced that the EU would hand Herzegovina over to the Bosniaks when S-For had expelled all the Croats – as 'proof' of this they quoted EUAM's more generous funding for the East Side. I wasn't rash enough to refer to the link between that generosity and the Croats' reduction of the East Side to rubble.

Mostar's public transport had not yet been revived and there were delightfully few private cars, which tempted motorists to do original things like backing out of side-streets at speeds that would have been reckless if driving forward, and executing stunt U-turns without warning on wide shopping streets. The Austrian-built West Side must once have been attractive, with its tree-lined avenues of rather pompous residences and its fine public buildings now restored by EUAM. Close to my lodgings stood a grievous blot on the cityscape, Mostar's 'innovative' Catholic cathedral; at first glance I mistook it for a deformed and oversized aircraft hanger.

Graffiti abounded on the few workers' blocks, towering over moribund factories: 'K-FOR=JNA' was the commonest inscription. No one had tried to erase the swastikas and an elaborate sketch showed a crucifix decorated with the chequerboard flag planted on a stack of rifles. Only the cheerful crudity of a football boast provided light relief: 'Kalemovac – WE ARE THE BEST WHO FUCK THE REST'.

Most of my time was spent East rather than West. The Croats' antipathy to expats was palpable – without any overt rudeness they could make one feel uncomfortable. The Šahovnica, Croatia's flag, flew everywhere; the bars boycotted Bosniak-brewed Sarajevsko beer, serving instead an inferior and more expensive import from Croatia; only kuna (and of course DM) were acceptable, BiH's konvertible mark provoking contemptuous exclamations or angry gestures. Could it be that Mostar was poised for the next round? One day a young acquaintance, a moderate Croat, glancing up at the USAF helicopters that regularly patrolled the skies, said, 'If S-For went we'd be fighting again after four minutes!' When I repeated his comment that evening, Mr Vip nodded and did not deride it.

The Dutch government, suffering from Post-Srebrenica Guilt Disorder, was funding the rebuilding of several villages which had for centuries supplied Mostar's food markets. But, said Mr Vip, only the Oldies wished to return home. The younger generations, newly addicted to urban life – though experiencing it under the direst of conditions – saw going 'back to the land' as a defeat of sorts. So now the Food Industry must supply Mostar (and many similar places), thus adding to our planet's deleterious food-miles.

The scale of Mrs Jakšić's breakfasts indicated that she was not very good at doing her sums. A DM25 B&B charge can hardly have covered those multi-course spreads of fruit juices (real), egg salad, cheeses, cold meats, honey, preserves, buns, bread and strong hot tea or coffee.

Before the war Mrs Jakšić owned a thriving souvenir shop near the Old Bridge – too near. By December 1993 it was a mere heap of stones. Mr Jakšić had run his own tailoring business, specializing in boys' clothes, also on the East Side and by now EUAM-rebuilt. However, as a Croat he couldn't feel relaxed about working in East Mostar 'while the tension is so high'.

Among my few fellow-guests were Hana and Fehim Pandža, a youngish Bosniak couple (both doctors) on a recce in their home town after seven years of self-imposed exile in Holland. We first met over breakfast and talked in a general way about the BiH tragedy. The Pandžas, who had arrived from Amsterdam the evening before, looked apprehensive. It was going to be quite a shock, said Hana, seeing their house – Fehim's family home – against a bombed background. Three days later, by which time we had become friends, I heard the whole story.

The Pandžas' motives for wishing to return, leaving well-paid jobs in Amsterdam, sounded genuine. They loved Mostar, they had never taken to the Western European pace of life, they knew their professional skills were urgently needed on the East Side. However, their neighbours were being unhelpful. The Pandžas belonged to an unpopular category: Bosniaks who had had the funds and the know-how to escape when the Croats turned nasty, leaving the unprivileged to defend the East Side as best they could. Such returnees, however well-motivated, were coldly received.

'This I don't complain about,' said Fehim. 'It's not unfair. We were young and with good qualifications and we did run away, after long thinking.'

'And feeling very sad,' interjected Hana.

'If we stayed we couldn't help much,' continued Fehim. 'Mostar was worse in some ways than Sarajevo, though it didn't go on so long. We had less help from outside – *no* medicines! The media paid less attention – it was too dangerous for them around here.'

'And for us,' said Hana. 'We were at more risk than most, the Croats copied the Serbs, trying to get rid of educated Bosniaks.'

'Clever!' exclaimed Fehim. 'The plan's working, all over BiH. The sort of Bosniaks who could help rebuild communities aren't there. UN agencies and NGOs have to give jobs to people who don't understand what they're supposed to be doing. In Holland we hear a lot about that but no one has a remedy.'

The Pandžas had found their home damaged but habitable – and inhabited by twenty squatters. The Dutch were rebuilding those villagers' houses yet not one squatter intended to leave Mostar. In theory, legal mechanisms existed to sort it all out. In practice such mechanisms were as yet inoperative. Next day the Pandžas would retreat to Amsterdam feeling rejected and hurt, as Hana admitted. Then she added, 'Always we'll come back for our holidays.'

Fehim nodded. 'Maybe some time things will change and we can stay.'

In 1987 a local architect and city planner, Amir Pašić, won an international award for his meticulously careful restoration of the long-neglected 450-year-old city now known as East Mostar. Every ancient craft tradition and historical detail was respected. Moreover, this was not a 'gentrification' that would squeeze out the poorer residents but an investment in their futures as well as in their Ottoman past. People were helped to open museums, cafés, shops (Mrs Jakšić's among them) and thereafter tourism flourished as coachloads daytripped from nearby Medugorje and Dubrovnik. The East Side began to look almost as prosperous as the West Side and attracted a few Croat mini-entrepreneurs which caused a frisson of unease but nothing serious.

Poor Mr Pašić! In May 1992 came the first Serbian artillery attacks from the mountains above, prompting him to leave for Istanbul with his detailed plans of Old Mostar, dating from the sixteenth century. There, initially to mend his own broken heart, he set up an institute dedicated to the rebuilding of Mostar and before long graduate students from many countries, including Serbs and Croats from BiH, were working with him.

By November 1993 the Croat forces (HVO) had completed what the Serbs had begun and much of Old Mostar lay in ruins. The incomparably beautiful Old Bridge (Stari most), constructed in 1561, was finally destroyed, after repeated attempts, on 9 November – the fifty-fifth anniversary of Kristallnacht, as a few elders remembered. This was not a military act – the bridge was of no strategic significance – but 'denigration by dynamite', akin to the Taliban's destruction of the Bamian Buddhas in March 2001.

Standing on the high embankment, looking down at the stone blocks recovered from the Neretva, carefully numbered and stacked on platforms ready for re-use, I wondered when the obstructive West Side authorities would allow reconstruction to begin. Despite the estimated cost ($15.4 million), funding was available. Turkey, Italy and the Netherlands have written large cheques and for the first time in its history the World Bank has backed a non-economic project, contributing $4 million.

A few months later I heard that site surveys had begun, after the election of a moderate Croat, Neven Tomić, as deputy mayor. A UNESCO team of local and foreign experts had reluctantly concluded that the original stones, so lovingly retrieved from the river-bed, were too shell-damaged for reuse. However, the 1,088 new blocks were coming from the Tenelija quarry, the source of their sixteenth-century predecessors. And they were being cut by Korčula men – the cultural, and in some cases biological, descendants of the original masons.

The East Side's commercial activity was scarcely perceptible in April 2000. Many business premises had been obliterated, many remained closed though rebuilt, and the few open stores had a huxter feel, offering a jumble of garments, agricultural implements, foods, toiletries, electronic goods, shoes, rope, fertilizer, plastic kitchenware, synthetic carpets – all imported from Croatia, Slovenia, Austria. Some of the little souvenir shops near the Stari most site were open, hoping for daytrippers from Dubrovnik where tourism was reviving. Their sparse stock looked as though it had spent several years buried under rubble – which may well have been the case.

Sitting with a tankard of Sarajevsko under a chestnut tree in a café's cobbled courtyard by the Neretva, I got into conversation with the waiter – something inconceivable in West Mostar. Simo's face was slightly misshapen; he had been in a bad car crash in the spring of 1992, followed by a year in a Zagreb hospital. Then came two years in England, where he wanted to settle and do computer studies and marry an English girl who seemed to love him. But alas! after Dayton he was deported and the girl didn't love him enough to move to Mostar – a severe test of love, he conceded, and he bore her no ill-will for failing it.

'Why a Zagreb hospital?' I wondered.

'Sarajevo already was under siege and it was before Croats fought Bosniaks. For me there was no problem in Zagreb. Now it would be different. Things have got worse very fast.' On his return from England Simo had been alarmed to hear of certain Mostar *imams* telling Bosniaks never to marry non-Muslims and urging Bosniak women to cover their heads in public. Also, Arabic had been introduced in Muslim-run schools where the pupils were forbidden to listen to Western pop music. This reminded me of Fehim's comment about Bosniak peasants tending towards conservatism. By terrorizing them into cities, the Serbs and Croats have helped those Arabian-schooled *imams* who want to 'reform' the more heterodox and find it easier to brainwash them *en masse*.

Simo, aged thirty-two, spoke of his tension-free schooldays and condemned the Croats' refusal (echoed by hardline *imams*) to resume integrated schooling. This was his main reason for being determined to settle elsewhere. 'I want to marry and have children but not here, where they grow up thinking about their *enemies* across the Neretva.'

Our British and Irish debates about asylum seekers and illegal immigrants rarely take into account Simo's sort of dilemma. He could not claim to be seeking asylum because his life was threatened. Yet his wish to rear children free of the new Mostar's prejudice, fear and suspicion seemed to me justification enough for becoming an illegal immigrant.

The symbolism of the Croat-destroyed bridge is corny yet vivid. That act of vandalism, like the Serbs' destruction of Sarajevo's libraries, expressed contempt not only for the Ottomans' cultural legacy but for a tradition of tolerance. In a sick way, the thinking is quite sophisticated and subtle, recognizing that unique manuscripts and superb feats of architecture buttress the 'enemy's' collective morale.

My last visit to the site of the Old Bridge coincided with the arrival of a school excursion from Sarajevo. While most of the teenagers stood in a group, gazing at where the bridge used to be, one girl sat alone on the cliff-top with tears silently streaming down her cheeks. Those tears would have pleased the HVO.

10

Clerical Extremists

The link between the Bosnian Church and the Bogomil heresy is a myth only recently refuted by scholars. Their indefatigable detective work, as lucidly disentangled in Noel Malcolm's *Bosnia: A Short History*, makes a gripping read. Bosnia did indeed have its own deviation from standard Christianity – either Western Catholic or Eastern Orthodox – but this was peculiar to the region, not an import from Bulgaria as originally suggested. Part of the explanation is mundane: local topography. Now that motor roads are everywhere, it is hard to imagine Bosnia-Herzegovina's medieval isolation. (This is where cycling helps; the cyclist is not quite as cut off as the motorist from times past, though s/he has it so easy when freewheeling for miles on tar.) Throughout the Middle Ages BiH's mountainous hinterland was more isolated than during Roman times when most of it, after A.D.9, belonged to the province of Dalmatia. Eventually the good Roman roads collapsed and the cut-off Bosnian villagers, lacking any formal religious authority in their everyday lives, happily merged pre-Christian beliefs and customs with their sketchy knowledge of Catholicism. Syncretism Ruled OK, as it did in many other countries from Tibet to Madagascar to Peru, and the Bosnians were content with their 'priestless folk-Christianity'.

Then, in April 1347, Bosnia's Ban, Stephen Kotromanić, wrote personally to the Pope requesting the dispatch to his territory of priests 'skilled in the teaching of the faith and not ignorant of the Slav language'. (It seems the Ban, born into the Orthodox Church, had recently changed sides.) Soon after, a group of Slav-speaking Franciscans arrived and Rome developed an obsession about 'the Bosnian heresy'.

In 1451 a papal legate to Bosnia reported back to Rome: 'In places inhabited by the heretics, as soon as the friars arrive the heretics melt away like wax before a fire.' By then the Franciscans had established sixteen monasteries, each restricted to a maximum of twelve friars. Initially they lived appropriately frugal lives, wearing peasant garb, touring remote villages on horseback to administer the sacraments and staying overnight with the locals who addressed them (and still do) as 'Ujak' (Uncle).

In 1459 King Stefan Tomaš was persuaded, by Rome and the friars, to persecute the schismatic Bosnian Church as the price to be paid for papal support
against the advancing Ottomans. The 'erring' clergy were told they must either
convert to Catholicism or leave their native land. Two thousand or so promptly
converted, a stubborn forty took refuge in the least accessible valleys of
Herzegovina and four years later the Ottomans occupied most of BiH.

Because the Bosnian Church's extirpation almost coincided with the Ottoman
conquest it was for long assumed that the majority of Bosnians quickly accepted
Islam to escape papal/Franciscan persecution. However, the friars had already
defeated the 'heretics' when the Ottomans arrived and in fact Muslims did not
become an absolute majority in BiH until the late sixteenth or early seventeenth
century. The Turks were non-proselytizing conquerors and throughout their
empire Christians and Jews were free to practise their own religions and impose
their own civil laws within their own communities. But higher taxes were
demanded of non-Muslims and very likely most Bosnians went over to Islam for
economic reasons.

As the centuries passed the friars' asceticism dwindled and some Ottoman beys
gave them a hard time, using various forms of coercion to squeeze money from
the order. They also had self-inflicted problems. In 1695 the Olovo Prior reported
plaintively to Rome that without a subsidy his monastery would have to be abandoned; for seven years the alms collector, Fr Stanić, had been embezzling the
parish tithes.

By the mid-eighteenth century Rome was feeling uneasy about the calibre of
BiH's Franciscans and foreign travellers were criticizing both the friars and the
Orthodox clergy, whose avarice had for long been a public scandal. In 1808 a
French consular official deplored the Franciscans' gratuitous meddling with villagers' lives and was alarmed by the rivalry between the Catholic and Orthodox
clergies 'who make horrible allegations about one another, provoking friction
between their flocks'. As Noel Malcolm observes:

> Without the urging of these interested parties, it is doubtful whether the Catholic and
> Orthodox peasants would have found much cause for antipathy between themselves;
> they spoke the same language, wore the same clothes, went sometimes to the same
> churches and shared exactly the same conditions of life.

Those words also fit post-Tito Yugoslavia, though there the 'interested parties'
were usually political rather than religious leaders.

During the 1880s, when the Habsburgs were reorganizing their newly-annexed
territory of BiH, Jesuits accompanied the many Austro-Hungarian immigrants
and within a decade the Franciscans had lost their 500-year monopoly, though
not their grip on the peasantry or their possessiveness towards BiH. In 1923,

despite Jesuit competition, they still ran twenty-nine monasteries, five seminaries, a few hospitals and sixty-three of seventy-nine parishes.

Then came the Second World War and the friars' most shameful hour, the Nazi/Ustasha/Franciscan alliance. On 6 March 1942 Nikola Rusinovic, Ante Pavelić's representative at the Vatican, met Cardinal Eugène Tisserant, a French Slavonic scholar and confidant of Pope Pius XII. As recorded by the Italian historian Carlo Franconi, the Cardinal told Rusinovic:

> I know for a fact that it is the Franciscans themselves, as for example Fr Simić of Knin, who have taken part in attacks against the Orthodox populations to destroy the Orthodox Church. In the same way you destroyed the Orthodox church in Banja Luka. I know for sure that the Franciscans in Bosnia have acted abominably and this pains me. Such acts should not be committed by educated, cultured, civilized people, let alone by priests.

The Cardinal must surely have shared his knowledge with the Pope. Yet exactly a month earlier, on 6 February, Pius XII had received in audience at the Vatican an Ustasha youth group and at the end of 1942 another group was granted the same honour.

In the late 1960s Carlo Franconi collected evidence throughout BiH that would nowadays have The Hague Tribunal clogged with Franciscans. The friars, often well-armed, played a leading part in many massacres; near Banja Luka one was seen brandishing his crucifix to bless a killer squad; at Alipasin-Most another danced around the bodies of 180 slaughtered Serbs. Operating individually, certain friars controlled Ustasha platoons which specialized in killing livestock, torching homes, pillaging villages and 'converting' Orthodox peasants to Catholicism. No wonder relations between the Catholic Church and the State were icy in post-war Yugoslavia.

During the early 1960s a slow thaw set in and the Bishop of Mostar began to seek a widening of his diocesan jurisdiction, a revision of the 1923 borders drawn by Rome. In 1966 he signed a secret agreement with BiH's administration and persuaded the Vatican to authorize a 'reapportionment', reducing the friars' jurisdiction to thirty parishes. Franciscan blood boiled – mutterings were dark – duplicity, greed and numerous other moral defects were imputed to His Lordship of Mostar.

Eight embittering years later Rome decided to present another five parishes to Mostar's Bishop. Franciscan blood boiled over and the Prior wrote to Rome – evidently a rude letter for it provoked his suspension. Bishop Žanic saw this punishment of his enemy as a green light and moved swiftly against the remaining Franciscan parishes. In response, the parishioners barricaded their churches and threatened or attacked any diocesan clergy who attempted to enter them. Thus the battlelines remained drawn for five years.

Then the Virgin Mary intervened, complete with shimmering lights and Fatima-echoing platitudes about World Peace. That was on 24–25 June 1981, on a Medugorje hillside, and the six child visionaries (four girls and two boys, all remarkably photogenic) gave their testimony to the Church authorities under the guidance of a local Franciscan pastor. Not for an instant did any friar question the authenticity of the visions, which recurred every evening at the same time in the pastor's parlour. When one of the children sought the Virgin's opinion about two friars who had been disciplined by Bishop Žanic she defended them and declared that the Bishop should apologize for his mistake. The transparency of this ploy might have been expected to abort Medugorje as a place of pilgrimage – but those who want to believe, will.

At this point Bishop Žanic condemned the visions as a 'collective hallucination', induced by Franciscan manipulators, and strove to have them denounced by the Vatican. But the local Franciscans' popularity, reinforced by the American Franciscans' power, defeated him. American friars immediately took over the marketing of the miracle, at the Franciscan Center in Steubenville, Ohio. Soon more than 6,000 pilgrims were arriving daily. By 1988 ten million had visited Medugorje's 'Three Spiritual Zones', as demarcated by the Steubenville salesmen. The ease with which so many have been persuaded to believe in the visions, though their sordid background is unconcealed, has inspired numerous academic studies. And the still more numerous Medugorje-related works of piety, on sale all over the world, generate royalties beyond reckoning.

Muslims everywhere have always revered the Mother of Jesus and in the early days many Bosniaks joined the Catholic pilgrims. This greatly displeased Croatia's politicians who, with enthusiastic support from the Franciscans, were intent on 'nationalizing' Medugorje. They chose to proclaim Croatia's independence on the tenth anniversary of the first apparition: 25 June 1991. Less than two years later Croat extremists warned: 'Anyone found sheltering Muslims in the Holy City (Medugorje) will have their homes blown up'. In the souvenir shops Nazi regalia then went on sale beside Madonna statuettes. At this stage even Zagreb's Cardinal Kuharić, a fervent Croatian nationalist, took fright. He wrote to Herzegovina's extremist leader, Mate Boban, cautioning that he and his hard-line Franciscan supporters were risking war-crime charges and suggesting 'peaceful coexistence' with Bosniaks. Boban wrote back: 'This is not a time of coexistence. It is a time for something else.'

Meanwhile Pope John Paul II was stirring uncomfortable memories of Pius XII's relationship with Ante Pavelić and his Ustasha death squads. In January 1993 the Pope presided over a Balkan 'peace-seeking' conference at Assisi, but neither he nor any other participant condemned the Herzegovina Franciscans' backing of the Boban faction. Those peace-seekers referred even-tonguedly to 'all the suffering peoples' of the region – a correct attitude, argued some, given the

Papacy's ostensibly apolitical role in the world. (Another echo from Pius XII's day.) Yet in Latin America John Paul II never had any inhibitions about reprimanding liberal theologians who opposed repressive governments. And a few weeks after Assisi the Pope was in the Sudan, loudly denouncing the military regime's persecution of Christians. A much shorter flight would have taken him to Mostar, somewhere considerably more open to papal influence. BiH's many moderate Croats, cowed and silenced by the extremists, would have been immensely strengthened, politically and emotionally, had the Pope visited them to condemn the persecution of Bosniaks and Boban's religion-coated nationalism.

In September 1993 Cardinal Kuharić appointed a new Bishop of Neum and invited Bosniak *imams* to attend his consecration which they gladly (and bravely) did. By this date the *imams* were aware of losing what little influence they once had within their community. The Bosniaks, though they had done nothing to provoke the two-pronged attack on BiH and are in general less aggressive than Serbs and Croats, were now committing their share of vengeful atrocities and the longer the campaigns against them continued the more uncontrollable became their retaliations.

BiH's disintegration aggravated the Franciscans' internecine war with Bishop Ratko Perić, successor to the retired Bishop Žanic. In October 1994 Bishop Perić told the BiH Synod of Bishops he hoped soon to restore ecclesiastical harmony in Herzegovina – after the Vatican had pronounced the apparitions inauthentic. (As I write, seven years later, the Vatican remains silent and we may assume it dares not utter, given the awkward fact that Medugorje's Virgin has laid a 24-carat egg. The region offers no alternative tourist attractions; it's those Three Spiritual Zones or nothing.) In reaction to this talk of 'inauthenticity', loyal friends of the Franciscans threatened to dynamite Mostar's cathedral (rather a good idea, if the motive were different) and tension rose higher by the day. This caused the Superior of the Franciscan Province of Bosnia, Fr Petar Andjelković, to join with Cardinal Kuharić and Archbishop Puljić of Sarajevo in a united public condemnation of Croatian atrocities. After that, Fr Andjelković needed a bodyguard. Herzegovina formed (and to an extent still forms) the vortex of the ultra-nationalist Croats' rabid religious bigotry. In Medugorje, Franciscans feed pilgrims a poisoned dish of anti-Bosniak propaganda blended with Ottoman horror stories – a dish indistinguishable from that served up elsewhere by the Serb Orthodox clergy.

In November 1995 the Pope directed Francesco Monteresi, his Nuncio to BiH, to organize a three-day meeting between Bishop Perić and the Franciscans and there was talk of withdrawing the friars from BiH if they refused to co-operate. Mgr Monteresi's task was to compel them to cede the parish of Čapljina to Mostar. Čapljina, a small town some fifteen miles from Medugorje, is another Franciscan stronghold, its name no longer associated with a very beautiful valley but with a particularly brutal HVO-run prison camp.

During this volatile meeting at Mostar's friary the doorbell rang and in walked Gojko Šusǎk, then President Tudjman's second-in-command and Minister of Defence, accompanied by the President's son, Dr Miroslav Tudjman, Director of Croatia's Intelligence Service (HIS). The friars had invited Mr Šušak, a vocal Bosniak-hater, to attend the session and show whose side he was on. As he often stayed with the Franciscans his arrival was not remarkable – though unexpected by the Nuncio, who lost the battle for Čapljina and fell silent on the subject of withdrawing the Franciscans from BiH.

Medugorje, I was to discover, is proud of Gojko Šušak, a local lad made bad whose photograph hung in several shops and cafés – and in the hallway of my lodging-house. Having emigrated to Canada – in Tito-time a favourite hardliners' refuge – he manufactured pizzas in Ottawa (an awful lot of pizzas) and eventually returned home to become one of Tudjman's chief advisers and most generous financial backers. In *The Death of Yugoslavia*, Laura Silber and Allan Little have exposed his 'stoking of tension and provoking of conflict' in the spring of 1991.

Many people with Balkan agendas were kept busy during November 1995. While President Clinton *et al.* were exerting themselves at Dayton, and the Papal Nuncio at Mostar, the International Criminal Tribunal (ICT) at The Hague was indicting two Croats: General Tihomir Blaškić and Dario Kordić, the latter chosen by Tudjman to lead Herzegovina's hardline nationalist party (HDZ), despite the availability of several less fanatical candidates. Both men were accused of having organized the massacre of all the inhabitants of fourteen Bosniak villages in the Lašva Valley. At Dayton, Tudjman immediately announced that he intended to promote the General and decorate Kordić – this was on 13 December, a few days after he had guaranteed to deliver ICT suspects to The Hague. Within a month Kordić had been trebly decorated in true Ruritanian fashion:

> For 'particular merits in advancing the international position and prestige of the Republic of Croatia and its relations with other countries' he was awarded The Order of Prince Branimir with Neckband.
>
> For 'a heroic deed in war' he was awarded The Order of Nikola Šubić Zrinski.
>
> For 'his contribution to the maintenance and development of the Croatian state-forming ideal, the establishment and betterment of the sovereign state of Croatia' he was awarded The Order of Petar Zrinski and Fran Krsto Frankopan with Silver Braid.

In December 1995 Tudjman released from jail Ivica Rajić, who had also been indicted for crimes against humanity, including the mutilation and incineration, while alive, of Bosniak children in the village of Stupni Do.

On the day I bought Ruairi in Zagreb the International Criminal Tribunal sentenced Tihomir Blaškić to forty years' imprisonment. Even my most moderate Croat friends were quietly unhappy about this sentence and many people angrily asserted that the HDZ, to protect 'their own', had made a scapegoat of the former

General by concealing evidence which would certainly have reduced his culpability in the eyes of the Tribunal. Six weeks later, in Mostar, I found that Bishop Perić had stirred the local pot of trouble by attacking the Tribunal through press interviews. Replying to the Bishop in an open letter, Judge Finn of the Office of the High Representative in Sarajevo agreed that His Lordship had grounds for concern, then suggested that it might be more helpful to Blaškić, and would certainly be more logical, were he to redirect his attack to the HDZ in Zagreb. This suggestion was not taken up – at least in public.

The weather forecast ('rain approaching') prompted me to leave Mostar before dawn. The first stage on the road to Medugorje was a serious corkscrew ascent, an hour's walk with Mostar now on my left, now on my right, its dim street lights switching off as the sun rose invisibly, behind sullen clouds. Then, where the road curved around two bare brown mountains, their snows recently thawed, I was looking down into deep canyons containing amorphous piles of war debris and West Mostar's garbage. From this pass there was no descent; ahead stretched an uneven karst plateau defiled by dynamited electricity pylons and the charred corpses of small industries. In the mortar-pummelled town of Kruševo the primary school had been repaired and dour-looking nuns in pre-Vatican II habits were rounding up their pupils. Coasting past, I waved at them – whereupon a dozen small boys and girls ran to the gateway to jeer at me. That school was defiantly flying the Croatian flag, as were the town's police station and Catholic church.

Not far from Medugorje, a memorial stone to three Italian journalists, killed on this spot by a mortar shell in 1993, had been rudely defaced. On the town's outskirts I passed a military base, S-For's Spanish Battalion headquarters. In 1981, when the six child 'visionaries' imagined their first apparition, Medugorje was a scattered village (population 3,000 or so) of which few traces remain. Its name means 'between the mountains' and now a bright, brash pilgrim resort occupies a dusty (or muddy) plain, semi-surrounded by pale limestone ranges. The first vehicle I saw in the main street was a parked luxury coach decorated with wreaths of green and orange shamrocks and inscribed 'PADDY TRAVEL: Medjugorje'. This purpose-built town has a tiny Irish colony, believers in both the apparitions and the opportunities arising therefrom. Slowly I pedalled past several big hotels, many *pensions* scarcely smaller, twenty restaurants, more than 200 souvenir shops, scores of cafés, pastry shops, pizza parlours, travel agencies – and a Teniski Klub. Most premises were closed. Then, seeing an open bookshop, I dismounted and was about to enter when a handsome, cheerful-looking young man emerged – Stefano, a part-time pilgrim guide who kept all Medugorje's statistics on the tip of his tongue. The 55 per cent of households offering bed did not offer breakfast because that would be bad for the café trade. At present more than 7,500 such beds were available at very low rates, this being a slack season. So far 2000 had been a disappointing year though advance bookings were up on 1999 when Nato's airwar put people off. Soon I was installed in my cheapest Balkan lodgings: £3.50 for an 'en suite' ground-floor room looking across flat fields towards a Spiritual Zone – the Hill of Apparition.

A noon rainstorm coincided with my arrival on that Hill where, according to the Franciscans' Information Office brochure, 'millions of faithful are able to satisfy all their spiritual and religious needs'. A tall conventional crucifix marks The Spot and amidst white boulders and straggly scrub stand many little wooden crosses, commemorating 'favours granted, prayers answered, diseases cured'. I was reminded of Mount Melleray grotto, eight miles from my home town, where in 1985 we had a similar phenomenon: a statue of the Virgin moved, talked to children, started a pilgrim rush. The Church ignored this apparition, though individual priests and nuns occasionally joined the coachloads who came to the grotto week after week and year after year, participating in all-night vigils and depositing considerable sums of money in a padlocked collection box. But most pilgrims were Irish and Melleray never became a multi-million-dollar industry. It seems our Tourist Board needs lessons from the Franciscan Center in Steubenville, Ohio.

Given Medugorje's genesis, can there be any validity in the claim that many lives are enriched when devotees gather here, in what they feel to be a 'holy place', and fervently pray together? I believe that devout crowds – be they Hindu, Buddhist, Jewish, Christian, Muslim – can generate positive energies in certain settings when united by reverence for something beyond humankind. But in Medugorje . . .? To me the place felt like what it is, a base con-trick, taking advantage of people's credulity. And therefore a sad place – as is the Melleray grotto.

Writing in 1994, Frances McCrea and Gerald Markle proposed that 'in the most general sense, the Medjugorje phenomenon – indeed all such apparitions – may be conceptualized as a revolt against modernity, a revolt against secularization'. This may well apply to some former Yugoslavs, made uneasy by their uncertain future, by the threat of fundamental changes – 1981 was the year after Tito's death. However, none of the American pilgrims with whom I spoke showed the slightest outward symptom of a revolt against modernity, even as it is manifested in their country's armed forces' use of depleted uranium and cluster bombs.

Symptoms of a revolt against secularization were to be found in all Medugorje's bookshops, their long shelves packed with Catholic fundamentalist volumes, the majority US-published and available in numerous translations: French, Italian, Spanish, Polish, Hungarian. A disproportionate percentage of the authors were Irish, Dark Agers who could no longer find a market in Ireland for their gay-bashings and rantings about evolution, abortion, single-purpose sex.

Hagiographies of Maria Goretti, Padre Pio and Archbishop Stepinac were conspicuously displayed, and amidst the pious and/or polemical volumes on Medugorje itself I spotted a French priest's 'study' of the Rwanda apparition which 'foretold' the genocide. According to him, President Habyarimana had been killed by 'inflamed Marxists' because he was a devout Catholic who had formally dedicated Rwanda to 'Christ and His Blessed Mother'. Parallels were drawn between Rwanda and Bosnia: both suffered as a direct result of ignoring the Virgin's advice. But what angered me, during those rainy hours of browsing, was the manner in which the controversy surrounding the apparitions was being used as anti-Bosniak propaganda. Then an unexpectedly jolly title caught my eye – *Randy England*. But alas! this proved to be the author's gigglesome name. His pulverizing attack on liberal theologians was entitled *The Unicorn in the Sanctuary*.

That night was memorable for a five-hour storm, the thunder loud enough to waken me repeatedly, the lightning a triumph of pyrotechnics, more spectacular than any millennial display. Next morning the gale was making wavelets on the flooded field outside my window and the rain continued torrentially.

At ten o'clock I attended the daily English-language Mass in Medugorje's surprisingly austere little church; its pleasing 1983 stained glass windows don't make the common mistake of trying to look medieval. Some two-thirds of the congregation were American, from octogenarians to schoolchildren, all wearing their tour badges and eagerly stuffing the collection baskets with dollars. A scowl greeted my pointed half-kuna. Three overweight and grey-bearded American friars concelebrated the Mass; an Irish priest preached at length. His mawkish clichés were so soporific – especially after a thunder-broken night – that I soon dozed off, but was roused by a scandalized matron from Chicago who jabbed me in the ribs and hissed, 'Listen to Fr Dempsey!'

Afterwards I approached several friars, feigning geniality, but they obviously smelt my hypocrisy (another of those hostile, probing sceptics!) and brushed me aside: 'No time to talk, we have a very full schedule.' Everybody who dealt officially with the Three Spiritual Zones, whether clerical or lay, had tight faces and hard wary eyes. In contrast, the ordinary townsfolk were friendly and welcoming. There was no overcharging, no touting and, amongst those I happened to meet, most revealed a seemingly genuine belief in the Apparition. Repeatedly people boasted that Medugorje had escaped any war damage because Gospa (their name for the Virgin, meaning simply 'Lady') was more effective than UN troops. All Serb shells aimed at Medugorje disappeared – fell nowhere. The various armies and militias must have done a deal (as they occasionally did, regarding other issues) to protect BiH's main source of foreign currency. Without some 'arrangement' this town could not possibly have escaped the damage inflicted on all others in Herzegovina.

In a large empty café opposite the church I endured my first and I hope last exposure to TV-commerce. On a gigantic TV set, flanked by portrait photographs of Tudjman and Šušak, odious salespersons were promoting (in mid-Atlantic English with German dubbing) a bizarre range of goods, all to do with beauty or slimness or fitness, the prices given in various European currencies. A gadget that might have fallen off a spacecraft was guaranteed, when applied to a woman's skin once every three months, to 'de-energize follicular activity' and we were told 'For 50 per cent of the female population hair removal is their biggest problem'. (But does it *have* to be? I wondered, thoughtfully stroking my moustache.) Next came an unintentionally comic machine called 'Eezifit' (£150). This promised to 'exercise the upper body and the lower body, while simultaneously providing cardio-vascular toning'. It could simulate uphill and downhill walking *and* it had 'an innovative feature – press this switch for a fresh, cool breeze'. Moreover, 'twenty minutes interaction with your Eezifit equals ninety minutes outdoor exercise' – leaving you seventy extra minutes per day to earn enough to pay for the Eezifit and similar follies, such as an 'electro-muscular stimulator' which, if attached to the middle spine as you do your everyday household chores, 'tones your whole body like you had been having hard exercise without the effort'. I can think of no better example of the dynamics of consumerism. First you buy labour-saving devices, then you buy other devices to compensate for the lack of muscle-toning labour in your life. All this is only superficially comic; a world so vulnerable to dodgy salespersons is far advanced on the road to environmental ruin. Not to mention the ruin of people's follicular, cardio-vascular and spinal bits.

All day it rained and I spent hours lying on my bed – the room was chairless – reading a Sarajevo purchase, Warren Zimmermann's *Origin of a Catastrophe*. Mr Zimmermann, the last US ambassador to Yugoslavia, wrote in his final chapter:

> We were watching a cultural genocide, an attempt to wipe out an entire culture – its civil institutions, its mosques, its libraries and schools, its future leaders. What wasn't eradicated had to be moved far away, and all incentives for return had to be destroyed. These war crimes weren't accidental. They were the direct result of the policies of Slobodan Milošević and Radovan Karadžić . . . UNPROFOR was out of its depth. I still find it perplexing why most of its commanders, especially General Rose and Canadian General Lewis MacKenzie, found the Bosnian Serb army so compatible and its contention that 'everybody commits atrocities' so convincing. Was it Serbian spit and polish when contrasted with the ragtag Bosniaks in tennis shoes? Or was it simply a failure to learn how this war had begun and what it was really about?

For me next day there was no escape from the visual and atmospheric evidence of 'cultural genocide'. At 6.45 I set out, the sky still cloudy, and all along my forty-mile route to Stolac the Croatian flag was ostentatiously displayed, sometimes as a banner stretching across village streets – or what remained of them. Most of the destroyed homes had been large newish houses, their owners having benefited from Yugoslavia's thriving tourist trade on the nearby coast.

At a T-junction, some eight miles from Medugorje, I gazed over the wide, long Trebizat valley, its beauty extinguished some time ago by industrialization. Far below, in the town of Ljubuški two large factories had been used as HVO prison camps; hereabouts were several, I had passed one just over the hill from Medugorje. Then I turned left to freewheel into springtime – the budding trees and bushes faintly green, the grass vivid, the joyous yellow of furze splashed over sheer, gaunt karst precipices, a profusion of wild flowers half-hiding the wayside litter. The sky had cleared and now the temperature rose perceptibly. Yet ahead of me were distant snowy ridges, with eccentric separate cloud formations gliding along their lower flanks.

In the Franciscans' stronghold of Čapljina wayside signs urged passers-by to visit their new chapel and shrine, visible on a nearby hillside, gleaming white and flying an outsize Croatian flag. Then my quiet little road crossed the busy E73 not far from Počitelj, a small town clinging to cliffs above the Neretva. Here a tall roadside cross – crudely carved and garishly painted – had recently been erected to celebrate the expulsion of Počitelj's Bosniaks and the destruction of the old town. My binoculars brought close the ruined medieval walls and narrow streets of fifteenth-century stone houses. In September 1993 five of the major buildings listed in Amir Pašić's *Islamic Architecture in Bosnia and Herzegovina* were dynamited in Počitelj. Now we can only look at pictures of them – the most magnificent being Hadži Alija's mosque (built 1562–3).

The town's surviving Bosniaks were imprisoned in the Dretelj camp near Čapljina where (as in the Chetniks' Omarska camp) they were sexually mutilated and forced to drink their own urine. Croat criminals from Ljubuški's jail were often given the doubtless pleasurable task of murdering Bosniaks. Meanwhile, in Medugorje, devout Christians were reciting their rosaries and singing their hymns and the friars – when not helping to run Dretelj – were preaching about Gospa's message of 'Peace to all men!' In Čapljina, in February 1996, the Herceg-Bosna authorities held a conference on 'The Historical Development of Croat Počitelj' and it was decided to build a church on the site of Hadži Alija's mosque.

I did not turn aside to mourn over Počitelj. By then I was punch-drunk on ruins and the empty spaces where once stood the Ottomans' most precious bequests to Europe. Quickly I pedalled on as distant thunder boomed and echoed amidst the mountains ahead and purple-black clouds obscured their snow-crests. I was planning to linger at Radimlje, a rare collection of *stećaks* (previously described as Bogomil tombstones) not far short of Stolac. But it had been foolish of me to look forward so much to this Bosnian Church necropolis; I should have foreseen the surrounding mine-warnings. Tantalizing glimpses of distant sarcophagus-like tombs only increased my frustration and on hearing myself literally grinding my teeth I realized that it was time to leave BiH.

When the Serb army occupied Stolac in 1992 a Croat-Bosniak alliance drove them out, whereupon they repeatedly shelled the town from the surrounding mountains. Within a year Croats were attacking their former allies and a UNHCR worker reported:

On 23 August 1993, four mosques in Stolac were blown up. That night, witnesses said military trucks carrying [Croatian] soldiers firing their weapons in the air went through the town terrorizing and rounding up all Muslim women, children and elderly. The cries and screams could be heard throughout the town as the soldiers looted and destroyed Muslim homes. The soldiers, who wore handkerchiefs, stockings or paint to hide their faces, took the civilians to Blagaj, an area of heavy fighting to the north-west.

My reaction to Stolac proved that I was not yet – not quite – punch-drunk. I almost wept over the rubble of that town, many of whose ancient family residences were buildings protected under Yugoslav law. Its four small, exquisitely proportioned mosques didn't need to be 'listed'; Bosnians of every religion and none were proud of them. In Yugoslavia 'multiculturalism' wasn't thought or talked about; it was the code by which people lived.

Those purple-black clouds went into action as I was approaching Stolac, a small town at the convergence of three narrow valleys. Its buildings are tightly packed between high, steep, rocky ridges, their bleakness relieved by clumps of pines and a few cypress groves. On the highest ridge stand the mighty remains of an Ottoman fortress and the Croatian flag was arrogantly flying from still sturdy battlements. In springtime the dull green Bregava river, which rises nearby, foams noisily through the town centre but by August is a mere trickle. On its right bank weeping willows half-hide the restored Stolac Motel where the surly receptionist objected to my dripping cape (motels expect dry guests, whatever the weather) and made difficulties about Ruairi's accommodation until a fellow-guest came to my linguistic rescue. Suzana was a young Bosniak from Mostar, an OSCE employee on election business in Stolac. We lunched together, at a window table within earshot of the Bregava, and exchanged potted biographies.

Suzana's Serb father was five years old when the Ustasha murdered his parents, in August 1941. A Mostar Bosniak family then adopted him; the two families had long been friends and professional colleagues. At university in Sarajevo he met and married a Stolac Bosniak and, after two years' hospital experience in Belgrade, they set up a joint medical practice in Mostar. But not for long; Suzana was only four and her brother two when a car crash left them fatherless.

Now Suzana was supporting three relatives. A shell fragment had permanently paralysed her mother during the siege of Mostar; her brother had taken to drink after eight months in an HVO prison-camp; her widowed octogenarian grand-aunt had obstinately returned to Stolac in 1997 and was sharing the one intact room in her eighteenth-century home with a family of four from some remote razed village. The lack of electricity and running water didn't bother the peasants, who were used to neither, but grand-aunt felt the privations. Yet she wouldn't leave Stolac, where she *belonged*. Suzana swore at the numbers of new mosques being built throughout BiH before the homeless were rehoused: 'Oil sheikhs showing off!' She also complained that in 1998, when tourists were back on the Dalmatian coast, 'they bought many precious looted things for bargains. Foreigners couldn't know where they came from – I don't blame them. In Dubrovnik my uncle saw a carpet from his Stolac home – unique and very old and the looters had treated it well. He had no money to buy it back though he loved it so much – his business was also destroyed. This makes me very angry when I think of it so I try not to, but that's hard. The looters knew they could display stolen goods publicly in Croatia and make big money and never be punished. "The culture of impunity" my American friends in Mostar call it. It puts down no good roots for a law-respecting democracy. This maybe is only a small detail and politicians like to think about big things. But if bad ones aren't punished we can have no security or stability.'

Suzana was another who feared that the Dayton Accord had merely initiated an interval of S-For supervised non-fighting far removed from real peace, while solving nothing politically. 'Look around here,' she said. 'The Croatian currency used, the Croatian flag flying from everything – and tomorrow in Trebinje you can't use the legal BiH currency and you'll see the Republika Srpska flag flying from everything. Still we're told BiH is an independent sovereign state internationally recognized with a seat at the UN. Does it look like that to you? And though it's all a sham we're told it's a great victory for US diplomacy – and does anyone outside know or care it's a sham?'

I told her that most of those who think about BiH's problems have always recognized the sham.

'Those *few*!' laughed Suzana. 'You needn't say it, I'm working with foreigners since '96. They come here knowing nothing about the country and many never bother to learn.'

I asked 'What about the older foreigners who really loved and knew Yugoslavia and say, "You recovered from the hatreds of the Second World War – you can do it again!" Perhaps you can?'

Suzana shook her head. 'No, never – this is terminal. The idea of Yugoslavia is gone. After '45 there was no choice, we had to recover from the hatreds. Tito was a clever social engineer, he bullied us into recovering. It was all different then. We got some economic support from outside but really we were on our own – people forget that. Once Tito broke with Moscow we were more on our own than any other European country except Albania. You in the West were putting your EU together, the East was a bloc run from Moscow – we were isolated, depending on ourselves. That was good, there was only one way to go: forget the past and pull together! "Brotherhood and Peace!" People my age laugh at that but it worked.

Now we're being helped and used by outsiders, helped to become *pretend* independent states that can't stand alone. Our helpers like that, they like to control the bits of what was Yugoslavia. It wouldn't have suited them if Tito II had followed Tito I and kept us separate and really independent. They want all European countries in the EU, in the OSCE, in the WTO, in Nato – all under their management.'

When discussing the Balkans, we all bring our personal convictions and prejudices on to somebody else's scene, as Vesna had remarked in Velika Kladuša. And, as Suzana's comments emphasized, the Great Powers bring their own complex ambitions and inappropriate methods and try to force 'democracy' on people who only treat it as a key to the international money-box. Hence the space Tito had for 'social engineering' is no longer available, as the 'bits' compete for funding and the Great Powers compete for Balkan 'spheres of influence'.

When the rainstorm had passed Suzana went about her ballot-box business and I walked to the Ottoman fort. BiH's battered towns had in common an aura of unease, lethargy, failure, regret/nostalgia – general disorientation. Despite all those Croatian or Serbian flags so triumphantly displayed, they felt like *defeated* places. And their physical destruction was mirrored in many unhappy eyes, betraying the destruction of hopes and ideals. The takeover by Croats or Serbs of Bosniak-majority towns and villages had been presented to the conquering minority as a victory. Yet among ordinary folk there was no rejoicing, which in a sterile way is consoling.

The long climb to the fort soothed me – and here was a 'natural' ruin, brought about by desuetude and time. Now the sun was out and a brilliant abundance of wild flowers, holding quivering raindrops, gave the cliff-face a festive air. Emerald moss carpeted the Ottomans' paved road, almost as flawless as the day it was built, despite the Serbian military traffic in 1992. But then, at the crumbling stonework of the main gateway – more mine-warnings. For one exasperated moment I was tempted to ignore them, as I had been at Radimlje. However, personnel mines are usually lavishly planted and who wants to be a one-legged or blinded septuagenarian? Grumpily I sat on a boulder in the warm sun, lit an anti-frustration mini-cigar and wrote in my notebook:

My different reactions to post-genocide Rwanda and the post-wars (or inter-wars?) Balkans make me feel guilty. Although Rwanda shattered me – often numbed me, emotionally – BiH seems to be affecting me more *personally*. So of course I suspect myself of Eurocentricity. Did I at some deep shameful level see the Rwandan tragedy as peculiarly African and therefore understandably incomprehensible? Whereas I feel it should be possible to comprehend fellow-Europeans . . . But no – I think I can honestly let myself off that guilt hook. What so grieves me about the former Yugoslavia is the sudden collapse into cruel anarchy of a state that under Tito had achieved a reasonable degree of stability. In contrast, Rwanda as an independent state had always lived on the brink of anarchy, its few years of apparent tranquillity deceptive. Thus the genocide was not the undoing of something achieved but the dreadful outcome of the failure to achieve . . . Yugoslavia's agonizing disintegration was the destruction of a good which existed, a state with many imperfections but in which the majority of people had learned how to live, frugally, in harmony. To that extent it was a model for us all – frugality is what every country must learn to accept, *soon*, if our planet is to remain habitable for human beings.

Why, given what Western Europeans did to one another during the first half of the twentieth century, have so many commentators labelled these Balkan wars 'un-European'? Perhaps because the methods of killing often seemed 'primitive'? Cutting people's throats, dumping old folk in forests where they must die of hunger or exposure, incinerating live children . . . Yet in my lifetime the carpet-bombing of cities incinerated thousands of live children. Why do some people think those Western European bomber-pilots were less primitive than the Balkan militia who built a bonfire and threw children on to it? *Were* the pilots less primitive? Could they have incinerated children *not* by remote control? Judging by those I myself have known, the answer is 'No'. But what does that tell us? It tells us that having the technological ability to be brutal by remote control turns men who could not be brutal one-to-one into men who can massacre on a scale unachievable by primitive militias. Modern warfare is de-civilizing us. Our culture breeds men who couldn't possibly throw live children on bonfires, but it allows the same sort of men to do much worse without feeling too bad about it.

Herzegovina's April weather is as unpredictable as Ireland's – but much more extreme. It was still raining at dawn, after another thunderstormy night, yet by eight o'clock I was pedalling out of Stolac in bright sunshine under a clear sky, with a cold gusty gale behind me. Beyond the town an almost traffic-free road at first rose gradually, between wide slopes blanketed in coarse pale brown grass. But soon I was on foot, beginning a two-hour walk.

After Stolac, I needed such a climb – revealing, in three directions, an ever-widening panorama of karst mountains. Some travellers find this rocky core of Herzegovina depressing – too forbidding, almost intimidating – but I rejoiced in its stern aridity, untamable and jagged and *free*. Here one can't cultivate, or pasture flocks, or fell trees, or build mega-dams, or in any way exploit or subdue these immense expanses of naked limestone.

Two-thirds of the way up, mine-warning tapes stretched along the verges for half a mile, preceding another 'WELCOME TO REPUBLIKA SRPSKA'. Around the next corner I was astonished to see – amidst these wild unpeopled mountains – two long, low, semi-derelict buildings, their original purpose uncertain, facing each other across the road. Nearby were parked ten lorries and vans crammed with squealing pigs, mooing calves, bleating sheep. ('Animal welfare' was not on their transporters' agenda.) This seemed a bizarre location for a livestock fair, if such it was. Only three men were visible, leaning against a wall, sharing a bottle of *rakija*; they ignored my greeting. Then two shaggy sheep-dogs rushed from behind a lorry barking possessively. I stood still, wondering if the men would call them off. They didn't, so I amiably addressed the two and slowly extended a hand. They stopped barking, dropped their tails and looked puzzled; the tone was right but the language was wrong. I judged it safe to proceed. Next day in Trebinje someone told me that this remote 'border' crossing is a favourite *rendezvous* for traders in stolen livestock.

Soon the gradient allowed pedalling, between high rounded mountains, erosion-smoothed, with deep intervening gorges holding tumbled chunks of whitish rock. Then Ljubinje appeared, scattered over a circular valley: yet another devastated little town, its burned factory roofless. A side valley was partially cultivated, the neat, thin strips of young green maize and rich brown ploughland forming a tweed-like pattern when seen from high above. But where were the cultivators? Ljubinje seemed depopulated, most of its houses looted if not torched.

The next long climb was gradual, around mountains thickly strewn with monstrous, bulbous, barn-sized boulders. Here I was overtaken by a four-vehicle OSCE convoy taking election monitors from Mostar to Trebinje. Then came a spectacular descent of brake-testing steepness, down and down and down, the Z-bends dizzyingly sharp and the astonishing Popovo *polje* opening out below me – long, narrow miles of flat fertile land with rock walls rising sheer, for thousands of feet, from its edges. A month earlier I would have seen here a shallow, fishful lake. But recently the water had sunk swiftly away into underground ghylls, leaving a deposit of freakishly generous reddish soil which commonly yields two (sometimes three) crops before the water rises again.

For twenty level miles the road followed the base of the mountains and close by, on my right, stretched the *polje*. Four hamlets had been established, centuries ago, where recesses in the cliff-wall allowed building on sloping ledges of cultivable land. Both the houses and the minuscule mosques were constructed all of stone, including the roofs, and it had not been possible to demolish their four-foot-thick walls with the artillery available to local Chetniks. Yet few families had returned and a melancholy loneliness marked this very lovely region. Each hamlet had its colossal stone cisterns; the little Trebišnjica river dries up completely in midsummer so drinking water must be stored. Down here the spring growth was well advanced: lilac, plum and apple blossoms overhung the road, primroses lined garden paths leading to empty homes, new grass glistened in tiny fields bounded by dry stone walls, fuschias blazed between boulders and in some pastures flat karst slabs lay on the grass like gravestones.

In mid-afternoon Trebinje appeared on the far side of a plateau dotted with small factories (mostly defunct) and encircled by low, drab ridges on which nothing visible grew. In this town the Austrian legacy is much more obvious than the Turkish. Two wide, straight streets, sporting several fanciful 'Venetian' façades, lead to spacious parks where hens were impatiently scratching through layers of litter beneath magnificent horse-chestnuts, the Habsburgs' arboreal hallmark. Residential suburbs that might have strayed from Graz scramble up the eastern ridge and an unusual number of formidable barracks mark Trebinje's importance as an Austrian military post. But a Habsburg ghost would be shocked. The poverty-stricken town had a squalid aura, its war damage comparatively slight outside of the Ottoman quarter but with ugly (in every sense) Chetnik graffiti defacing most buildings, including a derelict Orthodox church.

Once Trebinje welcomed tourists – coachloads came from Dubrovnik (only twenty miles away) to be shown 'a typical Muslim town' and herded to the 'Oriental Market' where the more gullible were fleeced and the rest took photographs (for a fee) of women traders in fake folk costumes. However, after its recent drastic population change it seems Trebinje does not welcome tourists; I have rarely visited such an unfriendly place. But perhaps allowances should be made for election fever. I had arrived on the eve of polling day and the Serbs' resentment of expat monitors disposed them to be hostile to any foreigner. Those new settlers were out in strength. Young men wearing quasi-military gear and Republika Srpska's recently invented 'crest' paraded the streets with drums and brass bands and banners, or got rowdily drunk, in cafés displaying 'Chetnik' insignia, to pre-celebrate their presumed election victory. When first I heard those drums, involuntarily I shuddered – the spirit of Drumcree seemed present.

Despite its lack of allure, I was to spend two nights in Trebinje; Merima had arranged an appointment for me with her close friend Haris – of whom more anon. A handsome Austrian bridge took me across the Trebišnjica river (here wide and shallow) to the Leotar Hotel on the quay, a standard 1960s eyesore where the staff were unhelpful to the point of rudeness. My bathroom tap (cold water only) couldn't be turned off and my french window had to remain closed, the room being too small for its two beds. There was no bedside lamp and the central bulb was fifteen watt. The dressing-table stool (no space for a chair) had a broken leg and the nylon carpet smelt of vomit.

From my window I watched five piebald goats devouring the shrubs' new buds in the hotel grounds with the apparent approval of their herd, an emaciated young woman clad all in black. Near a car park, the contents of three overloaded garbage skips were being scattered on the grass by scavenging crows and a small white terrier, having found a fragrant Pampers, rolled in it ecstatically and stood up looking brown.

Ten minutes later, seeing me crossing the car park, the goat-herd timidly approached and begged successfully for marks. Her timidity and thinness suggested that sheer hunger was driving her to overcome pride.

In the OSCE office I sought information about Zlatko Lagumdžija, leader of the

Croatian Social Democratic Party (SDP), who had recently been in contention with the OSCE for reasons unclear to me. The rather snooty expat staff were uncooperative but one of their interpreters, a charming young man also named Zlatko, agreed to meet me after work in a café opposite the old town walls. While waiting for him, sitting at a pavement table, I noticed a succinct summing-up of the US's role in the contemporary world. An advertisement for chewing-gum, stuck to a shop window across the street, said 'The GENUINE American gum!' And on an adjacent wall the graffiti read: 'AMERIKANS AR PIRATS!'

Zlatko had strong feelings about the Lagumdžija controversy and was more than willing to clarify the matter. Mr Lagumdžija, BiH's deputy prime minister during the wars, remained dedicated to the restoration of BiH unity and was seen as the one politician who, being so widely respected, just might be able to defeat the extremist Serb and Croat leaders. But that brought everyone back to Dayton's main defect. It insisted on a three-man BiH Presidency: a Bosniak, a Serb, a Croat. Therefore Federation citizens were restricted to voting for a Croat or Bosniak while Republika Srpska residents, whatever their preference, must vote for a Serb. When changes to Dayton were proposed by Mr Lagumdžija, to enable pro-moderate changes in BiH's constitution, the High Representative declared that only a two-thirds majority of the BiH Parliament could institute such changes. And here the whole situation ate its own tail, to use Zlatko's graphic phrase. No such majority was achievable because the extremist parties naturally upheld a constitution that perpetuates division along nationalist lines. Mr Lagumdžija then called for the resignation of the OSCE 'experts' who had drafted BiH's new electoral legislation and an OSCE spokeswoman referred to the 'complete irresponsibility' of the BiH Parliament. 'That's why,' concluded Zlatko, 'in our office we're not – how do you say? – not happy pussies.'

Republika Srpska had been without a President since March 1999 when the then High Representative, Carlos Westendorp, sacked the entity's President Nikola Poplašen because of his hardline attitudes. This strengthened Republika Srpska's comparatively moderate Prime Minister, Milorad Dodik. Mr Westendorp then offered to appoint Mirko Šarović as entity President, under IC-specified terms and conditions which Mr Šarović found unacceptable. In January 2000 a Šarović move to grab the entity's presidency was condemned by the High Representative's office as 'illegal and unconstitutional' and he was accused of working hard to 'destabilize the entity'. (He had Milošević's backing.) During the ensuing stalemate there was surprisingly little comment from the anti-Šarović factions and Zlatko explained why.

'I see we are having a big game here, with elections and democracy. Like children playing with being grown up, making a house in the garden. When any foreign High Representative man can sack a President and say for the media BiH's Parliament is irresponsible, how is it possible for Bosnian people to believe they have democracy? Nobody except *Germans* can sack the German President – right? The French Parliament doesn't have to obey foreigners – right? Poplašen and Šarović are bad men – very bad! That is one fact. What is second fact, Poplašen's followers vote for him and foreign monitors say this is "free and fair" vote. What is third fact, he behaves like his followers want and then the High Representative sacks him! This way, you can't teach people about democracy and how they must respect it. That is not only my thoughts, it is the thinking of many Bosnians – Serb, Croat, Bosniak. We get angry to be treated like playing children.'

I said, 'But at least Dayton stopped the killing. What alternative do you see?'

Zlatko then argued, predictably, that had the combined Croatian and Bosniak forces been allowed to continue fighting in the autumn of 1995 the Serbs would very soon have been defeated and Dayton need never have happened.

Franciscan support for Croat nationalism was matched by Orthodox support for Serb nationalism. In *The Bridge Betrayed*, Michael Sells records how the feast day of St Sava, founder of the Serbian Church, was celebrated on the eve of Trebinje's terrorization. The congregation heard a Chetnik paramilitary leader boasting of his murder squad's achievements and calling for a 'Christian, Orthodox Serbia with no Muslims and no unbelievers'. Those moderate Serbs, lay and clerical, who protested against the expulsion of Trebinje's Bosniaks and the destruction of its mosques were excoriated by Bishop Atanasije of Herzegovina. He also condoned atrocities condemned even by Vuk Drašković and Dobrica Ćosić, politicians whose popular writings consistently 'incited to violence'. Later, when 'cleansed' Foča was renamed Srbinje ('Serb Place'), several senior clerics attended the ceremony and Professor Vojislav Maksimović of Sarajevo University praised 'the Serb fighters from Foča and the region [who] were worthy defenders of Serbianness and of Orthodoxy'. (Arkan's Tigers were among Foča's 'defenders' and foreign cameramen were invited to film them kicking Bosniak corpses and stamping on the skulls with their high leather boots specially polished for this TV opportunity.) Metropolitan Nikolaj, BiH's senior Orthodox cleric, conducted his 1993 Easter Day service flanked by Karadžić and Mladić and referred to their leading the Bosnian Serbs along 'the hard road of Christ'. When both were indicted by the International Criminal Tribunal their Orthodox friends indignantly defended them; the Greek Orthodox Church had already invested Karadžić with the 900-year-old 'Knights' Order of the First Rank of Saint Dionysius of Xanthe', describing him as 'one of the most prominent sons of our Lord Jesus Christ working for peace'. Karadžić's guru, Jovan Rašković, caused much amusement by citing the Muslims' ablutions before prayer as proof of their 'anal-analytic' nature. The Orthodox Church's official journal printed the writings of Vuk Drašković and Dragoš Kalajić who claimed that 'Slavic Muslims do not belong to Europe, their culture is an unconscious expression of "semi-Arabic subculture" and the Slavic Muslims of Bosnia have inherited an inferior "special gene" passed on by the Ottomans from North African Arabs.'

Small wonder so many places of worship, including Orthodox churches in Kosovo, were targeted in all the recent Balkan wars – though so few 'former Yugoslavs' still believe in the faiths of their fathers.

On election Saturday – a sunny windless morning – the polling stations opened at 7 a.m. and within an hour many couples and groups were on their way to the ballot boxes; despite Zlatko's scorn for 'the game', most citizens obviously valued their right to vote. (All over BiH I had observed traffic signs, advertisement hoardings and signposts obscured by the election posters of a bewildering multiplicity of parties.) A few discreetly armed policemen dawdled around the entrance to each polling station but all day the town's atmosphere remained calm and quietly cheerful, despite the previous day's intimidating displays of swaggering, drumming and chanting. For this imposition of decorum the OSCE deserved most of the credit – according to Haris, when we met at noon.

Haris was tall, narrow-shouldered and much too thin, with prematurely grey hair, an aquiline nose, deep-set hazel eyes and a big smile revealing crooked teeth. For generations (Merima told me, in Sarajevo) his family had been prosperous Trebinje merchants but in 1985 Yugoslavia's declining economy prompted him to migrate to the US. There he taught Serbo-Croat in a school for immigrants' children while establishing himself as a freelance journalist.

'Then I swam against the tide,' Haris said. 'When so many were leaving I came back, in April '92, to Sarajevo, as an American war correspondent. A week later I'd dropped my new identity and become a Bosnian again. Listen carefully – a Bosnian not a Bosniak! Here in Trebinje all stayed calm right up to the end of '92, no matter what was happening other places. Our Bosniaks and Serbs were always really good friends – more Bosniaks than Serbs answered the first JNA call-up in 1990. The shock was terrible in January '93 when suddenly all Bosniaks – the majority population! – were ordered to leave Trebinje for good. I came from Sarajevo, disguised as an American in an Unprofor vehicle, to be with my parents. The town council said no local official had given this order – then everyone calmed down, didn't move. A few days later the outsider gangs arrived, looters and torchers, rapists and killers. Nobody tried to stop their robbing and burning. When they destroyed the Osman Pasha mosque, inside the old town walls, and began to go for the homes of leading Bosniak families, all Bosniaks took fright. Most didn't wait to be murdered – not after a few public executions. A good Serb friend of mine from our schooldays, a well-known actor, died in the hospital here from injuries after a punishment assault. He was punished for helping a Bosniak friend escape from one of Arkan's so-called militia. People were shot if caught carrying away more than one small bag of possessions. Everything else and their houses had to be left for the gangs – booty was their pay. Local bus owners got rich quick, charging DM280 for a single ticket to Denmark, Sweden or Turkey – countries that promised to welcome Bosniaks. People without marks had no choice but refugee camps, already overcrowded.'

Throughout BiH, said Haris, many Serbs and Croats ('*very* many!') helped Bosniaks at great risk to themselves. He was now collecting examples of such incidents 'to publish in the US and Europe in memory of my friend Srdjan, the actor. This is a story that *must* be told – and told by a Bosniak. Stereotyping is so dangerous, people can *become* as they are *presented*. All those reports of atrocities, year after year, about the *Serbs* did this, the *Croats* did that, the *Bosniaks* did the other – when most of them *didn't*! Most were victims and many were heroes. It's urgent to publicize this. All the nationalists want it suppressed, they need mutual hate to keep their pots boiling. That's why it's so hard for me to get material, people remain afraid to admit they opposed extremists. Those gangs and their guns haven't gone away. But I must have verifiable evidence, otherwise it's all dismissed as more propaganda. It's another big problem that so many I need to interview are displaced and hard to find.'

When I commented on Trebinje's unfriendliness Haris smiled sadly. 'Why are you surprised? You're not in a normal town. This whole entity is abnormal. In '94 Mladić, Karadžić and Arkan – desperate for more troops – sent agents around the refugee camps in Serbia, with Milošević's permission. They forced thousands to their front lines, gave them little or no pay and less food – they were stealing from each other and going AWOL looking for paid work. After the ceasefire they were told to stay here, to populate their new entity. By then half a million Bosnian Serbs had emigrated and about 150,000 were under the new Federation government. That's why we've this high proportion of young men in the RS towns, mostly unemployed – a time-bomb primed with testosterone. When they ran away from Croatia in '91, and BiH in '92 and '93, they were average peasant boys – maybe not too smart but smart enough to know they didn't want to do Milošević's dirty work against their neighbours. After they'd been through the Chetnik mind-bending machine, most became what you saw around Trebinje's streets yesterday.'

Haris and I corresponded occasionally on my return to Ireland and in May 2001 he wrote:

You must have heard about the mob attacks at the Trebinje and Banja Luka foundation-stone ceremonies for new mosques. I witnessed both and they frightened me more than being shelled in Sarajevo. This felt like proof our polarization is now set in concrete. While the fighting continued our situation was in transition and we were so near the days of harmony it didn't seem possible they couldn't be recovered.

In Banja Luka mob-rule organizers have it very easy with 70% of the residents dis-placed Serbs. They panicked when told the new mosque meant Bosniaks returning and wanting their homes back – leaving those Serbs again homeless. More than 2,000 Chetniks went on the rampage, waving Chetnik flags, singing Chetnik war chants. They badly beat up thirty Bosniaks and killed one elderly man. They slaughtered a pig on the site of the Ferhat Pasha mosque and hung the head on the door of the Islamic Community building, yelling anti-Islamic slogans. They burned seven buses that brought Bosniaks to the ceremonies, also a BiH TV team's vehicle and the car of Zlatko Lagumdžija, our Foreign Minister. He and the US ambassador and the head of the UN mission in BiH and 350 other foreign officials and government representatives were stoned and had to take refuge for hours in the Community building. S-For weren't around, though this event was being publicly planned for a month and everyone expected trouble. After, their British Commander said while the mob was controlling Banja Luka the Republika Srpska prime minister rang him to say he didn't want S-For troops getting involved, he wanted the local police to cope. While he was making that call he could see the local police standing by, doing nothing to restrain the Chetniks! The British ambassador accused the prime minister's party [the Serbian Democratic Party, Republika Srpska's largest parliamentary party] of directing the violence. The local leaders didn't intervene with the crowd until the British S-For officer on the ground threatened to deploy armoured vehicles to rescue all the big shots trapped in the Community building.

President Vojislav Koštunica's comments didn't help. He was in the US meeting Kofi Annan and announced the violence made him 'concerned and unhappy' and showed no new mosque should be built in BiH because 'such actions might provoke further inci-dents'! A classic Serb nationalist judgement – let the Bosniaks give in yet again to Serbian bullying!

The international community are slow learners. Chris Patten [EU External Affairs Commissioner] produced another classic – this one a patronising reprimand. 'EU tax-payers are spending huge sums to assist BiH, including Republika Srpska – the sort of medieval behaviour we saw yesterday had no place in modern Europe.' Do these people not realise how stupid they sound? Any violence in the Balkans has to be 'medieval' – we're such backward, uncivilized warring factions! But Nato's state-of-the-art violence, a clever airwar using cluster bombs and DU [depleted uranium] is OK in modern Europe.

To end I have some good news. The HDZ is dying in a corner. About six months ago they were plotting to set up an independent statelet – once you recognise the right of self-determination, where does it end? You could have every village independent, as it was for centuries in the Republic of Raetia until Napoleon forced them to join Switzerland. Now I'm straying off the point. So the HDZ tried to split the Federation Army by offering DM500 a month to every Croat officer and soldier who deserted. At first many wouldn't agree – then they were intimidated, quit their barracks and went home. Our new Defence Minister, Mijo Anić, moved smartly, promised more pay if they'd sign a pledge of loyalty. Meanwhile S-For woke up for long enough to raid the Hercegovacka Bank in Mostar, where the HDZ kept their stolen loot, and all their funds were blocked by Western auditors. Very soon 3,000 had signed that pledge, led by the two senior officers who organized the mutiny. Now the HDZ leader, Ante Jelavić, and some of his lieutenants are facing the possibility of arrest and quarrelling among themselves. Last week the newspapers quoted Petar Milić – a good guy, member of the Croat National Council – who said, 'Personal interests inside the HDZ are persuading members to return to the language of compromise and pragmatism'. Which is *very* good news!

11

Disconcerted in Montenegro

In Mostar various people had offered conflicting advice about where a visa-less Irish citizen should cross into Montenegro. For reasons best known to the Yugoslav Embassy in Zagreb I had been refused a visa in March and, as Montenegro remained part of the shrivelled Yugoslavia, in theory I did need one. In practice, however, it seemed the situation was 'fluid' – diplomatic-speak for chaotic. Everything depended, I was told, on who – if anyone – checked my passport. The Montenegrin police, loyal to their anti-Milošević President Milo Djukanović, would almost certainly admit a visa-less EU citizen without comment. The JNA, at that date regularly patrolling all Montenegrin borders, would quite certainly do one of three things: turn me back, admit me after payment of a heavy 'fine' or arrest me as a Nato/CIA spy. The third alternative would be legally justifiable, as several British, Canadian and Dutch visa-less travellers were to discover to their cost a few months later. But in Mostar the general consensus was that I'd not be noticed pedalling along the little-used, fifty-mile Trebinje-to-Nikšić road.

From Trebinje's outskirts this road follows the shore of a deep, still lake – jade green or black, according to the early morning play of light and shade – at the base of sheer rock mountains. From the far shore rise matching mountains, softened by patches of juniper. A gradual climb ended on a low pass from where I could see that mighty barrier – a stupendous complex of ranges – separating Montenegro from the rest of the world. During a two-mile freewheel to a fertile oval valley, the day's first vehicle overtook me – a dusty, dented Yugo with three pigs in the open boot.

Near the village of Lastva an unlovely new bridge spans the Trebišnjica. Beyond were many burned and/or shelled roadside dwellings, nor did the surviving homes look prosperous, despite the surrounding lushness.

At the Portacabin border post four Republika Srpska policemen stared at me disbelievingly for a moment before deciding 'harmless lunatic'. While one checked my passport another offered me a tin of Coca-Cola from their UN-embossed freezer box. My passport was not stamped. Perhaps an 'entity' is not a 'state', however much its police may enjoy 'playing border posts'?

A steep six-mile walk followed, the first stage around a succession of smooth-crested, boulder-strewn mountains, left naked and damp where snow had recently melted. On some sheltered slopes newly green expanses of pastureland, bright with daisies and dandelions – their homeliness seeming oddly incongruous – were being grazed by sadly few cattle and sheep. One deep valley held traces of an aborted dam project and large signs forbade photography. On the opposite mountain I counted nine small ruined homesteads, the patches of hard-won cultivable land beside them still discernible, enclosed by Connemara-type stone walls.

Onwards and upwards – until eventually I had the exhilarating satisfaction of being on a level with the highest summits, still snow-laden, gleaming beyond a tangle of lower peaks. These were all jagged and bare, displaying austere escarpments and isolated slender steles of black rock, hundreds of feet high. As the grandeur of this range overwhelmed me, I was suddenly on Cloud Nine, aware only of a fit body, a good bicycle, a warm sun, keen clear air, the deep blue sky of high places – and no traffic, no litter, *no ruins*.

Soon after, the altitude slowed me; even fit bodies need time to adjust to thinning air. I sat on a boulder, directly overlooking a stony gorge thousands of feet below, and ate a hunk of bread with Haris's present of goats' cheese. Nearby, in three directions, black crags – sharp and stern – stood out against that intensely blue sky. Montenegro – Crna Gora in Serbo-Croat – is a literal description of this region. The profound silence, solemn and soothing, was broken only by mewing falcons and croaking ravens. And theirs were the only movements in all that expanse of harsh beauty: the falcons circling, drifting, gliding, swooping – the ravens being aerobatic, tumbling and darting and swerving and soaring, showing off in the springtime.

Restored, I pushed on for another fifteen minutes – then unexpectedly found myself on the pass, where the road had been roughly blasted through a rock-wall. Ahead stretched a startlingly different landscape. To east, south and west lay an arid grey immensity of low (from my vantage point) rounded mountains, packed together, extending to far horizons. Inhospitable terrain: no wonder Montenegro is the most sparsely populated region of the former Yugoslavia. Here was no steep descent to match my climb; instead I freewheeled slowly, sometimes having to pedal and now feeling slightly tense. Would I meet the laid-back Montenegrin police or the paranoid JNA? Seeing two tiny police huts, I relaxed even before being politely welcomed. One officer merely glanced at my passport. The other spoke good English and remarked jokingly if rather ungallantly, 'You're too old for this sort of thing!'

The road switchbacked on through those strange grey-brown rocky hills with strips of fertile land at their bases, cultivated by the inhabitants of a few dismal hamlets. Soon fast cars, driven recklessly, became a hazard. Around one corner I was alarmed by a razor-wire-fortified JNA base. A conspicuous notice warned, in

Serbo-Croat and English, 'NO PARKING! NO LOOKING! NO PHOTOGRAPHY!' With eyes averted I sped past, conscious of being stared at by sentries. Soon after came the start of a long, precipitous descent to Nikšić, on a perilously broken surface.

At first I wondered if Nikšić was real – or was I having a nightmare about being in this place of immeasurable destitution and gloom? Once a bustling industrial success, where happy 'self-management' workers achieved high productivity rates, the town's iron works employed 30,000 as late as 1990. But now Nikšić was dead, a victim of Yugoslavia's 1980s economic collapse, then of UN sanctions, latterly of Milošević's closing of the Serbia-Montenegro border in an effort to bring down President Djukanović. I pedalled slowly through the suburbs, between sprawling deserted factories, some looted for building materials. In the centre, at three o'clock on a Monday afternoon, all the big stores and most small shops were closed. So were the cafés, apart from a cramped, dim room in a one-storey cottage standing on wasteland; and a Balkan town without any café life, however muted, really is dead. The pavements were cracked and weedy and littered with broken glass. Some of the apartment blocks were incomplete – four stories instead of eight, with bent steel rods decorating their roofs. Many blocks were literally falling apart, their balconies hanging loose, spray-gun graffiti on every wall. Post-Tito, Nikšić became notorious as one of Yugoslavia's most violent and lawless towns; it provided the majority of those Montenegrin reservists who in 1992 ran amok in and around Dubrovnik. In that campaign so many troops died within weeks that Montenegro quite quickly became anti-war, despite its martial traditions.

Personally I found Nikšić's few visible citizens friendly and helpful – and pathetic, as they plodded dejectedly along their potholed streets and shopped at corner kiosks. These displayed a few smuggled processed foods (Kellogg's cornflakes, Heinz tinned beans, Jacob's biscuits) and toiletries (Kolynos tooth-paste, Nivea cream, Lux soap). Later that day I learned that Nikšić also has 'outlets' offering more costly 'humanitarian aid' goods purloined from Kosovo and Albania.

In all the main streets three-man police road blocks were checking every vehicle and my antennae registered tension. A few days previously, a midnight bar fight between pro-Djukanović policemen and JNA recruits from Serbia had left three dead. Montenegro's police, it was said, were being rigorously vetted to ensure their pro-Western 'reliability'. And, it was also said, JNA recruits had been condi-tioned to treat 'Djukanović's police' as Nato collaborators. The President's enemies were accusing him of hiring police reinforcements from Western Europe and South America. This was among the various rumours I noted in my journal without being able to determine how many grains of truth they contained. But later, in Podgorica, I did observe an extraordinary number of foreigners, who could not possibly be mistaken for tourists, crowding the hotel restaurants and pavement cafés.

Nikšić's 'luxury' hotel, an empty monument to thwarted tourism, offered the only lodging. The minimum tariff was £40 for a large double room with TV, telephone, bedside radio (but no bedside lamp) and four enormous garish paintings of Montenegrin ski-slopes. The telephone and radio were out of order; I didn't test the TV.

As a foreigner, I was not allowed to drink alcohol (specifically) in either the non-residents' café or their restaurant – a weird restriction of uncertain provenance. To reach the residents' bar and restaurant I had to return to the street and walk around the block to another entrance. Then the door of the bar stuck on the carpet, needing two waiters to free it – after which I was rewarded by an excellent beer. Nikšić brewery has long been famous and was among Montenegro's few surviving industries. In one corner three silent men sat sipping *rakija* while lugubriously watching an angry TV debate about The Hague Tribunal. Kriegler, a Bosnian Serb leader who had just been captured and helicoptered to The Hague, comes from the Nikšić area.

The restaurant had glass external walls, many plastic pillars, triffid-like potted plants and seating for four hundred. At 7 p.m. two tables were occupied, one by Milana and Sanja, the other by myself. Soon we were sharing a table. Milana spoke perfect English, very precisely, without abbreviations or elisions. Tall, slim and dark-haired, she had a feline sort of elegance and a warm smile. Having recently returned from a two-year teacher training course in England, she was finding the contrast between High Wycombe and her run-down birthplace acutely depressing. Her friend Sanja, considerably older and a professor of metallurgy, was dowdy and dumpy but no less charming. Their salaries came to DM240 and DM280 per month, augmented by many hours of private tuition. Both were fiercely anti-Milošević and neither made any attempt to deny or excuse the atrocities committed by Serbian forces and their militia allies during the 1990s. Milana believed that in any country a minority could be incited to commit similar crimes – something I had realized in 1985, while writing about race relations in England.

Regrettably, my congenial companions had to eat quickly and hurry away to their respective pupils. But before we parted they gave me several Podgorica addresses.

Officially the Ottomans conquered Montenegro in 1499 but for centuries they made little effort to control the region. In exchange for the payment of a low poll tax the tribes were left to govern themselves and never experienced the *timar* system, which rewarded the *spahis* (the celebrated Ottoman cavalry) by giving them the right to demand from peasants a certain percentage of their crops or flocks. In fact Montenegrins rarely met Ottomans, apart from an occasional tax collector who usually failed in his mission. Most lived in the mountains, raising cattle and sheep, hunting and fishing, cultivating the art of cattle-rustling and relishing banditry when the opportunity arose. They jointly owned pastures and woodlands and scorned political borders; the adjacent mountainous regions of Albania and Herzegovina (where the population was then largely Serb) were regarded as part of their own land. The tribal chiefs saw themselves as Serbs, and on the whole supported Serbian 'causes', but when it came to territory they naturally put Montenegrin objectives first.

Eighteenth-century Montenegro was proud of being the only Serb land that had never lost its independence to the Ottomans. In pre-helicopter days its topography gave its warriors an insuperable advantage (forget the *spahis!*) and they often sallied forth into the wider Balkan world to oppose Turkish rule, as represented by Ottoman military commanders in Serbia and Macedonia and by the Muslim élites of Bosnia and Herzegovina.

In the first half of the nineteenth century the Montenegrins numbered about 120,000 of whom 20,000 were fighting men. Statistics recorded in the spring of 1875 sound grimly familiar. The latest phase of what was then known as 'the Eastern Crisis' had involved 30,000 Ottoman soldiers taking on 25,000 Montenegrin-led men who in our day would be called 'freedom fighters'. More than 200,000 refugees fled into Austrian territory (Croatia), an estimated 150,000 lives (mainly civilian) were lost and countless villages were looted and burned. There is no mention of rape, not because it didn't happen but because it was a taboo subject in the 1870s.

By then Montenegro had come to wield more political influence than seemed consistent with its size (smaller than Northern Ireland) and its underdeveloped state; and that remains true of twenty-first-century Montenegro. During the republican presidents' momentous deliberations in 1991–2 Milošević was dependent on the loyalty of Momir Bulatović, leader of Montenegro's Communist Party. In 1989 Bulatović and Milo Djukanović had been 'best buddies' and co-leaders of the group of young Communists who then took power in Montenegro. But soon their ways diverged. Bulatović presented himself as a Serb nationalist-cum-socialist, a man of the people solicitous for the welfare of peasants and factory workers. Djukanović presented himself as a cosmopolitan technocrat and sought followers among the urban middle class and the educated young. In Podgorica he kept the police and many business managers on his side and his home town of Nikšić provided a secure power base.

Then came the October 1997 OSCE-monitored elections for the Montenegrin presidency. In the second round a 67 per cent turnout gave Djukanović 174,745 votes to Bulatović's 169,257. The fury that followed was mainly verbal. Bulatović and his henchmen tried to organize violent demos but failed to gain popular support for this rejection of democracy, though several times they brought

Podgorica to the edge of the cliff. President Djukanović's inauguration took place
in Montenegro's old royal capital, Cetinje, on 15 January 1998.

Balkan main roads are not cyclist-friendly, especially in Montenegro, Kosovo and
Albania where beardless youths driving unregistered Mercedes strive to overtake
everything in sight without regard to the lie of the land. As my map showed no
alternative to the busy Belgrade–Podgorica *autoput* I had sought local advice from
Milana, who told me where to find the old road, restored by the Italians when
they annexed Montenegro during the Second World War but no longer used by
vehicles.

A few miles out of Nikšić, where I turned off the *autoput*, four policemen, break-
fasting in their hut, insisted on presenting me with four hard-boiled eggs – one
from each lunch box – and a bread roll. Said the English-speaker, 'On the
old road there is no place for getting food, you will be hungry, it is far to
Podgorica.'

As this road climbed high around the forested flanks of almost sheer mountains I could often see, on the next mountain, its supporting fortifications – vast
neat walls of stones built into the slopes, truly works of art, with a beauty never
to be attained by utilitarian concrete. The very broken surface prevented pedalling, even where the gradient would have allowed it, but I was happy to dawdle
through this uninhabitable terrain, rich in birdlife, with the first flowers of spring
– yellow, blue, scarlet – sprinkling the verges. Again and again the road twisted
around the heads of deep tree-filled gorges and the wide valley of the river Zeta,
on my right, seemed like the view from an aeroplane.

The junction with a narrow tarred road came as a surprise. Here a signpost
pointed up to Ostrog Monastery but having gone off Orthodox monks in the
Republika Srpska I freewheeled down – very steep descent – to the little village of
Bogeti. There the road widened before again descending, less steeply, to the long
fertile Zeta valley, all green and warm and quite densely populated. Its substantial farmhouses, some new, stood amidst tidy orchards and fat cattle grazed in
riverside pastures.

At Danilovgrad a wide modern bridge spanned the swift green Zeta; from here
the distant rush of *autoput* traffic was faintly audible. This town, fifteen miles north
of Podgorica by the old road, is small, quiet and dispirited, its centre overlooked
by Tito-era government buildings, its short streets broad and broken. Yet compared to Nikšić it seemed rather jolly. Groups of men sat in the afternoon sun at
pavement café tables and some of them were smiling. Women sold artificial
flowers from corner kiosks and a dozen chatting passengers stood around the
minibus taxi rank. Milana had advised me to stay here and make daytrips to

Podgorica; recent exotic additions to the capital's population had inflated lodging costs to a minimum nightly tariff of £70. However, the ramshackle Hotel Danilo was closed, permanently, though its restaurant remained open and provided the best food in town. This I learned from a tall young man whose tracksuit hung loosely on a bony frame and whose pallor was as unhealthy as his English was fluent. He introduced himself as Dragan and eagerly invited me to stay in his home. When I hesitated, wondering how his family would react, he added that his brother Petar, recently returned from fourteen years in Canada, 'likes foreigners to talk to because this town bores him'.

Dragan led me up a side street lined with pleasant little two-storey detached houses, doubtless built with *Gastarbeiter* assistance. Flower-filled front gardens indicated that despite Yugoslavia's economic collapse and Montenegro's uncertain future some citizens of Danilovgrad were keeping their upper lips stiff.

Petar greeted me with bemused delight. A small, lean, brown-haired man, he was not exactly handsome but had an interesting face: a high forehead, wide-set dark eyes, a prominent too-fleshy nose, a generous mouth, a square chin and mug-handle ears. His wife, still in Canada with their ten-year-old son, was Irish, from Co Cork, also of the Murphy clan. Petar at first insisted that I must be his guest but was easily persuaded to accept DM100 in advance for four nights' lodging.

The family consisted of Petar, Dragan and their father. Father was tall, stooped and white-haired, a retired postman-cum-police reservist who, explained Petar, had been afflicted by chronic depression since his wife's death in 1996. He spoke no English but with old-fashioned courtesy made me feel very welcome and insisted on providing sustaining breakfasts of bread and cheese. To accommodate me Petar moved into Dragan's room and I slept on the sofa in his bedsitter, its walls lined with Orthodox icons and portraits of semi-mythical Serbian sages and heroes. The upper storey had recently been converted to a flat, occupied by a young couple who ran a taxi service to Podgorica and a flower-stall by the taxi rank; both viewed me with deep suspicion.

Petar had arrived home to find his only sibling a heroin addict. 'Since he was born I've loved him to bits. He was only four when I left in '83 and I'd mothered him always, our mom got sort of invalided after she had him. I was sixteen then and I fed and washed him and changed his diapers and got him to sleep – he was like my own kid along with being the baby brother. Seeing him all destroyed when I got back was a trauma. Seems our pop never noticed, didn't want to know, only thought he was unhealthy. I bust myself trying to save him, got real tough and bullied him and sometimes cried over him. Seems he's clean now but I watch all the time, seeing who's he hanging out with, keeping him away from Podgorica.'

Petar was not at ease in his home town. He declined my invitation to dine that evening in the hotel restaurant and during the next few days I realized that he could relax only in Podgorica among his fellow neo-Chetniks, either in their homes or in one of the alarmingly numerous bars where the city's Chetnik élite (teachers, lawyers, journalists, doctors) were made to feel welcome.

The original Chetniks fought behind Turkish lines between 1904 and 1914. Other armed bands called 'Chetnik' emerged after 1920 – their motivation opaque – and during the Second World War these united to field 13,400 lightly armed warriors. When Yugoslavia collapsed in 1941, Colonel (later General) Dragoljub-Draža Mihailović recruited more Chetniks to his personal resistance movement. Mihailović, a pious Orthodox Christian, devoted to king and country (Serbia), had as a junior officer survived the Serbian army's 1915 retreat across Albania, one of the twentieth century's major endurance tests. His Chetniks developed their own Royalist cult, adopting several ancient Serbian symbols and designing a skull-and-crossbones flag inscribed 'Freedom or Death'. Many of them cultivated long beards and flowing locks in emulation of the eighteenth-century Hajduks, anti-Ottoman brigands of whom Alberto Fortis wrote in 1778: 'The greatest part of the Hajduks look upon it as a meritorious action, to shed the blood of the Turks; a mistaken zeal for religion, joined to their natural and acquired ferocity, easily leads them to commit such acts of violence; and the ignorance and natural prejudices of their priests are too apt to inflame their barbarous fanaticism.'

In July 1941 Tito's Partizans and Mihailović's Chetniks – two improvised armies at opposite ends of the ideological spectrum – united to fight the German invaders. But this alliance proved frail. Mihailović was determined to restore the Serb-dominated Kingdom of Yugoslavia, Tito was determined to establish a secular socialist federal state. As yet most Partizans were Serbs so a Russian-doll situation developed – a Serbian civil war being fought within a World War, while within both Partizans and Chetniks some splinter groups were arguing that it would make much more sense for everyone to fight on Hitler's side.

In 1946 Tito's government executed Mihailović, a formal court having convicted him of collaboration with the Nazis. 'Another show trial!' complained some contemporary Western commentators. But what would The Hague Tribunal have made of General Mihailović? On 1 January 1943 one of his commanders, Pavle Djurišić, reported that in East Bosnia and the Muslim Sandzak the Chetniks had distinguished themselves: 'The operations were executed exactly according to orders . . . All Moslem villages in the three above mentioned districts are entirely burnt. All property has been destroyed except cattle, corn and hay. The collection of fodder and food has been ordered so that we can set up warehouses for reserve food for the units which have remained on the terrain in order to purge it and to search the wooded areas as well as establish and strengthen the organization on the liberated territory . . . Complete annihilation of the Moslem population was undertaken. Victims: about 1,200 fighters and up to 8,000 others, women, old men and children.'

So far so bad – but Balkan cross-currents flow without ceasing, often forming those whirlpools into which so many Western military and political leaders fell with a loud splash during the 1990s. Not all Chetniks were Serbs and not all Ustashas were Croats. In some areas, soon after the German invasion, Muslim Ustashas slaughtered their Serb neighbours. Elsewhere certain Muslim villages became Chetnik to a man and western Bosnia produced a small crop of Croat Chetniks. By 1944 an estimated 8 per cent (4,000 or so) of Mihailović's men were Muslims.

At that date some 20,000 Chetniks were being cared for by the British in a prison camp in southern Italy where they wore British uniforms and were trusted to guard rations and munitions. Subsequently 12,000 of those emigrated to Canada, the US and Australia; the rest settled in Britain.

After 8 May 1945 thousands more Chetniks came down from the hills and tried to surrender to the Allies. The Ustasha captured and murdered any found crossing Croat-held territory and most of those who made it to Austria were no luckier. Together with thousands of other 'Yugoslav refugees' they were sent back to Yugoslavia by the British army, to be slaughtered on arrival by Tito's Partizans – not as enemy troops (the civil war, too, was over) but as political opponents. Nigel Nicolson, who participated in this operation as an Intelligence Officer with 5 Corps of the Eighth Army, later gave evidence:

We were ordered to tell these wretched men that they were going to Italy and that they would remain in British hands. And this was something that even at the time shocked us deeply. We had to put up a sort of façade. They were collected at this railway station. It took several days actually. These long, long trains with box cars and we used to put 30 men into the box cars. They were allowed to take their wives and children with them too. They were all shoved in, in rather a merry mood. They thought they were going to sunny Italy where they would be looked after and fed. We hid the Tito troops behind the station buildings. They only appeared at the very last moment and marched up and down and all the Chetniks started shouting and screaming and swearing at us. We hated it. It was so much against the tradition, particularly of the Brigade of Guards, to lie even to your enemies. They weren't really enemies. They were simple peasants. One mustn't think of these Slovenes and Chetniks as one would think of the German army. They were very young, some of them just boys with older men with their wives and some of them with their children. You were dealing not really with an army, you were dealing with thousands and thousands of civilians. I wrote a daily situation report. At the end of one of them I said that 'our soldiers carried out this odious task with great reluctance', which was perfectly true. But I got hauled over the coals for that. I shouldn't have said it. But I think this was one of the most disgraceful actions that British troops have ever been asked to carry out.

(From a BBC *Timewatch* programme, 3 January 1984)

This dispatching of more than 26,000 men, women and children to certain death began on 20 May 1945 and has been uneasily defended, by some, on the grounds that chaos then prevailed throughout Europe and people scarcely knew what they were doing – which is not at all the impression given by Nigel Nicolson's evidence. Certainly Field Marshall Alexander, Allied Supreme Commander in the Mediterranean, and his political adviser Harold MacMillan knew exactly what they were doing when they authorized the delivery of those anti-Tito prisoners to the Partizans. In exchange, Marshall Tito pulled his five divisions (lavishly equipped by the Allies) out of the provinces of Carinthia in Austria and Venizia-Giulia in Italy, which he was then absurdly claiming as part of Yugoslavia. Seemingly Alexander thought it prudent to forfeit 26,000 peasants by way of avoiding a Balkan postscript to the Second World War.

At breakfast time on my first morning in Danilovgrad I assumed Petar was teasing me when he observed cheerfully, 'The buds are unfolding, it's time for Balkan blood to flow.'

An hour later we heard that four local men had been killed during the night in fights with Milošević's paramilitary police. 'Told you so!' exclaimed Petar gleefully. 'The vines are budding, the blood is shed! We've been waiting long enough, it's time for action and this is the signal!'

Early every morning Petar and I took a minibus taxi to Podgorica, returning after dark. Given the peculiar nature of my Podgorica circle, I resigned myself to not contacting Milana's civilized friends and relatives. In Montenegro's tiny capital one is constantly aware of being watched, and in April 2000 it was a fearful city where many individuals and groups seemed poised to react to violence. On paper that statement looks fuzzy and unconvincing – was I being alarmist, or panicky, or fantasizing? I think not: in my antennae I trust. And being driven around by Petar's friends recalled those far-off days when occasionally it was impossible for me to avoid being driven around Belfast by paramilitary leaders who had already been assassins' targets.

In 1941 Podgorica was a small town of no importance, though useful to the Axis occupiers as an airbase. Allied bombers demolished it almost completely and it was reincarnated as 'Titograd', becoming the Montenegrins' symbol of all that is modern and progressive in their country. Less ugly than the average reincarnation within Communism's architectural sphere of influence, it has wide tree-lined boulevards but is devoid of 'tourist attractions', either natural or man-made. Parking is difficult; the pavements of this impoverished city are often obstructed by an improbable plethora of long, sleek, shiny new cars. Many have no registration plates, all are untaxed and uninsured. According to an OSCE official I met later in Pristina, approximately 80 per cent of cars in Montenegro, Kosovo and

Albania have been stolen in Western Europe and are driven by untested and unlicensed men (never women). Having bought your cut-price Mercedes off you go and if you happen to kill a cyclist or pedestrian so what? This is equivalent to killing a dog or cat and in most cases there is no penalty, beyond what the individual driver's conscience might impose. In recent years, it is alleged, certain car manufacturers have been colluding in this trade to help solve over-production problems. And indeed it is hard to see how the trade could thrive so outrageously without some 'insider' collusion.

Podgorica is not all drab angular blocks; near the centre are busy little streets of attractive one- and two-storey houses, some with dormer windows in their red-tiled roofs. The façades are brightly painted, the ground floors occupied by family shops, shoe-makers, barbers, legal and newspaper offices – and Chetnik-friendly bars frequented by bearded intellectuals. One newspaper editor, who liked my attitude to Nato, was determined to interview me on the subject. Foolishly I agreed; one tends not to disagree with determined Chetniks. Two months later, in Dubrovnik, I heard that the Chetnik website was presenting me to the world as a famous Irish cyclist and fervent supporter of Greater Serbia – not the image one would choose to project while pedalling across Croatia.

The psychological dynamics of those four days were intricate. Why was I accepted into this closed male world of manic Chetniks? Obviously I had got off to a good start as an Irishwoman and putative IRA supporter, despite my saying nothing to reinforce that misconception. More importantly, I was seen as a vehicle for conveying the Chetnik viewpoint to the outside world. I never conceal my vocation; to do so, while encouraging people to talk openly, would be sneaky. And those Chetniks, convinced of the rightness of their 'cause', rejoiced to find someone able to advance it if they could put it across convincingly. Also – the ultimate irony – our anti-Nato fellow-feeling was genuine, as was our shared fear of America's ambition to control the world for its own benefit.

By the end of Day Two I longed to escape from the Chetnik ambience. Then I told myself that it would be cowardly to reject this opportunity not only to observe but to feel in my very guts the source of the poison that had killed Yugoslavia. However, those days were uniquely stressful: and I do mean 'uniquely'. My companions were driven, obsessed, consumed and degraded by a white-hot hatred of Albanians, Bosnians, Croatians, Bulgarians, Greeks, Turks, Russians, Communism, the Catholic Church, the Protestant Churches, the UK, the US, the EU, the UN, Nato, their own President Djukanović and of course Slobodan Milošević – seen as a traitor who negotiated with the US at Dayton and surrendered Kosovo to end the airwar. One was aware of hatred as the cement that held their deranged personalities together, the fuel that gave them emotional energy. In their presence one felt the need for some sort of psychic protective clothing against the radiation from this hatred. Having written books about Northern Ireland's conflict, South Africa's agonies and Rwanda's genocide, I am no stranger to hatred. Yet nowhere have I been exposed to it in such a concentrated and irrational form as during those four days. Chetnik irrationality is truly terrifying. In Northern Ireland, South Africa or Rwanda one can discern reasons for what happened, not excuses or justifications but *causes*, circumstances that pushed people over the edge. Among the present-day Chetniks no such circumstances exist. Their wide-ranging hatred is free-standing, unrelated to reality, not provoked by any injustice or oppression, feeding only on a grotesque perception of Serbs as victims.

One of Petar's close friends, pony-tailed and heavily bearded Miga, insisted on my seeing a nearby Kosovo Refugee settlement, proof of the misery inflicted on Serbs by Albanians, Nato, the UN Mission in Kosovo *et al.* Miga drove us across the city at sickening speed in a scratched and dented 1982 Yugo with three bullet-holes in the driver's door. Like Petar, he lived close to the poverty line. However, his only child, a fine-featured but cold-eyed law student daughter with an impressive academic record, would provide for papa in his old age.

We arrived at the settlement just as word was getting around that 'gift clothes' were soon to be distributed. For some reason this alarmed Miga. He scowled and chewed his moustache, lit one cigarette off another, refused to leave the car, told me to take no photographs. Petar, however, urged me to take many: 'You must show the world what Nato has done to Serbs!' When I remarked that these refugees were Gypsies, not Serbs, he at first looked taken aback, then annoyed. 'It's the same!' he snapped. 'They've lived in Kosovo for years and centuries, taken Serb names and religion, helped to protect us from the Albanians – they're good people!'

Leaving the car, Petar and I walked twenty yards to where hundreds were assembling around a detached suburban villa, rented by an NGO. 'The clothes are inside,' said Petar. 'Some UN person will hand them out.' This was a shouting, angry, jostling crowd. Seeing me, a group broke away and surrounded us, young men and women waving ID documents which recorded how much aid each had received, and when. One man grabbed my shoulder, shook me roughly and told Petar to translate: since July 1999 he had been given no suitable clothes for his twelve children. A woman deliberately spat on my trouser leg and screamed that her asthmatic six-year-old daughter had been without treatment since August 1999 because Montenegrin Albanians had stolen all the donated medicines. Now Petar lost his nerve. 'They think you're UN!' he muttered. Seizing my hand he led me to the car at a trot while yelling over his shoulder, 'She's a tourist!'

Miga accelerated past the crowd and sped up the road to the settlement where more than 2,500 refugees lived in varying degrees of misery. The most salubrious quarter consisted of two rows of solid wooden tin-roofed huts (twelve in all), each about fifty yards long and fifteen feet wide, divided into rooms accommodating not less than twelve and not more than twenty-five (UNHCR regulations). Petar was eager to give me a conducted tour of the interiors but Miga vetoed that. Beyond the huts, on the same expanse of stony dusty wasteland, squatted a late-comers' shanty-village. Here were huddled those pathetic yet ingenious shelters seen the world over, constructed of scrap iron, rotten planks, plastic sheeting, cardboard boxes, old carpets and (an innovative touch) deceased motor vehicles. Worn-out tractor tyres kept the roofs in place, more or less, during winter gales. This smelly eyesore had mushroomed only yards from a large new housing estate, its red-tiled detached dwellings painted gleaming white, its windows neatly curtained and flower-filled. 'Here's a lot of friction,' observed Petar gloomily. I could believe him. When I noted a shortage of children he explained, 'Most are in an NGO-run school – or sort of school. There's not qualified teachers but it keeps them off the road for a few hours a day.'

We were about to depart when the angry father of twelve (aged thirty-five) came hastening towards us carrying a yellow plastic sack. As he flung it to the ground at my feet a dozen shanty-dwellers ran towards us and Miga urgently beckoned me to leave the scene. But Petar said, 'No! Listen to this man, I know him, he's Ivan from Suva Reka.'

Ivan then emptied his sack; its contents had probably been donated in Winchester or Cheltenham. He pointed to my camera and Petar said, 'Take a picture.' Obediently I photographed the little pile: four tweed hats, a pretty lace-edged white nightgown, a green velvet smoking-jacket, a Paisley scarf, a bra (M&S) and an outsize thick woollen cardigan. Petar translated: 'He asks what good are these for his twelve children? His wife says she wishes they'd stayed in Kosovo instead of being humiliated here like this.'

I made sympathetic noises while having ambivalent feelings; all those adult refugees were much better dressed than the average citizen of Nikšić or Danilovgrad. As Ivan stuffed his inappropriate gifts back into their sack we retreated to the car.

Petar, too, was angry and began to argue with Miga as we approached the NGO villa. In its front garden groups were comparing the contents of their gift sacks. Only then did it occur to me that those Gypsies were Displaced Persons from Kosovo (still part of the Federal Republic of Yugoslavia) and not refugees from a foreign country.

Petar turned to me and said, 'I want another shot, you can get it from the car.' Still scowling, Miga stopped opposite the villa and Petar indicated a large white van parked nearby. 'Get that quickly!' he ordered. As my camera shutter clicked Miga drove on – fast. Petar relaxed and smiled and asked, 'Did you see those two men beside the van? They're Albanians from Ulcinj.' (A town near the Albanian border.) 'They steal refugees' medicines and clothes and food and bedding and sell everything in their Sunday market. They've it all stitched up, the UN employs some of them.' Suddenly Petar took the camera off my lap, removed the film and put it in his jacket pocket.

I felt a frisson of fear. To what use would the van photograph be put? Trying to sound casual I said, 'Please, let me have that film. I prefer to develop them all in Ireland, the processing is better.'

Petar laughed. 'Nowadays it's the same everywhere but don't worry, you can have the negatives.' Earlier that day he had hurriedly borrowed the camera, apparently to photograph particular cars parked near the main Chetnik bar – a harmless foible, I thought at the time. Now I was not so sure.

Miga lived in a rambling dilapidated house in a district where high mud and stone walls enclosed every compound. A slavering red-eyed Rottweiler had to be chained to a verandah pillar before any visitor could be admitted through the eight-foot-high metal gate.

Petar's Uncle Miloš was waiting for us, a well-preserved octogenarian, florid and clean-shaven, wearing a black beret and sipping a heavy red wine from his son's vineyard. This veteran of Mihailović's campaign had been among those who fled to Austria in May 1945, surrendered to the British, then were deviously delivered to the Partizans. When the engine of his prison-train caught fire windows were broken and he escaped and hid in the mountains where he had fought as a Chetnik. 'He still hates the British,' remarked Petar. 'If he could get a nuclear bomb he'd use it on them. It upsets him that Queen Victoria was related to our royalty.'

Miga's living room had an unsettling atmosphere, like the chapel of some arcane and unwholesome cult. Just below the ceiling ran a wall-length frieze of Serbian kings from the tenth century to the present day – many of them imaginary. Among the insignia were the Order of the White Eagle (Serbia's coat of arms) and the Order of St Sava, Serbia's patron saint. Interspersed among numerous icons and photographs of monasteries and Patriarchs and religious ceremonies were other photographs of masked men drilling, and Arkan taking a salute, and Vukovar reduced to rubble with a Serb soldier grinning beside a destroyed bridge waving the Chetniks' very own flag. On a low table between two sofas stood a wooden crucifix, amidst bottles and glasses and cigarette packets, and beside it was the Chetniks' sinister pennant, hanging on a metal stand – a cross with four reversed 'Cs' between its arms.

Soon three other men had joined us, all in their forties, all eager to 'educate' me. During such sessions it was hard to disentangle truth from propaganda, propaganda from myth, myth from distortion. Much nonsense was talked, especially about the Serbian dynasty and the sacred significance of Kosovo to all Serbs and the fact that Serbs had never *ever* in all their history used violence except in self-defence. However, on one issue Uncle Miloš was simply being factual. During the Second World War, when the Italians' Albanian puppet, Verlaci, annexed Kosovo, the delighted Kosovo Albanians immediately turned on those Serbs who, during a bout of royalist social engineering, had been planted there between the wars. Many Serbs were murdered, many others fled. 'So now,' said Uncle Miloš, 'you know why the Albanians can claim to be in such a huge majority in Kosovo.

They did their own ethnic cleansing in the Forties.' This of course is not the whole story, of which more when I get to Kosovo. But as far as it went Uncle's accusation contained no distortion.

Amidst the pictorial displays on the living-room walls were postcards of Ostrog Monastery. I exclaimed at its dramatic setting and regretted not having visited it, whereupon Petar announced that next day we would 'do a pilgrimage'. His young friends Josif and Ljubomir, 'refugees from Kosovo', would be happy to accompany us there in Josif's new Mercedes.

Many Kosovo Serbs were living in Podgorica and the educated younger generation, equipped with entrepreneurial flair and mobile phones, seemed to be prospering in the crevices of Montenegro's shadowy business world. Josif and Ljubomir were among this minority and later that day Petar introduced me to them. Both were tall, fair, handsome – pleasant young men, well-dressed and well-groomed and, I intuited, not too comfortable among the Chetnik intellectuals. When we dined in the Crna Gora Hotel (reputedly a Chetnik-free zone) they relaxed visibly and talked volubly.

In Peć, their home town, Josif and Ljubomir had built up good businesses: Josif a restaurant and disco, Ljubomir a hardware and electrical shop. During the airwar they and their parents took refuge with friends in Skopje, returning to Peć on 12 June to find much of the town in ruins but their properties undamaged. Soon the Kosovar refugees also returned and, said Josif, 'Many stole our homes and businesses. Some were not real refugees but pretending, to get all the handouts.'

Ljubomir's father's café was seized on 18 June by an Albanian Albanian, a notorious heroin dealer who for years had been living in Belgium. His brother, from Tirana, took over Ljubomir's shop. When the café owner, after moving to Podgorica, contacted the returnee from Belgium and suggested the payment of some rent he was told, 'No rent, no deal of any sort and if you try to come back you're dead.'

Josif's restaurant was attacked on 20 June by four masked and armed men. In response to his sos, K-For and the KLA arrived together, the latter still armed though according to the 9 June Military Technical Agreement they should by then have been disarmed.

'But,' I interjected, 'that disarming schedule was ludicrously unrealistic.'

'So why did Nato promise to do what they couldn't do?' demanded Josif. The masked gang were allowed to get away, he claimed, because K-For feared a shoot-out. They had in fact done little damage; their purpose was intimidation, to be followed by a takeover of the premises. 'Now they make much money from it,' said Josif. 'They use a man who learned about cooking in Switzerland and have many expat customers.'

Within days of the 9 June Agreement being signed fifty-eight Serbs were murdered in Peć and fifty had disappeared. Then 300 hid in the Orthodox

Patriarchate, hoping to be able to emerge in safety when K-For had got a grip on the situation. After a month they became disillusioned and moved to Montenegro, leaving all their possessions behind. By mid-July tens of thousands of Serbs had fled from Kosovo.

Ljubomir said, 'Nato promised 50,000 K-For peace-keeping troops but what use are they to us? Why do the UN and Nato keep saying they want everyone to live happily together when they can't protect one community? They don't want to protect us. When one KLA leader was arrested by the UN police they found half a million dollars in cash in his apartment, and hand grenades and guns, but they released him after a few hours. The KLA is Nato's friend. Before the bombing, 2,500 police kept peace in Kosovo.'

I refrained from commenting on that last point; no Kosovar would describe as 'peace' what Milošević's police imposed on the province.

On 26 July 1999, three days after the murder of fourteen Serb farmers, Josif and Ljubomir and their families migrated to Podgorica, taking the contents of their homes with them in a hired truck.

Thus far the young men had been talking calmly, giving exact dates and precise figures, but as they recalled the move from Peć that artificial calm could no longer be sustained. Suddenly their feelings surfaced and my heart ached for them. Too easily the world's privileged minority overlooks the long-term effects of violent conflict and social dissolution. Josif and Ljubomir were comparatively lucky: uninjured, intelligent, educated, able to pick up the material pieces and start again. Yet both had lost relatives and friends in horrific ways, known extreme fear, seen dreadful sights, been uprooted from the territory where their families had lived for generations.

One night Josif had helped to give nine decomposing murder victims a decent burial; four of those had been his friends. Ljubomir had helped neighbours to search for missing children and seen three little bodies with their throats slashed. As our companions talked on Petar fidgeted impatiently, glancing at his watch – though I was being provided with such excellent anti-Kosovar ammunition. Sometimes the young men were incoherent, on the verge of tears. I didn't want to hear the sort of details they were remembering but for their sakes I was thankful so much was pouring out.

Finally Petar said, 'It's late, we must go, the last taxi leaves at nine.'

As we stood up Josif impulsively clasped both my hands and exclaimed, 'Sorry! Sorry! We have put too many bad things in your mind!'

'Don't be sorry,' I said, 'I'm glad you could tell me.'

The convergence in my life of the Chetniks and Ostrog Monastery was both unsurprising and confusing. Unsurprising because Chetniks tend to be devout

Orthodox Christians, odd as that may seem to outside observers, and confusing for reasons soon to be explained.

(Come to think of it, Chetnik religious fervour is no odder than the fervour of some Northern Irish paramilitaries, Orange and Green, who find nothing incongruous about their faith reinforcing their political ideology and vice versa.)

Viewing the monastery from the Zeta valley, one can see why Rebecca West dismissed Ostrog (she didn't visit it) as 'a bleak pigeon-hole in a Montenegrin cliff'. As we sped along the main road, Petar reminded me that in April 1941, when the Germans began their bombing of Belgrade, the Yugoslav government packed the very young King Peter off to Ostrog, partly because of its inaccessibility but mainly because of its closeness to Nikšić's airfield. Soon defeat loomed and the royal party was advised to wait at the airfield for a British plane to fly them to Janina in British-held Greece. The plane failed to appear and no other Yugoslav airfield could be contacted by radio – so one of the Italian Marchettis based at Nikšić was appropriated, and by chance this bold gamble came off. From Janina King Peter travelled to London, via Jerusalem and Lisbon. 'And Serbia will never have peace,' concluded Petar, 'until we get back our king!'

When Josif turned off the *autoput* and our extraordinary ascent began everyone fell silent. I wished I were walking – preferably not pushing a laden bicycle – as Josif negotiated innumerable tight hairpin bends more suited to pack-animals than to motor cars. The very narrow road was in urgent need of repairs, especially along the verges, and though Josif was driving carefully, and knew the road well, I only enjoy sheer drops of a thousand feet when afoot or awheel (two wheels). Much of this mountainside is handsomely wooded – old mixed woods – with occasional sloping grassy patches offering grazing to a few sheep or goats. What, I asked myself, happens when two vehicles meet on one of the really dodgy stretches? Mercifully experience did not provide an answer; no one else visited Ostrog that day.

Some argue that this monastery affects people so strangely because of its altitude – more than 6,000 feet above the valley – and its melodramatic site on a narrow ledge with bare rock precipices rising above it for hundreds of feet to the mountain top. Much of the monastery was not built but carved out of the rockface. Ostensibly it is a revered place of pilgrimage because here lies the body of St Basil, a seventeenth-century Montenegrin whose career is obscure but who is reputed to work miracles on a regular basis. Personally I believe that the magic of such places goes way, way back, having nothing to do with any of the organized religions, linking us to something eternally elusive but precious and important. My reaction to Ostrog reminded me of unexpectedly coming upon a minuscule temple in Nepal, guarded by three ancient sacred trees – not any famous place of pilgrimage, just of local significance, but quite overwhelming.

Unlike most 'Holy Places', Ostrog is only marginally commercialized. Where the road briefly runs level – far below the monastery though very far above the valley – an inoffensive wooden café stands opposite a few stalls selling minute wooden crosses, religious postcards and the sort of piously tawdry souvenirs universally engendered by pilgrimage sites. The monastery itself is notably unmaterialistic; visitors may leave a donation if they choose but nobody is watching. In a rock cavern near the entrance one pays a nominal sum for candles, to be lit and stuck in trays of sand – separate trays for the dead and the living – while naming aloud the person for whom a blessing is sought.

From the cavern we ascended flights of steps, passed under stone archways, entered the monastery proper – its façade white-washed – then climbed a stairway and followed a low corridor to the saint's cave-cell. On the way we saw no one and there was no sound but our own footsteps.

A monk sat beside St Basil, as motionless and silent as the mummified body. My companions took it in turns to kneel beside the open sarcophagus, repeatedly crossing themselves before kissing the saint's velvet robe. When Petar asked in a whisper if I would like a blessing I said 'Yes' (I could hardly say 'No') and the monk murmured something that to me felt irrelevant. Nor do I think the mortal remains of St Basil (meaning no disrespect) had anything to do with my dazed state as I left that cell – dazed but exhilarated and, most curiously, affected physically as well as emotionally. It was as though my body had been joyously shocked, the way it is during the best sort of love-making when body and soul are ecstatic together. If that sounds blasphemous and/or Freudian, too bad – I'm now striving to describe the indescribable. And perhaps what I'm saying is that Ostrog, for whatever unknowable reason, induces a mystical experience.

Then came the confusion, the surreal conflict of psychic currents when Petar met a mentor, a senior monk, in the semi-cave complex where the dark rough stone of the mountain enclosed us. With a blend of spontaneous affection and ritualistic reverence he embraced this tall, imposing, long-bearded figure, then introduced us. As the smiling, welcoming monk gripped my hand and stared into my eyes I recognized a dedicated Chetnik supporter. He and Petar talked for the next half-hour while Josif, Ljubomir and I ascended to the bell-tower and stood leaning on the railing, wordlessly overlooking one of Europe's most magnificent mountainscapes. I felt grateful to the young men for their understanding silence.

As we all descended to the car Petar told me excitedly, 'That great man married us and christened our son – here at Ostrog! My wife's like you – no religion – but she was stunned too in this place, the way I can see you are. She didn't know what to say, she didn't understand her own reaction. Fr X's prayers saved me in Canada when I was having problems. I kept Ostrog and that holy man always in my mind and that kind of sedated me. I didn't expect to see him today, I'd heard he was in his home town. He comes from Ulcinj where most people are Albanian but he knows how to deal with them. They run away when they see him coming!'

12

Slowly into Albania

Next morning I left Danilovgrad by pre-dawnlight, covered the fifteen unexciting miles to Podgorica in an hour, briefly got lost in mouldering industrial suburbs, then sped over ten even less exciting miles to Tuzi, where a narrow road branches off towards Albania. Tuzi's population is almost entirely Albanian; it is a small town but growing fast, the locals' prosperity fertilized by UN sanctions.

Just beyond Tuzi I paused to breakfast: cheese, bread, smoked ham, all wrapped up by Petar's father and secured to Ruairi's carrier the evening before. Looking up at the mighty mountains ahead, I suddenly felt exhausted. Instead of crossing them, I would have liked to lie down and sleep for twenty-four hours. While enduring the Chetniks' distilled and matured fanaticism I had been continuously tense, keeping myself going on surges of self-defensive adrenalin. No wonder I felt limp, drained and, unusually for me, not enthused by high mountains ahead. However, the mountains were there and wouldn't go away. I ate a lot and felt a bit better. And thirty minutes later I felt very much better; those mountains were exalting enough to counter every sort of weariness.

During the climb I passed no dwellings and met only two antique Yugos, being driven slowly by peasants who stared half-fearfully at the apparition with a bicycle. My map failed to show two unsignposted junctions where nothing indicates which way to Shkodra, but I chanced to guess right. Then I was again altitude-troubled. In the world's serious mountain ranges one goes up and stays up and gradually one's blood cells adjust; in the Balkans it's all up and down day after day. Resting amidst jagged crags and tender new grass I consulted James Pettifer's *Blue Guide to Albania* and read:

Visiting Montenegro from Albania is not particularly recommended at the time of writing [1996] . . . The Foreign Office strongly discourages crossing this border. Travel insurance may become invalid . . . The Lake Shkodra region has never really recovered from the savage fighting in the vicinity during the Balkan Wars (1912–13), subsequent depopulation and what many Albanian nationalists have seen as the mistaken delineation of the border with Montenegro.

That reference to the Balkan Wars sent a shiver through me. All those miles of deserted Bosnian countryside I had crossed *en route* from Zagreb – at the end of this century, will guidebook writers be referring to Milošević's Balkan Wars to explain their depopulation?

While crossing an uneven plateau the cool breeze dried my sweat until I could see salt gleaming on my arms. Grassy summits, dotted with weather-sculpted silver boulders, rose nearby on my right only a hundred feet above the road. On my left were lush but empty pastures, and patches of woodland, sloping down to a hidden valley. Then the descent began, between high, dense hedges all mistily green as their buds unfurled. A sharp turn revealed an inlet of Lake Shkodra, a sparkling expanse of blue far below – soon lost sight of as the road plunged downwards, its surface abruptly deteriorating.

That descent ended at a T-junction where two old women, wearing ankle-length black dresses and Manchester United shirts, were following a firewood-laden donkey. Around the next bend a solitary Montenegrin policeman, young and friendly with plump pink cheeks, manned a poplar-trunk frontier pole. He indicated that I should push Ruairi around it and didn't bother to open my passport.

By now the cool breeze had become a strong wind and over the next few lakeside miles I could hear wavelets slapping the rocky shoreline, below thick shrubbery – a popular car cemetery, though faded wayside notices proclaim 'THIS IS A NATIONAL PARK'.

Only a few ragged men and boys, loitering near the barrier pole, observed my arrival at Hani i Hoti; apart from the local peasants, most traffic avoids this official crossing point during daylight hours. Then I realized that one of the men was a police officer, his pot-belly extruding from a scruffy uniform, his unshaven face badly scarred. Shouldering his rifle, he approached and unsmilingly signed me to take my passport into a large derelict building. Most of the roof had fallen in, all the windows were broken, the floor was strewn with shattered glass and roof tiles, the concrete staircase had collapsed and sturdy weeds sprouted from cracked walls. In a corner, under what remained of the roof, I found four policemen, their rifles neatly stacked, their office equipment consisting of one small table, one stool and three upturned beer crates. An English-speaker politely addressed me as 'Sir'; evidently a solo female cyclist was beyond his ken. The Albanian embassy in London had got it wrong, he informed me. Irish citizens do need a visa, fee DM25 – a modest demand in the circumstances.

Back on the road, a Shkodra taxi-driver had arrived. When he tried to grab Ruairi a customs officer intervened on my behalf, then declined an invitation to examine the pannier-bags. His office was another derelict building.

Beyond the border, disappointment awaits those seeking to escape into a land where peasants live much as they did a thousand years ago. Clusters of UN sanctions-related petrol and diesel pumps appear every few hundred yards and soon I was passing an enormous new restaurant, long and low, securely fenced with an electronically operated metal gateway; a score of motor cars and 4 x 4s were parked in the forecourt.

The first *bunkere* caught my eye only yards from Hani i Hoti. In their excellent account of post-Hoxha Albania, Miranda Vickers and James Pettifer explain this phenomenon:

> The Communist leadership was worried, after the Soviet invasion of Czechoslovakia in 1968, that the same fate might befall Albania, and its response was to begin the bizarre and costly construction of over 400,000 pillboxes, the now notorious *bunkere*, throughout the country, a ludicrous expression of faith in the people's ability to resist the Soviets . . . These concrete bunkers were complemented by an equally bizarre 'do-it-yourself' air defence system against airborne invasion: units of Young Pioneers were taught how to fix long pointed spikes at the tops of trees to impale foreign parachutists as they descended onto the soil of Albania.

These 'precautions', though a lamentable waste of money, were the least harmful manifestation of the crazed Hoxha mindset. Now the *bunkere* seem rather comical, like bloated toadstools, and those not overgrown serve many useful purposes – as hen houses, public lavatories, bus shelters, garbage incinerators, dog kennels, hot-houses, manure stores and children's Wendy-houses.

At Tuzi I had glimpsed a railway, here it was again accompanying the road, a sad symbol of Balkan regression. Built to link Shkodra with Belgrade, it was opened in 1988 (a mile from the border a dour concrete monument celebrates this event) but closed within three years, a casualty of war and sanctions. On this main road the potholes were deep and wide but broken tar doesn't much bother cyclists. However, the relentless headwind did bother me as it blew unimpeded over a limestone plain, reducing Ruairi to walking speed.

Near the little market town of Koplik (originally Cinna, founded by the Romans) a colossal new mosque shocked me. This gift from Saudi Arabia looks offensively incongruous beside Koplik's destitution: here was a degree of poverty exceptional in the Balkans. To replace some of the hundreds of mosques and churches destroyed by the pathologically atheistical Hoxha is, I suppose, a good idea – but Koplik needed only a small simple mosque. Nine-tenths of those oil dollars would have been better spent on the town itself.

From the marketplace two boy cyclists followed me for a mile or so, then drew level – one on each side – and talked across me, eyeing the pannier-bags, before insolently demanding money. Their bicycles were old and inferior – Ruairi was new and superior – I was in top condition and we shared the headwind handicap. Soon they had been left behind. But they seemed a bad omen; elsewhere in the Balkans this sort of harassment is unknown. In the Bradt guide to Yugoslavia (1989), Piers Letcher notes: 'Yugoslavs are among the most honest people I've met

. . . The crime rate within Yugoslavia is unusually low and the normal minimum precautions are more than adequate.' Even now, after a decade of impoverishing conflict and social chaos, one feels safe throughout what was Yugoslavia. When you delete war-associated crimes, the region remains exceptionally law-abiding.

Beyond Koplik several hamlets were visible on distant mountain slopes to the east. Here the motor traffic became mysteriously hectic and extra-dangerous because mingled with so many galloping horse-carts. Where were all these vans and cars and trucks coming from or going to? I could only conclude that Koplik is a smugglers' depot; from there a number of cross-border pack-animal tracks are accessible. And perhaps smugglers lived in the fine modern houses scattered over the plain. Above ground, nothing remains to indicate that this area has been populated, cultivated and defended for at least four millennia.

Six miles short of Shkodra a new two-storey motel appeared, standing alone at a junction with a dirt track leading to Lake Shkodra. Exhausted by the head-wind, I decided to book in there and spend the afternoon bird-watching along the shore. The small bar-restaurant was empty, there seemed to be no reception desk and the man who emerged from a back room stared at me uneasily. Aged fortyish, slim and below average height, he had curly black hair and narrow green eyes; his waiter's attire, complete with bow-tie, was somewhat marred by pink-and-white trainers. Despite the language barrier I soon got the message: he was trying to persuade me to continue to Shkodra. It was impossible to explain in sign language that, since I wanted to explore the lake shore, it made more sense to stay here rather than return next day from the city. Anyway, why was the manager of a new motel trying to get rid of a DM-bearing foreign guest? (It was obtuse of me not to question the purpose of a new motel where tourists fear to tread.) When I persisted, Bow-tie at last agreed to provide a room and demanded DM15 on the spot – which low tariff puzzled me. Ruairi was then locked in a store-room beside a washing-machine not yet unpacked from its crate and I took off for the lake. Seeing me go, Bow-tie became inexplicably agitated, shouted after me and beckoned me back. I waved at him cheerfully and went on my way.

For a mile or so the track took me past several new farmhouses and a few old dwellings. In a neglected collective farmyard two small vintage tractors had been abandoned to the embraces of morning glory. Women and an occasional man were being assisted by small children and grandchildren while planting maize in red-brown soil with Illyrian-age implements. The adult toilers were silent and glum-looking; the children seemed to be enjoying themselves. My passing was ignored.

Where the track ended an expanse of marshland barred me from the shore. Here was no sign of human activity. By now the wind had dropped and beyond the lake's still sheen rose the mighty mountains of Montenegro, Mount Rurrulija their king.

Lake Shkodra, shared by Montenegro and Albania, is the Balkans' largest lake: twenty-five miles long, ten miles wide, on average thirty feet deep. It sustains a remarkable variety of fish; the commonest, a sardine of sorts, is netted for sale in local markets as it has been for 2,000 years or more. However, sanctions had recently provided the fishermen with much more lucrative (if more risky) employment. For this reason I had reluctantly left my camera and binoculars in the motel. But the birdlife is so abundant and, oddly, unafraid that when I sat as close as possible to the water's edge I didn't need binoculars to observe cranes, waders, herons and duck. No less numerous and various are the aquatic plants, though I could identify only yellow and white water-lilies, just beginning to bloom.

At sunset I returned to the motel where Bow-tie, looking baffled and angry, stood awaiting me in the doorway with Ruairi beside him. There had been a misunderstanding: I had rented a room for three hours, so why hadn't I used it? We confronted each other like beings from different planets. The language barrier was not the real issue; even had I been able to explain myself Bow-tie would not have understood my way of being, any more than I could understand his allergy to a guest. He was obviously unnerved by my presence – a foreigner who insisted on staying overnight when Shkodra's hotel was so close. But by then the sun had set and Shkodra was no longer within reasonable reach of a cyclist. Bow-tie gave in, asked for another DM25 and grumpily agreed to provide supper for DM10.

The bar-restaurant remained empty, its ten four-person tables bare but for plastic condiment sets. I was starting my second beer when the motel owner arrived and glared at me while Bow-tie defensively explained my presence. Mr Keci was a tall, bulky, fair-haired sixtyish man who later tried to invade my bed – yet another of that evening's grotesque features. Having closely considered my passport he handed it back with an unexpected smile and said something reassuring to Bow-tie.

The motel's strong double door was now – at 7 p.m. – locked, bolted and barred by Mr Keci. Watching him, I reminded myself that this was rural Albania where after dark men don't casually drop in to the bar at the crossroads. Meanwhile Bow-tie was preparing my supper: one slice of teeth-defying goat's meat, one tomato, three slices of cucumber and a hunk of stale white bread. That was a memorably uncomfortable meal as the two men silently sat opposite me at a small table, watching every move of my knife, fork and strenuously chewing jaws. Then, to my utter bewilderment, Bow-tie wheeled Ruairi to the foot of the stairs and carried him up to my room – spacious and comfortable and TV-equipped though not 'en suite'. Mr Keci told me, in Italian, that the bathroom and lavatory could not be used during the night. A basin was provided as a chamber-pot – curiouser and curiouser . . . When I reached for the key Mr Keci shook his head: I was to be locked in, it seemed, until morning.

By 8.30, having dealt with Mr Keci's tentative invasion, I was asleep. Four hours later loud noises woke me – shouting, vehicle doors slamming, air-brakes squeal-ing, many footsteps thudding up and down the stairs and hurrying along the cor-ridor. Until 4.40 the motel and its environs seethed with activity: trucks stopping and starting, hoofs clattering, ponies neighing, much arguing and laughing, glasses clinking in the bar below, uninhibited love-making in adjacent bedrooms. Then suddenly everyone departed and only crowing cocks broke the silence.

Punctually at 7 a.m., as arranged, Bow-tie appeared to release me. No break-fast was on offer and I set off through the warm windless air with a rumbling tummy.

I wondered then how many Shkodra folk speak Italian, for obvious reasons Albania's first foreign language. Talented linguists admit to finding Albanian difficult and I found it impossible. My vocabulary remained restricted to 'po' and 'jo' (yes and no). Even the Albanian 'Hello' – *tungjatjeta* – sounded to me more like a South-east Asian airline than a greeting.

When Ruairi's rear tyre went completely flat, without warning, my misfortune was noticed by a kind young man on a loudly rattling bicycle held together by imaginative innovations. He dismounted, examined the tyre, then beckoned me to follow him along an appalling track, partially flooded and strewn with large loose sharp stones. At a village half a mile off the road, a small notice saying 'BICICLI' was nailed to a high wooden gateway. There the young man beamed at me before quickly pedalling away, giving me no time to thank him.

The gate was ajar; when I knocked it creaked open to reveal an untidy yard, shaded by fig and plum trees, where hens and cheeping chicks pecked busily and Mr Koliqi was brushing his teeth over a drain. He stood upright and looked puzzled. Then, noticing Ruairi, he smiled, advanced to shake my hand and led me into his home, an old two-storeyed house constructed of wood and stone with a shingle roof. Although in some disrepair, it suggested that previous generations had been less impoverished than Mr Koliqi, a tall, well-built man with sunken cheeks and white hair. In the damp-stained living room I was invited to sit on a sagging sofa and while my host fetched the *rakija* (at 7.45 a.m.) I noted that this was a Catholic home. (Most of Albania's Catholics live in the north.) On every wall hung familiar pictures, mass-produced in Italy: the Sacred Heart, the Immaculate Conception, St Joseph with the Infant Jesus, St Francis of Assisi, Pope John Paul II and of course Mother Teresa, the most famous Albanian of them all.

After Mr Keci and Bow-tie, I needed Mr Koliqi's warm welcome and enthu-siastic interest in my journey. A little Italian can go a long way when it has to and perhaps the *rakija* on an empty stomach honed my sign-language skills. Soon Mr Koliqi knew where I was going in the Balkans – my map helped – and I knew that his wife had been killed while staying with her sister in Durrës after the pyramid collapse; she was caught in crossfire during a riot. His two grown-up children had menial jobs in Shkodra: much work, little money. He himself was jobless though an experienced truck-driver. Trucking, he hinted, was now controlled by those who ran the drugs trade and/or sanctions-busting. As Tim Judah reports in *Kosovo: War and Revenge*:

> With family connections in Turkey, Germany and Switzerland, some Kosovars began to play a linking role in the international drugs trade, coming to dominate, for example, the heroin business in Zurich. The opening of Albania itself since 1991, coupled with sanctions on Serbia in 1992, also meant that a major new drugs route, passing through Albanian-inhabited parts either in Macedonia, Kosovo, Serbia proper or of course Albania itself, now opened up.

After our third round of *rakija* food was indicated. Mr Koliqi apologized because he could offer only a dish of large fishes' heads, taken from a rust-spotted fridge that groaned and shuddered in one corner. With a spoon one dug in the crevices of these skulls for bits of flesh and brains and eyes.

Word of my presence had got around and while Ruairi was being seen to four friendly neighbours called in to meet me. One young man had taught himself basic English through the BBC's World Service. 'Albania is no good to anyone,' he pronounced – then added, 'Unless you can be rich to begin, then you will get richer.'

The young man thought I was crazy to cycle alone through Albania – and he was right. However, one has to find these things out for oneself.

Prehistoric settlements flourished throughout the Shkodra region long before the city (until recently known as Scutari) was founded by the Labeates *c.* 1000 BC. This Illyrian tribe remained in control for some 700 years – which indicates that, however brutish and short individuals' lives may have been, political entities were then remarkably durable. The Ardiaean tribe took over in the third century BC and became notorious pirates, involved in more or less permanent low-level warfare with the Romans. In 168 BC their last King was captured by a Roman general and Shkodra became a Roman town. Eventually it was inherited by the Byzantines, before being occupied by the Slavs (comparative newcomers to the Balkans) from 1040 to 1355. The Venetians took over in 1396 and in 1479, after a famously long siege, Mehmed Pasha conquered Shkodra for the Ottomans at the cost of 30,000 men.

As the centre of one of the Balkans' largest *sanjaks* (Ottoman administrative districts), Shkodra soon came to feel quite independent of Constantinople. Barbara Jelavich, in her magnificent *History of the Balkans* (vol. I), explains that in Albania

> by the end of the eighteenth century two centres of power had emerged. In the north, around the city of Shkoder, the Bushati family gained a dominating position . . . Their prime influence was established by Mehmet Pasha in the years between 1757 and 1775

. . . When he attempted to widen his political jurisdiction further and refused to forward the taxes he had collected, the Ottoman government had him poisoned. Although a conflict over succession followed, his son, Kara Mahmud, took his place . . . The Habsburg government was willing to recognise him as an independent ruler if he assisted Austria against the Porte . . . In June 1788 an Austrian delegation went to Shkoder to negotiate with him. The Albanian Pasha, influenced by the fact that the Turkish armies were winning at the time, massacred the delegation and sent their heads to the Sultan. Back in favour in Constantinople, Kara Mahmud was appointed governor of Skhoder. He subsequently fought for the empire in Montenegro and Bosnia.

Nineteenth-century Shkodra became Albania's largest city, an important commercial centre of 40,000 inhabitants. (Its present population is exactly twice that.) The twentieth century began ominously, marked in 1901 by the Albanian labour movement's first strike and by an assembly of 8,000 armed men who declared their resolve to use those arms should the Turks attempt to repress by force the Albanian national movement.

During the Balkan Wars, Hussein Riza Bey led the defence of Shkodra on behalf of the Turks against a combined Serbian and Montenegrin army. This last of the city's long sieges (October 1912 to April 1913) came to an inglorious end when Hussein Riza was assassinated by Essad Pasha who surrendered to an international naval force under Sir Cecil Gurney. Thereafter Shkodra's fortunes declined. It was too prominent for its own good during the northern tribesmen's rebellion against Zog in 1926. The city's police were slaughtered by the rebels, who in due course were slaughtered by Zog's mercenaries. Because the (self-appointed) King and his Italian allies consistently neglected the disloyal north, Shkodra soon became a mere market town for the locals.

It is not unfair to describe present-day Albania as a heavily-armed society with an inherited contempt for law and order as generally understood in modern Europe. Apart from political violence, the *Hakmarrje* (blood-feud) tradition, rooted in millennia of Albanian history, was revived within weeks of the country's liberation from Enverism. Around Shkodra alone, during the first half of 1992, nineteen blood-feud murders were recorded. (The murder rate for the mountainous hinterland is officially unknown.) President Berisha's government, under close international scrutiny and craving foreign investment, felt dreadfully embarrassed by the countrywide spate of *Hakmarrje* killings and robbery-related murders and decided to impose the death penalty with increasing frequency and publicity. To the discomfiture of those who deny its deterrent value, this perceptibly lowered the murder rate – though it remained high by Western European standards. Tirana saw fifteen executions in 1993; the men were swiftly convicted, marched to open graves, shot in the head, dumped in their coffins and briskly buried. In June 1992, in Fier, a globe-shocking event took place: Albania's first public execution since 1986. Two brothers, aged twenty-one and twenty-four, were convicted of murdering a family of five, including a seven-month-old baby, by battering them to death while robbing fifty dollars' worth of leks. Many Albanians travelled long distances to witness the brothers being hanged from city-centre plane trees. Their corpses were left dangling for eighteen hours while hundreds of men, women and children assembled to stare at them. According to James Pettifer 'President Berisha had his own personal video made of the event. The international community was horrified at such a "primitive" and "barbaric" act being permitted by a democratically elected European government.' Presumably on that occasion the 'international community' excluded the US.

Year after year, in country after country, I am exasperated by the West's pretence that an election (preferably monitored by some such institution as the OSCE) can of itself enable 'democracy' to flourish where it was never heard of before and where most people are either indifferent or hostile to it. Clearly the Rich World's main concern is the extension not of democracy but of the Free Market. A façade of 'democracy' satisfies, if behind it corporations may safely wheel and deal.

It took less than an hour for me to add Shkodra to my short list of 'Favourite Cities'. On the outskirts I observed three elderly cyclists leisurely pedalling abreast, animatedly conversing and ignoring the furiously hooting Mercedes behind them. Traffic lights were not needed but traffic police in twos or threes wandered around at the main junctions blowing whistles and vaguely waving their arms while everybody did his/her own thing. The internal combustion engine could scarcely be heard above the noise of trotting horses and squealing cart-wheels and the surfaces of most streets were so sensationally rough that cyclists and carts often overtook motorists. It was soothing to be amongst so many bicycles, ridden by both sexes and all age groups, their carriers usually loaded with goods or passengers or both.

Most people looked healthier than the Slavs, with rosy cheeks, strong white teeth and clear skins. Paradoxically, their poverty may explain this; the majority, unable to afford junk food and fizzy drinks, eat only real unprocessed food. Shkodra's citizens also struck me as being, in general, more spontaneous and cheerful than the Slavs, though in contemporary Albania they have little to cheer them. Later, when I mentioned this impression to Ferhet, my local mentor, he replied, 'Maybe so, but be careful! We are a psychopathic country now. Too many are violent and cruel, liking brigandage and anarchy.'

In the town centre Shkodra's only hotel reminded me of Nikšić's and I veered away, then saw a tiny sign pointing up an alleyway to 'Zimmer-Chambre-Room'. The short alleyway led to a large two-storeyed stone house, built in the 1890s by Mr

Rexhepi's grandfather. Mrs Rexhepi had to unbolt and unlock the door before opening it. She had a kindly smile but hesitated briefly and when I looked at myself as she saw me I could understand why. A weather-beaten, scruffy elderly female leaning on a bicycle does not accord with the Albanians' image of a bona fide tourist. Then all was well, the smile widened and for DM10 I enjoyed luxury accommodation plus excellent breakfasts: unlimited quantities of milky coffee, hot bread, home-made butter, cheese and jam.

My high-ceilinged room had three tall windows, gracefully draped, a glass-fronted bookcase containing many tomes on archaeology (Mr Rexhepi's hobby), an elegant *chaise longue*, a walnut desk supporting an IBM 196c typewriter (the twin of the machine on which this book is being typed) and a standard lamp between two single beds. In 1992, when Albania's tourist trade was freed from Albturist shackles, a shower and lavatory cubicle had been installed in one corner. But soon after political turbulence discouraged tourists.

This guest room opened off the family dining room where a long oak table matched a massive sideboard and the TV was never switched off; from there one door led to a landing at the head of a wide wooden staircase and another led into a small kitchen complete with sink (the water supply erratic), electric cooker, washing-machine and deep-freezer, the last unplugged because the family could not at present afford to stock it. The ground-floor flat was occupied by Ferhet, a high-school teacher of English and German, his timid wife and five-year-old daughter. Ferhet, the only English-speaker on the scene, was small and dark and both physically and mentally energetic. Within moments of our meeting he had suggested a walk next day to the Illyrian citadel at Gajtani, about three miles beyond Shkodra on the road to Tirana.

'You are seeing Albania's best first,' Ferhet informed me. 'Shkodra is like a person with a complicated personality. It is my birthplace, I love it, in other places I don't feel comfortable. I lived in Germany three years, '91 to '94, and I could have stayed there earning well. But Shkodra pulled me back – not Albania but Shkodra and the mountains, the Dinaric Alps, which are not like other mountains.' I knew what he meant; West Waterford pulls me back.

Ferhet offered to escort me round the corner to the money-changers, who hang out all day in little groups on the road opposite the newly-opened Mosque of El Zamil – a present from Egypt and Saudi Arabia. 'The biggest mosque in Albania,' Ferhet said proudly, 'and one of the biggest in the Balkans.' The fluted stonework of the minarets is exquisite but the stainless steel of the dome jars, as do the expanses of glass, a modern fetish peculiarly unsuited to mosques though a feature of most of the Balkans' 'presents from Arabia'. Ferhet informed me, 'This city had thirty-five mosques before 1939. Hoxha destroyed most of them. Now we have only seven *imams* but some young men are being trained in Saudi Arabia, Egypt and the Lebanon. This I don't like, we don't want Islamic extremism here,

Shkodra never had that sort of trouble. Albanians are always flexible, people changed their religions when that made political sense, in those times when Turks and Habsburgs were coming and going. Shkodra is the centre for Albania's Roman Catholics – about 350,000. It's also one of our main Islamic centres. In '91, when the anti-religion laws went, people all over the country started repairing or rebuilding mosques and churches and Shkodra was in the lead – Muslims and Christians helping one another. We don't want *imams* coming back from Saudi telling us Christians are wrong and bad.'

From among the money-changers one of Ferhet's friends stepped forward and we shook hands. There was no haggling; as in Serbia six months previously, banks were of no significance and everyone offered exactly the same rate. (Then, the equivalent of 100 leks to the pound sterling. Sterling was not of course acceptable in Shkodra: only US dollars, DM and Italian lire.)

Near the Hotel Rozafati I paused to admire a fine bronze statue of Luigj Gurakuqi (1879–1925) and asked Ferhet, 'Who was he?'

'A very clever man, he organized for Albania to use the Latin alphabet and led anti-Zog northern Catholics. And he worked hard for Kosova to join Albania. Zog paid someone to assassinate him in a Bari café. You know Zog wasn't really a king, he just liked the sound of it! As a dictator he could set up a special constitutional assembly and in 1928 he ordered it to make him king! He was thirty-three then – born the son of a chief in central Albania, very right-wing, happy collaborating with the Italians.' Ferhet was silent for a moment, frowning. Then he added, 'And now we have leaders happy to collaborate with the US! Have the Ottomans left us not able to govern ourselves except the Hoxha way, through oppression?'

I suggested a beer at the little café on the corner of the Rexhepi laneway. We sat outside, under a faded awning. On the far side of the street rose an empty three-storey block with cracked walls and boarded-up windows. 'Once that was our Hoxha museum, I remember having to go as a schoolboy and learning by rote about the achievements of Uncle Enver.' Ferhet broke off to summon a waiter, who turned out to be his first cousin. 'He must do this work because all, all the money went in the pyramid crash . . .'

An unregistered Mercedes passed, packed with young men, raising clouds of dust and hooting aggressively at a cycling mother, her large handlebar basket full of fish, two small children on the carrier. 'Kosovars,' commented Ferhet. 'Smugglers. Very rich, very rude. First they lived in Tirana as refugees and made good contacts there for sanctions-busting. When countries can't export or import, jobs are lost. Then guys without work find out fast they can make a lot more than their wages busting sanctions. People in top jobs in the UN should be smart enough to see something as simple as that!'

I asked, 'What d'you think about Kosovo now? Should it become independent or join Albania?'

Ferhet laughed. 'The Kosovars don't want to join us. They think we're too poor and primitive. They were always the poorest bit of Yugoslavia but they were much better off than us. Tito was better than Hoxha. I don't want Kosova. We can't run Albania the size it is – what would happen if it was bigger? I'm not an Albanian nationalist. I told you, I love Shkodra and our mountains. I'd like my territory to be less poor and violent, that's all I want.'

Suddenly I saw Ferhet as a pleasing anachronism. I seemed to be hearing an echo from the centuries before nationalism evolved, when people were content to identify with the familiar area where they felt rooted.

Later that evening there came a knock on my door and Ferhet appeared bearing his precious short-wave radio. 'I would like you to borrow,' he said, 'and be able to hear your BBC.' I was too touched to point out that, being an Irish citizen, I cannot claim the BBC as 'mine'. Besides, such a reaction would have been tainted with nationalism.

Next morning I bought two litres of (undiluted) milk warm from the cow. The pavement sellers, middle-aged women wearing long multi-coloured skirts and brilliantly embroidered bodices, took it in turns to transport by pony-cart their village's surplus milk and only early birds could catch those litres. On realizing how eagerly they were sought I restrained myself from further indulgence; no dairy produce of any sort was available in the numerous but poorly stocked shops. Apart from the twice-weekly market, on open ground near the base of the citadel, most trading took place along a wide street where peasants displayed live poultry in wicker cages. Here one could buy those shoddy household goods seen all over the Poor World, locally-produced fruits and vegetables, clothes originally donated for refugees and out-of-date antibiotics. As the only tourist in town I was often greeted with waves and smiles and, by Day Two, with some expressions of gratified surprise at my still being around.

I visited the Wednesday market, but not for long. The numerous kids and the very woolly lambs with black faces were scared and miserable, having just left their mothers. They cried most piteously while being tied by the feet and hung upside down on the handlebars of bicycles or made to curl up in cardboard cartons on carriers. One woman strode off with a lamb over her shoulder in a white cotton bag and its twin under her arm. An elderly bald man pedalled confidently between gaping potholes, through the mix of horse-carts and Mercedes, with a bleating kid draped around his neck and three squawking, flapping hens tied to his carrier. The tribeswomen, down from high villages and clad in traditional costumes, moved through the townsfolk with aloof dignity. In every corner tethered ponies, horses and donkeys were being fed, some from enormous nose-sacks. But the majority were far too thin, never groomed and white-flecked where saddle-sores had healed. Almost every animal I saw in Albania looked underfed.

In Shkodra's 400-year-old café, described by James Pettifer as 'one of the oldest continually occupied cafés in Albania', the décor and flooring have been grievously modernized but the original structure remains unaltered – solid, simple, yet sophisticated in the perfection of its proportions. An English-speaking waiter indignantly denied the café's Ottoman provenance. 'Everything in Albania was built by Albanians,' he asserted. 'This café was built in 1931. We did also build a famous citadel – you have seen it?'

The only other customer, sitting at the next table, overheard this exchange and introduced herself as Rosapha. 'I am called after the young woman who gave her name to the citadel. She was built into the wall, a sacrifice to the devil who tried to stop the construction work. Don't listen to this silly waiter, he repeats Communist school propaganda. My job is with Mother Teresa's nuns. I help with healthcare, in villages near Shkodra, translating.'

Rosapha was small, slight and olive-skinned with a pointed chin and enormous dark eyes that gave her a permanently startled expression. Her family, too, had run aground on a pyramid and been forced to sell their home in 1998, to a Kosovar back from Switzerland 'who got rich helping the KLA to buy guns'. Rosapha added, 'If you visited us before December '96 you would have seen Shkodra becoming better, getting shops with goods from Italy, Holland, Hungary, Bulgaria, Austria. We had new cafés opening and people showing hope for the future. Now, you see how it is – worse even than before!'

Shkodra's April temperature – like a hot midsummer day in Ireland – was a trifle too high for me. Frequent anti-dust hosings, outside shops and cafés, reminded me of Vientiane – as did the equally frequent whiffs from leaking sewers and piles of rotting garbage on which dogs and cats scavenged together, many of the females bulging with their next litter.

In such a mini-city the lack of public transport doesn't matter; Shkodra is easily walkable and, as one walks, its complex past unfolds around every corner. The old Ottoman shopping area offers sad evidence of the revival of commercial activity as 'freedom' dawned, followed by the abrupt collapse of small family enterprises. Nearby, low-rise Enverist apartment blocks, built of ill-baked bricks, have deteriorated more rapidly and less gracefully than the Ottoman homes around the next corner, their wooden balconies with delicately carved purdah screens overhanging narrow laneways. Most such dwellings have thick, stone-faced brick walls; the rest were constructed entirely of round stones, cleverly mortared. The Balkans' largest Catholic Cathedral (built 1856–98) is too grimly monolithic to be outwardly impressive yet given its history one has to be moved by the interior. Hoxha's vandals converted it to a volleyball court, with tiers of concrete seats obliterating its quasi-Romanesque arches, yet within a few years of liberation

Vatican-funded craftsmen had restored it. Now it is quite beautiful, uncluttered by its nineteenth-century accumulation of mass-produced incitements to piety. Beside it the palace of the Archbishop of Shkodra (also nineteenth-century) pretends to be a Renaissance *palazzo* and nearby is a 1970s Enverist military barracks, surprisingly open to the public, with a crumbling façade and male underwear hanging out to dry on the balconies. In tangled gardens shaded by vine trellises stand roomy bungalows (faintly Raj) and diplomatic residencies (faintly Habsburg), all dating from the latter half of the nineteenth century. High walls half-conceal a very splendid Albanian house with a tower at one end, said to have been built *c.* 1750 by the Prenk Bib Doda clan and still privately occupied. Finally I came to rest in the half-overgrown Christian cemetery, crowded with disintegrating monuments to eminent citizens of the pre-Balkan Wars era. And there I sat on a fallen angel and drank one of my litres of milk.

Ferhet was an intuitive young man. We much enjoyed our walk to the Illyrian citadel and I appreciated his guidance; the site is not conspicuous and the local villagers seemed considerably less affable than the townsfolk. However, he sensed my wish to be alone at Rozafat citadel and arranged for Mrs Rexhepi to provide me with a packed breakfast. 'But be careful,' he warned. 'You'll be near our Gypsy Quarter and they rob tourists.'

My immediate reaction was to bristle at this generalization but next day I felt what he meant. Vigilance was needed in that neighbourhood; twice efforts were made to distract me while small hands slipped into my empty pockets.

Two miles from the centre I turned left on to a track sloping up, past a few cottages, to the base of Rozafat's crag. Here the citadel's impregnability becomes awesomely evident; 500 feet above me its walls, following the contour of the outcrop's edge, were gold-tinged by the rising sun. The long Ottoman approach road, coiling steeply up the crag's south side, is magnificently paved with shiny cobbles; since the Ottomans' departure it has never, Ferhet informed me, needed repairs. It leads into a dusky vaulted passageway through the walls – and then I was in a serene pastoral world where wild flowers bejewelled the spring grass and herbs scented the air and the only sound was the immemorial music of sheep bells. From below I had seen a shepherd driving his flock towards the passageway and now he greeted me gravely with a silent nod and a movement of one hand that was almost a military salute. A white-haired ancient, he wore baggy pantaloons, a felt cloak and the Albanian males' distinctive close-fitting headgear – the *plish*. At 7 a.m. he and I had Rozafat to ourselves.

The walls' total length, including the eight protective towers, is more than half a mile and they enclose an oval space covering some twenty-three acres. From the second century BC to the First World War this citadel was of major military importance. Its impregnability made it the scene of several of Europe's bloodiest sieges and eventually Rozafat became a compact town in its own right, complete with cathedral – built in 1319 and consecrated as Shkodra's cathedral. When the Ottomans converted it to a mosque in 1479 it acquired a minaret and now, as a bleakly beautiful ruin, it dominates the whole citadel. Nearby is another more prosaic ruin, a sturdy edifice known as 'the prison' though its original purpose is uncertain.

I breakfasted sitting on the walls, overlooking the confluence of the rivers Buna and Kir; beyond stretched vividly green drained marshlands, and then the shimmering expanse of Lake Shkodra. On such a clear morning one can see for thirty miles or more, from every side of the citadel; to the north-east, distance did not diminish the shining ferocity of the Dinaric Alps. In 1479, after Shkodra's last stand against the Ottomans, 60,000 unburied bodies lay on the battlefield below; luckily for the survivors it was January, and very cold, and the feast on offer drew vultures from far and wide. This Turkish victory sent panic waves throughout Christendom – a panic one can still sense, looking at Veronese's 1585 frescoes in the Doge's Palace in Venice.

In the early fifteenth century a novel defensive system was constructed, incorporating an immensely high Venetian tower; from its top one gets the best view of Rozafat's complicated layout. The inner castle enclosed a long three-storey building, its walls massively thick – the Venetians' arsenal. The Turks also used it to store dangerous goods before it became the official residence of the Pashas of Shkodra. Now it has been demoted to café status and is the main source of Rozafat's lamentable litter problem. In horror I watched an adolescent café employee emptying trash-cans into one of the citadel's famous and revered (by antiquarians) cisterns. That was at noon, when a busload of Tirana youths arrived with ghetto-blasters to dissipate the tranquillity. My 6 a.m. start had been a wise move.

In our neurotically safety-conscious countries, Rozafat would by now have been drearily modified lest visitors might come to some harm; in Albania, one has to look out for oneself. On the walls loose masonry abounds and no one could survive the precipitous drops. Other hazards include some of the immensely deep underground cisterns, built to store water for those interminable sieges and now partially overgrown, and the romantic entrances to what once were secret passages leading down to the riverside.

Directly below Rozafat, standing alone amidst cultivated fields, is Shkodra's most beautiful building – in fact, the most beautiful building I saw anywhere in the Balkans. And we have the Hereditary Pasha Mehmet Bushati to thank for it – he who fiddled the tax returns and was poisoned by the Porte. In 1773–4 he ordered the construction of the Leaded Mosque in imitation of Istanbul's Great Mosque, a symbolic gesture of which the Sultan no doubt took note. Hoxha's vandal squads damaged this mosque only slightly; perhaps in some hidden corner of their sick psyches even they were susceptible to its beauty. And although it was the scene of much brutal violence during Albania's first 'democratic' election campaign, when the police aimed at worshippers as they prayed, skilful restorations have erased all signs of conflict. To my delighted surprise the main door was open, though there was nobody around, and I remember that afternoon as a fortifying interlude such as travellers need in the modern Balkans. Rarely, nowadays, does the over-expanded tourist industry allow one to enjoy so special a place in solitude.

13

Quickly out of Albania

A 'wrong key' mystery delayed my departure for Pukë (pronounced Pookay). The Rexhepi family slept on the ground floor and every evening the door at the foot of the stairs was locked and its Yale-type key hung on a nail to allow me to let myself out at dawn. But now that key didn't work – and we were without our interpreter who had gone to a teachers' conference in Tirana. Doggedly I struggled – manipulating, coaxing, even trying brute force while on the other side of the door Mrs Rexhepi shouted incomprehensible advice or instructions. Such moments fully expose the limitations of sign language. Then someone whistled piercingly outside the hall door and – inspired by a rare flash of genius – I rushed upstairs to peer out of the kitchen window. Mr Rexhepi stood staring up, looking un-amused; evidently he blamed me for this contretemps, or perhaps he was just feeling grumpy because Mrs Rexhepi couldn't get to the kitchen to prepare his breakfast. He waved a bunch of keys, then threw them up. At the second attempt I caught them but none of the five fitted. Now there were several arguing voices beyond the door, sounding angry with each other. I longed to be off, taking advantage of the cool morning hours, but giving way to impatience wastes energy so I sat on the bottom step and relaxed. Fifteen minutes later another whistle summoned me back to the kitchen window: Mr Rexhepi wanted the keys thrown down. He caught them deftly, leaped on to his bicycle and quickly pedalled away. Soon he was back, throwing up another bunch, one of which freed me. If only Ferhet had been there to elucidate.

By 7.45 I was jolting over Shkodra's main street, in warm sunshine under a cloudless sky. For the first few miles, on the smooth-surfaced Tirana road, the traffic was a menacing mix of horse-carts, trucks, bicycles and Mercedes. I rejoiced to escape on to the Pukë road, a narrow strip of broken tarmac winding through fertile land where many family groups were carrying green branches to a small ramshackle church – it was Palm Sunday, I then realized.

Beyond the wretched little town of Kozmac our climb began, into a magnificence of mountains exceeding even my great expectations of Albania; many hours were to pass before any other dwellings appeared. Far below the road,

Miridita tribeswomen in ankle-length black gowns and white headscarves looked like nuns as they moved across the rugged valley floor tending their flocks of sheep and goats – the goats' multicoloured coats long and silky. Numerous paths leading away from the road into folds of the mountains indicated an unseen population; then a bus from Shkodra overtook me, stopped a little way ahead, put down a young man and two sacks. His brother (judging by appearances) was awaiting him and together they loaded a donkey before setting off into the sort of terrain I wished I could trek through with one of those bargain pack-ponies (£50) available in Shkodra's market. Here I brunched off breed and cheese, while watching the brothers and their donkey grow smaller and smaller, strolling at donkey pace towards a distant village.

On this high plateau the road rose and fell between the bare crags of mountain summits, with grassy valleys wide and shallow on my right. Soon after brunch I passed five children (two girls, three boys) sitting with a granny-figure on a long slab of rock overlooking their grazing flock. When greeted, they stared at me with a blend of incredulity and excitement. Moments later, coming to a severe gradient, I dismounted and only then noticed that the children were pursuing me – as friendly and curious children have done in a dozen countries. These, however, were neither friendly nor curious but predatory. Crowding around me, they grabbed at Ruairi, demanding DM, and were only briefly deflected by the contents of my purse – a few hundred leks, thrown downhill. Luckily that incline was short but as I remounted they caught up with me, pushed me to the ground, and one lad tugged at the rain-cape strapped to the carrier. Standing up, I seized the pump and laid about me, striking two boys on their heads – whereupon they all fled. But they didn't flee far. When I had to dismount for the next steep climb they were already in position up the mountain on my left, from where they pelted me with sharp stones. I know they were sharp because one of them cut my scalp.

That encounter shook me, despite the brigands' age – seven to twelve-year-olds, I estimated. They had after all knocked me to the ground, my right elbow was grazed and aching and my scalp was bleeding. Moreover, I sensed that the granny-figure would have condoned their robbing me. Then, stopping to pee, I realized that they *had* robbed me; both pannier side-pockets were empty. This astounded me, given the design of those pockets, with strong zips concealed under tight rain-proof flaps. Going on my uphill way, I mourned the loss of my indispensable *Marco Polo* map, a plastic wallet holding precious addresses of people already met and contacts yet to be made in Kosovo, a leather photograph wallet, James Pettifer's *Blue Guide to Albania*, Misha Glenny's *The Fall of Yugoslavia*, Serbo-Croat and Albanian mini-dictionaries and phrase books, my spongebag-cum-first-aid-kit, a blank notebook, four unused films and a large packet of 'emergency rations' peanuts. Few of those items would reward the children's remarkable dexterity. By far the most serious losses were the map and the addresses. I hope those to whom I should have written gratefully on my return home will one day read these lines.

Reflecting on the child robbers' tactics, it seemed likely their behaviour was not unusual in these parts. I therefore armed myself with a stout stick and unpacked my Croatian coins.

The Shkodra to Pukë road goes twice from almost sea-level to more than 5,000 feet. Built by the Italians in the 1920s, and not since repaired, it rivals the worst tracks in the most neglected corners of Uganda, Tanzania, Malawi. Those thirty-five miles took me ten hours; bus journeys take two and a half hours. There is one small town *en route* and I met only two Shkodra-bound vehicles and three Pukë-bound. I must have walked more than twenty miles; on most of the dramatic descents the surface precluded freewheeling. Not that that mattered: amidst such splendour I am as happy walking as cycling – under normal circumstances.

At noon I turned the last hairpin bend of a long, long climb up a pine-clad mountain above an oval river valley which at each end became a gorge, a mere cleft between sheer precipices. Here the forest receded from the track and grass grew high around towering outcrops of silvery rock. As I relished the simple contrasting colours sheep-bells could be heard tinkling faintly in the distance – perfect background music. Then I saw a wisp of smoke rising from behind a house-sized boulder; someone was cooking lunch. I paused to take my stick off the carrier when a boy appeared. Seeing me, he summoned his companions and they all hurried to the roadside: three boys and a girl, in the nine to twelve age group. As I came closer they shouted in unison, demanding DM, and moved to block my way, holding hands. Smiling at them, pretending not to understand this 'game', I pushed through their barrier – whereupon they scrambled around me, the girl trying to thrust her hand into my trouser pocket, the smallest boy tugging at the camera pouch around my waist. When another boy fell behind I looked back to see him pulling my gloves and water-bottle off the carrier. Stick-wielding time had come and I struck him hard across the face – but he got away with his loot – and then struck the biggest lad who had taken hold of Ruairi's handlebars. Momentarily scared by my assaults they retreated, the girl running back towards their camp-fire. But the boys raced ahead of me and again I was stoned as I began to freewheel down a steep half-mile descent – not very fast, but fast enough to escape. That stoning left me with a throbbing lump behind my right ear and Ruairi with two bent spokes on the front wheel. By then I was thoroughly unnerved. It is hard to take seriously the threat emanating from a few pre-pubescent children – until you meet them in rural Albania where there is nothing to curb their inherited notion that robbing travellers is a respectable occupation.

The third attack came from four boys and two girls whose huge flock of sheep was grazing on a wide plateau overlooked from every side by gaunt rock peaks. When they spotted me near the edge of the plateau – more forested slopes lay ahead – I was slowly negotiating the gulleys that here criss-crossed the track. As they purposefully advanced I dismounted and armed myself. All these children, however short of cash their families may have been, were sturdy and well-built with clear complexions – very unlike the enfeebled products of urban slums. They were also adequately clothed and shod, though unwashed and uncombed. In contrast to the others, this slightly older gang did not immediately demand DM but sought to engage me in conversation, their friendliness blatantly false. They had a plan, I sensed – perhaps allies lurked nearby? Even without help the six could easily have overcome me. I amiably sustained my side of the sign-language conversation and, as we approached the descent, prepared myself to scatter kuna and leap on Ruairi, desperately hoping for a cycleable surface. But suddenly the biggest boy – he could have been thirteen or fourteen – grabbed my stick while simultaneously two others tried to separate me from Ruairi. I let the stick go, the better to secure my grip on the crossbar – then shouted '*Deutsch mark!*' and flung a fistful of kuna into the wayside grass. The bright coins glittered as they fell and while the sextet frantically searched for them I made my getaway – or so I thought.

This descent, through dense pine forest around several hairpin bends, was just cycleable: both brakes were needed all the way. Where it ended the next climb began; one could see the track zigzagging up a precipitous rock mountain scattered with low scrub. And here three of the boys confronted me, each armed with a stick; they had used a footpath short-cut.

That was a nasty moment – very nasty. Then, as the trio moved towards me in silence, I remembered my binoculars case sometimes being mistaken for an underarm holster – it was worth a try. Shouting angrily I swung the case from under my arm, made to open it and mimed firing a revolver. To my great astonishment the boys promptly fled, back into the forest whence they had come. In Pukë, when I articulated my astonishment, I was told, 'Albanians take guns seriously. If you'd really had one those boys would have expected you to shoot them dead.'

Also in Pukë, a local government official explained to me, in kindly tones, that I should have left Shkodra prepared to hand over modest amounts like DM50 (£20), thereby avoiding stones. This sounded like a sort of road toll imposed by child shepherds on foreign travellers, which the official seemed to think was not unreasonable. Funny place, Albania – funny-peculiar.

As I began that last climb (Pukë on its plateau was only a few miles ahead) I remained tense. Had my ploy terminally scared the boys? Or would they regain their nerve, realize that they had been duped and again pursue me? Happily this mountain's gradient allowed of no short cut; as I ascended I could observe lower stretches of the road and reassure myself that I was not being followed. After nine hairpin bends I came to level ground, agreeably wooded – beech, oak, fir, wild cherry – and soon Pukë appeared on a rise above the road, backed by a long, smooth-crested ridge with much higher summits in the near distance, sharp and snow-streaked.

The town of Pukë (population 7,000 or so) does not match its setting; it seems to epitomize all Albania's troubles and visually has no redeeming feature. Yet its warm-hearted population served as an effective antidote to the junior brigands.

By the time I arrived the town was expecting me; the drivers and passengers of those three Pukë-bound vehicles had observed my progress with fascinated amazement. A bus driver, relaxing on a café verandah with two policemen, invited me to have a beer (did I need it!) and within minutes Sokol and Hydajet had joined us. Both spoke English, mostly self-taught; Sokol's was the more fluent because he had recently spent two months in Ireland interpreting for an NGO which sponsors medical treatment for Albanian children. These two had been close friends for all of their twenty years ('we were babies together') but Sokol seemed the dominant – and less likeable – character.

Half an hour later Pukë's mayor was welcoming me – instructing the hotel owner to provide free accommodation and meals – arranging an interview with the local TV station for eight o'clock next morning. The mayor had the air of a tribal chief whose orders are not disputed, ever, by anyone. Despite my allergy to television I became next day Pukë's latest celebrity, greeted by all I met in the street, invited here, there and everywhere for *rakija* or coffee or what is euphemistically called 'juice' – a dire liquid allegedly derived from fruits but tasting only of chemicals.

The Albturist Hotel, once Pukë's pride and joy, had been literally falling to bits since the end of Enverism. Chunks of masonry lay in the corridors, three of the planks in my bedroom ceiling hung loose, there was no running water and cockroaches abounded. A single bed furnished my room, augmented by a cracked and cigarette-burnt plastic table borrowed from the terrace café to serve as my 'desk'.

That evening's TV news, translated by Sokol, only mildly interested the locals though in some parts of the world it might be considered sensational. During the forenoon two policemen, returning to Pukë from Fierzë by jeep, skidded on a hairpin bend and their vehicle ended up on its side mere inches from a 1,000-foot drop. ('Many fall off the road at that corner,' interjected Sokol.) The officers, only slightly injured, were trying to right the jeep when five youths appeared out of nowhere, overpowered them, seized their rifles and small arms, ammunition, mobile phones, uniforms, boots and thermos flasks. The police, tied up on the verge, witnessed two approaching vehicles, travelling in convoy, being robbed at gunpoint (their guns). Listening to this apparently commonplace news item, I realized how lucky I had been to meet only unarmed children. Earlier the mayor had been complaining that since the plundering of the state arsenals after the pyramid collapse armed children are no longer a rarity.

That evening I wrote in my journal:

This has been a surreally scarey day. All those, including James Pettifer in his *Blue Guide*, who advised against cycling alone through Albania were right. The surreality came of my molesters being children. What most scared me was the expression on their faces. They looked vicious, in an adult sort of way. I'm sure I'd have found them less upsetting – even less frightening – had they been older. As for the standard poverty excuse, I can't accept it. Most of my journeys have been through countries where any Westerner, even me on a bike, seems rich – yet never before have I met children like these. And now what about my ardent support for non-violent methods of conflict resolution?! How does that fit with my physically attacking children? Very quickly, under pressure, our ideals go phut and brute force seems the obvious response. I also ask myself – if the local peasants produce criminal children, capable of such well-organized attacks, what must the adolescents and adults be like? I'm not going to stay around to find out. Next stop Kosovo – by vehicle.

Since Roman times Pukë (then known as Epicaria) has been an administrative centre for a wide area. Given the surrounding terrain there isn't much choice and, having found this bit of level ground, the administrators stayed put for millennia. Before the Romans, the Pirust tribe mined copper hereabouts and became renowned metal-workers; examples of their art are on view in all Europe's great archaeological museums. In the whole municipality there are only 250 acres of arable land and always the forests have been the locals' main resource. For more than 2,000 years resin has been exported, to the Adriatic coastal towns and Kosovo and Serbia, and from the second to the fourth centuries this flourishing trade sustained a second town, Pezhve, some three miles south of Pukë. But now, to add to Pukë's other woes, the processionaria disease is rampaging through the pine forests. One can scarcely imagine this prosperous past, when Pukë was an important stopping place for merchants toing and froing between the Adriatic and the Danube. The Via Publica, from which Pukë is said to take its name, must have been much better maintained than today's track.

Other traditional products are a variety of medicinal herbs, honey, chestnuts, apples, cherries and – nowadays most important of all – forest mushrooms. These are not eaten locally but have become an important trade for Italian companies which pay the pickers a pittance. During the season most of Pukë's able-bodied inhabitants take off for the forests and annually collect some forty tons of various fungi.

The mayor saw fruit exporting as the way forward for Pukë, if outside investors could be persuaded to plant thousands of hectares with apple and cherry trees. He seemed genuinely concerned to help the area – but how to compel outsiders to deal fairly with indigenous workers?

In Pukë – as in Shkodra and, later, Kukës – there was much talk about Albania's need for foreign aid and investment but little awareness that donors and investors are waiting for the country to become less anarchic before they sign any more cheques. Ferhet saw this as a despair-inducing dilemma: unless more work becomes available, how to restore law and order without reverting to an Enverist reign of terror? Albania's unemployment rate is by far the highest in Europe and Ferhet reckoned (perhaps melodramatically?) that without remittances from exiles some Albanians would be dying of hunger. Given its sparse population and natural resources the country could of course survive and be healthy, in every sense, without foreign investment – under a government inspired by Richard Douthwaite. But that would involve rejecting Consumerism and the Albanians, like everyone else in our self-destructive age, crave the life-style depicted on satellite TV.

The mayor was proud of Pukë's association with Lek Dukagjin (1410–81). The Dukagjin chiefs ruled Pukë during the fifteenth century when Lek established the '*Kanun*', otherwise known as 'the Law of Lek'. Based on customary law dating back certainly to Roman and possibly to Illyrian times, the *Kanun* survived 500 years of Ottoman rule and 50 years of brutal Enverist oppression and still operates after a fashion – in so far as any legal system can be said to operate. (I was advised not to waste time reporting the junior brigands to Pukë's police.)

My live TV interview took place in the hotel bar with a wide-eyed audience of ten army conscripts, beardless youths who were enjoying diluted beer for breakfast – diluted by themselves.

Afterwards, Sokol said I must meet 'the best people in Pukë' – a nice accolade for his nun friends. In 1991 Mother Teresa set up her Missionaries of Charity Order headquarters in Bushat, a big village ten miles south of Shkodra, and a year later a six-nun congregation arrived in Pukë and built a shed-like church and simple bungalow-convent at the base of a mountain on the edge of the town. Their compound is securely fenced and guarded; in Albania missionaries of all stripes are now alarmingly numerous and not very popular.

Aosta-born Mother Angela, fair-haired and blue-eyed, described herself as the 'project leader'. A compact little figure, her aura combined energy, decisiveness and calm. The most junior sister, recently arrived from Cameroon, became moist-eyed on hearing that I knew her country. She had not yet ventured beyond the compound, the locals were being given time to adjust to the notion of a black-skinned person living in their midst. (Why post a Cameroonian to one of Albania's most isolated regions where strangers of any skin colour are viewed with suspicion?)

Middle-aged Mother Angela spoke fluent English. While Sokol and Hydajet dug in the garden – their only paid work – she entertained me in the simple convent parlour, its walls bare but for a copper bas-relief portrait of the Skopje-born Mother Teresa. We talked for more than three hours, sharing a small pot of coffee. The nuns' main project was to provide primary healthcare in remote villages in the once-Catholic hinterland. Only when closely questioned did Mother Angela admit that the early years were 'not easy'. Some villages lay a three- or four-hour walk from the motor road and the nuns took an armed bodyguard until 'unfortunate incidents' convinced them that they would be safer unguarded. They then got quite used to being robbed, before the villagers realized that the medical contents of their rucksacks were more beneficial to the community if administered by trained nurse-nuns. 'Now of course we're generally accepted,' said Mother Angela with a happy smile. 'We hardly ever get hassled.' She seemed genuinely unaware of having achieved anything remarkable and I felt my expressing admiration for the nuns' courage might embarrass her. Instead, I confessed that I was retreating from Albania in disarray, after my minor 'unfortunate incidents' on the way from Shkodra.

Mother Angela listened attentively, looking pensive, then nodded. 'Some of those children can be vicious,' she agreed. 'But don't forget they're victims, born into a totally traumatized society. Imagine people who've been in prison all their lives suddenly released and expected to live normally. They couldn't. And the rural Albanians can't. They are completely disorientated. Hoxha institutionalized them, forced them to accept one set of rules and never question it. Overnight all those were gone and not only gone but labelled "wrong". And there's nothing instead. The peasants have no one of their own to give them a sense of direction. Everyone was in Hoxha's mental prison, including the people who ran it. You mentioned poverty – have you travelled through famine areas? No? Then maybe you can't fully imagine how Albania was in '91 to '93 before the international community started feeding the people. Here in the north-east is the country's poorest region, some of the villages we visit simply don't have enough to eat – now, in the year 2000. But I agree poverty is only part of what we're talking about. The collective moral confusion is the main problem.'

We then discussed prostitution. Mother Angela was too sophisticated to worry about the standard version, the post-Hoxha re-establishment of brothels in Tirana, Durrës, Vlorë, Elbasan. What anguished her was the trade in very young girls who find themselves trapped in Italy or Greece, having been promised good jobs as barmaids, waitresses or domestic servants in rich households. Being illegal immigrants they must obey the *mafia* and having lost their virginity they know their marriage prospects back home are virtually nil. A minority do escape and return, risking *mafia* retribution and parental rejection. 'We have a refuge for them in Tirana,' said Mother Angela, 'but they can be so disturbed it's impossible for them to accept any restriction. They know they need our protection but they resent it. Then we're accused of kidnapping and proselytizing . . . It all gets very complicated. But this problem is not specially Albanian, it's global. Only Western women are liberated, the rest are exploited like never before.'

Next we tiptoed around the abortion issue – I was very conscious of Mother Teresa's views. Hoxha, like Ceauşescu, outlawed contraceptives and abortion to promote a high birthrate. By 1989 Albania's population had reached 2.8 million

– the highest ever – and at 2.1 per cent its annual growth rate was the second highest in Europe, after Kosovo. Two-thirds of the population were under twenty-six in 1990 and 40,000 were joining the work force annually – or trying to.

'At that time,' said Mother Angela, 'thousands were dying after illegal abortions.' She paused, then continued in a carefully neutral tone, 'The new government brought in the Abortion Law in January '92, allowing the operation before the twelfth week. In July '92 official statistics recorded 0.8 live births to one abortion for the previous six months.' The neutrality ebbed from the quiet voice. 'That is a tragic ratio! And caused by no family planning provisions and extreme poverty. Most of those mothers were married, Albania doesn't have a big unmarried mothers problem. Not yet – I dare say it's on the way.'

Before we said goodbye, Mother Angela lent me a photocopied map of Kosovo and asked Sokol to help me re-photocopy it. But we found that Pukë's one photocopier, in the municipal offices, had long since broken down.

As we returned to the town Sokol again reminisced about 'my Irish experience', which had filled him with a scorn for Albania that I found rather trying. Even my praise for the Balkans' Turkish dishes prompted the inane comment that Irish cooking is better than Turkish.

Deploring the Albanian repression of women, Sokol recalled nostalgically, 'In Dublin you can meet a girl for the first time in a pub, go to her flat for the night, then walk off next morning and never see her again! That's how it should be here.'

'So when you marry, you won't care how many men your bride has slept with?'

Sokol blushed and looked away and said nothing.

'He will care!' exclaimed Hydajet. 'He must have a virgin to marry!'

'So that's *not* how it should be here,' I observed.

Sokol recovered himself and hastened to repair his liberal image. 'Anyway I won't let my father choose my wife,' he declared defiantly. 'I'll go to Tirana and find the right girl for myself.'

Soon after, we passed two comely young women who smiled at me (the TV star) and nodded a greeting. Hydajet remarked, 'Those two are aged twenty-six but they won't ever marry, they always go round together.'

In my Western way I inwardly wondered, 'Lesbian?' Then Hydajet continued, 'They were silly when they were young, they used to talk to men.'

I stared at him. 'What d'you mean, "talk to men"?'

Both my companions laughed. 'This isn't Ireland!' said Sokol, who had quite recovered his composure. 'Here girls can't even *talk* to men. The guys those two talked to were lucky not to be shot by their brothers or fathers. My brother was shot because he talked to a girl in the hotel bar and bought her a juice. She was crying because her father was drowned in the dam. That's why my brother talked to her.'

'Your brother was shot dead?'

'Yes,' said Sokol.

I went silent. Was Sokol having his revenge, trying to shock me by presenting this stereotype of 'the stage Albanian'?

There was worse to come. When Sokol left us Hydajet took me on to his home, to meet his mother and older brother. I asked, 'Was that true, about Sokol's brother?'

Hydajet looked puzzled. 'Why would he tell you lies? Yes it's true. Then his father made the wife stop the baby, it wasn't wanted without a father.'

'You mean have an abortion?'

Hydajet frowned. 'I don't know that word – the baby was inside and you can kill it then.'

'That's an abortion,' I told him – whereupon, as was his wont, he took out a notebook and carefully inscribed this new word in capitals.

I asked, 'What happened to the widow?'

'Another word I don't know – but I can guess it! Nobody knows where she went, maybe to Tirana. Nobody wanted her.' He added, 'This abortion is dangerous, when my brother got dead in a car crash his wife did an abortion because she hated him so much and two days later she was dead – she never stopped bleeding.'

These vignettes of family life in Pukë were straining my credulity yet it was impossible to disbelieve them. I asked, 'Why did she hate him?'

Hydajet replied, 'It is sometimes happening in Albania, girls hating the man they marry. They have no choice, they must obey. Not now in cities so much but still is the way in towns and villages.' His sister-in-law, he explained, didn't go to the hospital for her abortion because his mother 'wanted the baby instead of my brother'. So the abortion was supposed to be spontaneous.

By then we were approaching Hydajet's block, one of a row of shoddy low-rise oblongs surrounded by weeds, rubble and garbage, the narrow concrete stairways unlit, the corridors dank. Wistfully my companion remarked, 'Sokol says in Ireland is not places like this, all has nice houses.'

Tartly I replied, 'So Sokol didn't visit inner-city Dublin.'

As Hydajet's mother and brother embraced me warmly he translated. 'They saw you on TV and they think you are their friend.'

This home was typical of several I visited in Pukë's blocks: three rooms so mini-mally furnished they seemed bigger than they were, with ill-fitting windows, inex-pertly laid floor tiles, damp-stained yellow-brown walls brightened by a few family photographs. Yet the electric cookers were usually luxury models and quite new, as were the TV sets and video recorders. Such goods are not on sale in the shops but many may be traced back (I was informed in Kukës) to the prodigious 1992 looting of Dubrovnik and adjacent towns by Milošević's Montenegrin 'Special Forces'. The market was so flooded that much of the loot eventually went on sale in Albania for a fraction of the normal price. When I commented that the Irish find cooking by electricity very expensive everyone laughed; in Pukë paying electricity bills went out of fashion in 1992. Ingenious things could be done to the cables – it was all part of being liberated and democratic.

My hostess was a small frail woman, full of kindness, who gave an impression of stoical inner strength, such as some people develop in reaction to every sort of hardship. Looking at her, I remembered – 'she wanted the baby instead of my brother'. Cruelty breeds cruelty. A woman forced to marry a hated man disregards the need of a bereaved mother. Mrs B—— was ten years my junior but afflicted by rheumatism, a heart condition and kidney stones. 'Our hospital has no help for her,' said Hydajet sadly. 'She says before were two good doctors but in '91 they went away. I think they went to some other country where they get more money.'

In one respect, this apartment was not typical. All the furniture had been made by Hydajet's brother, a gentle handsome thirty-year-old. The table at which I sat depicted around its edges, in finely carved detail, Pukë's battles against the Ottomans. Given such outstanding talent, this family should not have been destitute. Yet it does cheer one to meet a craftsman who finds joy simply in the creation of beauty.

Next day there was much discussion among my Pukë friends about the safest transport to Kosovo. One confab took place on the hotel terrace, overlooking the wide main street which runs down to shabby municipal buildings and an enormous ill-equipped school. The hotel owner opposed my taking the bus to Kukës, and then a minibus taxi to Prizren in Kosovo. He felt certain the Kukës *mafiosi* who swarm around the bus station would steal Ruairi and all thereon; as Sokol pointed out, the junior brigands had not stolen him only because children from remote villages cannot ride bicycles. I had already been offered a lift in Mr Quni's van, scheduled to leave for Prizren at 2 a.m. on the following morning – one didn't ask 'Why 2 a.m.?' Doubtless Mr Quni had his own good reasons for wanting to drive through Kukës in darkness and perhaps Sokol's father knew those reasons. Looking touchingly worried, he advised against this particular van on the grounds that it could run into big trouble. But to me the bus-station hazard seemed the greater. Reluctantly I chose the van, though travelling by night through the Dinaric Alps would be so frustrating.

Sokol and Hydajet escorted me to Mr Quni's home, some way beyond Pukë, to let him know my decision – only to find that his journey had been postponed until the following week. We were invited in to the Qunis' attractive stone cottage, built in 1998 at the base of a long rocky ridge opposite a pine-covered mountain. The carpeted living room was furnished with a sofa, several easy chairs, two long coffee tables, three standard lamps and a corner cabinet displaying a clutter of colourful ornaments. Evidently those trans-border journeys were worthwhile.

This was a happy family of two early teenage sons, a shyly smiling twelve-year-old daughter and a strikingly handsome mother with jet-black hair worn in a bun that showed her strong-boned face to best advantage. She settled down to talk while her daughter – in the adjacent kitchen, visible through an archway – brewed coffee and cut goats' cheese into cubes, to be eaten with spring onions. Meanwhile chubby cheerful Mr Quni was pouring a singularly potent distillation into tiny glasses for the males and the Irish female. The Albanian female drank juice.

Mrs Quni, having watched my lengthy TV interview, was vibrating with curiosity. How come my husband, brothers, sons allowed me to travel alone? And on a bicycle! Why did I not have a vehicle? Did Irish people not use cars and buses? What did writing books mean? Was I a university person?

Sokol, embarrassed at having to translate all this, muttered apologetically, 'Albanians are very ignorant, they don't know how other countries are.'

I retorted, 'Did you meet many in Ireland who know how Albania is?'

During Nato's airwar more than 20,000 refugees passed through Pukë on their way to Tirana and the coastal towns; all were provided with overnight shelter, basic rations and moral support. Some 3,000 from the Prizren area stayed in Pukë where the Qunis, and 266 other families, offered hospitality. Those who could not be accommodated *en famille* were cared for in camps by Arab, Austrian and Italian aid agencies. The Qunis' eight refugees were made welcome for seven weeks and on their return to Kosovo the family continued to keep in touch with them; ten months later they were still in a UNHCR Holding Centre. 'They had no strong men left to build new houses and the old were burned and smashed,' explained Mr Quni. 'Their three strong men were all in the KLA, after the Serb militia came they joined. They all got taken to Serb prisons.'

I was then shown a home-made video of the refugees' arrival, their first meal with the Qunis (plainly they were starving), their children's birthday parties during the exile, picnics by the river and finally their departure in mid-June, clutching small bags of food gifts. We live in a very odd economic environment. Making videos costs money; had the Kosovars not been videoed they could have received bigger bags of food gifts.

The Qunis' views on Kosovo's future were reassuring. While sympathizing with their fellow-Albanians they did not advocate a Greater Albania. Like Ferhet, they only wanted peace in their corner of the world, however it might come about.

As we were leaving, Mr Quni presented me with compensation for my transport disappointment – a large bottle of that singular distillation.

Sokol then suggested a detour to show me one of Hoxha's holiday homes, a simple villa on a secluded ledge semi-encircled by woodland. Surprisingly, it had not been vandalized during the phase of vengeful violence that followed Albania's emancipation. Hydajet saw its lack of security precautions as a measure of Enverism's successful population control.

Sokol's grandfather had been at school – and even shared a desk – with Hoxha; in 1991 the eleven-year-old grandson made a tidy sum selling copies of a unique school group photograph to the international press. Like many of their generation, my companions had no sense of history – only a flock of muddled myths about Albania's past fluttering around in their minds. As we strolled past buildings erected by the Italians between the World Wars, these were described as 'hundreds of years old'.

When Mr Kelmedi (Pukë's plutocrat) invited us to an evening meal Sokol for some reason declined the invitation. Seven-foot-high brick walls enclosed the Kelmedis' palatial new bungalow in its large garden where an armed guard lurked in the shrubbery. The parquet flooring had been over-varnished and the Italian furniture was trendy, expensive and memorably ugly. Mr Kelmedi offered Scotch whisky, London gin, Spanish sherry, Italian wines and was puzzled when I expressed a preference for Albanian beer. At first the conversation centred on my possible role as a stimulant for Irish investment in Albania. Perhaps I knew someone who might be interested in going into partnership with my host to develop commercial orchards around Pukë? When I explained that I don't move in such influential circles, that I live in a little town devoid of multinational tycoons, the Kelmedis looked nonplussed. Hydajet translated: 'When they saw you on TV they thought you were important.'

As we ate, Mr Kelmedi asked why the West so opposed independence for Kosovo when they seemed to favour it for Montenegro – with not much more than one quarter of Kosovo's population. I agreed that in this case 'the West's' motivation was obscure, then added that in fact there is no such *political* monolith, with united policies, but only a dissent-ridden hotchpotch of governments and institutions. The real monolith is corporate.

Our meal was the best part of that evening, cooked by Mrs Kelmedi, simple but delicious: a thin herby fish soup, rice and kebabs with an interesting salad (so interesting I could identify few of the ingredients) and a syrupy Turkish pastry pudding.

Pukë's only bus (second-hand, donated by the Swiss government and seeming incongruously affluent) took four and a half hours to negotiate the fifty-five miles to Kukës. This stretch of the Via Publica had deteriorated so perilously that foreign vehicles were then being advised not to use it. However, it would have presented no threat to a cyclist and I felt grievously thwarted as we climbed out of and descended into profound river gorges separating desolate mountains, their summits too often invisible from a bus seat. Occasional gigantic pylons marred this wildest of Europe's landscapes. We stopped only once, in a grisly small town whose roofless factories had been wrecked by starving workers in January 1991 as the old system and its economy collapsed. Here my strolling up and down the street provoked some inexplicably hostile glances. The shops were either closed or half-empty and the pavement stalls offered very little of anything, yet white satellite dishes marked almost every flat in each grim decaying block. As we all returned to our seats the bus driver – a kindly man of a blessedly cautious temperament – presented me with a 'juice' which politeness compelled me to drink. He then indicated that I should throw the empty carton towards the verge . . .

From a height the new Kukës is visible on the shore of a new lake covering more than eight square miles. The old Kukës has been at the bottom of that lake since 1976 when the Fierzë hydro-electric dam, on the Drin river, flooded its valley. James Pettifer notes: 'Kukës is a good centre for fishing and walking in the surrounding mountains but many visitors may prefer to wait until social and political conditions in the area are more settled before attempting to do either.'

In view of those social conditions, Sokol had asked the driver not only to deliver me to the Hotel Gjalica in the town centre but to escort Ruairi into the hotel. My arrival, wheeling Ruairi along a narrow hallway to the cramped reception cubicle, sent the numerous (rather unfriendly) staff into shock. In the Balkans one usually pays on departure and the tariff includes breakfast; here, DM75 were instantly demanded, an exorbitant charge for a damp, grubby bed, a waterless bathroom and no breakfast.

Perhaps the old Kukës had character; as a settlement it dated from Illyrian times. Then the Romans arrived in a small way, making it an overnight stop at a road junction. The southern road, now vanished, joined the famous Via Egnatia from Durrës to Constantinople, one of the Roman Empire's most important highways. Under the Ottomans Kukës became an insignificant market centre on the Shkodra–Prizren trade route but Turkish influence remained minimal. The twentieth century saw the town's status raised by a notch or two, firstly as King Zog's regional *gendarmerie* headquarters, then as a base for those legendary British SOE officers who supported Tito's Partizans from 1943 to 1945.

In the 1970s the Fierzë hydro-electric scheme brought an unprecedented cash flow into the region, stimulating a rare enthusiasm for Enverism and its planned economy. This led to much civil strife as the tyrant's system fell and the nearby Kalimash chrome mine, a major source of jobs, was closed. More unrest occurred in 1992 when it seemed the new government had forgotten its pre-election promises concerning the highly combustible issues of land compensation and reform. Some peasants had already been given cultivable plots, and ownership of their homes and outbuildings, but most state farms were left unused, forcing thousands to emigrate. Had all the state land been redistributed in 1992–3, Albania would now be much less poor. Miranda Vickers and James Pettifer have noted: 'As Albanians struggle to find enough cash to buy imported Greek fruit and olives, hundreds of thousands of olive and citrus trees have been abandoned.'

Since 1992 the population of Kukës, and its extensive, almost roadless hinter-land, has been steadily dwindling. This is among the few regions where Enverist provocateurs can still stir trouble, as they did in May 1994. Then representatives of 200 families displaced by the dam, and never compensated for their submerged properties, went on hunger strike, occupied the municipal building, blocked all its approach roads and eventually were dealt with, brutally, by the police. Things got so out of hand that Tirana took fright, President Berisha summoned the govern-ment to an emergency session and Premier Meksi instructed the authorities to grant all the reasonable demands of the displaced and dispossessed. However, he dismissed some demands as 'absurd and unaffordable' and six years later I heard angry complaints about the wide application of those adjectives.

Having locked Ruairi in my room I went walkabout and noted how quickly a modern town can come to look and feel derelict. My memory of Kukës is of a place uniformly grey. The cafés were few and subdued, the larger business prem-ises had long since been closed, the small shops opened only sporadically. Serious trading happened in a muddy, smelly, disorganized marketplace, its trestles shaded by the ubiquitous UN blue tarpaulins – relics of Kukës's brief exposure to the inter-national spotlight when tens of thousands of refugees were camped all around.

On the bleak shore of the lake (very obviously artificial) stands the imposing Mosque of Salim Ben Mahfuz, a 1995 gift from Egypt, all blue crenelated con-crete and airy open terraces. It seems to have gone astray; one feels it should be surrounded by hot sand and date palms. Instead, as I turned back towards the town, the famous *Bora* suddenly sprang up – a gusty gale-force wind peculiar to this corner of the Balkans. It brought masses of purple-black cloud sweeping over the Vikut summit and moments later icy rain drove me into the OSCE building.

There a pleasant surprise awaited me. The Director, Jim, was a compatriot who promptly invited me to stay; he held the Hotel Gjalica in low esteem and the OSCE offices-cum-residence had three spare bedrooms. Accepting his invitation for the following night, I wished I hadn't already booked into the Gjalica. But then I might never have met Ibrahim and Migjen, my fellow-guests, with whom I talked for hours in the dreary hotel restaurant. For some reason they did not want to be seen associating with a foreigner in the more congenial – to me – surroundings of a café.

Ibrahim – aged thirty-four, an ex-teacher employed by a Tirana UN agency – was in Kukës 'to write a report'. His twenty-nine-year-old cousin, Migjen, had emigrated to America during Tirana's 1991 riots. He was visiting Europe to gather material for his thesis on 'The Uses and Abuses of Humanitarian Aid to the Balkans'. On this subject the cousins did not think alike.

Said Migjen, 'In 1992 armed gangs were regularly looting Red Cross food trucks. Hoards of starving people – all sorts, not only peasants – were raiding food aid storage centres. In Durrës port between 2,000 and 2,500 tonnes of EC food aid were unloaded every day for the Italians' humanitarian mission, "Operation Pelican", organized to stop Albanians invading and ransacking Italy. The frozen meat from EC dumps was so old it poisoned hundreds who didn't know how to defreeze. Between all the aid agencies, 800 tonnes of medical supplies, bedding, footwear, garments were handed out monthly. But gangs grabbed most of it for sale on Tirana's black market. You can't run a rescue mission like that without basic roads, bridges, telecommunications and some sort of police control and local administration. It's possible . . . '

'You're wrong!' interrupted Ibrahim. 'Look at the size of the problem – those guys did a great job in a short time. What would have happened without them? How many would have died of hunger, cold, disease? OK, the gangs grabbed a lot – but it was *there* in the country, and the people who bought it *needed* it. We're not talking about luxury items. You weren't here, you don't know how much our situation improved for a while. In '94 the Italians went home and most NGOs pushed off to Bosnia. It wasn't the aid agencies' fault the pyramids collapsed. It was our fault we were back by '97 to square one – or square zero.'

At that stage I went off to hunt for another round of beers and eventually tracked down three waiters and three chamber-maids watching TV in the manager's office. When the adolescent waiter tried to overcharge me by 100 per cent Ibrahim angrily reprimanded him. Then he turned to me and declared, 'We've lost our identity! This is not how real Albanians treat guests!' He gestured in the general direction of the lake. 'You see how Kukës is now – not the real Kukës, that's under the water, destroyed twenty-five years ago. Albanians are the same, destroyed after years submerged in fear and hate and no compensation now for lost pride. We don't believe in Albania any more, we just want to escape, to anywhere. Peasants risk their lives – often lose them – trying to get past the border guards to Greece or Italy. People with education would kill – sometimes do – to get to the West. We hated that man so much we seem now to hate Albania, not to trust ourselves. We're not able to believe in our country's future because of its past. Can you understand?'

'I'm trying,' I replied, 'but it's hard. Somehow Albania's experience seems disconnected from anything else I've encountered. I don't mean worse, many others have suffered even more and for longer. But different . . .'

'We were always different,' said Ibrahim quickly and proudly. 'We never really belonged to Europe, or anywhere. We were Albanians – that's it! Yes there were influences: Greek, Turkish, Italian, Slav, I've read about them all in English books. But we stayed alone, they were only on the outside, not getting into us to change us.'

Ibrahim and Migjen shared Jim's strongly held opinion that I should have ignored local advice and reported my misadventures to the Pukë police. Ten days previously an aid worker driving alone on the same road in an NGO landcruiser had had her windscreen shattered by stones and was then physically restrained while children robbed the vehicle of everything portable. (I might have recognized those children.) She, too, had failed to report this much more serious crime. Yet, as Ibrahim rightly observed, 'If foreigners don't show they expect the police to do a good job, the OSCE is wasting its time here.'

The OSCE's regional mandate was to supervise the performance of the Albanian police and the Italian K-For troops in charge of cross-border security, and to report daily to Vienna, by e-mail, on the local crime rate. Migjen wondered what those daily reports achieved, apart from enabling some bureaucrat in Vienna to compile statistics, carefully tabulated, about the nature and number of crimes committed in a remote district of Albania.

The OSCE employs many well-paid thousands, often on such short-term contracts that their contributions to projects are rendered almost useless. And they enjoy diplomatic status perks, to the chagrin of some NGO workers. However, the Kukës folk, Ibrahim claimed, know they will be listened to by the OSCE if they report crimes – as they may not be listened to by their own police. And the police know the OSCE has some influence in Tirana regarding promotion and demotion.

'That's very important,' said Migjen. 'Last month an area director – he's from Germany – had two senior officers sacked: one for blackmail, one for drug-dealing. He told me he wasn't too scared about retaliation, they live so far away from his base. But it was a brave thing for him to do – this is a very small country. Last week we saw a reverse case, two newly-appointed police chiefs assassinated for being too efficient and honest. They'd got their jobs after the OSCE insisted and gave the government a lot of hassle. What's most unpopular is the big push to stop the stolen car trade and have all cars registered and licensed.'

Another important step towards reform, said Ibrahim, would be salary increases. Senior officers received only US$400 monthly, juniors less than US$100.

While doing his research in Priština Migjen had been shocked by the number of Albanian men who were masquerading as Kosovar refugees and living off their wits, plus aid.

'For this you need to be clever,' remarked Ibrahim. 'I mean *clever*, not educated. The educated don't need to pretend, they get jobs with aid organizations and make foreign friends who can help them get visas and work permits.'

'Is that your plan?' asked Migjen.

For a moment Ibrahim stared at him in silence, leaning forward across the table. Then he said, 'So you don't know your cousin! I hate Albania the way it is so I'll be staying around to change it. I'll be around long after you've gone back to America!'

Until dawn the *Bora* blustered. At 9.30 – the street gutters still running with grey rainwater – I wheeled Ruairi OSCE-wards under a low untidy sky of ragged grey clouds. For this quarter-mile journey I hadn't bothered securing the pannier-bags: they were hanging from the carrier by their top clips.

Less than fifty yards from the OSCE gate, and twenty yards from a pair of traffic police on duty at a junction, I felt Ruairi suddenly lose weight and looked around to see a boy aged twelve or thirteen sprinting away with my rain-cape under one arm and a pannier swinging from the other hand. A dozen witnesses were standing nearby, outside a huxter's shop; frantically I appealed for help – obviously I couldn't myself pursue the thief, abandoning Ruairi. Nobody moved, though the boy ran past several men who could easily have intercepted him before he disappeared between two blocks. Presumably he had dared to rob me in broad daylight in the town centre only because he knew any witnesses would be on his side.

Moments later I was in the OSCE hallway yelling – 'Jim! I've been robbed again!'

For an instant Jim thought I was joking – then he swung into action as only a retired Gardai Special Squad officer could. Within five or six minutes the entire OSCE staff had been mobilized. Two Land Rovers were driving at speed up the rough laneway between the blocks, with Jim in the lead. And Astrid, a charming young woman from Tirana, had radioed the police headquarters, another thirty yards up the same street.

The police response was a familiar one: before they could take any action I must make a full statement, signed and witnessed, giving a detailed description of all the missing items. Astrid looked apologetic but unsurprised. Jim had anticipated this and left Martin to accompany me to the Criminal Department – Martin (also from Tirana) being the OSCE's special liaison officer with the police. In the headquarters' entrance hall we pushed our way through a large unruly crowd of tense-looking men with passport problems. An officer directed us to a small office, ill-lit by a grimy window and furnished only with a little table and one chair. After a ten-minute delay, during which I seethed with impatient rage, the Chief of the Criminal Department arrived, shook hands cordially, removed his overcoat and seated himself behind a manual typewriter to take down my statement, very slowly, with two fingers. He spoke no English and along the way asked many questions – not all relevant. This seemed a lowly task for one of his rank but it transpired that most of the local police were only semi-literate. Then the Chief decided that he needed a second copy; I must have one, that was the proper procedure. My suggestion that we should photocopy it in the OSCE office clearly offended his professional and/or national pride. At which point Astrid arrived, bright-eyed and breathless, with the news that four small boys had brought the pannier to the OSCE gate and were waiting there for a 'reward'.

I felt quite dizzy with relief; the loss of that pannier would have spancelled the rest of my journey. As we hastened to the gate Martin instructed me (unnecessarily) to give no reward – but not to refuse it before checking the bag's contents. The children's implausible yarn deceived nobody. Happening to glance out of their schoolroom window, they had seen an unknown boy throwing the bag into bushes and promptly got their teacher's permission to retrieve it. But who, seeing a worn old bag being discarded, would suspect it of containing anything worth retrieval? (Like a £300 tent and other equipment to the value of some £260.) Examining the contents, while the boys (all younger than the thief) stood smiling and expectant, I found many items missing: my heavy-duty cycling trousers, thermal underwear, a shirt, torch, repair kit, belt, spoon and fork. Everything had been thoroughly searched for cash, then the tent and space-blanket (probably both baffled the thief) had been stuffed back clumsily. And what about my raincape, for which I had recently paid £55? (It was very state-of-the-art.) The boys' smiles faded as Martin spoke sternly to them. Then their blond, blue-eyed leader muttered something and they scuttled away. 'Maybe you'll get something else back,' said Martin. 'They didn't expect robbing a cyclist would bring Jim's flying squad on their heels.'

Three hours later the boys reappeared with my trousers minus the incongruously fancy belt I had bought in Sarajevo from a pathetic Chinese hawker. Although so blatantly the thief's accomplices, they were still cheekily demanding a reward and the gate guard had to get quite tough before they sullenly moved off. I was reminded of an incident recorded by James Pettifer: 'In 1993 the BBC sent a World Service publicity bus to travel around Albania promoting the newly-restored service. The inhabitants of Kukës appeared bemused by the BBC bus which was besieged by children and adults alike, desperate to grab publicity pens and other material and appearing to mis-identify the bus as an aid truck. Staff were obliged to lock the doors and make a hasty retreat.'

That afternoon Jim again came to my rescue. Nowhere in the Balkans, at that date, was there any hope of replacing my stolen map, and Kukës is not (or was not then) within telephonic reach of the outside world. However, Jim nobly put the OSCE e-mail system at my disposal and luckily my publisher's e-mail address had been scribbled on the cover of my journal at the last moment. John Murray VII could therefore be pressed into service as many John Murrays have been, by many travellers, throughout the centuries. (The twenty-first century is the fourth to be graced by a John Murray.) Jim warned me that e-mails from Kukës do not always do what they are supposed to do so I crossed my fingers and toes while begging John to send a replacement map to the OSCE head office in Priština.

To celebrate the recovery of most of my stolen goods, which would certainly not have been recovered without Jim's Rapid Reaction Force, I invited the OSCE team out for an evening meal. On our way to the American Bar we met the Police Chief and the Chief of the Criminal Department who asked me into their headquarters for a coffee. Instead, I asked them to join our party and a good time was had by all. 'The American Bar' is a misnomer; one couldn't imagine anything less American than this simple wood and stone restaurant where delicious fish meals are served after a long alcoholic interval. The Chiefs were keen to impress me with their detection skills – unused, in my case. I was tempted to ask why no effort had been made to arrest the thief, whose identity was certainly known. But such a tiresome question might have marred this celebratory occasion.

Jim insisted on driving me to Prizren; he was not, I intuited, averse to escaping, however briefly, from Kukës. As it was Easter holiday time Astrid and Martin came too. The road from Kukës to the border is plagued by armed gangs – often KLA (Rtd) – who commonly leave their victims standing by the wayside in their underpants (or lying dead by the wayside, if they have been foolishly uncooperative). But expat vehicles are rarely attacked.

Here the landscape is still mountainous, but these are comparatively gentle mountains and their lower slopes and shallow fertile valleys sustain several villages. Groups of women, not often assisted by a man, were preparing the slopes for planting, turning over the heavy intractable soil with short spades. Occasionally burnt-out vehicles by the wayside defaced this pastoral scene. And in several fields huge craters marked the spots where Nato bombs had fallen on the wrong side of the border. Given the Alliance's cosy relationship with Tirana, these are no doubt known as 'friendly bombs'.

Soon we came to the border post, manned (and womanned) by German K-For troops, Ghanaian and Nepalese UN Police and sundry other IC representatives, all bristling with arms. Jim waved his diplomatic passport and we zoomed past half-a-dozen queuing vehicles into Kosovo, where canary-yellow tape fences enclosed minefields.

This premature departure saddened me – I had been so looking forward to a month amidst Albania's mountains. Yet I also felt a sense of relief; landmines and unexploded cluster bombs are easier to avoid than juvenile criminals.

14

In and around Prizren

When the Serbian and Montenegrin armies seized Kosovo in 1912, at the end of the First Balkan War, some 20,000 Kosovo Albanian men, women and children were slaughtered and countless thousands fled. A year later, during the Second Balkan War – when the victors of the First were fighting each other – rumours of extreme savagery caused the American Carnegie Endowment to send a commission to the battlefield to investigate what was really going on. Its much-quoted report included

> . . . whole villages reduced to ashes, unarmed and innocent populations massacred *en masse*, incredible acts of violence, pillage and brutality of every kind – such were the means which were employed and are still being employed by the Serbo-Montenegrin soldiery, with a view to the entire transformation of the ethnic character of the regions inhabited exclusively by Albanians.

In 1915 the Kosovars took their revenge when the defeated Serbian army was retreating to the Adriatic coast via Kosovo, Montenegro and Albania. Three years later the survivors of that army accompanied the victorious allies northwards, reoccupied Kosovo and in November 1918 set fire to hundreds of homes, destroyed grain stores and livestock and massacred many more thousands. (Nobody recorded exactly how many.) Subsequently the Kingdom of the Serbs, Croats and Slovenes (known as Yugoslavia from 1929, and which rapidly became a royal dictatorship) assisted more than 70,000 Serbs and Montenegrins to settle in Kosovo and broke a promise to compensate the dispossessed Kosovars, leaving them with no option but to emigrate. The majority went to Turkey. Noel Malcolm has estimated that between 90,000 and 150,000 left during the interwar decades.

In 1937 Vaso Čubrilović, a widely respected Belgrade historian, gave some advice to his government in a paper entitled 'The Expulsion of the Arnauts' (Kosovars). Dismissing the colonization scheme as inadequate, he wrote:

> The only way to cope with them is the brute force of an organised State. If we do not settle accounts with them at the proper time, within 20–30 years we shall have to cope

with a terrible irredentism, the signs of which are already apparent and which will inevitably put all our southern territories in danger . . . The law must be enforced to the letter so as to make staying intolerable for Albanians: fines, and imprisonments, the ruthless application of all police dispositions . . . There remains one more means, which Serbia employed with great practical effect after 1878, this is by burning down Albanian villages and city quarters. [A reference to the expulsion of about 100,000 Albanians from Serbia in 1887–8.]

Čubrilović conceded that France and Britain might oppose his plan but argued:

At a time when Germany can expel tens of thousands of Jews and Russia can shift millions of people from one part of the continent to another, the shifting of a few Albanians will not lead to the outbreak of a world war.

The Second World War, followed by Titoism, stymied this plan.

In July 1989, exactly two weeks after Milošević's speech at the Kosovo Polje rally to commemorate the six hundredth anniversary of the battle, I chanced to be travelling by train to Macedonia to visit my daughter, then living in Skopje. From Belgrade southwards I shared a carriage with two Kosovar university students who had grown up in that uneasy decade when Yugoslavia's economy was in decline and Serbian ultra-nationalism was gaining strength. On the basis of Milošević's utterances over the past two years, those young men foretold in outline what would happen to Kosovo during the 1990s. Not knowing that the JNA would be otherwise engaged from 1991 to 1995, they expected heavy repression sooner than it came and predicted, without enthusiasm, the emergence of a guerrilla movement, a direct descendant of past resistance movements supported by certain elements in Albania and abroad. Rather to my surprise, they were not thirsting for independence; were Kosovo's autonomy fully restored, and the Serbs off their backs, they would be happy to remain Yugoslavs as well as Kosovars.

Both young men were proud of having joined the miners' famous fifty-mile march, from Trepča to Priština and back, during the previous November – part of Kosovo's answer to the rabble-rousing rallies Milošević was then organizing all over Serbia. Week after week he presented the Kosovars as the Serbs' chief enemies: rapists, poisoners of wells, stealthy murderers of children, desecraters of monasteries, violent savages uncontrollable by any non-military means. The miners' march brought hundreds of thousands of Kosovars on to all the region's roads; by day and by night they marched, through snow and ice, quietly and purposefully – one of their purposes being to prove to the world that they were capable of the non-violent resistance preached by Dr Ibrahim Rugova. This was an angry population yet not one incident of destruction or vandalism or assault marred their protest against the abolition of Kosovo's autonomy. They carried huge pictures of Tito, waved Albanian and Yugoslavian flags symbolically tied together and chanted their praise of the 1974 constitution which had given them, for the first time in their history, genuine self-rule and the right of veto in the Yugoslav federation of six republics and two provinces. The withdrawal of Kosovo's and Vojvodina's autonomy in fact destroyed the federation as a legally constituted entity, which momentous development went largely unnoticed by the outside world. This, ironically, was the last time (in Priština of all places, in 1988!) that a pro-Tito, pro-Yugoslavia demonstration was held.

During 1990–91 what had been autonomous Kosovo was taken apart: the administration dismantled, the security forces and police disarmed, industrial enterprises and all public property taken over by Belgrade, the mass media brought to the Serbian heel. All Kosovars employed by the management bodies of cultural institutions and social sector firms were dismissed and the Albanian language department of Priština University was closed down. Readers interested in the details of what happened next are directed to Appendix II.

As an introduction to Kosovo, Prizren misleads. An old town of great charm, it escaped major war damage and looked bright, clean and cheerful. Its streets were lined with cafés, ice-cream parlours, small *lokantas* serving delicious Turkish food and restaurants catering for expats and the local élite. On those warm spring evenings its citizens, young and old, enjoyed their *korzo* by the little Prizrenska Bistrica river – the young, at dusk, spontaneously forming groups to dance their national dances in front of the imposing Sinan Pasha mosque. Opposite this, across the river, is the pleasant four-storey Hotel Theranda. The Romans of course were here, their town called Theranda.

Young German K-For troops, heavily armed and assertive, controlled the traffic – not difficult – and had occasional confrontations with their local contemporaries. On my first night I heard and saw two youths, who had broken the midnight to 6 a.m. curfew and cheeked K-For, being beaten up under my window. That same night a bar store-room was looted and, as I breakfasted next morning, the waiter derided the Turkish UN police who had witnessed the crime but done nothing.

During the thirteenth and fourteenth centuries, when Kosovo was at the geographical centre of the Serbian state, the Nemanjićs' kingdom extended into Montenegro, and across northern Albania, and Prizren was an important trading centre on the route from the Adriatic. Its flourishing colony of Ragusan merchants probably built the Catholic church and from the 1330s to the 1380s Prizren was the seat of a Catholic bishopric, one of those bishops being an Englishman from Nottinghamshire.

The Nemanjić kings constructed the Ribnik, a mighty fortress on a long, high, green ridge overlooking the town. Landmine warnings deterred me from fully exploring the ruins – KLA-laid landmines, said the locals, because Serbs would otherwise have used the fort as a safe sniper base for aiming at Kosovar homes on the slopes below. But now those mines endanger Kosovar children who, ignoring the warnings, take their goats to graze amidst the chunks of fallen masonry.

From Ribnik, a strange three-peaked mountain is conspicuous to the west. This was once the site of an annual two-day festival, celebrating the Assumption of the Virgin Mary, which for centuries attracted pilgrims of all religions. Noel Malcolm quotes a 1681 visitation report of the Catholic Bishop of Skopje, Pjeter Bogdani: 'They spend all the night there, with drums, whistles, dancing and singing – Muslims, Serbians and Greeks . . . walk round the peak of the highest mountain for three hours in bare feet (with some of the leading Muslims on horseback).'

Like Ireland's Croagh Patrick pilgrimage, this celebration seems to have had pagan roots. At dawn the Bishop celebrated Mass on the summit, preaching to his mixed congregation in Albanian, then lunched with Prizren's Orthodox Bishop.

The town's most famous church is Sv Bogorodica, built 700 years ago on the site of an earlier basilica and one of King Milutin's forty-two foundations. (Milutin has the unique distinction, among Serbian kings, of having made it into Dante's Divine Comedy, as the scorned counterfeiter of Venetian silver coins contaminated with a base metal.) This church's exterior is an extraordinary blend of Greek, Serbian and Romanesque, with five cupolas and a belfry. Like all Kosovo's Orthodox churches in this embittered era, it was surrounded by razor-wire and guarded twenty-four hours a day by K-For soldiers perched on an APC. A large notice proclaimed 'KFOR AREA!' and warned in German, English, Albanian and Serbo-Croat: 'Prohibited area! Danger, authorized use of firearms.' Presumably this meant K-For troops were authorized to fire on anybody who ventured beyond the razor-wire. When I asked one of the surly youths atop the APC if tourists could get permission to enter he snapped, 'Kosovo is no more a tourist zone!'

As J.A. Cuddon was visiting Sv Bogorodica in 1967 he made an observation most poignant from the 2000 perspective:

> Two elderly Albanian tribesmen came in [and] spent a long time there, strolling round, looking at the frescoes and discussing them . . . I was much impressed by their reverence and sense of propriety and the proudly unassuming way in which they viewed works of art alien to their religion yet a cherished element of their past.

Those men were closer in spirit to the Assumption festival of 1681 than to contemporary Kosovo.

On Easter Saturday morning long processions of jolly schoolchildren, wearing bright green aprons and blue peaked caps, marched around the town centre. Their many banners bore prayers for peace – 'Bless all who live in harmony' – and environmental exhortations – 'Plant more saplings for our Kosovo!', 'Keep

Kosovo clean!' There were also grateful messages – 'Thank you INTERNATIONAL COMMUNITY! Now We Must Help Ourselves!' A young Albanian-American woman informed me that this was the UN's Earth Day, the launching of a 'Greening of Kosovo' campaign to end on 5 June – Environment Day. Every week local companies would sponsor street-washing and each member of UNMIK's staff had donated DM20 to buy saplings to plant along the river. One wearies of the UN's plethora of 'Days' but this particular campaign made a lot of sense and Prizren was looking the better for it.

The Albanian-American, Rebeca, and her Tirana-born colleague Rosa were treating themselves to an unauthorized Easter break in Prizren – unauthorized because their US NGO employer forbade staff to enter Kosovo. 'That's neurotic!' said Rebeca. 'When you're posted to Albania you gotta get out! And Prizren – after Tirana Prizren is like Manhattan!'

I saw her point. Kukës and Prizren – only thirty miles apart – could be on different continents. It was hard to believe that twelve months previously the airwar had made most of Prizren's residents refugees. Albania received the majority and they had brought back mixed memories. One woman expressed it graphically: 'The people in front of you were giving and sharing so much it made you cry, while the people behind you were all the time trying to steal the few things you'd brought from home.'

Rebeca and Rosa worked for some hare-brained NGO which was sending retired American farmers ('all very good Christians') to teach Albanian farmers how to grow vegetables (mainly onions!) more efficiently. One despairs of these patronizing though well-meaning projects, being set up all over the Poor World by ignorant zealots.

Both young women referred to their families having been seriously injured by the pyramid crashes. However, Rebeca argued that no one could be blamed for investing. She had put in US$500 and six months later taken out $1,500. 'Then I kept it out – I knew a World Bank guy working in Tirana and he told me it was all shit. But if you'd nobody to tell you, sure you'd go on putting more and more in with that sort of profit.'

This was the twenty-year-old Rosa's first venture outside Albania and she seemed rather uneasily in awe of her Americanized colleague who smiled openly at passing men and used words like 'shit'. When I sought her opinion about a Greater Albania, incorporating Kosovo, she replied, 'Maybe only quarter of us want it. The rest of us are afraid of the Kosovars – they have too many links with international crime. Unity would make our security situation even worse.'

Later, several Kosovars were to give me the same reason, in reverse, for their not being keen to join Albania. Rebeca believed there was no general enthusiasm in favour of a Greater Albania because both peoples feared 'unification' would mean having to share donated goodies.

By this time a local journalist had joined us at our café table on the hotel terrace. He informed me, 'Eighty percent of Kosovo's population is still depending on regular humanitarian aid, only twenty percent have jobs. Most don't want independence, we'll need K-For's protection for at least thirty, maybe fifty years.'

I wondered then (to myself) 'Are those observers right, who argue the present régime suits Kosovo's *mafia*?' In a constitutional and legal limbo they can receive international sustenance while operating freely, emboldened by their 'protectors'' aversion to body-bags.

That afternoon I again ambled through the steep, narrow, cobbled laneways of ancient Prizren, the quarter below Ribnik where high walls conceal brown-tiled Ottoman dwellings in tree-shaded courtyards, entered through nail-studded double doors. Outside most doors are stone mounting-blocks, rubbed smooth by generations of boots. Here the only damaged buildings were Serbs' homes, attacked post-airwar by Kosovar returnees. As I stood gazing at one half-burnt house, a man in his forties approached and asked, 'Are you a journalist? I saw you writing and writing outside the hotel – you come from UK?' When I had explained myself, Naim invited me to 'drink coffee'. He was a small nimble man with black receding hair and an aquiline nose; he wore corduroys and a green polo-necked sweater.

In Naim's 'Turkish' home we sat in a spacious first-floor room, its brick walls whitewashed, a long, low divan running below the windows, overlooking central Prizren. My host smiled when I admired the tall carved cupboards for storing bedding, the burnished brassware hanging along one wall, the leather-covered ottomans, the low ornamental wooden tables, the faded goat's hair carpet – 'locally woven and dyed,' explained Naim. 'But now those arts and crafts are not valued. To be fashionable we must import.'

Naim prepared the coffee himself; his wife, an UNMIK translator, was doing overtime that weekend.

Returning from the kitchen, Naim laid a pewter tray on one of those low tables and said, 'I talked to you because you looked so sad, staring at that burnt house. And I feel so sad myself, I thought maybe we could be sad together.'

As Naim paused and poured our coffees I felt some reply was needed and said feebly, 'It's not just Prizren – the Balkans generally has become so sad-making. Especially for those who can remember Tito's Yugoslavia.'

'Yet I shouldn't be complaining,' continued Naim as though I hadn't spoken. 'People think I'm lucky. Myself and my wife have jobs good enough to feed and educate our children. And I can get promotion. But I don't want to stay here, Kosova's not now real for me. Most people are happy being protected by K-For, UNMIK, OSCE – they only want no more Serbs, they don't think about what it means to be a "protectorate". You could say we were an Ottoman protectorate for 500 years – without the present perks. But that was different. The Turks didn't smash our Albanian culture and we absorbed a lot of theirs – look around this room! Most of our best brains went to Constantinople and got top jobs with the Porte, helping to run the empire. Albanians didn't have to feel inferior the way we do now. If I must live as people do in the West I want to be in the West, not in the ruins of my own culture watching it fall to bits under pressure from outside. My job now is collaborating with the protectorate and I don't like it. If I migrate with my family I'll have some small job – I won't be as important as I am in Prizren. But I can begin again, be myself. Now I'm not myself, working for a system I can't respect. If we had leaders who could take us into a really independent Kosova I would never want to leave – I only want to leave because I love my home place too much.'

I said, 'You have my sympathy, my own small country has recently lost most of its identity. But could a really independent Kosovo work? If Serbia had a civilized government, wouldn't you be better off with your autonomy restored? It's not so long since the Trepča miners were marching against Milošević carrying the Yugoslav and Albanian flags entwined.'

Naim lit another cigarette and said, 'A few months after that march Milošević's tanks crushed Titoism in Kosova. A Federal Republic of Yugoslavia without Slovenia, Croatia, Bosnia, Macedonia – what is it but Serbia under another name? No more autonomy! Only fools could believe it would be genuine, like before. When we set up our parallel state in '90 we proved we could run an improvised economy on our own. It was exciting to see what we could do. Milošević thought when he sacked 70 per cent of employed Albanians they'd mostly migrate. Instead they opened more than a thousand shops and mini-markets and set up wholesale networks. A few months later the private sector had taken over the supplying of goods – and cafés, restaurants, travel agencies, transport. Civil servants who'd been paid about US$100 a month could make three times that much. Sacked miners and policemen and factory workers registered hundreds of vehicles and took over public transport in and between towns – and got it so well-organized and cheap the state-run services nearly went bankrupt. Money from abroad helped – about 25,000 Kosovars were working in Western Europe. Also rich Albanian-Americans supported our parallel education system. And people here gave 3 per cent monthly from their earnings as a voluntary tax. By '95 we were educating more than 300,000 junior school pupils and nearly 60,000 in sixty-five secondary schools. We ran two schools for the handicapped and twenty small colleges for more than 12,000 third-level students. I don't pretend academic standards were high but we were proving we wouldn't be demoralized. Now between the "Protectorate" and the KLA *mafia* our skills and initiative are being discouraged. We're getting like an African country, sitting back waiting for help. I was not for independence till '97, I'm not really a nationalist. I hoped Rugova's non-violence could work but no one took him seriously – only force works! For years I was deceiving myself and now I see the reality I want to run away from it.'

· I said, 'But the threat to Kosovo's culture isn't unusual. All over the world small countries – and big ones too – are being homogenized. We're told the majority everywhere want "globalization" – which of course is untrue. Most people have no choice, don't know what's hitting them.'

Swiftly Naim replied, 'But most countries have governments to defend their own traditions – Kosova's helpless!'

On this issue I had the last word. 'When the globalizers pounce, governments provide no defence. Politicians are easily subverted.'

We talked on until sunset, mainly about the controversy surrounding the Serbian state's legal claim to Kosovo. Repeatedly the region was forgotten when various treaties were being signed, but not ratified by all parties: the London Treaty of 1913, the Treaty of Bucharest (also 1913), the 1914 Treaty of Istanbul, the 1920 Treaty of Sèvres, the 1925 Treaty of Ankara. In 1925 Turkey did recognise Kosovo as part of Yugoslavia – but not of Serbia.

Naim insisted on escorting me downhill through the twilight, then introduced me to a brother-in-law who invited me to supper and later confided his theory about Naim's wish to emigrate. That burnt Serb home belonged to a lifelong friend and professional colleague – but Naim's adolescent son had led the gang of arsonists in August 1999.

The Theranda Hotel overlooks two short, narrow bridges, less than a hundred yards apart. On the newish one a pair of unmanned APCs were permanently parked – ugly incongruous intrusions on Prizren's mellow symmetry. ('A traffic calming measure,' replied the young German officer I questioned.) The other, Ottoman bridge is among the town's chief glories, its golden-brown stones arching gracefully over the shallow rushing Bistrica. On my way out of Prizren at sunrise on Easter Sunday I paused to photograph it, then pedalled away past unlovely administrative buildings, now occupied by UNMIK, the OSCE and the UN Police.

Naim had suggested that I go next to Peć before his brother, who would offer hospitality and 'local information', left for Germany. On the main road to Djacovica, marked 'Horse' by K-For, shell and bomb damage made the potholes seem trivial. Not far from Prizren the Albanian flag flew high above a new roadside KLA cemetery in the course of being developed as a place of pilgrimage. A kiosk selling badges, postcards and refreshments was not yet open. Gravel had recently been spread on the muddy ground between the rows of graves, each marked by a simple headstone and a framed photograph nailed to a three-foot-high stake. Enormous wreaths of artificial flowers, enclosed in transparent plastic, were piled on and around the few score mounds of earth. The home village of these young men was visible in the distance, beyond level green pastures and clumps of poplars. My binoculars showed many ruined houses, some being repaired, others being replaced. In the background rose snowy summits – the KLA's stronghold on the Albanian border.

To the local farmers Western Christendom's Easter Sunday meant nothing. By 7 a.m. many were driving to their fields on tractors old and new, some drawing trailers full of women and children clutching hoes and spades. Quite likely the new tractors were 'aid' from an Irish NGO which should have known better. In Prizren I had discussed this 'regional project' with its leader, a smooth-talking young man not long down from university with a degree in Development Studies. He looked puzzled when I queried the provision of large tractors and combine harvesters. Given the quality of the local soil, the level of the local water table, the poverty of the villages and an 80 per cent unemployment rate, would it not be more practical to provide new ploughs and draught-animals which could help to fertilize the land? How, when 'aid' disappears, will these peasants pay for fuel and maintenance? How soon will their gleaming machines be rusting in a corner or undergoing cannabilization for the benefit of those who can afford spare parts?

By now the young man was looking irritated. Sharply he reminded me, 'We're not here to push these farmers *backwards*! Besides, men here treat machines as exclusively their concern, so tractors and combines make less work for women.'

I said no more. But are we who have become so alarmingly physically lazy right to regard as penitential those tasks which for millennia have been taken for granted by cultivators on every continent?

In Priština I came upon NGOs suffering from an *embarras de richesses*. The excessive publicity focussed on Kosovar refugees (excessive given the extent of other peoples' needs) brought a tidal wave of funding to Kosovo and some NGOs found themselves hurriedly devising inappropriate projects. There could be no question, I was informed, of transferring the surplus to some region of extreme privation, like Bangladesh. The rules do not permit money donated for one area to be spent elsewhere.

All day Albania's magnificent mountains were tantalizingly close, and it didn't help that my recent abrupt separation from them had been caused, really, by my own obstinacy. Had I put aside my preference for travelling alone and acquired an Albanian escort I could probably have travelled safely to the remotest corners of the land. But would an escort have been willing to walk or cycle?

Here I was on the edge of Kosovo's central plain where the gentle landscape – arable pasture, woods – is only lightly scarred by industrialization but grossly defiled by every sort of litter: agricultural, domestic, industrial, commercial, military. It is also defiled by something invisible and far more disturbing – depleted uranium (DU). For details of Nato's use of DU, see Appendix III.

The traffic soon became a threatening medley of APC convoys, fast cars, slow tractors, racing French army jeeps, manure-laden horse-carts and wide Russian army trucks overloaded with glum-looking youths. As the vehicles swerved to avoid the deeper shell craters, or accelerated to overtake on corners, I felt my nerve going.

Near Djakovica a small wayside memorial – a flower-draped square of wood – named the fifty-six men, women and children killed here on 14 April when Nato repeatedly bombed a bona fide refugee convoy of tractor-trailers, horse-carts and cars. I remembered then the dismissive comment of a us army officer met in Sarajevo: 'Fighting an airwar, you have to make mistakes.'

On the outskirts of Djakovica I turned on to a quiet secondary road and the twenty-five miles to Klina wound through undulating farmland where poplar groves and minarets marked distant villages and small fields had high hedges, as in Ireland. For much of the way a disused – because bombed – railway line ran close to the road and a mile or so from Klina Italian troops were regulating one-way traffic across a temporary K-For-built bridge.

Klina, on the edge of the Drenica district, is known as 'the KLA's capital' – Drenica having been the main Serb versus Kosovar battleground in 1998–9. Arriving at noon, I sought lodgings but could find none. Yet here was another many-roomed OSCE base: given such an acute housing shortage, how can expats justify grabbing so much space? In this misfortunate once-industrialized town the few open cafés served no food and the shops were sold out of bread and offered nothing that could be eaten uncooked. Burst water mains – long since burst – were flooding the unpaved main street to a depth of nine or ten inches. The war damage was extreme: 31 per cent of houses completely destroyed and 27 per cent severely damaged, according to the International Management Group, the Rapid Village Assessment and various other 'shelter agencies' which together swarmed on to the scene in June 1999. (Statisticitis is endemic among aid agencies.) The population looked spaced out and the atmosphere felt uncomfortably tense with an APC parked at almost every corner. That evening in Peć a young Kosovar OSCE employee accused K-For of heightening Klina's tension by 'acting pro-Serb'. He looked baffled when I observed that a failure to protect the town's 5,600 Serbs from its 66,000 Kosovars would create tension of another sort – but not less tension, unless the elimination of all Serbs brought a harmonious homogeneity to the place.

North of Klina the placid countryside was bright with the pale green of budding beech woods, the glinting of a musical little river, the glowing of wild flower patterns on sloping pastures. But all this springtime beauty merely empha-sized the desolation of the man-made scene: fifteen harrowing miles of pastures ungrazed, villages savaged by mortar bombs and flames, mosques demolished – beside one mound of rubble lay a minaret, freakishly intact. For my generation of locals, the recent conflict must have revived ghastly childhood memories.

Hereabouts, during the Second World War, Kosovars of a vengeful disposition had an opportunity to punish those Serbs who between the wars had been planted in Kosovo by the royalist government. After April 1941 most of the province was controlled by the Italians whose 'Civil Commissioner', Carlo Umilta, later reported on what he had seen between Djakovica and Peć: ' . . . villages where not a single house has a roof, everything had been burned down . . . There are headless bodies of men and women strewn on the ground . . . The Albanians are out to exterminate the Slavs who beg passing Italian lorries to take them to safety.' The figures for that period are no more reliable than our own but at least 3,000 Serbs and Montenegrins were killed and by April 1942 more than 70,000 Serb 'displaced persons' had registered in Belgrade.

Approaching Peć, several wayside notices advertised the NGOs responsible for funding a clean-up of both town and river. Yet here I saw the ultimate in littering: at intervals along the Bistrica garbage had formed dams, flooding the banks.

Peć is an ancient town crouching at the convergence of two massive mountain ranges dramatically separated by the Rugovo Gorge. To the Serbs it is (or was) a place of enormous spiritual and emotional significance – the seat, since the fourteenth century, of their Orthodox Patriarchate. Otherwise it is of little significance, an isolated, impoverished and now uneasy town which suffered war damage comparable to Klina's. However, reconstruction was happening less slowly here and someone had given schoolchildren a morale-boosting task – to decorate many of the town centre ruins with jolly frescoes in brilliant colours. A few Ottoman corners survive, in unhappy juxtaposition to Titoesque developments, and I found myself warming to the place as I pushed Ruairi through a maze of short irregular streets, in search of Naim's brother's house; I was equipped with directions written in English and Albanian.

Unfortunately Mr Qemalit had had to change travel plans and leave for Germany that morning. Nobody else in the household spoke English but his frail elderly mother invited me in for coffee and handed me a note. It read:

> Dear Irish Woman – I regret it is not possible to spell your name. Please come back after May 7 and be my guest for as long as pleases you. Now is no room.
>
> After that date 12 of my family will be gone to Germany. Please come back.
>
> My brother has said to me you are a nice peculiar person. Yours respectfully . . .

Mr Qemalit's house was spacious but packed with thirty-seven relatives and in-laws from shattered villages. I decided then to continue to Priština next morning; I would be in Peć again on my way back to Montenegro.

The town's only surviving hotel, multi-storeyed and pretentious, was built in 1981 by the owner's father. Mr Istogu, having lived for five years in Acton, spoke perfect English and his adolescent son had a strong London accent. The Istogus

also spent some time in Tirana during the transition from Enverism – an experience about which father and son had much to say, of startling interest but not
repeatable. That was after our haggle – Mr Istogu reckoned DM100 a reasonable
charge for a cramped room and a waterless bathroom. As he wore a Rolex watch
and diamond tiepin and drove a new Volvo (registered), I suggested DM30 and we
finally agreed on 50. My only fellow-guest was a congenial Sri Lankan ICRC
official on a Balkan tour.

Elsewhere, such expensive hotels provide substantial buffet breakfasts. Here the
ration was one cup of lukewarm tea, one stale bread bun and a one-egg omelette
(a pullet's egg, at that). When the Sri Lankan diffidently asked for butter and jam
these came in airline containers and he was charged extra.

15

The Kosovo Experiment

It would have been impossible to cycle against the gale that blew me over the fifty miles from Peć to Priština in two and a quarter effortless hours. Even on slightly uphill slopes it was hardly necessary to pedal. Much of this plain is patchily wooded – beech, oak, ash, birch – and but for its garbage quota might be described as pleasant though not exciting. To this quota K-For dump-trucks were scandalously contributing, some thirty yards off the road. In the few little towns, I noticed many families engaged in DIY rebuilding.

From afar, Priština's factory chimneys and high-risery can be seen starkly prodding the sky – seeming irrelevant, this being the capital of an essentially rural province. During its autonomous phase, Kosovo lacked leaders able to guide its peasants towards some modest prosperity through increasing agricultural production. Always this region had been Yugoslavia's poorest, with an average per capita income of US$795 in 1979, when the national average was US$2,635 and the Slovenian average US$5,315. Tito insisted on wealth redistribution and in Serbia people had complained to me about the Kosovar leaders' stealing and squandering of those generous subsidies. Then in Kosovo I heard people protesting against the injustice of their province never having been allocated its fair share of Yugoslavia's wealth, much of it derived from Kosovo's Trepča mines. Whatever the truth, Tito's perceived 'pampering' of Kosovo enraged Slovenia and Croatia – why was so much of their hard-earned wealth being handed over to the lazy, thieving Shiptars? (In this context, 'Shiptar' is the equivalent of 'nigger').

On the outskirts of Priština packs of mangy feral dogs were scavenging and snarling around high mounds of household refuse. Seeing an enormous UN compound – 'Engineering Depot' – I stopped to seek advice about lodgings. A cheerful young Kosovar mechanic in oversized dungarees spoke adequate English and explained that the numbers of homeless villagers now living in the capital had doubled its population and I would be unlikely to find B&B accommodation. He then kindly wrote out a list of Priština's few hotels, added a neatly drawn street plan and recommended me to start with Hotel Dia (DM60) on the far side of the city.

That gale did nothing to enhance my first impression of Kosovo's capital;

flurries of litter whirled high above the rooftops while choking clouds of dust mingled nastily with the sweat on my face and arms. The pavement cafés were deserted and when I paused for a beer a friendly waiter invited Ruairi inside because 'There are many thieves, they try to take the shoes off your feet, be always watching!'

Priština looked much less bombed than Belgrade – or Peć. Only 4 per cent of dwellings were destroyed and 2 per cent moderately damaged. I wheeled Ruairi across the town (it's not really a city) and soon came to a wide expanse of waste-land – old rubble mingled with new grass – where two buildings, standing a hundred yards apart, brought me to a stupefied halt. One was the university library, built in 1980 and by far the ugliest building I have ever seen, anywhere. Picture an agglomeration of scores of concrete oblongs each about the size of a shipping container, with sides of dark metal grilles – all piled irregularly, some sur-mounted by smallish, greyish domes (instead of windows), the whole hideous mass being supported by squat square concrete pillars forming a sinister shadowy verandah. To compound this intrinsic ugliness, every accessible surface had been black spray-painted with Chetnik-style slogans and symbols.

When I turned towards the other building, a not-quite-finished Orthodox cathe-dral, its red brick and conventional design soothed my tortured eyes. Razor-wire surrounded it and near the sentry-box by the gateway, on a tall flagstaff, the Union Jack flapped vigorously in the gale. A lone English soldier, well-armed and very young, strolled to and fro behind the wire barrier, looking resigned. When I stopped to chat his face lit up and soon he was showing me photographs of his German fiancée: 'We'll marry in October, when I get out of this tip.' Within the cathedral a tent had been pitched by the four-man unit who guarded Priština's most provoca-tive building day and night. It was so provocative because, during the autonomy era, this land had been officially presented to Priština University as a site for various badly-needed extensions. Then came the Serbian confiscation of all Kosovo's pub-licly owned property and the erection of a new Orthodox cathedral to celebrate that takeover. The university was offered no alternative site. In an independent Kosovo – I was later informed – the cathedral would be promptly razed.

From the town centre I ascended a long, very steep street lined with small shops, derelict offices and one-storey dwellings behind high walls. It led to a semi-rural suburb where bony cows grazed in a former municipal park; morning and evening these were led to nearby houses to be milked in small front gardens or on the pavement. By then I was beginning to warm to Priština; from almost every vantage point its surrounding grassy hills are visible.

Hereabouts my street plan failed me and I approached a fair-haired middle-aged woman to ask the way to Hotel Dia. It was close, she said, at the foot of another steep hill. The sprawling pile flew two enormous flags from the rooftop: the Union Jack and the Stars and Stripes. I didn't get as far as reception; in the otherwise empty foyer sat an exceptionally off-putting character. He looked up from his laptop only for long enough to convey contempt for a cyclist and tell me, 'Our tariff is DM150, minimum.'

Back on the hilltop, I was wondering where to go next when that amiable woman reappeared, looked puzzled, then asked, 'Was the hotel full?' 'Too expensive!' I said – and at once she offered to introduce me to friends who had a half-built upper storey. If I wasn't looking for comfort I could perhaps stay there, her friends would be glad of a few extra DM; they had lost much of their property when Serbian militiamen raided their home in April 1999.

Mrs Ndrecaj led me down another steep hill – this street quiet, leafy, very respectable. Soon we passed Mr Ibrahim Rugova's unostentatious home with an electronic security system but – rather to my surprise – no armed guard. 'Mr Rugova doesn't like armed men,' said my companion. 'Good for Mr Rugova!' said I.

The Zejanullahus' detached unfinished house, set in a small flowery garden, bore the scars of that Serbian attack: bullet marks on the façade, two boarded-up windows. When Mrs Ndrecaj had explained me Vera and Feti extended a traditional Balkan welcome. Coffee was made, *rakija* poured, a tray of *burek* came warm from the oven. And Vera's sister, who lived across the road, was summoned to join us.

Feti had been a well-known professional musician in the good old autonomous days; now he was a high-school teacher earning monthly what I paid the family for five nights' accommodation – DM200. He was still mourning his beloved guitar, stolen by the militia. It had cost the equivalent of £500 in 1975 and was irreplaceable. Vera, teaching in a primary school, earned DM150 monthly. Yet this family, who could no longer afford a motor car or a telephone, seemed to have been saddened rather than embittered by their misfortunes.

A raw concrete staircase, without banisters, led to the unfinished upper storey and my tiny but adequate bedroom. The shiny new bathroom lacked water, a common Priština inconvenience at that date, but it didn't take long to fetch a pailful from a nearby standpipe. Although the modest tariff did not include meals, Vera or Feti insisted on inviting me into their living room for refreshments whenever I returned to base. During my nine days as an adopted member of this endearing family I also got to know several of their relatives and neighbours and, through them, other groups elsewhere in Priština. Soon I came to realize how much ordinary citizens were suffering from Kosovo's prevailing anarchy – and how much it grieved them when foreigners' ill-considered remarks seemed to brand all Kosovars as 'criminals'.

A chronic condition of legal chaos had been encouraging crime since the Trio (UNMIK, OSCE, K-For) took over in July 1999. At first UNMIK's chief administrator decided, as a logical consequence of accepting Yugoslavian sovereignty, to uphold those Yugoslav laws assumed to have been valid pre-OAF. However, his decision was swiftly overruled by Kosovar judges who maintained that all laws applied after the loss of Kosovo's autonomy were discriminatory and invalid. UNMIK then pronounced that those laws should nevertheless be applied while a group of 'experts' were 'considering the matter'. Meanwhile K-For was capturing hundreds of suspected murderers and other dangerous criminals and containing them in detention camps – from which the Kosovars were expeditiously released by Kosovar judges and the Serbs by Serb judges. This surprised nobody. Nato's military commanders and their political bosses well knew that without effective police support, and a normally functioning judiciary, armies cannot reduce crime to an 'acceptable' level.

If asked to put my impressions of 'Kosovo 2000' in a one-word nutshell I could only say 'unreal'. Pretence permeated the atmosphere. The pretence that all KLA members could be either disarmed or converted to a socially responsible Civil Defence Force. The pretence that the ragbag UN Police were willing and able to perform as a cohesive, disciplined unit. The pretence that the Trio could persuade the Kosovars to roll out 'WELCOME' carpets for Serb returnees, that both communities could be induced to 'co-exist and collaborate in an atmosphere of mutual tolerance'. The pretence that because the Security Council opposed an independent Kosovo it could be kept off the agenda for ever. The pretence that *one man* was the problem and post-Milošević all would be well. And the central pretence that the Trio formed a resolute, caring, united team.

The creation of this fantasy land was made possible by the UN's assumption of all administrative powers in Kosovo, Yugoslavia's sovereignty having in practice been suspended by Nato's illegal use of force – obliging the UN to delegate Nato to maintain law and order. (Readers confused by this line of reasoning may be assured that they are not alone.) Security Council Resolution 1244 required Kosovo's interim administration to prepare the province for its reincarnation as a peaceful 'multi-ethnic' democracy. This notion that outsiders could impose a régime based on genuine reconciliation between Serbs and Kosovars was an ominous example of how neo-imperialistic the Great Powers have become. Day after day Trio representatives droned on about a harmonious multi-ethnic Kosovo in which everybody would live happily ever after, forgiving and forgetting. In pursuit of this mirage, UNMIK was attempting to establish stable political and economic structures. The OSCE was attempting to set up sound legal and democratic systems and foster independent media, free of intimidation and refraining from 'incitements to hatred'. (In the Kosovo context these are often successful incitements to murder.) The Nato-led K-For was attempting to prevent armed conflict, find illegally held weapons, protect all minorities and generally guarantee 'security'. Of the three institutions, K-For seemed to many the least ineffectual. Its task was the most straightforward (though complicated by an over-developed instinct of self-preservation) and its leaders were less prone to involvement in the ferocious in-fighting which dominated the UNMIK/OSCE relationship, semi-paralysing both institutions.

The IC's humanitarian wing is slow to learn from its mistakes, usually rooted in a refusal to look beyond the 'aid crisis' effect to the political cause. Among the most notorious of such mistakes was its support for the organizers of Rwanda's genocide when they migrated, amidst hundreds of thousands of Hutu, to the refugee camps of Zaire and Tanzania. There the relevant UN agencies and countless NGOs elevated their 'neutrality' above all other considerations and allowed the genocidal leaders to run the camps, thus enabling them to reinvigorate and re-arm their soldiers. Many of those weapons, purchased with the assistance of Rich World innocents who responded generously to NGO appeals, were subsequently used to destabilize Rwanda's new government and kill uncounted thousands in the Democratic Republic of the Congo.

In Kosovo the post-conflict situation was of course much less dire, but the Trio made a similar mistake. On arrival they were hijacked by certain KLA leaders who presented themselves as the Kosovar representatives best qualified to co-operate with the new administration. Shamefully, these men were taken at face value and the competent, experienced, moderate Kosovar and Serb community leaders got no opportunity to prove their worth. Moreover – and for many this was the ultimate exasperation – the Trio perversely declined to co-operate with those units of the KLA which had the will, knowledge and capacity to assist them in a campaign against the Albanian *mafiosi*.

Apologists for the Trio point out that Resolution 1244 presented them with a uniquely daunting task: totally to reform a society and to do it *now*, with no time allocated for preliminary studies either of the background or the foreground. The Kosovo protectorate, they argue, is an experiment, the sort of thing that has to be tried out on the way to inventing a New World Order.

It is astonishing now to recall that as late as March 1998 Shkelzen Maliqi, a distinguished Kosovar polymath, could write: 'Recently the [Kosovo] Albanian population lost patience and groups calling themselves the Kosova Liberation Army began to appear. Guerrilla actions have been mounted against the Serbian police but the KLA does not seem to represent a crucial factor that could substantially change the balance of power.' Oddly, Mr Maliqi appears to have overlooked this organization's deep roots in Albanian/Kosovar history. As they went into action against Milošević's Special Forces many guerrillas sang songs celebrating the heroes of old and containing such lines as, 'If you don't die for your homeland, / You'll never rise from the dead!', 'I was taught how to shed my blood by my old grandpa!' and 'If you don't have a gun, / Attack him with your teeth!'

In Priština it can be tactless to question expats – especially Americans – about the KLA. Are they now 'terrorists' or gallant Nato allies? But a few K-For officers admitted to being exasperated by Kosovo's many political parties (actually competing clans, transformed by modern life into competing gangs) led by KLA 'heroes' who voiced strident demands for independence in lieu of outlining policies. Several of those 'heroes' were known to Interpol as mature *mafia* leaders, deep into the intercontinental drugs trade. Some of their juniors longed to emulate them and were already in the same business in a small way. When first I heard the KLA being associated with organized crime (not confined to drugs-dealing: they also traffic in girls and tobacco) I dismissed such talk as Serb propaganda. But it isn't.

A few of my new Priština friends obviously feared to discuss the KLA, but others had much to say on the subject, about which they frequently and vehemently disagreed. Many emphasized how misleading this umbrella term had become. Prolonged negotiations followed the Trio's arrival; then the KLA formally handed over to K-For 27,000 grenades, 10,000 weapons and 5.5 million rounds of ammunition. Simultaneously they announced that they were retaining, in Albania, a considerable (unspecified) proportion of their weaponry and that they wished the 5,000-strong Kosovo Protection Corps (KPC), which is led by ex-KLA officers, to be regarded as independent Kosovo's embryonic army. As one K-For officer dryly remarked to me, 'They're half disarmed and wholly rearmed.'

In October 2000, in the province's first free 'official' elections, with an 85 per cent turnout, Ibrahim Rugova's moderate party gained 58 per cent of the votes, as against 35 per cent won by three 'splinter' parties backed by various KLA factions. Shkelzen Maliqi then observed, 'The KLA might have won more votes had some of its staff been less violent and arrogant in the build-up to the polls.'

My friends also emphasized the difference between the 'professional' KLA and the 'amateur' recruits who fought only to defend their villages from Milošević's thugs. Inevitably some amateurs (usually the youngest and poorest) joined the professionals. But most such units voluntarily disbanded themselves when the Serbian forces withdrew, being interested only in picking up the pieces of their shattered family lives as best they could.

On 25 April the 'UNMIK News' announced: 'An eight-member mission of the Security Council will visit Kosovo from 27 to 30 April, in order to see first-hand the work of UNMIK in the troubled province and send a strong message on the need to reject violence. . . . The current President of the Security Council, Ambassador Robert Fowler of Canada, said the delegation wanted to observe the UN operation on the ground in order to "comprehend better the difficult challenges faced by UNMIK".'

From 27 to 30 April thousands of Kosovars proved eager to help illustrate those 'difficult challenges' by staging well-organized anti-UNMIK demos and blocking all road access to Priština for eight hours each day. Very obviously the KLA (now again an illegal organization) was helping to run this operation; all cafés, shops, offices and schools had been ordered to close. Only those cafés and restaurants favoured by expats and guarded by K-For (the 2nd Battalion of the Royal Artillery, fresh from Belfast and wishing they were back there) remained open. A *burek* shop foolish enough to defy the diktat was stripped of all its furniture and equipment after the owner had been shot dead, by two gunmen, at 3 p.m. on 28 April.

Early on the morning of 27 April I noticed the absence of motor traffic – then came upon a novel sight, at one end of Priština's main thoroughfare, recently expediently renamed Mother Teresa Street. All across this wide street men lay in sleeping-bags, some still asleep, some yawning and rubbing their eyes, others reaching out for coffee provided by the women who were running a nearby 'camp kitchen'. Scores of other demonstrators had taken over the broad, shallow steps leading up to Priština's theatre and had covered its façade with posters. Strong emotions were powering this protest against UNMIK's failure to secure the release of more than 1,000 Kosovar political prisoners, still being held illegally in Serb jails. One prisoner's name and photograph were particularly prominent: Dr Flora Brovina, a celebrated paediatrician and poet who had worked for years in Kosovo on behalf of the Belgrade-based Humanitarian Law Centre founded in 1992 by Nataša Kandić, an outstandingly courageous Serb woman. When the bombing started, Nataša drove alone from Belgrade to tour Kosovo and see for herself what was really going on. As I had discovered in Belgrade, the Humanitarian Law Centre is one of the few sources of unbiased, detailed, precisely accurate information about (among other issues) the Kosovo conflict. In March 1999 Dr Brovina was sentenced to twelve years' imprisonment for 'terrorist activities carried out during a state of war'. Many demonstrators carried enlarged placard photographs inscribed 'FLORA', showing a strong, serious, benign face. Many other photographs, held aloft by prisoners' relatives and friends, included Bekim Istogu, aged seventeen, detained in Sremska Mitrovica prison – infamous for its maltreatment and torture of all prisoners but especially Kosovars. As no criminal proceedings had been brought against him his detention broke Federal law. Another placard listed eight Kosovars sentenced to fifteen years' imprisonment in February 2000 for 'terrorism and seditious conspiracy'. Arrested by the JNA in Montenegro in April 1999, they had confessed, while in military custody, to killing sixteen policemen in the villages of Prilep and Ločani. Subsequently they told the court that their confessions had been made under torture and the local police gave evidence that none of their colleagues had been killed on the relevant dates. All these details were available on the bilingual (English and Albanian) posters, but when I sought more information I was rebuffed, evidently seen as a Trio hanger-on with whom nobody wished to communicate. Kosovo's initial adulation of the Nato-led Trio was waning.

Now the sleepers arose, rolled up their bedding, combed their hair, moved off to the 'kitchen' – and were immediately replaced by a row of junior schoolchildren, neatly dressed boys and girls who sat cross-legged on the street, completely blocking it. They sat quite still, not talking; one felt they had been well trained. From the background this scene was being impassively observed by several British four-man foot-patrols and three pairs of UN Police sitting smoking in those large gas-guzzling vehicles whose two-tone colouring has inspired their local nickname – 'Coca-Colas'. Overhead a helicopter circled low, round and round and round, watching the wasteland space where, it was rumoured, the Security Council mission would soon land. Although all was so quiet, apart from the 'copter, one could sense the tension rising.

Groups were coming on foot from every direction, assembling in bigger groups at all the street corners. Hundreds quickly became thousands, of all ages and conditions. Impeccably groomed young women carried babies in slings; other young women wearing ill-fitting 'donated' clothes looked underfed and exhausted. Toddlers rode on paternal shoulders, gum-chewing teenagers sported flashy gear, expensively tailored middle-aged men twirled canes, stout matrons with tight dyed perms wobbled in unsuitable shoes. Bent old village women, wearing ankle-length skirts, held the hands of small grandchildren wearing vulgar T-shirts and the very latest in luminous trainers. And a number of dreadfully maimed young men in invalid chairs were being pushed by their luckier comrades, defiantly wearing battle fatigues and KLA insignia. This was 'Kosovo 2000' in microcosm, a fractured and uncertain society briefly united by their support for the prisoners' anguished families.

When the march began the tension eased; by then one knew the security forces had been directed not to intervene. Placard-bearing relatives, their faces movingly worry-worn rather than angry, led the silent, slow procession down Mother Teresa Street, past the Grand Hotel, past the unfinished Orthodox cathedral and the university library – looking from a distance like something left behind by aliens. This display of People Power was all the more impressive for being silent: no songs or chanted slogans, nothing gimmicky, simply a demonstration of anxiety, grief and controlled frustration – the frustration expressed on the placards.

After the march, when the Protest had been handed in to UNMIK's headquarters and KLA marshals were no longer imposing discipline, the mood changed. Most marchers were under-twenty-fives, reflecting Kosovo's population pattern (unique in Europe) and suddenly there was an amorphous menace in the air, a feeling that anything could happen. In the centre, thousands were strolling the streets, 'making a day of it', and hundreds sat on the low walls along Mother Teresa Street. Nearby kiosks sold fast foods and fizzy drinks and cartons of leaflets were being distributed, giving details of the prisoners' cases.

As I turned towards the Kukri café (not my favourite but K-For guarded) a running youth kicked my arse, hard – then glanced back to observe my reaction.

He must have been disappointed; outwardly there was no reaction though inwardly I felt both scared and outraged. During the week ahead I had to adjust to this unpleasant local custom. According to Belda, a friendly waitress at the Kukri who witnessed that incident, I was likely to be mistaken for a Serb in Priština and therefore should avoid the more lawless districts and never go on foot after dark. I took her advice. When I queried why anyone should mistake me for a Serb, in a city swarming with expats from five continents, Belda pointed out that expats never walk further than from their office doors to their vehicles. But I remained baffled; although one might instantly label a person Latin or Scandinavian, Serbs are not so distinctive.

In Serbia, too, I had often been mistaken for a Serb: people stopped me to ask the time, or for directions, or (once) if I knew of a cheap hotel. There the error seemed mildly amusing; in Priština it had disagreeable consequences. Five times youths kicked me as they raced past and frequently I was spat on and/or verbally abused by people of all ages and both sexes. Then I remembered being mistaken in Romania for a Romanian, though with happier results. Oddly enough, I found being spat on, with hatred, much more upsetting than being sworn at or kicked.

The Kukri was said to be the only café in Priština safe for Serbs to use, allegedly because K-For snipers were permanently posted in an upstairs room. It was directly opposite the main entrance to UNMIK's colossal headquarters, and UNMIK employs most of Priština's surviving Serbs. In Belgrade I had heard all Serbs who work for the Trio described as 'traitors'. Presumably their Trio-standard pay-packets – some ten to twenty times what they could earn in Serbia – compensated them for having the worst of both worlds, in terms of social acceptability. They lived in a dismal ghetto of flats known as 'the Yu Project', K-For guarded day and night yet rocket-attacked at intervals. None dared leave the block's courtyard without armed protection and K-For bussed their children to school in one of the Serbs' rural enclaves.

When Belda had brought me a *pivo* I settled down to diary-write with my precious (DM8) tin of mini-cigars on my lap; one learns fast in Priština and I knew better than to leave them exposed on the table. Soon one of the small boys loitering nearby begged, 'Cigara Cigara!' When I ignored him he darted forward and made to grab the tin – contemptuous of the five UN Police sitting at the next table. These were Nigerian, Malayan and Kuwaiti, all English-speakers. Holding the child by the arm I called them but they pretended not to understand and ordered another round of beers. As I released the boy his companions fell about laughing at the silly old woman who had imagined the 'Coca-Colas' would exert themselves. Then all four sat on the low wall surrounding the café terrace, jeering at me.

In Kosovo, as elsewhere, the overpaid UN Police were a public scandal. All Priština could count how many hours they spent slouched at café tables or enjoying multi-course meals in restaurants. When 'working' they cruised aimlessly around the city, wasting incalculable dollars on fuel for their luxury vehicles while polluting the atmosphere. The New York City contingent were risible – many long since retired, pot-bellied, white-haired. Nor was it confidence-building to over-hear three Canadian Mounties mocking the UN High Commission for Human Rights as they entertained a colleague with an account of helping K-For to search a Priština flat for arms: 'So we were doin' what we had to do when these fuckers came nosin' round – Fred saw the vehicle and we told the Albs we'd do more than we had to do if they whined. Who sent them "Human Rights" bull-shitters here? They're a fuckin' disgrace, they should keep out, they believe every lie those bas-tards tell them!'

The Kukri and a much bigger adjacent café provided fertile eavesdropping ground; the tables were close-packed and many Trio expats have to speak English loudly and clearly.

I was about to move on when three outgoing young Kosovar women, OSCE employees, came to sit at my table and soon were telling me how angry it made them to see Serbs in control of Northern Mitrovica. Said one, 'If K-For are real soldiers why are they afraid to fight? And if they won't control that situation why won't they let the KLA look after their own people?'

Another said, 'My home is there but we can't return to it safely. This way of behaving – so scared of the Serbs – makes us think differently about Nato. They're not such great guys as they looked last year!'

All three women came from previously well-off professional families now largely dependent on their daughters' earnings. They described the 1990s as 'a nightmare decade, to buy medicines in the pharmacy we had to pretend to be Serbs! We made up the smeary way they do and dyed our hair to try to look Serbian. We felt like hunted rats, hated and despised. Outsiders talk nonsense about our future. There's only one answer now – independence!'

My companions were warmly friendly until I showed some sympathy for the Kosovo Serbs now confined to protected enclaves. Then the temperature dropped abruptly and soon they departed, having asserted that most Serbs voted Milošević into power and supported his anti-Kosovo campaign and must be treated accord-ingly and should stop complaining.

That afternoon UNMIK issued a 'MEDIA ALERT – URGENT SCHEDULE CHANGE – SECURITY COUNCIL VISIT – The Press BUS scheduled to leave Priština at 0600, 28th April to Prizren has been cancelled . . . All media hoping to travel to Vucitrin and Mitrovica on 28 April by private vehicle to cover the Security Council visit are reminded that UNMIK cannot guarantee them access to media opportunities in these areas . . .'

No mass demo had been organized for 28 April but the schoolchildren were back on traffic-stopping duty and a silent sit-down vigil was staged near the Security Council mission's Grand Hotel base. Throughout the mission's three-day visit

K-For snipers occupied nearby roofs and a wide area around the hotel was barred to traffic and the general public. To gain access to the Grand, one had to explain oneself, then the white-tape barrier was lifted by one of Kosovo's new police force, the TMK, on duty here in partnership with the British Military Police and Italian Carabiniere. Some amusement was caused by UNMIK's choice of TMK representatives – smiling handsome young men and smiling beautiful young women, unarmed, smartly uniformed and graciously polite to all those for whom they lifted the tape. One could imagine the Security Council delegates (from Bangladesh, Argentina, Canada, China, Ukraine, Jamaica, Malaysia, Russia) noting in their reports how successfully the Trio had converted the KLA to a civil defence force.

That morning I arrived early at the Plaza, a would-be 'ornamental' public space between the Grand and UNMIK's headquarters. Here the vigil-keepers were camping out under a huge colourful awning – a hundred or so, including six girls still asleep under quilts in one corner. Several elders, wearing the Albanian *plish*, were squatting in the early sun, drinking coffee and relishing their first cigarette. But the majority were sullen-looking young men. One was already on sentinel duty, a conspicuously tall and well-built 'marshal'', wearing a black shirt and pants with a red ribbon on his left arm. For hours he stood erect, his fists clenched by his sides, his gaze fixed on the middle distance. One of his duties was to scare off the media attached to the Security Council circus and assumed to be pro-Trio – a pathetic example of political immaturity. First you organize a truly impressive demo to coincide with the arrival of the world press, then you refuse to explain your motivation to journalists and threaten to shoot TV cameramen – how not to win allies.

I had a breakfast appointment with twenty-three-year-old Melina, an UNMIK employee who had emerged from Kosovo's 'parallel' education system speaking fluent English. 'My father taught me,' she explained. 'He's a scholar, he translates English classics.' She was a good-looking lass, raven-haired and green-eyed, tall but small-boned, her shoulders and hips very narrow – a not unusual physique in the Balkans. Sometimes I wondered about the alleged genetic separateness of Slavs and Albanians who have been sharing territory for so long.

We met at the UNMIK café, so called because of its clientele rather than its ownership. Even before sitting down Melina condemned the demo. 'K-For should stop all this disruption, the *mafiosi* are running it, it's only damaging our economy. We don't need any more protests, Nato has liberated Kosovo, we're no longer part of Serbia. In Priština we're tired of having our city changed by all these villagers moving in. They could go back to their home places, UNHCR gives them money to rebuild, but they prefer city life – it's easier to be criminal in a city!'

In Melina's view the US provided the best K-For troops who did most for Kosovo, though they numbered only 12,500 out of K-For's 45,000. She eulogized Camp Bondsteel, their gigantic military base near Uroševac and the Macedonian border. The biggest US base to have been built since the Second Indochina War, it incorporates a state-of-the-art helicopter base, permanent housing for 5,000 troops and the sort of luxury facilities expected by the sort of soldiers who rely on their government not to expose them to any serious risk. 'Bondsteel gives so many jobs!' enthused Melina. 'It's transformed the whole area. And it means the Americans will always be here to protect us from the Serbs.'

At our previous meeting Melina had naively boasted of Kosovo having no hard drugs problem and no prostitution, divorce or promiscuity because of its strong Islamic tradition of united families. She looked at first disbelieving, then uneasy when I warned her that in Kosovo Bondsteel will do what US army bases always do – breed hard drugs dealing and a wide variety of brothels including paedophiliac 'fun-rooms'.

Melina went on to recall Nato's press conferences during the airwar, regularly televised at 3 p.m. 'Daily we lived for that moment! Jamie Shea – he kept our spirits alive! We cheered and clapped him every afternoon and when he visited us we all wanted to hug and kiss him! We were imprisoned in our homes waiting for the Serbs to attack and rob and kill us and he gave us courage, made us feel hopeful saying the Serb army was smashed! I never feared death, only rape. I knew if they came they would rape me and my mother in front of my father and brother before killing us all – that is how Serbs are.'

When I commented on Mr Shea's economy with the truth Melina laughed and said, 'I know, he told us afterwards! He said propaganda lies are part of all wars and we told him they were good for us. We loved Bill Clinton, too, and Tony Blair and General Clark and Mr Solana – and Mr Robertson with the funny voice who talked from Italy. We'll always love them!' Then Melina glanced at her watch, exclaimed and stood up. But she was only forty-five minutes late for work – a peccadillo by UNMIK standards.

Priština remained eerily hushed until 3 p.m. when the juvenile barricaders quietly went home under marshals' orders and traffic flowed again. In contrast to the previous day's milling throngs, only small groups of youngsters drifted to and fro on the main thoroughfare. At noon, on my way to visit a flat beyond the university, I paused to photograph one of the barricades; eight high-school pupils were sitting across the road at an intersection under the benevolent gaze of three British Tommies. Then I continued up a dual carriageway lined with four-storey concrete apartment blocks. Given the numbers of K-For troops in the vicinity, with some of whom I was by then on first-name terms, I felt relaxed despite my 'Serb' aspect. I hadn't yet got the measure of Priština. Not long before, a wellarmed UN policeman, sitting in his vehicle outside the UN Police headquarters, had been robbed of his waist-pouch, containing DM8,000, by two unarmed youths.

Suddenly my right arm was seized and a fist struck my shoulder. The boy – aged perhaps fifteen – had crew-cut brown hair and wore a fawn combat jacket and a horrible expression: he looked both slightly mad and very bad. (Afterwards I repented of this instant judgement; he may well have been exposed to some ghastly soul-distorting experience like seeing his family slaughtered.) Probably he had noticed me taking that photograph; his quarry was the strong plastic carrier-bag containing my camera. My journal, as always, was in the cloth bag worn around my neck – though post-Albania I did wonder if that tactic was unwise, perhaps inviting strangulation.

What followed might be described as a trotting battle, myself and the lad struggling as we trotted. With one hand I held the camera close to my chest, with the other I tried to fend off repeated blows. Several nearby groups of young men – student types – ignored my appeals for help. Then a 'Coca-Cola' came slowly cruising towards us – the only vehicle in sight. I trotted faster, still dodging those fists, the blows now accompanied by shouted demands for money. When the police driver noticed what was happening he speeded up, at which point the lad raced away into a narrow alley between slummy apartment blocks.

This 'Coca-Cola' team consisted of two amiable Zambian officers who spoke halting English, a very young TMK recruit who spoke none and a Kosovar interpreter.

The senior Zambian beckoned me to enter the vehicle and got out his note-book: 'Now you give statement. Name?'

Crisply I retorted, 'First you find the boy, then I give statement.'

The Zambian pondered this novel approach to crime control. 'You know the fellow? You can identify?'

The interpreter muttered to me, 'They fear to go into such places, our village people don't understand Africans.'

I turned towards the alley and said, 'Let's go! Let's waste no more time!'

The junior Zambian had to guard the vehicle; even those distinctive 'Coca-Colas' are stolen and within hours repainted and driven out of Kosovo. The interpreter led the rest of us between graffiti-daubed walls over piles of garbage into a courtyard littered with broken glass and rusted scraps of cars. There was no one around but many faces appeared at windows, peering suspiciously down. Now the interpreter, too, seemed a trifle nervous and the TMK youth was visibly trembling. Of course we didn't find the lad; the residents were rudely unco-operative and after some fifteen minutes we retreated. The interpreter said apologetically, 'Here people are not used to helping police – for too long our police were Serbs.'

Back in the vehicle a detailed statement was taken from me by the senior Zambian and written down by the interpreter who explained, 'It's just for the record' – lest I might imagine further efforts would be made to arrest the culprit. He warned me not to walk around Priština – a futile warning. There was then no public transport, no taxi service, and I certainly wasn't going to risk Ruairi's being stolen while I went about my business.

The 'Coca-Cola' kindly delivered me to the Kukri where it was eavesdropping time again. At the next table an obese Chinese-American K-For press officer was telling a young English journalist, newly arrived, 'There's no story in mines or cluster bombs, that's all part of war. You're only a baby if you fuss about that kinda detail.'

The newcomer blushed – no doubt conscious of being an almost beardless youth – then stoutly challenged the K-For line. 'It's ironical, isn't it, that Nato has refused to clear its unexploded cluster bombs? Didn't they come here to protect Kosovars? Now those bombs will be killing innocent peasants.'

The press officer chuckled, his treble chin quivering, and lit a fat cigar before replying. 'You know what? Those peasants, they'd all be dead already but for Nato! You gotta put some logic in there, get your priorities right – OK? But you've lotsa time to learn, get real, quit the pussy-footing. Kosovo's for men, not mice!'

The Kukri's chairs did not long remain unsat on and soon I was talking with Miranda, a forceful grey-haired Argentinian woman (OSCE). Her research showed a high proportion of returnees (and 'displaced persons') squatting in Priština simply because their destroyed villages still lacked schools and clinics, promised by the Trio ten months previously. She believed the Kosovars would never 'get things together' until left on their own. 'They have many practical skills and remittance cash comes pouring in from their diaspora. They could be self-sufficient but our aid skews the scene.' She paused, then added, 'I can feel guilty here about not getting *positively* emotionally involved. This is my seventh posting and mostly I enjoy different cultures – adjusting and participating. I'm not one of those expats who never mix with locals. But I do find these Balkan people generally unattractive – greedy and cruel, calculating and rigid.'

Then Miranda was joined by her Swiss friend Elsa, also OSCE. As we discussed the demo she remarked, 'Yesterday was good for our Swiss VIPs – taught them a lesson! They arrived to see the Kosovo schools we fund but had to fly home from Skopje after seeing nothing but road-blocks! Often those people think our difficulties here, trying to get things done, are imagined or exaggerated.'

The Swiss Department of Defence was planning Alpine holidays for rural pupils. One group of eight children, having heard rumours of this, were waiting outside their school with bags packed, expecting to fly off with the VIPs. 'I fight against such schemes,' said Elsa. 'It's only to make us feel better. We try to soothe our rich consciences giving hospitality like that and all sorts of goodies. But what does two weeks in Switzerland really do for those peasant children? Makes them more fed up with life at home – already there's too many only thinking about how to get out and stay out. Or maybe that's the Final Solution for Kosovo? If enough leave, the Serbs can have it all to themselves.'

Later that day, in a large flat on the outskirts furnished with much more money than taste, I met a notorious *mafioso* character. Since the new year he had run two

European NGO directors out of town; in the course of safeguarding their own projects they were threatening to interfere with his way of life. He had been born in
Tirana, spent some years in Switzerland, then moved to Kosovo when the Trio's
input of dollars made it interesting. Our meeting was at his request, which slightly
disquieted me. However, his cross-examination indicated that he merely wanted
to establish my real motive for visiting Kosovo. He was, I gathered, allergic to
investigative journalists.

16

A Daytrip with Compatriots

Almost every morning in Priština I breakfasted at a tiny four-table *burek* eatery run by Geoje and his brother. In August 1999 the two young men had returned from a five-year exile in London, having saved up enough to start their own business. 'Our mother died during the war,' said Geoje with a catch in his voice. 'She died of hardship in the forest. Then our father became too sad and in poor health and we wanted to help him.'

Before leaving Britain the brothers were mistaken for refugees and the local authorities investigated their ability to look after themselves when they arrived home, closely questioning them about Kosovo to test their authenticity. In the UK, Geoje estimated, some 80 per cent of asylum-seeking 'Kosovars' were Albanian and when these failed the questions test they were deported without benefits of any sort. Therefore a group of Kosovars set up an agency (£5 per hour consultation fee) where such Albanians could go for priming on the Kosovo area they were claiming as their birthplace – a classic example of Balkan private enterprise.

Geoje complained about Kosovars being given a bad name by drug-dealing and girl-trafficking Albanians. 'Same as all places we have our criminals but they're not as bad or as many as in Albania.' Macedonia's Albanians too, were denounced for forming too many alliances with the Albanian *mafiosi*.

The demo had also angered these brothers. Afterwards they said, 'Why make business stop? Life is hard enough for people trying to work honestly to live. Why didn't K-For control the gangsters and let us earn? If you have a small business you have little cash, if for three days you can't work you get hungry.'

Geoje dwelt wistfully on the UK's credit system. 'It's like magic, nobody using money! Only you need a job to borrow money for a house, a car, all electronic things, all furniture and clothes – everything! No problem! Here you must have cash to buy materials and then build your home yourself. In UK are so many good jobs, I had ten in five years all with restaurants where I could save tips. The English don't like to work, they get so much from the government for doing nothing. The government even pays girls with no morals. In the flat next ours lived one aged twenty with three children from different fathers and the government gave her a free flat and much money. Here such behaviour is not possible. Her father would kill a girl trying to behave this way.'

In Mitrovica, the brothers' home town, 'our people now are suffering much trouble. And K-For keep out of it. Last Saturday I was there and saw the trouble and where were the French troops? They were in restaurants where you pay DM10 for one hamburger, drinking and singing and dancing with their own women. They've let the Serbs chase all the Northern Mitrovica Kosovars out of their homes over the bridge.' Geoje made no mention of the Kosovars having chased all the Southern Mitrovica Serbs over the bridge in the other direction. As I was going on to Mitrovica from Priština he gave me his uncle's address.

In April Priština's apple and lilac trees are laden with fragrant blossoms and tattered plastic bags. On 21 April the Interim Administrative Council (IAC) had issued a press release from the co-heads of the Department of Health and Social Welfare on how 'to deal with the problem of tularaemia, informing the public on the preventative actions and methods to be taken to avoid contamination'. Maybe that department would do better with one head instead of two. The widespread outbreak of tularaemia was owing to the IAC's failure to deal with Priština's garbage, despite the lavish funding at its disposal. This disease is (I quote from Black's *Medical Dictionary*) 'of rodents such as rabbits and rats and spread either by flies or by direct inoculation, for example, into the hands of a person engaged in skinning rabbits. In man the disease takes the form of a slow fever lasting several weeks, with much malaise and depression, followed by considerable emaciation. It is found widely in North America and Europe but not in Great Britain.' Early every morning, as I walked into the city centre, I passed an unofficial dump along the edge of a small overgrown wooded park. The high mound of garbage blocked the footpath and people held handkerchiefs to their noses as they hurried past. This was in one of Priština's more salubrious districts, only a few yards from the handsome house occupied by the UNCHR and fifty yards from the Park Hotel. At intervals municipal workers attempted incineration, which made the stench even worse without deterring the rodents. Never have I seen so many sleek, squealing rats assembled in one place. At daybreak, before pedestrians and vehicles sent them scuttling home to digest their large meals, they swarmed by the hundred over that mound. And many others like it befouled Priština. Then dogs and cats replaced them – some obviously feral, others family pets who could, and too often did, contaminate their owners with the tularaemia bacillus. When, people desperately wondered, would the co-heads of the relevant department get around to organizing garbage collection as a 'preventative action?'

Priština's traffic chaos provided another, minor grumbling-point. This chaos, said the grumblers, could have been avoided had the UN Police, or the Italian Carabiniere, or the British Military Police bestirred themselves. Priština's main thoroughfares are wide and straight, its traffic lights usually work, the numbers of vehicles were not then excessive, yet prolonged crises happened on a daily basis.

My favourite writing haven was the Restaurant Afridita, little used by expats and raised high above pavement level at a junction of three main streets, affording a clear view of some of the more comical snarl-ups (comical for the onlookers). One afternoon I watched a twenty-five-minute blockage, with all three furiously hooting tail-backs extending out of sight. When one lane of a dual carriageway was briefly cleared two huge trucks did u-turns to escape by driving on the wrong side and came up against a flow just released by traffic lights. This hopelessly compounded the confusion, which was being observed by two 'Coca-Colas' and three K-For military police jeeps – themselves entrapped.

Why did no police officers emerged from their vehicles to unravel this preposterous tangle? A waiter remarked that only when drivers at the invisible ends of the queues sought alternative routes would the problem be solved. 'But,' he added, 'in Kosovo we don't like to back off!'

Eventually two Nepalese UN Police did emerge, were joined by three British officers – and all five had an acrimonious argument about how to proceed. Failing to reach agreement they retreated to their vehicles and awaited developments. The waiter grinned and said, 'These nations are not united!'

Moments later a serious fight broke out, just below the Afridita, between the frustrated drivers of a small van and a Mercedes, backed by their total of five passengers. No police intervened though violent blows were being exchanged. At last the logjam was shifting and the bleeding van driver sped away, pursued by the Mercedes. My companion foresaw the fight being resumed elsewhere and possibly ending in murder. 'The police should know this,' he said, 'and chase them. Maybe they do know but they're scared, though they could easily get more men on their radio.' He was commenting quite casually, not being dramatic. In defence of the police I pointed out that their use of weapons is restricted, as the Kosovars' is not. But that scene illustrated why no one had been brought to justice for the 900 murders committed in the ten months since Kosovo became a Nato protectorate.

The Afridita served tolerable food at reasonable prices and its friendly staff more than compensated for grubby tablecloths. It was a tactful place to suggest when Kosovar friends wished to entertain me; the Kukri or UNMIK restaurant prices were three to five times higher for similar meals. I eschewed the Grand Hotel, probably ten to twenty times higher and no more palate-titillating. Kosovo is not a gourmet destination.

One day Mr Adem Qosja stood me lunch – a small compact man with unhealthy skin, thinning grey hair, an habitually compressed mouth and deep-set brown eyes that met one's gaze steadily. He spoke fluent English and was among several Kosovar husbands who mentioned their wives' being linguistically challenged as the reason for meeting me in a café.

In 1991 Mr Qosja had sent his seventeen-year-old son to Britain to avoid Milošević's call-up but he refused to believe that thousands of Serb draft-dodgers went into exile at the same time. No people should be sweepingly condemned, asserted Mr Qosja – except Serbs, who are all guilty, who all share their leaders' lust for domination and over the centuries have always been the bullies of the Balkans. And he had heard witnesses' accounts of Gypsies helping Serbs to slaughter villagers in exchange for some of the loot. (My mind darted back to that Gypsy settlement outside Podgorica and Petar's claim, 'they are like us now'.) As for Kosovo's tiny minority of Turks, some also sided with the Serbs though most were pro-Kosovar even if afraid to show it. Serbia's then opposition parties were dismissed as 'fake democrats trying to get on America's good side, many are even worse than Milošević'. The Trio's multi-ethnic Kosovo ideal he described as 'crazy day-dreaming. Our Serbs can stay and have all human rights but no power, ever. And they must forget Serbia – swear allegiance to Kosovo. They needn't worry about security, there's no KLA problem – that's all Serb propaganda.' Mr Qosja boasted of being apolitical, standing aside from all parties and factions. 'I've no faith in any of our leaders, they don't know about modern politics in a democracy. But maybe America will find us a good leader – it could be someone from our Albanian community in the States which is very rich.' Mr Qosja, it transpired, was being cultivated by the State Department and dazzled by US flattery. Photographs showed him at a party given in Washington DC by 'America's richest Albanian'; his fellow-guest of honour was an Orthodox priest from southern Albania. When I asked, 'Would you attend such a mixed party in Kosovo?' Mr Qosja pretended not to hear.

Mr Qosja's malleability in the hands of a Great Power was unsurprising. The leaders of two of Kosovo's numerous political parties revealed a juvenile gratification at having been invited to sessions of the European Parliament, wined and dined by Euro MPs, interviewed by German and French newspapers, photographed with and praised by x, y and z. These conversations depressed me. The longing to join Nato and the EU ('our family of nations'), shared by the governments (though not necessarily the peoples) of ex-Communist countries, has motives other than a devotion to democracy.

Most Priština conversations, whether with locals or expats, brought forth a crime story. Recently, it was said, Albania's Minister for the Interior attended an international conference on law and order in Sofia and on his return journey Bulgaria's border police checked his engine number and found that the ministerial car had been stolen in Switzerland. They confiscated it, leaving him to hitch home. This is such a good story I found it hard to believe but my informant assured me it was the unvarnished truth.

The other stories were only too credible. Near Djakovica a routine K-For patrol stopped a heavily laden NGO landcruiser, forced the reluctant Kosovar driver to reveal the contents and found forty boxes of hand grenades.

A few days after my departure from Prizren, a demining NGO's vehicle was attacked near the town by ten armed men who got away with wage-packets worth DM900,000.

At the end of April an NGO office in Peć was broken into by someone who knew when it would be unguarded for thirty minutes; the carefully hidden safe was stolen, but none of the valuable electronic equipment.

The week before Easter a Serb family ventured out of their enclave, guarded round the clock by Swedish troops. The mother was driving, a grandmother and two small boys sat in the back. Soon a gang of young men attacked and burned the car; when the Swedes arrived the family was being kicked on the road. All were seriously injured; the grandmother died next day.

From another enclave, in March, a young couple and their three children set out to visit friends in Macedonia, less than twenty miles away, but were soon identified as Serbs and shot dead. In Kosovo modern technology was helping law-breakers more than law enforcers; youths equipped with mobile phones watched the periphery of Serb enclaves and when a vehicle left unescorted (against K-For orders) they contacted murder squads which set up ambushes.

In early April the Kosovar owner of a flat in a newish (1982) building tried unlawfully to evict a Serb tenant to free the property for letting to an NGO at DM5,000 per month. Two of the elderly man's family had been murdered in September 1999, four had been 'dispersed' – intimidated out of Priština. The Kosovar couple in the flat below, neighbours for fifteen years, shopped for him because he feared to go out alone and generally kept a kindly eye on him. They advised him to move but he doggedly refused to leave his home – where could he safely go, alone as he was? A week later he was pushed from a window of his fourth-floor flat and died instantly. From the courtyard below one of his Kosovar friends – the wife – witnessed the crime and was warned to keep quiet or she too would be killed. The landlord told the UN Police his tenant had committed suicide – a plausible story, the suicide rate being then understandably high among elder Serbs. However, a few days later the Kosovar wife spoke indiscreetly and within twenty-four hours both she and her husband had been shot dead. None of the security forces took effective action, though the case was much discussed in Priština and seen as further proof that criminals had little to fear in Nato's protectorate.

The density of Kosovo's expat population had cruelly inflated rent prices, to the delight of property owners (already rich) and the despair of the homeless (already poor). One NGO's spacious luxury flat (DM4,000 per month) was used only occasion-ally, by staff living elsewhere in Kosovo, as a weekend R&R base. The planting of rich expat colonies in impoverished societies does immense economic and psycho-logical damage – as I've noted in other books, but the point bears repetition.

When Milošević's forces withdrew there came another invasion – 600 or so foreign NGOs, each with its urgent need for residential and office accommodation, for local staff and for 'projects'. It doesn't follow that because an NGO arrives promptly on a scene of misery it knows how to go about helping, or even how to avoid worsening the situation. Kosovo's situation was certainly worsened when so many uninformed and unfocussed aid workers joined the Trio's bloated bureaucracies. By global standards this 'humanitarian crisis' was minor and – as Miranda had remarked – potentially capable of being dealt with by the diaspora-funded Kosovars themselves, had outside aid not blunted their initiative and sharpened their cupidity.

A remarkable Canadian also frequented the Afridita. Duncan, an Albanian-speaking Quaker in his fifties, had been living in Kosovo since May 1998 and remained there throughout the bombing. He had tried, without much success, to protect the more scatterbrained NGOs when he saw them being deftly milked by some of their Kosovar staffs, working in cahoots with KLA (or, later, TMK) relatives and friends. Such 'co-ops' stole supplies, siphoned petrol, fiddled the books and, when lent landcruisers at weekends (by misty-eyed expats who thought they deserved the 'bonus' of taking their families for a Sunday drive), smuggled arms, drugs and cigarettes.

Said Duncan, 'Every day NGO funds are being squandered while Kosovar teachers get starvation wages. Sometimes literally starvation, I've seen men too hungry to have the mental energy to teach. But NGO "mandates" don't allow them to supplement those wages. And UNMIK and the OSCE spend so much sustaining themselves there's not enough left over for basic things like schooling.'

On four continents, for nearly forty years, I have been listening to and participating in criticisms of NGOs. But nowhere have those criticisms been as harsh as in Kosovo, so very little was there to show for the US$2.2 billion immoderately poured into a region half the size of Wales with a population of less than two million. The establishment of Nato's protectorate was of course a political rather than a humanitarian act so perhaps it was predictable that the Trio and the NGOs would fight for their 'fair shares' of those billions while the garbage remained uncollected, the teachers underpaid, the hospitals understaffed and the criminals unimpeded.

Over our next beer Duncan and I discussed Mr J. Dienstbier. In Prizren I had been given a copy of his 'Report on the situation of human rights in Kosovo, Federal Republic of Yugoslavia', presented by Mrs Mary Robinson to the United Nations Commission on Human Rights on 30 March 2000. His summing-up included the flat statement that, 'In Kosovo, under current conditions, no one enjoys freedom of movement, safety, security, or the rule of law.' At this the Trio took umbrage and on 21 April UNMIK issued a press release:

The Interim Administrative Council today issued the following statement: The IAC distance [sic] itself from the statement on Kosovo of Mr Jiri Dienstbier . . . to the United Nations Commission on Human Rights on 29 March, as well as the recent report of the

International Crisis Group. We will answer substantively to them. The IAC also under-lines that the recent article by *Der Spiegel* on the administrative and political situation and on individual political organizations in Kosovo do not accurately describe the situation on the ground. In this respect, the IAC notes that UNMIK Police deny the claim that they have underway criminal investigations against top-level Kosovar political leadership.

'I can believe that denial,' commented Duncan.

At this point six Tommies came racing towards the OSCE headquarters, almost opposite the Afridita, to defend it from a mob of angry adolescents. Then a convoy of four APCs appeared and the mob fled as the Brits swung their guns. Duncan observed, 'This protectorate might be better protected if all K-For troops were Brits.'

On the following morning I stood for half an hour, awaiting a friend, in the foyer of UNMIK's headquarters, watching the staff toing and froing. Here, indeed, was the 'international community' in all its multi-coloured and multi-featured diversity – Nigerian, Mexican, English, Bangladeshi, Swedish, Russian, Peruvian, Australian, Indian, Italian, Kenyan, Japanese, Polish, Egyptian, Bulgarian, Argentinian . . . Each was labelled according to country of origin and most were young, prepared to endure a Priština posting to enhance their CVs as they aimed upwards. This is job creation on a global scale – what would all these men and women be doing in a UN-free world? The majority could certainly not find equally well-paid jobs at home. At the UNMIK cafe I often talked with a representative cross-section and was disheartened by their lack of interest in the Balkans. Nor did they display any real concern about Kosovo's present or future. Like Christianity and Communism, the UN is a beautiful idea that on the whole hasn't worked because too few people have been committed to making it work. Yet one of its agencies can claim a mighty achievement; apparently the WHO has freed all the world from smallpox and much of it from polio.

Towards the end of my stay in Priština K-For's Irish contingent, the 2nd Transport Company, treated me to a day out, an action-packed fourteen hours. My genial host, Commandant Michael McDermott, picked me up outside the Grand Hotel in his personal jeep, flying the Irish flag and equipped – he being the CO – with mysterious communications paraphernalia which took up most of the back space. I had already been to a very jolly evening party at the Irish base, organized to break the monotony for the 103 men whose entertainment was confined to playing Bingo in their dreary camp on flat land fifteen miles south of Priština. No K-For troops could be let off the leash lest they might cause 'inter-national incidents'. They were rich young men, in the eyes of their local contem-poraries, and that could cause tension – or worse. Also their relaxed 'Western' attitude to the opposite sex, however innocently manifested, might have been mis-interpreted by the sort of Kosovar male who still regards women as 'property'. And then there were all those Kosovars who denounced K-For's allegedly pro-Serb bias: its protecting of enclaves, escorting of school buses, provision of secure transport to the border for Serbs needing hospital treatment in Belgrade.

What contributed significantly to that party's jollity was the relationship between officers and 'other ranks'. When off duty they were simply comrades enjoying themselves together, something unimaginable in a British army context. Not for the first time, I rejoiced to have been born into a genuinely democratic – in this sense – republic. (Not that Ireland was officially a republic in 1931 – but in spirit it was.)

The CO – Mike to his friends – had planned my day to provide glimpses of Kosovar life at the level where he and his men had become integrated; most of their spare time was dedicated to welfare work.

We began by visiting Štimlje's Mental Institution; an army minibus loaded with badly-needed clothes, collected by Mike in Ireland, followed our jeep. Once such institutions were known as 'lunatic asylums'; of late the politically correct have renamed them 'residences for the intellectually challenged'. This establishment, government-run in the old Yugoslavia, is now partly subsidized by a Swedish NGO. A staff of 104 young women (they seemed kindly) looked after 340 patients, some 60 per cent of whom have been here for twenty years or more. In 1999, when rampaging Serbs raped a few of the women patients, the rest were disguised as boys. The enormous building looked less grim than I had expected: not unlike a nineteenth-century Irish convent, surrounded by grassy slopes, many trees, flowering shrubs – and inmates can see the world go by through a highish peri-meter fence.

This Institution had been adopted by the Irish troops several months previ-ously and their arrival caused much excitement. Clothes, sweets, cigarettes and picture magazines were handed out to appropriate recipients. But more impor-tant was the distribution of affectionate sympathy, Mike and his men having established relationships that obviously brought comfort to many. They were of all ages and varying stages of mental disability, from half-crippled youths crouch-ing alone in corners, mumbling and dribbling, to perfectly coherent middle-aged men afflicted by clinical depression, to crazed old women who wandered around naked from the waist down, frenziedly muttering and wringing their hands. Others, permanently locked in their rooms, gazed silently down at us from high barred windows. The place looked reasonably clean and tidy but the food served in the vast canteen was – Mike told me – very inadequate. These patients were from all over the former Yugoslavia and their refuge may well be the only corner of contemporary Kosovo where one's place of origin doesn't matter. Here there is neither Bosnian nor Croatian, neither Serb nor Albanian.

Between Štimlje and Račak I saw a cheering sight unrelated to Kosovo. From the balcony of a new, neat bungalow hung three flags: a large Irish tricolour flanked by two smaller Union Jacks. In that bungalow lived some of the Trio's RUC contingent, whom I had met at the Camp Clark party.

Our Kosovar interpreter, who spoke five languages, hoped to become a doctor. I noticed the troops were quite wary of what they said in his presence; often in Kosovo there is a hidden agenda and almost certainly he was keeping the Irish camp under surveillance for the KLA. Even the mildest implied criticism of Kosovo irked him. When I exclaimed at the numbers of unregistered cars on this road he replied huffily, 'The registration process is now moving out from Priština but these procedures take time and we have much bigger problems.' One couldn't divine his real attitudes and opinions which may well have been fluid, depending on circumstances and opportunities. By then I had reason to regard many Kosovars as arch-opportunists – an essential survival mechanism, given their history. With it goes an admirable clan system of mutual support, both immediate and remote.

Račak, our next stop, is a tiny village which became of large significance on 15 January 1999. In Priština I had spent an afternoon talking to a young Račak man now living, with twelve other displaced Kosovars, in a two-roomed flat. His recollection of the local atmosphere at the time of 'the Račak massacre' was not quite in accord with the authorized version. Eloquently he described the terrified confusion, the villagers feeling almost as fearful of the KLA as of the Serbian forces. By then the KLA were giving priority to goading Nato into action on their behalf, to obtain independence for Kosovo – even if that meant sacrificing some of their own people to arouse international public concern and leave the anti-action lobby with no more wriggle-room. My informant asserted (and US military intelligence agreed with him) that the KLA's killings of numerous Serbian policemen in 1998–9 were calculated to provoke revenge attacks on villagers. The media then focussed on those tens of thousands, driven out of their homes and living in misery on high mountains. By implication the KLA were the gallant defenders of their terrorized fellow-Kosovars.

Near Štimlje we passed two villages where the KLA had ambushed and killed three Serbian policemen on 8 January and another on 10 January. The authorities then announced a major assault on the Štimlje-Račak area and, trailed by a TV crew, both the paramilitary police and the Yugoslav army moved in on 12 January. On the morning of 15 January some of the police and troops were taken on by the KLA around Račak village. When the guerrillas withdrew after a few hours, having lost nine men, the Serbian police found thirty men and boys hiding in a cellar and set the boys free. The twenty-three men may have been executed at 3 p.m. when distant shooting was heard in the woods above the village. Subsequently forty-five bodies were recovered there, lying close together and including several old men, three women and a twelve-year-old boy.

Throughout the day a Kosovo Verification Mission (KVM) team had been nearby – *how* near remains a matter for dispute. Following the Holbrooke/Milošević Agreement in October 1998, the 2,000-strong verification team had been deployed – and identified by the Serbs as a Trojan horse containing Nato spies. On 8 January 1999 they were proved right when the Mission leader, William Walker, told a State Department news conference that within the team 'sizeable numbers have military backgrounds. A lesser number, but also a sizeable number, have police backgrounds. I hope everyone on my mission is trying to gather as much intelligence as they possibly can. A lot of it comes back to Washington, but it goes to all the Nato capitals.' Not long before, the US Senate had passed a Bill calling for the overthrow of Milošević – and a CIA document, leaked on 12 January 1999, revealed that US$35 million was to be made available to FRY's opposition parties.

Warning lights flashed when the OSCE chose William Walker to lead its Verification Mission. A career diplomat, he had been special assistant to Eliot Abrams, who helped Lieutenant Colonel Oliver North in the White House's operation to overthrow the Nicaraguan government. During his time as US Ambassador to El Salvador, from 1988–92, military death squads, trained at the US Military School of the Americas at Fort Benning, near Columbus, had terrorized the country. On 6 May 1996 Mr Walker conducted a ceremony in Washington to honour the 5,000 undercover US soldiers who had fought in El Salvador while he was insisting there were only fifty US 'military advisers' in the country.

The 'unauthorized version' of the Račak killings claims that twenty-two were victims of that morning's fighting around the village. Allegedly, when the Serbs withdrew, those bodies were moved to the execution site in the woods where they were displayed next day, by the KLA, to Walker and his verifiers, accompanied by a CNN crew who filmed his emotional reaction to all those corpses and recorded his condemnation of this 'Serb crime against humanity', 'this unspeakable atrocity committed by Serbs with no value for human life'.

The cold-blooded massacre of forty-five panic-stricken villagers overtaken by ruthless Serbs as they fled through the woods has a resonance different from the execution of twenty-three captured men (war crime though that is) and the piecemeal deaths of twenty-two elderly men, women and a boy in the course of a gunbattle and heavy shelling. Many elements within Milošević's forces enjoyed indiscriminately massacring Kosovars (and others). But the seven boys found hidden in the cellar were freed before the men were taken away to be murdered, which suggests that indiscriminate killers were not in charge on 15 January.

Whatever the truth may be, 'the Račak massacre' had momentous consequences. The media coverage – including close-ups of blown-apart heads being viewed by a stricken Mr Walker – aroused worldwide horror and began to prepare the way for a general acceptance of OAF's inevitability. This atrocity was depicted and written up with few references to its complex background. Thus isolated, as an example of Serbian barbarity, it acquired a propaganda value denied to the Kosovars' killing, a month earlier, of six Serbian teenagers as they played pool in the Panda café in Peć. Or to the occasional murders by the KLA of Kosovars too vocally supportive of Dr Rugova's non-violent policies.

According to villagers who found the bodies at 4 a.m. on 16 January and testified to Human Rights Watch, 'It was clear that most of these men were fired upon from close range as they offered no resistance. Some of them were apparently shot while trying to run away.' In mid-February Dr Helena Ranta, who led an EU forensic team to investigate the killings, reported, 'There were no indications of the people being other than unarmed civilians.' However, within days a host of question marks had come to hover over Račak and they haven't gone away. The KVM's deputy leader, Gabriel Keller – a former *chargé d'affaires* at France's Belgrade embassy, whose reciprocated detestation of his boss was no secret – alleged that Walker had distorted the account of the massacre given to the world via CNN and other US media. A group of Italian military verifiers, writing anonymously in the geostrategic review *LiMes*, accused the US of 'sabotaging the OSCE mission' and of using it 'to give the world the impression that everything had been tried and thus create grounds for public consent to the aggression we perpetrated'. A Swiss verifier, Pascal Neuffer, noted, 'We had the very sharp impression of doing espionage work for the Atlantic Alliance.' Other verifiers complained that Walker controlled the mission's information flow, encouraged the KLA to provoke Serbian attacks and taught them how to guide bombers to their targets.

Viewed from the slope on which the massacre victims are buried, Račak's scattered red-roofed houses, newly white-washed, gleamed against a background of lush pastures and the mosque's slender minaret shone silver. Beyond stretched long, low wooded ridges, with gentle blue hills rising in the middle distance. On and around each grave were piled wreaths of artificial flowers and above this grassy ledge – not a formal cemetery – the Albanian flag fluttered high and defiant. Here, as so often in the Balkans, natural beauty heightened one's sense of the sheer futility of war. Kosovo's peasants, blessed by a fruitful land providing wholesome food, clean water, ample fuel and a healthy climate, should have been able to enjoy a social stability unknown to hungry billions on other continents. Granted, the ownership of Kosovo's territory has long been contentious and Albanians are prone to endemic clan feuding. Yet left to their own devices, including the archaic but serviceable Law of Lek, the Kosovars would never have had to endure such a turmoil of bloodshed, torture, fear and hate.

Mike and a corporal stayed with the vehicles, talking to a shyly excited group of malnourished children, while the rest of us ascended a long steep hill, knee-high in grass, to the wooded mountainside where the bodies were found. We climbed an unsteady old wooden gate at the edge of the forest, then continued up and up through a wondrous springtime richness: dog-roses budding, bracken uncurling, new-leaved beeches shimmering in the noon brilliance, no sound but birdsong, the narrow path stony – and then some stones were paint-daubed, to mark where bodies had lain. We could go no further (land-mines?) and looking back over Račak's tranquil valley, now far below, I tried not to imagine how the murdered men must have felt during their last moments on that January afternoon.

Several teams of Irish soldiers with building skills contributed voluntary labour to Mike's rehousing scheme, a private initiative (partly supported by Ireland's Ministry for Defence) to help the most destitute of Camp Clark's neighbouring communities. We visited one miserable Serbian enclave – previously a group of prosperous villages – guarded by Swedish troops. (Traditionally Serbs were Kosovo's most productive farmers; some say they had been given the best land, some say they were the most hard-working, others say 'it was a bit of both'.) The enclave's reactions to our K-For vehicles were interesting. Nato is both the enemy who defeated (sort of) the Serbs and the protector who now makes their survival in Kosovo possible – albeit under barely tolerable conditions. Young men gave us many hard angry looks but there were a few friendly waves and smiles from small children and elders sitting in the sun. Undercover JNA agents were known to lurk here, and also a sprinkling of criminals – both war criminals and the 'ordinary decent' sort. Mike remarked that when a conflict, as in Kosovo, has not been resolved no army retreats without leaving agents behind. When I asked if we might stop, for me to buy a box of matches at a crossroads kiosk, I was escorted to it by Sergeant Noel McCarthy with his rifle at the ready. My change for a DM10 note came in dinars, a currency valueless outside FRY since the Trio decided that Kosovo's currency should be the DM. However, I didn't choose to argue despite my armed guard. As we drove slowly along the rough, narrow, twisting roads, between neglected orchards and farmyards, no one was completely relaxed.

A muddy boreen (the jeep got stuck at one point) led to our destination. Amidst a group of semi-derelict dwellings, barns and stables stood an ancient stone house on the verge of collapse. The roof was leaking, the back wall bulging ominously, the insecure outside stairs and balcony were of rotting wood, the pine floor was also rotting fast and sloping perilously. Here lived a family of six, befriended by the Irish; nearby stood a solid, spacious brick bungalow, well insulated, with large windows and high ceilings, soon to be completed by one of the volunteer teams. Previously this family had lived in a Priština apartment. Then the refugees returned, the revenge killing of Serbs started and their Kosovar neighbours, at great personal risk, drove them to this village, the husband's birthplace, where they were now largely economically dependent on his father. In Priština he had been a street-sweeper, in the enclave he could find work only occasionally, as a farmhand paid by the hour. The six had been living for nine months in one small damp draughty room, furnished only with three collapsing sofas (their beds) and a wood-stove too rusty to work properly. They lacked most normal possessions, apart from the 'kitchen' equipment one might take for a Spartan camping weekend. I felt concerned for the mother, a squat unshapely woman with a broad ravaged face who wept continuously and uncontrollably while holding Mike's hands and thanking him for their new home. Very likely she had been through horrors never spoken of – not exorcised. And her father-in-law, said Mike, made her feel unwelcome. Her four quite beautiful children must have taken after pappa who did not appear.

Elsewhere in this enclave we stopped to admire other of the teams' achievements: badly burned homes perfectly restored with placards hanging in the windows saying 'THANK YOU IRISH TRANSPORT COY' – 'THANK YOU IRISH ARMY' – THANK YOU ALL THE PEOPLE IN CORK'. Noel, who comes from Youghal, had spent some of his home leave fundraising in Cork.

The sun was declining as we approached Janjeva. This mainly Catholic little town – Croatian and Albanian Catholics – adheres to the steep green slopes of two mountains at the end of a road where other forested mountains crowd around. From the late thirteenth century Janjeva was one of Kosovo's three main gold, silver and lead mining centres, the others being Trepča and Novo Brdo. The Croats first arrived here in 1303, possibly as miners. They no longer speak Serbo-Croat, only dialects of Albanian and Turkish, and there has been much intermarriage over the centuries; many Albanian clan names have Serbo-Croat suffixes. All the town's inhabitants – Croats, Albanians, Turks – have for centuries had the reputation of being honest, industrious, peaceable. And they were outstandingly talented craftsmen and women. Narrow cobbled laneways lead very steeply upwards between high stone and mud walls – two- and three-storeyed houses have tiny iron-barred windows at street level and wooden balconies above – superbly carved stone archways lead to hidden courtyards. No normal motor vehicle could cope with these gradients; a tethered horse wearing a wooden pack-saddle (almost identical to the one I used in Baltistan) panicked and tried to bolt as we passed. Near one summit stands a small simple church and on this Monday evening scores of men, women and children were slowly walking up to evening Mass. The women wore baggy pantaloons, intricately woven aprons, richly embroidered bodices and colourful headscarves – their everyday garb. From here we were overlooking all of Janjeva, hundreds of red-tiled, grey-walled houses jumbled higgledy-piggledy on those precipitous slopes. Tragically, many are now empty and disintegrating. In 1991 Janjeva's Croats numbered more than 4,000; in 2000 only 742 remained. The rest have 'gone to Zagreb'; when the Serbs attacked Croatia they felt it would be dangerous to stay where their ancestors had been rooted for 700 years.

Back at Camp Clark, Mike apologetically explained that the bar did not open until 8 p.m., after Mass – regularly attended by most of the troops. This piety suggests that the Irish army no longer represents a cross-section of the population. One engaging NCO in his early thirties had visited Medugorje twice while stationed in Bosnia and recalled, 'You know, Our Lady said she'd always protect the place – and she did, during the war!' I smiled politely and refrained from mentioning the vested interests involved in protecting Hercegovina's tourist industry.

After supper Noel drove me back to Priština; not even geriatric females are allowed to stay overnight at Camp Clark.

The collecting of my replacement map became a cliff-hanger because of Priština's 'civil unrest' (a curious term for an agitation that had produced some very uncivil behaviour). In all I paid eleven visits to the courier's office near the Grand Hotel; post-bombing, one couldn't ring up to check. My Priština OSCE friend had authorized the DHL chief to hand the 'item' directly to me. By 3.30 p.m. on Friday 28 April I was in despair; yet another 'event' had prevented travel to and from the airport. The approaching weekend included Labour Day on the Monday so nothing would be functioning until Tuesday, when I wanted to be in Mitrovica. However, the courier office staff advised me to return at 4.45 – they closed at 5.00 – on the off-chance their van might be able to negotiate the various barricades. At 4.40 I returned and YES! the 'item' had come – and been instantly delivered to the OSCE headquarters, which would also be closing at five. I sprinted there and arrived sweating and panting at 4.55. But no DHL packet had been delivered for Dervla Murphy – so said the young Kosovar man at reception. The packet was clearly visible on his desk, just out of reach beyond the security bars, but still he insisted – 'This not for you, this for a man called John Mur-RAY.' Frantically I demanded to see my friend, but he of course had long since departed; expat weekends tend towards elasticity.

'On Tuesday or Wednesday your friend can help you,' said the young man soothingly.

I lost my temper then, since there was nothing to be gained by remaining calm at 4.59. Hesitantly the young man allowed me to inspect the package, holding one end lest I might run away with it, and triumphantly I pointed to my name – which admittedly was much less conspicuous than the sender's. And so there was a happy ending at 5.01.

17

Tension in Mitrovica

The Greeks mined some silver and lead around Mitrovica and the Romans extracted vast quantities of both metals. These Trepča mines, worked by Saxon settlers, provided much of the wealth enjoyed by Serbia's medieval kingdom and the early Ottomans maintained production; at the end of the sixteenth century they were collecting annually more than 800,000 troy ounces of silver. Then for a few centuries the disorganized Turks more or less abandoned Kosovo's mines.

In the 1920s a British company redeveloped Trepča and during the 1930s one of Kosovo's few Communist Party cells took root there. In 1937 and 1939 these pioneers inspired their fellow-workers to strike in demand of less medieval working conditions. By July 1941 Germany's war industries were receiving every day 500 tons of Trepča's lead and zinc concentrate (some 40 per cent of the Reich's wartime lead consumption) and the Communist miners' amateur efforts to sabotage this enterprise failed ignominiously.

In the 1960s, it was established that this mining area contained 56 per cent of Yugoslavia's lead and zinc reserves, 50 per cent of its magnesite, 100 per cent of its nickel and large deposits of chrome, bauxite and iron ore. While Milošević was proclaiming the Serbs' passionate devotion to Kosovo – their 'Jerusalem', the fount of their spiritual sustenance – Robert Fisk characteristically shone a spotlight on reality:

Goodbye to monasteries and churches, Serb Orthodox graves, mosaics, frescoes and Byzantine temples. Goodbye to the spiritual strength of Kosovo. For here, deep in the mines of Trepča, lies the tangible value of this dangerous province for Slobodan Milošević , the richest piece of property in the Balkans, the vault of Serbia, whose worth in demonstrated and estimated reserves of lead, zinc, cadmium, silver and gold is a full three billion pounds. Even if the Field of Kosovo – the meadow laced with poppies where the Turks defeated Mediaeval Serbia – were to be abandoned to the Albanians [Kosovars], who comprise 90 per cent of the population of Kosovo, what Serb would ever renounce the Trepča mines?

Under the Trio, Trepča's future looks uncertain. Like all Kosovo's state-owned mineral resources and factories, it is claimed by both Kosovars and Serbs. Belgrade fancies partition, a little border adjustment which would move Mitrovica and Northern Kosovo into Serbia. The Kosovars' reaction to this idea may be imagined. The fact that Belgrade had already sold off large chunks of both the Trepča mining complex and Kosovo Telecom (KT) to French and Greek companies worsened the confusion surrounding their legal status. And similar complications arose because of the merging, after 1990, of many of Kosovo's industries and businesses with Serbian companies.

To the Kosovars, the UN mission in Kosovo seemed ill equipped to disentangle their economy from Yugoslav jurisdiction. The administration had made a smelly mess of the granting of rights to foreign mobile phone companies. The original network, covering only part of Kosovo, was owned by the Serbian Mobitel. When UNMIK and KT agreed to build a parallel network, KT chose the German company, Siemens, to construct it. UNMIK, however, decided the contract should go to the French company, Alcatel, which would transfer a large part of the profits to its base in Monaco, leaving only a small slice of cake for KT. Kosovar experts analysed the two contracts in detail and pointed out that the Siemens deal would be far more profitable for KT, whose managing director then refused to sign the contract with Alcatel. When UNMIK replaced this managing director by decree, awarding the contract to Alcatel, Kosovo's media responded by accusing UNMIK of arrogance.

The twenty-five miles to Mitrovica, through wide expanses of young wheat and ungrazed grassland, were not enjoyable. On this main road (there's no alternative) traffic is heavy and a strong gusty crosswind (surprisingly cold) increased the hazards. At 7.30 the first large white OSCE vehicle overtook me – and was followed, during the next hour, by twenty-two others. I counted them with mounting incredulity. Each held one or at most two passengers though they can comfortably carry ten. The pollution involved, the waste of fossil fuel and cynical squandering of taxpayers' money doubly enraged me when I observed that all were bound for the same OSCE enclave not far from Mitrovica. Apparently each expat must have his/her own status-boosting vehicle – a virus which has infected the bigger NGOs. In Priština I witnessed two colleagues from the same aid workers' office taking off for Prizren, forty-six miles away, in separate landcruisers carrying only the driver and a passenger. One vehicle left the compound at 8.15, the other at 8.30; one returned at 4.50, the other at 5.20. Both men had spent the day in Prizren town, which can be walked across in fifteen minutes. The fires of my rage are stoked when I see heart-rending fundraising photographs and remember the proportion of donations misspent.

Mitrovica sprawls amidst industrial wasteland overlooked by magnificent mountains. The famous mines are in those mountains, six miles beyond the turn-off for the town, but the road to Trepča was blocked by sandbags, razor-wire and ten surly French soldiers. Without a Special Permit I could go no further.

For a mile, from the main road to a 100-metre tunnel, the verges were heaped high with fetid garbage. Beyond the tunnel lay a charmless broken-down town ignored by the guidebooks and in May 2000 extremely tense. However, many of the locals were friendly and the traffic consisted mainly of K-For vehicles. The only hotel was inaccessible, on the north (Serbian) side of a bridge elaborately barricaded and guarded by two tanks. Here also one needed a Special Permit.

Tension had been high since the end of February when some 60,000 Kosovars marched on Mitrovica to demand that all displaced Kosovars should be allowed to return to their homes in the northern – always mainly Serbian – district. On the south side 220 Green Jackets were deployed to somehow dissuade 60,000 angry Kosovars from crossing the Ibar. The marchers pushed the soldiers back on to the bridge, where they were rescued by Danish and French riot police arriving from the northern side. So much tear gas was used to disperse the Kosovars that the Green Jackets unavoidably absorbed some – but it must have seemed very much the lesser of two evils.

Turning back from the bridge, I consulted a Canadian UN Policewoman who advised me to ask about lodgings at a particular café where, she assured me, the young men were 'dependable and not anti-K-For'. This assurance struck me as rather odd; I had not yet seen the recent K-For Civil Military Cooperation (CIMIC) report expressing Nato's concern about its forces 'having lost substantial credibility in the eyes of both the international and local communities'. The young men were indeed amiable but knew of no available lodgings. Mitrovica, like Priština, was overcrowded with homeless villagers. They could only suggest my asking local staff at the UN Police headquarters.

On the headquarters forecourt I chanced to hear Mrs Dedaj, a not-so-young Kosovar woman, talking English to Pierre, a very young Frenchman whose NGO was by way of 'reforming' the town bakery. (This sort of project raises Kosovar eyebrows – and sometimes hackles.) As Mrs Dedaj had a kind face I explained my need and at once she invited me to the bakery. One of its employees, Mr Foniqi, would certainly be glad of a lodger's DMs – Ruairi could ride in the NGO jeep.

The bakery was an enormous rambling building where I spent an hour in Pierre's office, furnished only with a small desk and two camp chairs, waiting for Mr Foniqi to come off his night shift. It transpired that he could not offer me accommodation – a cousin's family had just returned from Germany – but his brother-in-law, Mr Azemi, had several spare rooms. As we drove to the far side of the town, in an ancient rust-eaten car, Mr Foniqi excoriated the French and Russian troops for what he perceived as their pro-Serb bias.

At the end of a long dual carriageway, lined with small shops, shoddy apartment blocks and empty offices, we unexpectedly turned into Mitrovica's Hampstead. Here narrow streets wound between pleasant houses, some shaded by mature walnut or fig trees, most set in colourful gardens – tulips, roses, lilac, plum blossom. On the edge of this district stood Mr Azemi's three-storey brick villa, the third floor as yet unfinished – OAF interrupted construction.

Mr Azemi – tall and lean with thick black hair – had a long scar dramatically bisecting his left cheek. Mrs Azemi was also tall but portly and blonde and expansively good-natured. The eldest of their six children was a strikingly beautiful seventeen-year-old daughter. This was an affectionate, united family, though not without its problems.

My host insisted on Ruairi's being locked to an iron strut in his doorless garage and gestured towards children playing in the street, implying that they might steal this fine bicycle – though two of them were his own. Then he locked my panniers and other possessions in the first-floor drawing room, which seemed a bit extreme. However, when I disobediently left that door open, later on, my binoculars and Ruairi's pump vanished. I felt miserably guilty, poor Dad was so embarrassed. He gave his ten-year-old son a verbal thrashing and threatened him with a physical one if the stolen goods were not immediately returned – they were. Both parents, looking deeply ashamed, explained that even in this respectable neighbourhood the young had become compulsive thieves. Nothing was safe, not even their parents' property.

In the Azemis' case, that property was quite something. The ground-floor living room and the first-floor drawing room were stuffed with obese sofa suites (powder blue upstairs, blushing pink downstairs) and grossly gilded glass-topped occasional tables. Glass-fronted cupboards from Italy held shelves of Turkish copperware and brand new furry toys with TV associations. Tall veneered corner cabinets displayed showroom quantities of cut glass with the labels still on. The wall-to-wall carpeting came from Japan and the kitchen end of the L-shaped living room was at the cutting edge of domestic technology – though Mitrovica's erratic electricity supply, post-OAF, often sent Mrs Azemi back to her wood-stove. Mr Azemi operated an international trucking company, which explained a lot.

At noon I walked back to the town centre to keep an appointment with Agim, the son of a Priština friend. We were to meet at the café nearest the bridge and there, under a wide awning, sat a pale thin young man wearing the prearranged sprig of lilac in his shirt pocket. He stood up and began to apologize for not being able to offer me a room; foreseeing this I had been keen to find accommodation before our meeting.

Agim worked as a translator for a demining NGO; a family disaster had prompted him to seek that job. Two of his cousins, a brother and sister aged four-teen and twelve, had triggered a mine in October 1999, while collecting firewood near their village in the mountains above Mitrovica. Both lost both legs. Their father was among the thousands of Kosovar men still missing and presumed dead, though no one said so. Within a week of the accident their mother had a mental breakdown and was being cared for by her septuagenarian parents in Peć. Until she recovered the children would stay with Agim's mother, their aunt. 'But she gets no better,' said Agim sadly. 'For all these six months she only wants to stay alone in a room, not talking. The doctor gives her pills to sleep but he can't make her eat enough.'

Kosovo is not nearly as contaminated by landmines and unexploded ordnance (UXO) as are, for instance, Laos, Afghanistan and Angola. Yet between June and October 1999 more than 300 Kosovars were killed or severely injured. Nato dropped thousands of cluster bomb units despite the long-established fact that 10 to 30 per cent fail to detonate as planned. Cluster bomb units (CBUS) can hold different varieties of bomblets, the number in each unit ranging from 147 to 247. Once dropped, CBUS dispense their bomblets at a predetermined height and each is meant to have three effects. A fragmented metal body explodes into hundreds of shards that rip through soft targets like human beings; a shaped charge capable of penetrating tank armour explodes on impact; a zirconium incendiary coating creates additional effects – like carbonizing human bodies. In one small area near Mitrovica, Agim's team found 46 unexploded bomblets, in another area 108, some caught in the branches of trees, some hidden by dense vegetation or half-buried in soft wet ground, their protruding 'parachutes' beckoning curious child-ish fingers.

Near Musa village, a few miles from Mitrovica, a group of children returned home one evening full of excited chat about a fascinating bright yellow cylinder seen in a field. They were warned not to touch it but next day a young man noticed them crowding around the bomblet, discussing whether or not to pick it up. Angrily he ordered them to leave the field at once. Then, lest they might again be tempted to play with the device, he decided to move it and was killed instantly. The children were already at some distance but one boy suffered serious fragmen-tation injuries and lost a hand. In the same village, Serb-laid fragmentation mines killed 122 cattle within weeks of the refugees' return.

'We were everybody's victims,' said Agim, 'including the KLA's.'

During our conversation I had been keeping under surveillance the French troops on duty near the bridge. Some stood slumped against a wall, picking their teeth. Others were drinking cans of Coke and smoking as they sauntered to and fro. Occasionally one would hand his weapon to a buddy before nipping into a café for a quick brandy. Sauntering groups of youths sniggered at them – then laughed aloud when their sniggering provoked shouted abuse. The French were the least impressive K-For contingent. Throughout southern Mitrovica one could sense an alarming mutual hostility between troops and townsfolk.

'In Priština it's better,' remarked Agim. 'The British are the best. They behave politely and you never see them drinking and smoking on duty. The Italians are next best but not so friendly.'

When Agim went back to work I went shopping. Mrs Azemi wouldn't even consider accepting DM from a guest (albeit an uninvited one) so I had to go shopping; an appropriate amount of coffee seemed the safest choice, which led to my meeting Mr Pajaziti. His tiny aromatic shop occupied a corner at a Y-junction in Mitrovica's oldest district where the streets were narrow and the buildings decrepit in a mildly romantic way. He sold only coffee – the beans from a dozen countries, the roasting and grinding done to order to please individual palates. (Younger and linguistically depraved generations would no doubt describe this as 'personalized coffee'.) On realizing that I meant to bulk-buy Mr Pajaziti gestured towards a chair and requested his assistant to organize a tasting session. He was a dapper little man with a bald pate, shrewd twinkling blue eyes and fluent English; he seemed more like a professor than a coffee merchant.

Mr Pajaziti had never entertained any illusions about the Trio. He leant back in his chair, stretched out his short legs, lit another cigarette and said tolerantly, 'You can't blame them, they're lost in Kosovo, they've no mental map. They only have satellite phones and spy planes and e-mails – nothing to help them communicate with Balkan people. Surely they have good intentions about giving us stability and democracy and communal harmony and so on. It's a shame they can't understand how reality is, they're wasting a lot of money here. Nobody can *give* democracy to other people. People have to make it for themselves, when they're ready. The OSCE thinks it's "creating the conditions for democracy to take root". But it isn't, it can't. That's a K-For job – or a UN Police job but they're dysfunctional. And K-For doesn't have the mandate to get rid of our anti-democratic forces. They're not allowed to shoot the gangsters who don't want democracy. K-For have to be restrained, thinking about everyone's "human rights" while criminals run wild knowing they can get away with it.'

I said, 'But what you're suggesting would be a mini-war on the ground and Nato won't risk being hurt themselves.'

'That's unkind!' protested Mr Pajaziti. 'They mean to help, to show us a more civilized way of living. The problem is, they can't see there's no peaceful short cut to civilizing the Balkans. You have to go the long way round, through blood and more blood. The West's new ways of thinking can't control our old ways of acting.'

Back with the Azemis, I discovered that my first impression of Mr Pajaziti was correct; he had been a professor of philosophy in Belgrade until his philosophy diverged too openly from Milošević's.

As the sun declined we moved up to the third-floor balcony and sat on lengths of foam rubber sipping countless glasses of Turkish tea and nibbling very salty peanuts – served by the beautiful seventeen-year-old who was all the time running up and down the steep flights of stairs, bearing trays. In the near distance, beyond several half-built houses, stretched a low green mountain ridge beneath a subtly-tinted, ever-changing sky.

Soon twenty-four-year-old Nevrija joined us – dark-haired, sallow-skinned, sad-looking, the youngest of Mrs Azemi's family of seven sisters and one brother. She used to live in Djakovica, where she saw her husband being murdered by Serbian paramilitaries outside their apartment block. The couple's one-year-old son was also present – 'But he's OK now, he didn't understand.' According to Mr Azemi, 'There was no reason for this killing, only rage and hate.'

We talked about the difficulties of rearing children in a shattered society. Mrs Azemi worried about the long-term effects of fear, the sort of fear her children experienced when the bombing started and they fled to their Montenegrin holiday home in the mountains above Rožaj. Pre-OAF, while Serbian forces were repressing parts of rural Kosovo, the conflict was perceived as being between those forces and KLA-dominated villages and the apolitical Azemis in their quiet suburb didn't feel much at risk. Only when the bombing started did panic spread; then the Serbs treated all Kosovars as allies of the bombers.

Mr Azemi believed one effect of extreme fear felt in childhood could already be seen: a mindless indiscriminate aggression rooted in insecurity.

When I remarked that Mitrovica reminded me of Mostar – the river dividing communities, the atmosphere of bitterness, tension and suspicion – the Azemis looked at me blankly. Bosnia was not in their sights. Although so near in miles, its problems were remote and ill-understood. Kosovo's Muslims do not think of Bosnia's Muslims as natural allies and vice versa. Whatever fellow-feeling may exist is based on a shared anti-Serbness rather than Islamic solidarity; it would be impossible to find less 'fundamentalist' Muslims than those bred in the Balkans. As Noel Malcolm has observed, 'So untroubled are the Kosovars by religious politics that no one thinks it strange to have a "Christian Democrat" party in which the overwhelming majority of the members are Muslims.' Yet Serbian nationalist propaganda would have us believe that the Orthodox Slavs were being menaced by 'an Islamic crescent' stretching from Kosovo through the Sandak to Bosnia.

Twelve miles from Mitrovica a bombed bridge over the river Klina cut the road to Peć. Reconstruction work had just begun and a kind foreman directed one of his team to help Ruairi and me to negotiate the high, steep embankments. (The Klina itself was easily forded at the expense of wet trousers.) Then came forty traffic-free miles through a sparsely inhabited, unlittered countryside that was moving from springtime's promise to summer's bounteousness. And close by on my right rose the fortress-like 7,000-foot Mokra Gora range, marking the Montenegrin border. Some three miles out of Peć I joined a main road and was back in Litterland, amidst crazed drivers and dead dogs and cats.

In the town centre I stopped a well-dressed young man to ask the way to an Irish NGO residence where I had been invited to stay. His reaction was startling; ignoring my request for directions, he condemned the NGO in question for 'helping Serbs in their enclaves'. Such NGOs, he insisted, were being dishonest. 'They pretend they come here to help Kosovars and people give them money for Kosovars – not for Serb murderers and rapists!' He then introduced himself as Shaqir, a medical student, and expressed a wish to discuss 'the ethics of revenge'.

'Why not?' I said. 'But let's move to that café – I need a beer.' This encounter would never have happened had I been stopping my landcruiser to ask the way.

Shaqir seemed rather shocked by my beer-absorption rate – but then he hadn't just pedalled fifty-five miles. He made clear his 'ethical' position by asserting that after recent events any Kosovar is entitled to kill any Serb who stays in Kosovo. The region needs to be 'purified', blood must wash away 'the genocide'. I was about to dispute the use of this term in any Balkan context when our discussion was interrupted by the arrival of Shaqir's brother, several years older with a gaunt face and a permanent frown.

Hamdi was not talkative; he had recently been diagnosed, Shaqir explained, as 'clinically depressed'. In May 1999 he had seen a cousin and two friends shot in his village, after a torture session, by 'the criminals from Serbia'. All the victims were uniformed – but at the time unarmed – KLA members, as was Hamdi. He had bought his life with DM500 – which took me back to Rwanda, where similar deals were done during the genocide. The money, said Shaqir, had arrived from Germany the day before. 'Our sister works there, she's secretary for one of our big businessmen. In Germany live many rich Kosovars but now it's too hard to get a visa. You must prove you need asylum and they say we don't need it any more – K-For protects us. But K-For only protects Serbs!'

Hamdi's depression dated from that trauma. He feared to sleep, so tormenting were his guilty nightmares. That four-man KLA unit had been close-knit; only he had DM500.

Part of the Balkan tragedy has to do with peasant populations being so easily indoctrinated and roused to violence – and people like Shaqir do the indoctrinating and rousing. Most of the Kosovar fanatics I met were, like the Montenegrin Chetniks, educated middle-class men – or, occasionally, women.

Later that day I asked a likeable young Kosovar woman doctor why so many fine Serb homes had been vandalized in Peć by homeless returnees who could have lived in them. Crisply she replied, 'It was necessary to destroy those houses to tell all Serbs, everywhere, they can never, any of them, come back to Kosovo. When we get independence we will welcome other people, especially Americans who helped us with bombs. But Serbs will be killed if they try to come back. Maybe you think that's not right – maybe it isn't right. But they will be killed. Now Kosovo is only for us, not for sharing ever again with Serbs.'

In a village near Peć I met a Kosovar peasant mother of four daughters, aged twenty-four to fourteen, who had seen her sixteen-year-old KLA son being shot. The Serbs, having captured him elsewhere, brought him home to execute him in front of his family and neighbours. Through an interpreter his mother said to me, in her daughters' presence, 'I don't like girls, I didn't want girls, I only cared about my son – my only son!' This woman, hearing of the Trio's plans to encourage local Serbs to return, vowed that she, personally, would strangle with her bare hands any Serbian children who appeared in her village. I didn't doubt for a moment that she meant what she said.

In another once-mixed village a mother informed me that she would call the KLA to kill any Serbs who returned; her two sons were missing presumed dead. She derided claims that the KLA had been disbanded; she knew where to find them – they would always be available when needed. Uneasily I contrasted these attitudes with the reactions of so many Northern Irish parents who, after the murders of their children, appealed for 'no retaliation, no more killing'.

When Mr and Mrs Gashi invited me to supper I didn't expect to end up at a Divine Assembly prayer meeting. Mrs Gashi, a teacher, was Mr Qemalit's sister-in-law and her husband ran a thriving DIY store in the enormous basement, lit only by oil-lamps, of a badly bombed government building. (Post-OAF, all Kosovo's DIY stores were thriving.) In March 1999, when the Gashis took refuge with relatives who lived just over the Macedonian border, they met Linda and Alan, a young English couple dispensing aid to refugees. The aid was provided by their church or sect, the Divine Assembly – not an NGO, Mr Gashi informed me, but 'a group of the best Christians who spend their own money and don't collect from other people'. When the refugees went home Linda and Alan followed them and, since all their 'converts' came from Peć, rented a rickety old house near the centre and settled down, hoping to enlarge their congregation. By then the Gashis were, apparently, devout believers – 'Before we had no religion, we grew up under Tito, thinking atheism was the sensible way.'

After supper, Mr Gashi insisted on my accompanying himself and his wife and a seven-year-old son (the youngest of three) to their weekly prayer meeting. Linda and Alan, it seemed, were expecting me and I intuited the Gashis would lose face if I didn't appear. We drove across town in an elderly Mercedes ('Not stolen!' laughed Mr Gashi) and by torchlight climbed an outside stone stairway; firewood was stacked under the house. In a long, simply furnished living room the rest of the congregation had already assembled: ten young men and a young woman who shared interpreting duties with Mr Gashi.

Linda and Alan, a good-looking young couple, exuded the sort of determined cheerfulness often found amongst proselytizing evangelists. Fruit juice and herbal tea were served and bowls of nuts passed around. Then the proceedings opened with a short prayer of toe-curling sentimentality, followed by Alan's homily. He employed the 'softly softly' approach, no heavy fundamentalist stuff and no tackling of the currently topical issue of 'Christian forgiveness'. Next came 'Revelation Time'. As a teenager, Alan revealed, he had received the gift of faith through witnessing a miracle – a real miracle, like the miracles in the Bible. When a school friend developed a life-threatening ear abscess he was cured not by any medical treatment but by fervent prayer. As this was being translated I looked around the room, studying expressions; every face remained impassive. 'What', I asked myself, 'is going on here?' Was the Divine Assembly helping possibly traumatized young men in ways incomprehensible to me but none the less valuable for that? When Alan announced 'Discussion Time' and urged people to ask questions – to argue if they felt like it – there was a long silence, broken only by foot-shuffling. Alan tried again and the young woman began to say something, then stopped.

'Yes?' encouraged Alan. 'Is there something you don't agree with?'

A young man harshly intervened. 'If she doesn't agree with us she can go home!' He glared at the young woman who blushed crimson and looked down at her hands.

Alan couldn't cope with this jolt to the meeting's gentle rhythm. Hastily he stood up and led the closing prayer, after which Linda came to sit between Mr Gashi and me. From the ensuing conversation I learned that the Divine Assembly was helping to fund an extension to the Gashi home, to enable them to increase their income by letting a flat to expats. Given the family's comparative affluence, this could only be a ploy to bind them to the sect. Feeling increasingly ill at ease, I soon exercised my elder's privilege and suggested that it was time to go home.

Razija, a lawyer in her early thirties, could not under the prevailing conditions earn a living as a lawyer and was instead translating documents for UNMIK. 'Big money, much boredom! Is this good for Kosova? Is it right to have most professional people doing unproductive jobs near the bottom of UNMIK's ladder? Shouldn't we be helping to lead the country, to reform it? Not necessarily lead it politically, but intellectually, doing what we're qualified to do. In Kosova now are UN human rights lawyers – my age and even younger – from Norway, Kazakhstan, Tunisia. Why? They know nothing about the country, won't learn the language – how can they do a better job than I could?'

Razija was tall, slender, dark-haired, her hazel eyes deep-set. We were walking to the ruin of her home, through the narrow laneways of a once-prosperous suburb at the base of a towering mountain. More than half the visible houses were too war-damaged to be habitable.

Razija said, 'Here in Peje, Serbian savagery started with the bombing. Before that, it was one of the places least affected by "counter-insurgency" or our "war of independence" – however you like to call it. Then the Serbs said, "You and your KLA asked for Nato, now you've got it – so get out!" We were at their mercy and they had no mercy. The most terrifying thing was knowing so many had been released from mental homes and prisons. They enjoyed torturing and killing Kosovars. That wasn't KLA propaganda. If you met them on the street you could see the madness in their eyes.'

In 1988 Razija's teacher parents had invested all their savings in a handsome three-storey house set in a spacious garden behind high mud-brick walls. As Razija unlocked the metal double gate I noticed her jaw muscles tightening. She paused before pushing the gate open and said, 'I hope I don't cry. I do sometimes, even now.'

The family had left their home intact but returned to a fire-ravaged shell. However, being built of concrete it was restorable – 'If ever we can afford it!' said Razija. The Serbs had looted everything movable, including windows and doors – everything except the books. Mr Loxha had been bibliomanic since boyhood: over 2,000 volumes were burned. The charred remains of the larger volumes lay scattered about the floor. On his return, their grief-stricken owner had exclaimed, 'You can replace a house but never a library!' My heart ached for him. Razija said, 'I really, truly don't want to hate Serbs but now I can't stop myself . . .'

The long, high-ceilinged rooms had french windows and wide balconies and the remaining fragments of the banisters allowed me to appreciate how superbly they had been carved, in a style similar to Hydajet's brother's work in Pukë. In what was once a thoughtfully laid out and lovingly tended garden (Mrs Loxha's hobby) flames had leaped to the vine trellises but the fig, plum and pear trees survived. The basement provided ample storage space for home-made wine and *rakija*, grain and dried fruits, smuggled (sanctions-breaking) petrol and firewood. There the Loxhas cowered while hoping the airwar would be over in a few days – as forecast when it started. Ten Gypsies joined them, a clan who for years had supplied their firewood and who foolishly imagined that with 'rich people' they would be safe.

On 3 April, ten days after the bombing started, a platoon of Milošević's Special Police swarmed over the wall and ordered everyone to leave Kosovo, without delay. The Gypsies walked up the Rugovo Gorge, carrying their small children. Serb neighbours – old friends – gave the Loxhas shelter for one night while they were deciding what to do. They had been allowed to take nothing with them; the masked 'platoon' included local criminals wearing stolen uniforms. Razija hadn't heard of JNA troops being involved in such operations but by then they seemed no longer in control, except perhaps indirectly. It was widely believed that some 'understanding' between professional soldiers and thugs restrained the latter from indiscriminately murdering Kosovars. 'We think,' said Razija, 'the army chose to ignore all the looting and burning. But if too many Kosovars had been killed, instead of driven away, the army might have interfered with the looting.' Never having ventured out from their basement, the Loxhas hadn't realized that by 3 April most Peć Kosovars had fled in terror.

At dawn on 4 April seven Loxhas plus a baby set out for Rožaj, just over the border in Montenegro, in a small aged Škoda. The road was still crowded with refugees: thousands on foot, other thousands in horse-carts or tractor-trailers. 'Some walkers we recognized and felt so awful, having no room for them. We were sick with fear – Nato planes bombing and Serb paramilitaries on the road shouting – "Go back to Albania! You're not wanted in Montenegro!" We didn't know then what I've mentioned – the restraint on killing us. Every Serb with a gun we thought might shoot us all or worse. We heard about Nato telling the world they were helping us, preventing a disaster. It didn't feel like that. The confusion made the fear worse. Nobody knew what was happening or why, there didn't seem to be any plan or pattern. It wasn't a war, it was an upheaval. An "airwar" is just a game and later we heard the JNA had lots of fun getting Nato to waste millions of dollars bombing dummy tanks and so on. We nearly fainted with relief when we got to Rožaj. It's a small town, mostly Muslim, and people were kind though the place was chaotic, nothing organized for refugees – nearly 70,000 went to Montenegro. We knew nobody except the Peje friends we met. We were put in a small chalet up on the ski slopes and shared it with them – thirty-three people in two little rooms! But it was beautiful all around and we spent most of the day outside. After two weeks it seemed the bombing would never end and we moved down to Ulcinj where my mother has relatives – on that journey we pretended to be Serbs. We went by bus, leaving the car in Rožaj – it would have given us away.'

On 11 June, immediately after the Serbs withdrew from Kosovo and the Trio took over, Razija came back first on recce. 'Even though I expected what I saw it was a shock. The English phrase "heart-broken" is true, I could feel the pain in my heart.'

That day Razija found an empty, fully-furnished Serb house whose owners had departed with the JNA. At once she put a notice on the gate claiming the property (this quickly became the procedure, informal but accepted) and sent a message by an Albanian-Montenegrin bus driver urging her family to return. Next day an eighteen-strong village family arrived back from a camp in Macedonia and also claimed this house but somehow Razija retained possession. (Here the narrative got a bit fudgy and I sensed it might be tactless to seek clarification.)

At first Mr Loxha protested that he couldn't live in a Serb home amidst a Serb family's intimate possessions. 'But there was no alternative,' said Razija, 'and by now he's settled down.' Her mother had stayed in Ulcinj. 'She's still stressed, she won't ever recover. Many older women are like that when their homes are gone with all the things they collected and loved.'

Only a week previously the Serb had written from his new home in Podgorica to assert his ownership of the Loxhas' new home. 'We sent a message saying he couldn't have it though there's no proof he did anything wrong. Eighteen months ago we would not have behaved like this. We've changed. Many people have – and not for the better.'

Then Razija suggested a walk around the nearby mountain on a high level path from which one could see how grievously Peć had been damaged – by Nato, by Serbian forces and, to a lesser extent, by Kosovar returnees. I told Razija then about the three unappealing Kosovar men I had met in a café the day before. One spoke enough English to boast about the three Serb homes they had burned on their return because Serbian police had burned their village homes in April 1999. When I asked, 'Why didn't you move into those houses instead of burning them?' their spokesman replied, 'The UNHCR are giving us materials to build new homes.'

Those men took pride in their vengefulness. Razija commented, 'It's very Albanian. Now people call us "Kosovars" but our cultural roots are Albanian. It's foolish to forget that – can even be dangerous.'

Our path was directly above a straggle of old farmhouses with grey-brown tiles and ramshackle outbuildings. Some had been burned, some shot at or shelled. The mountain on our left rose steeply – pasture, merging into beech woods. A little way up from the path stood a solitary three-storey farmhouse with an old couple sitting on the first-floor balcony, gazing towards the horizon; the husband wore a loose turban, his wife a tight headscarf. Their son overtook us then: tall, thin, raggedly dressed and followed by a twelve-year old daughter carrying a pail of frothy milk. He saluted us, addressed me in rusty but serviceable English, invited us in to drink milk. His name was Ismail.

Entering the ground-floor room, we saw that this house, too, had been torched and looted though the massive rough-hewn roof beams were merely scorched and the stone walls smoke-blackened. But the looting had left this family destitute, one cow their only remaining asset. They were camping in their home, like that Serb family near Priština, Mike's enclave protégés. On the balcony Granddad welcomed us graciously but Grandma scarcely registered our arrival. 'Like my mother,' murmured Razija. 'She's still in shock. Maybe what they looted here wasn't so much but had the same importance.'

The daughter, pale and unsmiling, brought us our glasses of milk. Ismail accepted a cigarette from Razija and summoned his sixteen-year-old son; we had glimpsed him curled up asleep on the floor under a ragged quilt. He slouched on to the balcony, yawning and bleary-eyed, greeted us sullenly – then sat cross-legged beside his grandmother and looked up at her closed unhappy face with a tender smile that transformed him.

This family had trekked up the Rugovo Gorge three days after the bombing started, not fearing the bombs but greatly fearing the Serbs' reactions to them. The grandparents, in their late seventies, walked all the way to Andrijevica – at their pace a six-day journey. Before they left, Ismail killed a four-month-old calf and hunks were grilled every evening. His wife, a diabetic, died on the way. She was buried below the Čakor pass and it worried him that because the ground was so hard her grave was too shallow.

As we were leaving I whispered to Razija, 'Should we give the children some-thing?' She shook her head and afterwards explained, 'It would have been an insult, these are very traditional people and we were their guests, we didn't ask for milk.'

I wondered, 'Is there no help for such a family from all the millions – actually billions – of dollars sloshing around Kosovo?'

Razija vigorously kicked a stone: there was a lot pent up inside her. 'It seems they don't fit into any aid agency's "qualifying category". They have a home and a cow and a share in a small field. Aid bureaucrats like their categories. The three arsonists you mentioned earlier fit nicely into the UNHCR's "Category 5: Houses considered uninhabitable, irreparable and requiring reconstruction".'

We parted on the bridge, having spent a few moments gazing down at the narrow river's early summer turbulence. The Pećka Bistrica, bisecting the town, makes an important contribution to Peć's subtle charm. Racing out from the confines of the Rugovo Gorge it is strong, snow-cold, loudly insistent – an ani-mated affirmation of Nature's continuity, never mind how human beings are behaving. Thus it flowed when the Illyrians were around, when the medieval Serbian kingdom flourished and a monastery was built on its banks in the twelfth century, when the Turks came, when the Austrians attacked, when the Turks went, when later kingdoms came and went, when the Nazis came and went, when Tito came and went, when Nato came . . .

18

Enclaves at Risk

The 'humanitarian ethic' requires all aid workers to sound and act neutral at all times in the course of their duties. But in Kosovo personal bias occasionally surfaced, especially if individuals or groups with whom expats worked were involved in 'incidents'.

Some NGO workers showed rare courage by regularly visiting Serbian enclaves. To 'aid' them is one thing, to visit them unguarded is quite another; in Peć I heard threats being made against one named expat, seen as 'pro-Serb'. And of course there could be no question of my cycling to any of the local enclaves. Apart from K-For's ban on unauthorized visitors, I was told it might be unwise to be seen fraternizing with Serbs. In Prizren I would have dismissed such a warning as one more manifestation of Balkan paranoia but the intervening weeks had taught me much. So I travelled to the largest enclave in a style to which I am not accustomed, sitting beside the brave Kosovar driver of Pam's NGO jeep; Pam and her equally brave interpreter sat in the back.

For ten miles we followed a narrow green-hedged road running level towards Albania's mountains, their highest peaks still wearing coronets of luminous snow. We met only military traffic; this road is a *cul de sac*, ending just beyond the enclave, and these Serbs no longer run cars – there is nowhere they can safely go. The UNHCR was at that time planning an inter-enclave minibus service, to be escorted around Kosovo by armoured vehicles.

The Italian K-For roadblock was elaborate; barrels of concrete required vehicles to edge between them at walking speed, massed razor-wire writhed and glittered in the morning sun, two gigantic tanks with manned guns seemed grotesquely belligerent against a background of (apparent) rural peacefulness. These menacing monsters could have no possible function as a deterrent to stealthy murderers. Were they in situ lest the JNA might decide to return? Our familiar jeep was waved on and soon we reached a scattered village.

About 3,000 remained in this enclave where there was a ten-to-one preponderance of women; most were mourning menfolk either killed in combat, having joined Milošević's 'Specials' after the airwar began, or murdered by Kosovar returnees. The paramilitaries had used these amateur soldiers as cannon fodder – Nato-fodder – and forced Gypsies wearing JNA uniforms to bury Kosovar bodies.

This village, set amidst extraordinary natural beauty, had once been prosperous. A busy little river, sparkling through its centre, turned old mill-wheels in the shade of fig, walnut and mulberry trees. A maze of rough tracks linked sturdy old houses, built of alternate layers of wooden beams and neat mud bricks, and new homes modelled on German des.res. In a mini-lake, encircled by willows and alders, a myriad frogs were croaking their mating chorus – one could hear them half a mile away. Surrounding pastures were possibly mined and therefore unstocked; a few bony cattle, tethered in neglected-looking farmyards, munched fodder cut from the safe (demined) verges. Many houses had been demolished by the KLA, some had been abandoned and then vandalized, others were bullet-pocked but occupied.

We paused to greet one of Pam's colleagues who was trying to organize the re-roofing of the shelled community centre. As he could find no Serbs skilled enough to do the job, heavily guarded Kosovar workmen would have to be brought in, if any were willing to take the risk. This meant a loss of precious wages for the enclave and one of the aims of such NGO projects is to inject cash into impoverished communities while encouraging them to help themselves.

Even here the Serbs did not allow misfortune to unite them. A few days previously, the Orthodox Patriarch from Belgrade – a frail little man aged eighty-eight – had travelled to the enclave in an APC on a morale-boosting Easter mission. Outside the crumbling village church he was booed and verbally abused by an aggressive mob of about a hundred men and youths. Some said these were the last dregs of the local Communist party, resentful of church interference in Kosovo affairs; the Patriarch was reputed to favour discussions with Ibrahim Rugova's 'anti-violence' party. Others thought they recognized Chetniks recently emerged from the woodwork and contemptuous of Patriarchal moderation. Yet others alleged a Communist/Chetnik alliance – surely by now wildly improbable. Most villagers were mortified by this insult to their religious leader and people wondered why K-For could not keep the mob away from the Patriarch. They didn't understand about 'mandates'.

We visited four families and Pam's arrival brought smiles to prematurely lined faces. In each farmyard we sat outside (it was the beginning of the al fresco season) and coffee was served in due course; happily there is nothing 'instant' about Balkan coffee. Two households proudly produced communal bowls of their own fragrant honey and we dipped in with our coffee spoons. As Pam checked what she had to check I wandered around nearby orchards (plum, pear, cherry, apple) and noticed small boys playing – like their contemporaries all over Kosovo – with realistic-looking toy guns. Dangerously realistic, I remembered Mike saying. In

Kosovo's circumstances these should be banned; one could too easily imagine a nervous young K-For squaddie over-reacting . . .

More horror stories were told in these farmyards than I wanted to hear: but for some women telling them to the visitor from Ireland, through our interpreter, seemed necessary (therapeutic?). One tall, well-built woman with a strong square-jawed face had seen her nineteen-year-old son being knifed to death in the centre of Peć on 30 June 1999. She seemed to mistake me for a person of importance (my whitening locks can have that effect) and asked rather truculently why Kosovo's new rulers had not brought one person to justice despite the murder rate during their time in control. I tried to explain that they were not fully in control but were playing a game called 'State Construction'.

Coping with personal tragedies must be all the more difficult when there is too much time for brooding, when the routine activities of daily life cannot be resumed because one is not free to move, free to trade, free to seek education, medical care or entertainment beyond an enclave's confines. And the enormous Italian military base within this enclave was uncalming, a reminder of the take-over of FRY territory by forces which not long before were bombing the land. The only ray of hope shone from Italy where, according to one woman, Albanians are hated, whether they come from Albania or Kosovo or Macedonia. In contrast – she alleged – 'Italian people like to help us because they know we are innocent.' A few Italian tycoons and corporations had offered to pay for academically prom-ising boys to complete their education in Belgrade or Italy. When I asked, 'Only boys? No girls?' the women looked mildly amused at the quaint notion of their daughters going to university. This was not quite a twenty-first-century village.

At the end of the track, where the snow crests seemed close, we were overlook-ing steep grassy slopes, being stroked and silvered by the breeze. Here a small newish bungalow served as a spinning and weaving centre where a dozen not very skilled women – elders teaching youngsters – produced blankets, tapestries, table-mats. Pam's NGO had provided looms, spinning-wheels, wool and encouragement but in Peć there was no sale for work easily recognizable as 'Serbian'. Pre-OAF, Peć had the highest percentage of Serbs of any Kosovo city or town; now none was left, though many had moved only as far as Northern Mitrovica and were hoping soon to return – or so they announced. 'They'll be lucky!' our interpreter said grimly, through compressed lips. Pam did her best to sell the women's weavings among Peć's multitude of expats but admitted this was 'uphill work'.

Outside the weavers' centre 'the Professor' appeared, a gentle middle-aged man, erudite and charming, speaking fluent English – a person displaced by Milošević. He had been born in this village, had migrated to Belgrade at the age of eighteen with an Orthodox Church scholarship and there achieved academic distinction. Then he became a victim of Milošević's infamous 1998 Belgrade University purge and, when that failed to silence him, a target for assassination.

Even without the assassination threat, I could well understand his returning to the enclave, where he had inherited a few fields – enough to sustain himself and his wife. I had not forgotten those other purged academics met in Belgrade, transformed into hungry pavement hawkers.

Pam mentioned our plan to visit the Patriarchate on the morrow and invited the Professor to accompany us. He hesitated, looking wistful, then explained that were he recognized in the NGO jeep on the way to the Patriarchate we might all be ambushed on the way back. This depressing conversation was interrupted by one of the weavers, dressed all in black – the village women's uniform – who wanted me to know about her two sons. They had been beaten to death *en route* for Serbia and safety, beaten to pulp with blocks of concrete and iron bars – she couldn't tell them apart in the mortuary. They died in Priština hospital but only because the anti-Serb medical staff let them die – she was certain they could have been saved.

'I don't believe that,' said the Professor. 'For one thing, most of the staff were Serb at the date she's talking about. But the poor woman is half-mad with grief. The tragedy is she'll go on stoking her own and other people's anti-Kosovar hate with this illusion she has.'

Pam had offered to get me a permit to visit the Patriarchate of Peć, known somewhat hyperbolically as 'the Serbian Church's Rome' and in times past Peć's only 'tourist attraction'. It is now as closely guarded as the White House and a Visitor's Pass is issued only after detailed consultations between the Patriarchate's bureaucracy, the Italian K-For Commanding Officer and the applicant's guarantor – in my case Pam. Our negotiations were not expedited by Kosovo's communications deficit – a Nato bequest.

Pam and I presented our passports at the Italian base where none of the gate-guarding soldiers was authorised to admit us. We had to wait some ten minutes for a captain, summoned by radio – a cheerful, helpful young Venetian. The base's nucleus is a former shoe factory which not long ago, when the enclave's population was over 9,000, provided many jobs. K-For had added a townlet of prefab bedrooms and offices and planted rows of acacias around the blessedly litter-free compound. (Military discipline does have its uses.) In an office full of wireless equipment the captain offered us coffee before instructing a sergeant to begin the arduous task of communicating with the CO and the Patriarchate, putting the two in communication with each other and with Pam, and disseminating my passport details. After half an hour, during which nothing much happened, we were invited to lunch in the canteen where hundreds of tables occupied the factory floor. The menu was predictable: all the troops' food, and their drinking water, comes from Italy – for a good reason.

Of the 31,500 depleted-uranium-tipped weapons dropped on Kosovo, 14,180 fell between Djakovica and Peć in K-For's Italian zone. Those figures were publicized by Valerio Calzolaio, Italy's Deputy Ecology Minister, following the deaths from leukaemia of twenty-eight-year-old Giuseppe Pintus and twenty-three-year-old Salvatore Vacca in September–October 1999. Both men had served in BiH – where DU-tipped weapons were also used – from November 1998 to April 1999.

On 22 November 1999 Robert Fisk wrote in *The Independent*:

A growing number of doctors and scientists suspect that an explosion of cancers in southern Iraq is caused by the US use of DU during the 1991 Gulf War . . . Italian K-For troops now manning a checkpoint only a few feet from the craters of a Nato DU bombing at Bistrazin have no idea that depleted uranium dust was scattered over the ground around them seven months ago . . . A [K-For] British ordnance officer told me, 'I give three pieces of advice to my men if they think they are near DU munitions explosions: stay away, stay away and stay away'.

Four months after my visit, two soldiers from the Italian base were rushed to a Rome hospital with 'leukaemia-like' symptoms. In Peć on that occasion Colonel Gianfranco Scalas, Nato's spokesman, announced reassuringly that 'examinations of the field had repeatedly shown that the present radioactivity was within normal limits'. In April 2000 the Belgian government began a medical check on their 14,000 K-For troops and six months later André Flahaut, Belgium's Defence Minister, admitted that those troops were 'suffering from a continuous deterioration of their health condition'. He proposed setting up a special life-insurance system for 'peace-keepers' but avoided mentioning DU. Both DU and cluster bombs, as 'weapons of indiscriminate effect', violate Article 51 Protocol 1 of the Geneva Convention.

Within an hour of our returning to that patient sergeant in the radio office, all was well – everybody had communicated with everybody else and the Patriarchate and its 'defence force' were prepared for my arrival.

In all the Balkans' conflicts, religious buildings and monuments have been major targets because they are felt to symbolize the 'other's' rootedness in the disputed territory. In BiH more than 1,000 mosques were destroyed. In Kosovo, between June and December 1999, approximately one hundred Orthodox churches and monasteries were viciously vandalized, or burned or dynamited to rubble. Most of those buildings dated from the fourteenth century and one – blown up by the KLA immediately after the JNA withdrew – contained a precious library of manuscripts dating from the fourteenth to the eighteenth century. No wonder the Serbian Patriarch concluded: 'These acts of vandalism cannot be called acts of individual and blind revenge. It is becoming increasingly evident that there is a systematic strategy in the background to annihilate once and forever all traces of Serb and Christian culture in Kosovo.'

When I talked about Kosovo's enclaves on my return home people looked baffled and asked, 'Why do any Serbs hang in there? Why not move to the safety of Serbia? What can be their children's future?' But Kosovo's Serbs know the score; grim as life is in their enclaves, it is measurably less grim than the conditions being endured by many displaced Serbian peasants in Serbia.

The Trio's inability to create conditions in which Serbs may safely lead a normal life underscores the limitations of militarism; with all the most up-to-date weaponry in the world you cannot change one man's prejudices. Nato's KLA protégés are determined to drive all Kosovo's Serbs out of the province – their home territory, where they have every right to remain. Would it not be kinder and more practical to stop the 'Let's pretend' game and re-settle those Serbs who cannot fend for themselves in various Rich World countries? The majority would certainly jump at any opportunity to shake the Balkan dust off their feet forever.

That evening the Irish army invaded Peć, as my fellow-guests at the NGO residence. It was good to see Mike and his men again – twenty of them, plus their chaplain, the Rev. Michael Murphy, recently retired from missionary work in South Africa. As a caring CO, Mike regularly took batches of twenty to relaxing weekend parties in comparatively luxurious surroundings. (Wherever NGOs proliferate, so do parties; teams based in areas like Kosovo have to be self-entertaining.)

During the evening, Pam and Mike went into a huddle about the Professor. Plainly he had longed to accompany us to the Patriarchate; a visit to that 'significant place' would sustain him spiritually and he surely needed such sustenance. However, as K-For was not mandated to organize spiritual sustenance for individuals he could not request an Italian armed guard. But Mike was happy to help; the success of Irish soldiers as UN 'peace-keepers' has much to do with their humane flexibility. On the following afternoon an Irish K-For minibus, in which the Professor could travel unseen, would fetch him from the enclave.

I had already walked out towards the Patriarchate, a mile or so from the town, tucked away between wooded foothills where the river emerges boisterously from the Rugovo Gorge and overlooked by an Italian road-block-cum-camp. Terraced fields behind the monastery compound, sloping up to the base of a cliff sprouting dwarf oaks, are now perforce neglected – too vulnerable to snipers. The Patriarchate's site is visually more impressive than its three little churches, their cupolas so inconspicuous a motorist could easily pass by without realizing that here is the faintly beating heart of Serbian Christianity. As J.A. Cuddon wrote in his *Companion Guide to Yugoslavia*: 'Between them the three churches form the Canterbury of Serbia but the whole group would fit into Canterbury Cathedral five or six times, and in St Peter's would look no bigger than a summer house.'

Noel Malcolm claims that the Patriarchate is here by chance:

Kosovo was not the main focus of the church-building activities of most medieval Serbian rulers, although important churches and monasteries were built there, particularly in the fourteenth century. One factor only made Kosovo central to the Serbian Church: the location of the seat of the Archbishopric, and then Patriarchate, in Peć. This was largely the consequence of a chance attack on the monastery of Žiča in the 1290s by a marauding force of Tatars and Cumans. Had those raiders taken another route, perhaps Kosovo would never have acquired the significance which it has gained for modern Serbs.

The oldest structure, the Church of the Apostles, was probably built in the early thirteenth century by the Patriarch Arsenius at the request of St Sava, the founder and first archbishop of Serbia's national Church. At the beginning of the fourteenth century two more churches were added and Archbishop Danilo II's biographer records that he wished to build a shared narthex 'worthy of much talk' – which he did, in about 1340. It was famed for its beauty, but during restoration work in the 1560s its external archways had to be filled in for safety reasons and it is now a mere architectural curiosity. Further seventeenth, eighteenth, nineteenth and twentieth century restorations have inexorably diminished the Patriarchate's aesthetic appeal.

In 1346, half a century after that raid on Žiča monastery, the Serbian Church moved its seat to Peć. In the same year the Archbishop, having been promoted to Patriarch rank, crowned Tsar Dušan in Skopje – assisted by the Greek Archbishop of Ohrid and the Bulgarian Patriarch – anointing him Emperor of the Serbs, Greeks and Albanians.

In 1459, soon after the fall of Smederevo – marking the final overthrow of the Serb state by the Ottomans – the Serbian Patriarchate was abolished and its spiritual power transferred to the Greek Archbishops of Ohrid. Almost exactly a century later it was revived by Mehmed Sokolović, one of many Serb Bosnians who had accepted Islam and risen high in the Sultan's court. He had in fact risen to the top and, as Grand Vezier, he appointed a relative (some say a brother) as Patriarch Makarije of Peć – which became once more the Serbs' cultural and national centre.

After Makarije's death a succession of Patriarchs turned political and began a national liberation struggle through unwise negotiations with Austria, Russia and even, in their desperation, the Pope of Rome (not an obvious ally for Orthodox clergy). In the mid-seventeenth century the Patriarchate bonded with the Russian Orthodox Church; senior monks travelled to Russia and brought back cash gifts, liturgical accessories, printed books and moral support. That last was badly needed towards the end of the century when Austro-Turkish hostilities involved the Patriarch; he had been inciting rebellion against Ottoman rule in Hercegovina and encouraging Serbians to join the Austrian forces. In 1688 the Patriarchate's priceless treasures, collected over four centuries, were hidden in the dome of Gračanica monastery – but someone tipped off the Turks, who needed nine pack-horses to transport their loot. There followed the Serbs' Great Migration of 1689 to Austrian-held territory, led by Patriarch Arsenije III. The migrants included Kosovo's most prosperous and best-educated Serbs; it was a Balkan equivalent of Ireland's Flight of the Earls. And soon many thousands of Albanians came down from their high, bare, ungenerous mountains to settle on the deserted fertile land between Peć and Prizren. The Pasha of Peć then annexed the Patriarchate's land, but after much hassle it was bought back in 1720.

Another Austro-Turkish war (1737–39: they were two-a-penny in the eighteenth century) required another Patriarch, Arsenije IV, to flee from the Ottomans; he, too, had been 'promoting treason', as the Turks saw it. (And as the Austrians were to see it pre-1914, when the Serbs encouraged BiH to rebel after its 1908 annexation by the Habsburgs.) In 1766 the Patriarchate was again abolished and until the Serb uprising of 1804 only Greeks were appointed as higher clergy in the Serbian lands under Ottoman rule.

During the Ottomans' decline their empire was for generations on a life-support machine provided by the British and the Austrians, who then valued Turkey as a barrier between Russia and the Near East. Meanwhile the Balkans sank deeper and deeper into a poverty from which the Patriarchate was not immune. As its own guidebook puts it, 'At this time there was no important artistic activity'. That is an understatement. The painters then employed, who superimposed their own daubs on glorious fourteenth-century frescoes, did damage to make you weep.

In 1924 the first Patriarch of the new kingdom was enthroned in Peć and seven years later extensive restoration work began under the architect Djurdje Bošković. All the monastery and guest-house buildings are comparatively modern, dating from the nineteenth and twentieth centuries.

To fetch the pilgrim – as I thought of him – we drove in convoy to the enclave: Mike and Fr Murphy in the jeep, Pam and I and the armed escort in the minibus. The Professor, standing outside his house with a friend, asked if the friend could come too. Stefan, aged fortyish, thin, dark-skinned, unshaven, poorly dressed, was just back from a Belgrade Displaced Persons' Centre. Although the enclave offered him nothing much it was better, he reckoned, than the Centre. On our way back to Peć he seemed very tense and the Professor explained that he was worried about his house, bought fifteen years ago when he married and started a bakery business. Had it survived when the JNA withdrew? We did a detour to pass it and saw a burnt-out ruin. Stefan said nothing but his grief was angry. I thought then of Razija, coming back to her burnt-out ruin. Her home attacked by Serbs, Stefan's by Kosovars: this was not war but criminality unrestrained, a social sickness rather than a political/ethnic crisis. Razija and Stefan were both civilized human beings victimized by their society's collapse into anarchy and then morally degraded, provoked into hating 'the other'. Given a Tito-style law-and-order régime, Peć's Serb and Kosovar communities, whatever they might have muttered about each other in private, would never have been tempted – or dared – to burn each other's homes.

Despite all those ritualistic radio negotiations at the Italian base, and Mike's rank, the sentries in their boxes at the Patriarchate gate would not admit us, or even allow us to approach the gate, until they had checked within to make sure we were expected and not KLA in disguise. There must have been a communications failure; we had arrived punctually at the prearranged time.

Looking across the river, I saw a level path running along the mountainside, not far above the water. This is much used by Kosovar villagers who, as they pass, shout abuse and make threatening and/or obscene gestures whenever any resident of or visitor to the Patriarchate is seen at the gate. (Nobody can be seen within the high perimeter walls.) A target so exposed to attack from both mountainsides can be only partially protected. At the turnoff, where a little track runs down to river level from the road, K-For maintains a sandbag-fortified camp and a round-the-clock guard. Here all IDs are checked and car boots opened but, given the nature of the terrain, this is little more than 'gesture security'. Several Kosovars remarked to me that K-For's 'Serb Protection programme' was, as one Priština intellectual put it, 'laying emotional mines for the future'. 'Protecting Serbs' looks like 'distrusting Kosovars', which generates hostility between K-For and the majority of Kosovars who feel no impulse physically to harm Serbs. And it can be seen as a challenge by that minority who consider themselves entitled – even obliged – to seek vengeance. But given the corner into which the Trio has backed itself, what is the alternative to this programme? When I asked that question in Priština there was a one-word answer – 'Migration!' (of Serbs).

Two Italians escorted us through the high arched gateway and formally delivered us to a youngish handsome monk speaking fluent English. His long black robe emphasized extreme tallness and slimness – an enchanting coincidence, such figures being common in fourteenth-century frescoes. (Or had he been hand-picked for the job by some imaginative superior with a nice sense of the appropriate?) His long beard was a shade darker than his very long golden-brown pony-tail, his nose was Grecian, his eyes sapphire-blue. He apologized for not being able to stay with us – he was just then in charge of someone Very Important – later he would be at our disposal.

In the monastery garden water whispered: rills were running through stone channels from an ancient sparkling fountain. Vivid green grass, too long to be called a lawn, was bordered by white-painted stones and aromatic shrubs. Over all presided a gigantic walnut tree, reputedly more than 550 years old. It seemed a fanciful sculpture in wood, an artist's deviation from a tree, wild and dark and eccentric, its contorted branches thrusting and twisting this way and that at unlikely angles, obeying none of the laws laid down by Nature for the development of trees. Suspending disbelief, I sent my mind back 550 years; in 1450 it would have been a sapling – perhaps planted by order of Tsar Dušan?

An elderly monk who spoke German but no English conducted us through the churches. The narthex, once Archbishop Danilo II's pride and joy, is now a drab enclosed space; little has survived of the original frescoes and only a fragment remains of a reddish marble baptismal font placed in the traditional south-west corner. Within the churches one is frustrated by dim lighting, faded colours, crumbling plaster, clumsy restorations or additions. To appreciate the frescoes' multiple messages one would need to be knowledgeable about the politics and theology of the contemporary background, and how these influences mutated from century to century. One would also need at least eight hours and a strong electric torch.

We were invited then to view the fish-farm, a 1980s commercial enterprise still flourishing despite all and an important source of income – as is the honey from a row of beehives shaded by spreading mulberry trees. These monastic products are popular with expats. We were admiring the four large ponds, full of the fattest trout I have ever seen, when three nuns joined us – still wearing, unlike their Roman Catholic cousins, habits (black) and coifs (white). They bore, I noted with interest, trays of bottles and glasses. The Patriarchate is noted for more than one kind of spirituality and the bottles contained home-made *šljivovica* (plum *rakija*), *komovica* (grape *rakija*), *travarica* (herb *rakija*) and *orahovac* made from walnuts – a new experience for me. Everyone was encouraged to sample each of these distillations. Pam backed off after the *šljivovica* but the Irish army and I proved equal to our task. (The Professor and Stefan had stayed in the churches, in their sacred space; here they were pilgrims, not sightseers.) The Patriarchate also owns venerable vineyards from which came wines famous throughout the Balkans; but K-For could not guard that land and Kosovars had appropriated it. However, a few cows, many fowl and a vegetable garden made the monastery almost self-sufficient in food.

The youngest nun, a twenty-six-year-old from Belgrade, hoped it would be possible to spend the rest of her life in the Patriarchate's convent; she believed the world is doomed unless the majority in every country recognize the power of prayer and the need for frugal living to protect the environment. She had a long pale face, level dark eyebrows and an aura of detached serenity. Then suddenly she laughed quietly. 'You look puzzled!' she said. 'You don't understand why a young woman chooses to be locked in here? But I like thinking and this is a good place for thinking.' (I was reminded of Mujica on his mountain above Sarajevo.) As we talked on she referred to the Patriarch's recent analysis of the Kosovars' anti-Orthodox campaign. 'I feel he left out something important. This campaign is not coming spontaneously from inside Kosovo. It's an import from Enver Hoxha's Albania. Kosovo's Muslims always had respect for our churches and shrines, often came to Christian holy spots praying for help with barren women or harvest problems. But you know how it was in Hoxha's Albania, people driven to hatred of all religions and this infected the KLA leadership.'

It was coffee-time – sobering-up time. (The nuns, I should make clear, do not drink alcohol.) Descending to the garden, we joined our fellow-guests: three Russian UNMIK bureaucrats and a Portuguese UN policeman with an interesting face who told me, 'I come here every Sunday to unwind in this tranquillity.' Rather a false tranquillity, I thought, given that all the residents are prisoners.

The lay residents, already sitting at a trestle-table under an acacia, were half a dozen devout elderly women whose Peć homes had been destroyed. They now lived in the guest-house, being cared for by the nuns. One was knitting nonstop and at intervals declaimed fiercely: 'Communism of all sorts is a veer-us! Every sort is a veer-us!' She glared at me, as though suspecting I might disagree, and repeated, 'A veer-us! People thought it was a better sort under Tito but they were wrong. Everywhere, always, Communism is a catastrophic veer-us – a catastrophe!'

Another woman – the youngest of this group – had persuaded her only surviving son (his brother, a JNA officer, had been killed in a KLA ambush) to stay with her in the Patriarchate where she watched him closely. But one day he eluded her and walked into Peć for a haircut and (one imagines) a bit of café life. Two months later his decapitated body was found by chance, because of the stink: it had been loosely covered with rubble in the ruins of the family home, not far from the Patriarchate. His head was never found.

Rebecca West dropped two clangers in one sentence when describing a meeting in this garden, in 1937, with Serb women who 'were old enough to remember the bad days in Petch when the Turks had so encouraged the Albanian Moslems to ill-treat their Christian fellow-Slavs that at every Serb funeral the corpse was pelted with stones and filth.' Apart from Albanians not being Slavs, there is no historical evidence, as distinct from anti-Turkish legends, that the Turks routinely encouraged their Balkan subjects to ill-treat one another. The Ottoman ideal was an empire inhabited by peaceable, hard-working taxpayers; the last thing they wanted was sectarian turmoil. As Stevan Pavlowitch explains in his *History of the Balkans: 1804–1945*:

The Ottomans rarely took the Orthodox Church seriously as a potential danger. Fanatics roused a Muslim rabble now and then, and there was haphazard persecution, but in general the authorities did not object to the practice of Christianity so long as Christians remembered their inferior status. Its very weakness as an organization ensured the survival of the Orthodox Church. It was kept alive by the fact that most Christians clung to their faith. It learned to endure humiliations passively.

Perhaps that passivity partly explains why I found the Patriarchate lacking in the emanations one might expect. There is no feeling of continuity – naturally enough, in view of its history. And its present circumstances – reviled by the town's citizens, guarded by alien troops, inhabited by embittered displaced persons, cynically exploited by irreligious politicians as the main reason why Kosovo must remain part of Serbia – all this can only create an unquiet atmosphere. But possibly I would have reacted differently had I been alone, able to wander around for a few hours in silence. I am not good at group sight-seeing, however congenial the group.

For bedtime reading I borrowed a newly-arrived *Spectator* (22 April 2000: only a fortnight late) and read Samuel Brittan's verdict on contemporary Kosovo:

> More Kosovan Albanians – let alone Serbs – were killed after the war started than before . . . We now have an anarchic and violent aftermath. The agreed division of labour was that the Americans would bear the brunt of the fighting, but that the Europeans would bear the brunt of reconstruction and policing and the formation of legitimate civil authority. Predictably they have failed to respond adequately. Even after a lot of prodding they can only talk of grandiose aid schemes and capital projects to gratify European construction companies. Meanwhile the Danube is still blocked and . . . Serbia, which was one of the richer Balkan republics, has now achieved the distinction of a lower GNP per capita than Albania.

Experienced Peć friends advised me on my choice of route into Montenegro. The alternatives were a traffic-demented main road to Rožaj and a little-used track through the Rugovo Gorge and over the Čakor Pass to Andrijevica. Since the spring thaw Serb military activity had increased along the border, tension was rising in Montenegro and Andrijevica's 100-bed hotel had been taken over by Milošević's 'Specials'. However, parts of the Rugovo track have deteriorated to danger point for vehicles ('in poor condition' warned my map) and this region, never densely populated, had recently been almost completely depopulated. With luck, I would get through to Andrijevica unhindered.

At 6 a.m. I set off – the air cool, the sun just up, the cloudless sky pale blue. As I passed the Patriarchate the Italians were brushing their teeth outside their tent. They paused to stare at me in wild surmise, then recognized the mad Irishwoman and allowed me to pedal on unchecked. Mike had kindly provided an Irish army tricolour badge to pin on my shirt and an Irish K-For disc to hang around my neck: the contemporary version of a protective talisman.

'The Rugovo Gorge' is a misnomer, an oversimplification. The road to the Čakor Pass, built in 1925, twists its way for twenty-four miles through a complex mountain massif offering extreme contrasts: the fierce barrenness of the first gorge (there are two) – open sunny pastures – antique pine woods, dense and dark

– the even fiercer second gorge – then treeless grasslands at 6,000 feet where in mine-free days shepherds lived in reed-built hamlets tending their flocks throughout the summer.

Viewed from the Patriarchate, the massif ahead seems impenetrable. Then suddenly one is in the Gorge, the Bistrica in spate double-echoing back from soaring rock walls, creating a curious booming sound. On a few high ledges solitary pines had grown to maturity; they only looked like dwarfs because of the Gorge's immense scale. Here again I noticed that when cycling upstream, close to fast-flowing water, one seems to be expending more energy than is required by the gradient – a strange illusion. Over the first ten miles this gradient was easy enough and the surface tolerable – for a cyclist.

Where the Gorge widened slightly, burgeoning shrubs and saplings filled clefts near track level, their exuberant growth emphasizing the silver nakedness of the battlements above. Occasionally brown streams from melting glaciers leaped down precipices to discolour the green Bistrica; as one passed them the air temperature dropped perceptibly. Then a newish wooden farmhouse appeared on a strip of grassy riverbank; beside it two cows and their calves were tethered under a tree. This was the only occupied home I saw all day.

As the track wound around the base of a beech-wooded mountain I was overlooking on my left a narrow, shallow sunlit valley from which broad pastures, alternating with patches of pine forest, rose steeply towards snow-streaked rock summits. A few isolated abandoned dwellings clung to grassy precipices; given politically settled conditions, this now-deserted region could support a thriving peasantry. Often I paused, to marvel at my surroundings, and it was 9.15 when K-For's border checkpoint appeared ahead, a little camp at a junction with a pony-track. The four bewildered-looking but polite young Italians glanced at my passport, offered me a drink of bottled water and wished me well.

Now the track briefly descended, curving around a lowish ridge until the camp was out of sight. Here I was in Gorge II, in no man's land, beyond K-For's control yet far from Montenegro, beginning an eight-mile push – no more pedalling. Sheer cliffs rose thousands of feet from the permanently shadowed river. '4,000 feet', guessed J.A. Cuddon, but that was an exaggeration. I reckoned 2,000 or so – which is still overwhelming, when you stand, feeling very tiny, and look up. Sometimes the track became an ankle-deep stream of melted snow coursing over pretty multi-coloured pebbles – jewel-like in the brilliant sunshine – before cascading into the turbulent torrent on my right, a river halfway to being a waterfall. Thirteen months previously, thousands of terrorized refugees had fled this way and left their imprint – many wayside trees mauled for firewood, much pathetic litter strewn around overnight campsites. Even in May the temperature dropped as I ascended and amidst the twilit pine woods snow glimmered in gullies. When the Kosovars were struggling upwards, the nights must have been perilously cold.

I remembered too the Second Serbian Army which in 1915 retreated through the Gorge in an exceptionally severe midwinter, accompanied by many of their womenfolk and children. In 1915 this track was no more than a pony-trail and the rivers had to be forded. Near Peć they had destroyed or buried their heavy guns and military equipment, to deny them to the Austrians, and had reorganized themselves into mountain warfare platoons. They were marching towards the Adriatic coast and Corfu, where the British gave succour to their surviving Balkan allies. Thousands died of hunger and cold or were killed by Albanians.

After a few miles I crossed the Bistrica, loudly foaming around boulders on a partially blown-up and clumsily repaired small bridge. Beside it stood the remains of a JNA armoured vehicle – very blown up. Soon I could see the end of Gorge II directly ahead, a dramatic bastion of rock mountain (this one not far off 4,000 feet) forcing the track to swing away from the river and begin a climb so steep that frequent pauses were physiologically as well as aesthetically necessary. At this height the beeches had only begun to bud though down on the plain they were in full leaf. A series of hairpin bends (their verges crumbling over 1,000-foot drops) took me above the treeline; here were severe escarpments and phallic peaks surrounded by rich grassland, now mined and cluster-bombed. These meadows displayed an extravagant glory of wild flowers. Sheets of cowslips covered some slopes; otherwise I could identify only foxgloves five feet tall, outsize buttercups, hellebore, cyclamen, violets, broom, peppermint. A few days later, at a similar altitude in Montenegro, I strolled through a meadow and counted twenty-seven varieties of flowering plants.

Rounding yet another hairpin bend, I could see in the distance a substantial two-storey building on a wide ledge below the track – and, in an adjacent field, a solitary figure leaning on a long stick. Moments later, I realized that the figure was a cleverly constructed scarecrow. And the building was a derelict bullet-riddled police barracks.

Up and up zigzagged the track, its gradient but not its surface now less punishing. Approaching the pass, I could see a glittering snowline – and soon I was on it, the track blocked for some forty yards. That was daunting; I didn't have much energy left for dragging a laden bicycle through two feet of spring-softened snow. And beyond that challenge came another, much more serious. Two Serbian paramilitaries sat smoking in their parked jeep – hard-faced middle-aged men, listening to a politically correct tape of Montenegrin folk-music.

At first the advantage was mine; I had been half-expecting this contretemps whereas the paras had certainly not been expecting the arrival of a cyclist. Momentarily they looked almost scared, as though I were some threatening incarnation of a malignant mountain spirit or the ghost of a slaughtered Kosovar granny. Then one man got out to confront me, pointed to my K-For disc and shouted, 'Here is Yugoslavia, Nato cannot come!' I should have foreseen that hereabouts Mike's talisman would have a negative effect, contradicting my claim to be an innocent tourist – which anyway was implausible, given the shortage of tourists on the Čakor Pass in May 2000. Having scrutinized my passport, the para triumphantly accused me of having no tourist visa for Yugoslavia. But I was already – was I not? – in Yugoslavia. By Belgrade's reckoning, Kosovo is very much part of Yugoslavia, so why did I need a visa to proceed into another part of Yugoslavia? But my captor was unwilling to discuss such delicate matters. Curtly he ordered me to wait for 'the Captain' and returned to the warmth of his jeep.

Sitting on a boulder I shivered in my sweat-soaked garments and snow-soaked boots, then stood up and groped in a pannier for my emergency flask of *rakija*. This felt like a genuine emergency, justifying *rakija* consumption at noon. As I moved, so did my captor – taking his revolver from its holster lest I might be fetching a weapon. Sweetly I smiled at him, took a swig and offered him one. He stared, then grabbed the half-litre flask and retreated to the jeep where his companion was laughing raucously. Something else I should have foreseen: Serbian paras are not into reconciliation.

On the 6,500-foot pass, once an Ottoman frontier post, nothing man-made marred the jagged arrangement of lower mountains on which I gazed in suspense. Would I be allowed through them? To the south-west rose the Prokletije range, shared by Albania and Montenegro, its dominant peaks – Bogićevica, Maja Rozit, Djaravica – all between 7 and 8,000 feet. No motorable track connects the Čakor area and Albania but several convenient pony-trails do. When the UN imposed sanctions on Yugoslavia the pony- and mule-loads of cigarettes and drugs were augmented by petrol. But even the sturdiest pack-animal cannot carry very much liquid and only rich Montenegrins could afford the fuel thus transported.

After an hour and twenty minutes the Captain arrived – tall and so grossly obese that his small jeep looked unequal to carrying him up mountains. My K-For talisman didn't become an issue; he must have had the wit to realize that Nato spies don't wear Nato discs. But in a manic way he ranted about Ireland's refusing visas to Serbs and supporting the UN sanctions and boycotting the Yugoslav soccer team. Then he noticed my 1999 Serbian visa – expiry date 18 November – and accused me of overstaying by six months. This was getting ridiculous – I pointed to my Zagreb entry stamp for 27 February 2000. Finally we got down to business: a DM100 fine was demanded. I tried to explain why I had no visa: it was all the fault of the Yugoslav consul in London, who had assured me I could get one in the Zagreb embassy where in fact they only issue visas to Croatian citizens. But the DM-centred mood of the moment was not conducive to a consideration of my plea. I accepted that I was in the wrong, legally, yet I could not accept that these paras were legally empowered to fine me. I thought fast. If I paid up, would they allow me to continue? That seemed unlikely, given the hostility being shown by all four. (The Captain's driver was singularly unpleasant.) I therefore refused to pay and turned Ruairi towards Peć, whereupon the Captain informed me that I was under arrest and would be imprisoned in Andrijevica; his driver was ordered to load Ruairi into a jeep, which he promptly did. Equally promptly I took out my purse and handed over the 'fine', then pretended to assume that I could now enter Montenegro. The Captain tucked my DM into his wallet, gestured to the driver to release Ruairi and shouted 'No! You go back to your Nato friends!' Perhaps the paras really did feel vindictively anti-Irish? Yet in Serbia, six months previously, being Irish had saved me from being ostracized. But then I was dealing with normal Serbs.

As I recrossed the snow obstacle both jeeps moved off, doubtless heading for the nearest café and a rave-up at my expense. I reflected then that I had been lucky; the paras could have robbed me of everything – journal-bag, money-belt, camera, binoculars, Ruairi and the panniers. Perhaps Mike's talisman had worked, suggesting some status which might provoke a fuss were I to be seriously molested.

Three months later, in the same area, two Englishmen and two Canadians were less lucky. Then, probably for the first time in its history, the little town of Andrijevica hit the (inner page) international headlines when the four were jailed there, preparatory to being shown on Serbian TV as 'undercover agents', suspected of having entered Montenegro illegally to teach the local police how to organize anti-Serbian 'terrorist actions'. The two Englishmen were working for the OSCE in Priština, the Canadians were an uncle and nephew employed by the Meridian road construction company; all were without visas. Explosives were found in the Canadians' vehicle – because, explained uncle, they had left for their Montenegrin holiday in a hurry and he forgot to remove them. No wonder they ended up in jail.

I don't like, on my travels, to be defeated, to have to turn back. I longed to continue to Andrijevica, doing a six-mile detour to Lake Plav en route. And I dreaded being traffic-tormented on the main road to Rožaj. On such occasions my obstinate streak and my cautious streak collide. I thought – why not sleep in the deserted police barracks and cross into Montenegro before dawn, when the hungover paras were unlikely to be on duty?

Descending to the ledge, I peered through shattered windows and saw bloodstained walls and floors. A door stood open but I decided against entering; such a building could well be booby-trapped. Sitting on short grass – the ground around me strewn with spent bullets – I ate bread and cheese and toyed with the idea of putting up my tent, despite the incompatibility of tent-pegs and landmines. But bread and cheese are calming foods; they nourish caution rather than obstinacy. Then a surge of parsimony clinched the matter. Supposing I were to make that dawn crossing, spend a few hours around Lake Plav, arrive during the afternoon in Andrijevica – and there find myself paying another DM100 to the Captain . . .

By 6 p.m. I was back in Peć, where a friend remarked that DM100 seemed a mild fine – almost kindly, perhaps linked to the current Balkan perception of cyclists as wretchedly poor folk, unable to afford even a stolen Mercedes.

19

The Uniqueness of Montenegro

Before sunrise I was on the newish 'highway' to Rožaj, pedalling past bombed and burned dwellings and shops and barns and a shelled mosque. Outside the little village of Vitomirica – almost a suburb of Peć – I counted thirty-two trucks parked by the roadside, their drivers still asleep at 6.15; K-For would man this checkpoint at 7 a.m. These colossal articulated monsters bring aid from Western Europe and planks for rebuilding from Montenegro. In theory K-For prevents weapons-smuggling; in practice, here as elsewhere, that is easier said than done.

At first the climb was gradual and on either side verdant flower-bright meadows lay beyond those 'Irish' hedges so often seen in Kosovo – ash plants soaring above dog-roses and woodbine. Then, at the base of the mighty Mokra Gora – its lower slopes fragrant with mimosa and acacia – my fifteen-mile walk began. This is a well-graded road, its tar not too broken and the traffic flow less dire than I had feared. Many hairpin bends led to a false pass where the Italians have a big camp. As something had gone wrong with their communication system no traffic was being allowed past a roadblock. Twelve trucks stood in the 'departure' queue and countless others, visible in the distance, formed the lengthening 'arrivals' queue. I paused to rest near a three-sided, chest-high sandbag enclosure protecting a weapons-laden youth who viewed me with a mixture of suspicion and ridicule. His CO soon came striding down the road, saluted smartly and said, 'You may be on your way – I think you have no drugs to sell!'

As I continued, almost all of Kosovo became visible: the familiar mountains along the Albanian border – the central plain – Priština's smudge of polluting smoke – the Star Planina range on the Macedonian border. Remembering the deprivation I had witnessed throughout Serbia it seemed outrageous that 243 aid agencies still remained in this tiny province, while Serbia's eight million were being ignored (*punished*) by most aid providers. According to three Priština-based aid workers, representing different agencies, helping Serbs was simply *not on*. So successfully had they been demonized, to justify OAF, that few donors would support 'Serb Relief Programmes'. Even worse, many donors might be alienated from an agency that 'helped all those bad people'. This discrimination directly flouted the 'humanitarian community's' traditional ethos. And what a contrast to K-For's protection of the Serbian enclaves!

After a short descent the road rose again, much more steeply, through stony mountains supporting only scattered pines and sparse rough scrub. Snow lay in the many deep gullies, still gleaming white on 9 May, and whenever the sun was briefly enclouded the cool air became cold. Kosovo's early summer lushness seemed very far away. For miles ahead I could see my road blasted out of pale grey cliffs, blatantly a creation of modern technology, wounding the landscape – unlike the Rugovo Gorge road, a mere improvement of an ancient track. Despite its wounds this was an exhilarating landscape, wild and open – a continuous ascent around mountains that didn't seem as high as they were because machines had found the easiest way through. Soon came a sign in six languages saying 'YOU ARE NOW LEAVING KOSOVO. KFOR TROOPS TURN BACK.' A thin line of red paint on the road surface marked the border – but why here? I could see no topographical or other feature that made any sense of this particular spot as a 'frontier'.

Towards noon the traffic increased, laden vehicles descending the severe gradients at 15 k.p.h., their brakes squealing and groaning, audible miles away – the returning empty trucks rattling quickly uphill. By then the bare rock peaks on my left were close and jagged, beyond a narrow, shallow valley of coarse shaggy grass, still winter-yellow, where tall rough boulders thrust out of the earth at odd angles. The brilliant sunshine had lost its heat and when I paused to rest I found myself shivering. Approaching the pass, the road ran level for a mile or so between slopes no longer naked: their scattering of dwarf pines seemed black amidst glistening expanses of snow. My map leaves this pass nameless and gives no altitude; but my lungs told me it is, by European standards, a high one.

On 3 May 1999, between 11.45 a.m. and 1.30 p.m., Nato repeatedly attacked this road near the pass, dropping numerous cluster bombs and firing three Cruise missiles. Seventeen passengers in a civilian coach travelling from Djakovica to Podgorica were killed and forty-four injured, some so severely that they have been crippled for life. Several bomb craters are visible. To the west stretched many miles of valuable summer grazing, now too dangerous to use. I was not tempted to linger on the pass; it is a favourite truckers' picnic spot with consequences that can (or perhaps cannot) be imagined.

Now distant stretches of Montenegro's fertile lowlands could be glimpsed between a magnificent multitude of intervening mountains. Then the road plunged into pine forests, covering near-precipitous slopes for mile after mile. These were mighty trees, not crowded and puny as in sterile, silent commercial plantations but allowing undergrowth to flourish and joyous with birdsong. It didn't matter that here the surface was wrecked; I wouldn't have wanted to speed downwards. Eventually beech woods replaced the pines, steep fields appeared, and then the first dwellings I had seen since sunrise, old stone farmhouses with shingle roofs. Another bend brought into view a dramatically deep valley, seeming from above a mere cleft, separating towering mountains and scarcely wide enough to accommodate both the road and the infant river Ibar which rises nearby as a noisy, speeding, sparkling stream. In a hamlet on its left bank trucks were being checked by four Montenegrin police who showed no interest in my passport; I got the impression they wished to pretend they hadn't seen me.

The remaining few miles to Rožaj sloped gradually down; here some shingle roofs had been replaced by tin – uncommon in the Balkans – and glossy cattle and ponies grazed in small fields. The surly locals did not return my greetings; from their children I picked up rather unfriendly vibes.

Soon I could see below me an oval green valley, perhaps ten miles by six, its encircling mountain ridges of varying heights – to the south-west rose snow giants. The road became very steep through Rožaj's 'suburb' of solid two-storey homes in what I thought of as 'German wages style'.

Reaching level ground, on the busy main road from Novi Pazar to Berane, I stopped at the first café. That pass had left me with but a single thought – *pivo*. Sitting on a raised terrace, within sight of Ruairi, I was welcomed by Hashim, the elderly owner, his eyes wide with curiosity. Having heard my story he sat beside me and proudly declared, 'Here in Rožaj all can be friendly – is not like Kosovo!' Around this one table, he pointed out, were a young Serbian woman (his waitress), a Rožaj Muslim trader, a Kosovar refugee from Peć who had chosen to settle here and practise his tailoring craft, a Croat truck driver employed by UNHCR – and Hashim himself, a Bosniak-Montenegrin cross who had moved from Mostar as a youth. He repeated, 'In Rožaj all are friends, Montenegro has no problem only from outside people try to make problems for us – between us. They are bad ones who need for themselves all the power.'

I found this factually inaccurate statement strangely moving: at least Hashim had wholesome aspirations. It saddened me to look at my companions' faces – here were individuals bred in Yugoslavia, ordinary people not really knowing why their country had disintegrated, gathered around this table by chance in an amity that was not feigned. Hashim wouldn't let me pay for my three bottles of *pivo* and as I left he presented me with a banana and a bouquet of lilac from a bush hanging over the balcony.

In the not-so-distant past, demented architects roamed loose in Yugoslavia and gave birth to monsters like Rožaj's hotel: broad at the base, immensely tall, narrowing storey by storey and culminating in a beak-like roof. Inside, one couldn't escape from full-length mirrors. Everywhere were mirrors: in the foyer, behind the reception desk (but there wasn't a receptionist, the manager or owner doubled), on each landing, along the corridors, in the loos, on each side of each square pillar in the many-pillared restaurant. Why? Above all, why in the restaurant? Who wants to watch their reflection chewing very tough steak, an activity that enhances nobody's appearance? Before long I felt threatened by loss of identity; given so many mes, was there a real one?

My DM50 room overlooked a green space where children played merrily until after dark and the animated chatter and laughter of strolling adults mingled with distant Montenegrin folk music. Many youths wore apparently expensive 'fudbal' gear which puzzled me until someone explained that these were obsolete club 'strips' discarded by Western Europe's over-indulged youths while still almost new, then donated to 'refugees', stolen by Balkan entrepreneurs and sold at locally affordable prices.

Rožaj is mainly Muslim but with a handsome Orthodox church; it was a relief to see it unguarded and to be in a town unblemished by war damage – though an air of destitution prevailed. The contrast with Kosovo was obvious and disturbing. In the Trio's 'protectorate' aid dollars were creating an artificial prosperity not based on internal resources or endeavours, yet making many Kosovars seem well off compared to most Montenegrins. As one Priština-based UN volunteer bluntly put it, 'We're breeding parasites here and what will they feed off when we go?'

Another contrast with Kosovo was pleasing. There everyone warned me that Ruairi needed maximum security; in Rožaj the hotel manager assured me that he would be safe if left unlocked just inside the main door – 'OK, no problem for thieves here, all is honest!' After that, I felt it might be taken as an insult if I locked him – and even in the twenty-first century one has to be careful not to insult Montenegrins.

In this 100-bed hotel I had only one fellow-guest, a heavily-built, tight-lipped, grey-haired man who dined facing the wall in a far corner of the vast restaurant. Dinner was predestined; the waiter looked embarrassed when I asked for a menu. A small steak, overcooked to leather consistency, was accompanied by a small tomato – sliced on a separate plate but undressed – and one repulsive white bread roll resembling melted plastic.

The middle-aged waiter, small, slim and sandy-haired, had rotting teeth, bulging pale blue eyes and enough English to convey his hatred of Nato and his support for Milošević. 'Before the bombs I had no politics, now all Serbs must have support for our leader. In Montenegro we are all Serbs – you know that? In this town you meet other people but they are not Montenegrins. Now Nato wants us to say we're different from Serbs and want our own country but this is not true. They want to weaken Serbs by dividing them. First they take Kosovo with bombs – Kosovo, our sacred place, our first home! Now they want also Montenegro, then next Vojvodina, then Serbia, all to make a fine new colony for America, to give control of oil from Central Asia. We know this game, we are not stupid! They want to make a war here, two bits of Montenegro fighting – then they come saying they protect us and teach us democracy and peace! And here maybe is easier than

Kosovo, here now they have their puppet – and more like him if we kill him which we will if the fighting starts . . .'

The waiter didn't bother to listen to my response; he knew what he thought and he was sticking with it.

Not far beyond Rožaj I took a rough track to Berane, climbing gradually around grassy mountains, their lower slopes dotted with red-roofed farmhouses set amidst blossoming orchards. Then came two hours pedalling on a soft carpet of pine needles near the crests of ridges where the air was richly resinous and birdsong the only sound. Eventually the track narrowed to a mere path and a long descent followed, the surface too broken for cycling. But I was happy to walk, slowly, prolonging my time in this Paradise. The path, clinging to almost vertical slopes, overlooked a series of ravines – a thousand feet deep or more – and from those profound depths to the high summits stretched a flawless covering of beech, birch and hazel trees in all their springtime glory. Often I paused to sit in warm sunshine on the flowery edge of a precipice, watching raven aerobatics, listening to the silence, relishing the solitude of this most lovely hidden place. Each journey provides certain enduring memories, days or hours set apart from all the rest when everything converges to create pure enjoyment – something more often attained through music. That detour, from the moment I left the main road, was one such occasion.

Gradually the ravines widened, then became uneven grassy valleys where a few little houses were built on hillocks. Here the path retrieved its 'track' status and for miles the rock cliffs from which it was hewn displayed extraordinary and very beautiful colours – glistening bottle-green and blue-green and turquoise, the fallen slabs and slivers by the verge looking as though highly polished.

When the scattered village of Trpezi appeared, far below, the track suddenly acquired a new tarred surface and I met a motor car – just one, but enough to break the spell. Swiftly I freewheeled down and down, no braking needed for the easy curves and Ruairi having a rare opportunity to prove himself a racer in disguise. Our descent ended on a tiny stone bridge across a lively stream. Here the noon heat felt oppressive but oaks and sycamores shaded the steep climb out of that cleft.

At a junction two friendly young roadblock policemen invited me to sit on their bench, offered me a mini-carton of juice, asked for my passport and map and showed me where I could not go – which was where I wanted to go . . . (In Berane I learned that my preferred route was then being controlled by Milošević's Special Interior Ministry police.) One officer pointed to his home on the far side of a wide valley and urged me to view it through my binoculars. 'It is fine good house, yes?' There he lived with his parents, his wife and their newborn baby. His father had recently retired after working for thirty years in Hamburg while his mother brought up two children and farmed five hectares. No wonder the population dwindled, with so many dads spending so much time abroad, coming home only at four-or five-year intervals for a brief holiday.

Soon I was pedalling again, across gently hilly arable land where several substantial farmhouses stood by the roadside and the grandmothers wore calf-length black skirts and headscarves, the mothers and little girls Bermuda shorts, the little boys 'fudbal' gear. Soon those long skirts will be seen no more. Throughout this area, and between Berane and Kolašin, I noticed an astonishing number of identical male twins.

During the final steep descent, around craggy mountains, I realized that I was ravenously hungry; Rožaj's hotel served no breakfast. The usual industrial (or post-industrial) mess disfigured the outskirts of Berane, a large bedraggled town retaining a few traces of dignified nineteenth-century prosperity but by now only marginally less depressing than Nikšić.

Food was not easy to find. At 3 p.m. the wide streets were almost deserted, most of the little restaurants and *burek* shops were closed and the few open 'supermarkets' sold nothing that could be eaten raw. Under the awnings of pavement cafés sat small groups of men, looking uncheerful. In the open-air market, where stallholders were packing up, I found a hand of bananas and ate them on the spot. By then I had registered tension in the air – not the exciting sort generated by a specific crisis but a low-level unease, a sense of waiting for some nebulous but unpleasant development. Yet in general the natives were diffidently – almost furtively – friendly. And one woman was positively outgoing.

I met Ana when at last I came upon an open café-cum-*burek* shop – a cabin of a place, five little tables crammed together. She was eating a dry bread roll with her coffee (she couldn't afford *burek* at the equivalent of 25p a slice) and on seeing a foreigner she stood up to shake my hand, welcome me to Berane and ask why I was travelling by bicycle. A Serb from Knin, in her forties, she was tall and thin with a bad complexion and dull black hair. She spoke fluent English and told me her parents still lived in Knin – 'They refused to be ethnically cleansed, they are brave!' She hadn't seen them since 1995. 'Their hearts are broken because they have missed my daughters growing up – two daughters, twelve and fourteen. My parents love them very much, they have no other grandchildren, they have missed them every day since 1995.' Ana knew it would now be safe to visit Knin but she couldn't afford the fares – more than DM1,000. And her parents were almost destitute; the Croat army had reduced their home and business premises to rubble and 'they are too old to start again'. Ana had three jobs: doctor's receptionist in the forenoons, private secretary to a local politician in the afternoons, English teacher in the evenings and at weekends. Her average monthly earnings came to DM250. Before we parted she gave me her parents' address and begged me to visit them. 'To see you will make them happy because you have seen me. Tell them, please, I look well and all is fine for me . . .'

The present Berane (Ivangrad in Tito-time) is a recent development, dating from 1862. The Lim river rises nearby at the foot of the Čakor Pass and is Berane's saving grace – wide, shallow, swift, sparkling a clear emerald green, spanned by two modern bridges. I had crossed one on my way into the town and now I crossed the other to reach the Category B 200-bed Hotel Berane. This barracks-like structure – five storeys high, fourteen bedrooms long – is separated from the Lim by a complex of ugly, angular restaurants and cafés, now unused. (Previously Berane, like Rožaj, was a popular tourist resort – national rather than international.) Graffiti artists had been busy here and litter lined the empty swimming pool. A bronze statue of a naked ballerina (originally a fountain, spitting water towards the sky) had greatly offended the local Orthodox clergy when it first appeared. So I was informed that evening, by an off-duty police captain. He added, 'Sometimes, when our young men get very drunk, they try to use that woman – it is funny to see!'

Directly behind the hotel are sloping green fields with bushy hedges and in every other direction rise Berane's guardian mountains. Six cows were grazing on the former lawn, their herd an ancient woman squatting under a mulberry tree. She wore a filthy but colourful traditional costume and was smoking what seemed to be a homemade cigar of notable pungency. She smiled at me toothlessly, waving a greeting.

I thought I had become immune to the ugliness of Balkan hotels but Hotel Berane proved me wrong. The shudder-making foyer – very long, wide and high – sported rows of shiny brown imitation-wood pillars, bile-coloured circular floor rugs, fat orange leatherette chairs on thin metal pedestals, twee little tiger-striped stools, hideously 'innovative' pseudo-chandeliers and lurid murals depicting Lake Plav at all seasons. Symptoms of neglect were everywhere; tourism had died and the Tourist Union of Yugoslavia could not afford to maintain all this pretentious vulgarity in a pristine state. The friendly staff spent most of their time relaxing in those repulsive chairs, coffee-sipping, chain-smoking and chatting. However, my DM35 room was inoffensively utilitarian.

I had planned to avoid a day on the main road by going to Kolašin via Andrijevica and Mateševo, through the Biogradska National Park. But that whole area had recently been taken over by Milošević's 'Special' forces and on the edge of Berane a massive sandbag barrier, unmanned at 6 a.m., blocked the road to Andrijevica. Obviously my karma did not include a visit to that town.

For the first twenty miles out of Berane the E65 runs due north, beside the Lim – then for fifteen miles due west, climbing steeply, before the Bjelasica massif allows it to turn due south for Kolašin and Podgorica. This region presents a different sort of beauty around every corner. Sometimes ferocious naked rock mountains formed the backdrop to placid riverside pastures where lines of shimmering pussy-willows hid the Lim and women were milking cows into wooden pails. Elsewhere rugged red-brown cliffs loomed close on both sides – or immense expanses of pastureland swept up and up to the base of stern silver escarpments – or hillsides were smothered in blossoming orchards, looking like pink-white clouds that might at any moment float away. And everywhere the verges were radiant with variegated wild flowers, in the early morning all dewy and twinkling.

At 11.30 I passed the small town of Mojkovac and noticed a contingent of 'Specials' who had taken over the hotel and were patrolling its environs with rifles at the ready. Abruptly I changed my mind about pausing to explore this fourteenth-century town.

Two hours later a torrential downpour began without warning as I was approaching a disintegrating 'MOTEL'. This building, huddled under a grassy cliff half a mile short of the turnoff for Kolasin, was literally falling apart (recalling Pukë's hostelry) and DM10 seemed a reasonable tariff for an adequate room with hot water '*en suite*' between 5 and 7 p.m.

When the rain stopped at 2.30 the crests of Kolašin's surrounding mountains remained lost in dense cloud and the air felt damply cold – quite like home. Hungrily I set off from the motel on foot, passing three affable Montenegrin policemen, crouching inside their minuscule sentry-box where a bridge over the river Tara joins the E65. Kolašin, on the left bank of the Tara, was a winter sports centre in happier times. Its name means 'St Nicholas' in Albanian – oddly enough, given the Balkan penchant for changing place names to suit political evolutions and revolutions. In medieval times Serbs settled here, as their empire expanded, subduing or banishing the original Albanian residents. Then Catholic Albanians recaptured the town (their home territory is close, as the raven flies) and in due course the Ottomans took it and established a strongly fortified outpost. During the eighteenth century, as happened in other corners of Montenegro, thousands of Muslim Albanians were absorbed by the Serbs and adopted both their religion and their language. The unabsorbed Muslim Albanians frequently attacked those renegades, until in 1858 an alliance of several neighbouring Serbian tribes overran Kolašin and slaughtered all who had retained their Albanian identity.

The 'Specials' had also requisitioned Kolašin's 150-bed hotel, and its adjacent rows of tourist chalets, and had sealed off a public park overlooking the Tara. (Another demented architect – or maybe the same one? – had designed this hotel; its eaves reached almost to the ground and its roof was dotted with fake portholes.) A score of 4 x 4s marked POLICIJA were parked outside the hotel and vicious-looking, heavily-armed foot-patrols prowled about the town centre. As elsewhere

in Montenegro, the regular police – neatly uniformed, equipped with long trun-
cheons and side-arms – were continuously sauntering around, always in threes,
seeming on excellent terms with the general public.

During the afternoon I met five English-speakers but none, understandably,
wished to discuss Montenegro's tensions with a stranger. Only one little restaurant was serving food; there I devoured a tomato omelette and two stale bread
rolls. My fellow-customer – a very old man, white-bearded – poured *rakija* into a
local red wine. Both he and the elderly waitress were listening attentively to an
inflammatory radio speech being given by a Milošević henchman about Kosovo,
Serbia and Montenegro. At intervals the speaker was cheered for minutes on end:
not a difficult sound effect.

Back at the hotel, the lavatory didn't flush and hadn't flushed for a long time – a
bathroom not '*en' suite*' would have been preferable. The owner spoke some English
but was uncommunicative. His wife, haggard and sour, glared at me with outright
hostility. In the restaurant (no food served) a few men drank excessively after sunset
and the two waitresses seemed – in p.c. parlance – intellectually challenged.

Next morning I made an extra-early (5.15) start and at first was pedalling uphill
through dense mist: visibility fifty yards. But by six, as I reached a pass, the sky at
the zenith was a pale milky blue. From here the road descended gradually, for
many miles, around forested mountains, and on my left were wide deep valleys,
filled near ground level with a pure white immobile ocean, the sort of cloudscape
normally seen only by air passengers. Rising out of this dazzling mass, like cliffs
from the sea, were long, vividly green wooded promontories – the lowest mountain spurs. Thousands of feet above towered bare, sheer rock peaks, their multi-
coloured layers distinct as slanting sun rays struck them – black layers and yellow,
grey and dusky pink, nutmeg brown and rust red. Then, as the sun asserted its
power, the cloud ocean slowly shifted and rose and became separate, sinuous
clouds, coiling and creeping up the valleys' sides, assuming ever stranger shapes.
I walked downhill, stopping often. The contrast between the soft, evanescent,
insubstantial clouds and the sharp, austere, immutable rock peaks was almost
eerie. For over an hour the display lasted; then wisps of silver vapour drifted gently
across the road and I freewheeled on. Such experiences make one feel grateful
(but to whom or what?) for the privilege of having been born.

Down and down and down we went; the depth of the Tara Canyon (3,900 feet)
is exceeded only by Colorado's Grand Canyon. In the still shadowy confines of
other profound side-gorges speedy young rivers foamed and sang between perpendicular cliffs. By 8 a.m. the heavy traffic was increasing, most of it bound for
Kosovo, including a convoy of white ICRC trucks preceded and followed by pairs
of ICRC jeeps. Here are many narrow, unlit tunnels, their lengths specified on

wayside signs. Given my new tunnel phobia, the 115-metre test felt quite scary. And I funked a 284-metre test, having ventured in far enough to discover that the edges of the road were wide drainage channels – one couldn't walk close to the wall. Hastily I retreated to a nearby natural layby where the Moracă river hundreds of feet below made loud music, amplified by mountain walls thousands of feet high, their ledges and crevices supporting wind-twisted miniature trees and tall clumps of lupins.

I had resigned myself to waiting indefinitely for some kind person driving an appropriate vehicle but mere moments later a likely-looking van appeared and responded to my thumbing – one more in that long string of coincidences which tempt me to believe in guardian angels. The driver's teenage son spoke enough English to reassure me: all the subsequent tunnels were short. Neither he nor his father could understand my determination not to be driven all the way to Podgorica – another twenty miles. To explain the joys of cycling in sign language is impossible.

Amidst this chaos of mountains vast chasms are spanned by road and rail bridges of seemingly superhuman dimensions – staggering feats of engineering. No wonder the Ottomans, for all their architectural ingenuity and logistical expertise, couldn't get around in Montenegro.

Suddenly I was out of the gorges and could see the road for miles ahead, descending through cultivated land between brown-green hills that in Ireland would seem like high mountains. Here a few wayside cafés and two petrol stations signalled the nearness of Podgorica. At noon in that low-lying city it was very hot. Avoiding the centre, I diary-wrote in a small dingy café until 2.30 – then sought the Cetinje road.

A long ascent took me through dusty, semi-rural suburbs of comatose factories and new villas. Then came a short, steep descent – and Ruairi began to wobble badly. I diagnosed a loose back wheel and considered my options: a seven-mile walk back to Podgorica or a fifteen-mile walk on to Cetinje. (All my tools had been stolen in Albania.) Fifteen uphill miles would take at least four hours and it was then 3.30; yet I chose that option, though it is not my habit to travel in Europe after dark. (To do so in rural Africa or Asia is safe enough but Europe has degenerated.) If I failed to find lodgings I could camp out.

Progress was slow and energy-consuming; that loose wheel acted as a brake while making a nasty noise, something between a squeal and a snarl. Ahead of me lay a new world: no more lush pastures, dense forests, sparkling streams. In this Mediterranean climate zone (the transition is dramatically abrupt) a thin covering of dull scrub stretched over miles of stony broken land to the base of Mount Lovćen's arid foothills. Rough tracks led to distant hamlets but the only roadside structure was a police-post hut in whose shade three officers were playing cards. Then suddenly a new restaurant appeared, long and low, with a large brightly painted bungalow to one side. The friendly proprietress, her looks spoiled by that peculiarly unattractive crimson-tinted hair so popular in the Balkans, was happy to offer me a cell-like room (DM10) occasionally used by truckers. As I attended to my *pivo* level we conversed in a limited polyglottal fashion, fumbling with phrases of German, English, Italian, Serbo-Croat. Times were very hard, my hostess lamented. She and her husband, now deceased, had returned from Germany in 1990 and invested all their savings in this restaurant and dwelling. Then the curtain came down on Yugoslavia's tourist industry. And now, though tourists were flocking back to the coast, they rarely ventured inland.

How does one define a 'country'? If a region lacks demarcated, recognized boundaries, any judicial or administrative structures, any independent source of revenue or generally accepted leader (never mind a constitution), and if the majority of its inhabitants concentrate on fighting, brigandage and stockbreeding, in that order, might it not more accurately be described as So-and-So's 'territory'? Anyway – such was the condition of Montenegro until comparatively recently.

Cetinje was founded in 1482 when Ivan Crnojevic, the ruler of Zeta, in retreat from the Ottomans, moved the seat of his metropolitan diocese from the Ostrog heights to a hidden plateau below Mount Lovćen. He built a modest stone palace, and a fortified monastery, and for more than two centuries Montenegro was ruled by Cetinje-based bishops – in so far as the tribes recognized any authority.

As 'heads of state', these bishops worked hard to establish relations with powerful countries and became experts at soliciting what we would now call 'international aid'. Venice was the first donor; subsidies were paid to various tribal leaders to bring them onside. When the Treaty of Karlowitz (1699) granted the whole of Dalmatia to Venice, Montenegro became a next-door neighbour and during Venice's 1714–18 war with the Ottomans bigger subsidies were forthcoming. In 1717 the Doge appointed a civil governor for Montenegro, a post always to be held by a member of the Radonjić clan, a branch of the Njeguš tribe to which the bishops' Petrović clan also belonged. The bishop and the governor were supposed to be elected by an assembly of tribal chiefs but both offices soon became hereditary, the celibate bishop's mitre passing to a nephew.

For centuries Montenegro, as a political unit, played a part on the international stage out of all proportion to its tiny size and backward condition. The explanation was its geostrategic location, close to the important Adriatic ports of Ulcinj and Bar and sufficiently inaccessible to ensure its *de facto* independence – however often the Ottomans might invade, or assert that it formed an integral part of their empire.

After 1718 Venice gradually lost interest in Montenegro and its subsidies dwindled. The joint rulers, having failed to attract Austrian support, then concentrated on strengthening bonds with Russia – already a provider of 'aid'. Thrice Bishop Vasilije visited St Petersburg, hoping to persuade the Empress Elizabeth to declare Montenegro a Russian protectorate. In 1754 he published his own *History of Montenegro* in Moscow, by way of arousing enthusiasm for this protectorate scheme; but the Russians remained unenthused.

When the Cetinje rulers prudently refrained from helping Russia in her 1768 war with the Porte – fearing Ottoman retaliation if Montenegro took sides – many of the tribal chiefs were outraged; possibly they felt passionately pro-Russian, possibly they apprehended a diminution of 'aid'.

Eleven years later the Empress Catherine caused a minor frisson in diplomatic circles by declining to receive a Montenegrin mission to St Petersburg; Russia had recently decided to co-operate with the Habsburg Monarchy and steer clear of the volatile western Balkans. Again Montenegro switched its attentions to Vienna, offering to raise special troops to fight for Austria. But the Habsburgs, who as yet knew next to nothing about the Cetinje régime, were underwhelmed by this offer. However, they did dispatch an officer, Colonel Paulic, to suss the place out. His 1781 report unflatteringly described a roadless region without currency or cuisine, headed by a bishop who couldn't control numerous chronically fractious tribes. Moreover, the Venetians and the Ottomans were equally opposed to any Habsburg meddling in Montenegrin affairs.

In 1785 came a threat from Albania where Kara Mahmud, whom we have already met in the Shkodra context, was trying to set up an autonomous principality in which he hoped to include Montenegro. Some tribes supported his first attack, enabling him to reach Cetinje where his troops demolished the monastery before being repulsed by tribesmen loyal to the Bishop. His anti-Porte attitude, and military successes against the élite janissaries, impressed both Russia and Austria, then hatching their own separate anti-Porte plots. This alarmed Montenegro, though needlessly: with another war against the Ottomans imminent, Russia's Montenegrin policy had shifted once more. All Balkan Christians were urged to support the Russians when the fighting started in 1787 and now Montenegro was in the happy position of being cultivated simultaneously by Russia and Austria. Military advisers arrived from St Petersburg and Vienna, bearing substantial gifts – and followed by Hercegovinian volunteers and Austrian conscripts, to reinforce Montenegro's warriors.

Many machinations and battles later, in 1796, Kara Mahmud – by then reconciled with the Porte – again invaded Montenegro. He reckoned it would be easy prey this time, Austria and Venice having just been vanquished by France – a fatal miscalculation. At the Battle of Krusi he was defeated and beheaded, after which Montenegro considerably increased its territory by annexing the adjacent region of Brda, previously dominated by Albanian tribes.

By the end of the eighteenth century the debilitated Porte had lost its grip on the rival Muslim Pashas of Sarajevo, Travnik, Mostar and Shkodra. What if those rivals chose to unite against Christian Montenegro? Reacting to this external threat, Bishop Petar I attempted in 1798 to form a central administration and induced most tribal chiefs to accept, in theory, rule from Cetinje – for the sake of effectively co-ordinating their country's defence. This chiefs' assembly also assented to the establishment of a central court, the *Kuluk*, with both administrative and judicial functions. In practice, however, nothing much changed. As the nineteenth century dawned Cetinje still consisted only of the rebuilt monastery and a few stone houses; many of Montenegro's 240 villages were bigger than its capital. The tribesmen were as reluctant to pay taxes to Cetinje as to the Porte, therefore no army could be organized or administrative system set up. And Petar I could do nothing to halt tribal warfare, the raiding and looting of Ottoman lands and blood-feuding. That last tradition had existed from time immemorial, as J.A. Cuddon records:

> One of the most famous Montenegrins of this century – Milovan Djilas, formerly a colleague of Marshal Tito – tells how, for centuries . . . relationships in the clan and tribe were regulated by many archaic customs, the most deep-rooted of which was the blood feud which demanded satisfaction by death for injury, insult or murder. He describes how his own family suffered from these barbarous traditions. His brothers, his father, an uncle, his two grandfathers and his father's grandfather were all killed in the payment of debts of honour. This may seem quite incredible in one family, but it was by no means uncommon and was quite recent. In fact feuds were still going on after the last war.

And in Albania they are still going on at the dawn of the twenty-first century.

By our standards, blood-feuding seems an irrational barbarity. The Montegrin tradition of brigandage is easier to understand; it was a survival mechanism, an activity built into the Montenegrin way of economic life. The territory could not support its steadily growing population and, had the Ottomans not been in control of so much of the Balkans, Montenegro's surplus people would, in the natural course of events, have moved to more cultivable areas. As things were, the price of retaining personal independence was the development of brigandage as a way of life. Meanwhile, emigration to Serbia, Russia and the Habsburg Empire increased throughout the nineteenth century.

In 1830 Bishop Petar I was succeeded by Rade, a seventeen-year-old nephew who had been given no schooling and was not a monk. His selection provoked a vigorous Petrović versus Radonjić power struggle. The former won, the office of governor was scrapped, the Radonjić clan members were either murdered or banished and Cetinje's new bishop ruled as the unchallenged religious and secular leader of Montenegro. As custom dictated, the not very religious Rade became a monk, took the name Petar II Njegoš and in due course gained fame as an exceptionally gifted poet.

In 1831 two Russian envoys (themselves Montenegrins) arrived in Cetinje to advise the young ruler on how to set up state offices that would actually work and for which the Russian government would pay. Although Petar II took their advice the offices in question never did work. In 1833 yet another determined effort was made to collect taxes – at a very low rate – but when a few of the braver tax-collectors had been beheaded, and several others threatened with beheading, this effort, too, was abandoned. Russian subsidies remained one of the Bishop's few financial resources. His much-praised administrative abilities were therefore largely wasted; without the backing of a police force, militia or army he could do no more than his forebears to restrain those who resented his authority and some-times allied themselves with his enemies. During his reign, as throughout the pre-vious century, Montenegro's foreign policy gave priority to the securing of an outlet to the Adriatic.

Every history, travel and guide book remarks on Petar II's height: six foot eight inches. He was stunningly handsome, an advantage emphasized by his sartorial idiosyncrasies, and a serious student of philosophy and literature – fluent in Latin, Russian, French and German. Sadly, he died of tuberculosis in 1851, having appointed as his successor a Russian-educated nephew.

This Danilo declined to become a celibate bishop and obtained the approval of St Petersburg and Vienna for the secularization of his office. In 1852 he pro-claimed himself 'Prince', which did something to increase his influence over the tribes. As the Great Powers wove their dangerous web of pre-Crimean War intrigues, Prince Danilo adopted the neutrality policy of his ally, the Serbian Prince Alexander Karadjordjević. He also transformed thousands of guerrilla fighters into a regular army and imposed a new legal code that severely punished brigandage and blood-feuding.

By mid-century, as a result of certain fundamental reforms, the Ottomans had regained control of Bosnia's rebellious beys and the newly appointed governor, Omer Pasha Latas, tried to undermine the Piperi tribe's loyalty to Cetinje. In 1853 this provoked the Montenegrins to attempt to seize Zabljak on Lake Shkodra, which gave Omer Pasha an excuse to invade – leaving Danilo no choice but to call for help. Vienna promptly rallied round, preferring Montenegrin to Ottoman possession of this Dalmatian borderland. The Habsburg Empire deliv-ered an ultimatum to the Ottoman Empire, whereupon Omer Pasha was recalled and Montenegro's captured territory restored to the Prince. All the Great Powers then reassured Danilo, directly or obliquely, by guaranteeing not to permit any future Ottoman military interventions.

To some chiefs, the Crimean War looked like God's gift to tribesmen: now was the moment to seize chunks of Ottoman territory. They seemed not to under-stand that France and Britain, allies for the first time in 200 years, were campaign-ing to protect the Porte from the Tsar. When Vienna (reluctantly on the Allies' side) leant on Danilo he proved himself to have gained an unprecedented degree of control over even the most unruly chiefs. Then, while Russia looked weak, he tried to form closer ties with France, though Napoleon III loathed Orthodox Christianity. However, those ties were not needed after the war when Russian influence was soon restored and subsidies from St Petersburg continued to be the main prop of Cetinje's administration.

In 1858 the Ottomans put the Great Powers' guarantee to the test by again attacking Montenegro – a rash move. With the assistance of Christian Herzegovinian forces, Danilo's modernized army defeated the invaders and captured the Herzegovinian town of Grahovo. Both Russia and France then put pressure on the Porte in support of Montenegro and for the first time a boundary was fixed between the principality and all the surrounding Ottoman territories, Grahovo being included in Montenegro.

In 1861 Prince Danilo's very beautiful Dalmatian wife, Darinka, felt unwell and her doctor recommended sea-bathing at Kotor. Danilo escorted her down to the coast, ignoring warnings that he would be at risk within Austria's jurisdiction. One evening, in a seaside public garden, a Montenegrin shot him in the back and he died by his wife's side. The assassin, it was assumed, belonged to a colony of Montenegrin exiles who, resenting Danilo's reforms, had settled in Dalmatia where they lived on pensions from Vienna.

A nineteen-year-old grand-nephew of Peter II succeeded Prince Danilo. Nikola I, Montenegro's last ruler, was a vile character – 'educated in France but bred in Hell,' as one of his victims put it. A skilful politician and military tactician, he spoke six languages fluently and continued Cetinje's time-honoured policy of annually extracting considerable sums of money from the Russians. He also obtained generous loans from the Habsburg Monarchy and audaciously requested and received intermittent funding from the Porte. Yet he never became anyone's puppet.

Most of Prince Danilo's reforms died with him and during the following decades the Montenegrins contributed more than a mite to the western Balkans' restlessness, persistently raiding and looting over the newly-drawn border. An ever-growing population desperately needed more agricultural land and the tribes shared in Serbia's longing for territorial expansion – and, on the emotional level, for a formally recognized end to the last symbolic vestiges of Ottoman sovereignty over Serbia.

Bosnia's 1875 revolt against the Ottomans sent a terrified scramble of refugees into Montenegro where many died of hunger. It attracted some outside assistance, including 5,000 or so Russian volunteers – mainly incompetent alcoholics – and unnumbered cohorts of Montenegrins eager for loot. The Ottomans, weakened by more domestic problems, failed to cope with this uprising and soon Bulgaria was emulating it – whereupon the Porte despatched the dreaded *bashi-*

bazuks, Turkish irregulars infamous for their cruelty. The resulting 'Bulgarian massacres' shocked and enraged public opinion, especially in Russia and Britain – though few British had ever before heard of Bulgaria (just as few had heard of Kosovo in January 1998).

In April 1877 Russia declared war on the Ottomans – who then made another rash attempt to subdue Montenegro, as a source of ferocious support for the Russians. At the end of this conflict the Montenegrins were triumphantly occupying the coast from Budva to the river Bojana, a strip of land coveted by Cetinje for generations. The principality was doubled in size by the Treaty of Berlin (1878), which also recognized Montenegro's independence (and Serbia's and Romania's) and granted Cetinje its longed-for outlet to the sea, the port of Ulcinj. However, there were strings attached – really steel hawsers. The Treaty excluded all warships from Montenegrin waters and Austria-Hungary was delegated to police the Montenegrin shore. Vienna dreaded Russia's acquiring an Adriatic port – as did France and Britain, whose recurrent nightmares had the Russian navy poking its prow into the Mediterranean. Montenegro was also forbidden to develop a fleet – a very remote possibility, but the Powers visualised Russian warships flying the Montenegrin flag of convenience.

The Berlin settlement allowed the Habsburg occupation of BiH and the *sanjak* of Novi Pazar, so Montenegro was now bounded on three sides by Habsburg-ruled lands. This drastically reduced the tribesmen's scope for raiding expeditions and internecine conflicts multiplied. Enough foreign aid was now being lavished on the principality to keep destitution at bay and give every child basic schooling – but Nikola deflected this funding into other channels. By 1912 at least one-third of Montenegrin men were being hunger-compelled to leave home in search of seasonal work or to emigrate permanently, usually to the United States. As in Ireland at the same period, exiles' remittances enabled their families to survive. (But, unlike Ireland, Montenegro – its present population is about 640,000 – does not have the economic foundation on which to build an independent modern state.)

Nikola's foreign policy was designed around his daughters. He acquired useful diplomatic toeholds by marrying them off in significant directions: two to Russian Grand Dukes (both Grand Duchesses soon achieved influence in the St Petersburg court), another to Prince Petar Karadjordjević (she unfortunately died before he inherited the Serbian throne), the fourth to Victor Emmanuel III – that poor lass led a miserable life as Queen of Italy. In 1910 Nikola proclaimed Montenegro a kingdom and caught up with his Italian father-in-law. During the Balkan Wars and the First World War he manipulated this royal connection in a manner that caused incalculable trouble and confusion among the Great Powers.

Franz Lehar's parody of Nikola's principality in *The Merry Widow* (1905) was not too exaggerated, though its première brought protesting Montenegrin students on to the streets of Vienna. Cetinje was then a town of 5,000 inhabitants, accessible only by horse and pack-animal and known throughout Europe's diplomatic circles as 'the capital with thirteen legations and a hotel'. Montenegro's total population of about 250,000 (less than the Habsburg city of Prague) contributed 50,000 warriors to Nikola's army. Italian entrepreneurs, having won a monopoly on Montenegro's tobacco crop, had been granted the right to develop the port of Bar and build Montenegro's first railway, opened in 1909, from there to Virpaza. Both the Habsburgs and the Italians knew that Nikola would always co-operate with them for a (large) consideration.

In 1910 famine hit the brand-new kingdom and Russia's annual subsidy, which paid most military and administrative expenses, was raised from 800,000 to 1.6 million kronen, supplemented by a massive gift of wheat which Nikola at once sold to the highest bidders for his own profit. Three years later 20,000 Montenegrin soldiers lost their lives during the seven-months siege of Shkodra, when Nikola surrendered the town after making a fortune on the Viennese *bourse* by abusing his foreknowledge of the surrender.

In 1914 – Nikola's fifty-fourth year in power – he telegraphed to Belgrade on the outbreak of war, promising King Petar that he and his people would stand by Serbia in all circumstances. Yet when the Montenegrin and Serbian troops together invaded Bosnia, and were about to take Sarajevo, Nikola suddenly withdrew his men, leaving the Serbs with no alternative but to forego their gains. In 1915, during the Serbs' midwinter retreat to Corfu across the mountains, Nikola ordered his soldiers and police to prevent Montenegrins from selling or giving food to the starving army and its wretched civilian followers. In January 1916 Nikola's son, Prince Petar, surrendered Mount Lovćen to the enemy while his father manoeuvred 50,000 Montenegrin troops into a corner where they could not escape the Austrians. Although then on bad terms with Vienna, he had betrayed his own men because he feared their escaping, like the Serbs, over the sea to Corfu, where the British might help them to dethrone him. After the war he 'emigrated' to France and died in exile in 1921. By then Montenegro was part of the new Kingdom of the Serbs, Croats and Slovenes – to the chagrin of its traditionalists and the joy of its educated exiles. Those exiles had formed the Montenegrin Committee for National Unification and on 28 November 1918 deposed Nikola's Petrović dynasty, by majority vote, and proclaimed unification with Serbia. A staid ending to the turbulent tale of a land that for five centuries had remained free and individualistic when all around were subservient to Venetians, Ottomans or Habsburgs.

20

From a Former Royal Capital to a Former Republic

On the long walk up to Cetinje I no longer felt irritated and frustrated by Ruairi's noisy disability – though I did feel worried about finding a reliable bicycle mechanic. A loose back wheel is no trivial complaint and Cetinje's setting does not encourage cycling as a popular hobby.

This road wriggles through an extraordinary landscape. Sharp-edged silver-grey rock formations tower nearby – of varying heights, from 100 to 1,000 feet – the limestone blocks seemingly laid one on another by Inca stone-masons reincarnated as giants. In contrast, untidy expanses of tumbled dark rock recall the much-quoted Montenegrin legend: 'As God was flying over the Balkans during Creation Week, carrying an enormous sack of stones, the Devil pursued him and slit open the sack – and out fell Montenegro!' Yet 'barren' does not describe this region. Between its disarray of crags and boulders and sloping slabs – like collapsed dolmens – grow many small trees and scented shrubs and flaring patches of broom. And in the cool stillness of early morning, before traffic fumes intrude, one gets frequent whiffs of thyme and sage. The volume of traffic is indicated by an unbroken trail of litter befouling both verges and by the numbers of dead creatures on the road. I lost count of the frogs, hedgehogs and snakes – one more than five feet long. A horribly smashed tortoise was the biggest I have seen since camping on the Galapagos and finding myself one sunrise eyeball to eyeball with a specimen bigger than my tent. (I wasn't hungover and hallucinating; I have a photograph to prove it.)

Very far below the road cowbells chimed faintly in small hidden valleys where fields of alfalfa, wheat and potatoes surrounded red-tiled dwellings and shingle-roofed barns. Above those minute pockets of fertility rose sheer karst mountains and, because the road was carved out of equally sheer precipices, I had to move to the left verge to look into the valleys. A motorist could drive through this region believing it to be uninhabited. In places, as I gained height, the extreme tip of Lake Shkodra was visible, glinting away in the distance – a thin tongue of blue.

I noticed an above-average number of flower-bedecked memorial plaques, all recording the deaths of young men. While resting in view of a particularly dangerous curve, marked by outsize 'NO OVERTAKING!' signs, I observed within ten minutes three drivers doing just that. Do those signs have a negative effect? Some argue they are interpreted as a gauntlet being thrown down by Fate. Alternatively, a young man who heeded them might see himself – or be seen by others – as wimpish. And that would never do, in Montenegro.

Some four miles from Cetinje a tunnel confronted me, its length unspecified but its exit invisible from the entrance. Noxious fumes drifted out and combined with the thunderous rumble of vehicles to revive sickening memories . . . I stood where approaching drivers could see me thumbing from 200 yards away but my guardian angel was off duty. For two hours and forty minutes I was ignored, though many vans and empty taxis raced past. When at last a taxi stopped the driver peered at me suspiciously for a moment, as though half-expecting me to pull out a pistol and hijack his limousine. Then he began to negotiate: DM30 to Cetinje. We settled on DM20.

Cetinje's site is as improbable as its history: a flat plain covering two and a half square miles and entirely surrounded by harshly handsome 3,000-foot karst mountains, their grey serrated crests like ancient fortifications. As we have seen, they served precisely that purpose and the Ottomans found Cetinje unconquerable. Given the region's infertility, they couldn't provision a major campaign and the Montenegrins, aided by their terrain, repeatedly slaughtered the inadequate forces deployed against them. This food problem also explains Cetinje's remaining for so long a village, despite its 'capital' status; in 1860 only thirty-four small thatched houses stood around the monastery and palace. Until roads allowed the bulk transportation of food, few could be fed on the local produce grown between boulders.

Outside Cetinje's motel my guardian angel came back on duty. A lanky youth was riding his shiny new racing bicycle round and round the open space in front of the motel, where concrete paths enclose squares of lawn – surely he would know of a cycle repair shop. He didn't, but he himself enjoyed taking bicycles to bits and putting them together again. Trustingly I followed Danilo through an alleyway between the motel and the adjacent JNA barracks, then up twisting streets of pleasant little houses clinging to precipices.

Mr and Mrs Pandurović were sitting on their verandah doing something complicated with dried leaves – sorting and blending them, Danilo explained, for the herbal medicines they distilled. They were a likeable couple, though at first understandably thrown by me as a phenomenon.

Coffee was brewed, *rakija* poured – and, unexpectedly, Mrs Pandurović participated in the repair work, acting as an adviser when it came to the tricky matter of aligning gears. Both she and her husband spoke better English than Danilo; for years they had worked in Dubrovnik hotels. Soon Mrs Pandurovic was apologizing for not having sleeping space to offer me; Serb refugees from Peć, an elderly woman and her daughter and two granddaughters, were occupying the spare room. Their menfolk were missing, possibly still being held as hostages by the KLA in Albania. But Mrs Pandurović feared they were dead.

Both Danilo and his father wore tiny wooden crosses around their necks, the Orthodox equivalent of the medals and scapulars worn by most Irish Catholics in my youth. Mr Pandurović fingered his cross while expressing his determination to join the Serbian invasion forces which one day would drive Nato out of Kosovo. 'I am aged only forty, I am young enough to fight – and Danilo is old enough to fight!'

When I ventured to ask, 'Is Serbia strong enough to defeat Nato?' Mr Pandurović laughed and replied, 'To keep Kosovo we must win! God will help us. We will fight for God's kingdom of justice and truth, for Serbia's unity and freedom – so we will win! Nato is afraid of death, we are happy to die to keep Kosovo. That makes us stronger than Nato.'

This rhetoric sounds to us like so much superstitious nonsense; a secular mindset makes much more difficult any understanding of the residual mythical/religious underpinning of 'The Kosovo Problem'. Yet as Mr Pandurović talked on, I realized that here was no homicidal fanatic in the Chetnik mould but a pure-bred Montenegrin with a mission. He believed in his people's descent from those defeated Serbian warriors who fled into the mountains in 1389 – a people destined to recover control of the 'sacred territory' of Kosovo from the Albanians, now misrepresented as successors of the hated Turks.

Among ordinary folk, down the centuries, the Kosovo myth (described as a 'cult' by many, including the Serb historian Olga Žirojević) retained more influence in Montenegro than in Serbia. It exasperates most outsiders; if peoples could go around claiming the territories their forefathers owned six centuries ago much of the Caucasian-inhabited world would be up for redistribution. However, those who cherish such politico-religious myths are rarely open to argument.

After Danilo had scoured his oily hands more coffee appeared and I observed that the Pandurović family was quite unusual; not only did the wife possess superior mechanical knowledge but the sixteen-year-old son felt free to challenge his father's views in the presence of a stranger – of course politely, not with teenage truculence. Mrs Pandurović considerately translated the essence of their debate. In brief, Danilo was not prepared to fight for Kosovo and sturdily advocated Montenegro's complete independence, a concept abhorrent to his father who, though implacably anti-Milošević, defined himself as a Montenegrin Serb who would be severed from his roots by the proposed independence. Mrs Pandurović, while showing me to the loo, whispered, 'I stay neutral!'

As I prepared to leave, Danilo asked, 'Do you think Yugoslavia was real?'

I parried the question: 'Who am I to say?'

Danilo persisted. 'Was it real for you, before, when you visited so long ago, when my parents were babies? Did it feel like a real country, one country?'

'Yes,' I said, 'it felt just as real as Italy or Germany. They too became one country quite recently, unlike France or Spain or England.'

'But it wasn't real!' exclaimed Danilo. 'When Milošević pushed it, it collapsed!' He then asked – suddenly shy, blushing slightly – if he might bring some of his friends to the motel to meet me. 'They have interest in foreigners and now Cetinje has no more tourists.' I assured him that to meet his friends would be a privilege.

Cetinje is not used to being tourist-deprived. As Vesna Goldsworthy points out in her immensely entertaining and informative *Inventing Ruritania*, the town was on a nineteenth-century beaten track:

> The then capital of Montenegro was relatively accessible from the Adriatic Coast and received a steady trickle of visitors from England. The narrow track winding up from the Austrian-controlled coast to the Montenegrin border . . . acquired a certain mystical resonance as one of those points at which the English traveller stepped out from the 'known' West into the unknown 'real' Balkan world in which the feudal European past and the Orient overlapped in a kind of Ruritanian enchantment. Many report the chilling warnings they received from Dalmatian ships' officers and townsmen before they entered the land of the Black Mountain, contributing to the theme-park quality it possessed for upper middle-class British tourists of the day. Among those circles in Britain which admired the martial verve of mountain peoples such as the Pathans and Gurkhas, Montenegrins appealed as Christian equivalents in Europe's backyard, a role to which they were more than happy to play up.

Cetinje's two hotels (one reputedly the best in Montenegro) closed years ago and the surviving motel retained certain animated nineteenth-century features: bedbugs thrived under my mattress and cockroaches were everywhere. The DM30 tariff seemed excessive, given a shared 'toilet' and washroom in which only cold water trickled from stiff taps into filthy basins hanging out from the wall – which posture impeded the water's exit. The bedroom walls were cardboard-thin partitions and on the first night, in a neighbouring room, two greybeards talked loudly into the small hours. One fancied himself as a mimic and his performances were rewarded by his friend's prolonged spasms of hoarse laughter, invariably ending in a bout of productive coughing. When at last they slept one snored like a trumpet and his bed was very obviously beside mine. I could even hear him scratching in his sleep as the bedbugs feasted. Next morning I observed that both men were aurally challenged. On the following nights insomniacal and argumentative mobile-phone addicts occupied that same room. However, those minor drawbacks were counterbalanced by a cheerful and helpful young staff, two of whom spoke English.

During 1999, the receptionist told me, not a single tourist had set foot in

Cetinje and hopes were not high for 2000. The week before, one American had checked in, but when introduced to the 'facilities' he demanded his money back and took the first bus for Podgorica. Recounting this, the receptionist looked puzzled and aggrieved.

It was *pivo* time. Sitting outside the motel, under a tattered Marlboro canopy, I was greeted by a fellow-guest, a middle-aged man with a crew-cut and a drooping moustache which contradicted each other. He wore a paramilitary-style khaki shirt and trousers, had a bulge under one arm and introduced himself as Obrad, from Belgrade, in Cetinje to supervise the restoration of the National Art Gallery. Although it was temporarily closed, I should be able to gain entrance by presenting myself as 'a foreign writer on a Balkan tour of culture'. But could I keep a straight face while thus presenting myself? I did try, next day – to no avail.

Obrad frankly despised the Montenegrins. 'All are idle, dirty, dishonest and the young men don't want work. They want only to play American music very loud and drive stolen cars very fast!'

I made no comment. There are many hard-working, well-groomed, honest young Montenegrins like Danilo and his friends, yet the other sort are indeed more obvious – but so they are in every country, having a life-style designed to draw attention to itself.

Obrad, too, insisted that Serbia must recover Kosovo. 'We need to be in control there to civilize those Albanian people – and also the Kosovo Serbs, they are not much civilized. I am a fair man, I see faults both ways in that backward place – it is very primitive.'

As for Nato's intervention – there had been no 'humanitarian catastrophe'. 'It was our counter-insurgency against terrorists – same you have in Ireland, I hear.' The JNA was a strictly disciplined force, there had been no atrocities, all was Nato propaganda.

Clearly Obrad's interest in Kosovo was geopolitical and economic; he showed no sign of being, like Mr Pandurović, emotionally and religiously entangled in the myth. He made me feel disputatious, as Mr Pandurović had not. I asked, 'Do you really believe what you're saying? Have you never heard of the Special Interior Ministry police? Or the released criminals in Arkan's murder squads? Or the incinerated and stabbed women and children?'

Obrad smiled at me condescendingly. 'You people are all the time fooled by Nato!'

That goaded me to state the obvious: 'However things unfold, whatever international juggling may go on, it's certain Kosovo will never again form part of Serbia.'

Surprisingly, Obrad did not contest this; one suspects the pragmatic wing of Serbdom inwardly accepts it as a fact, while outwardly they nourish the illusions of hard-line Chetniks and pious sentimentalists.

Switching tracks, Obrad declared that if Nato tried to 'colonize' Montenegro the world must prepare for yet another Balkan bloodbath. Like the waiter in Rožaj he thought the CIA might well provoke a civil war. Before we parted he magnanimously offered to lend me his can of insecticide spray at bedtime.

One has to admit that Cetinje – unlike its setting – is not beautiful. Trees are the town's best feature: horse chestnuts (flowering abundantly in May) around the edges, lofty pines encircling the monastery, stately planes lining the long, wide 1930s boulevards (their width seeming rather absurd), eight fine limes shading the paved central square. This space is presided over by a classical figure in flowing robes standing on a high pedestal above four open-mouthed lions' heads – a fountain that must have been attractive when splashing. Desuetude had lowered it to litter-bin status.

Cetinje's patina of dereliction – neglect verging on squalor – had an egalitarian quality. Everything was affected, from the baroque Government House, built in 1910 and at that time the largest building in Montenegro, to the workers' apartment blocks built when Tito's determination to industrialize every corner of Yugoslavia reached Cetinje. This decay was not of the pleasing sort, as when ancient towns are gently mouldering away; apart from the monastery (itself much restored) there is nothing ancient here. On a grassy hill above the monastery stands the ruin of Tower Tablja, raised by Petar II to house cannons for the monastery's defence. It is now an unlovely sight – the usual garbage dumped around its base, the usual menacing political graffiti defacing its stump. Until the 1880s it had a secondary use, as a display point for janissaries' heads. I like the anecdote about Marshal Marmont, Napoleon's envoy to the Balkans, who reproached Bishop Petar I for tolerating this lamentable custom. The Bishop wondered why it should seem shocking to a Frenchman, whose people had done the same thing to their own king and queen.

In the spring of 2000 there was no good reason why any of Cetinje's five museums should be open and only one was – by appointment with the curator. The English-speaking guide arrived half an hour late, a small, thin, sallow, raven-haired woman, obviously irritated by my existence. I would have much preferred to wander around unguided but that was not allowed for 'security reasons'. This State Museum, formerly King Nikola I's palace, is an agreeable building no bigger or grander than the average Irish country house. I could tell you more about the exhibits had the guide not rushed me through it in fifteen minutes, leaving only blurred memories of military banners, costumes, armaments, medals – and bedrooms and drawing rooms and dining rooms over-furnished (mostly Louis Quatorze) and enlivened by portraits of over-armed Montenegrin warriors and gorgeously apparelled members of the Petrović family. Before leaving I bought an obsolete pamphlet – 'Cetinje and its Museums' – for its poignant sentimental value: graphics done in Zagreb, research in Montenegro, photography by a Bosnian, published in Belgrade . . .

The implacably closed ethnographic museum, in the Biljarda, would have interested me far more. Petar II's palace has always been known as the Biljarda because of the poet-bishop's billiard table; several mules were needed to carry it up from Kotor, in sections, and this import evidently made such a deep impression on the locals that the new (1838) ruler's residence was named accordingly. It doesn't look even remotely like a palace – more like a barracks, long and low, with round towers at the corners of its enclosing walls.

At least half of Cetinje's business premises were closed – some with broken boarded-up windows. A baffling number of the open stores catered for small children only: clothes and toys. The shop names and descriptions were in Roman script, the new signposts in Cyrillic. Opposite my favourite café was a 'Dragstor' – replacing, as too often now in the Balkans, the 'Apoteka'. Most people bought their basic goods in cramped little huxters' shops, recalling my home town in the 1950s. The large open-air market was extra-depressing: only one-third of the stalls in use, the few available goods adulterated (if edible) and shoddy (if wearable). As elsewhere in Montenegro, the currency situation was idiosyncratic – heavily skewed in the Montenegrins' favour. Dinars were unacceptable from a foreigner and all marked goods were priced in DM. Yet one's change came either in dinars or in kind – a packet of six paper handkerchiefs, a box of matches, a bar of chocolate, three disposable picnic mugs. To protest was useless; recently the Podgorica government had publicly abandoned the dinar in an attempt to ease the pain caused by UN sanctions.

By 7 a.m. Cetinje's numerous cafés were open – several dotting the main square – and within an hour the sun was hot, daily papers were being eagerly read and much vigorous political argument contrasted with the somnolence otherwise prevailing in Montenegro's cultural capital. (I could tell it was political by the names being bandied about.) The trios of policemen were less obvious here than elsewhere, there was no perceptible 'Specials' presence and the handsome young officers who emerged from the JNA barracks seemed on excellent terms with the locals. (One of them was on intimate terms with the best-looking of the motel's graceful young waitresses.)

Feeling at ease and happy in Cetinje, I spent three days wandering around, communing with the past – and also with the future, as represented by Danilo's friends and others among his generation who were curious about my journey. Cetinje's youths seemed intellectually linked to the outside world as their contemporaries I had met elsewhere in Montenegro were not. Most held strong, often conflicting, views about which turning their country should take at this crossroads in her history. Yet their arguing was never aggressively confrontational;

minor points were graciously conceded, opposing attitudes respected. Listening to – and learning from – my youthful companions, I wished they could influence the world's 'mature' politicians. Incidentally, their all being male was no coincidence; outside of Podgorica, young Montenegrin women do not participate in café life.

In 1904 Edith Durham was, for once, defeated – by the Lovćen Pass. Not by the crossing of it (as a traveller nothing defeated her) but by the describing of it. She wrote: 'The road from Cattaro [Kotor] to Cetinje has been so often written of that it is idle to describe it once again, nor can any words do it justice.' That being the case in 1904 I needn't feel obliged, a century later, to attempt the impossible. (This crossing is even more overwhelming, and for a cyclist much less strenuous, done the other way round, from Cetinje to Kotor.)

Cetinje folk are not early risers; only the cockroaches were stirring when I set off through an opaque dawn, its greyness matching and softening the plain's karst battlements. For an hour the narrow tarred road was cycleable, wriggling this way and that as it sought to ascend those battlements. The sun rose – swollen and crimson, for a moment looking as though impaled on a crag – before the plain was lost to view. By then I was pushing Ruairi around steep bends where at intervals a vehicle skeleton could be seen rusting away between small trees and feathery silver-green shrubs. Soon after came an outburst of furious barking and around the next bend were four houses. My passing provoked the chained watchdogs – mongrel hounds of fearsome aspect – to hysterical, salivating rage. On the precipitous slopes below those houses, between colossal outcrops of karst, a few minuscule terraced fields had been created, reminding me of the 'made' fields on the Aran Islands. Nearby were the ruins of several tall fortified houses such as I had seen, still occupied, in Albania; one might easily not notice them, so well did their immensely thick stone walls blend with their surroundings. No doubt they explained why a village is marked here on my map.

A level stretch followed, along a mountainside densely bushy or lightly wooded – the birdsong mellifluous, the wild flowers iridescent. The next climb, long and steep, rounded rock peaks rising from wide slopes bright with broom and patches of short new grass. Sometimes a fifty-mile expanse of lower mountains was spread below me, irregular valleys divided by rugged ranges, every detail clear in the brilliant morning light – until fading to a powder-blue blur along the far horizon.

Suddenly, after an extra-steep climb, the road was overlooking an oval valley, thousands of feet below, mountain-enclosed on every side, some five miles wide and eight miles long. That descent was vertiginous – the hairpin bends so tight, the gradient so extreme, the road so narrow, that I found myself wobbling if I glanced into the valley; so I walked down, the better to enjoy this magnificence. A faded sign informed me that hereabouts Montenegro's favourite hero, the poet-bishop Petar II, was born. Had I arrived thirty years earlier I would have left Ruairi with a villager and climbed Mount Lovćen – a summit now best avoided. In 1971 it was desecrated by a gigantic and surpassingly ugly mausoleum to 'honour' the remains of Petar II. At the time, Yugoslavia's historians, artists and poets united to oppose the erection of this monstrosity but the bureaucrats won. As contemporary Ireland is learning the hard way, those who have the final say in such matters often come from the very bottom of the yob pile. My own once-beautiful home town is now a heart-breaking example of what happens when EU 'Heritage Town' funding is at the disposal of officially-sanctioned vandals.

In the village groups of women and girls, fetching water from standpipes, seemed startled to see me. This fertile valley's farmhouses were surrounded by fields of alfalfa, decorated with seeding dandelions looking like a powdering of silver fluff. A few cows and herds of goats grazed in securely fenced pastures.

I breakfasted not far beyond the village, sitting on a slab of rock. All around me grew minute unfamiliar flowers: orange and pink and yellow and every shade of blue. As I exercised my jaws on what passes for salami in Cetinje, the day's third car appeared, then stopped. The driver leant out to offer me a lift – an elderly man with kind eyes. He looked both worried and perplexed when, having expressed much gratitude, I declined his offer.

This reminded me of the Zagreb friend who had investigated me on the inter-net and discovered a derogatory review of *South from the Limpopo*. The reviewer wondered, 'Why does the author travel by bicycle? What is she trying to prove?' Sadly, there now exists a generation too motor-dependent to be capable of under-standing a cyclist's motivation. *I* often wonder, 'Why do people travel by car/bus? What's the point?' Had some misfortune compelled me to cross the Lovćen Pass by motor transport, a few stops to 'admire the view' would not have consoled me. Cyclists know the joy of being *with* a place, rather than glimpsing it from inside a speedy machine.

I expected another long climb out of this valley but soon the road entered a hitherto invisible cleft – and then I was overlooking the Gulf of Kotor 5,000 feet below, with the Prevlaka Peninsula, long and narrow, rising high from the dazzling blue-green Adriatic. High – yet from my vantage point seeming insignificant. 'One of the most remarkable natural phenomena in Europe', writes J.A. Cuddon with splendid restraint. The Gulf of Kotor, suddenly seen from the top of the Lovćen Pass, is literally heart-stopping. But here, following Edith Durham's sen-sible example, I rest my pen.

Before beginning the descent I counted eight hairpin bends, precisely aligned, directly below me like the steps of a stairs; and there were twenty-four more. J.A. Cuddon again: 'The Lovćen mountain soars almost sheer for nearly 6,000 feet . . .

When you look up the side of it, it does not seem possible that anything could be built on it . . . To go up or come down is a memorable if alarming experience.'

Lovćen's precipices – emphatically not slopes – are quite densely forested: mostly pines on the higher ground, then oak, hazel, beech, juniper, cypress. Some trees have grown *through* vast smooth slabs of rock split by the 'power of plants'; others protrude from the precipices at grotesque angles, between massive out-crops that make them seem like weeds. This was my most dramatic ever descent with a bicycle. (Trekking descents, amongst serious mountain ranges, are in another league.) I write 'with a bicycle' because I chose to walk down; in certain places, even bicycles are too speedy.

A long flat plain, several miles wide, separates Lovćen's base from the coast. At one point I could see what had been a busy industrial zone; now there were few or no vehicles in the workers' car parks, spread below me like features in a child's game. Approaching the first small dwellings, where the precipice became a slope, litter reappeared on the verges and plastic bags fluttered in the bushes.

Then came the anti-climax, seven trafficky miles across the plain to Tivat ferry. I had considered spending a few days around Kotor but hereabouts tourism has revived and only for Dubrovnik's sake would I attempt to overcome my tourist allergy. A free ten-minute ferry trip, where the Bay of Kotor is at its narrowest, put me on the road for Dubrovnik, with the Gulf on my left and the long Radovici peninsula beyond. Hercegnovi, eight miles up the coast, did not tempt me to linger. Once this ancient town was a tranquil place of dignified beauty; now vile hotels overlook a gravel beach concreted over for the convenience of sun-seeking multi-tudes who lie in rows on inflated mattresses. The mind boggles: what would one not pay to avoid lying on concrete amidst a multitude surrounded by high risery?

Beyond Hercegnovi and its satellite spa of Igalo (much more high risery) the traffic dwindled and soon the ridge-top border post could be seen above a deep forested valley. Bilingual legends over the huts read: 'POLICE OF THE REPUBLIK OF CRNA GORA' and only Montenegro's flag was flying. A policewoman smilingly waved me on, wishing me 'a happy journey'; the customs and immigration officers showed no interest in me, nor did their Croatian counterparts a hundred yards further on. Just over the border men were spraying wayside flowers and grasses with an ominously odorous chemical – is this a requirement for entry to the EU? In Ireland I regularly observe the same insanity. Here the traffic was light, all the vehicles registered and the road surface well maintained. But I was back in a war zone where brightly painted new houses alternated with stark black roofless ruins.

In the autumn of 1991 Montenegrin reservists, mostly from Nikšić, were deployed to secure the Prevlaka Peninsula, commanding Kotor Bay and soon to become the Yugoslav navy's new base. These were not beardless youths but tough, well-trained men of the Sava Kovačević Fifth Proletarian Brigade – tribesmen recently converted to industrial work and genetically programmed to be more effective on battlefields than in factories. Following the besieging by Tudjman's forces of Zagreb's JNA barracks, and others throughout Croatia, reprisals began in this Konavle region. It is a vulnerable sliver of Croatia, a strip of farmland between the Adriatic and the mountains of Herzegovina, now only two or three miles away on my right. Numerous journalists have recorded the Montenegrins' spectacular orgy of looting and arson, for which General Kadijević subsequently disclaimed all responsibility, protesting that his regional COS had disobeyed orders by crossing a certain line on the map. Another orgy marked the reservists' retreat in September 1992.

At the first hamlet a petrol-station-cum-shop and a large restaurant-cum-al fresco-café faced each other across the road with the glossy anonymity of all such places throughout the overdeveloped world. The contrast with Montenegro was striking. And perhaps this is how Montenegro will soon be – and Albania, and everywhere else awaiting conquest by 'globalization'. My granddaughters will grow up deprived, in a monotonous world where prosperity is equated with TNC-imposed homogeneity. However, at least Konavle was billboard-free until I joined the main road to Dubrovnik. There, ten miles from the city, a cottage-sized Benetton advertisement obscured what would otherwise have been a superb view of the curving coast. Does it never occur to advertisers that by defiling the landscape they might be antagonizing potential customers?

Dubrovnik (previously Ragusa) is newish by Dalmatian standards, founded in the seventh century AD when Slav invaders sacked Epidauros (now Cavtat) and its Latin-speaking population moved a few miles north, across the bay. A Slav settlement gradually expanded nearby but the two communities merged only when it became necessary to construct a shared system of fortifications in 1272. Soon after, the first Slav names (mainly women) appeared in the roll of the Ragusan nobility.

Ragusa's sailors were famed for their courage, when they had to fight, but the Republic's noble families had achieved their status through trade, not war; from Constantinople to London their merchant-adventurers were active and respected. Is there a lesson here for us? What one might call the moral development of this society – a free and independent city for more than eight centuries – says a lot about the civilizing effects of basing one's security on diplomacy rather than militarism, of glorifying traders rather than warriors. Lovett F. Edwards lists the benefits enjoyed by Ragusa's citizens:

A system of state medical assistance was decreed in 1301, a public apothecary in 1318, a hospital for the poor in 1347, a hostel for foreign visitors in 1423 and a foundling hospital in 1432. Torture as a legal procedure was abolished at the end of the seventeenth century. The inquisition never set foot in the city, and there is no example in its history of any person being burnt alive. The excesses of the slave trade were modified in 1312 and the trade itself abolished in 1416. It is only necessary to compare these dates with parallel ones among the neighbouring Turks and Venetians, or even contemporary France and England, to see how much this tiny republic was ahead of its times.

Moreover, at the beginning of the fifteenth century Ragusa established a reliable supply of drinking water and introduced Europe's first garbage collection system – and anyone who polluted the town was heavily fined. Bring back the Ragusans, say I!

A century before mass tourism blighted our planet Dubrovnik had a foretaste and since the 1960s it has been a major target of the packaged. Therefore I did not expect its contemporary citizens, for all their civilized inheritance, to differ from other tourism-dependent populations. But I could not have been more wrong; almost everyone I met was courteous, relaxed, quietly welcoming. To me the city seemed awash with visitors but Tomislav, my B&B host, saw it as practically empty; throughout the previous week, he informed me, there had been a nightly average of only one tourist for every hundred beds.

Tomislav and Latinka, both high-school teachers, lived near the crest of a ridge so steep that its houses were approached by very many steps, rather than streets. My accommodation consisted of a large comfortable bed-sitting room – a bathroom in which the bath had a stopper, illimitable hot water and large soft towels – a kitchenette complete with coffee-making equipment and a refrigerator – a private patio surrounded by cherry, lemon, orange, fig and palm trees, with wisteria and bougainvillea pouring over the walls and tall bushes of old-fashioned red roses scenting the air. Best of all, my bedroom window directly overlooked the Old Town and that night there was a full moon . . . I couldn't remember when last I had encountered such luxury. And all for DM25 – less than the tariff in Cetinje's bugful motel.

Tomislav, though a notably unmilitary type, had fought with the Croat National Guard in the defence of Dubrovnik. Proudly he told me, 'The JNA never got into the Old City because a thousand men were afraid of thirty heroes poorly armed!' (Presumably this claim is a trifle hyperbolic.) He condemned JNA atrocities and lack of discipline; with his own eyes he had seen senior Montenegrin officers looting on a grand scale. However, he viewed the original attack on Dubrovnik as not planned and directed from JNA headquarters but as one more example of the extent to which the army ran amok under 'gangster cos'. He was evasive about Croat misdeeds – not least among them the setting up of small artillery emplacements on the precious town walls, deliberately inviting JNA shells. Turning the conversation, he admitted he found it difficult to forgive the West for standing aside while Vukovar was being totally destroyed and Dubrovnik 'sent to hell'.

Latinka recalled fleeing to the island of Korčula in October 1991, with a toddler and three-month-old baby; there they remained for eighteen months. 'The worst was the worry about Tomislav – and our city. Really there were very few deaths, compared to what happened in other places. But we didn't realize that at the time and there was this horrible fear of disease – the water shortage, the sewage system breaking down, the poor diet . . . We were lucky but it didn't feel that way then, with Tudjman exaggerating all the damage. When Tomislav sent messages saying "It's fine, it's OK" I didn't believe him, I thought he was just trying to keep me cheerful!'

Tomislav had a seventeen-year-old daughter by his first wife, a Hungarian from Novi Sad. During the wars he couldn't see her for four years; now both travelled to Budapest once a month for a weekend together – an expensive stratagem forced on them by the closing of the Serb-Croat border.

As a Dubrovnik liberal, Tomislav conceded that many Serbs were genuinely if ineffectively anti-Milošević. Yet he had wholly approved of OAF though his liking for Kosovars was not perceptible. He explained, 'I'd prefer to see Nato's troops in there instead of Serbia's. My ex-wife says bombing the Serbs was unfair, punishing innocent civilians. I say I'm sure they'd good strategic reasons for taking out all Novi Sad's three bridges. A big powerful organization like Nato has smart guys running it.'

Perhaps fortunately, I was by then too sleepy to argue.

Next morning I hoped to walk the walls alone, as the sun rose; but there was no admission until 9 a.m. so I watched the sunrise from the foot of St John's Fortress and then went wandering. Structurally, Dubrovnik is not all that ancient – not a higgledy-piggledy medieval maze of twisting streets and individualistic dwellings. In 1667, on 6 April (Easter Sunday), an earthquake killed more than two-thirds of the citizens, levelled most of their homes, cracked even the massive fortifications and destroyed most of the famous buildings – among them the cathedral, to whose building fund Richard *Coeur de Lion* had lavishly contributed. This disaster quickened the Republic of Ragusa's decline, which had begun a century or so earlier. Slavs moved in to replace the dead and rebuild the city; increasingly Slav names appeared in the roll of the nobles. The Major Council (the government) decreed that all new buildings must be of stone, conform to a certain design and be laid out in an orderly pattern; this was among the earliest and most successful of Europe's town planning endeavours and it explains the Old Town's mathematical formality.

As an outsider, one cannot discern 'a patricians' district' and 'an artisans' district' – apart from the telltale family crests engraved over some entrances. Now most houses are divided into flats and in this celebrated city ordinary life goes on: women hanging out their washing on exquisite wrought-iron balconies high above the narrow streets – children laughing and squabbling (oddly reassuring to overhear) – men putting out garbage-sacks beside time-worn stone steps – cats dozing on window sills – people hurrying off to work carrying brief-cases or tool-kits, ascending steep flights of scores of steps with an agility rarely seen nowadays in motorized cities. Were it not for this rhythm of normal living the Old Town would by now have become, in spirit, no more than tourist bait. But the dread developers, those Attilas of our time, yearn to 'improve' it – so I was told that evening, sitting in a small quiet café talking to a charming octogenarian whose agitation visibly increased as he unburdened himself.

The developers were planning a complex of artists' studios and tourist apart-ments – a modern art centre – night clubs and pizza parlours – toilets for tourists. And the cost, in human terms, would be the enforced displacement of 700 working-class residents who have nowhere else to go and are so attached to their homes that throughout the shelling of Dubrovnik they refused to be moved to the comparative safety of a DP camp.

By 8.50 a.m., at the entrance gate to the walls, a package of Austrians was already patiently queuing, complete with voluble guide, and behind them were two score giggling and scuffling Zagreb schoolchildren. Again I retreated, to 'do' some of the sights of Dubrovnik. The herd instinct is strong and from 1.00–2.30 p.m. I had the walls to myself, while lunchtime smells wafted up from open-air restaurants.

Looking down on the town's roofs, one can see many replacements, exactly copying the originals. Dubrovnik's post-war restoration was generously funded and, on the whole, skilfully done. If not told where to look, newcomers would scarcely notice the JNA-inflicted damage – at the time exaggerated by the Croats who regarded as their propaganda trump card the Serbs' monumentally stupid shelling of this 'jewel of the Adriatic'.

The walls' modifications are regrettable: concreted steps, concrete smoothed over rocky paths, waist-high concrete walls – all to safeguard tourists, nowadays assumed not to have the wit to safeguard themselves. Here, too, as down in the town, there is some incongruously crude pointing, apparently done by amateurs in a hurry. And the graffiti gangs have been at work: 'Fuck the ARMY!' in English was a popular legend. ('Which army?' I wondered.)

Towards sunset, having 'done' a few more sights, I sat with a *pivo* in the Stradun, the Old Town's only wide street – of polished stone, lined with tall, gravely impos-ing buildings. And there Dubrovnik's free evening entertainment mesmerized me: thousands of swifts giving a dizzying display of aerobatics, circling high in the sky, then swooping and darting low between the buildings, their speed and flock coor-dination something to marvel at, their shrill frenetic twitterings so loud I had to raise my voice when ordering another *pivo*.

Looking up and down the Stradone, I mentally congratulated the successors to the Major Council: no plastic disfiguring of shop façades is allowed and only café table sunshades – Coca-Cola and Marlboro – marred the Adriatic's most famous thoroughfare. The authorities deal with litter-louts almost as sternly as their ancestors did. (Yet there is a carpet of cigarette butts despite numerous specially designed ashtray bins.) Music in public places, including cafés, must be muted. Only delivery vans and small lorries to do with reconstruction are permitted to enter the Old Town – briefly in the early morning – and beyond the walls a municipal mobile crane patrols the streets, at once confiscating any illegally parked vehicle. Here the pavements are unobstructed and pedestrians may safely walk.

In 1990, less than 7 per cent of Dubrovnik's citizens were Serbs, most of whom fought with their Croat fellow-citizens against the JNA. Yet I found myself resenting the city's being now so tightly embraced by the Hrvatska Turistička Zajednica (Croatian National Tourist Board). Their literature presents Dubrovnik as 'a rich part of Croatia's inherited cultural greatness', ignoring the Republic of Ragusa's former independence of Croatia – and everyone else. Dubrovnik must have fitted more naturally into Yugoslavia's wide patchwork than it does into Croatia's narrow new nationalism.

21

Ruairi's last lap – Through the Krajina

It was by now (mid-May) hellishly hot at sea level and the coast road from Dubrovnik to Split is a dangerously busy unshaded motorway, linking many tourist resorts, camp-sites and caravan parks. Happily there was an alternative; the Dubrovnik-Rijeka car ferry departs daily at 8 a.m. from the port of Gruž.

A splendidly rugged coastline allowed Dubrovnik's not-very-New Town to be built out of sight of the Old Town and its inconspicuous apartment blocks are set amidst tall trees on steep slopes. Gruž's severely shelled port has been restored and its few Renaissance palaces along the waterfront seem, oddly, to have escaped damage.

The shoebox-shaped car ferry was less than one-sixth full – so the captain announced, by way of explaining why the restaurant was closed and why meals would be available in the self-service cafeteria only from 12.30 to 1.30. (The one dish on the menu consisted of tinned spaghetti Bolognese and 'salad' – two slices of tomato on a yellowing lettuce leaf.) Most passengers were German, English or French. A few rich Dubrovnik motorists were on the overnight trip to Rijeka, bound for Western Europe, and a very rich Croat-American returnee soon engaged me in conversation.

Punctually at 8 a.m. we sailed and this Zagreb entrepreneur, standing beside me at the prow, remarked complacently, 'Croats are as efficient as Germans, that's why Germany backed our independence, they knew we'd make good trading partners and they were right. Have you seen the changes in Zagreb? It's another world now, part of the First World!' This uncongenial character had lived in Chicago for twenty-five years and just sold his share in a Dubrovnik hotel to an American brother-in-law. I considered drawing his attention to those high-rise slums, not far from what he would call 'downtown Zagreb', where thousands endure a level of deprivation unknown in Tito-land. But some arguments are not worth starting.

The Adriatic must be polluted but doesn't look it; those emerald waters seemed as clear as in the days when argosies sailed from Ragusa, and pirate boats from north Africa, and galleons from Venice, and warships from Constantinople. Our first stop was at Korčula, reputedly the most beautiful of all the Dalmatian islands – so tantalisingly beautiful, from offshore, that I promised myself a holiday there if one January I was neither on a journey nor writing a book.

The four packages who disembarked were replaced by others – and by a few solo travellers, including a retired Serbian army officer whose company I enjoyed for the rest of the voyage. He had moved to Korčula when tourism's collapse lowered the rents – 'Also I can fish every day for free food.' He was surviving on a monthly pension of DM250, having retired in 1988. 'This was an early retirement but I could see what was coming. I'm a Yugoslav, I was born one and I'll die one. I joined the Partizans as a teenager and stayed in the army to defend my country, not to kill my countrymen. Some think I'm brave, to live in Croatia now. But many still recognize and respect a Yugoslav, even if we don't officially exist! I've no problems with my Croat neighbours – why should I? My mother was a Croat, half my nephews and nieces are Croats. Today I go to a Rijeka hospital for tests, paid for by a nephew living in Zagreb. The JNA, or someone acting for them, killed two of his closest friends in Vukovar but he doesn't want revenge on me!'

The new Split, developed in a rush during Tito-time, has almost obliterated the old Split, founded by the Emperor Diocletian. As the ferry glided slowly into an overcrowded harbour we had a depressing view of the city's shapeless ugliness, crawling and sprawling all over arid slopes. But then I lowered my eyes and saw Diocletian's Palace, its grey southern wall nearly 600 feet long, seventy feet high, eight feet thick – the only reason I planned to spend a day in Split. The Emperor was born nearby, in 245, and when he voluntarily abdicated in 305 his palace had just been completed. To build it took ten years. To appreciate its ruins, seventeen centuries later, takes a day.

As I pushed Ruairi out of the ferry's belly, a woman of about my own age, with fuzzy faded hair and a plump creased face, placed a hand on my forearm and offered a room for 300 kuna (£30). I disliked her at first sight – an insincere smile, crafty eyes – but the desperation of her touting suggested a particularly hard-hit victim of tourism's collapse. Quickly we negotiated down to 180 kuna and she beckoned me to follow her on an allegedly 'twenty-minute walk'. Within ten minutes she had become alarmingly flushed and breathless; normally she would take a bus with her captured lodgers. At the next bus-stop she leant against the shelter, panting, and indicated that I should pedal in pursuit of her No. 16. From there, at her pace, it would have been at least an hour's walk to our horrible destination. I overtook the bus at each stop and could see Mrs Stipe anxiously peering out, then waving at me vigorously. We were following a wide thoroughfare through Split's apparently limitless and utterly featureless suburbs. Mrs Stipe left the bus quite close to her block, approached from street level via a long, steep flight of broken concrete steps. I tried to use this obstacle as a valid excuse to say goodbye but Mrs Stipe summoned the only person in sight, who chanced to be a stalwart young man. Moments later Ruairi was on a rubble-strewn walkway – and eventually in a lift where he had to be held upright, standing on his hind wheel, as it were.

Mrs Stipe lived alone in a large, well-appointed flat where I was given a tiny room, not '*en suite*', and recommended to admire the fine view from my ninth-floor window. Between nearby kindred blocks, segments of a beach, furnished with tourist amenities, could be glimpsed. Before I had time to mop my sweaty brow, Mrs Stipe demanded her 180 kuna. Having as yet no kuna, I gave her a DM50 note and awaited my change. She seized the note, refused to understand that she owed me 20 kuna and asked for my passport. Foolishly I handed it over, warning her that she would have to be up early to return it.

Mrs Stipe insisted on showing me the nearest mini-market and when I bought only a bottle of wine, pretending not to hear her pleas for fruits, salami and coffee, she put those items in my basket as I queued. I removed them with a sharp reprimand which attracted the check-out girl's smirking attention but left Mrs Stipe unfazed. Back in the flat, she produced two glasses and a corkscrew and invited me to relax in her sitting room. Having filled both glasses, I curtly explained that I had work to do. In one gulp Mrs Stipe emptied her glass then made to grab the bottle as I reached out to pick it up. At that point I thought better of leaving the pannier-bags exposed overnight in the hallway, where Ruairi was parked for lack of space in my room. A sullen Mrs Stipe watched in silence as I unhooked them.

At dawn my hostess was up and dressed and in blackmailing mode. Ruairi had been taken hostage – he was nowhere to be found in the flat – and neither he nor my passport would be returned without the payment of 300 kuna. This, according to Mrs Stipe, was the price we had agreed on: and she blandly denied having already received DM50. As Croat police officers do not inspire confidence, I produced one of my secret weapons. Purposefully unzipping my money-belt, I drew out an expired Royal Geographical Society Life Fellow's card. (The current one always remains safely at home.) This tiny bit of worthless plastic, if wielded with a certain set of gestures, facial expressions and tones of voice, has a conveniently intimidating effect on those to whom it is incomprehensible. Within five minutes I was pocketing my passport and Mrs Stipe was scuttling down the long corridor to retrieve Ruairi from her son's flat.

It didn't take long to find alternative, congenial lodgings with a friendly young couple living not far from Diocletian's Palace. For some mysterious reason, the magic of these ruins has not been dissipated by mass tourism; in my experience they are in this respect, as in several others, unique.

*

Inland from Split is the Knin Krajina, scene of one of the Balkans' most vicious (and internationally least noticed) forced uprootings, which in August 1995 drove some 200,000 Serbs into permanent exile.

During the seventeenth and eighteenth centuries the Habsburgs encouraged various groups of Serbs who had incurred the wrath of the Ottomans to settle in Croatia. There they were given land, in exchange for a long-term commitment to defend the frontier between Christendom and Islam. This became known as the Military Frontier (Vojna Krajina) and extended for a thousand miles into present-day Romania, varying in width from twenty to sixty miles. Here the Serbs enjoyed autonomy; they were not ruled, like their Croat neighbours, from Zagreb, but directly from the Imperial capital.

In Serbia under the Ottomans, and later under their own nineteenth-century rulers, the Serb peasants were in general peaceable and stoical – almost placid. In the Krajina, as armed freemen liable to be called upon to serve in any Habsburg war, they soon developed a warrior cult, heroism being judged by battlefield standards and weapons being revered – even by women. Otherwise, they became Croatian in language-use, script, dress, diet, customs, folk music, behaviour, house-building methods – everything except religion.

By the nineteenth century the Krajina Serbs were caught between three ruling powers – Austria, Hungary, Croatia – whose interests did not always coincide. Loyal to their Habsburg masters, they came to be depicted by some Croatian viceroys as an 'undesirable element' and this attitude soon turned them into a touchy, bigoted and aggressive community, increasingly introverted.

In April 1941, when Ante Pavelić declared a Nazi-sponsored Independent State of Croatia, he made plain his intention to eliminate all Serbs – 'Kill a third, expel a third, convert a third (to Catholicism).' However, many of the Krajina warriors survived by rallying to the Chetnik flag and fighting back.

Fast forward to early 1990 when the Krajina Serbs, understandably alarmed at the prospect of living in a Tudjman-led independent Croatia, formed the Serbian Democratic Party (SDS). Although never a united party, from it sprang armed rebellion and a 'Republic of the Serbian Krajina.' This 'entity' owed its potential for disruption to Knin's vital strategic importance as the rail junction between the interior and the Dalmatian coast. Whoever controlled Knin, controlled Croatia's economy.

Many books describe the confused and violent four-year history of that notional 'republic' which 'occupied' one-third of Croatia's territory. In *Burn This House* Ejub Štitkovac, a Bosniak *imam*, has written:

In an attempt to place the Krajina under Croatian control, Croatia maintained a state of low-level warfare throughout 1992 and 1993. In September 1993, Croatian forces attacked the so-called Medak pocket, a group of villages in the Adriatic hinterland just north of Zadar. On September 17, the territory was handed over to the United Nations, but not before it had been completely emptied of its Serbian population, which offered no resistance. All houses were torched, livestock slaughtered, farming equipment destroyed, wells poisoned . . . By the beginning of 1994 Slobodan Milošević was ill inclined to risk his status as a peace negotiator by helping the Serbs in Croatian Krajina. From that point on, every Serb in Croatia had every reason to feel infinitely more threatened than at any time since World War II.

On 4 August 1995 the Croatian army launched 'Operation Storm', an all-out attack on the Knin region. The poorly armed Krajina warriors retreated in disarray, leaving a terrified civilian population to escape into BiH and Serbia as best they might. Within forty-eight hours the Krajina, home to those Serbs for four centuries, had ceased to exist as a human community. The Croatian troops shelled the fleeing peasants and murdered any Serbs they came across who for reasons of age or infirmity had been unable to escape. Some were burned in their homes, others were tortured before being killed. This 'tidying up' continued throughout the autumn. The Helsinki Human Rights Committee in Zagreb estimates that approximately 6,000 civilians were killed during Operation Storm and 1,000 or so in the months that followed.

A Croatian Roman Catholic priest commented that environmentalists would organize worldwide protests if 200,000 birds were driven from their natural habitat but few seemed to notice 200,000 Serbs being driven into permanent exile.

Milorad Pupovac, moderate leader of Zagreb's Serb minority, commented: 'The attack on the Serbs of the Krajina has given a legitimacy to the practice of ethnic cleansing and the creation of ethnically pure states. Krajina as a multi-ethnic community is finished.'

Carl Bildt, a former Swedish prime minister and the EU's mediator on the former Yugoslavia, commented: 'If we accept that it is all right for Tudjman to cleanse Croatia of its Serbs, then how on earth can we object if Yeltsin cleanses Chechnya or if one day Milošević sends his army to clean out the Albanians from Kosovo?'

Three and a half years later Nato's spokesmen were declaring that Kosovo and Serbia must be bombed because 'We can't stand by again and watch more ethnic cleansing.' Many voices were then raised, for and against OAF, but few asked, in plain English, 'What has converted the US administration to "humanitarianism" since it collaborated in ethnic cleansing in 1995?'

A Kerryman going to Knin wouldn't start from Split's old town. Of EU-style signposts there were many but not one mentioned Knin. And the few pedestrians available at sunrise looked blank, shook their heads, smiled weakly and left me to it. I began to wonder if some collective-guilt-inspired amnesia was at work – Knin a place best forgotten.

As I pedalled this way and that, through the suburbs, a police car pulled up and two officers, shouting together, hectored me for not using the 'cycle-path' – unmarked as such and anyway within an hour it would be blocked for the day by parked cars. Eventually I realized that the Knin road must branch off from the very new (1999) Split to Zagreb highway which I had examined with distaste as we sailed into the harbour. It forms a livid scar on the steep grey immensity of Split's encircling karst mountains and my binoculars revealed curving miles of metal fencing and many straight soulless bridges spanning rifts in the barren lime-stone. Seen from offshore, the speeding vehicles seemed insect-sized. And now came a ninety-minute walk on this *autoput*, against a gale-force wind. But at least the five tunnels were high, wide and well-lit, with sos telephones on either side and footpaths on which a laden bicycle could be pushed in comfort.

Approaching the pass, I gazed in awe at the ruins of Klis, dominating the coast below and the islands of Čiovo, Brač and Šolta. Built on this strategic saddle some sixteen centuries ago, the fortress was held in turn by Avars, Turks, Venetians, Austrians. I longed to climb around it but dared not leave Ruairi unguarded.

Still there was no signpost for Knin but my map told me where to escape on to a narrow, little used road. For a few miles it descended through rocky wildness to a heartbreaking plateau. Here were wide, boulder-strewn pastures, no longer grazed – occasional stands of mixed woodland – a dreadful number of burnt-out homes and abandoned vineyards. The vines, though strangled by other creepers and weeds and tall grasses, were laden with fruit. What happens now, I wondered, when the grapes ripen? Since the 1690s these vineyards have been producing a white wine respected throughout the Balkans.

Here that gale-force wind was behind me and Ruairi seemed to have an engine. At the northern end of this plateau stands Drniš, on the banks of the river Čikola, overlooked by a karst ridge – a shockingly shattered town of steep winding streets and many fine Ottoman buildings, including the ruins of a bastion. At noon the town centre was deserted, apart from a procession of schoolchildren being shep-herded by a frowning nun. Bizarrely, three banks were open though none was doing any business; they all regretted being unable to change DM. In the two cafés, where small groups of men silently played cards, no food was served. Most of the shops were either closed or in ruins; finding a survivor, I bought three tins of sar-dines but not a crust remained of the day's bread delivery.

Near the Habsburg town hall (partially restored) one intact bench remained in a neglected public garden. There I sat devouring sardines and wishing I had bought bread in Split. Then a frail elderly man, who needed his walking stick, came to sit beside me and observed, 'You are very hungry! Why are you here with a bicycle?' He spoke English precisely; he was a retired science teacher.

I tried to explain myself and Mr Pervan said, 'You should go to some other country. Now is nothing to say about Yugoslavia. Many people write books about us but there is no more to say. You see this town – my town. It was beautiful and peaceful. Now it is as you see it. But you see only the buildings destroyed. You can't see how the people are destroyed. I don't mean the people who are dead, but peoples' way of living together is ended.'

The Bosnian Serb commander, Ratko Mladić, directed the JNA attack on Drniš in the autumn of 1991 when the town was held by Croatian forces. Mr Pervan asked, 'Why is Nato not able to capture Mladić? Are they afraid of his bodyguards? Are they not really soldiers but only government officials dressed in uniforms?'

I said, 'They prefer to offer bounties, to pay gangsters to kidnap war criminals.'

We walked together to the street and when I offered my hand to Mr Pervan he bowed to kiss it; somehow I wasn't surprised, that gesture matched the dignified ruins of Drniš.

The road to Knin curved around the base of stony hills and on my right stretched the contrasting fertility of the plateau. Here were quite a few new houses, built on sites once occupied by the banished Krajina Serbs. According to Mr Pervan, some families had chosen to move out of Drniš rather than reconstruct amidst the sad wreckage of their town. I had asked him about the abandoned vine-yards; the thought of all those wasted grapes troubled my frugal soul. 'But they must be wasted,' he replied. 'To pick them would bring misfortune on the person.'

Suddenly I heard a grinding, snarling noise – and, rounding the next bend, saw a giant yellow machine, shiny new, taking up more than half the width of the road while one of its huge whizzing blades ripped branches off the graceful wayside willow trees and another mowed down the abundant wayside flowers whose brilliance and variety had been my consolation all morning. This outrage was so totally unexpected that I felt physically shocked. Here was no question of road-side growth being a traffic hazard, but I knew the explanation. A Zagreb friend had condemned the importing of these machines as part of a 'tied aid' deal. And of course no one tried to restrain the local authorities from using them indiscriminately, with gusto, glorying in them as symbols of 'progress'.

Half an hour later the road climbed into wilder terrain where cliffs towered on my left and below the road lay wild hilly country, densely wooded in the clefts, scrubby along the ridgetops. By now the sky had clouded over and those clouds were black and low. When the downpour came I was on a hilltop, close to Knin, and a solitary shelled house offered shelter. The roof had collapsed but one room retained its ceiling. I sat on the rubbly floor amidst the intimate débris of family life: a hairbrush, a rusty egg-beater, a child's sandal depicting Mickey Mouse, several broken coffee cups – the pretty sort housewives produce with pride – a large wedding photograph evidently torn out of a looted frame, the young couple's features no longer discernible. Very likely this home was abandoned on

4 August 1995. Marcus Tanner has recorded: 'As soon as the bombardment started the Serb troops fled the frontlines, provoking a panicked flight into Bosnia by thousands of civilians, who left their houses with washing on the line and meals half-eaten on kitchen tables.'

Within fifteen minutes the downpour had stopped but the road was a racing sheet of water. One sees Knin's fortress, standing high above a narrow gorge, while most of the town is still hidden behind a mountain spur. Here is another mighty structure that for a thousand years has been fought over at intervals by the usual *dramatis personae*: Hungarians, Bosnians, Ottomans, Venetians, French, Austrians. I lingered on a little bridge over a little river, gazing up at the outsize Croatian flag draped over the battlements. On 5 August 1995 Tudjman hastened to Knin to kiss this flag and announce that the task of creating an independent Croatia had now been completed. I could see soldiers pacing to and fro, seeming toy-sized. A notice warned that this historic monument is no longer a tourist attraction – it's back in business.

Girding my emotional loins, I continued into the bomb-ravaged centre of what was, until recently, a notable medieval town. Its trees survive almost unscathed: stately rows of planes and chestnuts and poplars. But little restoration work has been done and the now sparse population seemed apathetic, not exactly unfriendly but indifferent to the stranger. Independent Croatia hasn't done much for 'liberated' Knin.

In Berane Ana had written the names and address of her parents in large block letters but it took time to find them. The address was obscure; with several other doughty Serb families they lived in a corner of a three-quarters-destroyed apartment block on the edge of the town. When I delivered recent photographs of their granddaughters they embraced me with tears in their eyes. Neither spoke any English but a young Croat woman, Staka, was summoned to interpret; I got the impression she had 'adopted' the Ivančevićs and become a surrogate daughter. She explained that this little community had no running water or electricity; during Knin's very cold winters they spent most of the day in bed.

Both Mr and Mrs Ivančević had memorable features, the sort of strong, definite bone structures often seen in the Balkans, not exactly 'handsome' or 'beautiful' but striking. And I soon realized that they were not only brave, as Ana had described them, but wise. When I asked why they had remained in Knin, Staka translated Mr Ivančević's reply with a verve that expressed fellow-feeling. 'If all the Serbs left Knin, how could there be reconciliation? For centuries the Krajina was mostly Serb. If all the Serbs run away, that's wrong. Now the fighting is over and Tudjman is gone, people can talk. I can talk and say my family is here in the Krajina for three hundred years and it is right we stay here. It is right Hungarians stay in Vojvodina and Albanians in Kosovo. We are all where history has put us and we don't have other homes. In other places in Yugoslavia we are like foreigners. We must not be frightened and run away because politicians send soldiers saying "run away"!'

At the end of July 1995, when Croatia's army was closing in on the Knin region, the Ivančevićs had been invited to take refuge with Staka's grandparents, old friends of theirs who lived in Klis. In April 1996 they returned to Knin – as did 10,000 or so other Serbs, during that year. A similar number of Croats, uprooted from Serbia, BiH and Kosovo, have moved into abandoned Serbian homes.

As I left the apartment block, heaving Ruairi over piles of rubble, the black clouds reassembled and I had been well washed by the time I reached Knin's small two-storey motel, a few miles beyond the town. Its superb site, below the Bosnian border mountains, was an advantage lost on its architect. From the bar balcony, facing a row of concrete block garages and store-rooms, the mountains were invisible; and my bedroom window looked on to a nearby blank wall. The middle-aged couple in charge spoke English and were polite – but distantly so. All evening they remained resolutely uncommunicative, though I was the only guest.

Next morning, uncertain of what nourishment sources might lie ahead, I waited for breakfast and got off to a late start under a cloudy sky – high silvery clouds, showing patches of blue. For an hour the ascent was gradual, through narrow green valleys separating a tangle of mountains – quite challenging, though lacking the craggy ferocity of the Dinaric Alps. Ash trees and bramble hedges bordered meadows glowing with buttercups, beautiful to look at but not conducive to the region's agricultural revival. Amidst weed-conquered fields and orchards stood many charred and/or shelled houses.

The village of Strmica was almost deserted; it had had fine schools and several large, centuries-old, magnificently constructed stone houses. Here wayside notices claimed that the UNDP, EU *et al.* were engaged locally in 'rehabilitation programmes'. Of these there was no trace apart from the toing and froing, later in the day, of several white 4 x 4s. The fertility hereabouts surprised me; my reading had led me to expect much harsher and bleaker terrain along the 'Military Frontier'.

Not far beyond Strmica the road abruptly left the valley to climb a steep forested slope and my four-hour walk had begun. Around the second hairpin bend a tiny wooden hut, manned by two underworked policemen, served as the Croatian border post. The English-speaker asked if I wanted a stamp in my passport? Travellers continuing to Serbia preferred not . . . I said 'Yes, please' and was then offered a swig of *rakija*. 'To make you warm,' said the officer. 'Up there is very cold' – he jerked his head towards the pass. There was no BiH border post but more ruins disfigured the next bend: two houses, a petrol station, a small restaurant (tourists used to come this way). Between there and the pass lay only uninhabited heights and depths.

The road curved up and up, from one almost sheer mountain to the next, and every slope, throughout this range, wore a seamless covering of forest: pine, oak, beech, acacia and unknowns. For two hours the valley behind me was visible at intervals and eventually Knin could be seen again, beyond the foothill summits. Now the sky was cloudless, the sun warm, the acacias' rich scent vying with resin, the birdsong continuous; no other sound broke the stillness. Sometimes, in the depths of the valley on my right, I caught glimpses of a river; but those depths were so profound no water music reached me.

A few miles below the pass naked karst peaks rose from wide bright empty pasturelands. My binoculars showed several shepherds' shelters, lean-tos of woven branches, in the lee of gigantic boulders. And now, from the west, came a mass of black cloud, inexorably rolling towards me at eye-level, obscuring the mountain flanks I had just traversed. Distant thunder rumbles echoed boomingly through the valleys and suddenly a gale was blowing, gusty and very cold.

The pass was a broad, level saddle, its short grass strewn with chunks of karst and solitary pines a few feet high – and also with sofas, beds, cookers (gas and electric), carpets, washing-machines, display cabinets, tables, chairs . . . Who knows what logistical difficulty compelled Croatian soldiers to jettison some of their loot just here?

Ahead lay a vast elevated plateau, broken by low grassy hills and ridges. As I began the descent those clouds hit the pass – an icy deluge. Within moments my windproof – but not waterproof – jacket was soaked through while overhead the thunder roared and reverberated. Moments later two houses appeared in a dip between ridges, facing each other across the road – one a ruin, one partially restored. A man was hurrying home wearing a plastic sack over head and shoulders. In his doorway he paused for an instant to stare at me – then slammed the door. One end of the ruin was dry and there I wrapped myself in my space-blanket and sat shivering in what had evidently been the utility room. Washing-machine instructions in Italian and English remained on a wall above the scars of the relevant fittings and broken glass carpeted the concrete floor. Even the light-switch and the interior door had been looted. Outside many plum trees flourished and between thunderclaps a chorus of birds celebrated the rainstorm.

As the downpour continued I decided to press on to the small town of Bosansko Grahovo, the only town in these mountains. It was much closer than expected – over the next ridge – but I foresaw an accommodation problem. The phrase 'ghost town' springs to pen. When the Croatian army seized this Krajina Serb stronghold in July 1995, as one of the bases from which to launch Operation Storm, they destroyed 80 per cent of the buildings and restoration has been minimal. To arrive in Grahovo soaked to the skin, numb with cold and ravenously hungry was unfortunate. Then I noticed a faint little sign saying 'Motel' – could it by any chance be amongst the intact 20 per cent? It was – an ugly edifice on the outskirts. In the bar my hands were too numb to open my purse. Four unshaven, ill-dressed young men sitting in a corner sniggered at my handicap but the teenage bar-girl was sympathetic. However, my requesting a room dismayed Astrid and she disappeared for fifteen minutes. Exploring, I realized that only the bar was functioning: the bedrooms, restaurant, disco hall and foyer were locked and shuttered. I had resigned myself to sleeping on the bar floor when Astrid returned, beaming and bearing keys. She led me upstairs to a fetid bedroom and made apologetic noises about the lack of water. But at that stage all I wanted was to get out of my wet clothes.

An hour later the rain stopped though the sky remained low and dark. I went food shopping and in the course of a half-hour walk through devastated streets saw only four inhabitants and one open shop. I bought six tins of sardines, a dozen bread rolls and a large bar of chocolate imported from Austria so long ago that it smelt like mildewed hay. Many roadside aid agencies' hoardings detailed their (purely aspirational) commitment to this district. All had been angrily defaced, a form of protest rarely seen. I thought then of Dubrovnik, its structures promptly restored because of its cultural status and economic importance and its population now poised to resume normal life. In contrast, what does the future hold for such places as Grahovo, Knin and Drniš?

At 6.30 a.m. the sky was clear but the temperature close to freezing. After a brief descent from Grahovo the road ran level for miles across flowery meadows. To left and right were lightly wooded, rough-crested mountains, seeming low because of this plateau's altitude. I met no traffic; the burnt-out remains of cars were to be seen beside demolished houses.

S-For mine warnings marked the plateau's edge and frequently thereafter the skull-and-crossbones reappeared. The next forty miles took me over two magnificent passes but numerous deserted homesteads and almost deserted villages made this a harrowing day.

The first long descent was dramatic, around mountains forming one wall of an abyss – the other wall perpendicular red-brown cliffs a thousand feet high. In places those cliffs had been riven (by an earthquake?) to create narrow shadowy chasms where ravens nested. Then I could see Drvar, another battle-scarred, depopulated town, scene of a famous confrontation between Tito's Partizans and the German invaders. It straggles down the middle of a long valley, the ranges on either side rising abruptly from green fields mostly uncultivated.

After the steep ascent from Drvar I was pedalling for miles through shallow valleys full of tall, pink-tinged grass, rippling in the wind, and beech woods carpeted with bluebells, and expanses of emerald turf displaying a dazzle of wild flowers. No livestock appeared, anywhere, unless one counts two pairs of glossy chestnut horses pulling firewood-laden carts towards Drvar. The only other traffic consisted of a ten-vehicle convoy of rowdy Spanish policemen; had it not been 9 a.m. I would have diagnosed intoxication.

Near the second pass, outside an abandoned village, stood that Balkan rarity – an attractively designed hotel, all of wood, now half-burned. Hereabouts, too, were the charred or savagely vandalized remains of simple holiday homes, set inoffensively amidst the pines. Now this area's only residents were unkempt soldiers occupying a large semi-derelict school building. From here the long descent to a wide, flat plain corkscrewed through mature forests of oak and Scotch fir.

Down on the level, I wilted in the midday heat, crossed the E761 *autoput* (Sarajevo to Bihać) and pedalled hungrily into Bosanski Petrovac at 1.15. This must once have been a pleasant little town, with its two old mosques (recently over-zealously restored) and Habsburg public buildings. It escaped extensive structural damage but around every corner one can see how much economic damage was done. While seeking a restaurant I passed a new graveyard for 1992 victims and paused to read the inscriptions; several were babies' graves. In the town centre stands a clumsy marble memorial to the many local men who died in combat. At last I found a brand-new Pizzeria – so new that the kitchen was not yet operational and the pizzas came from the owner's home in the next street.

Because of the heat, I had abandoned my plan to continue to Bihać, only thirty-five miles further, and in Petrovac's inexplicably enormous hotel I spent the afternoon on my room balcony reading a Split purchase, Dubravka Ugrešić's *The Culture of Lies*. That slim volume of essays taught me more about the disintegration of Yugoslavia than any of the other books listed in my bibliography.

By nine o'clock next morning I was sitting – breathless – in one of those tiny sheep-on-spit eating-houses common in BiH and not describable as restaurants because there's nothing else on the menu and no cutlery is provided. My breathlessness was owing to a race with a rainstorm. For most of the way from Bosanski Petrovac the *autoput* ran level across a plain where small patches of wheat had been planted amidst miles of lush unused meadows. Beside this road, much travelled by expats and visiting VIPs, the ravaged homes had been 'tidied' in the course of NGO-funded 'Remove War Debris' projects. These ruins – roofless and windowless but with fine stone walls left standing – somehow seemed all the more macabre because of their lack of hanging beams and surrounding rubble. For thirty miles a cool crosswind blew and the sun shone pleasantly warm from a clear sky. Then suddenly, as I began the long descent to Bihać, black clouds gathered above the massif to the west and soon I could see a curtain of rain moving towards the town. Giving Ruairi his head, I sped down to the flat land, then for a mile or so raced that curtain to the suburbs where the rain and I arrived simultaneously and the eating-house offered shelter. My sprint had been observed by the proprietor and his wife who cheered me as I dragged Ruairi up the wooden steps of their verandah.

Mrs Alajbeg didn't wait for me to order a plate of mutton: it was at once placed before me. I must have looked as hungry as I felt; the Petrovac hotel kitchen staff were not early risers. This was a two-spit establishment, each under its tin 'roof', the fireplaces of stone. While meat was being hacked off one sheep, the other elderly ewe (past lamb-bearing) continued to revolve over glowing logs. Ideally, the wood should never flame and Mrs Alajbeg reproved her husband if he allowed a log to do so. He, apologizing for the toughness of the meat, explained that he sold all his lambs to Bihać's hotel, army barracks and rich families.

The Alajbegs (in their late fifties) were a friendly couple and stoically cheerful though life was hard and unpredictable. They looked on the bright side: all their immediate family – a daughter, a son, their own siblings and nephews and nieces – had survived the Nineties. Which meant, as Mr Alajbeg pointed out, that they had been unusually lucky.

Both Alajbegs spoke some English, German, French and Italian. Their language school had been a Swiss hotel where from 1975–90 they worked throughout the skiing season (grandparents cared for the children), returning annually in April to farm their ten acres.

As I finished my second large plate of mutton Mr Alajbeg produced a family photograph album, held together with strips of sticking plaster, and said, 'I can show you little bits of history!' There was his great-grandfather, posing in a studio in September 1914 before going off to be killed – a Muslim fighting shoulder to shoulder with the Krajina Serbs against the Serbian Serbs. And there were his grandfather and father, Partizans wearing stern expressions and long moustaches and proudly clasping guns. The Ustasha killed his grandfather but his father survived. 'Otherwise,' said Mr Alajbeg, 'I wouldn't be here – isn't that a funny thing to think?' Finally there was his Uncle Abdul who in 1954 had been one of the leaders of the Cazin Peasants' Revolt. I wanted to know more about this unique event in post-war Europe but my questions embarrassed Mr Alajbeg. The methods used to put down the Cazin rebels showed Tito's regime at its most ruthless; even those who had fought bravely with the Partizans were not spared. Therefore Mr Alajbeg wanted to talk about the Revolt only as an example of how Serb, Croat and Muslim peasants collaborated naturally when not being led astray by politicians.

At 12.30 the downpour dwindled to a drizzle and I went on my way, Mrs Alajbeg having firmly refused any payment for those two plates of mutton. However, on the *pivo* side of the ledger I had been a good customer.

Within the Croatian kingdom Bihać was a royal free city but few traces remain of its medieval importance. In 1592 the Ottomans razed it, all the surviving inhabitants fled and the rebuilt city – its Gothic cathedral converted to a mosque – became an island of Ottoman culture and trade in a mainly Serbian sea of peasants. Yet its comparative nearness to Zagreb and distance from Sarajevo, and its Krajina hinterland, gave it a distinctive flavour.

When Tito's military strategists decided to put BiH at the centre of Yugoslavia's 'defence system', the most important of its four military airfields was bestowed on Bihać. According to Stipe Sikavica, the Croatian journalist who was for many years a Belgrade-based defence correspondent:

> The Bihać airway had five runways, each from 7,500 to 10,000 feet long. An electronic state of the art hangar had been provided in four underground tunnels for about 100 planes and their maintenance. Its many additional underground facilities made this airfield among the best-fortified air bases in Europe. A system of thick, vertical steel pipes, deeply sunk over every 150 feet of the entire installation, could be filled with explosives if the danger of the base falling to an enemy ever became imminent. When the fighting started in BiH the army (JNA) . . . filled the pipes with explosives and on 16 May 1992 the airfield and its underground facilities, built at the cost of eight billion dollars, were destroyed in one mega-explosion lasting only minutes.

Here is militaristic folly on the Nato-esque scale: first you spend eight billion dollars on one of the best-fortified air bases in Europe – then when the fighting starts you recognize it as a rogue white elephant and blow it up.

As a Bosniak enclave surrounded by Serb-held territory, Bihać gained unwanted fame during the recent conflict. Yet it suffered relatively little structural damage, though many bullet-pocked and shrapnel-scarred buildings contribute to its generally dismal ambience. IC vehicles abounded but the town showed few signs of having benefited from their owners' presence. Soon I was crossing my old friend the River Una, flowing wide and jade-green through the centre and decorated with three swans – one white, two black – enclosed in a 'safe area' beside the park. (Many Bihać citizens remain underfed.) That park is renowned for its majestic Habsburg-planted trees, their height and girth awesome. During the terrible winter of 1992–3, when Bihać's famished population had to fell most other trees, these were spared by common consent – which says much for the town's sense of community. The 500-bed Park Hotel was three-quarters closed and I had to wait fifteen minutes while a gorgeously-uniformed doorman searched for the receptionist.

Going walkabout in the drizzle, I noticed that some streets had recently been renamed in honour of military units and the town was swarming with skinny adolescent recruits wearing new uniforms and shiny boots that looked too big for them. Where one might expect to see Tourist Board information displayed, there were 'Join the Army!' photographs. These showed jolly young men around camp fires with weapons stacked nearby – frowning young men crouching in bushes aiming at the enemy – agile young men scaling cliffs with knives in their mouths – keen-eyed young men poring over maps – solemn young men standing to attention at their passing-out parade. This recruitment campaign was part of a 'peace-keeping' operation. It's known as the Equip and Train (E&T) programme and was set up by Nato to make Bosnia's Federation Army 'a viable force'. So reports Zoran Kušovać, Zagreb correspondent for *Jane's Defence Weekly*. He goes on to explain: 'A US consultancy, Military Professional Resources Inc., was contracted to guide the transformation of the Federation Army in line with NATO doctrine and standards . . . Only a unified military structure would enable Bosnia's entry into NATO's Partnership for Peace (PfP) programme.'

Commerce was not flourishing in Bihać but, encouraged no doubt by E&T, two shops offered a wide range of military and paramilitary gear, including handcuffs, laser pointers and a gruesome array of 'hunting' knives – some made in China and labelled, in English, 'For Self-protection'.

Later I observed an extraordinary convoy holding up the city centre traffic for forty minutes. A tourist coach packed with sleeping troops was followed by hundreds of aged private cars (or so they seemed), each carrying two soldiers, with guns and camping gear piled on the back seats; a second coach formed the rearguard. Back in the hotel bar I was informed, 'They were returning from manoeuvres in the field. We haven't got around yet to giving them troop-carriers.'

My informant ('call me Burt, short for Halliburton') was a retired US army officer, now an E&T consultant. He reckoned the training was going well ('Those guys are born fighters!') but the quality of the donated equipment angered him. 'You wanna good fighting force, you gotta spend!' He complained first about the tanks: 'No way can you run a war with five different designs – *five*! That way you need five different training programmes!' Worse still, the thirty-year-old helicopters had weak tails and couldn't fly high enough to clear the Balkan mountains. And the obsolete communications equipment should have been donated to a museum.

I asked, 'When you've equipped and trained them, who are these recruits supposed to fight?'

Burt stared at me, genuinely puzzled. Then he explained that E&T is a programme to keep the peace; if Bosniaks, Croats and Serbs are all equally well armed and trained no one will attack anybody else – end of problem. 'This system is called "deterrence",' he added, speaking slowly and clearly, in the manner of a kindly teacher addressing a pupil with learning difficulties.

I asked, 'Do you ever think about the link between Nato's expansion, and its emphasis on "interoperability", and the armaments industry?'

'Sure I think about it,' said Burt. 'We're in the same defence business – they make it, we use it! We got more than a link, we're one team.'

I persisted. 'But have you thought about Nato's role in setting the pace for global spending on armaments? Don't we need a world in which governments admit that arms spending doesn't benefit the majority of people? That it deprives them of basic necessities?'

Burt laughed and patted me on the shoulder. 'You shouldn't be worrying your-self about this kinda stuff! Sure, we'd all like to live in that dreamworld – but we've gotta live in the world the way it is. And there's too many bad guys out there for Nato to go soft. We've gotta be ready for more Kosovos – right?'

I asked, 'Do you think Nato's bombing of Kosovo and Serbia was a war?'

'Whatcha mean? Sure it was a war, against that bastard Milošević!'

'But can you so describe it when war was not declared and the aggressor so organized things that nobody got killed on his side?'

Burt looked mightily affronted. 'But Milošević was the aggressor!'

'Not against any Nato country,' I reminded him. 'And in '99 there were several other leaders around the world treating their own people far worse than Milošević was treating the Kosovars. How much had the bombing to do with controlling future oil and gas routes?'

Again that puzzled look – and it wasn't feigned. 'Watcha mean? You been watchin' too much espionage stuff on TV!'

I didn't elaborate; GUUAM's significance would probably have been lost on Burt. But I couldn't resist telling him that I have never possessed a television set. His reaction was predictable. 'Hey! – so that's why you got your head messed up about Kosovo! You never saw those refugees sufferin' – and how they thanked us when they got back home! And like I said, there's more Kosovos comin' – we gotta keep out aheada the rest.'

'But what about that system called "deterrence"? Moments ago you said the way to avoid war was to arm everyone equally. If so, isn't it dangerous for Nato to keep out ahead of the rest?'

Burt shook his head. 'You don't get it! There's rogue states out there – Iraq, North Korea, maybe Libya, Afghanistan, Iran – who knows? Would you give those guys as much weaponry as Nato has?'

Unkindly I remarked, 'Some people – actually a lot of people – include the US on their list of rogue states. And I'm suggesting less weaponry for Nato, not more for anyone else.'

This time Burt's smile was rather strained. 'It's a messy world out there,' he observed. 'You need doin' some real hard work to get to understand it.'

By way of signalling a truce we discussed the local weather – all those sudden rainstorms! – before parting.

Burt was not, obviously, an aggressive or callous man, yet his role on the interna-tional stage was destructive. For him and his like soldiering is a career that extends, very lucratively, far beyond retirement. Both Nato and the armaments industry need Military Professional Resources and similar Incs. To prosper, such men don't have to bother about how the guys at the top are thinking. A rapidly multiplying species, they are assisting militarism to take over the world and I find them more scary, because much more influential, than the psychopathic mercenaries.

From Bihać a busy main road accompanies the Una to Ostrožac's bridge. The long climb to Cazin, the last such of this journey, took me into a dense cold cloud which sat on the mountains until mid-morning, limiting visibility while numbing my hands. Here Ruairi was retracing his wheel-marks and it cheered me to see how much home-building had been accomplished since early March. But the battered town of Velika Kladuša looked no less dispirited in bright summer sunshine.

Near the apparently unmanned BiH customs and immigration offices some optimistic entrepreneur had opened a 'Duty Free' store in a mobile home. Down the road, Croatian customs officers were checking the boots of three BiH cars but showed no interest in my panniers. Just over the border, there is a junction: I had come from Zagreb via Glina and Topusko, I would return via Vojnić and Gvozd.

As I bumped over a severely shell-damaged surface, through placid lush countryside, the sad symbolism of those borders hit me yet again. In 2000 they seemed as artificial and tragic as on that December day, in 1991, when I bussed from Ljubljana to Zagreb. The outside world, while registering shock/horror as Yugoslavia disintegrated, too readily accepted the ultra-nationalists' propaganda and vaguely concluded, 'Oh well, the Balkans are like that . . .' In fact, throughout the centuries, when the former Yugoslavs fought they were usually either defending themselves against outsiders or being recruited by outsiders to fight on their behalf. Moreover, Yugoslavia was not – as so many people, including some Yugoslavs, imagine – a mere ragbag of imperial off-cuts. Its foundations had been laid in the nineteenth century by a coming together of South Slav leaders who dreamed of uniting their people in an independent state.

Given the bloody turmoil of the 1990s it is tempting to scoff at the Titoist rallying call – 'Brotherhood and Unity!' But it did work. Building on those nineteenth-century foundations, Tito constructed a new stable Yugoslavia by doing what the leaders of divided societies are repeatedly advised to do – 'Look forward, don't let past dissensions and grievances destroy the present, build for the future on the common human desire to live in peace.' The defects in his construction that left it vulnerable to the megalomaniacs have been dissected and analysed in many books by a wide variety of 'experts'. One influential theory is that Tito-land was foredoomed to fail, being based on the repression of post-war (Second World War) animosities that needed to be acknowledged, considered and countered as part of the process of reconciliation. The firm imposition of 'Brotherhood and Unity!' was not enough, it is argued, to secure long-term peace and stability; it was too simplistic, too totalitarian, too heedless of the vengefulness inherent in human nature. Recent events seem to bolster this argument yet the attitudes of very many former Yugoslavs confound it. Also, given the challenge confronting Tito in 1945, unity could not have been achieved by setting up some sort of Truth and Reconciliation Commission and encouraging people to study how best to go about healing the wounds they had inflicted on one another. Life wasn't like that, in post-war Yugoslavia. A democratic leader who organized elections, leaving everyone free to remain within their mutually hostile mental camps, harking back to wartime atrocities in their electioneering campaigns, could not possibly have restored peace. A dictator who insisted on 'Brotherhood and Unity!' and gave people no choice but to be Yugoslavs, rather than Chetnik-tainted Serbs, Ustasha-tainted Croats and so on was being pragmatic and humane. (I'm not suggesting that Tito would ever have considered the democratic option; he was a fervent Communist, though unorthodox enough to cut the Communist cloth to fit Yugoslavia.) Of course in Tito-land there were stresses, prejudices, corruptions and inequalities. But so there are today in the world's most respected demo-cracies and at least Yugoslavia's inequalities were fewer and milder.

Remembering my last crossing into Croatia, from Montenegro, I marked the difference: here were no shiny petrol stations and well-stocked shops. But then Dalmatia has always been different. This lonely expanse of countryside felt like a discarded corner of the new free-market-dominated Croatia – most dwellings in ruins, most fields untilled, the few inhabitants elderly. I noticed an uncommon number of nineteenth-century traditional wooden farmhouses (all abandoned) with skilfully carved shutters, balconies and porches. Over some doorways the names of husband and wife, and the date of their marriage, were engraved. Unpruned vines had crept from verandah trellises through broken upstairs windows and feral vegetables could be seen amidst the weeds in gardens that once fed a family. These were among the 20,000 Serbian homes destroyed and looted during Operation Storm; terrorism directed against civilians was an integral part of this campaign. In the words of Laura Silber and Allan Little, 'it brought about the biggest single forcible displacement of people in Europe since the Second World War'.

When commentators described Nato's 1999 airwar as 'the Alliance's first ever military action' they were forgetting Operation Storm. (This is but one of many expedient memory lapses in relation to the Yugoslav tragedy.) On 4 August 1995, as the Croatian army attacked Knin, the Serbian forces' communications systems were bombed to bits by Nato warplanes. At the time Colonel Leslie of the US army was stationed in Knin with Unprofor. Having observed the Croats' strategy, he reported: 'It was a textbook operation, though not a JNA textbook. Whoever wrote that plan of attack could have gone to any Nato staff college in North America or Western Europe and scored an A-plus.' When will The Hague Tribunal turn its attention to those who organized Operation Storm? Or does some arcane chemistry turn forcible uprooting into 'a just war' when the Great Powers are participating?

I joined the Karlovac-Sisak main road at Vojnić, a smallish shell-scarred town. Hereabouts the phoney four-year-old 'Serbian Republic of Krajina' made a futile last stand in August 1995 as the Serbian forces elsewhere were retreating in disarray. My final ten miles wound through low hills, their Maytime beech woods lustrous in brilliant sunshine, and over grassy downlands only occasionally defaced by car cemeteries. The traffic was mainly commercial and most truck drivers indulged in that popular Balkan sport of passing a cyclist with inches to spare.

Gvozd, scattered around a T-junction, consisted of a few blocks of low-rise apartments, a school with shell craters in the playground and a motel long closed. No residents were visible and the atmosphere felt curiously oppressive. Sitting outside the only café – empty at 4.15 – I asked the young man who brought my *pivo* if any lodgings were available. When I had slowly repeated my question he understood and emphatically said 'No!' before hurrying back to a televised soccer match. However, having covered eighty-five miles since leaving Bihać, in Gvozd I put my trust. Despite those odd vibes, it felt like a safe place for sleeping out.

I was diary-writing when a car stopped and Mr Kosinožić, after a moment's hesitation, asked if he might share my table – the only one al fresco. He was tall and middle-aged with friendly eyes and a bad limp. He spoke fluent English and was openly curious about the solo cyclist. We talked for hours and drank all the café's *pivo*.

As the district's chief veterinary officer, Mr Kosinožić had had responsibility, before the wars, for TB-testing some 50,000 cattle. Now fewer than 1,000 remained.

'Who will come back, or be resettled here?' I asked. 'So much rich grazing land – and so beautiful – it broke my heart today to see it deserted.'

'Think then how broken *our* hearts are! For sure the Serbs won't come back – and around here they were good, quiet, hardworking people. My mother was one of them, you passed her childhood home today. They were not like those aggressive Serbs living around Knin. Tudjman said "all not guilty of war crimes are welcome back". We knew that was only for outsiders to hear, specially his German and American friends. *He* knew, the day he was saying it, what his own forces were doing and what he wanted them to do – burning and vandalizing Serbian homes, shops, offices, churches. Some say the Herzegovina Croats will come here, their land is so poor and stony. But we don't need any of the fanatics they have down there, we've too much of that sort already in Croatia. And now who owns this land that those Krajina Serbs were on for centuries? People chased away in war, don't they have rights when peace comes? Shouldn't those refugees, wherever they are now, get money from Croats or whoever settles here? It's too complicated! We hear there are new laws about these matters but we don't see them used. Maybe our government will again ask Serbs to come back – and mean it this time. Our new President Stipe Mesić is a good man, they could trust him. Or after all that happened, could they ever trust Croats again? For me that makes the worst tragedy. Not what happened in '91 or '95 but what it could still be doing to our grandchildren in thirty, forty, fifty years . . .'

At sunset Mr Kosinožić invited me to stay in his Vojnić home, a much appreciated gesture. But I had to make a dawn start, to cover the fifty-five miles to Zagreb by noon, in time to confirm my return flight to Dublin.

'As you leave this area you will be cheered up,' said Mr Kosinožić. 'Soon you'll see livestock in the fields and people out in the meadows making hay. But not enough young people, they get bored doing hard work outside in the heat and the cold. I believe it's the same all round the world. There's nothing different about the Balkans.'

Before we parted, Mr Kosinožić persuaded the youth in the café (still empty) to cook me chips and fried eggs. And he explained that the lady from Irska would be camping nearby. An hour later I was asleep beside Ruairi on a patch of grass behind the school.

Let four 'former Yugoslavs' have the last words. Milan Milošević, a leading Serbian political commentator, wrote in his essay 'The Media Wars: 1987–1997' in *Burn This House* (edited by James Ridgeway and Jasminka Udovički):

A mental conversion was necessary before the majority of Yugoslavs could tolerate nationalist slogans. Despite the claims of foreign journalists and politicians, in the former Yugoslavia mutual trust was in ample supply. For the war to become thinkable, trust that had steadily grown since the Second World War despite some tensions between the ethnic groups had to be rooted out first, and confusion, doubt and fear implanted in its stead. That is what Belgrade television achieved over three and a half years preceding the war in 1991. TV studios proved to be colossal laboratories of war engineering.

Stipe Sikavica, one of Croatia's best known freelance journalists, made the same point in his essay 'The Army's Collapse':

Although the devastation of Vukovar might appear a wanton act of madness, an underlying logic did exist. With its mixed population living in harmony, Vukovar was targeted, as were many towns after that, with the intention of eradicating every possibility that Serbs and Croats would continue to live as neighbours.

Ejub Štitkovac, a Bosniak *imam*, poet and novelist, recalled in his essay, 'Croatia: the First War':

Many Serbs in Croatia were against the war and refused to be turned against their Croatian neighbours. For this, many paid with their lives. Others, under explicit threat that their families would be wiped out, ended up joining the paramilitaries. Sometimes, however, Serbs and Croats fought side by side against either Croatian or Serbian attacks on their homes. Sometimes they fled together.

And Dubravka Ugrešić, at the end of *The Culture of Lies*, poignantly recorded:

A few years ago my homeland was confiscated, and along with it my passport. In exchange I was given a new homeland, far smaller and less comfortable. They handed me a passport, a 'symbol' of my new identity. Thousands of people paid for those new 'identity symbols' with their lives . . . My passport has not made me a Croat. On the contrary, I am far less that today than I was before . . . Being an ethnic 'bastard' or 'schizo-phrenic' is my natural choice, I even consider it a sign of mental and moral health. And I know that I am not alone. Violent, stubborn insistence on national identities has pro-voked a response: today many young citizens of former Yugoslavia, particularly those scattered throughout the world, stubbornly refuse any ethnic labels.

Appendix I

The EU in Mostar

I quote from the European Union Administration of Mostar's own report:

On 19 April 1994 a two-man Advance Party, consisting of the Diplomatic Adviser and the Chief of Staff, was established in . . . a small town some 30 kms South-West of Mostar. The aim of this Advance Party was, in close consultation with the EU Presidency, to make the necessary arrangements for the start of the EUAM. This included such matters as supervising the build-up of the members of the staff, making recommendations on the necessary logistic staff required, devising the administrative budget for the first six months, finding a base for the EUAM in Mostar and establishing relations with political leaders in Mostar . . .

The functioning of the EUAM was based on Articles 8 and 9 of the MoU. One of the first tasks of the Administrator was to establish the Advisory Council (Article 8) which, reflecting the national composition at the time of the 1991 census, consisted of five Croats, five Bosniaks, three Serbs, one Jew and finally one off-spring of a mixed marriage. This Council normally met once a month to discuss a wide range of matters. Discussions centre around the monthly report given by the Administrator on achievements to date, future plans and current problems.

In accordance with the MoU the Advisory Council appointed three Principal Counsellors . . . to advise the Administrator on a daily basis. These three Principal Counsellors were the Mayor of Mostar West, the Mayor of Mostar East and one of the three Serbs who used to serve for one month each as a Principal Counsellor . . .

In accordance with the MoU, seven Departments were established, each headed by a EU national seconded by his or her government. These Departments were:

City Administration
Finance and Taxes
Reconstruction
Economic and Transport Infrastructure
Education and Culture
Health and Social Services
Public Order

In due course an eighth Department was formed as the Education and Culture Department was split into two. This eighth Department was Cultural Life, Youth and Sports.

Additionally, the Administrator had eight Advisers. These were the:

Diplomatic Adviser (in due course joined by the Political Counsellor)

Refugee Adviser

Military Adviser

Press Adviser

Legal Adviser

Humanitarian Co-ordinator

Telecommunications Adviser

Chief of Staff

It was envisaged that the Administrator would be assisted in his task by a WEU Police element (of up to 182 officers) whose fundamental task would be to supervise the formation of a unified police force of Mostar.

In addition a EU Ombudsman was established and a Unprofor Liaison Officer was attached to the EUAM. The Administrator had daily meetings with all his Advisers and Heads of Departments to discuss current problems and plans, and to give advice and guidance. (A diagrammatic organization of the EUAM is at Enclosure C, together with a diagram of the internal administrative organization.)

We have now arrived in cloud-cuckoo-land – a movable territory, to be found on all continents when the IC rides to the rescue. The reactions of Mostar's population to this EU edifice could have been predicted by the cats on the rooftops. *Why* does the IC, in its various institutional incarnations, imagine that a Mostar-type problem can be solved by importing a bureaucracy?

This EU Joint Action strategy required the Administrator, Herr Hans Koschnik, to accept, as his senior staff, people chosen by their own government – without reference to him. Those experienced in such matters estimate that it takes at least a year for an *ad hoc* multi-national team to achieve the minimum of efficient co-ordination. (More often they never achieve it.) Also, the 'gravy-train' aspect of multi-national interventions means that one can't trust all governments to select those best qualified to fill particular posts. However, the EUAM team undoubtedly deserved some danger money. They were seen as targets by both Croats and Serbs and their headquarters – the Hotel Ero, near the former confrontation line – was occasionally hit by Serb shells. Around midnight on 12 September 1994 an anti-tank rocket was fired at the Administrator's flat. (A few Croat suspects were arrested but soon released.) On 7 February 1996, following the announcement of a boundary decision displeasing to the Croats, Herr Koschnik's vehicle was attacked by a large, well-organized lynch mob who would almost certainly have killed him had the vehicle not been an armoured car. Eleven days later, at an EU meeting in Rome, his decision was overturned at the Croats' request – whereupon he 'returned his mandate as Administrator' (EU-speak for 'resigned') and was replaced by Señor Perez Casado from Spain.

EUAM's aim was to unify the city of Mostar. West Mostar was then an unofficial 'entity' run by rich, powerful, utterly ruthless gangsters, men who had gained control during the wars and were not going to be deprived of it by 182 WEU policemen. They so terrorized the Croat political leaders that few would support EUAM's schemes, to all of which the gangsters were implacably opposed; their aim was to keep Mostar divided. It didn't help that Serbo-

Croat is not a popular language in EU schools. Therefore even the most delicate negotiations depended on the fluency and integrity of local interpreters who, given the city's fractured state, could not be expected to function without prejudice. And some were of course 'planted' by the gangsters.

Stage One of EUAM's special housing project, to enable Displaced Persons to return home, required Bosniaks to guarantee the safety of Croats who settled back into their East Side homes. This the Bosniaks eagerly did, such projects serving to promote their own unification policy. However, those displaced Croats either feared to move back or were forbidden to do so. Meanwhile the gangsters continued to expel hundreds of Bosniaks from their West Side flats and there was absolutely nothing EUAM's eight Departments and platoon of Advisers could do to prevent this. Their Report notes gloomily:

> In two and a half years, virtually no progress had been made in returning DPs to their previous sides of the former confrontation line. The sum total of returnees was 18 old ladies who were moved from East to West Mostar to join their families . . . Nevertheless, the EUAM housing authority did carry out the most comprehensive registration of Mostarians wishing to return. Over 9,000 applications from all three sides were received and built into a database which was later transferred to the Commission for Real Property Claims.

Happy are those bureaucrats who can build a database!

For health reasons, a municipal dump was high on EUAM's agenda and they chose a site, recommended by earlier studies, near a village east of the river but in Croat territory. Many months and discussions later this plan had to be discarded because the Croats demanded a site West of the Neretva – where none, in rocky Herzegovina, could be found. Finally an old dump on the East Side (for decades Mostar's main dump) was made temporarily usable again; but the Croats refused to use it, instead dumping by the roadside.

Then there was the HEP issue. (HEP is EU-speak for hydro-electric power plant.) The Croats alleged that after the February 1994 cease-fire one of the Neretva's five HEPs, Salakovac, was illegally appropriated by the Bosniaks despite having been placed in the demilitarized buffer zone. When asked by President Zubak to cope with this potentially very dangerous controversy, the EUAM Administrator devised a compromise both ingenious and just; without going into details, suffice to say that it involved generous EU funding for HEPs and was interwoven with EUAM's daydream about a unified Mostar. After five months of angry arguing the project had to be abandoned; the Bosniaks were allergic to the 'conditionality' prudently placed on the funding. It later emerged that they had sought and found World Bank funding for Salakovac behind EUAM's back – without 'conditionality'.

Every fortnight, when the Freedom of Movement hot potato came on the Administrator's menu, the Croats accused EUAM of being pro-Bosniak. This made sense since nobody was impeding the Croats' freedom of movement. They however restricted the number of East Mostar residents allowed daily across the confrontation line to 250 women, children and men over military age (seventy). As only forty-five or so Croats still lived in East Mostar, while some 6,000 Bosniaks remained in their traditional quarter in West Mostar, this restriction penalised only Bosniaks. And it was relentlessly enforced; at almost every

West Side street intersection Croat police maintained checkpoints. All EUAM's protestations and pleas, arguments and lectures, could not change this. Until the signing of the Dayton Accord in November 1995, 250 remained the daily quota.

MoU's most pathetic Article (No. 12) stated: 'A single police force, unified at all levels, will be established under the authority of the EU Administrator . . . The WEU Police element will be entitled to organise, administer, direct and supervise some police functions . . . It will supervise and monitor other police functions.' Two and a half years later the Report was ruefully noting: '[Often] the WEU officers had to turn their efforts to the preservation of order and not unification.' Almost all the Croat police had served in one of Croatia's armies and many of them were the gangsters' work-mates, men who early in '92 had retreated into Herzegovina with their private supply of weaponry to continue their lucrative careers as gunmen. The entire force simply refused to co-operate with their Bosniak would-be-colleagues.

The Office of the EU Special Envoy in Mostar (OSEM) opened in August 1996. The Report understates: 'It was appreciated that the time remaining of the mandate of the EUAM did not give sufficient time for the stabilisation of the political process in Mostar . . .' Another Joint Action was therefore initiated and an exceptionally patience-testing series of negotiations took place in a whirlpool of animosities; the hard-line Croats' party, HDZ, had furiously rejected an Ombudsman decision affecting the outcome of the 30 June elections. On 7 August, when it was agreed to establish OSEM for four months, EUAM's Chief of Staff was renamed EU Special Envoy. Immediately other post-election problems proliferated – in April 2000 I could still feel their after-shocks. On 31 December 1996 OSEM departed, leaving behind what it engagingly described as 'a small Rear Party'.

Of EUAM's eight departments, only Reconstruction was allowed to achieve enough to justify its existence. The Ombudsman also made his mark in minor but helpful ways. History does not record how the other departments' staffs, and the advisers, passed their time. No doubt they attended many meetings, and wrote many reports, and built many databases.

I can't help feeling some sympathy for EUAM; the rare honesty of its Report disarms one. Yet sympathy is misplaced. The Advance Party arrived on the scene more than three months before the comic opera Inauguration of the Administrator in the presence of Presidents Izetbegović and Tudjman. How come that Party failed to find out the most elementary facts of Mostar life? Such IC-sponsored debacles expose institutions alarmingly unplugged from reality, dreaming up foredoomed operations in Brussels, Geneva, New York – and wasting prodigious amounts of (in this case) EU tax-payers' money. The Ottoman Empire's slow decline began when the Porte's 'departments' became too influential and our own civilization's more rapid decline may be partly owing to the same imbalance. Because the bureaucratic mindset paralyses common sense 'setting up structures' too often satisfies the IC's urge to 'do something'. This urge may have the noblest of motives (e.g., helping to reunify BiH or Kosovo) but down on the ground where real life is lived (or lost) noble motives butter no parsnips.

In Mostar EUAM learnt many lessons but will those be heeded when next the EU is considering a Joint Action? Mr Vip thought 'Probably not.'

Appendix II

Kosovo, Serbia and Nato's Airwar

After the abolition of their autonomy the Kosovars set up a parallel state – born on 2 July 1990 with a Declaration of Independence, baptized by the Proclamation of the Constitution of the Republic of Kosova on 7 September 1990, confirmed by the election of a multi-party Parliament on 24 May 1992. Most Kosovars backed this parallel state but the Great Powers, while deploring Serbia's takeover, in effect supported Milošević by insisting that Kosovo must remain within the Federal Republic of Yugoslavia (FRY).

Although Kosovo was now enduring a repressive paramilitary occupation, serious violence did not break out until 1997, partly because of Dr Rugova's non-violent stance, partly because the Kosovo Liberation Army (KLA) took time to get organized and attract outside assistance.

Unfortunately the multi-party Parliament was far too multi to be healthy. A population of two million or so spawned fifteen or seventeen parties competing for power and profit – not that much of either was then available to Kosovars. The number of parties depends on how you count the Social Democratic Party of Kosovo and the National Democratic Party of Kosovo, both of which had divided into two factions by 1995.

The Democratic League of Kosovo (LDK), founded in December 1989, acquired thousands of members within weeks, reflecting the widespread respect felt for Dr Rugova – though admiration for non-violent policies is not something one immediately associates with Albanians of any region. His party established a network of branches throughout Kosovo and the Albanian diaspora in the US and Western Europe. Its aim was a Pan-Albanian front, modelled on the old Socialist Alliance, in which the whole population, including women and children, could participate. The status of Kosovo was the party's main concern and in the September 1991 referendum (boycotted by Kosovo's Serbs) 99.87 per cent voted for independence. Dr Rugova then called for the establishment of a temporary protectorate in Kosovo under a UN mandate but no one listened. (And now Kosovo does have protectorate status, too many bloody years after it was first suggested.) The Kosovars soon after set about organizing their own schools and medical services as best they could, without the Serb-annexed buildings and facilities or any funding to pay staff.

In December 1992 came the first rattle of Nato's sabre when George Bush, at the end of his presidency, warned: 'In the event of conflict in Kosovo caused by Serbian action, the US will be prepared to employ military force against Serbians in Kosovo and Serbia proper'. The Bush administration feared conflict in Kosovo more than in Croatia or BiH, lest it might extend to Macedonia, then to Bulgaria and – the nightmare scenario – to Greece and Turkey, two Nato allies.

When Albania imploded in 1996–7, temporarily ceasing to exist as a functioning state, many of its security forces became gun-toting civilians with criminal tendencies and from government arsenals the citizenry helped themselves to more than 750,000 AK47s – a lot of rifles when distributed among a population of less than 3.5 million in a country about the size of Wales. The borders with Kosovo and Macedonia were now wide open and the KLA began to coalesce – at first almost unnoticed. Being an irregular force, it never achieved a generally recognized command hierarchy but by February 1998 it was giving Kosovo's Serb oppressors an excuse to be even more oppressive. Also, a few of its leaders, and some of their rich supporters among the influential Albanian diaspora, were indulging in bouts of fiery eloquence about a 'Greater Albania'. In Kosovo itself those men made little impression yet now the spectre of mass Albanian irredentism moved out of the shadows to terrify the Americans, who endowed it with much more substance than it had.

At a press conference in Priština, in February 1998, Robert Gelbard, the US Special Envoy to Belgrade, publicly denounced the KLA as 'a terrorist organization', words widely interpreted as a signal to Belgrade condoning whatever measures the Serbs might think necessary to eliminate their 'domestic terrorist threat'.

A month later Dr Rugova organized elections for the parliament and presidency of the 'Republic of Kosova', that political entity recognized only by Kosovars. The KLA angrily protested that no elections should be held while the country was at war and called for a boycott. But although the Kosovars were proud of the KLA's guerrilla successes they were not prepared to submit to its political diktats and the vast majority – rural and urban, rich and poor – went to the polls and voted for Rugova, the advocate of non-violent opposition to Serbian repression.

Soon after Milošević simultaneously put his 'counter-insurgency' plans into operation and offered to negotiate one to one with Rugova about Kosovo's future. The LDK leader rejected this offer, ostensibly because he considered a foreign mediator essential. More likely he felt it would be unwise to begin negotiations about Kosovo's autonomy when his party had recently promised its supporters independence. It might also be dangerous; the KLA already had a deserved reputation for assassinating 'traitors' and talking with Milošević, as the 'War of Independence' gained momentum, could well be seen as traitorous.

From March to September 1998 the US and Milošević were effectively allies, behind Washington's verbal anti-Milošević smokescreen. Throughout that summer, as Serbian forces terrorized thousands of Kosovars, no loud condemnations came from the US, the EU or the Russian government. According to Britain's then Foreign Secretary, Robin Cook – when it was his turn to justify Operation Allied Force – Milošević's forces 'behaved with extreme brutality' between October and December 1998. The *Agence Europa Bulletin* reported a meeting of EU Foreign Ministers' General Affairs Council on 9 December: 'At the close of its debate on the situation in the Western Balkans, the Council mainly expressed its concern for the recent "intensification of military action in Kosovo", noting that "increased activity by the KLA has prompted an increased presence of Serbian security forces in the region".' Was this meant to convey that the EU tended to blame the KLA for the 'intensification of military action'? Milošević may have chosen to think so.

Meanwhile negotiations were fitfully continuing between the US State Department, the Yugoslav President in person, and representatives of Dr Rugova. President Clinton's most esteemed Yugoslav 'experts' were Richard Holbrooke and Christopher Hill, but the former had recently left the political scene and the State Department now chose to negotiate through Robert Gelbard – who had already antagonized Milošević. Soon both Rugova and Milošević were requesting Holbrooke's return to the Balkans as 'a mediator without preconditions'. (Holbrooke and Hill advocated a 'twin track strategy' for exorcizing the Greater Albania spectre: counter-insurgency against the KLA, plus autonomy talks.)

In 1920 David Lloyd George complained that negotiating with Eamonn de Valera was like trying to pick up mercury with a fork. Chancing to overhear him, de Valera retorted, 'Then why don't you try using a spoon?' Eventually Holbrooke used a spoon and in October 1998 the Holbrooke-Milošević Agreement set up the Kosovo Verification Mission (KVM). This allowed unarmed American-led OSCE monitors to 'observe' limited Serbian counter-insurgency operations throughout Kosovo. But the agreement was Holbrooke's personal initiative and inconsistent with the State Department's ambition to force Milošević to accept a Nato-led 'compliance force' (as distinct from a UN 'peace-keeping force') to supervise the departure of all Serbian troops and police from Kosovo and the restoration of the province's autonomy. At this stage Nato military intervention was frequently threatened and, when Christopher Hill put the compliance force proposal to Milošević in December 1998, it was angrily rejected.

At Dayton, in 1995, the US President had found the Yugoslav President 'someone he could do business with', though Milošević's 'war crimes' were by then common knowledge. The Dayton Accord did nothing to restrain Milošević in Kosovo; by accepting Republika Srpska, it suggested that Serbs could get away with mass murder in the course of 're-arranging' populations. However, after those years of lethal fumbling in BiH some representatives of the 'international community' were guilt-laden. From that group emerged numerous 'airwar' supporters who urged: '*This* time we must be really tough!' So again Milošević became a demon, though in fact the Serbian forces had thus far been less demonic in Kosovo than elsewhere. In *Winning Ugly* by Ivo H. Daalder and Michael E. O'Hanlon, published by the US Brookings Institute, the authors comment on the Serbs' 'relative restraint . . . by the standards of many civil and ethnic wars'.

On 20 December 1998, when Serbian forces reappeared in strength in Kosovo, the IC accused Milošević of 'bad faith'. Seemingly none of the high-powered negotiators or UN and OSCE advisers had foreseen that a withdrawal of most Serbian forces, after the Holbrooke-Milošević Agreement, would leave the way clear for the KLA to consolidate its positions, train its numerous new recruits and import more weapons from Albania – activities which could be observed, but not deterred, by unarmed monitors. The Alliance now had its collective underpants in a serious twist. The KLA were 'terrorists', Kosovo was 'an integral part of the Republic of Serbia (FRY)', the Serbs were reasserting their right to defend their territorial integrity and the Alliance/UN was denying them that right while agreeing that Kosovo belonged to Serbia though it should be granted autonomy . . . This central paradox, not often remarked on by the media, was to render Operation Allied Force surreal. Politically, the military contestants agreed on a pivotal issue: the Kosovars must be denied their independence, though they formed 90 per cent of the province's population and had voted for it overwhelmingly. So 'democracy-defending' Nato was bombing Kosovo and Serbia to force Serbia to oppress Kosovo in a Nato-approved manner by opposing the independence-seeking KLA – while granting the Kosovars that autonomy they had peacefully rejected through the ballot box . . .

So skilfully did Nato's political leadership 'manage' the English-language media that to this day many people remain unaware of the ambiguities surrounding the February–March 1999 Rambouillet conference. For instance, Chapter 7, Appendix B of the proposed Agreement made preposterous demands. I quote:

> The Nato force occupying Kosovo must be immune from all legal process, whether civil, administrative or criminal . . . Nato personnel shall enjoy . . . with their vehicles, vessels, aircraft and equipment, free and unrestricted passage and unimpeded access throughout the Federal Republic of Yugoslavia, including associated airspace and territorial waters . . . Nato is granted the use of airports, roads, rail and ports without payment of fees, duties, tolls or charges. The economy shall function in accordance with free market principles.

This Pentagon-drafted Appendix B was at once published in full in *Le Monde Diplomatique* but was not published in the UK or the US until two days after the signing, on 9 June, of the Military Technical Agreement which brought OAF to an end.

During OAF Satish Nambiar, the Indian general who led the UN mission in Yugoslavia in 1992–3, commented:

> The Yugoslav government had, after all, indicated its willingness to abide by nearly all provisions of the Rambouillet 'agreement' . . . but they would not agree to station Nato forces on the soil of Yugoslavia. This is precisely what India would have done under the same circumstances. Nato's massive bombing appears no different from the morality of the actions of the Serb forces in Kosovo.

However, Timothy Garton Ash, writing in the *New York Review of Books* (21 September 2000) dismissed the 'conspiracy theory' that the Rambouillet proposals were designed to be rejected by Milošević. He concedes that Appendix B 'may have been arrogant and foolish' but insists that 'it was not a cause of war'. This view is based on his conversations with 'senior Western negotiators' who assured him that neither the Serbian team at Rambouillet nor Milošević himself identified Appendix B as 'an obstacle to an otherwise achievable agreement'. But is it likely that those 'senior Western negotiators' would have confided all the facts to an internationally influential writer on Balkan affairs?

As several European allies were at first unenthusiastic about bombing Milošević out of Kosovo, the US State Department disseminated two items of misinformation, allegedly collected by Nato's intelligence services. One hinted that Milošević hoped for a brief bombardment which would enable him to accept the compliance force without losing face. The other mentioned a possible anti-Milošević military coup which could be precipitated by a short sharp Nato attack. In fact the Pentagon had foretold a protracted and hard-to-manage airwar and the CIA had predicted a catastrophic exodus of refugees.

Soon the tendentious claim that '100,000 Kosovo Albanians are dead or missing' was widely believed in Nato countries, leading to acceptance of the argument that to protect Kosovars the Alliance must bomb their homeland, plus Serbia.

On 23 March 1999, by which date all were primed for war, the Belgrade parliament requested the OSCE and the UN to facilitate a peaceful diplomatic settlement. It called for

> . . . more negotiations leading toward the reaching of a political agreement on a wide-ranging autonomy for Kosovo, with the securing of a full equality of all citizens and ethnic communities and with respect for the sovereignty and territorial integrity of the Republic of Serbia and the FRY. The Parliament does not accept the presence of foreign military troops in Kosovo but is ready to review the size and character of the international presence in Kosovo for carrying out the reached accord.

This move was reported on the major wire services yet scarcely mentioned by the media at the time. The fact that there was a last-minute Serbian peace plan on offer, which had not even been considered, was unknown to the general public on 24 March as the first bombs fell. Then millions reacted emotionally and generously to TV pictures of suffering refugees. Nato's media allies had not of course pointed out that Operation Allied Force would leave its target areas strewn with unexploded cluster bombs, saturated with deadly chemicals and dusted with depleted uranium.

The 9 June Agreement was a cross between the Serbian peace plan and the Rambouillet proposals, Nato having dropped its Appendix B demands and Serbia having agreed to 'an international security presence with substantial Nato participation . . . deployed under UN auspices'. The 'security presence' was strictly excluded from Serbia and Montenegro. Political control of Kosovo was delegated to the Security Council, which remains responsible for maintaining an 'interim administration'.

Military leaders are not always the most dangerous militarists. Nato's more intelligent military leaders knew that an airwar could not solve Kosovo's problems but the politicians (and those who control them) insisted on *action*. Then, while the Alliance 'projected air power', Serbian thugs, goaded rather than impeded by the bombing, ran amok. It is a double paradox that while militarism as an ideology rampages across the globe, in response to arms industry and oil industry pressures, realistic generals can be overruled by civilian leaders who worship their armed forces without understanding the limitations of military power. Operation Allied Force called into question one of democracy's most revered principles: soldiers must always obey politicians. If Nato's political leaders continue to behave as though the possession of a superior war machine entitles them to impose their will on other states, regardless of social and economic complexities, the twenty-first century will be even bloodier than the twentieth.

Nato's 'first real war' has to be seen in the context of Nato's expansion. Throughout the 1990s, the Alliance's *raison d'être* was being frantically revised. It's awkward for a 'defensive alliance' when the enemy evaporates. The logical reaction is another evaporation: no more Soviet threat, no more US-led defensive alliance. Instead, there was talk of expansion and the Chairman of Lockheed became chairman of a US advocacy organization frankly named the Committee to Expand Nato. Opponents of expansion included William Perry, who retired as US Secretary of Defence in spring 1997, Michael Mandelbaum, an influential US strategic analyst, and numerous senior diplomats, notably George Kennan and most former US ambassadors to Moscow. But this distinguished coalition was defeated and on the very eve of the airwar Nato expanded into the Czech Republic, Poland and Hungary. Look at the map – what then lay between Hungary and the Nato member states of Greece and Turkey? Only the Federal Republic of Yugoslavia.

Often I am asked, 'But what was the alternative to bombing, in March 1999?'

That question prompts a Kerryman answer. When the lost motorist asked 'Which way to Dublin?' the Kerryman replied, 'If I was going to Dublin I wouldn't start from here.' And had I wished to 'protect' the Kosovars I wouldn't have started in March 1999. I would have started in September 1991, when Dr Rugova sought a temporary protectorate under a UN mandate. Or a belated start could have been made in January 1998 when the Contact Group, representing Britain, France, Germany, Italy, Russia and the US, urged the Serbian and Kosovar leaderships to 'begin a meaningful dialogue'. That was seven weeks before the Serbian forces' first major attack on the Kosovars made *meaningful* political dialogue a mere daydream. Had the Great Powers acted swiftly and decisively then, to secure a UN mandate to establish a temporary (non-Nato) international protectorate in Kosovo, Operation Allied Force could surely have been avoided.

OAF's ostensible military objectives were summed up by the US administration as 'The Three Ds: Demonstrating Nato's resolve – Deterring attacks on Kosovar civilians – Degrading the Serb capacity to inflict harm on the Kosovars.' Simultaneously President Clinton stated that no ground troops would be used, though it is not usual for a Commander-in-Chief thus to reassure the enemy. Already it was obvious that Nato's declared military and political objectives were out of alignment. Its resolve to deter attacks on civilians and 'degrade' the Serbian military machine could only be demonstrated by the use of ground troops. As several commentators noted, a Serb armed with a knife, a half-pint of petrol and a cigarette-lighter could not be deterred by a Stealth bomber costing one billion dollars.

Five days after Nato flew into action its chief spokesman declaimed: 'We are on the brink of a major humanitarian disaster in Kosovo, the likes of which have not been seen in Europe since the closing stages of World War II. There is a campaign under way to ethnically re-engineer the make-up of Kosovo.' Dutifully General Clark, Nato's commander, echoed that – 'Milošević is working very, very fast, trying to present the world with a fait accompli, to change the demographics of Kosovo.'

In the year before Operation Allied Force, some 2,000 Kosovars were killed during counter-insurgency operations. During the seventy-eight-day airwar, approximately 10,000 more (mostly civilians) were killed, plus one or two thousand Serbs, military and civilian – according to Nato figures. With OAF exacerbating instead of halting a 'humanitarian catastrophe', Nato desperately needed a military reason to maintain its 'mission of mercy'. In *Winning Ugly*, Ivo H. Daalder and Michael E. O'Hanlon explain Milošević's Operation Horseshoe, said to have been based on Mao's tactic of draining the sea in which the fish swam. It involved isolating the KLA by driving their supporters out of their villages over 'a broad swathe of territory in the shape of a horseshoe'. It also involved forcibly uprooting Kosovars from the capital, Priština, and the major towns of Prizren and Peć. Another alleged objective was to destabilize Macedonia and Albania by flooding them with refugees. 'In short,' concluded Daalder and O'Hanlon, 'Operation Horseshoe was an audacious plan.'

But did it ever exist? In September 2000 a retired German general, Heinz Lockwei, published his account of events. In *The Kosovo Conflict*, and in numerous interviews, he offered proof (never refuted) that Operation Horseshoe had in fact been invented by the German Minister for Defence, Rudolf Scharping, as his personal contribution to Nato's propaganda arsenal. Until summer 2000 Heinz Lockwei had been Germany's representative at the OSCE head office in Vienna but after the publication of *The Kosovo Conflict* he lost this job. Remembering his accusation, it is interesting to read, in *Winning Ugly*, that Operation Horseshoe was first mentioned publicly in the *Washington Post* on 11 April 1999, when things were going very badly for Nato. A footnote records that the Alliance first heard of Operation Horseshoe in late February when German intelligence sources produced 'a copy of the plan apparently obtained from Austrian and possibly Slovenian sources'. Its contents could not be verified before 'it was proved accurate – when Serb forces accelerated the plan's implementation in late March'. By late March the Serbian forces had gone berserk in reaction to Nato's bombing. By 11 April the publicizing of Operation Horseshoe served a useful purpose.

The US State Department hawks had hoped to put a crushed Milošević on display at Nato's fiftieth 'birthday party' at the end of April. As things turned out, this celebration happened midway through the airwar when various Alliance members were registering ill-disguised hostility to their US overlord. Tactless questions and barbed remarks diminished the gaiety of that extravaganza, sponsored by Boeing (makers of fighter aircraft), Lockheed Martin (makers of the Stealth bomber), United Technologies (makers of Sikorsky helicopters), Raytheon (makers of laser-guided missiles) and Lucent Technologies (makers of army radios). However, the hawks' insistence on playing the Kosovo card did in the end convey an important message to the world. A sustained attack on a sovereign European state, without a clear UN mandate or any formal declaration of war (as international law requires), proved that the UN is never to be allowed to thwart the US. Operation Allied Force also illustrated a point made by Admiral Eugene Carroll (US Navy) in a BBC interview on 20 November 2000: 'Nato won't ever give up its dominance of Europe, military and political.'

The authors of *Winning Ugly* make the same point while arguing that Operation Allied Force did the right thing, though not in the right way. They explain that 'making war while accepting political constraints that impede sound military preparations can be a prescription for defeat – and nearly was in this case'. Having described the US as 'the Alliance's undisputed leader', they maintain that it was 'bad policy' to accept Alliance political constraints instead of 'working to mold them in support of the US perspective . . . Western countries need to learn as much as they can from Operation Allied Force . . . This war will not be the last time that Nato governments use force to save lives.'

So there we have it from the Brookings horse's mouth. The US, as Nato's undisputed leader, must 'mold' its European allies into abandoning their tiresome political constraints and going for the military option – which will not always have to do with saving lives.

Nato gave itself an interesting fiftieth birthday present – GUUAM. This new alliance of Georgia, Ukraine, Uzbekistan, Azerbaijan and Moldova, to be armed, trained and given 'security advice' by Nato, shares a common interest: Caspian oil and gas. Estimates of the oil deposits vary, but it is known that the Tengiz field represents the biggest oil discovery anywhere since 1975. It is also known that BP Amoco's gas find, forty-three miles south of Baku, holds at least fifteen trillion cubic feet and possibly twice that.

Back in January 1996, A. Cohen, then senior policy analyst of the US Heritage Foundation, noted that:

> Control over these [Caspian] energy resources and export routes out of the Eurasian hinterland is quickly becoming one of the central issues in post-Cold War politics. On 21 September 1997 the *New York Times* urged its readers to:
> 'Forget mutual funds, commodity futures and corporate mergers. Forget South African diamonds, European currencies and Thai stocks. The most concentrated mass of untapped wealth known to exist anywhere is in the oil and gas fields beneath the Caspian and the lands around it . . . The strategic implications hypnotize Western security planners as completely as the finances transfix oil executives.'

On 9 November 1998 the *International Herald Tribune* quoted the then US Energy Secretary, Bill Richardson:

> This [Balkan conflict] is about America's energy security . . . It is also about prevent-ing strategic inroads by those who don't share our values. We are trying to move these newly independent countries toward the West. We would like to see them reliant on Western commercial and political interests rather than going another way. We've made a substantial political investment in the Caspian and it's very important to us that the pipeline map and the politics come out right.

The pipelines and tankers in question must use routes that would be threatened if the southern Balkans' instability got out of hand. From the Black Sea, tankers sail through the Bosphorus and around the Greek and Turkish coasts. In April 1999 the Baku-Supsa pipe-line was opened. Another, from Azerbaijan to Ceyhan, had been planned – but the Azeri government created obstacles. However, in late June 1999, a fortnight after the airwar ended, the US Trade and Development Office (TDO) announced that another option was being considered: a trans-Balkan pipeline, from Bulgaria's Black Sea port of Burgos via Macedonia to an Albanian port. The TDO Director explained:

> The continuing conflicts in Yugoslavia have made the proposed trans-Balkan pipeline appear impractical in past years. But the prospect that the US government would guar-antee security in the region . . . now makes it a much more attractive proposition. This grant represents a significant step forward for this policy of multiple pipeline routes and for US business interests in the Caspian region.

The grant mentioned – us$588,000 – was to go to Bulgaria to pay for a pipeline feasibility study. The establishment of the Kosovo 'protectorate' must have greatly gratified Zbigniew Brzezinski – former us National Security Adviser, vigorous advocate of Nato's expansion, Chief Guru to Madeleine Albright, spiritual father to GUUAM and mentor to a consortium of twelve oil companies, the Azerbaijan International Operating Company.

Appendix III

The Use of Depleted Uranium (DU) in the Balkans

On 7 February 2000, Nato's then Secretary General, Lord Robertson, wrote to the UN Secretary General, Kofi Annan:

> I can confirm that DU was used during the Kosovo conflict . . . during approximately 100 missions. The GAU-8/A API round is designated PGU-13/6 and uses a streamlined projectile housing a sub-calibre kinetic energy penetrator machined from DU, a non-critical by-product of the uranium refining process . . . A total of approximately 31,000 rounds of DU ammunition was used in Operation Allied Force. The major focus of these operations was in an area west of the Peć-Djakovica-Prizren highway . . . However, many missions using DU also took place outside of these areas. At this moment it is impossible to state accurately every location where DU was used.

Before that admission, Finland's Minister of the Environment, Satu Hassi, issued a statement:

> I think the EU should make an initiative: military use of DU should be forbidden. Depleted uranium is a waste from the nuclear industry. In the industry itself, the handling of DU is strictly regulated and controlled, and waste is kept in guarded areas. But in military use, in combat situations and test shooting, the very same waste is dispersed into the environment, where the spread follows a haphazard pattern. Munitions containing DU are now part of the armament of many countries. I am of the opinion that the use of DU should be banned . . . It will permanently contaminate the areas where it is used with toxic heavy metal.

DU is seen by the Pentagon as manna from heaven. Nuclear waste costs next to nothing, the supply is unlimited and uranium-tipped 'tank-busters' have extra 'penetrative power'. Therefore when the DU controversy arose after the Gulf War, and refused to go away, the Pentagon became even more secretive than normal. Like all debates which leave the public dependent on the competence and integrity of scientists, this one often generated more heat than light. The topic's vulnerability to journalistic oversimplifications assisted the Pentagon and the arms industry, which share a determination to obstruct or subvert DU research. When the US government commissioned a Rand report, in response to growing public disquiet, its authors omitted to mention DU's most dangerous feature, its trans-mutation into ceramic aerosols.

In August 1999 this phenomenon was explained by Dr Rosalie Bertell, an epidemiologist with thirty years' experience of studying the health effect of exposure to ionizing radiation.

> DU is radioactive waste, and it attains special deadly properties when it is fired in battle. Because of its density and the speed of the missile or bullet containing it, DU bursts into flame on impact. It reaches very high temperatures, and becomes a ceramic aerosol which can be dispersed 100km from the point of impact. Because the radiation dose to the person depends on the strength of the source of the radiation, and the time duration of the exposure, this ceramic aerosol formation is important. Ceramic (glass) is highly insoluble in the normal lung fluid, and when inhaled, this ceramic particulate will remain for a long time in the lungs and body tissue before being excreted in urine . . . Much of the ceramic DU aerosol is in respirable size particles and it stays in the lungs for upward of two years . . . Ingested uranium is excreted in faeces, basically never entering into the human blood and lymph system. In contrast, the DU ceramic aerosol released in war enters directly into lymph and blood through the lung-blood barrier and circulates throughout the whole body . . . Women (because of their radiation sensitive breast and uterine tissue) and children (because their bones are growing, thus able to pick up more DU than adults) will be most at risk from the delayed DU weapon action . . . DU is also a heavy metal and is chemically toxic to humans . . . The aerosol can be resuspended in wind or when disturbed by traffic and this inhaled DU represents a seriously enhanced risk of damaged immune systems and fatal cancers.

Luckily most of the JNA 'tanks' attacked with DU-tipped shells were dummies, therefore many tank-busters hit sand or clay, penetrating the ground – which meant fewer ceramic aerosols being created. (The JNA left Kosovo with most of its military equipment intact.)

In a charitable mood one might assume that the military use of DU was embarked on in ignorance of the long-term medical consequences. Possibly the inventor of the 30mm Penetrator missile didn't know that depleted uranium, relatively harmless if secured in a nuclear waste dump, becomes an agent of mass destruction when incorporated in a weapon – including the destruction (deformation) of children as yet unconceived. And now, though the original ignorance (if such it was) has been dispelled, the militarists cannot bear to be without the *power* (and such cheap power!) of their penetrators.

On 1 July 1999, three weeks after OAF's ending, a 'Hazard Awareness' document was issued by the US Joint Chiefs of Staff and passed to all K-For commanders. It warned that spent ammunition and other DU-contaminated materials, such as the heads of anti-tank shells, should be touched only by those wearing masks and protective clothing – items not readily available to the Kosovars then returning to their fields. All K-For troops were advised to take special precautions, like importing their drinking water and fresh vegetables. But Robert James Parsons has reported:

According to Frederick Barton, deputy high commissioner for refugees, the UNHCR's efforts to draw the civilian population's attention to the risks of contamination met with tremendous resistance both from [Kosovo] Albanian politicians and from Nato and UNMIK administrators. (*Le Monde Diplomatique*, February 2001)

However, UNMIK warned its own officials and UN agencies not to send pregnant women to Kosovo. Some NGOs, reacting to DU's close association with birth defects in the US and Iraq, offer their women staff of child-bearing age the option of not serving in the Balkans.

A UNEP Balkans Task Force (BTF) report, dated 23 September 1999, recorded that on 17–18 August Nato informed its DU fact-finding unit that information on the use of DU was classified. The BTF was led by Finland's former environment minister, Pekka Haavisto, a man determined to include DU in his investigation. But the UNEP, like WHO and all other UN agencies, is controlled, regarding matters nuclear, by the International Atomic Energy Agency (IAEA) – itself a UN organization founded to promote the nuclear industry. Since 1959, when an agreement was made between the IAEA and WHO, the latter has been prevented from dealing with radiation as a public health issue.

The BTF report, entitled 'The Kosovo Conflict: Consequences for the Environment & Human Settlement', was to have been released at a press conference in Geneva on 8 October 1999. At the last moment it was announced that it would be released instead in New York on 11 October. And so a group of Geneva-based journalists particularly interested in DU had no opportunity to question Mr Haavisto. Moreover, the report had been edited by Robert Bisset, a senior UNEP official, who reduced the last chapter from 72 pages to two.

Immediately after OAF, Nato applied pressure all round. Julia Taft, the US Under-Secretary of State for Population, Refugees and Migration, arrived in Geneva to tell the UN Economic and Social Council that this 'humanitarian war' had been a great success, a triumph for Nato in its new role as defender of underdogs. Then, during a press conference at the Palais des Nations on 14 July, she had to confess she didn't know what depleted uranium was – why were some people getting so angry about it?

Meanwhile IAEA and WHO representatives were describing DU as 'perfectly harmless' and a former Swedish prime minister, Carl Bildt – Kofi Annan's Special Envoy to the Balkans – curtly dismissed it as a 'non-issue'.

In December 2000, eighteen months after the end of the 'airwar', UNEP – now under pressure from various agitated governments – sent another team of fourteen scientists to Kosovo. They reported 'remnants of DU ammunition accessible to playing children and animals.' In Priština, a Nato representative implausibly argued that K-For's 44,000-strong force did not have enough manpower to fence off all 112 DU-contaminated sites – then he added that one-third or so were already fenced off, being minefields.

Various governments had become agitated because of the deaths and cancerous illnesses of numerous young soldiers – Italian, French, German, Portuguese, Spanish, Dutch, Belgian – all of whom had served in Kosovo or BiH, where Nato also used DU in 1995. When a young Portuguese soldier, Corporal Hugo Paulino, died three weeks after returning from Kosovo the military medics diagnosed 'herpes of the brain' and the Nato-cowed Defence Ministry refused to release his body to his family for radiological testing and an autopsy. Later, to calm Portuguese public fury, the government sent a specialist team to test the ground in and around Klina where higher than normal levels of radiation were found.

However, the time-scale was puzzling – would DU damage so quickly manifest itself? This seemed unlikely. But in mid-January 2001 a US Defence Department spokesman, Kenneth Bacon, admitted that a year earlier traces of plutonium, neptunium and americium had been detected in DU munitions. He explained, 'These are very, very small amounts and as soon as they were discovered as indicating a flaw in the production process, the Nuclear Regulatory Commission suspended the operation for three months at this munitions plant in Paducah, Kentucky.' Not even Nato disputes the fact that inhaling one-millionth of an ounce of plutonium can cause a fatal cancer. So those 'stray elements' (Mr Bacon's phrase) being in 'very, very small amounts' is not soothing.

A few weeks before this confession, the world press had enjoyed a double leak. Until 9 January 2001 the relevant US 'Hazard Awareness' document had remained inaccessible to the public. Then an anonymous 'military official from a European country' showed it to the *New York Times*. Days later the British press acquired a document entitled 'The Use and Hazards of Depleted Uranium Munitions'. It had been prepared in March 1997 by Britain's MoD medical experts and it concluded: 'Inhalation and ingestion of uranium compounds may have occurred [during the Gulf War]. All personnel should have a full medical history taken and be counselled appropriately. They should be aware that uranium dust inhalation carries a long-term risk to health.'

This greatly embarrassed Lord Robertson, previously a British Defence Secretary. He had just announced at Nato's headquarters in Brussels: 'I want to reassure our troops, civilian back-ups and families that there is nothing to fear from this particular type of munitions. People must understand that when we act, we act with the interests of our troops and civilians very much in mind.'

Now a Nato spokesman rode to his lordship's rescue – on a lame horse. He said, 'Updated medical studies show no link between the use of DU and the recent deaths of military personnel'. A British MoD spokesman obediently echoed him. But increasing scepticism was expressed by the EU Commission President, by Italy's president and prime minister, Portugal's prime minister, Russia's foreign minister, the Belgian, French, Greek and Italian defence ministers and the German Chancellor, Gerhard Schröder, who called for the banning of DU-tipped weapons. Bluntly Herr Schröder stated, 'I don't consider it right to use munitions that can damage our own troops when they are fired'. (The inference being that damage to other people, now and in the future, is not so important – even unimportant?)

There followed a brief period of media concentration on DU, on its potential as a killer and its threat to Nato unity. Then its news value expired; those activists dedicated to its outlawing are still beavering away but to no appreciable effect. As usual the US ignored its allies' concerns and protests, foreseeing no real threat to Nato unity. Words had been used in large quantities, registering disapproval of DU, deploring deaths, demanding investigations, requesting information, suggesting discussions. But we Europeans seem to assume that nothing can ever be *done* to oppose the US.

Somewhere near the Albanian border, amidst the bowels of the mountains, Tito built underground concrete military installations lest Hoxha might one day decide to invade Yugoslavia. Robert James Parsons quotes a Swiss military analyst who visited this complex in Tito's time and who now judges that 30mm Penetrators would merely chip the concrete. However, DU-reinforced Cruise missiles might do the job. And, according to the British military analyst Dennis Flaherty, 'One of the aims of the Kosovo war was to test such missiles equipped with a new technology (known as Broach) allowing as many as ten Penetrators to be fired at a time in order to penetrate underground bunkers more effectively'.

Acronyms

APC	Armoured personnel carrier
APWB	Abdić Forces
ARWB	Autonomous Region of Western Bihać
BiH	Bosnia-Herzegovina (Serbo-Croat abbreviation)
BTF	Balkans Task Force
DU	Depleted uranium
EU	European Union
EUAM	European Union Administration of Mostar
FRY	Federal Republic of Yugoslavia, name adopted by Serbia and Montenegro in 1992
GUUAM	Nato-inspired alliance of Georgia, Ukraine, Uzbekistan, Azerbaijan and Moldova
HDZ	Croatian Democratic Union, a hardline Croat nationalist political party
HLC	Humanitarian Law Centre (Serbia)
HOS	Croatian Defence Force, military wing of the HSP
HSP	Croatian Party of Rights
HV	The Croatian Army
HVO	The Bosnian Croats' Army
I-For	Implementation Force, UN troops deployed in BiH until 20 December 1996
IAEA	International Atomic Energy Agency
IC	International Community
ICRC	International Committee of the Red Cross
IMF	International Monetary Fund
IWCT	International War Crimes Tribunal at The Hague
JNA	Yugoslav National Army
K-For	Kosovo Protection Force, Nato-led international security force stationed in Kosovo after the airwar
KLA	Kosovo Liberation Army
KOS	Yugoslav Military Counter-Intelligence
KVM	Kosovo Verification Mission
LDK	Democratic League of Kosovo (Ibrahim Rugova's moderate party)
MoD	Ministry of Defence (UK)

MoU	Memorandum of Understanding
MUP	Federal Yugoslav Police Force
Nato	North Atlantic Treaty Organization
NGO	Nongovermental organization
OAF	Operation Allied Force, Nato's bombing campaign against Serbia
OHR	Office of the High Representative, set up to implement the Dayton Accord in BiH
OSCE	Organization for Security and Co-operation in Europe
OSEM	Office of the EU Special Envoy in Mostar
RS	Republika Srpska (BiH)
RSK	Republika Srpska Krajina (Croatia)
RUC	Royal Ulster Constabulary
S-For	Stabilization Force, UN troops deployed in BiH after December 1996
SDP	Party of Democratic Change (Croatia)
SDP	Serbian Democratic Party (BiH)
SDS	Serbian Democratic Party (Croatia)
SIM	Special Police of Serbian Interior Ministry
SOS	Serbian Democratic Party (the Krajina)
TDO	Trade and Development Office (US)
TMK	Kosovo's new police force
TNC	Transnational corporation
UNDP	United Nations Development Programme
UNEP	United Nations Environmental Protection agency
UNHCHR	United Nations High Commission for Human Rights
UNHCR	United Nations High Commission for Refugees
UNICEF	United Nations International Children's Emergency Fund
UNMIK	United Nations Mission in Kosovo
Unprofor	United Nations Protection Force deployed in Croatia and BiH
UNSC	United Nations Security Council
UXO	Unexploded ordnance
WHO	World Health Organization

Bibliography

Ali, Tariq (ed.), *Masters of the Universe? Nato's Balkan Crusade*, Verso, London, 2000

Allcock, John B., *Explaining Yugoslavia*, Hurst & Co., London, 2000

Bassett, Richard, *Balkan Hours*, John Murray, London, 1990

Blaskovich, Jerry, *Anatomy of Deceit*, Dunhill, New York, 1997

Bosnia: What Went Wrong? A Foreign Affairs reader, 1998

Carver, Robert, *The Accursed Mountains*, John Murray, London, 1998

Clark, Victoria, *Why Angels Fall*, Macmillan, London, 2000

Cornwell, John, *Hitler's Pope*, Viking, London, 1999

Daalder, Ivo H. & O'Hanlon, Michael E., *Winning Ugly: Nato's War to Save Kosovo*, Brookings Institute Press, Washington DC, 2000

Duijzings, Ger, *Religion and the Politics of Identity in Kosovo*, Hurst & Co., London, 2000

Emerson, Peter, *A Bosnian Perspective*, December Publications, Belfast, 1993

—— *From Belfast to the Balkans*, De Borda Institute, Belfast, 1999

Foretić, Miljenko (ed.), *Dubrovnik in War*, Matica Hrvatska, Dubrovnik, 2000

Fyson, George (ed.), *The Truth About Yugoslavia*, Pathfnder Press, New York, 1993

Glenny, Misha, *The Fall of Yugoslavia*, Penguin, London, 1992

Goldsworthy, Vesna, *Inventing Ruritania: The Imperialism of the Imagination*, Yale University Press, London, 1998

Gutman, Roy & Rieff, David (eds), *Crimes of War*, Norton & Co., New York, 1999

Hukanović, Rezak, *The Tenth Circle of Hell*, Basic Books, 1996

Jelavich, Barbara, *History of the Balkans, Vol. I: 18th and 19th centuries, Vol. II: 20th century*, Cambridge University Press, Cambridge, 1993

Judah, Tim, *The Serbs*, Yale University Press, London, 1997

—— *Kosovo: War and Revenge*, Yale University Press, London, 2000

Little, Allan & Silber, Laura, *The Death of Yugoslavia*, Penguin/BBC Books, London, 1995

Malcolm, Noel, *Bosnia: A Short History*, Papermac, London, 1996

—— *Kosovo: A Short History*, Papermac, London, 1998

Maliqi, Shkelzen, *Kosova: Separate Worlds*, Dukagjini, Priština, 1998

Markle, Gerard E. and McCrea, Frances B., 'Medjugorje and the Crisis in Yugoslavia' in Swatos, William H. (ed.), *Politics and Religion in Central and Eastern Europe*, Praeger, London, 1994

Meir, Viktor, *Yugoslavia – A History of its Demise*, Routledge, London, 1999

Mihaljčić, Rade, *The Battle of Kosovo*, BIGZ, Belgrade, 1989

NATO Crimes in Yugoslavia: Documentary Evidence, Vol.I: 24 March–24 April, Vol. II: 25 April–10 June, Belgrade, 1999

Nešić, Tihomir (ed.), *An Open Book Against Aggression*, Beleg Series, Belgrade, 1999

Nikić, Gorazd (ed.), *Croatia Between Aggression and Peace*, AGM, Zagreb, 1994

Omrćanin, Ivo, *Forced Conversion of Croats to the Serb Faith in History*, SAMIZDAT, Washington DC, 1985

—— *Finis of the Independent State of Croatia*, Dorrance & Co., 1983

—— *Holocaust of Croatians*, SAMIZDAT, Washington DC, 1986

—— *Anglo-American Croatian Rapprochement*, SAMIZDAT, Washington DC, 1989

O'Shea, Brendan, *Crisis at Bihać*, Sutton Publishing, 1998

Pavlowitch, Stevan K., *A History of the Balkans: 1804–1945*, Longmans, London, 1999

Pettifer, James & Vickers, Miranda, *Albania From Anarchy to a Balkan Identity*, Hurst & Co., London, 1997

Popov, Nebojša (ed.), *The Road to War in Serbia*, Central European University Press, 2000

Prentice, Eve-Ann, *One Woman's War*, Duckworth, London, 2000

Ramet, Sabrina Petra, *Balkan Babel*, Westview Press, Colorado, 1996

Rieff, David, *Slaughterhouse – Bosnia and the Failure of the West*, Simon & Schuster, New York, 1995

Ridgeway, James & Udovički, Jasminka (eds), *Burn This House: The Making and Unmaking of Yugoslavia*, Duke University Press, London, 1997

Robertson, Geoffrey, *Crimes Against Humanity*, Allen Lane, London, 1999

Rohde, David, *A Safe Area: Srebrenica*, Pocket Books, New York, 1997

Rose, Michael, *Fighting For Peace*, Harvill Press, London, 1998

Schopflin, George, *Nations – Identity – Power*, Hurst & Co., London, 2000

Sells, Michael A, *The Bridge Betrayed*, University of California Press, Berkeley, 1996

Softić, Elma, *Sarajevo Days, Sarajevo Nights*, Key Porter Books, 1995

Sommelius, Torgny, *The Iron Gates of Illyria*, Rupert Hart-Davis, London, 1955

Spotlight Report No. 28, Humanitarian Law Centre, Belgrade, 1999

Tanner, Marcus, *Croatia: A Nation Forged in War*, Yale University Press, London, 1997

Thomas, Robert, *Serbia Under Milošević*, Hurst & Co., London, 1999

Thompson, Mark, *A Paper House: the Ending of Yugoslavia*, Pantheon Books, New York, 1992

Tomić, Novo, *The Twilight of the West*, Hoboctn, Belgrade, 1999

Ugrešić, Dubravka, *The Culture of Lies*, Phoenix House, London, 1998

Weine, Stevan M., *When History is a Nightmare*, Rutgers University Press, Piscataway NJ, 1999

West, Rebecca, *Black Lamb and Grey Falcon*, Macmillan, London, 1940

Williamson, Samuel A. Jnr., *Austria-Hungary and the Origins of the First World War*, Macmillan, 1991

Zimmermann, Warren, *Origins of a Catastrophe*, Random House, 1999

GUIDEBOOKS

Introducing Yugoslavia, Lovett F. Edwards, Methuen, London, 1954

Companion Guide to Yugoslavia, J.A. Cuddon, Collins, London, 1968

Rough Guide to Yugoslavia, Routledge & Kegan Paul, London, 1985

Yugoslavia: Mountain Walks and Historical Sites, Piers Letcher, Bradt Publications, Chalfont St Peter, 1989

Blue Guide: Albania, James Pettifer, A & C Black, London, 1996

Acknowledgements

I owe a special debt of gratitude to those who befriended me in the Balkans and patiently sat by me while I jotted down in my notebook the information they so generously provided.

Ailsa Moore and Peter Emerson shared with me their helpful contacts.

Several compatriots, who might prefer not to be associated with some of my views, offered lavish hospitality when I wandered on to their scene.

Mirabel and Hugh Cecil provided practical and moral support at critical moments.

Back home, I received much essential additional information from Jo Murphy-Lawless, Kate Thompson and David Keating.

When I wanted to bin the whole typescript my daughter Rachel came to the rescue with calming encouragement and constructive criticisms.

Diana Murray's shrewd editorial interventions were invaluable, as they have been for the past thirty-eight years of my writing life.

Vesna Goldsworthy generously undertook the tedious task of providing the diacriticals and also rescued me from the edge of numerous linguistic and other Balkan pitfalls.

My publisher John Murray VII, by now accustomed to the flawless productions of computerized authors, struggled through my archaic typescript, defaced by manuscript corrections, with a tolerance probably unique in the twenty-first-century publishing world.

My editor, Anne Boston, brought order out of chaos in several chapters. For the remaining chaos only I am to blame.

INDEX

Index